Fundamentals of Financial Instruments

T0313846

Fundamentals of Financial Instruments

An Introduction to Stocks, Bonds, Foreign Exchange, and Derivatives

SUNIL PARAMESWARAN

Second Edition

WILEY

Other Wiley Editorial Offices

John Wiley & Sons, 111 River Street, Hoboken, NJ 07030, USA
John Wiley & Sons, The Atrium, Southern Gate, Chichester, West Sussex, P019 8SQ, United Kingdom
John Wiley & Sons (Canada) Ltd., 5353 Dundas Street West, Suite 400, Toronto, Ontario, M9B 6HB, Canada
John Wiley & Sons Australia Ltd., 42 McDougall Street, Milton, Queensland 4064, Australia
Wiley-VCH, Boschstrasse 12, D-69469 Weinheim, Germany

Library of Congress Cataloging-in-Publication Data is Available:

9781119816614 (Hardback)
9781119816645 (ePDF)
9781119816638 (ePub)

Cover Design: Wiley
Cover Image: © naqiewei/Getty Images
Author photo: Courtesy of Sunil Parameswaran

To my students in India, Australia, Singapore, and the United States over the past 30 years.

Contents

CHAPTER 3
Equity Shares, Preferred Shares, and Stock Market Indices   78

CHAPTER 5
Money Markets

Preface

Readers the world over have appreciated the first edition of this book, which appeared over a decade ago. Some people pointed out that I should include more material on financial institutions and the key features of the markets in which financial products trade.

Consequently, I have included a detailed chapter on mutual funds, pension funds, and exchange-traded funds. There is also a new chapter on orders and exchanges, which deals with continuous markets in detail, with a brief focus on call markets as well. Macroeconomic issues are key for understanding financial markets, and hence there is a new chapter on such issues. The chapter is by no means exhaustive, and people wishing to acquire a more detailed perspective would have to look for an economics text.

Interest rate derivatives are perhaps the hardest product to explain in futures and options. Consequently, while the book continues to have three separate chapters on futures, options, and swaps, I have opted to include a chapter on interest rate derivatives and on financial products with such derivatives built in, such as callable bonds and putable bonds.

Excel has many useful functions for students and professionals in the field of Finance. I have described the use of many of these functions at key places in the book.

The previous edition had some statistical information on markets, and certain qualitative descriptive features, which I felt were better to remove. I have eliminated such features in the second edition. I feel that a chapter on clearing and settlement may be relevant for the kind of audience that this book aims to address. I will bring that in if and when there is a third edition.

Readers are welcome to share their comments and suggestions with me. Constructive advice and criticism is welcome and will be incorporated while undertaking revision of the material in future. My email is: tarheelconsulting@gmail.com

I hope that the book serves as a source of pertinent and comprehensive knowledge for readers everywhere.

Sunil K. Parameswaran
Director & CEO
Tarheel Consultancy Services
Manipal, India
November 2021

Preface to the First Edition

This book grew out of my lecture notes used for corporate training programs in India and abroad. The feedback from participants has been invaluable in polishing and refining the exposition. The eventual flow and clarity that I believe I have been able to achieve is in no small measure due to the critical and incisive inputs of my students as well as professional acquaintances.

There is typically no course exclusively on financial instruments in most MBA curricula. Consequently, this topic invariably gets combined with material on financial institutions as part of a course on Financial Markets. I, however, believe that there is a strong case for offering a comprehensive course on financial instruments for second-year MBA students. However, care should be taken to ensure that material which is covered in traditional courses like Financial Derivatives and Fixed Income Securities is not repeated any more than is necessary. Many students who take such a course may not be majoring in Finance and consequently may not take specialized courses such as Derivatives. For them therefore the specter of substantial overlap is less of an issue. Even for students of Finance, despite the inevitable repetition of facets of topics such as Bonds, Futures, and Options, a course on instruments is a comprehensive and integrated offering that will serve them in good stead in the future.

The book starts from first principles and builds in intensity. Exposure to one or more courses on Financial Management will certainly be useful for the reader as he or she navigates through the material. While the book is a standalone treatise on the subject, readers may like to augment it with standard texts on issues in Finance such as Security Analysis, Bond Markets, Futures & Options, and International Finance.

The issues covered in this book are universal and of relevance for students of Finance as well as market professionals irrespective of where they may happen to be located. However, most of the illustrations and examples pertain to markets in the developed world, particularly the United States, and the products that trade in them. Consequently the book should have appeal for readers in all parts of the world.

Readers are welcome to share their comments and suggestions with me. Constructive advice and criticism is welcome and will be incorporated while undertaking revision of the material in future. My E-mail ID is: skp@tarcon.org

I hope that the book serves as a source of pertinent and comprehensive knowledge for readers everywhere.

Sunil K. Parameswaran
T.A. Pai Management Institute
Manipal – 576104
Karnataka, India

Acknowledgments

I am indebted to all my students in India and Australia who went through this material and offered ideas for embellishing the content and polishing the exposition. The participants at my Executive Education programs offered invaluable advice. Because most of them were non-Finance professionals, primarily from the Information Technology field, they had unusual and interesting perspectives which helped augment the more traditional feedback from business school students and associates.

I am extremely grateful to John Wiley & Sons, Singapore, for giving me the opportunity to develop and promote this book. In particular I owe a tremendous debt to my former publisher, Nick Wallwork, for taking a chance with an unknown Indian academic. Gladys Ganaden, who subsequently took over, has been an enormous source of support and encouragement. She is the primary force behind the second edition of the book, for she perceived the need and inspired me to write it. I am indebted to her.

The editorial team of Purvi and Pradesh has been very supportive of this project right from the outset and I owe them an enormous debt. Donna, who was the copyeditor, has done a wonderful job, and has provided invaluable support at the copyediting and typesetting phases.

And finally, I am indebted to my mother for her patience and moral support.

About the Author

Sunil K. Parameswaran is the director and CEO of Tarheel Consultancy Services, a corporate training and management consultancy firm set up by him in 2004.

Sunil is a Visiting Faculty at some of the leading business schools in India, where he anchors courses in the area of Finance. His primary areas of interest are Securities Markets; Financial Derivatives; Fixed Income Securities; and International Finance.

For the past 20 years Sunil has been active as a corporate trainer and management consultant. He has delivered training programs on Global Securities Markets and Global Banking to some of the multinational IT firms located in India. Sunil also has over 30 years of teaching experience and has taught at leading business schools in the United States (University of Iowa), Singapore (National University of Singapore), Australia (La Trobe University), and India.

His past clients include WIPRO Technologies, HCL, Capgemini, Accenture, Microland, and JPMC.

Sunil obtained his PhD in Finance from the Fuqua School of Business at Duke University in North Carolina. He obtained his MBA from the Indian Institute of Management, Bangalore, and holds an undergraduate degree in Chemistry from St. Stephen's College, New Delhi.

A prolific writer, he has published several books with John Wiley & Sons in Singapore and DeG Press in the United States. His most recent book is *Fixed Income Securities*, published by DeG Press, Boston/Berlin.

CHAPTER 1

An Introduction to Financial Institutions, Instruments, and Markets

THE ROLE OF AN ECONOMIC SYSTEM

Economic systems are designed to collect savings in an economy and allocate the available resources efficiently to those who either seek funds for current consumption in excess of what their resources would permit, or else for investments in productive assets.

The key role of an economic system is to ensure *efficient allocation*. Efficient and free flow of resources from one economic entity to another is a sine qua non for a modern economy. This is because the larger the flow of resources and the more efficient their allocation, the greater is the chance that the requirements of all economic agents can be satisfied, and consequently the greater are the odds that the economy's output will be maximized.

The functioning of an economic system entails making decisions about both the production of goods and services and their subsequent distribution. The success of an economy is gauged by the extent of wealth creation. A successful economy consequently is one that makes and implements judicious economic decisions from the standpoints of production and distribution. In an efficient economy, resources will be allocated to those economic agents who are able to derive the optimum value of output by employing the resources allocated to them.

Why are we giving so much importance to the efficiency of an economic system? The emphasis on efficiency is because every economy is characterized by a relative scarcity of resources as compared to the demand for them. In principle, the demand for resources by economic agents can be virtually unlimited, but in practice, economies are characterized by a finite stock of resources. Efficient allocation requires an extraordinary amount of information as to what people need, how best goods and services can be produced to cater to these needs, and how best the produced output can be distributed.

Economic systems may be classified as command economies or as free market economies. This definition refers to the two extreme ends of the economic spectrum. In practice, most modern economies tend to display characteristics of both kinds of systems, and they differ only with respect to the level of government control.

A COMMAND ECONOMY

In a command economy, such as the former Soviet Union, all production and allocation decisions are taken by a central planning authority. The planning authority is expected to estimate the resource requirements of various economic agents, and then rank them in order of priority based on their relevance to social needs. Production plans and resource allocation decisions are then made so as to ensure that resources are directed to users in descending order of need. In practice, communist and socialist systems, which were based on this economic model, ensured that citizens complied with the directives of the state by imposing stifling legal, and occasionally, coercive measures.

The failure of the command economies was inherent in their structure. As we have discussed, efficient economic systems needed to aggregate and process an enormous amount of information. When this task was entrusted to a central planning authority, this not only proved to be infeasible in practice, but the quality of information was also substandard. The central planning authority was supposed to be omniscient and was expected to have perfect information as to what resources were available and what the relative requirements of the socioeconomic system were. This was necessary for them to ensure that optimal decisions were made about production as well as distribution.

Command economies were in practice plagued by blatant political interference. The planning authority was often prevented from making optimal decisions due to political pressures. The system gave the planners enormous powers that permeated all facets of the social system and not just the economy. One of the hallmarks of such systems was the absence of pragmatism, and a naïve idealism that was out of touch with realities. Planners used their authority to devise and impose stifling rules and regulations. These regulations, which were in principle intended to ensure optimal decision making, sometimes went to the ridiculous extent of imposing penalties on producers whose output exceeded what was allowed by the permit or license given to them.

Such economies were a colossal failure in practice and were characterized by an output that was invariably far less than the ambitious targets that were set at the outset of each financial year. When confronted with the specter of failure the planners tended to place the blame on those who were responsible for implementing the plans. The bureaucrats in charge of implementation passed the buck back by making allegations of improper decision making on the part of the planners. Eventually the contradictions in the system lead either to the total repeal of such systems or else to substantial structural changes that brought in key features of a market economy.

A MARKET ECONOMY

Such economies work in principle as follows. Economic agents are expected to make the most profitable use of the resources at their disposal. What is profit? Profit is defined as the revenues from sales less the costs of production of the goods sold. Thus, profit is a function of the prices of the inputs or the factors of production, such as land, labor, and capital, and the prices of the output. An optimal economic decision is defined as the one that maximizes profit. Economic agents who generate surpluses of income over expenditure will obviously be able to attract more and better resources. Failure, as manifested by sustained losses, will result in those economic agents being denied access to the resources being sought by them.

In such systems the prices of both inputs and outputs are determined by factors of supply and demand. These economies, in contrast to command economies, are characterized by decentralized decision making. In principle, agents are expected to make a rational decision by evaluating competing resource needs based on their ability to generate surpluses. In practice, every decision maker will have a required rate of return on investment. The threshold return, or the return exceeding which the venture will be deemed to be profitable, is the cost of capital for the decision maker. A project is deemed to be worth the investment only if the expected rate of return from it is greater than the cost of the capital that is being invested.

As can be surmised, the key decision variables in these economies are the prices of inputs and outputs. Hence, for such economies to work in an optimal fashion, it is imperative that prices accurately convey the value of a good or a service, from the standpoints of producers who employ factors of production and consumers who consume the end products. The informational accuracy of prices results in the efficient allocation of resources for the following reasons. If the inputs for the production process, such as labor and capital, are accurately priced, then producers can take optimal production-related decisions. Similarly, if the consumers of goods and services perceive their prices to be accurate, they will make optimal consumption decisions. The accuracy of input-related costs and output prices will manifest itself in the form of profit maximization, which is the primary motivating factor for agents in such economies to engage in economic enterprise.

How do such systems ensure that prices of inputs and outputs are informationally accurate? In practice, this is ensured by allowing economic agents to trade in markets for goods and services. If an agent has the perception that the price of an asset is different from the value that he places on it, he will seek to trade. If the prevailing price is lower than the perceived value, buyers will seek to buy more of the good than the quantity on offer. If so, the market price will be bid up due to demand being greater than the amount on offer. This demand supply disequilibrium will persist till the price reaches the optimal level. Similarly, if the price of the good is perceived to be too high relative to the value placed on it by agents, sellers will seek to offload more than what is being demanded. Once again, the supply-demand imbalance will cause prices to decline till equilibrium is restored. Thus, differing perceptions of value will manifest themselves as supply-demand imbalances; resolving these will ultimately help ensure that the prices of assets accurately reflect their value.

Opinion: While free market economies have to a large extent been more successful than command economies, no one would advocate a total absence of the government's role in economic decision making. Unfettered capitalism is unlikely to find acceptance anywhere. There are disadvantaged sections of every society whose fate cannot be left to the market, and whose well-being must be ensured by policy makers to promote overall welfare. While societies characterized by command economies have historically not permitted free speech, in a country like the United States, even mild criticism of the market is considered to be heresy.

CLASSIFICATION OF ECONOMIC UNITS

Economic agents are usually divided into three categories or sectors:

- The government sector
- The business sector
- The household sector

The government sector consists of the central or federal government of a country, state, or provincial governments, and local governments or municipalities. The business sector consists of sole proprietorships, partnerships, and private as well as public limited companies. Sometimes business units are broadly subclassified as financial corporations and nonfinancial corporations.

Proprietorships: A proprietorship, also known as a sole proprietorship, is a business owned by a single person, and represents the easiest way to start a business. The owner may do business in their name or else in a trade name. For instance, a consultant named John Smith may run the business in his name, or choose a name like "Business Systems." The owner is fully responsible for all debts and obligations of the business. That is, creditors, or entities to which the business owes money, may stake a claim against all assets of the proprietor, whether they are business-related assets or personal assets. In legal parlance this is referred to as *unlimited liability*, as opposed to a corporation where the owners have *limited liability*, which we will shortly discuss in greater detail.

The start-up costs of a sole proprietorship are usually lower than those of other forms of business. Unlike a corporation, however, such businesses face relative difficulties in raising additional capital when they choose to expand the scope of their operations. Usually, in addition to the owner's personal investment, the only source of funds is a loan from a commercial bank.

Legally, the proprietorship is an extension of the owner. The owner is permitted to employ other people. The net profits from the business are clubbed with the proprietor's other income, if any, for the purpose of taxation. The lifespan of these entities is uncertain. For instance, if the owner were to die, the business would cease to exist.

Partnerships: A partnership is a business entity that is owned by at least two people or partners. One of the partners may be a corporation, which we will explain next. Legally, the partnership is an extension of the partners. Like a proprietorship, a partnership is permitted to employ others, and can conduct a business under a trade name. For instance, two lawyers named John Smith and Mike Jones may conduct their business as Smith & Jones, or else under a trade name such as "Legal Point." In a general partnership the partners have unlimited liability, and the partners are personally responsible not only for their own acts, but also for the actions of other partners and employees.

There are two categories of partnerships in many countries: *general partnerships* and *limited partnerships*. A general partnership is what we have just discussed. In a limited partnership there are two categories of partners: general partners and limited partners. The general partners are usually a corporation and have management control. They are characterized by unlimited liability. The limited partners, on the other hand, are like the shareholders of a corporation. Their potential loss is limited to the investment that they have made.

Like a sole proprietorship, a partnership is also easy to establish. However, unlike a proprietor, who is the sole decision maker, partners must share authority with the others. Consequently, it is important to draw up a partnership agreement at the outset, where issues such as profit sharing are clearly spelled out. Compared to corporations, partnerships also find it relatively difficult to raise capital to expand their businesses.

Corporations: A corporation or a limited company is a legal entity that is distinct and separate from its owners, who are referred to as shareholders or stockholders. A corporation may and usually will have multiple owners as well as many employees on its payroll. It must necessarily do business under a given trade name. Because a corporation is a separate legal entity, it has the right to sue and be sued in its own name. Shareholders of a corporation enjoy limited liability. Unlike a proprietorship or partnership, the ownership of a company can easily change hands. Each shareholder will possess shares of the company that can be usually bought and sold in a marketplace known as the stock exchange. While such share transfers may result in one party relinquishing majority control in favor of another, the transfers per se have no implications for the corporation's continued existence or its operations. Unlike proprietorships and partnerships, corporations find it relatively easier to raise both debt or borrowed capital, as well as equity or owners' capital. In most countries, however, corporations are extensively regulated, and are required by statutes to maintain extensive records pertaining to their operations. The cost of incorporation, and the costs of raising equity through share issues, can also be substantial. While owners of a corporation may be a part of its management team, very often ownership and management are segregated by entrusting the management of day-to-day activities to a team of professional managers. In some countries there exist entities known as Private Limited Companies. These companies cannot offer shares to the public, and consequently the shares cannot be traded on a stock exchange. However, the shareholders continue to enjoy limited liability and hence the name. The disclosure norms for public limited companies are generally more stringent than those for private limited companies.

During a given financial year, every economic unit, irrespective of which sector it may belong to, will get some form of income from its operations, and will also incur expenditure in some form. Depending on the relationship between the income earned and the expenditure incurred, an economic unit may be classified into one of the following three categories:

- A balanced budget unit
- A surplus budget unit
- A deficit budget unit

A balanced budget unit (BBU) is one whose income in a period is exactly equal to its expenditure. It must be reiterated that a balanced budget unit is impossible to observe in practice and consequently exists only in the realm of textbooks. For it is virtually impossible for a business or government to ensure that its scheduled income during a period is perfectly matched with its scheduled expenditure during the same period. In practice an economic unit may be a surplus budget unit (SBU) or a deficit budget unit (DBU). A surplus budget unit is one whose income exceeds its expenditure while a deficit unit is one whose expenses exceed its income. Usually, in most countries, governments and businesses invariably tend to be deficit budget units, whereas households consisting of individuals and families generally tend to be savers, that is they tend to have budget surpluses. By this we do not mean that all households and individuals are savers or that all governments and businesses have a budget deficit. What we mean is that while it is not impossible for a government or a business to have a surplus in a financial period, taken as a group, the government sector and the business sector generally tend to be net borrowers. By the same logic, it is not necessary that all households should save, although the category generally has a budget surplus in most periods. Finally, a country may have a budget surplus or a budget deficit.

AN ECONOMY'S RELATIONSHIP WITH THE EXTERNAL WORLD

The record of all economic transactions between a country and the rest of the world is known as the Balance of Payments (BOP). It is a record of a country's trade in goods, services, and financial assets with the rest of the world or, in other words, a record of all economic transactions between a country and the outside world. The transaction may be a requited transfer of economic value or an unrequited transfer of economic value. The term *requited*, in this context, connotes that the transferor receives a compensation of economic value from the transferee. On the other hand, an *unrequited transfer* represents a unilateral gift made by the transferor.

For instance, if Microsoft exports software to Germany in return for a payment in euros, it is a requited transaction of economic value. On the other hand, if the Gates Foundation were to donate $10 million to a charity in Zimbabwe, it is an unrequited or unilateral transfer.

Economic transactions can be classified into the following five basic categories. First is the import and export of goods and services in return for a payment in financial terms. For instance, a company in Houston imports crude oil from Saudi Arabia and pays in US dollars. The second category may be illustrated as follows. Sometimes an import or export of a product may be paid for by an equivalent export or import of another. A party in India imports crude oil from Nigeria by paying in the form of wheat. This is nothing but a barter transaction in simple English. The third type of transaction entails the exchange of one financial asset for another. For instance, a party in London buys US Treasury Bonds as an investment and pays the equivalent amount in dollars. The last two categories pertain to unilateral transfers, inward and outward, respectively.

The BOP is typically broken up into three major categories of accounts, each of which is further subdivided into various components. The major categories are:

The Current Account: This accounting head includes imports and exports of goods and services, factor incomes and payments, and unrequited transfers in both directions.

The Capital Account: Under this head we have the transactions that lead to changes in the foreign assets and liabilities of a country.

The Reserve Account: The reserve account is similar to the capital account, in the sense that it also deals with financial assets and liabilities. This account, however, deals only with reserve assets, which are assets used to settle the deficits and surpluses that arise on account of the other two categories taken together.

A reserve asset is one that is acceptable as a means of payment in international transactions, and which is held by and exchanged between the monetary authorities of various countries. It consists of monetary gold, assets denominated in foreign currencies, Special Drawing Rights (SDRs), and reserve positions at the International Monetary Fund (IMF). If there is a deficit in the current and capital accounts taken together, then there will be a depletion of reserves. However, if the two accounts show a surplus when taken together, there will be an increase in the level of reserves.

The balance of payments is an accounting system that is based on the double-entry system of bookkeeping. Consequently, every transaction is recorded on both sides, that is as a credit and as a debit. All transactions that have led to or will lead to a flow of payments into the country from the rest of the world will be shown as credits. The payments themselves should be shown as the corresponding debit entries. Similarly, all transactions which have led to or will lead to a flow of payments from the country to the rest of the world should be recorded as debits, and the corresponding payments should be recorded as credits.

The accounting principle can also be stated as follows. Any transaction which leads to an increase in the demand for foreign exchange should be shown as a debit, whereas any transaction which leads to an increase in the supply of foreign exchange should be shown as a credit. Thus, capital outflows will be debited, whereas capital inflows will be credited.

Why would the residents of a country demand foreign exchange? First, they may wish to pay for imports of goods or services. Second, they may want to make a dividend or interest payment to a party abroad. Third, they may want to repay a loan taken from an entity abroad. Unlike a company, a country does not have shareholders. Thus, all liabilities of the latter represent debt. It should also be clarified that a company's debt is what it owes to its banks or bondholders. In the case of a country, however, if a foreign entity were to take an equity stake in a domestic company, it would be treated as a part of the country's external debt.

Now let us analyze the receipts of foreign exchange by residents of a country. First, they may have exported goods or services. Second, they may have received dividend or interest payments from parties abroad. Third, they may have taken a loan from an entity abroad or may have liquidated a foreign financial asset.

A payment received from abroad will increase the country's foreign assets. Thus, an increase in foreign assets or a decrease in foreign liabilities will be shown as a debit. On the other hand, when a payment is made to an external party it will either reduce the country's holding of foreign assets or show up as an increase in its liabilities. This will obviously be shown as a credit.

The equivalence with corporate accounts: An export of goods and services by a country is equivalent to a sale by a company. It will be recorded as a credit, and the corresponding payment received or to be received will be recorded by debiting the cash account or the receivables account, if the sale is made on credit. Similarly, an import of goods and services is like a purchase by a company. It will be recorded as a debit and the payment, if made immediately, will be shown by crediting cash, or by crediting the creditor's account if the counterparty has supplied on credit. Dividends and interest payments made to foreign parties are equivalent to expenses for a company and will be debited. Inward dividends and interest are equivalent to income and will be credited. As we said earlier, a country has only creditors and no shareholders. Consequently, foreign liabilities will go up with credits and down with debits. Unlike a company's reserves, which belong to the shareholders and are consequently a liability for it, a country's reserves are an asset for it. Thus, a country's reserves will increase with debits and decline with credits.

Unrequited or unilateral transfers may be perceived as follows. Inward transfers are like purchases by a company, where the supplier has extended a 100% discount. On the other hand, outward transfers are like sale transactions, where the company concerned has offered a 100% discount.

Clearly, the balance of payments must always balance. Thus, a current account deficit must be matched by a surplus in the capital account or by a depletion of reserves, or both. A surplus in the capital account would indicate that the country's foreign liabilities have gone up, or, in other words, that it has borrowed from abroad. In the case of a company, if the net income for a period is negative, then either its liabilities must correspondingly increase, or its assets must decline. However, If the net income were to be positive, it would manifest itself as a reduction in the entity's liabilities or as an increase in its assets.

While analyzing the BOP, it is customary to study several subcategories of accounts. We will now look at two of the most important sub-classifications.

THE BALANCE OF TRADE

The balance of trade is equal to the total of merchandise exports and imports. It consists of all raw materials and manufactured goods bought, sold, or given away. If it shows a surplus, it indicates that exports of goods from the country exceed imports into it, whereas if it shows a deficit, it would obviously indicate that imports exceed exports. The balance of trade is a politically sensitive statistic. If a country's balance of trade shows a deficit, industries that are being hurt by competition from abroad will typically raise a hue and cry about the need for a level playing field to take on the foreign competition.

THE CURRENT ACCOUNT BALANCE

The current account balance refers to the total of the following accounts:

- Exports of goods, services, and income
- Imports of goods, services, and income
- Net unilateral transfers

Services include tourism, transportation, engineering, and business services. Fees from patents and copyrights are also recognized under this category. Income includes revenue from financial assets, such as dividends from shares and interest from debt securities. Unilateral transfers are one-way transfers of assets, such as worker remittances from foreign countries and direct foreign aid.

The net foreign assets of a country may be defined as its foreign assets minus its foreign liabilities. If the net foreign assets are positive, then the nation may be deemed to be a creditor nation; otherwise, it is a debtor nation. The change in the current account is equal to the change in net foreign assets.

$$\Delta \text{ Current Account} = \Delta \text{ Net Foreign Assets}$$

$$= \Delta \text{ Foreign Assets} - \Delta \text{ Foreign Liabilities}$$

If a country has a current account surplus, either its foreign assets will increase or its foreign liabilities will decline. On the contrary, if a country has a current account deficit, either its foreign assets will decline or its foreign liabilities will increase.

Opinion: Finance can be made incredibly complicated in the form of exotic securities and sophisticated mathematical models. But the core issue in an economy is that some entities have more than what they want, whereas others want more than what they have. The former transfer their surplus wealth to the latter, which issues securities in return. The securities themselves, and the businesses that deploy the resources, are vulnerable to different types of risks. Consequently, risk mitigation instruments, such as financial derivatives – which, incidentally, can also be used to speculate on risk – come into existence. But if we sift through the theories and the formulas, the underlying core transaction is a transfer from a Surplus Budget Unit (SBU) to a Deficit Budget Unit (DBU).

FINANCIAL ASSETS

"A financial asset is a claim against the income or wealth of a business firm, a household, or a government agency, which is represented usually by a certificate, a receipt, a computer record file, or another legal document, and is usually created by or is related to the lending of money."[1]

A financial claim is born in the following fashion. Whenever funds are transferred from a surplus budget unit (SBU) to a deficit budget unit (DBU), the DBU will issue a financial claim. It signifies that the party transferring the funds has a claim against the party accepting the funds. The transfer of funds from the lender may either be in the form of a loan to the borrower, or may constitute the assumption of an ownership stake in the venture of the borrower. In the case of loans, the claim constitutes a promise to pay the interest either at maturity or at periodic intervals and to repay the principal at maturity. Such claims are referred to as debt securities, or as fixed income securities. In the case of fund transfers characterized by the assumption of ownership stakes, the claims are known as equity shares. Unlike debt securities, which represent an obligation on the part of the borrower, equity shares represent a right to the profits of the issuing firm during its operation, if there is a profit, and to such assets that may remain after fully paying all creditors in the event of liquidation of the venture. It should be remembered that claims are always issued by the party that is raising funds and held by parties providing the funds.

To the issuer of the claim, the claim is a liability, for it signifies that it owes money to another party. To the lender, or the holder of the claim, it is an asset, for it signifies that the holder owns an item of value. The total of financial claims issued must be

---

[1]See Rose (2000).

equal to the total financial assets held by investors, and every liability incurred by a party must be an asset for another investor.

Why do investors acquire financial assets? Financial assets are essentially sought after for three reasons.

- They serve as a store of value or purchasing power.
- They promise future returns to their owners.
- They are fungible, in the sense that they can be easily converted into other assets and vice versa.

In addition to debt securities and equity shares, we will also focus on the following assets:

- Money
- Preferred shares
- Foreign exchange
- Derivatives
- Mortgages

MONEY

Money is a financial asset because all forms of money in use today are claims against some institution. Contrary to popular perception, money is not just the coins and currency notes handled by economic agents. For instance, one of the largest components of money supply today is the checking account balances held by depositors with commercial banks. From the banks' standpoint, these accounts obviously represent a debt obligation. Banks have the capacity to both expand and contract the money supply in an economy. Currency notes and coins also represent a debt obligation of the central bank of the issuing country, like the Federal Reserve in the United States. In today's electronic age, newer forms of money have emerged, such as credit, debit, and smart cards.

Money performs a wide variety of important functions, thus it is sought after. In a modern economy, all financial assets are valued in terms of money and all flows of funds between lenders and borrowers occur via the medium of money.

MONEY AS A UNIT OF ACCOUNT OR A STANDARD OF VALUE

In the modern economy, the value of every good and service is denominated in terms of the unit of currency. Without money, the price of every good or service would have to be expressed in terms of every other good or service. The availability of money leads to a tremendous reduction in the amount of price-related information that is required to be processed.

Take the case of a 100-good economy. In the absence of money, we would require $^{100}C_2$ or 4,950 prices.[2] However, if a currency were to be available, we would

---

[2]Obviously, the price of good A in terms of good B is the reciprocal of the price of good B in terms of good A.

require only 100 prices, a saving of almost 98% in terms of the required amount of information. Think of the saving for a modern economy, which has billions of goods.

MONEY AS A MEDIUM OF EXCHANGE

Money is usually the only financial asset that every business, household, and government department will accept as payment in return for goods and services.

Why is it that everyone is willing to readily accept money as compensation? It is primarily because they can always use it whenever needed to acquire any goods and services that they may desire. Thus, due to the existence of money, it is possible to clearly separate, in time, the act of sale of goods and services from any subsequent acquisition of goods and services. In the absence of money, we would have to exchange goods and services for other goods and services, a phenomenon which is termed as barter or countertrade.

MONEY AS A STORE OF VALUE

Money also serves as a store of value, or as a reserve of future purchasing power. However, just because an item is a store of value, it need not necessarily mean that it is a good store of value. In the case of money, inflation (the erosion of its purchasing power) is a virtually constant feature.

For instance, take the case of a good that costs $2 per unit. Thus, if an investor has $10 with him, he can acquire five units. However, if he were to keep the money with him for a year, he may find that the price in the following year is $2.50 per unit and hence he can acquire only four units. This is a manifestation of inflation, which may be considered to be a silent killer of wealth.

MONEY IS PERFECTLY LIQUID

What is a liquid asset? An asset is defined to be liquid if it can be quickly converted into cash with little or no loss of value. Why is liquidity important? In the absence of liquidity, market participants will be unable to transact quickly at prices that are close to the true or fair value of the asset. Buyers and sellers will need to expend considerable time and effort to identify each other, and very often will have to induce a transaction by offering a large premium or discount. If a market is highly liquid at a point in time, it means that plenty of buyers and sellers are available. In an illiquid or thin market, a large purchase or sale transaction is likely to have a major impact on prices. A large purchase transaction will send prices shooting up, whereas a large sale transaction will depress prices substantially. Liquid markets therefore have a lot of depth, as characterized by relatively minimal impact on prices. Liquid assets are characterized by three attributes:

- Price stability
- Ready marketability
- Reversibility

In these respects, money is obviously the most liquid of all assets because it need not be converted into another form to exploit its purchasing power.

However, liquid assets come with an attached price tag. The more liquid the asset in which an investment is made, the lower the interest rate or rate of return from it. Thus, there is a cost attached to liquidity in the form of the interest forgone due to the inability to invest in an asset paying a higher rate of return. Such interest that is forgone is lost forever, and consequently cash is the most perishable of all economic assets.

Consider a financial surplus of $100,000 that is available with an individual. The most liquid way to keep it would be in the form of cash, but there will be a nil return. If the person were to park the surplus funds in a savings account, he would have to sacrifice by way of liquidity, but would get a return. If he were to move the funds to a time deposit, he would lose even more liquidity, but would earn a greater return as compared to a savings account.

EQUITY SHARES

Equity shares or shares of common stock of a company are financial claims issued by the firm, which confer ownership rights on the investors who are known as shareholders. All shareholders are part owners of the company that has issued the shares, and their stake in the firm is equal to the fraction of the total share capital of the firm to which they have subscribed. In general, all companies will have equity shareholders, for common stock represents the fundamental ownership interest in a corporation. Thus, a company must have at least one shareholder. Shareholders will periodically receive cash payments from the firm called dividends. In addition, they are exposed to profits and losses when they seek to dispose of their shares at a subsequent point in time. These profits/losses are referred to as capital gains and losses.

Equity shares represent a claim on the residual profits after all the creditors of the company have been paid. That is, a shareholder cannot demand a dividend as a matter of right. The creditors of a firm, including those who have extended loans to it, obviously enjoy priority from the standpoint of payments, and are therefore ranked higher in the pecking order.

Equity shares have no maturity date. Thus, they continue to be in existence as long as the firm itself continues to be in existence. Shareholders have voting rights and have a say in the election of the board of directors. If the firm were to declare bankruptcy, then the shareholders would be entitled to the residual value of the assets after the claims of all the other creditors have been settled. Thus, once again, the creditors enjoy primacy as compared to the shareholders.

The major difference between the shareholders of a company, as opposed to a sole proprietor or the partners in a partnership, is that they have limited liability. That is, no matter how serious the financial difficulties facing a company may be, neither it nor its creditors can make financial demands on the common shareholders. Thus, the maximum loss that a shareholder may sustain is limited to his investment in the business. Hence, the lowest possible share price is zero.

DEBT SECURITIES

A debt instrument is a financial claim issued by a borrower to a lender of funds. Unlike equity shareholders, investors in debt securities are not conferred with ownership rights. These securities are merely IOUs (an acronym for "I Owe You"), which represent a promise to pay interest on the principal amount either at periodic intervals or at maturity, and to repay the principal itself at a prespecified maturity date.

Most debt instruments have a finite lifespan, that is, a stated maturity date, and hence differ from equity shares in this respect. Also, the interest payments that are promised to the lenders at the outset represent contractual obligations on the part of the borrower. This means that the borrower is required to meet these obligations irrespective of the performance of the firm in a given financial year. Quite obviously, it is also the case that in the event of an exceptional performance, the borrowing entity does not have to pay any more to the debt holders than what was promised at the outset. It is for this reason that debt securities are referred to as *fixed income securities*. The interest claims of debt holders have to be settled before any residual profits can be distributed by way of dividends to the shareholders. Also, in the event of bankruptcy or liquidation, the proceeds from the sale of assets of the firm must be used first to settle all outstanding interest and principal. Only the residual amount, if any, can be distributed among the shareholders.

While debt is important for a commercial corporation in both the public and private sectors of an economy, it is absolutely indispensable for central or federal, state, and local (municipalities) governments when they wish to finance their developmental activities. Although such entities can raise resources by way of taxes, and in the case of the federal government by printing money, they obviously cannot issue equity shares. For instance, a US citizen cannot become a part owner of the state of Illinois.

Debt instruments can be secured or unsecured. In the case of secured debt, the terms of the contract will specify the assets of the firm that have been pledged as security or collateral. In the event of the failure of the company, the security holders have a right over these assets. In the case of unsecured debt securities, the investors can only hope that the issuer will have the earnings and liquidity to redeem the promise made at the outset. In the United States, secured corporate debt securities are known as bonds, while unsecured debt securities issued by corporations are termed as debentures. In certain countries the terms *bonds* and *debentures* are used for both categories of debt securities. Also, the world over, government debt securities are known as bonds.

Debt instruments can be either negotiable or nonnegotiable. Negotiable securities are instruments which can be endorsed from one party to another, and hence can be bought and sold easily in the financial markets. A nonnegotiable instrument is one which cannot be transferred. Equity shares are obviously negotiable securities. While many debt securities are negotiable, certain loan-related transactions, such as loans made by commercial banks to business firms and savings bank accounts of individuals, are examples of assets that are not negotiable.

Debt securities are referred to by a variety of names such as *bills, notes, bonds, debentures,* etc. US Treasury securities are fully backed by the federal government, and consequently have no credit risk associated with them. The term *credit risk* refers to the risk that the issuer may default or fail to honor their commitment. Thus, the interest rate on Treasury securities is used as a benchmark for setting the rates of return on other, more risky securities. The US Treasury issues three categories of marketable debt instruments – T-bills, T-notes, and T-bonds. T-bills are discount securities also known as zero-coupon securities. That is, they are sold at a discount from their face value, and do not pay any interest. They have a maturity at the time of issue that is less than or equal to one year. T-notes and T-bonds are sold at face value and pay interest periodically. A T-note is akin to a T-bond but has a time to maturity between 1 and 10 years at the time of issue, whereas T-bonds have a life of more than 10 years.

PREFERRED SHARES

Preferred stocks are a hybrid of debt and equity. They are similar to debt in the sense that holders of such securities are usually promised a fixed rate of return. However, such dividends are payable from the post-tax profits of the firm, as in the case of equity shares. On the other hand, interest payments to bondholders are made from pre-tax profits, and therefore constitute a deductible expense for tax purposes.

If a company were to refrain from paying the preferred dividends in a particular year, then the shareholders, unlike the bondholders, cannot take legal recourse as a matter of right. In practice, most preferred shares are *cumulative* in nature. This implies that any unpaid dividends in a financial year must be carried forward, and the accumulated dividends must first be paid before the company can contemplate the payment of dividends to equity shareholders.

Preferred shareholders have restricted voting rights. That is, they usually do not enjoy the right to vote unless the payment of dividends due to them is in arrears. In the event of liquidation of the firm, the preferred shareholders will have to be paid off before the claims of the equity holders can be entertained. Thus, the order of priority of the stakeholders of the firm from the standpoint of payments is bondholders first, followed by preferred shareholders, and then equity shareholders. Within the category of bondholders, secured debt holders get priority over unsecured debt holders. The term *preferred* arises because such shareholders are given preference over equity shareholders, and not because the shareholders prefer such instruments.

FOREIGN EXCHANGE

The term *foreign exchange* refers to transactions pertaining to the currency of a foreign nation. Thus, foreign exchange markets are markets where foreign currencies are bought and sold. The conversion of one currency into another is termed as *exchange*. A foreign currency is also a type of financial asset, and consequently it will have a price in terms of another currency. The price of one country's currency in terms of that of another is referred to as the *exchange rate*. Foreign currencies are traded among a network of buyers and sellers, composed mainly of commercial banks and large multinational corporations, and not on an organized exchange. Thus, the market for foreign exchange is referred to as an *over-the-counter* or OTC market. Physical currency is rarely paid out or received. What happens in practice is that currency is transferred electronically from one bank account to another.

DERIVATIVES

Derivative securities, more appropriately termed as *derivative contracts*, are assets which confer upon their owners certain rights or obligations, as the case may be. These contracts owe their availability to the existence of markets for an underlying asset or a portfolio of assets, on which such agreements are written. In other words, these assets are derived from the underlying asset. If we perceive the underlying asset as the primary asset, then such contracts may be termed as derivatives, as they are derived from such assets.

The three major categories of derivative securities are:

- Forward and futures contracts
- Options contracts
- Swaps

FORWARD AND FUTURES CONTRACTS

A typical transaction, where the exchange of cash for the asset being procured takes place immediately, is referred to as a cash or a spot transaction. As soon as the deal is struck, the buyer hands over the payment for the asset to the seller, who in turn transfers the rights to the asset to the buyer at the same time. In the case of a forward or a futures contract, however, the actual transaction does not take place at the moment an agreement is reached between the two parties. What happens in such cases is that at the time of negotiating the deal, the two parties merely agree on the terms on which they will transact at a future point in time. The actual transaction per se occurs only at a future date that is decided at the outset, and at a price that also is decided at the beginning. Thus, no money changes hands when two parties enter into such contracts; however, both the parties to the contract have an obligation to go ahead with the transaction on the predetermined date, as per the agreed terms. Failure to do so will be tantamount to default.

EXAMPLE 1.1

WIPRO Technologies, an Indian company, has imported products from Frankfurt, and has entered into a forward contract with HSBC to acquire EUR 500,000 after 60 days at an exchange rate of INR 72.50 per euro. This is clearly a forward contract, for while the terms and conditions, including the exchange rate, are fixed at the outset, the currency itself will be procured only 60 days after the date of the agreement. Sixty days hence, WIPRO will be required to pay INR 36,250,000 to the bank and accept the euros. The bank as per the contract is obliged to accept the Indian currency and deliver the euros.

Forward contracts and futures contracts are similar in the sense that both oblige the buyer to acquire the underlying asset on a future date, and the seller to deliver the asset on that date. And in the case of either kind of security, both the buyer and the seller have an obligation to perform at the time of expiration of the contract. There is one major difference between the two types of contracts, however. Futures contracts are standardized, whereas forward contracts are customized. The terms *standardization* and *customization* may be understood as follows. In any contract of this nature, certain terms and conditions need to be clearly defined. The major terms which should be made explicit are the following:

1. The number of units of the underlying asset that have to be delivered per contract.
2. The acceptable grade or grades that may be delivered by the seller.
3. The place or places where the seller is permitted to deliver.
4. The date or in certain cases the time interval, during which the seller has to deliver.

In a customized contract, the preceding terms and conditions have to be negotiated between the buyer and the seller of the contract. Hence, the two parties are at liberty to incorporate any features that they can mutually agree to. Forward contracts come under this category. In standardized contracts, however, there is a third party that will specify the allowable terms and conditions. The two parties to the contract have to design the terms and conditions within the framework specified by the third party and cannot incorporate features other than those that are specifically allowed. The third party in the case of futures contracts is the futures exchange, which is the trading arena where such contracts are bought and sold.

OPTIONS CONTRACTS

As mentioned, both forward and futures contracts, despite the differences inherent in their structures, impose an obligation on the buyer and the seller. Thus, the buyer is obliged to take delivery of the underlying asset on the date that is agreed upon at the outset, while the seller is obliged to make delivery of the asset on that date and accept cash in lieu.

Options contracts are different. Unlike the buyer of a forward or a futures contract, the buyer of an options contract has the right to go ahead with the transaction, subsequent to entering into an agreement with the seller of the option. The difference between a right and an obligation is that a right need be exercised only if it is in the interest of its holders, and if they deem it appropriate. Thus, the buyer or holder of the contract does not face a compulsion to subsequently go through with the transaction. However, the seller of such contracts always has an obligation to perform if the buyer were to deem it appropriate to exercise that right.

EXAMPLE 1.2

Peter Norton has acquired an options contract that gives him the right to buy 100 shares of ABC at a price of 42.50 per share after three months from Mike Selvey. If the price of ABC shares after three months were to be greater than $42.50 per share, it would obviously make sense for Peter to exercise his right and acquire the shares. Otherwise, if the share price were to be lower than $42.50, he can simply forget the option, and buy the shares in the spot market at a lower price. Notice that he is under no compulsion to exercise the option, for it confers a right on the holder, and does not impose an obligation. If Peter were to decide to exercise his right to buy, however, Mike would have no choice but to deliver the shares at a price of $42.50 per share. Thus, options contracts always impose a performance obligation on the seller of the option, if the option holder were to exercise that right. The reason is that when two parties enter into an agreement for a transaction that is scheduled for a future date, then at the time of expiration of the contract, a price move which translates into a profit for one of the two parties will obviously lead to a loss for the other. Hence, we cannot have a contract that confers both the parties with the right to perform, for the party who is confronted with a loss will simply refuse to perform. Thus, either we can have contracts that impose an obligation on both parties, such as forward and futures contracts, or we can have a contract that confers a right on one party and imposes an obligation on the other, which is essentially what an options contract does.

When a person is given a right to transact in the underlying asset, the right can obviously take on one of two forms. That is, that person may either have the right to buy the underlying asset, or the right to sell the underlying asset. Options contracts that give the holder the right to acquire the underlying asset are known as Call options. If the buyer of such an option were to exercise that right, the seller of the option is obliged to deliver the underlying asset as per the terms of the contract. Peter, in the previous example, obviously possesses a call option.

There exist options contracts that give the holder the right to sell the underlying asset. These are known as Put options. In the case of such contracts, if the holder were to decide to exercise his option, the seller of the put is obliged to take delivery of the underlying asset.

Options give the holder the right to buy or sell the underlying asset. If the contract were to permit exercise only at the time of expiration, the option, whether a call or a put, is known as a European option. If such an option were not to be exercised at the time of expiration, then the contract itself would expire. There exists another type of contract, where the holder has the right to transact at any point between the time of acquisition of the right and the expiration date of the contract. These are referred to as American options. Quite obviously, the expiration date is the only point in time at which a European option can be exercised, and the last point in time at which an American option can be exercised.

An options contract, whether a call or a put, requires the buyer to pay a price to the seller at the outset, for giving the right to transact. This price is known as the option price or option premium. This price is nonrefundable if the contract were not to be exercised subsequently. If and when an options contract is exercised, the buyer will have to pay a price per unit of the underlying asset if exercising a call option, and will have to receive a price per unit of the underlying asset if exercising a put option. This price is known as the *exercise price* or the *strike price*. The difference between the two prices is that while the option premium has to be paid at the very outset, the exercise price enters the picture only if the option is exercised subsequently. Thus, the exercise price may or may not be paid/received eventually. Futures contracts are termed as *commitment contracts*, for they represent a binding commitment for both parties. Options, on the other hand, are termed as *contingent contracts* for they will be exercised by the holder only in the event of it being profitable. In the case of calls, this will be contingent on the asset price being greater than the exercise price, whereas in the case of puts, it will be contingent on the asset price being lower than the exercise price.

Futures and forward contracts, however, do not require either party to make a payment at the outset, because they impose an equivalent obligation on both the buyer and the seller. The futures price, which is the price at which the buyer will acquire the asset on a future date, will be set in such a way that the value of the futures contract at inception is zero, from the standpoint of both the buyer as well as the seller.

SWAPS

A swap is a contractual agreement between two parties to exchange cash flows calculated on the basis of prespecified terms at predefined points in time.

The cash flows being exchanged represent interest payments on a specified principal amount, which are computed using two different yardsticks. For instance, one interest payment may be computed using a fixed rate of interest, while the other may be based on a variable benchmark such as the T-bill rate.

A swap where both payments are denominated in the same currency is referred to as an Interest Rate Swap. The motivation for such a transaction may be understood as follows. Consider the case of a commercial bank that has entered into a fixed rate loan with one of its clients. It may now be of the opinion that interest rates are going to rise. Renegotiation of the loan may not be feasible. Even if it were, it would involve substantial legal and administrative efforts. It would be much easier for the bank concerned to enter into a swap transaction with an institution, perhaps another commercial bank, wherein it pays a fixed rate of interest and receives a variable rate based on a benchmark such as LIBOR. By doing so it would have converted its fixed rate income stream to a floating rate income stream and would stand to benefit if interest rates rise as anticipated. Thus, in a nutshell, the objective of a swap is to enable a party to dispose of a cash flow stream in exchange for another cash flow stream. Diagrammatically we can depict the above transaction as follows (Figure 1.1).

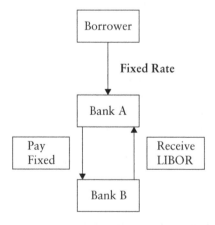

FIGURE 1.1

There also exist swaps where two parties exchange cash flows denominated in two different currencies. Such swaps are referred to as Currency Swaps.

MORTGAGES AND MORTGAGE-BACKED SECURITIES

A mortgage is a loan that is backed by the collateral of specified real estate property. The borrower of funds, the mortgagor, is obliged to make periodic payments to the lender, the mortgagee, to retire the debt. In the event of the mortgagor defaulting, the lender can foreclose the mortgage, which means that the lender can take over the property to recover the balance due.

A mortgage by itself is an illiquid asset for the party that makes the loan to the home buyer. Such lenders are called originators. To rotate their capital, lenders will typically pool mortgage loans and issue debt securities backed by the underlying pool. Such securities, the cash flows for which arise from the payments made by borrowers of the underlying loans, are referred to as mortgage-backed securities. The process of converting an illiquid asset such as a home loan into liquid marketable securities is referred to as *securitization*. The process of securitization, although it is common in the case of mortgage lending, is not restricted to such loans. In practice, receivables from automobile loans and credit card receivables are also securitized. The securities generated in the process are referred to as *asset-backed* securities.

HYBRID SECURITIES

A hybrid security combines the features of more than one type of basic security. We will discuss two such assets, namely convertible bonds and warrants.

A convertible bond is a debt security that permits the investor to convert the bond into shares of equity at a predetermined rate. Until and unless the investor converts the bond, it will continue to trade in the form of a standard debt security. The interest rate on such bonds will be lower than the rate on securities without the option to convert because the conversion feature will be perceived as a sweetener by potential investors. The rate of conversion from debt into equity will typically be set in such a way that the conversion price is higher than the market price prevailing at the time of issue of the debt. For instance, a bond with a principal value of $1,000 may be convertible to 25 shares of equity. In this case the conversion price is $40, and the share price prevailing at the time of issue of the convertible will be less than $40.

A warrant is a right given to investors which allows them to subscribe to the equity shares of the company at a future date at a predetermined price. Such rights are usually offered along with debt securities to make the bonds more attractive to investors. Once issued, the warrants can be detached from the parent security, and can be traded in the secondary market.

PRIMARY MARKETS AND SECONDARY MARKETS

The function of a primary market is to facilitate the acquisition of new financial instruments by investors, both institutional and individual. Thus, when a company goes in for an issue of equity shares to the public it will be termed as a primary market transaction. Similarly, if the government were to raise funds by issuing Treasury bonds, it will once again be termed as a primary market transaction.

Once a financial asset has been created and sold to an investor in the primary market, subsequent transactions in that instrument between two investors are said to take place in the secondary market. For instance, assume that GE went in for a public issue of five million shares out of which Frank Reitz was allotted 10,000 shares. This would obviously be termed as a primary market transaction. Now assume that, six months hence, Frank sells the shares to Mike Pierce on the New York Stock Exchange. This would obviously constitute a secondary market transaction. Thus, while primary markets are used by governments and business entities to raise medium- to long-term capital for making productive investments, secondary markets merely facilitate the transfer of ownership of an asset from one party to another.

Primary markets by themselves are insufficient to ensure the functioning of the free market system. That is, secondary markets are a sine qua non for the efficient operation of the market economy. Why is this so? Consider an economy without a secondary market. In such an economy, an investor who subscribes to a debt issue would obviously have to hold on to it until its date of maturity. In the case of equity shares, the problem will be more serious, for such securities never mature. Consequently, acquirers of shares in a primary market transaction and future generations of their family would have no option but to hold the shares for ever. In practice, no investor will make an investment unless they are confident there exists an avenue for a subsequent sale if they were to decide they no longer required it.

The ability to trade in a security after acquiring it in a primary market transaction is important for two reasons. First, one of the key reasons for investing in financial assets is that they can always be liquidated or converted into cash. In practice, such needs can never be perfectly predicted, and consequently investors would desire access to markets that facilitate the ready conversion of securities to cash and vice versa. Second, most investors do not hold their wealth in the form of a single asset but prefer to hold a basket or portfolio of securities. As the old adage says, "Don't keep all your eggs in one basket." Thus, a prudent investor would seek to diversify wealth among various asset classes such as stocks, bonds, real estate, and precious metals such as gold. In practice this kind of diversification will usually be taken a step further in the sense that the entire wealth that an investor has earmarked to be held in stocks will not be invested in the shares of a single company like IBM. That is, a rational investor will diversify across industries, and within an industry they will choose to invest in multiple companies. The logic is that all the companies are unlikely to experience difficulties at the same time. For instance, if the workers at GM were to be on strike, it is not necessary that workers at Ford should also be on strike at the same point in time. Consequently, if one segment of the portfolio were to be experiencing difficulties, the odds are that another segment would be doing well and will hence tend to pull up the performance of the portfolio.

Secondary markets are critical from the standpoint of holding a diversified portfolio of assets. In real life, investors' propensity to take risk does not stay constant over their life cycle. We know that debt securities promise contractually guaranteed rates of return and are paid off on a priority basis in the event of liquidation. On the other hand, equity shareholders are residual claimants who are entitled to payments only if there were to be a surplus after taking care of the other creditors. Thus, the risk of a debt investment will be lower as compared to an equivalent equity investment. Young investors who are having steady and appreciating income usually have a greater capacity to take risk, and consequently tend to invest more in equity securities. Even from the standpoint of equity shares, young investors are less concerned about steady dividend payments and tend to focus more on the odds of getting significant capital gains in the medium to long term. Senior citizens, on the other hand, want predictable periodic income from their investments and have little appetite for risk. Such investors therefore tend to hold a greater fraction of their wealth in debt securities. If and when such investors acquire equity shares, they display a marked preference for high-dividend-paying and less risky stocks.

Thus, as they grow older, investors periodically make perceptible changes in the composition of their portfolios. Young single investors who have recently secured employment may be willing to take more risks and would probably put a greater percentage of their wealth in equities. Later, as the family grows and investors approach middle age with children ready to go to college, they will probably distribute wealth more or less evenly between debt and equities. A similar redistribution of wealth across asset classes is observed when an investor approaches retirement. Elderly investors tend to have their wealth primarily in the form of debt securities. There is a saying in financial markets that an investor should allocate a percentage of his wealth to equity shares that is equal to 100 minus his age. That is, a person who is 30 years old should have 70% of their wealth in equities, whereas a person who is 70 years old should have 30% of their wealth in equities. Another way of stating this is that the percentage of wealth that is invested in debt securities should be equal to the investor's age.

Hence, from the standpoints of providing liquidity and permitting portfolio rebalancing, it is important to have active secondary markets. The absence of such markets would severely affect individuals' willingness to save, and consequently lower the level of investment in the economy.

EXCHANGES AND OVER-THE-COUNTER (OTC) MARKETS

A securities exchange is an organized trading system where traders interact to buy and sell securities. Thus, a securities exchange is a secondary market for securities. Public traders cannot directly trade on these exchanges but are required to route their orders through a securities broker who is a member of the exchange. Historically, trading took place on a trading floor, where member brokers would congregate and seek to match buy and sell requests received from their clients. These days most exchanges are electronic markets. Traders do not get to interact face-to-face but are required to key in their orders into a computer terminal which conveys the orders to a central processing system. The procedure for matching and executing orders is coded into the software.

There are two types of orders that can be placed by an investor. In the case of market orders, investors merely specify the quantity they seek, with the understanding that they will accept whatever price is offered. However, investors who are very particular about the price they pay or receive will place what are known as limit orders. The limit orders require not only the specification of the quantity sought, but also a limit price. The limit price is a ceiling in the case of buyers, that is, it represents the maximum amount that the investor is willing to pay. In the case of sell orders, the limit price is a floor, which represents the lowest price at which the investor is willing to sell. To ensure that traders are given access to the best available prices, all limit buy orders are ranked in descending order of price, while limit sell orders are ranked in ascending order of price. This is known as the price priority rule. Thus, potential buyers are given access to the lowest price on the sell side while potential sellers are given access to the highest price on the buy side. If two or more limit buy or sell orders were to have the same limit price, then the order that came in first would be ranked higher. This is known as the time priority rule.

The newer exchanges like EUREX in Frankfurt are fully automated electronic systems. Some of the older exchanges have changed with the times and have abandoned their trading rings or floors and have embraced electronic trading platforms. However, some of the other older exchanges continue to operate with a hybrid model. The New York Stock Exchange and the CME Group continue to run floor-based and screen-based trading platforms in parallel.

An over-the-counter or OTC network is an informal network of securities brokers and dealers who are linked by phone and fax connections. Most deals on such markets tend to be institutional in nature and are of sizeable volumes. The foreign exchange market globally is an OTC market, and most of the trading in bonds also takes place on such markets.

BROKERS AND DEALERS

A broker is an intermediary who arranges trades for clients by helping them to locate suitable counterparties. The broker's compensation is in the form of a commission paid by the client. Brokers do not finance the transaction, in the sense that they do not carry an inventory of the asset(s) being sought. They are merely facilitators of the trade, who receive a processing fee for the services rendered. Brokers are very common in real estate markets. For instance, if we were to contemplate the purchase of a house, we would approach a realtor, who will have a list of properties whose owners have evinced interest in selling. Realtors do not own an inventory of houses they have financed.

A dealer, on the other hand, is a market intermediary who carries an inventory of the asset in which he is making a market. Thus, unlike a broker, a dealer has funds locked up in the asset. Effectively, a dealer takes over the trading problem of the client. If the client is seeking to sell, the dealer will buy the asset from them in anticipation of the latter's ability to resell it subsequently at a higher price. Similarly, when a client wishes to buy the asset, the dealer will sell the asset from their inventory in the hope of being able to replenish their stock subsequently at a lower price. Thus, in order to ensure profits from trading activities, a dealer has to be a master of the art of trading. In developed countries, dealers will usually specialize in narrow segments of the securities market. That is, some will handle Treasury bonds, while others may choose to specialize in municipal debt securities. This is because, considering the volumes of transactions, skill is of the essence, and even small errors could lead to huge losses, given the magnitude of the deals.

How do dealers make money? Obviously, the price they quote for acquiring an asset will be less than the price at which they hope to sell to another party. The price at which a dealer is willing to buy from a client is called the bid and the price at which the dealer is willing to sell to a client is called the ask. The difference between the bid and the ask is called the bid–ask spread, or quite simply *the spread*. Dealers seek to make money by rapidly rotating their inventories. A purchase at the bid followed by a subsequent sale at the ask will result in a profit equal to the spread. Such a transaction is termed as a *round-trip transaction*. Dealers doing many round-trip transactions can survive on a lower spread. However, if transactions are few and far between, then the spreads will be high. In other words, if the volumes are high, then margins can be low. However, if the volumes are low, then the margins need to be high.

Many dealers don the mantle of both brokers and dealers. Thus, in certain transactions they will act as trade facilitators who provide services in anticipation of a commission, while in other cases they will position themselves on one side of the trade, by either buying or selling securities. Such dealers are called dual traders. A transaction where the dealer functions merely as a broker is referred to as an agency trade. However, a trade where the dealer is one of the parties to the transaction is termed as a proprietary trade.

Dealers who undertake to provide continuous two-way price quotes are referred to as market makers. Their role is to create a liquid secondary market. On the New York Stock Exchange (NYSE) there is only one market maker for a security. However, one dealer may make a market in multiple securities. This monopolist market maker is referred to as a *specialist*, and is also known as an *assigned dealer* because that role has been assigned by the exchange. When a company seeks to list its securities on the exchange, a number of potential market makers will express their desire to act as the specialist for the stock being introduced. They will be interviewed by representatives of the company as well as the exchange, and finally one of them will be selected as the specialist for that particular stock. There are also interdealer brokers who act as intermediaries for trades between market makers.

THE NEED FOR BROKERS AND DEALERS

Why do we require market intermediaries such as brokers and dealers? The reason is that when investors seek to buy or sell assets in the secondary market, they have to locate a suitable counterparty. Thus, a potential buyer needs to locate a seller and vice versa. Second, not only should a counterparty be available, there should be compatibility in terms of price expectations of the two parties, and the quantity that each of them is seeking to transact. Every trader seeks to trade at a price that is good from their own standpoint. Buyers will therefore be on the lookout for sellers who are willing to offer securities at prices which are less than or equal to what they are willing to pay. Similarly, sellers will seek to locate buyers who are willing to offer a price which is greater than or equal to the price at which they are willing to sell. As we have explained earlier, limit orders are arranged in descending order of the limit price on the buy side and in ascending order of the limit price on the sell side. Thus, buyers are guaranteed access to the lowest prices quoted by sellers while sellers are guaranteed access to the highest prices quoted by buyers. In addition, it is important that the quantity on offer matches the quantity being demanded. Often a large buy or sell order may require more than one trader to take the opposite position before execution.

On an organized exchange it is necessary to go through a broker or a dealer for certain reasons. First, access to the exchange is provided to only registered brokers and dealers. For exchanges that are totally automated, only brokers and dealers will have terminals through which orders can be routed to the central processing system of the exchange. Thus, it is essential for a public trader to go through a licensed market intermediary. Of course, big institutional investors may be provided with order routing systems so that they can seamlessly send orders to the exchange via the intermediary. Similarly, Internet brokers facilitate the access of electronic exchanges by retail clients. On exchanges with floor-based trading, only regular traders will be familiar with the jargon and protocol required for trading. Allowing a novice to step in would cause unnecessary chaos and confusion.

The other reason why exchanges insist on dealing with market intermediaries is to reduce the possibility of settlement failure. The term *settlement* refers to the delivery of securities from the seller to the buyer and the delivery of cash from the buyer to the seller. Default on the part of either party to a transaction can substantially dent the public's confidence in the system. To prevent settlement failure, exchanges have elaborate risk management systems in place. Market intermediaries are required to post performance guarantees or collateral called margins with the exchanges to rule out the possibility of a failed trade. Obviously, it makes sense for a party to have such a financial relationship with the exchange only if trading regularly and in large volumes. For public traders who trade relatively infrequently, it will not be practical to develop such an arrangement with the exchange. However, brokers and dealers who either trade regularly on their own account and/or have a large number of trades routed through them will find it worth the cost and effort to have such a financial relationship with the exchange.

The brokerage industry has now been deregulated in most countries. Prior to deregulation, a minimum brokerage fee was specified by the authorities. What was therefore happening in practice was that institutional clients were subsidizing retail clients. That is, institutional clients were paying more than they ought to have, considering the magnitude of their transactions, while retail investors were paying less than what they ought to have paid. The immediate impact of deregulation was a sharp increase in retail brokerage rates. However, a brand-new industry was born as a consequence, which is termed as *discount brokerage*. A regular broker, referred to as a *full-service broker*, will sit one-on-one with the client seeking to ascertain their investment objectives in order to provide suitable recommendations. The broker will also provide extensive research reports to facilitate decision making. A discount broker, on the other hand, will offer no advice. This broker's only task is to execute orders placed by clients. There is also a category of brokers referred to as deep-discount brokers. These brokers also provide no investment-related advice, but they insist on transactions of a substantial magnitude and charge commissions that are even lower than what are levied by discount brokers.

TRADING POSITIONS

Traders are said to have a long position when they own an asset. An investor with a long position will gain if the price subsequently rises and will lose if it were to fall subsequently. A rise in price will constitute a capital gain at the time of sale, whereas a price decline would be termed as a capital loss. The principle behind the assumption of such a position is: buy low and sell high. Investors who take long positions in anticipation of rising prices are said to be bullish in nature and are termed as bulls.

All traders in the market need not be bullish about the future. Some may be of the opinion that prices are going to decline. Such investors will assume what are termed as short positions. Traders are said to have taken a short position when they have sold an asset they do not own. In practice, this is accomplished by borrowing the asset from another investor. Such a transaction is called a short sale. In such cases, traders will have to eventually purchase the asset and return it to the lender. If their reading of the market is correct, and prices do decline by the time the asset is bought back to close out the position, they stand to make a profit. When someone with a short position acquires the asset, they are said to be covering their position. Short sellers, therefore, seek to sell high and buy low. Short-selling is considered a bearish activity and such investors are termed as bears.

THE BUY-SIDE AND THE SELL-SIDE

The trading industry can be classified into a buy-side and a sell-side. The buy-side consists of traders who seek to buy the services being offered by the exchange. The traders on the sell-side are those who are offering the services of the exchange. Thus, the terms buy-side and sell-side have no implications for the purchase and sale of securities. Traders on both sides of the market regularly buy and sell securities.

Of all the services offered by the exchange, the key is liquidity. The sell-side traders sell liquidity to the buy-side traders by giving them the opportunity to trade whenever they desire. The buy-side consists of individuals, investment funds, institutions, and governments that use the markets to achieve objectives like cash flow management and/or risk management. The sell-side consists of brokers and dealers who help buy-side traders to trade at their convenience.

INVESTMENT BANKERS

An investment banker is an investment professional who facilitates the issuance of securities in the primary market. These institutions help the issue process in two ways. First, they help the borrower to comply with various legal and procedural requirements that are usually mandatory for such issues. For instance, a prospectus or an offer document must accompany any solicitation efforts for the issue. Most issues have to be registered with the capital markets regulator of the country, which is the Securities and Exchange Commission (SEC) in the United States. Finally, most issues are listed on at least one stock exchange. Listing is a process by which an exchange formally admits the issue for trading between investors, after the securities have been allotted. An IT firm or an automobile manufacturer will be clueless about the latest regulations and procedures. Hence, they require professional advice to facilitate a successful issue of securities, and this is where investment banks can help.

Second, investment bankers provide insurance to the issuer by underwriting the issue. This means that they stand ready to buy that portion of the issue which remains unsubscribed, if the issue were to be undersubscribed. Underwriting helps in two ways. First, it reduces the risk for the issuer. Second, it sends a positive signal to the potential investors about the quality of the issue, since the investment banker stands ready to buy whatever they choose not to subscribe to. To give an example, consider an issue that has been underwritten by UBS. This means that if investors do not subscribe to the entire amount on offer, UBS will accept the remainder. This would reassure a potential investor, for obviously a bank like UBS would not give such an undertaking without doing its homework. In certain cases, an investment bank may not desire to take upon itself the entire risk of a new security issue, for the issue may be very large, or else may be perceived to be extra risky. Consequently, a group of investment banks may underwrite the issue together, thereby spreading the risk. This is called syndicated underwriting. The chief underwriter is referred to as the lead manager. The next rung of investment bankers are referred to as co-managers. There is also a selling group associated with most issues. It consists of relatively smaller investment banks, who do not underwrite the issue, but who have been roped in because of their expertise in marketing such issues in their zones of influence.

At times the investment bank, instead of underwriting the issue, will offer to sell it on a best efforts basis. That is, the bank will merely offer to do its level best to ensure that the issue is fully subscribed. In these cases, the investment bank merely performs a marketing function without providing the insurance that characterizes the process of underwriting. Consequently, the bank's commission in such cases will be lower.

Most public offerings are usually underwritten because issuers are more comfortable with such arrangements. This is because the investment bank has a greater incentive to sell the securities when there is a risk of devolvement. What is devolvement risk? It is the risk that the bank may have to buy the unsold securities in the event of undersubscription. Such an eventuality will inevitably lead to a loss for the bank, in the sense that the shares so acquired will have to be subsequently offloaded in the market at a price that is lower than the issue price. This is because devolvement is a clear sign of negative market sentiments about the issue, and an issue that fails will experience a fall in price on listing.

DIRECT AND INDIRECT MARKETS

In a direct market, the surplus budget units in the economy deal directly with the deficit budget units. That is, funds flow directly from the ultimate lenders to the ultimate borrowers. For instance, if 3M were to be making a public issue of shares and an investor were to purchase them, then it would be termed as a direct market transaction. Similarly, if the government were to issue bonds to individual as well as institutional investors, it too would constitute a direct market transaction. In practice, an issuer of equity shares or debt securities can do so either through a public issue or through a private placement. A public issue entails the sale of the issue to a large and diverse body of investors, both retail and institutional. Such issues are usually underwritten by an investment banker. In the case of private placements, which are more common for debt issues, the issuer will sell the entire issue directly to a single institution or a group of institutions.

In the case of indirect financing the ultimate lender does not interact with the ultimate borrower. There is a financial intermediary who in such markets comes in between the eventual borrower and the ultimate lender. The role of such an intermediary is, however, very different from that of a broker-dealer or an investment banker, who too are financial intermediaries albeit in a different sense.

A classic example of a financial intermediary in an indirect market is a commercial bank. Take the case of a bank like BNP Paribas. It raises deposits from individual and institutional investors. From the standpoint of the depositor, who is the surplus unit in this case, the bank is the corresponding deficit unit. The bank will issue its financial claims to the depositors for whom these claims will constitute an asset. A bank passbook, or computerized statement, or a certificate issued in lieu of a longer-term deposit, is a manifestation of such a claim. The rate of interest on such claims is the rate of return for the depositors. The risk for such depositors is that the bank could fail. If so, they may lose all or a part of their deposits. In the United States bank deposits up to $100,000 are insured by the Federal Deposit Insurance Corporation (FDIC).

After accumulating funds by way of deposits, the bank will then lend to corporate and noncorporate entities in need of funds. For such borrowers, the bank is the surplus budget unit, and for the bank they constitute the deficit units. The bank will hold claims issued by such borrowers in return for the funds lent to them and will be entitled to all cash flows emanating from them. Obviously, the bank is exposed to the risk that the borrowing entities could go bankrupt.

As can be seen, the link between the ultimate lenders and the ultimate borrowers is broken by a financial intermediary such as a bank in the case of indirect markets. The ultimate lenders, that is, the deposit holders at the bank, have no claim on the assets of the eventual borrowers, nor do they have a claim on the cash flows generated by such assets. It is the bank that has a claim on such assets and the corresponding cash flows. The depositors have a claim solely against the bank and are dependent on its performance in order to get the promised return on their savings. Besides commercial banks, other financial intermediaries in indirect markets include insurance companies, mutual funds, and pension funds.

MUTUAL FUNDS

A mutual fund is a financial intermediary in the indirect financial market. It is a collection of stocks, bonds, and other assets that are purchased by pooling the investments made by a large group of investors. The assets of the fund are managed by a professional investment company.

When investors make an investment in a mutual fund, their money is pooled with that of other investors who have chosen to invest in the fund. The pooled sum is used to build an investment portfolio if the fund is just commencing its operations, or to expand its portfolio if it is already in business. The investors receive shares of the fund in proportion to the amount of money they have invested. When a fund is offering shares for the first time, known as an Initial Public Offering or IPO, the shares will be issued at par. Subsequent issues of shares will be made at a price that is based on what is known as the Net Asset Value (NAV) of the fund. The Net Asset Value of a fund at any point in time is equal to the total value of all securities in its portfolio less any outstanding liabilities, divided by the total number of shares issued by the fund.

There are two broad categories of mutual funds, open-ended and closed-ended. Open-ended funds permit investors to acquire and redeem shares at any point in time, at the prevailing NAV. Thus, the capital of these funds is variable. Closed-ended funds make a one-time issue of shares to investors; however, such funds are usually listed on a stock exchange, which ensures that investors have the freedom to trade. Shares of such funds may be priced above or below the prevailing NAV.

The NAV will fluctuate from day to day as the value of the securities held by the fund changes. On a given day, from the perspective of shareholders, the NAV may be higher or lower than the price they paid per share at the time of acquisition. Thus, just like the shareholders of a corporation, mutual fund owners partake in the profits and losses as well as in the income and expenses of the fund.

One of the advantages of a direct market transaction is that the borrower and lender can save on the margin that would otherwise go to the intermediary to the transaction. After all, how does a depository institution like a bank make profits? Obviously, the rate of interest it pays to its depositors will be lower than the interest rate it charges borrowers who avail of loans. This profit margin is called the Net Interest Margin. So, if the borrowing firms could directly interact with parties who would otherwise deposit their funds with a bank, then they could profitably share the spread, which would otherwise constitute income for the bank. We will illustrate this with the help of an example.

EXAMPLE 1.3

First National Bank is accepting deposits at the rate of 3.50% per annum and is lending to companies at 4.50% per annum. Thus, the bank has a margin of 1% of the transaction amount. Now assume that the borrowing companies opt to directly issue debt securities to the public, with an interest rate of 4.00% per annum. If so, the investors would be getting 0.50% more than what they would were they to deposit their funds with a bank. The issuing companies too stand to incur an interest cost that is 0.50% less. Thus, both the parties to the transaction stand to benefit. What we have essentially done is that the profit margin of 1% which was going to the bank has been split 50/50 between the lending public and the borrowing firm. In practice the split need not be 50/50. All that is required is that the total benefit to the two counterparties should be 1%. Hence, a borrower with a high credit rating can directly tap the capital market without going through an intermediary.

Of course, if direct markets were to be all about advantages, then obviously indirect markets will fail to exist. There are certain shortcomings of such markets. One of the major problems in the case of direct markets is that the claims the borrower wants to issue are often not exactly of the type that individual investors want. Such problems could arise with respect to the denomination of the issue, or the maturity of the issue, or both.

For instance, take the case of a firm that is issuing securities with a principal value of $5,000. It will automatically lose access to investors who seek to invest less than that amount. This is known as the denomination problem. Second, in practice, borrowers like to borrow long-term. This is because most projects tend to be long-term in nature, and entrepreneurs would like to avoid approaching the market at frequent intervals in order to raise funds. But lenders usually prefer to commit their funds for relatively shorter periods. Thus, a company issuing debt securities with twenty years to maturity may find that it has few takers if it were to approach the public directly. This is referred to as the maturity problem.

Yet another problem with direct markets is that they are highly dependent on active secondary markets for their success. If the secondary market were to be relatively inactive, borrowers would find it difficult to tap the primary market. This is because most individuals who invest in debt and equity issues place a premium on liquidity and ready marketability, as manifested by an active secondary market. In times of recession, the secondary markets will be less active than normal, and such periods are therefore usually characterized by small and less frequent issues of fresh securities.

Besides, for an issuer of claims, the cost of a public issue can be high. Such issues require a prospectus and application forms to be printed and also require aggressive marketing. This is obviously not cheap. The investment banker has to be paid his fees, which can be substantial in practice. Finally, the issuing firm needs to hire other professionals like lawyers, CPAs, and public relations firms, whose services will also have to be paid for.

As we have discussed, companies that issue financial claims directly to the public find that many potential investors find the denomination and/or maturity of the securities offered to be unsuitable. Financial intermediaries, however, are able to resolve these issues, for they have the ability to invest relatively large amounts and for long periods of time. This is despite the fact that for a depository institution such as a bank, the average deposit may not be for a very large amount, and most deposits tend to be for relatively short periods. We say that such intermediaries are able to perform denomination transformation and maturity transformation.

Intermediaries like banks are able to effect such transformations because they sell their own claims to the public and, after pooling the funds so garnered, purchase financial claims from the borrowing entities. A large commercial bank will have many depositors ranging from those who deposit a few dollars to those who deposit a few million dollars. Similarly, a mutual fund will have investors ranging from those who seek to buy 100 shares to those seeking to acquire 100,000 shares. Since these institutions cumulatively receive funds on a large scale, they can profitably transform the relatively smaller amounts deposited with them into large loans for commercial borrowers. This is the essence of denomination transformation.

As mentioned earlier, most borrowers prefer to borrow long-term due to the nature of the projects they are executing. Lenders, on the contrary, like relatively short-term liquid assets that can be converted to cash on demand. Banks can pool short-term deposits and package them into medium- to long-term loans. They are in a position to do so because the deposits will periodically get rolled over, either because of renewal by existing depositors or on account of new depositors. Similarly, in the case of an open-ended mutual fund, share redemptions during a given day will be accompanied by fresh investments by either existing or new investors.

Financial intermediaries in the indirect market are also able to provide their depositors with risk management and risk diversification. All rational investors dislike risk and are said to be risk averse. This does not, however, mean that people will not take risks while investing. For, after all, every financial market transaction is fraught with a degree of risk. It is just that the magnitude varies from transaction to transaction and from instrument to instrument. The term *risk aversion* connotes that, for a given level of expected return, an investor will prefer that alternative that has the least risk associated with it. Put differently, while considering an investment in assets with the same degree of associated risk, an investor will choose the security that has the highest expected return. Alternatively, if the choice is between two assets with the same expected return, the investor will choose the one that has lower risk.

Intermediaries like banks have considerable expertise in dealing with risk as compared to individual investors. Thus, investors who lend indirectly through a bank can be assured that their funds will be deployed by the bank after doing a more thorough evaluation of the credit worthiness of the borrower than what they themselves could have done had they chosen to lend directly.

There is another dimension to the role played by banks from the standpoint of risk. We have already discussed the principle of diversification. That is, it is optimal to hold one's wealth in a portfolio of securities. However, in reality it is not easy for an individual investor to construct a well-diversified portfolio. Most individual investors will have a relatively small corpus of funds at their disposal and extensive diversification will be neither feasible nor cost-effective considering the magnitude of transactions costs that they are likely to incur. An intermediary like a bank has a large pool of funds at its disposal and therefore invests across a spectrum of projects from the standpoint of risk. Thus, depositors are assured that every dollar they deposit is effectively being lent to multiple borrowers, thereby ensuring diversification.

Financial intermediaries are also able to derive substantial economies of scale. That is, their fixed costs of operation get spread over a vast pool of transactions and assets. They are therefore able to ensure that they are relatively cost-efficient, and this benefit will be passed on to the depositors to a degree. We will illustrate the concept of economies of scale with a simple illustration.

EXAMPLE 1.4

Take the case of a business operation that costs $5,000 to mount and $2.50 per unit that is processed. If 2,000 units were to be processed, the cost per unit would be $5. If the number of units processed were to be 20,000, however, then the cost per unit would be only $2.75. Of course, the cost per unit cannot be reduced beyond a limit. This is because as the production volume increases, at a point in time the fixed costs will have to be incurred again, for a given production structure can support output only up to a point.

MONEY AND CAPITAL MARKETS

One of the ways of classifying financial markets is based on the original term to maturity of the financial claims that are traded. The market in which instruments with one year or less to maturity are traded is called the money market, whereas the market in which medium- to long-term instruments are traded is called a capital market. Obviously, all money market securities have to be debt securities since equity shares never mature. Capital market securities can be equity securities or medium- to long-term debt securities.

The two markets differ fundamentally from the standpoint of their roles in a market economy. Money markets provide a means for economic agents to adjust their liquidity positions. As we discussed at the outset, every economic agent will receive some form of income in a financial year and also incur some form of expenditure; however, for any economic unit, it will rarely be the case that cash inflows and outflows are perfectly matched with respect to their timing. The mismatch between inflows and outflows leads to short-term deficits and surpluses, which are bridged by borrowing and lending in the money market.

Consider the case of a government. Revenue comes primarily in the form of taxes and is lumpy in nature. However, expenses are incurred on a daily basis. Consequently, if the government were to have a budget surplus, which is rare in practice, for most governments have budget deficits, during most of the year there will be a deficit. Consequently, governments need to constantly borrow to meet the shortfalls. Similarly, a business may have a substantial profit in a financial year but may have a cash deficit on most days. Thus, it would need to borrow periodically to bridge the shortfall.

A capital market, on the other hand, performs a very different economic function. The purpose of a capital market is to channelize funds from people who wish to save to those who wish to make long-term investments in productive assets in an effort to earn income. Thus, when a government or a municipality needs to finance developmental activities that are long-term in nature, such as building a metro railway or putting up an oil refinery, or when a business wants to expand or diversify, it will approach the capital market for the required funds.

THE EUROCURRENCY MARKET

The development of the Eurocurrency market was one of the early factors in the growth of international investment. A eurocurrency is a freely traded currency deposited in a bank outside its country of origin. For example, Eurodollars are dollars deposited outside the United States while Euroyen are yen deposited outside Japan. The term *euro* refers to the fact that the funds are placed with an institution outside the country to which the currency belongs. The institution need not be located in Europe. While London, Zurich, and Frankfurt are major financial centers for such deposits, so are Singapore, Tokyo, and Hong Kong in the Far East, and Dubai and Bahrain in the Middle East.

The rapid growth of the Eurodollar market can be attributed to the following factors.

- After World War II the US dollar became the preferred currency for international trade, displacing the British pound, which was the primary vehicle for commercial transactions prior to the war.
- All countries sought to keep dollar balances to finance their imports. The former Warsaw Pact countries (satellites of the Soviet Union) were no different. However, they were reluctant to hold dollars with banks in the United States. A cold war was going on, and there was a legitimate fear that such deposits could be impounded by the US government. Thus, these countries began depositing their dollars with European banks. As trade grew, the European banks soon

discovered that there was a ready demand for these dollars by parties based outside the United States. As a consequence, an active Eurodollar market came into existence.

■ Due to capital market controls imposed by the US government. In the 1960s, through a legislation called regulation Q, the US government imposed low interest rate ceilings on US banks, and simultaneously imposed significant reserve requirements.

An interest ceiling meant that banks could not offer depositors more than the rate that had been mandated by the law, even if prudent business practices required them to do so. The implications of bank reserves may be explained as follows. When a unit of currency is deposited with a bank, only a fraction of it can be lent out. The balance has to be kept either in the form of approved securities or as cash. This amount is known as a reserve. The lower the reserve ratio, the more will be the money available with the bank for commercial lending. Consequently, the lower the reserve ratio, the higher will be the rates paid on deposits and the lower will be the lending rates, for the larger the amount of funds available for lending, the smaller will be the net interest margin that banks can afford to operate with.

As a consequence of these two factors, depositors became reluctant to park their funds with American banks, for these institutions could not offer attractive interest rates. At the same time, borrowers too were disenchanted, for the rates on loans were very high.

■ Lack of government regulations on Eurodollar deposits: Eurodeposits are relatively unregulated. For instance, the Federal Reserve, which is the central bank of the United States, does not regulate dollar deposits maintained outside the borders of the United States. Besides, such deposits do not suffer from statutory reserve requirements. Even if there is no statutory reserve requirement, however, banks by themselves usually maintain voluntary reserves as a measure of caution.

■ Due to the large flow of Petrodollars into international banks from the Oil Producing Export Countries (OPEC): There was a war in the Middle East in 1973 after which the oil-exporting countries recognized the full worth of their oil reserves as an economic weapon. Rising crude oil prices ensured that these countries were flush with funds, and the Euromarket, due to its lack of reserve requirements, and relatively low cost of operation due to economies of scale, was instrumental in recycling these so-called Petrodollars.

THE INTERNATIONAL BOND MARKET

The international bond market provides borrowers with a source of medium- to long-term funds. Borrowers include multinational corporations, domestic corporations, governments, national, and supranational financial institutions. It gives investors in the debt markets a way to diversify their portfolios over several different currencies. We have already highlighted the wisdom of not putting all one's eggs in one basket. But it is not necessary that all the securities chosen should be from the same country. Transnational diversification enables investors to take the diversification process a step further. The market consists of two broad segments: Eurobonds and Foreign Bonds.

Eurobonds are bonds denominated in one or more currencies other than the currency of the country in which they are sold. For example, bonds denominated in a currency other than the Japanese yen that are sold in Japan would be called Eurobonds.

A bond denominated in the currency of the country in which it is sold, but issued by an entity from a foreign country, is called a foreign bond. For example, if a US company were to sell yen-denominated bonds in Japan, it would be classified as a foreign bond.

Thus, bonds may be classified into three categories: domestic bonds, foreign bonds, and Eurobonds. If Sony were to issue yen-denominated bonds in Japan, it would be categorized as a domestic bond, for the issuer and the currency of issue are local. But if IBM were to issue yen-denominated bonds in Japan, it would come under the category of a foreign bond. This is because although the currency is local, the issuer is from a foreign country. Finally, if either IBM or Sony were to issue US dollar–denominated bonds in Japan, it would be categorized as a Eurobond issue, because the currency is foreign. In this case, the nationality of the issuer is irrelevant.

Foreign bonds are known by nicknames. Bonds sold in the United States are called Yankee bonds; those sold in Japan are called Samurai bonds; and those sold in the United Kingdom are called Bulldog bonds.

The Eurobond market has grown much more rapidly than the foreign bond market. This is due to several reasons.

Eurobond issues are not subject to the regulations of the country in whose currency they are denominated. Consequently, they can be brought to the market quickly and with less disclosure. This gives the issuer of the bonds greater flexibility to take advantage of favorable market conditions. Consider a bond issue from the issuers' perspective. The greater the regulations, the greater the time lag between planning and implementation; thus there is a greater chance of missing favorable market conditions. Consequently, issuers, and the investment banks that advise them, prefer markets characterized by minimal regulations. On the other hand, domestic securities issues are regulated by the market regulator of the country. In the United States it is the Securities and Exchange Commission (SEC).

The origin of the Eurobond market was fueled by the imposition of a tax called the Interest Equalization Tax, which was imposed by the US government in 1963 on the interest received by American investors from Yankee bonds. What had happened was that due to the interest rate ceiling in the United States, domestic institutions were unable to pay a high rate of interest to investors. Foreigners sought to take advantage of this situation by issuing Yankee bonds with relatively higher rates of return. The objective of the Interest Equalization Tax was to ensure that American investors did not perceive Yankee bonds to be attractive, despite their higher interest rates. The motivation for this measure was to arrest the perceived flight of capital from the United States. As a consequence, foreigners were forced to relocate their dollar borrowings to outside the United States.

Eurobonds offer favorable tax status. They are usually issued in bearer form, that is, the name and address of the owner are not mentioned on the bond certificate. There are two broad categories of securities: registered securities and bearer securities. In the case of the first category a record is maintained of the owners at any point in time, by an entity known as a registrar or share transfer agent. Each time the security is transferred from one investor to another, the records are updated; however, in the case of bearer securities, physical possession is the sole evidence of ownership. These securities are like currency notes. If one were to drop a hundred dollar bill on the floor, it is impossible to prove that it belongs to us. Such securities are easier to transfer and offer investors the potential freedom to avoid and evade taxes. Thus, holders who desire anonymity can receive interest payments from such securities without revealing their identity. Also, interest on Eurobonds is generally not subject to withholding taxes, or tax deduction at source.

Because of their unique features, investors are willing to accept a lower yield from Eurobonds than from other securities of comparable risk, but which lack the favorable tax status.

Eurobonds are not usually registered with any particular regulatory agency but are, however, listed on a stock exchange, typically London or Luxembourg. Listing is done not so much for the purpose of facilitating trading, but to circumvent restrictions imposed on certain institutional investors like pension funds, which are prohibited from purchasing unlisted securities. Most of the trading in Eurobonds takes place OTC.

GLOBALIZATION OF EQUITY MARKETS

Compared to debt markets, equity markets have been relatively slow to globalize. However, the winds of change are blowing across the world and markets are increasingly becoming modernized as well as integrated. The doctrine of LPG – Liberalization, Privatization, and Globalization – is gaining currency across the world. New developments in communications technology, coupled with deregulatory changes, and greater awareness of the benefits of international portfolio diversification on the part of investors, have led to rapid integration of equity markets in recent years. Some of the major deregulatory measures in the past two decades are the following:

- On 1st May 1975, the United States abolished fixed brokerage commissions.
- In 1985 the Tokyo Stock Exchange started admitting foreign brokerage firms as members.
- In 1986 the London Stock Exchange (LSE) eliminated fixed brokerage commissions and began admitting foreign brokerage houses as full members. This event is known as the "big bang" in financial circles. These changes were designed to give London an open and competitive international market. Until the end of World War II, London was the center of global financial activity. For obvious reasons, the center of postwar economic activities moved across the Atlantic to New York. London is, however, critical for global financial activities, for it lies in an ideal time zone. The city is located in between the capital markets of North America and those of Singapore and Tokyo. Consequently, it is the middle link for what is effectively a 24-hour market.
- In 1987, financial institutions in London were permitted to participate in both commercial and investment banking.
- In 1999 the Glass-Steagall Act, which sought to segregate commercial and investment banking activities in the United States, was repealed. The Act was a product of the Great Depression and sought to insulate commercial banks from the vagaries of the stock market. Once this Act was enacted, institutions were given

a clear choice. Either they could accept deposits and make loans, or they could provide underwriting and broker-dealer services. Thus, US institutions in the business of deposit taking and loan making were precluded from trading and market making in securities. For instance, Morgan Stanley was formed as a splinter from JP Morgan. While JP Morgan continued as a commercial bank, Morgan Stanley went into the areas of securities dealing and investment banking. In 1999 the Financial Services Modernization Act, known as the Gramm-Leach-Bliley Act, did away with this restriction and paved the way for giant financial conglomerates who could undertake both investment banking as well as commercial banking activities.

DUAL LISTING

Dual or multiple listing allows the shares of a company to be traded on the exchanges of many different countries. Foreign equity is traded in global markets, in the form of Depository Receipts (DRs). On the US exchanges, they are traded in the form of American Depository Receipts (ADRs). Such securities are special shares of foreign equity that are priced in US dollars. The issuance of such assets facilitates the ownership of foreign equity by American residents. An ADR is essentially a receipt issued by a depository bank in the United States that is backed by foreign shares that are deposited with a custodian bank in the country of issue of the original shares. ADRs are quoted and traded in US dollars just like domestic US shares.

The mechanism of issuing ADRs is as follows. A US depository bank will acquire shares of the foreign company in its domestic market. These shares will then be deposited with a local custodian bank in the foreign country. The US depository bank will then issue ADRs to the investors in the United States, where each ADR will correspond to a specified number of foreign shares.

Shareholders receive dividends in US dollars. The depository takes on the task of collecting dividends in the foreign currency, converting the dividends to dollars, and making payments.

An ADR may represent either a fraction or a multiple of the underlying shares, packaged in such a way that it will trade at the appropriate price range in the United States. This can be illustrated with the help of an example.

EXAMPLE 1.5

Take the case of a company based in India that is being traded at INR 60.00 per share, at a time when the exchange rate is INR 75 per US dollar. If an ADR were set to be equal to one Indian share, it will trade for approximately 80 cents in the United States. In order to ensure that the ADRs trade at a more respectable price, one ADR may be made equivalent to 10 domestic shares, thereby ensuring that it trades at approximately $8.00.

On the other hand a share may be trading at a very high price in its home country. For instance, if a share is trading at INR 37,500 in India, it will trade

(continued)

> (*continued*)
>
> at approximately $500 in the United States, assuming a 1:1 issue ratio and an exchange rate of INR 75 per dollar. In such circumstances one ADR may be set equal to 0.05 Indian shares, thereby ensuring that it trades at approximately $25 in the United States.

The ADR market is growing from the standpoints of both supply as well as demand. Foreign companies are being increasingly attracted to the US market for it is the largest in the world and is arguably the most efficient. Unlike other nations, the United States presents fewer barriers to entry. Compared to other countries the United States has more High-Net-Worth Individuals (HNWIs) who are not only better endowed financially, but are more aware of the benefits of international diversification and willing to take the attendant risks.

Although an American investor can always acquire a share that is traded on a foreign stock exchange, it is a lot simpler in practice to invest in an ADR. There is no need to locate a foreign broker or be conversant with the systems and practices of a foreign stock exchange and its related institutions. Besides, acquiring a foreign security will expose the investor to exchange rate risk. In most countries reporting standards are not as stringent as those prevalent in the United States. Consequently, companies abroad are able to get away with less disclosure, which may not be adequate for an American. A practical difficulty from the standpoint of trading foreign shares is that such transactions can be undertaken only when the overseas market is open, and the timings of these trading venues usually do not overlap with American market hours.

One of the advantages of ADRs is that an ADR may offer greater liquidity in the United States than the underlying shares do in their domestic market. Moreover, certain US pension funds and investment managers have a strong preference for ADRs because they are legally required to invest in ADRs while investing in non-US securities. Many institutional investors prefer investing in securities that are listed for trading in the US market rather than investing directly in foreign equity markets.

In order to list its shares on the exchange of a developed country, the issuing company must meet the securities market regulations of the foreign country as well as those of the stock exchange on which the shares are to be listed. This very often requires the company to comply with stringent disclosure norms. For instance, in order to list on the New York Stock Exchange (NYSE), it is necessary to comply with US GAAP (generally accepted accounting principles). For companies based in developing countries, such compliance has ensured more transparency in their operations, leading to the benefit of not just global investors, but also the domestic shareholders. However, after issues like the ENRON collapse, it is arguable as to whether the disclosure norms in the United States are as commendable and effective as once believed. Besides, many other countries have considerably beefed up their security-related regulations to a large extent, as a response to financial scams and scandals.

Foreign listing provides a multinational corporation (MNC) with indirect advertising for its product brands in the foreign market. It also raises the profile of the company in international capital markets, making it easier for it to raise finances in the future, and provides greater mileage for its international marketing efforts.

Take the case of an Indian company which is seeking to raise a bank loan in London. It will have greater credibility in the eyes of the international lending community if it were to be listed on an exchange in the developed world. Besides, when a firm's equity is held by shareholders across the globe, the risk of a hostile takeover of the firm may reduce somewhat.

There could be instances where foreign investors put a higher premium on the issue than do domestic investors. This could be the case, for instance, if the foreign market were to have greater experience in dealing with a particular industry. As Geddes points out, there was a flood of issues by international mining companies on the Toronto Stock Exchange in the mid-1990s.[3] This is because it was felt that Canadian investors had greater experience in evaluating shares of such firms.

At times a firm may go in for a global issue because it perceives its domestic market to be too small for an issue of the size it is contemplating. In Europe, for example, this fact has compelled Scandinavian and Eastern European firms to access markets across their borders.

There are two broad categories of ADR programs: sponsored and unsponsored. In the case of a sponsored program, the exercise is initiated by the foreign firm whose shares are sought to be traded in the United States. In the case of an unsponsored issue, the process will typically be initiated by an investment bank in the United States that has acquired shares in a foreign market.

FUNGIBILITY

Fungibility means the ability to interchange with an identical item. ADRs may be one-way fungible or two-way fungible. If an ADR is one-way fungible, then a US investor can sell the ADR back to the depository in the United States and have the equivalent number of underlying shares sold in the home country. However, if the ADRs were to be two-way fungible, then an investor could also surrender shares to the custodian bank in the home country and acquire ADRs in lieu. The problem with one-way fungibility is that it makes ADRs less attractive for American investors, because it has the potential to reduce the liquidity and the floating stock of ADRs in the United States. Besides, two-way fungibility is essential to preclude arbitrage opportunities.

ARBITRAGE

What is arbitrage? The term *arbitrage* refers to the strategy of making costless, riskless profits by simultaneously transacting in two or more markets. This is one of the fundamental principles underlying modern finance theory. One of the basic tenets of finance is the concept of risk aversion; that is, an investor will demand a risk premium for bearing a certain level of risk, and the higher the risk associated with an investment, the greater will be the premium demanded over and above the riskless rate of interest.

---

[3]See Geddes, 2001.

Arbitrage may be defined as the presence of a rate of return greater than the riskless rate on an investment devoid of risk or, equivalently, as the specter of a positive rate of return from a trading strategy that entails neither an investment nor an assumption of risk.

Take the case of a city like Mumbai, which has two major stock exchanges, namely the Mumbai Stock Exchange (BSE) and the National Stock Exchange (NSE). Assume that a share is trading at INR 100 on the BSE and at INR 100.75 on the NSE. An arbitrageur will place a buy order for 500,000 shares on the BSE while simultaneously placing a sell order for an equivalent amount on the NSE. Before accounting for transactions costs, he is assured of a profit of $500,000 \times (100.75 - 100) =$ INR 375,000. Considering the fact that he did not have to invest any money and was able to implement the strategy without taking any risk, such an opportunity should not exist.

There are certain practical issues to be considered while evaluating what looks like an opportunity for free money. First, can the trader make a profit after factoring in transactions costs like brokerage commissions? Most retail investors will have to incur such expenses; however, a securities dealing firm has a tremendous advantage for it does not have to pay such transactions-related charges. Consequently, such strategies that appear infeasible for retail traders may be profitable for institutions.

The second issue is that in this example both the exchanges have a T+2 settlement cycle. That is, if an investor were to trade on a particular day, the payment of cash to the seller and the delivery of securities to the buyer will take place two business days later. Thus, the arbitrageur cannot wait to take delivery on the BSE before giving delivery on the NSE. Consequently, to capitalize on such opportunities a potential arbitrageur needs access to a stockpile of cash as well as a long position in the security right at the outset.

In practice such opportunities will not remain for long. As arbitrageurs start buying on the BSE the price there will be driven up by the increasing demand. Similarly, as they start selling on the NSE, the increased supply will push prices down. After a brief while such opportunities will not be apparent.

In practice such opportunities exist for fleeting moments. They can be exploited by players who are always in the thick of the action such as financial institutions. The issue may be viewed as follows. A mispriced security offers a potential arbitrage opportunity. The possibility of making arbitrage profits ensures that securities are not mispriced in practice. To ensure that such avenues for profit are seized and exploited, traders increasingly rely on automated systems. One well-known type of arbitrage is Stock Index Arbitrage, which entails the exploitation of deviations from the postulated pricing relationship between stock indices and futures contracts based on them. This is not easy in practice, for if we take an index like the Standard and Poor's 500 (S&P), 500 constituent stocks have to be either bought or sold in the right proportions. Thus, the availability of a computer becomes imperative, and consequently the implementation of such arbitrage strategies is referred to as Program Trading.

ARBITRAGE WITH ADRs

Mispriced ADRs will be exploited by arbitrageurs. We will illustrate this with the help of an example.

Let's assume that shares of the Indian information technology company Infosys Technologies are quoting at INR 1,500 on the National Stock Exchange (NSE) in Mumbai, and that Infosys ADRs, where each ADR represents 20 domestic shares, are quoting at $410 on the NYSE. The current exchange rate is INR 75 per USD.

Quite obviously the ADRs are overvalued, for the dollar equivalent of 20 shares should be $400. An arbitrageur will short sell the ADRs in New York, acquiring 20 shares on the NSE for every ADR that is sold short, and then deliver them to the custodian bank in Mumbai, which will inform the depository bank in New York. On receiving intimation from Mumbai, the bank in New York will issue an ADR which can be used to cover the short position. The cost of acquisition of 20 shares in Mumbai will be INR 30,000 or $400. The proceeds from the short sale in New York will be $410. Consequently, an arbitrage profit of $10 can be earned.

Now let's examine a situation where ADRs are undervalued. What if the price of the Infosys ADR were to be $390? If so, an arbitrageur would acquire an ADR for $390 and deliver it to the depository bank in New York with instructions to sell the underlying shares in Mumbai. The sale proceeds will amount to INR 30,000 or $400. Once again, the arbitrageur will realize an arbitrage profit of $10.

J.P. Morgan was a pioneer in the creation of ADRs. They created the first ADR in 1927 to facilitate investment in foreign companies by American investors. An ADR is considered to be an American security, and consequently is freely tradable in the United States. It is akin to any other domestic security for the purpose of clearing and settlement.

GDRs

While ADRs are the most common type of depository receipts, there are other similar securities called GDRs. A global depository receipt (GDR) differs from an ADR in the sense that it is offered to investors in two or more markets outside the issuer's home country. Most such issues will include a tranche for US investors, as well as a separate tranche for international investors.

EDRs or Euro Depository Receipts represent ownership of shares in a corporation that is based in a country outside the European Monetary Union (EMU). While depository receipts are primarily issued to facilitate ownership of overseas equity, they can also be structured to permit investors to take a stake in a foreign debt issue. An American Depository Debenture (ADD) is a security that is based on a debt security issued by a foreign company.

RISK

Risk is defined as a position whose outcome is uncertain, and which has the potential to give rise to a loss for the holder. Assume that you are offered a security that will give a 20% return with a probability of 50% and a 40% return with the same probability. This is not a risky position, for, although the outcome is uncertain, there is no possibility of a loss. Similarly, take the case of an investment that is guaranteed to give a return of –10%. This too is not a risky position, for while there is a loss for the investor, there is no uncertainty regarding the outcome. So, what is an example of a risky position? Take the case of an investment in a share that will give a return of 0%

with 25% probability, –10% with 25% probability, and 10% with 50% probability. This is clearly risky, for the outcome can take one of three possible values, one of which would lead to a loss for the investor. Financial securities are exposed to multiple types of risks.

- Credit Risk: This is the risk that the deficit budget unit, which raises funds, may not make payments as promised to the investor. For instance, a business may issue bonds to the public with a face value of $1,000, and an assured interest rate of 10% to be paid every year. At the end of a financial year, however, it may be unable to make the promised interest payment. Or else, at the time of maturity of the security, it may be unable to repay the principal in full. Similarly, a financial institution like a bank, which makes loans to borrowers, is also faced with the specter of nonpayment. Such risk is also termed as default risk.
- Price Risk: Price risk or market risk is the risk that the price of the security at the time of purchase may be higher than its price at the point of a subsequent sale. In other words, it is the risk that there could be a capital loss for the investor. All marketable securities are subject to such risk.
- Reinvestment Risk: Whenever investors receive a cash flow from a security, they should reinvest it in the market, in order to ensure that they get an anticipated compounded rate of return. There is always a risk, however, that the prevailing market interest rate may be lower than what was expected at the outset. If so, the investor will have to settle for a lower than anticipated compounded rate of return. Such risk is termed as reinvestment risk.
- Inflation Risk: Inflation, or the erosion of purchasing power of money, is associated with every investment. Every investor will have a required rate of return that will include a premium for the anticipated rate of inflation; however, if the rate of inflation were to be higher than anticipated, the effective rate of return in terms of the ability to buy goods and services may be lower than expected. The return from a security in the absence of inflation is termed as the *real rate*. All investors will obviously demand a positive real rate of return. They will add a mark-up to this for the expected inflation, to arrive at what is called the nominal or money rate of interest. If inflation is higher than anticipated, however, the real rate received at maturity may be less than expected and can possibly be negative. The anticipated interest rate is referred to as the ex-ante rate. The interest rate that is eventually received is termed as the ex-post rate. In the absence of default, the ex-ante nominal rate will be equal to the ex-post nominal rate. However, because of inflation, the ex-post real rate may be lower or higher than anticipated and may possibly be negative.

  For instance, assume that the ex-ante real rate is 4% per annum and the expected inflation is 2.5% per annum. Thus, the nominal rate will be set at $1.04 \times 1.025 - 1 = 6.60\%$. However, if the actual rate of inflation is 4% per annum, the ex-post real rate will be only 2.5% per annum. If the actual rate of inflation were to be 8% per annum, the ex-post real rate will be a negative 1.30% per annum.
- Liquidity Risk: We have already expounded on this issue. Whenever funds are blocked in an investment, there is always the risk that at the time of its subsequent sale, the market may not be as liquid as it was at the time the securities were

acquired. If so, the seller may have to make a substantial concession by way of a reduction in price in order to complete the transaction. It must be remembered that if a transaction takes a considerable amount of time for execution, there is an associated cost, for time is money. Thus, the absence of an adequate number of buyers or sellers poses a risk for a party seeking to sell or to buy.

- Foreign Exchange Risk: This is a risk that is associated with an investment in a foreign country. If the domestic currency were to appreciate with respect to the currency in which the assets are denominated, there could be a loss for the investor.

   Assume that a US investor makes an investment of $100 in an Indian security when the exchange rate is INR 75 per dollar. At the end of one year, the price of the asset has increased from INR 7,500 to INR 7,800. Thus, there is a 4% return in rupee terms. However, the exchange rate at the end of the year is INR 80 per dollar. That is, the rupee has depreciated or the dollar has appreciated. Now, if the funds are repatriated to the United States, the American investor will receive only $97.50. Thus, there is a loss of 2.50% for him in dollar terms.

- Sovereign Risk: Such risk is associated with the structure of foreign economies and governments. Assume that a bank makes a loan to a party in Latin America, which subsequently defaults. In such cases, the lender may not have access to the same legal means of redressal that prevail in the United States. Besides, foreign governments may not be democratically elected or legally accountable. In certain countries, governments may suddenly impose exchange controls for instance, which could preclude a foreign company from repatriating the funds invested by it. It is not only foreign corporate securities that pose such risk; foreign government securities too are risky. There is always a likelihood that a Latin American government, for instance, which has issued bonds denominated in US dollars, may default. Such parties need not default on debt securities denominated in their own currencies, for they have the freedom to print money; however, such countries cannot print foreign currencies like the dollar or the euro.

AFTER THE TRADE – CLEARING AND SETTLEMENT

After a trade has been matched by a trading system, a post-trade process called clearing and settlement needs to commence in order to ensure that the seller receives the cash that is due to him, while the buyer receives the securities that he has acquired.

Clearing refers to all the post-trade processes other than final settlement, where the term *settlement* refers to the payment of cash to the seller and transfer of ownership of the securities from the seller to the buyer. Settlement is the last step in the post-trade process.

Different security types have different settlement cycles. Money market securities such as negotiable CDs and commercial paper settle *for cash*, that is on the same business day. Most US Treasury securities settle on the next business day. Most foreign exchange transactions settle *for spot*, that is two business days after the trade date (T+2 settlement). Equity and municipal bond transactions in the United States settle three business days after the trade date (T+3) settlement.

DEMATERIALIZATION AND THE ROLE OF A DEPOSITORY

A depository is a facility for holding securities in electronic form so that the purchase and sale of shares can take place via a process of book entry. The shares may be either *dematerialized* or *immobilized*. The term *dematerialization* refers to the replacement of physical share certificates by electronic records. On the other hand, if the securities were to be immobilized, an electronic record would be created without destroying the original physical certificates, which would continue to be held in secure storage.

The function of a depository is akin to that of a commercial bank. We will illustrate the similarities with the help of a simple tabular format as shown in Table 1.1.

The benefits of holding securities with a depository in dematerialized form are as follows.

1. It offers a safe and convenient way to hold securities.
2. It facilitates immediate transfers of securities.
3. No stamp duty is payable in most cases when securities are transferred in dematerialized form.
4. Transfer of shares in physical form has certain attendant risks such as
   (a) Bad delivery
   (b) Fake certificates
   (c) Delays
   (d) Thefts
   These can be eliminated by holding securities in dematerialized form.
5. There is considerable reduction of paperwork involved in the transfer of securities.
6. There is a reduction in the transactions costs involved in securities trading.
7. The concept of lot size has no meaning. Even one share can be bought or sold.
8. Nomination facility is available.
9. A change of address of holders gets registered with all the companies in which they hold securities. This eliminates the need for them to correspond with each company individually.
10. If there is a corporate action such as a stock dividend or a stock split, the shares are automatically credited to the investor's account.

TABLE 1.1   Commercial Banks and Depositories (Similarities and Differences)

Commercial Bank	Depository
1. Holds funds in an account	1. Holds securities in an account
2. Enables fund transfers between accounts after receiving instructions from the account holder	2. Enables transfers of securities between accounts after receiving instructions from the account holder
3. Facilitates transfers of funds without having to handle money	3. Facilitates transfers of share ownership without having to handle securities
4. Facilitates safekeeping of money	4. Facilitates safekeeping of securities

CUSTODIAL SERVICES

A custodian bank, a.k.a. a custodian, is a financial institution entrusted with the responsibility of safeguarding the financial assets of an individual or, more commonly, an institutional investor. The custodian typically performs one or more of the following functions:

1. It holds stocks and bonds in safekeeping.
2. It arranges for settlement whenever securities are purchased or sold. In the event of a purchase it ensures that securities are credited and cash is debited, while in the event of a sale it ensures that securities are debited and that cash is credited.
3. It collects dividends on shares and interest on bonds and ensures that the investor's account is credited.
4. It provides information related to the companies whose securities are being held by the investor, such as the schedule of their annual general meetings (AGMs).
5. It provides foreign exchange transactions if required.

Global custodians hold assets for their clients in multiple locations around the globe, using their own local branches or other local custodians. The advantage of employing a global custodian is that a settlement instruction needs to be sent to a single destination. Investors may also opt to use a network of local custodians, one in each financial center where they undertake trades.

If a custodial facility is availed of, the shares will be held in the name of the custodian, with the investor continuing to remain as the beneficial owner of the securities. The advantages of employing the facilities of a custodian may be summarized as follows:

1. It makes it easier and quicker to trade securities, particularly international shares.
2. It simplifies the management and reporting of share transactions. At the end of every financial year, the investor will receive a single consolidated statement giving details of purchases and sales, and any dividend or interest income received during the period.
3. The custodial facility also makes it easier to track the performance of the investor's portfolio.

GLOBALIZATION – THE NEW MANTRA

The word *globalization* indicates international integration of markets and economies, whereby they become interdependent and interconnected. In today's world, large corporations obtain financing from major money centers around the world in many different currencies to finance their global operations. The major money markets in the world include New York, London, Singapore, and Tokyo. The global nature of operations also forces many corporate treasurers to establish international banking relationships and place short-term funds in several different currencies. The effective management of foreign exchange risk is therefore an integral part of the duties of a modern treasury department. Individual investors too have started investing in the securities of many different countries to take advantage of the better performance potential from internationally diversified portfolios of financial assets.

The integration of financial markets around the world is due to four major factors.

Many countries have deregulated their money and capital markets substantially. The developed and some of the developing countries allow foreign brokerage firms to operate in their domestic stock exchanges to facilitate greater competition. The majority of countries have eliminated the structure of fixed brokerage commissions which used to exist. Commissions are now largely negotiable between the brokers and the clients and very often are a function of the trading volume and the quality of service that is sought. Interest rate ceilings have been largely removed, and offshore banking facilities (international banking facilities, or IBFs, in the United States) are available.

IBFs allow US banks to use domestic branches to service foreign customers with international transactions, both deposit and loan services, free of reserve requirements and interest rate regulations. Other countries have followed suit. The objective was obviously to make US banks competitive with respect to players outside the United States who were accepting deposits denominated in dollars and making loans in dollars.

Many countries have also sought to do away with the distinction between Commercial Banking and Investment Banking, and thus move toward Universal Banking. Most major banks these days are giant financial conglomerates that serve as one-stop financial solutions providers.

EXAMPLE 1.6

(An Illustration from India)

Take, for instance, the case of ICICI Bank, which is India's second largest bank. It is a traditional commercial bank on the one hand, in the sense that it accepts deposits from the public and makes loans. It has, however, an Asset Management Company that manages mutual funds in collaboration with Prudential Plc. ICICI Prudential is into Life Insurance. ICICI Lombard is into General Insurance. ICICI Home Finance is a subsidiary that makes real estate loans.

Constant product and process innovations are a major feature of the modern financial market. Innovations have manifested themselves in two forms: (1) many new products have been created and (2) new methods have been devised to facilitate the transfer of risks.

Of course, none of the observed advances in global markets would have been feasible without the developments in telecommunications, computer hardware, and software that we have witnessed in the recent past. They have helped develop systems where links can be instantly established, and funds and securities can be transferred safely and quickly. Companies like Bloomberg now provide round-the-clock access to prices and news from financial centers round the world. Most exchanges are now fully automated and electronic.

Today's markets are also characterized by the increasing sophistication of investors and borrowers. Multinational corporations and, surprisingly, even governments have become more sophisticated. Corporate treasurers, fund managers, and bureaucrats are highly educated and aware. Today's markets also tend to be largely dominated by institutions. These giants can take advantage of economies of scale worldwide. They can also afford to employ large teams of highly qualified experts.

CHAPTER 2

Mathematics of Finance

INTEREST RATES

Interest on money borrowed and lent is a feature of our daily lives. Most people have paid and received interest at some point in time. It is a common practice to make investments by buying bonds and debentures, and opening checking, savings, and time deposits with institutions like commercial banks. Bonds and debentures pay interest on their face value or principal. We refer to this as the coupon. Banks, while they do not pay interest on checking accounts, pay interest on savings and time deposits.

In today's consumer-driven economy, it is also a common practice to buy products and services on loan. Borrowing to buy residential property, which is referred to as a mortgage loan, is a major component of the debt taken by individuals and families. People also borrow to fund their academic pursuits in the form of student loans. Retail borrowing to finance various purchases such as automobiles and consumer durables (white goods) is a feature of today's society.

Interest may be construed as the compensation that a lender of capital receives. Why should a lender charge for making a loan? In other words, why not give an interest-free loan? It must be remembered that if you part with your money in order to extend a loan, then you are deprived of an opportunity to use the funds while they are on loan. The interest that you charge is consequently a compensation for this lost opportunity. In economic parlance we would term this as rent. Capital like land and labor are factors of production, and consequently those who seek to use the resources of others must pay a suitable compensation. To give an analogy, take the case of a family that gives its house or apartment to a tenant. It would obviously require the tenant to pay a monthly rent, because as long as he is occupying the property, the owners are deprived of an opportunity to use it themselves. The same principle is applicable in the event of a loan of funds. The difference is that the compensation in the case of property is termed as *rent*, whereas when it comes to capital, we term it as *interest*. In the language of economics, both constitute rent, albeit for different resources.

THE REAL RATE OF INTEREST

The price of a factor of production may be set or regulated by the government or may be left to be determined by market forces. In a free market, interest rates on loans are determined by the demand for capital and its supply. One of the key determinants of interest is what is termed as the *real* rate of interest.

What exactly is the real rate? The real rate may be defined as the rate of interest that would prevail on a riskless investment, in the absence of inflation. What is a riskless investment in practice? A loan to a central or federal government of a country may be termed as riskless, for these institutions are empowered to levy taxes and print money. As a consequence, there is no risk of nonpayment. In the United States, securities such as Treasury bonds, bills, and notes, which are backed by the full faith and credit of the federal government, may therefore be construed as riskless from the standpoint of nonpayment.

Even these Treasury securities, however, are not devoid of risk from the point of view of protection against inflation. What exactly is inflation? Inflation refers to the change in the purchasing power of money, or the change in the price level. Usually inflation is positive, which means that the purchasing power of money will be constantly eroding. There could be less common situations where inflation is negative, a phenomenon that is termed as deflation. In such a situation, the value of a dollar, in terms of the ability to acquire goods and services, will actually increase. We will illustrate our arguments with the help of an example.

EXAMPLE 2.1

Take the case of an investment in a Treasury security with a face value of $1,000. Assume that it will pay $100 by way of interest every year. When the security is acquired, the price of a box of chocolates is $10, and we will assume that the price remains the same until the end of the year. Consequently, the investor can expect to buy 10 boxes after a year when he receives the interest.

In this example, the rate of interest in terms of dollars is 10% per annum, since an investment of $1,000 yields a cash flow of $100. In terms of goods, which in this case is chocolates, our return is also 10%, for the principal corresponds to an investment in 100 boxes of chocolates and the interest received in dollars facilitates the acquisition of another 10 boxes. The rate of interest as measured by our ability to buy goods and services is termed as the real rate of interest.

In real life, however, price levels are not constant, and inflation is a constant fact of life. Assume that the price of chocolates after a year is $12.50. If so, the $100 of interest that will be received as cash will be adequate to buy only eight boxes of chocolates. The principal itself will be adequate to buy only 80 boxes of chocolates, which means that the investor can acquire only 88 boxes in total. Thus, while the return on investment in terms of money is 10%, in terms of the ability to buy goods, it is –12%.

Assets such as Treasury securities give us returns in terms of money, without any assurance as to what our ability to acquire goods and services will be at the time of repayment. The rate of return yielded by such securities in dollar terms is termed as the *nominal*, or the money rate of return. In our illustration the investor got a 10% return on an investment of $1,000. In the situation where the price of a box of chocolates remained at $10, the ability to buy chocolates was enhanced by 10% and consequently the real rate was also 10%. However, when the price of chocolates rose to $12.50 per box, an initial investment of $1,000, which represented an ability to buy 100 boxes of chocolates at the outset, was translated into an ability to buy only 88 boxes at the end of the year. Thus, the real rate of return in this case was negative or was –12% to be precise.

The relationship between the nominal and real rates of return is called the *Fisher Hypothesis*, after the economist who first postulated it.

THE FISHER EQUATION

Let us consider a hypothetical economy which is characterized by the availability of a single good, namely chocolates. The current price of a box is P_0. Thus, one dollar is adequate to buy $1/P_0$ boxes of chocolates at today's prices. Let the price of a box after a year be P_1. Assume that while P_1 is known with certainty right from the outset, it need not be equal to P_0. In other words, although we are allowing for the possibility of inflation, we are assuming that there is no uncertainty regarding the rate of inflation. If the price of a box at the end of the year is P_1, one dollar will be adequate to buy $1/P_1$ boxes after a year.

Let us assume that there are two types of bonds that are available to a potential investor. There is a financial bond that will pay $(1 + R)$ next period per dollar that is invested now, and then there is a goods bond which will return $(1 + r)$ boxes of chocolates next period per box that is invested today. An investment of one dollar in the financial bond will give the investor dollars $(1 + R)$ next period, which will be adequate to buy $(1 + R)/P_1$ boxes. Similarly, an investment of one dollar in the goods bond or $1/P_0$ boxes in terms of chocolates will yield $(1 + r)/P_0$ boxes after a year.

In order for the economy to be in equilibrium, both the bonds must yield identical returns. Thus, we require that

$$\frac{1+R}{P_1} = \frac{1+r}{P_0}$$

$$\Rightarrow (1+R) = (1+r) \times \frac{P_1}{P_0}$$

Inflation is defined as the rate of change in the price level. If we denote inflation by π, then

$$\pi = \frac{P_1 - P_0}{P_0} \Rightarrow \frac{P_1}{P_0} = (1+\pi)$$

Therefore

$$(1+R) = (1+r)(1+\pi) \Rightarrow R = r + \pi + r \times \pi$$

This is the Fisher equation. R or the return on the financial bond is the nominal rate of return, while r or the rate of return on the goods bond is the real rate of return. Thus, the relationship is that one plus the nominal interest rate is equal to the product of one plus the real interest rate and one plus the rate of inflation. If the real rate of interest and the rate of inflation are fairly small, then the product $r \times \pi$ will be of a much smaller order of magnitude. For instance, if $r = 0.03$ and $\pi = 0.03$, then $r \times \pi = 0.0009$. If so, we can ignore the product term and rewrite the expression as

$$R = r + \pi$$

This is called the approximate Fisher relationship.

In Example 2.1, the nominal rate of return was 10% while the rate of inflation was 25%. Thus, the real rate was $(1.10)/(1.25) - 1 = 0.88 - 1.0 = -.12 \equiv -12\%$.

SIMPLE INTEREST & COMPOUND INTEREST

Before analyzing interest computation techniques, let us first define certain key terms.

Measurement Period: The unit in which time is measured for the purpose of stating the rate of interest is called the measurement period. The most common measurement period is one year, and we will use a year as the unit of measurement unless otherwise specified. That is, we will typically state that the interest rate is $x\%$, say 10%, where the implication is that the rate of interest is 10% per annum.

Interest Conversion Period: The unit of time over which interest is paid once and is reinvested to earn additional interest is referred to as the interest conversion period. The interest conversion period will typically be less than or equal to the measurement period. For instance, the measurement period may be a year, whereas the interest conversion period may be three months. Thus, interest is compounded every quarter in this case.

Nominal Rate of Interest: The quoted rate of interest per measurement period is called the nominal rate of interest. For instance, in Example 2.1 the nominal rate of interest is 10%.

Effective Rate of Interest: The effective rate may be defined as the interest that a dollar invested at the beginning of a measurement period would have earned by the end of the period. Quite obviously the effective rate will be equal to the quoted or nominal rate if the length of the interest conversion period is the same as that of the measurement period, which means that interest is compounded only once per measurement period. However, if the interest conversion period is shorter than the measurement period – or in other words, if interest is compounded more than once per measurement period – then the effective rate will exceed the nominal rate of interest. Take the case where the nominal rate is 10% per annum. If interest is compounded only once per annum, an initial investment of $1 will yield $1.10 at the end of the year, and we would say that the effective rate of interest is 10% per annum. However, if the nominal rate is 10% per annum, but interest is credited every quarter, then the terminal value of an investment of one dollar will definitely be more than $1.10. The relationship between the effective rate and the nominal rate will be derived subsequently. It must be remembered that the term *nominal rate* of interest is being used in a different context than in the earlier discussion where it was used in the context of the real rate of interest. The potential for confusion is understandable yet unavoidable.

Variables and Corresponding Symbols

$P \equiv$ amount of principal that is invested at the outset

$N \equiv$ number of measurement periods for which the investment is being made

$r \equiv$ nominal rate of interest per measurement period

$i \equiv$ effective rate of interest per measurement period

$m \equiv$ number of interest conversion periods per measurement period

Simple Interest

Take the case of an investor who makes an investment of $\$P$ for N periods. If interest is paid on a simple basis, then we can state the following.

- The interest that will be earned every period is a constant.
- In every period interest is computed and credited only on the original principal.
- No interest is payable on any interest that has been accumulated at an intermediate stage.

Let r be the quoted rate of interest per measurement period. Consider an investment of $\$P$. It will grow to $\$P(1 + r)$ after one period. In the second period, if simple interest is being paid, then interest will be paid only on P and not on $P(1 + r)$. Consequently, the accumulated value after two periods will be $\$P(1 + 2r)$. In general, if the investment is made for N periods, the terminal value of the original investment will be $\$P(1 + rN)$. N need not be an integer, that is, investments may be made for fractional periods.

EXAMPLE 2.2

Katherine Mitchell has deposited $25,000 with Continental Bank for a period of four years. The bank pays interest at the rate of 8% per annum on a simple basis.

The growth of Katherine's deposit may be viewed as follows. An investment of $25,000 will become

$$25{,}000 \times 1.08 = \$27{,}000$$

after one year. Thus, the interest for the year is $2,000. At the end of the second year, interest for the year will be paid only on the original principal of $25,000, and not on the previous year's terminal value of $27,000. Consequently, the accumulated value after two years will be

$$25{,}000 \times 1.08 + 2{,}000 = \$29{,}000$$

Extending the logic, the terminal balance after three years will be $31,000, and the final balance after four years will be $33,000.

$$33{,}000 = 25{,}000 \times (1 + 0.08 \times 4) \equiv P(1 + rN)$$

Notice the following.

- The interest paid every year is a constant amount of $2,000.
- Every year interest is paid only on the original deposit of $25,000.
- No interest is paid on interest that is accumulated at an earlier stage.

EXAMPLE 2.3

Alex Gunning deposited $25,000 with International Bank for four years and nine months and wants to withdraw the balance at maturity. The bank pays 8% interest per annum on a simple interest basis. The terminal value in this case is given by:

$$P(1 + rN) = 25,000 \times (1 + 0.08 \times 4.75) = \$34,500$$

Notice that N, in this case 4.75 years, need not be an integer.

Compound Interest

Let us take the case of an investment of $P that has been made for N measurement periods. However, we will assume this time that interest is compounded at the end of every year. Notice, we are assuming that the interest conversion period is equal to the measurement period, namely a year. In other words, the quoted rate is equal to the effective rate.

In this case, an original investment of $P will become $P(1 + r)$ dollars after one period. The difference as compared to the earlier case, however, is that during the second period the entire amount will earn interest and consequently the balance at the end of two periods will be $P(1 + r)^2$. Extending the logic the balance after N periods will be $P(1 + r)^N$. Once again you should note that N need not be an integer.

Thus, the following observations are valid if interest is paid on a compound interest basis.

- Every time interest is earned it is automatically reinvested at the same rate for the next conversion period.
- Interest is paid on the accumulated value at the start of the conversion period and not on the original principal.
- The interest earned every period will not be a constant but will steadily increase.

EXAMPLE 2.4

Assume that Katherine Mitchell has deposited $25,000 with Continental Bank for four years, and that the bank pays 8% interest per annum compounded annually.

The initial investment of $25,000 will become

$$25,000 \times 1.08 = \$27,000$$

(continued)

(*continued*)

after one year. The difference in this case, as opposed to the earlier example (2.2) where simple interest was considered, is that the entire accumulated value of $27,000 will earn interest during the second year. Thus, the accumulated value after two years will be

$$27,000 \times 1.08 = \$29,160$$

By the same logic the balance after four years will be

$$25,000 \times 1.08 \times 1.08 \times 1.08 \times 1.08 = \$34,012.2240 = 25,000 \times (1.08)^4 \equiv P(1 + r)^N$$

The growth pattern is illustrated in the following table.

Notice the following. In the case of simple interest, the interest paid every year was a constant amount of $2,000. In the case of compound interest, however, the amount is steadily increasing, as can be seen in the last column of Table 2.1.

TABLE 2.1 The Compounding Process

Year	Balance at Beginning of Year	Balance at End of Year	Interest for Year
1	25,000.00	27,000.00	2,000.00
2	27,000.00	29,160.00	2,160.00
3	29,160.00	31,492.80	2,332.80
4	31492.80	34,012.22	2,519.42

EXAMPLE 2.5

Alex Gunning deposited $25,000 with International Bank for four years and nine months. The bank has been paying interest at the rate of 8% per annum on a compound interest basis. Let us calculate the terminal balance.

$$P(1 + r)^N = 25,000 \times (1.08)^{4.75} = \$36,033.20$$

In the earlier case, when we assumed simple interest, we got a value of $34,500.

As can be seen from the examples, compounding yields substantially greater benefits than simple interest. And since the rate of interest is taken to the power of N, the larger the value of N, the greater will be the impact of compounding. In other words, the earlier one starts investing, the greater will be the returns.

EXAMPLE 2.6

Jesus was born approximately 2,000 years ago. Assume that an investment of $1 was made in that year in a bank that has been paying 1% interest per annum since then, compounded annually. What will be the accumulated balance in the year 2000?

$$1 \times (1.01)^{2000} = \$439,286,205$$

PROPERTIES

- If $N = 1$, that is, an investment is made for one period, both the simple and compound interest techniques will give the same accumulated value.

  In the case of Katherine, the value of her initial investment of $25,000 at the end of the first year was $27,000, irrespective of whether simple or compound interest was used.

- If $N < 1$, that is, the investment is made for less than a period, the accumulated value using simple interest will be higher. That is

$$(1 + rN) > (1 + r)^N \text{ if } N < 1$$

For instance, assume that Katherine deposits $25,000 for nine months at a rate of 8% per annum compounded annually. If interest is calculated on a simple interest basis, she will receive

$$25,000 \times (1 + 0.08 \times 0.75) = \$26,500$$

On the other hand, compound interest would yield

$$25,000 \times (1.08)^{0.75} = \$26,485.48$$

- If $N > 1$, that is, the investment is made for more than a period, the accumulated value using compound interest will always be greater. That is

$$(1 + rN) < (1 + r)^N \text{ if } N > 1$$

As can be seen, if Katherine were to invest for four years, simple interest will yield $33,000 at the end, whereas compound interest will yield $34,012.2240.

Note 1: The word *period* used here to demonstrate the properties of simple and compound interest should be interpreted as the interest conversion period. In our illustrations, the interest was compounded once per year, so there was no

(continued)

(*continued*)

difference between the measurement period and the conversion period; however, take the case where interest is paid at 8% per annum compounded quarterly. If so, the above properties may be stated as follows.

- If the investment is made for one quarter, both simple and compound interest will yield the same terminal value.
- If the investment is made for less than a quarter, the simple interest technique will yield a greater terminal value.
- If the investment is made for more than a quarter, the compound interest technique will yield a greater terminal value.

Simple interest is usually used for short-term or current account transactions, that is, for investments for a period of one year or less. Consequently, simple interest is the norm for money market calculations. The term *money market* refers to the market for debt securities with a time to maturity at the time of issue of one year or less. In the case of capital market securities, however – that is, medium- to long-term debt securities and equities – we use the compound interest principle. Simple interest is also at times used as an approximation for compound interest over fractional periods.

EXAMPLE 2.7

Take the case of Alex Gunning, who deposited $25,000 with International Bank for four years and nine months. Assume that the bank pays compound interest at the rate of 8% per annum for the first four years and simple interest for the last nine months.

The balance at the end of four years will be

$$25,000 \times (1.08)^4 = 34,012.22$$

The terminal balance will be

$$34,012.22 \times (1 + 0.08 \times 0.75) = \$36,052.96$$

In the earlier case when interest was compounded for four years and nine months, the accumulated value was $36,033.20. Thus, simple interest for the fractional period yields an additional benefit of $19.76. The reason why we get a higher value in the second case is that for a fractional period simple interest will give a greater return than compound interest.

Effective Versus Nominal Rates of Interest

We will first illustrate the difference between nominal rates and effective rates using a numerical illustration and will then derive a relationship between the two symbolically.

EXAMPLE 2.8

ING Bank is quoting a rate of 8% per annum compounded annually on deposits placed with it, whereas HSBC is quoting 7.80% per annum compounded monthly on funds deposited with it. A naïve investor may be tempted to conclude that ING is offering better returns, as its quoted rate is higher. It is important to note, however, that the compounding frequencies are different. While ING is compounding on an annual basis, HSBC is compounding every month.

From our earlier discussion, we know that since ING is compounding only once a year, the effective rate offered by it is the same as the rate quoted by it, which is 8% per annum. However, since HSBC is compounding on a monthly basis, its effective rate will obviously be greater than the rate quoted by it. The issue is, is the effective rate greater than 8% per annum?

7.80% per annum corresponds to $7.80/12 = 0.65\%$ per month. Consequently, if an investor were to deposit \$1 with HSBC for a period of one year, or 12 months, the terminal value would be

$$1 \times (1.0065)^{12} = 1.08085$$

Consequently, a rate of 7.80% per annum compounded monthly is equivalent to receiving a rate of 8.085% with annual compounding. The phrase *effective annual rate* connotes that effectively the investor who deposits with HSBC receives a rate of 8.085% compounded on an annual basis.

Thus, when the frequencies of compounding are different, comparisons between alternative investments ought to be based on the effective rates of interest and not on the nominal rates. In our case, an investor who is contemplating a deposit of say \$10,000 for a year would choose to invest with HSBC despite the fact that its quoted or nominal rate is lower.

Note 2: It must be remembered that the distinction between nominal and effective rates is of relevance only when compound interest is being paid. The concept is of no consequence if simple interest is being paid.

A SYMBOLIC DERIVATION

Let us assume that an investor is being offered a nominal rate of $r\%$ per annum, and that interest is being compounded m times per annum. In the earlier example, since HSBC was compounding on a monthly basis, m was 12. The effective rate of interest i is therefore given by

$$1 + i = (1 + r/m)^m$$

We can also derive the equivalent nominal rate if the effective rate is given.

$$r = m[(1 + i)^{1/m} - 1]$$

We have already seen how to convert a quoted rate to an effective rate. We will now demonstrate how the rate to be quoted can be derived based on the desired effective rate.

Assume that HSBC Bank wants to offer an effective annual rate of 12% per annum with quarterly compounding. The question is what nominal rate of interest should it quote?

In this case, $i = 12\%$, and $m = 4$. We have to calculate the corresponding quoted rate r.

$$r = m[(1 + i)^{1/m} - 1]$$

$$\Rightarrow r = 4[(1.12)^{0.25} - 1] = 11.49\%$$

Thus, a quoted rate of 11.49% with quarterly compounding is tantamount to an effective annual rate of 12% per annum. Hence HSBC should quote 11.49% per annum.

PRINCIPLE OF EQUIVALENCY

Two nominal rates of interest compounded at different intervals of time are said to be equivalent if they yield the same effective interest rate for a specified measurement period.

Assume that ING Bank is offering 10% per annum with semiannual compounding. What should be the equivalent rate offered by a competitor, if it intends to compound interest on a quarterly basis?

The first step in comparing two rates that are compounded at different frequencies is to convert them to effective annual rates. The effective rate offered by ING is:

$$i = (1 + 0.05)^2 - 1 = 0.1025 \equiv 10.25\%$$

The question is, what is the quoted rate that will yield the same effective rate if quarterly compounding were to be used?

$$r = 4[(1.1025)^{0.25} - 1] = 0.0988 \equiv 9.88\%$$

Hence 10% per annum with semiannual compounding is equivalent to 9.88% per annum with quarterly compounding, because in both cases the effective annual rate is the same.

CONTINUOUS COMPOUNDING

We know that if a dollar is invested for N periods at a quoted rate of $r\%$ per period and if interest is compounded m times per period, then the terminal value is given by the expression

$$(1 + r/m)^{mN}$$

In the limit as $m \to \infty$

$$(1 + r/m)^{mN} \to e^{rN}$$

where e = 2.71828. Known as the Euler number or Napier's constant, e is defined by the expression:

$$e = \text{Lim}_{n \to \infty}(1 + 1/n)^n$$

This limiting case is referred to as continuous compounding. If r is the nominal annual rate, then the effective annual rate with continuous compounding is $e^r - 1$.

EXAMPLE 2.9

Nigel Roberts has deposited \$25,000 with Continental Bank for a period of four years at 8% per annum compounded continuously. The terminal balance may be computed as:

$$25,000 \times e^{0.08 \times 4} = 25,000 \times 1.3771 = \$34,428.19$$

Continuous compounding is the limit of the compounding process as we go from annual, to semiannual, on to quarterly, monthly, daily, and even shorter intervals. This can be illustrated with the help of an example.

EXAMPLE 2.10

Sheila Norton has deposited \$100 with ING Bank for one year. Let us calculate the account balance at the end of the year for various compounding frequencies. We will assume that the quoted rate in all cases is 10% per annum.

The answers are depicted in Table 2.2. As can be seen, by the time we reach daily compounding, we have almost reached the limiting value.

TABLE 2.2

Compounding at Various Frequencies Compounding Interval	Terminal Balance
Annual	110.0000
Semi-annual	110.2500
Quarterly	110.3813
Monthly	110.4713
Daily	110.5156
Continuously	110.5171

FUTURE VALUE

We have already encountered the concept of future value in our discussion thus far, although we have not invoked the term. What exactly is the meaning of the future value of an investment? When an amount is deposited for a certain time period at a given rate of interest, the amount that is accrued at the end of the designated period of time is called the *future value* of the original investment.

For instance, if we were to invest $P for N periods at a periodic interest rate of r%, then the future value of the investment is given by

$$\text{F.V.} = P(1 + r)^N$$

The expression $(1 + r)^N$ is the amount to which an investment of $1 will grow at the end of N periods, if it is invested at a rate r. It is called the *FVIF* (Future Value Interest Factor). It depends only on two variables, namely the periodic interest rate, and the number of periods. The advantage of knowing the FVIF is that we can find the future value of any principal amount, for given values of the interest rate and time period, by simply multiplying the principal by the factor. The process of finding the future value given an initial investment is called *compounding.*

EXAMPLE 2.11

Shelly Smith has deposited $25,000 for four years in an account that pays interest at the rate of 8% per annum compounded annually. What is the future value of her investment?

The factor in this case is given by FVIF(8,4) = $(1.08)^4 = 1.3605$

Thus, the future value of the deposit is $25,000 × 1.3605 = $34,012.50

Note 3: Remember that the value of N corresponds to the total number of interest conversion periods, in case interest is being compounded more than once per measurement period. Consequently, the interest rate used should be the rate per interest conversion period. The following example will clarify this issue.

EXAMPLE 2.12

Simone Peters has deposited $25,000 for four years in an account that pays a nominal annual interest of 8% per annum with quarterly compounding. What is the future value of her investment?

8% per annum for four years is equivalent to 2% per quarter for 16 quarterly periods. Thus the required factor is FVIF(2,16) and not FVIF(8,4).

$$\text{FVIF}(2,16) = (1.02)^{16} = 1.3728$$

Thus the future value of $25,000 is 25,000 × 1.3728 = $34,320

> **Note 4:** The FVIF is given in the form of tables in most textbooks, for integer values of the interest rate and number of time periods. If, however, either the interest rate or the number of periods is not an integer, then we cannot use such tables and would have to rely on a scientific calculator or a spreadsheet.

PRESENT VALUE

Future value calculations entailed the determination of the terminal value of an initial investment. Sometimes, however, we may seek to do the reverse. That is, we may have a terminal value in mind, and seek to calculate the quantum of the initial investment that will result in the desired terminal cash flow, given an interest rate and investment horizon. Thus, in this case, instead of computing the terminal value of a given principal, we seek to compute the principal that corresponds to a given terminal value. The principal amount that is obtained in this fashion is referred to as the *present value* of the terminal cash flow.

The Mechanics of Present Value Calculation

Take the case of an investor who wishes to have $\$F$ after N periods. The periodic interest rate is $r\%$, and interest is compounded once per period. Our objective is to determine the initial investment that will result in the desired terminal cash flow. Quite obviously

$$\text{P.V.} = \frac{F}{(1 + r)^N}$$

where P.V. is the present value of $\$F$.

EXAMPLE 2.13

Patricia wants to deposit an amount of $\$P$ with her bank in order to ensure that she has \$25,000 at the end of four years. If the bank pays 8% interest per annum compounded annually, how much does she have to deposit today?

$$P = \frac{25,000}{(1.08)^4} = \$18,375.75$$

The expression $1/(1 + r)^N$ is the amount that must be invested today if we are to have \$1 at the end of N periods, if the investment were to pay interest at the rate of $r\%$ per period. It is called the *PVIF* (Present Value Interest Factor). It too depends only on two variables, namely the interest rate per period and the number of periods. If we know the PVIF for a given interest rate and time horizon, we can compute the present value of any terminal cash flow by simply multiplying the quantum of the cash flow by the factor. The process of finding the principal corresponding to a given future amount is called *discounting* and the interest rate that is used is called the *discount rate*. Quite obviously, there is a relationship between the present value factor and the future value factor, for assumed values of the interest rate and the time horizon. One factor is simply a reciprocal of the other.

HANDLING A SERIES OF CASH FLOWS

Let us assume that we wish to compute the present value or the future value of a series of cash flows, for a given interest rate. The first cash flow will arise after one period, and the last will arise after N periods. In such a situation, we can simply find the present value of each of the component cash flows and add up the terms in order to compute the present value of the entire series. The same holds true for computing the future value of a series of cash flows. Thus present values and future values are additive in nature.

EXAMPLE 2.14

Let us consider the vector of cash flows shown in Table 2.3. Assume that the interest rate is 8% per annum, compounded annually. Our objective is to compute the present value and future value of the entire series.

TABLE 2.3   Vector of Cash Flows

Year	Cash Flow
1	2,500
2	5,000
3	8,000
4	10,000
5	20,000

The present and future value of the series is depicted in Table 2.4. As can be seen, we have simply computed the present and future value of each term in the series, and summed up the values.

TABLE 2.4   Present and Future Values of the Cash Flows

Year	Cash Flow	Present Value	Future Value
1	2,500	2,314.8148	3,401.2224
2	5,000	4,286.6941	6,298.5600
3	8,000	6,350.6579	9,331.2000
4	10,000	7,350.2985	10,800.0000
5	20,000	13,611.6639	20,0000.0000
	Total Value	33,914.1293	49,830.9824

While computing the present value of each cash flow we have to discount the amount so as to obtain the value at time "0." Thus the first year's cash flow has to be discounted for one year, whereas the fifth year's cash flow has to be discounted for five years. On the other hand, while computing the future value of a cash flow we have to find its terminal value as at the end of five years. Consequently, the cash flow arising after one year has to be compounded for four years, whereas the final cash flow, which is received at the end of five years, does not have to be compounded.

There is a relationship between the present value of the vector of cash flows as a whole and its future value. It may be stated as:

$$F.V. = P.V.(1 + r)^N$$

In this case

$$49,830.9824 = 33,914.1293 \times (1.08)^5$$

THE INTERNAL RATE OF RETURN

Consider a deal where we are offered the vector of cash flows depicted in Table 2.4, in return for an initial investment of $30,000. The question is, what is the rate of return that we are being offered? The rate of return r is obviously the solution to the following equation.

$$30,000 = \frac{2,500}{(1+r)} + \frac{5,000}{(1+r)^2} + \frac{8,000}{(1+r)^3} + \frac{10,000}{(1+r)^4} + \frac{20,000}{(1+r)^5}$$

The solution to this equation is termed as the Internal Rate of Return. It can be obtained using the IRR function in EXCEL. In this case the solution is 11.6106%.

Note 5: A Point About Effective Rates
Let us assume that we are asked to compute the present value or future value of a series of cash flows arising every six months, and are given a rate of interest quoted in annual terms, without the frequency of compounding being specified. The normal practice is to assume semiannual compounding. That is, we would divide the annual rate by two to determine the periodic interest rate for discounting or compounding. In other words, the quoted interest rate per annum will be treated as the nominal rate and not as the effective rate.

EXAMPLE 2.15

Consider the series of cash flows depicted in Table 2.5. Assume that the annual rate of interest is 8%.

TABLE 2.5 Vector of Cash Flows

Period	Cash Flow
6 months	2,000
12 months	2,500
18 months	3,500
24 months	7,000

The present value will be calculated as

$$P.V. = \frac{2,000}{(1.04)} + \frac{2,500}{(1.04)^2} + \frac{3,500}{(1.04)^3} + \frac{7,000}{(1.04)^4} = \$13,329.5840$$

Similarly the future value will be

$$F.V. = 2,000 \times (1.04)^3 + 2,500 \times (1.04)^2 + 3,500 \times (1.04) + 7,000$$

$$= \$15,593.7280$$

However, if it were to be explicitly stated that the effective annual rate is 8%, then the calculations would change. The semiannual rate that corresponds to an effective annual rate of 8% is $(1.08)^{0.5} = 1.039230$. The present value will then be given by

$$P.V. = \frac{2,000}{(1.039230)} + \frac{2,500}{(1.039230)^2} + \frac{3,500}{(1.039230)^3} + \frac{7,000}{(1.039230)^4} = \$13,359.1103$$

Similarly, the future value will then be given by

$$F.V. = 2,000 \times (1.039230)^3 + 2,500 \times (1.039230)^2 + 3,500 \times (1.039230) + 7,000$$

$$= \$15,582.0372$$

The present value is higher when we use an effective annual rate of 8% for discounting. This is because the lower the discount rate, the higher will be the present value; obviously, an effective annual rate of 8% is lower than a nominal annual rate of 8% with semiannual compounding. Because the interest rate that is used is lower, the future value at the end of four half-years is lower when we use an effective annual rate of 8%.

In this case, if we were to calculate the IRR for the given cash flow stream, we would get a semiannual rate of return. We would then have to multiply it by two to get the annual rate of return. The IRR for this cash flow stream, assuming an initial investment of $12,500, is 6.2716%. The IRR in annual terms is therefore 12.5432%.

EVALUATING AN INVESTMENT

Kapital Markets is offering an instrument that will pay $25,000 after four years in return for an initial investment of $12,500. Alfred is a potential investor, who requires a rate of return of 12% per annum. The issue is, is the offer attractive from his perspective? There are three ways of approaching this problem.

The Future Value Approach

Let us assume that Alfred buys this instrument for $12,500. If the rate of return received by him were to be 12%, he would have to receive a future value of $19,669. This can be stated as:

$$F.V. = 12,500 \times (1.12)^4 = \$19,669$$

If Alfred were to receive a higher terminal payment, his rate of return would be higher than 12%, else it would be lower. Because the instrument offered to him promises a terminal value of $25,000, which is greater than the required future value of $19,669, the investment is attractive from his perspective.

The Present Value Approach

The present value of $25,000 using a discount rate of 12% per annum is:

$$P.V. = \frac{25,000}{(1.12)^4} = 25,000 \times 0.6355 = \$15,888.15$$

The rate of return, if one were to make an investment of $15,888.15 in return for a payment of $25,000 four years hence, is 12%. If the investor were to pay a lower price at the outset, he would earn a rate of return that is higher than 12%, whereas if he were to invest more, he would obviously earn a lower rate of return. In this case Alfred is being asked to invest $12,500, which is less than $15,288.15. Consequently, the investment is attractive from his perspective.

The Rate of Return Approach

If Alfred were to pay $12,500 in return for a cash flow of $25,000 after four years, his rate of return may be computed as:

$$12,500 = \frac{25,000}{(1+r)^4}$$

$$\Rightarrow (1+r)^4 = 2 \Rightarrow r = [2]^{0.25} - 1 = 0.1892 \equiv 18.92\%$$

Since the actual rate of return obtained by Alfred is greater than the required rate of return of 12%, the investment is attractive.

Not surprisingly, all three approaches lead to the same decision.

ANNUITIES: AN INTRODUCTION

An annuity is a series of payments made at equally spaced intervals of time. If all the payments are identical, then we term it as a Level Annuity. Examples include insurance premiums and monthly installments on housing loans and automobile loans, which are paid off by way of equal installments over a period of time.

If the first payment is made or received at the end of the first period, then we call it an ordinary annuity. Examples include salary, which will be paid only after an employee completes his duties for the month, and house rent, which will be usually paid by the tenant only at the end of the month. The interval between successive payments is called the *payment period*. We will assume that the payment period is the same as the interest conversion period. That is, if the annuity pays annually, we will assume annual compounding, whereas if it pays semiannually we will assume half-yearly compounding. This assumption is not mandatory and, in practice, we can easily handle cases where the payment period is longer than the interest conversion period, as well as instances where it is shorter.

Consider a level annuity that makes periodic payments of $A for N periods. On a timeline the cash flows can be depicted as shown in Figure 2.1. The point in time at which we are is depicted as time 0.

FIGURE 2.1 Timeline for an Annuity

Assume that the applicable interest rate per period is $r\%$. We can then calculate the present and future values as shown here.

Present Value

$$P.V = \frac{A}{(1+r)} + \frac{A}{(1+r)^2} + \frac{A}{(1+r)^3} + - - - - + \frac{A}{(1+r)^N}$$

Therefore,

$$P.V(1+r) = A + \frac{A}{(1+r)} + \frac{A}{(1+r)^2} + - - - - + \frac{A}{(1+r)^{N-1}}$$

$$\Rightarrow P.V[(1+r) - 1] = A - \frac{A}{(1+r)^N}$$

$$\Rightarrow P.V = \frac{A}{r}\left[1 - \frac{1}{(1+r)^N}\right]$$

$\frac{1}{r}\left[1 - \frac{1}{(1+r)^N}\right]$ is called the *Present Value Interest Factor Annuity (PVIFA)*. PVIFA(r,N) is the present value of an annuity that pays $1 at periodic intervals for N periods, computed using a discount rate of $r\%$. Thus, like the factors that we studied earlier, it too depends on the interest rate and the number of periods. The present value of any annuity that pays $A per period can therefore be computed by multiplying A by the appropriate value of PVIFA.

EXAMPLE 2.16

Alpha Technologies is offering a financial instrument to Alfred that promises to pay $2,500 per year for 25 years, beginning one year from now. Alfred requires an annual rate of return of 8%. The question is, what is the maximum price that he will be prepared to pay?

PVIFA(8,25) = 10.6748. Thus the value of the payments is:

$$2{,}500 \times \text{PVIFA}(8{,}25) = 2{,}500 \times 10.6748 = \$26{,}687$$

Future Value

Similarly, we can compute the future value of a level annuity that makes N payments, by compounding each cash flow until the end of the last payment period.

$$\text{F.V} = A(1 + r)^{N-1} + A(1 + r)^{N-2} + A(1 + r)^{N-3} + ----- + A$$

Therefore,

$$\text{F.V}(1 + r) = A(1 + r)^N + A(1 + r)^{N-1} + A(1 + r)^{N-2}$$

$$+ ----- + A(1 + r) \Rightarrow \text{F.V}[(1 + r) - 1]$$

$$= A(1 + r)^N - A \Rightarrow \text{F.V} = \frac{A}{r}[(1 + r)^N - 1]$$

$\frac{1}{r}[(1 + r)^N - 1]$ is called the *Future Value Interest Factor Annuity (FVIFA)*. This is the future value of an annuity that pays $1 per period for N periods, where interest is compounded at the rate of r% per period. The advantage once again is that if we know the factor, we can calculate the future value of any annuity that pays $A per period.

EXAMPLE 2.17

Paula Baker expects to receive $2,500 per year for the next 25 years, starting one year from now. Assuming that the cash flows can be reinvested at 8% per annum, how much will she have at the point of receipt of the last cash flow?

FVIFA(8,25) = 73.1059. Thus the future value is:

$$\text{F.V} = 2{,}500 \times \text{FVIFA}(8{,}25) = 2{,}500 \times 73.1059 = \$182{,}764.75$$

ANNUITY DUE

The difference between an annuity and an *annuity due* is that in the case of an annuity due the cash flows occur at the beginning of the period. An N period annuity due that makes periodic payments of $A may be depicted as follows

FIGURE 2.2   Timeline for an Annuity Due

Present Value

$$\text{P.V.} = A + \frac{A}{(1+r)} + \frac{A}{(1+r)^2} + - - - - + \frac{A}{(1+r)^{N-1}}$$

Therefore,

$$\text{P.V}(1+r) = A(1+r) + A + \frac{A}{(1+r)} + - - - - + \frac{A}{(1+r)^{N-2}}$$

$$\Rightarrow \text{P.V}[(1+r) - 1] = A(1+r) - \frac{A}{(1+r)^{N-1}}$$

$$\Rightarrow \text{P.V} = \frac{A}{r}\left[1 - \frac{1}{(1+r)^N}\right](1+r)$$

Hence $\text{PVIFA}_{AD}(r, N) = \text{PVIFA}(r, N) \times (1+r)$

The present value of an annuity due that makes N payments is obviously greater than that of a corresponding annuity that makes N payments, because in the case of the annuity due, each of the cash flows has to be discounted for one period less. Consequently, the present value factor for an N period annuity due is greater than that for an N period annuity by a factor of $(1 + r)$.

An obvious example of an annuity due is an insurance policy, because the first premium has to be paid as soon as the policy is purchased.

EXAMPLE 2.18

David Mathew has just bought an insurance policy from MetLife. The annual premium is $2,500, and he is required to make 25 payments. What is the present value of this annuity due if the discount rate is 8% per annum?

$$\text{PVIFA}(8,25) = 10.6748$$

$$\text{PVIFA}_{AD}(8,25) = 10.6748 \times 1.08 = 11.5288$$

Thus the present value of the annuity due is:

$$2,500 \times 11.5288 = \$28,822$$

Future Value

$$\text{F.V.} = A(1+r)^N + A(1+r)^{N-1} + A(1+r)^{N-2} + ----- + A(1+r)$$

Therefore,

$$\text{F.V}(1+r) = A(1+r)^{N+1} + A(1+r)^N + A(1+r)^{N-1}$$

$$+ ----- + A(1+r^2)$$

$$\Rightarrow \text{F.V}[(1+r) - 1] = A(1+r)^{N+1} - A(1+r)$$

$$\Rightarrow \text{F.V} = \frac{A}{r}[(1+r)^N - 1](1+r)$$

Hence

$$\text{FVIFA}_{\text{AD}}(r, N) = \text{FVIFA}(r, N) \times (1+r)$$

The future value of an annuity due that makes N payments is higher than that of a corresponding annuity that makes N payments, if the future values in both cases are computed at the end of N periods. This is because, in the first case, each cash flow has to be compounded for one period more.

Note 6: It should be reiterated that the future value of an N period annuity due is greater than that of an N period annuity if both the values are computed at time N that is after N periods. The future value of an annuity due as computed at time $N - 1$ will be identical to that of an ordinary annuity as computed at time N.

EXAMPLE 2.19

In the case of Mathew's MetLife policy, the cash value at the end of 25 years can be calculated as follows.

$$\text{FVIFA}(8,25) = 73.1059$$

$$\text{FVIFA}_{\text{AD}}(8,25) = 73.1059 \times 1.08 = 78.9544$$

Thus the cash value of the annuity due is:

$$2,500 \times 78.9544 = \$197,386$$

PERPETUITIES

An annuity that pays forever is called a perpetuity. The future value of a perpetuity is obviously infinite. But it turns out that a perpetuity has a finite present value. The present value of an annuity that pays for N periods is

$$\text{P.V} = \frac{A}{r}\left[1 - \frac{1}{(1+r)^N}\right]$$

The present value of the perpetuity can be found by letting N tend to infinity. As follows:

$$N \to \infty$$

$$\frac{1}{(1+r)^N} \to 0$$

Thus, the present value of a perpetuity is A/r.

EXAMPLE 2.20

Let us consider a financial instrument that promises to pay $2,500 per year for ever. If investors require a 10% rate of return, the maximum amount they would be prepared to pay may be computed as follows.

$$\text{P.V.} = 2{,}500/0.10 = \$25{,}000$$

Thus, although the cash flows are infinite, the security has a finite value. This is because the contribution of additional cash flows to the present value becomes insignificant after a certain point in time.

THE AMORTIZATION METHOD

The amortization process refers to the process of repaying a loan by means of regular installment payments at periodic intervals. Each installment includes payment of interest on the principal outstanding at the start of the period and a partial repayment of the outstanding principal itself. In contrast, an ordinary loan entails the payment of interest at periodic intervals, and the repayment of principal in the form of a single lump-sum payment at maturity. In the case of an amortized loan, the installment payments form an annuity whose present value is equal to the original loan amount. An *Amortization Schedule* is a table that shows the division of each payment into a principal component and an interest component and displays the outstanding loan balance after each payment.

Take the case of a loan which is repaid in N installments of $A each. We will denote the original loan amount by L, and the periodic interest rate by r. Thus this is an annuity with a present value of L, which is repaid in N installments.

$$L = A \times \text{PVIFA}(r, N) = \frac{A}{r}\left[1 - \frac{1}{(1+r)^N}\right]$$

The interest component of the first installment

$$= r \times \frac{A}{r}\left[1 - \frac{1}{(1+r)^N}\right]$$

$$= A\left[1 - \frac{1}{(1+r)^N}\right]$$

The principal component

$$= A - A\left[1 - \frac{1}{(1+r)^N}\right]$$

$$= \frac{A}{(1+r)^N}$$

The outstanding balance at the end of the first payment

$$= \frac{A}{r}\left[1 - \frac{1}{(1+r)^N}\right] - \frac{A}{(1+r)^N}$$

$$= \frac{A}{r}\left[1 - \frac{1}{(1+r)^{(N-1)}}\right]$$

In general, the interest component of the 't'*th* installment is

$$A\left[1 - \frac{1}{(1+r)^{N-t+1}}\right]$$

The principal component of the 't'*th* installment is

$$\frac{A}{(1+r)^{N-t+1}}$$

and the outstanding balance at the end of the 't'*th* payment is

$$\frac{A}{r}\left[1 - \frac{1}{(1+r)^{N-t}}\right]$$

EXAMPLE 2.21

Sylvie has borrowed \$25,000 from First National Bank and has to pay it back in eight equal annual installments. If the interest rate is 8% per annum on the outstanding balance, what is the installment amount, and what will the amortization schedule look like?

Let us denote the unknown installment amount by A. We know that

$$25{,}000 = \frac{A}{0.08} \times \left[1 - \frac{1}{(1.08)^8}\right]$$

$$\Rightarrow A = \$4{,}350.37$$

We will analyze the first few entries in Table 2.6 in order to clarify the principles involved. At time *0*, the outstanding principal is \$25,000. After one period, a payment of \$4,350.37 will be made. The interest due for the first period is 8% of \$25,000, which

TABLE 2.6   An Amortization Schedule

Year	Payment	Interest	Principal Repayment	Outstanding Principal
0				25,000
1	4,350.37	2,000.00	2,350.37	22,649.63
2	4,350.37	1,811.97	2,538.40	20,111.23
3	4,350.37	1,608.90	2,741.47	17,369.76
4	4,350.37	1,389.58	2,960.79	14,408.97
5	4,350.37	1,152.72	3,197.65	11,211.32
6	4,350.37	896.91	3,453.46	7,757.86
7	4,350.37	620.63	3,729.74	4,028.12
8	4,350.37	322.25	4,028.12	0.00

is $2,000. Consequently, the excess payment of $2,350.37 represents a partial repayment of principal. Once this amount is repaid and adjusted toward the principal, the outstanding balance at the end of the first period will become $22,649.63. At the end of the second period, the second installment of $4,350.37 will be paid. The interest due for this period is 8% of the outstanding balance at the start of the period, which is $22,649.63. Thus the interest component of the second installment is $1,811.97. The balance, which is $2,538.40, constitutes a partial repayment of principal. The value of the outstanding principal at the end should be zero. As can be seen, the outstanding principal declines after each installment payment. Because the payments themselves are constant, the interest component will steadily decline while the principal component will steadily increase.

Thus, in the case of such loans, the initial installments will consist largely of interest payments. As we approach the maturity of the loan, however, the corresponding installments will consist largely of principal repayments.

AMORTIZATION WITH A BALLOON PAYMENT

Julie Tate has taken a loan of $25,000 from First National Bank. The loan requires her to pay in eight equal annual installments along with a terminal payment of $5,000. This terminal payment that has to be made over and above the scheduled installment in year eight is termed as a balloon payment. The interest rate is 8% per annum on the outstanding principal. The annual installment may be calculated as follows.

$$25,000 = \frac{A}{0.08} \times \left[1 - \frac{1}{(1.08)^8} \right] + \frac{5,000}{(1.08)^8}$$

$$\Rightarrow A = \$3,880.2950$$

Obviously the larger the balloon, the smaller will be the periodic installment payment for a given loan amount. The amortization schedule may be depicted as shown in Table 2.7.

TABLE 2.7   Amortization with a Balloon Payment

Year	Payment	Interest	Principal Repayment	Outstanding Principal
0				25,000
1	3,880.2950	2,000.00	1,880.30	23,119.70
2	3,880.2950	1,849.58	2,030.72	21,088.99
3	3,880.2950	1,687.12	2,193.18	18,895.81
4	3,880.2950	1,511.66	2,368.63	16,527.18
5	3,880.2950	1,322.17	2,558.12	13,969.06
6	3,880.2950	1,117.52	2,762.77	11,206.29
7	3,880.2950	896.50	2,983.79	8,222.50
8	8,880.2950	657.80	8,222.50	0.00

THE EQUAL PRINCIPAL REPAYMENT APPROACH

Sometimes a loan may be structured in such a way that the principal is repaid in equal installments. Thus, the principal component of each installment will remain constant; however, as in the case of the amortized loan, the interest component of each payment will steadily decline, on account of the diminishing loan balance. Therefore, the total magnitude of each payment will also decline.

We will illustrate the payment stream for an eight-year loan of $25,000, assuming that the interest rate is 8% per annum (Table 2.8).

TABLE 2.8   Equal Principal Repayment Schedule

Year	Payment	Interest	Principal Repayment	Outstanding Principal
0				25,000
1	5,125	2,000	3,125	21,875
2	4,875	1,750	3,125	18,750
3	4,625	1,500	3,125	15,625
4	4,375	1,250	3,125	12,500
5	4,125	1,000	3,125	9,375
6	3,875	750	3,125	6,250
7	3,625	500	3,125	3,125
8	3,375	250	3,125	0.00

TYPES OF INTEREST COMPUTATION

Financial institutions employ a variety of techniques to calculate the interest on the loans taken from them by borrowers. Thus the interest rate that is effectively paid by a borrower may be very different from what is being quoted by the lender.[1]

---

[1] To rephrase a famous Microsoft claim, in this case "What You See Is NOT What You Get."

The Simple Interest Approach

If the lender were to use a simple interest approach, then borrowers need only pay interest for the actual period of time for which they have used the funds. Each time they make a partial repayment of the principal, the interest due will come down for subsequent periods.

EXAMPLE 2.22

Michael has borrowed $8,000 from a bank for a year. The bank charges simple interest at the rate of 10% per annum. If the loan is repaid in one lump sum at the end of the year, the amount payable will be:

$$1.10 \times 8,000 = \$8,800$$

This consists of $8,000 by way of principal repayment and an interest payment of $800.

Now let us consider a case where Michael repays the principal in two equal semiannual installments. For the first six months, interest will be computed on the entire principal. So the first installment will be:

$$8,000 \times 0.10 \times 0.5 + 4,000 = \$4,400$$

The second installment will be lower, for it will include interest only on the remaining principal, which in this case is $4,000. So the amount repayable will be:

$$4,000 \times 0.10 \times 0.5 + 4,000 = \$4,200$$

The sum of the two payments is $8,600. In the first case the interest payable was $800, whereas in the second case it is only $600. Quite obviously, the more frequently principal is repaid, the lower will be the amount of interest.

The Add-on Rate Approach

This approach entails the calculation of interest on the entire principal. The sum total of principal and interest is then divided by the number of installments in which the loan is sought to be repaid. As should be obvious, if the loan is repaid in a single annual installment, the total interest payable will be $800 and the effective rate of interest will be 10%. However, if Michael were to repay in two equal semiannual installments of $4,400 each, the effective rate of interest may be computed as follows:

$$8,000 = \frac{4,400}{\left(1 + \frac{i}{2}\right)} + \frac{4,400}{\left(1 + \frac{i}{2}\right)^2}$$

$$\Rightarrow \frac{i}{2} = 6.5965\%$$

$$\Rightarrow i = 13.1930\%$$

The Discount Technique

In the case of such loans, interest is first computed on the entire loan amount. It is then deducted from the principal, and the balance is lent to the borrower, who has to repay the entire principal at maturity. Such loans are usually repaid in a single installment. Let us take the example of Michael.

The interest for the loan amount of $8,000 is $800. So the lender will give him $7,200 and ask him to repay $8,000 after a year. The effective rate of interest is:

$$i = \frac{8,000 - 7,200}{7,200} \times 100 = 11.11\%$$

LOANS WITH A COMPENSATING BALANCE

Many banks require borrowers to keep a percentage of the loan amount as a deposit with them. Such deposits, referred to as compensating balances, earn little or no interest. Obviously such requirements will increase the effective rate of interest, and the higher the required balance, the greater will be the rate of interest that is paid by the borrower.

Assume that in Michael's case, the bank required a compensating balance of 12.50%. So while he will have to pay interest on the entire loan amount of $8,000, the usable amount is only $7,000.

The effective rate of interest is:

$$i = \frac{800}{7,000} \times 100 = 11.4286\%$$

TIME VALUE OF MONEY–RELATED FUNCTIONS IN EXCEL

We will first demonstrate how to compute effective rates given nominal rates, and vice versa.

EXAMPLE 2.23

Mary has borrowed money from a bank, which is quoting a rate of 6.4% per annum compounded quarterly. To calculate the effective annual rate, we use an Excel function called EFFECT. The parameters are:

- Nominal_rate: This is the nominal rate of interest per annum.
- Npery: This is the frequency of compounding per annum.

The nominal rate is 6.40% or 0.064 in this case. The frequency of compounding per annum is 4. Using the function, we get the effective annual rate of 6.5552% per annum.

$$EFFECT(0.064, 4) = 6.5552\%$$

(continued)

(continued)

If we are given the effective rate, we can compute the equivalent nominal rate using the NOMINAL function in Excel. The parameters are

- Effect_rate: This is the effective rate of interest per annum.
- Npery: This is the frequency of compounding per annum.

Assume that the bank is quoting an effective annual rate of 7.2% per annum with quarterly compounding. What is the equivalent nominal annual rate? In this case the effective rate is 7.20%, and the frequency of compounding is 4. Thus,

$$\text{NOMINAL}(0.072,4) = 7.0134\%$$

The Future Value (FV) Function in Excel

To compute the future value using Excel, we need to use the FV function. The parameters are:

- Rate: Rate is the periodic interest rate.
- Nper: Nper is the number of periods.
- Pmt: Pmt stands for the periodic payment, and is not applicable in this case because there are no periodic cash flows. Thus, we can either put a zero, or an extra comma in lieu.
- Pv: Pv stands for the present value, or the initial investment. We input it with a negative sign in order to ensure that the answer is positive. In many Excel functions, cash flows in one direction are positive while those in the opposite direction are negative. Thus, if the investment is positive, the subsequent inflow is negative, and vice versa. In this case, if we specify a negative number for the present value, we get the future value with a positive sign. If, however, the present value is given with a positive sign, the future value, although it would have the same magnitude, would have a negative sign.
- Type: This is a binary variable, which is either 0 or 1. It is not required at this stage, and we can just leave it blank.

EXAMPLE 2.24

Rosalyn has deposited $20,000 with a bank for five years. The bank has agreed to pay 4.8% interest per annum compounded annually. How much can she withdraw at the end?

We will invoke the function as, FV(.048,5,,−20000) and the answer is $25,283.45. In this function we are inputting an extra comma in lieu of the value for Pmt. As an alternative we could have given the value as zero.

Now assume that the bank is quoting a rate of 4.8% per annum with quarterly compounding. The periodic interest rate is 1.20%, and the number of quarterly periods in five years is 20. The future value may be computed as follows.

$$FV(0.012,20,,-20000) = \$25,388.69$$

The Present Value Function in Excel

The required function in Excel is PV. The parameters are:

* Rate
* Nper
* Pmt
* Fv
* Type

Fv stands for the future value. The other parameters have the same meaning as specified for the FV function.

EXAMPLE 2.25

Sharon Oliver wants to accumulate $25,000 in her bank account after five years. The bank agrees to pay 5.40% per annum compounded quarterly. How much should she deposit today?

$$PV(.0135,20,,-25000) = \$19,118.99$$

COMPUTING THE PRESENT AND FUTURE VALUES OF ANNUITIES AND ANNUITIES DUE IN EXCEL

EXAMPLE 2.26

Allegra is offering an instrument that promises to pay $4,000 per year for 10 years, beginning one year from now. If the annual rate of interest is 5.40%, and interest is paid annually, what is the present value of the annuity?

We can use the PV function in Excel. The parameters are: Rate = 0.054, Nper = 10, Pmt = −4,000. There is no need to input parameters for Fv and Type. This is because there is no lump-sum terminal cash flow, and so there is no need to input a value for the future value. Type needs to be input only for annuities due.

$$PV(0.054,10,-4000) = \$30,295.65$$

(continued)

(*continued*)

The future value of this annuity may be computed using the FV function.

$$FV(.054, 10, -4000) = \$51,260.92$$

Now assume that the above annuities are annuities due. The present and future values may be computed as follows.

$$PV(0.054, 10, -4000,,1) = \$31,931.62$$

$$FV(0.054, 10, -4000,,1) = \$54,029.01$$

$$31,931.62 = 30,295.65 \times 1.054$$

And

$$54,029.01 = 51,260.92 \times 1.054$$

AMORTIZATION SCHEDULES AND EXCEL

Lorraine has taken a loan of $500,000 which has to be paid back in eight annual installments. The interest rate is 4.80% per annum. The periodic installment can be computed using the PMT function in Excel. The parameters are:

- Rate
- Nper
- PV
- FV
- Type

The values for PV and FV should have opposite signs.
For the first period, PMT(0.048, 8, −500,000) = $76,736.66.
Now consider the second period. There are two ways in which the PMT function can be invoked. We can specify the same set of parameters as for the first period. Or we can specify the Nper as 7, and the PV as the outstanding balance, which is $447,263.34.

$$PMT(0.048, 8, -500000) = PMT(0.048, 7, -447263.34) = \$76,736.66$$

Now consider the interest and principal components of each installment. We can use a function in Excel called IPMT to compute the interest component of an installment and another function called PPMT to compute the principal component of the installment. The parameters, for both, are

- Rate: This is the periodic interest rate.
- Per: This stands for period.
- Nper: This represents the total number of periods.

- Pv: This is the present value.
- Fv: This is the future value.
- Type: This has the usual meaning.

Consider the interest and principal components of the first installment.

IPMT(0.048,1,8,−500000) = $24,000. While computing the interest component of the second installment, we can invoke IPMT as IPMT(0.048,2,8,−500000) or as IPMT(0.048,1,7,−447263.94). Both will return a value of $21,468.64. Similarly, the principal component of the first installment is PPMT(0.048,1,8,−500000) = $52,736.66. For the second period,

$$PPMT(0.048,2,8,−500000) = PPMT(0.048,1,7,−447263.94) = \$55,268.02.$$

IPMT and PPMT can be used with two sets of parameters. We can keep the total number of periods at the initial value, specify the present value as the initial loan amount, and keep changing Per to compute the interest and principal components. For the first installment, Per = 1, and for the nth installment, it is equal to n. The alternative is to re-amortize the outstanding amount at the beginning of each period over the remaining number of periods. Remember that each time we re-amortize, we are back to the first period. Thus, after every payment, we are back to the first period of a loan whose life is equal to the remaining time to maturity, and whose principal amount is equal to the remaining outstanding balance.

CHAPTER 3

Equity Shares, Preferred Shares, and Stock Market Indices

INTRODUCTION

Equity shares, or shares of common stock of a company, are a type of financial claim issued by the firm to investors, who are referred to as shareholders. In return for their investment, the shareholders are conferred with ownership rights. A firm must have a minimum of one shareholder, and there is no limit to how many shareholders a firm may have. Correspondingly, there is no restriction on the total number of shares that may be issued by a firm. Large corporations have a large number of shares outstanding, and consequently their ownership is spread over a vast pool of investors. Shareholders are part owners of the company to whose shares they have subscribed, and their stake is equal to the fraction of the total share capital of the firm to which they have contributed.

At the outset, when a firm is incorporated a stated number of shares will be authorized for issue by the promoters. The value of such shares is referred to as the *authorized capital* of the firm; however, the entire authorized capital need not be raised immediately. In practice, often a portion of what has been authorized is held for issue at a later date, if and when the firm should require additional capital. Thus, what is actually issued is less than or equal to what is authorized and the amount that is actually raised is referred to as the *issued capital*. The value of the shares that is currently being held by the investors is referred to as the *outstanding capital*. In most cases, the outstanding capital is synonymous with the issued capital. In the event of a company buying back shares from the public, however, the outstanding capital will decline and consequently will be less than what was issued.

Shareholders are entitled to share the profits made by the firm, as they represent the owners of the venture. A firm will typically pay out a percentage of the profits earned by it during the financial year, in the form of cash to its shareholders. These cash payouts that shareholders receive from the firm are referred to as *dividends*. In practice, the entire profits earned by a firm will usually not be distributed to the shareholders. Most companies will choose to retain a part of what they have earned to meet future requirements of cash on account of activities such as expansion and diversification. The profits that are retained or reinvested in the firm are called *retained earnings*. The earnings that are retained will manifest themselves as an increase in the Reserves and Surplus account and will show up on the liabilities side of the balance sheet of the firm. Retained earnings can be a major source of capital for a corporation.

Shareholders are termed as *residual claimants*, and this categorization is valid in two respects. Every firm will have creditors to whom it owes money on a priority basis. For instance, it is a common practice to raise borrowed capital from investors in the form of what are known as bonds or debentures, a topic that we will cover in the next chapter. Creditors always enjoy priority over the owners of the firm when it comes to receiving payments. Thus, a firm may declare a dividend only after all payments due to its creditors have been made. Consequently, dividends are not contractually guaranteed, and can in principle fluctuate significantly from year to year. Being a residual claimant, a shareholder cannot demand a dividend as a matter of right. It is up to the board of directors of a firm to take decisions pertaining to dividends. Shareholders, of course, indirectly influence the dividend policy of the firm, because they have the power to elect the board of directors.

Shareholders may be said to be residual claimants from another perspective as well. At times sustained losses could lead to a situation where a firm is forced to file for bankruptcy. In such cases the assets of the firm will be liquidated and the proceeds from the same will be used to compensate the stakeholders. Once again the order of priority is such that the creditors will have to be paid first. If any funds were to remain after the creditors have been fully paid, then and only then will the shareholders be entitled to a return of capital.

Equity shares have no maturity date. That is, in practice, no entrepreneur will incorporate a company with a termination or winding-up date in mind. Thus the shares issued by the firm will continue to be in existence until and unless the firm itself is wound up. In contrast, most bonds and debentures, as we will see in the next chapter, are issued for a specified term to maturity.

Unlike the owners of a sole proprietorship or a partnership, shareholders of a corporation enjoy limited liability. That is, if a firm were to face serious financial difficulties and consequently be unable to pay what is due to its creditors, neither it nor its creditors can make financial demands on the shareholders by asking them to commit more capital. On the other hand, if a partnership were to go bankrupt, its creditors can come after the partners personally and stake a claim on their personal assets. Thus, the maximum financial loss shareholders may suffer is limited to the investment they made in the process of acquisition of shares at the outset. That is, the market price of a share has a lower limit of zero in principle, and if this limit were to be reached, the shares will be totally worthless, and the investors would have lost the entire amount they invested.

PAR VALUE VERSUS BOOK VALUE

Common stock usually has a par value also known as the face value or the stated value. The par value has no significance in practice, and in countries like the United States it can be fixed at a low and arbitrary level. Many companies in the United States choose to issue stocks with very low par values because, as per the regulations of certain states, the cost of incorporating a firm is based on the par value of the shares being registered. Hence such fees can be minimized by assigning low par values.

In the case of shares with a nil par value, the creditors of the firm cannot ask the shareholders to contribute additional capital. This may be explained as follows. Assume a firm is authorized to issue 250,000 shares with a par value of $10 each, and that it has chosen to issue 150,000 shares. Thus, the authorized capital is

$2.50 million while the issued capital is $1.50 million. At times, the company may ask the shareholders to pay up a fraction at the outset and call for the balance later. In such situations, the paid-up capital, which is the amount paid per share multiplied by the number of shares issued, will be less than the issued capital. If we assume that the shareholders have been asked to pay $8 per share, the paid-up capital is $1.20 million. If the firm were to subsequently experience financial difficulties, the creditors can demand that the shareholders pay up the difference between the issued capital and the paid-up capital, which is $300,000 in this case; however, if the shares have a zero par value, the entire contribution from the shareholders will be treated as the share premium, and such a demand cannot be made.

In the case of a no-par stock, the board of directors will assign a value to the stock each time they raise capital. Such stocks are popular with small organizations where the owners issue themselves a number of shares and simply infuse money into the corporation when needed. Such stock gives more flexibility to the corporation. Because there is no stated price for the stock, the directors can raise the price when the firm becomes more valuable.

The issue price of a share need not be equal to its par value and will often be in excess of its par value. This is true for companies that are already established at the time of issue. The excess of the issue price over the par value is referred to as the *share premium*. For instance, assume that Alpha Corporation is issuing 100,000 shares with a par value of $5 at a price of $12.50 per share. If the issue is successful, the company will raise $1,250,000 from the market. In the balance sheet, $500,000 would be reported as share capital and $750,000 would be reported as the share premium.

ACCOUNTING FOR A STOCK ISSUE

If shares are issued at the par value, the transaction would be recorded as follows. Assume 100,000 shares are issued at a par value of $10 each. Common stock, which is a liability for the firm, will be credited with $1,000,000 and cash, which is an asset, will be debited with $1,000,000. However, if the shares are issued at a premium of $10 each, then the common stock account will be credited with $1,000,000 and the additional paid-in capital account will be credited with $1,000,000. Cash will of course be debited with $2,000,000.

The book value is the value of a firm as obtained from the balance sheet or books of account, and hence the name. The term refers to the value of the assets behind a share, as per the balance sheet. In practice, it is derived by adding up the par value, the share premium, and the retained earnings and dividing by the number of shares issued by the firm. The book value can obviously be very different from the par value of the shares. A third term that is used in practice is the market value of a firm. This is the value assigned to the shares of the company by the stock market and is determined by multiplying the number of shares issued by the firm with the current market price per share.

VOTING RIGHTS

Investors who choose to acquire equity shares of a firm are conferred with voting rights, which includes the right to elect the directors of the company. The most common arrangement is to give a shareholder one vote per every share of stock being held; however, in practice, shares with differential voting rights can be issued.

If a firm were to issue multiple classes of shares, which differ from the standpoint of the voting rights bestowed on the holders, the categories of shares are usually otherwise similar to each other. That is, all shareholders, irrespective of their voting privileges, have an unlimited right to participate in the earnings of the corporation. They also have an equal right on the assets of the company upon liquidation, after all the other creditors and prioritized security holders have been paid off. All shares in a given class or category have equal standing, irrespective of the point in time or the price at which they are issued. For instance, if Alpha Corporation were to issue three years after its IPO, another 100,000 shares at $17.50 per share, then the newly issued shares will rank at par with the 100,000 shares issued earlier. In legal terms the two tranches are said to rank *pari passu*.

At times equity shares are divided into two or more classes with differential voting rights. One or more categories may have subordinated voting rights, and at times a category may be issued with no voting rights. The purpose of such an exercise is to vest the voting powers with a minority of shareholders who can consequently control the company with less than a 50% equity stake.

A group of shareholders can exert considerable influence over the affairs of their company if they satisfy one of these criteria:

- They own more than 50% of the voting shares.
- When they have one or more representatives on the board of directors.
- When they themselves are directors of the company.

In practice, minority shareholders have very little say in the affairs of their company, despite the fact that they do enjoy voting rights. This is particularly true when the company is controlled by a majority shareholder.

Statutory Versus Cumulative Voting

Every share of stock held by an investor corresponds to one vote for each director position that is up for voting; however, the votes may be apportioned in two different ways. Assume that a shareholder has 1,000 shares and that there are four vacancies on the board. If statutory voting were to be applicable, the shareholder can cast a total of 4,000 votes in all; however, not more than 1,000 votes can be cast in favor of any one candidate. On the other hand, if cumulative voting were to be applicable, then the votes could be apportioned in any way that the shareholder chooses. In this case too, a total of 4,000 votes can be cast. One shareholder may decide to cast 3,000 votes in favor of one candidate and 1,000 in favor of a second, without giving any votes to the remaining candidates. Alternatively, another shareholder in a similar situation may cast 1,000 votes in favor of each of four candidates. Cumulative voting is designed to give minority shareholders the opportunity to elect at least one candidate of their choosing, for it gives them the power to concentrate the votes on a candidate.

Proxies

In order to enjoy the right to vote, an investor must be a shareholder *of record*. What this means is the following. The registrar of a firm will be maintaining a record of its current shareholders. Only those listed on the corporation's register of shareholders as of a date known as the *record date* are eligible shareholders, from the standpoint of being eligible to cast a vote. The *record date* is usually a few days prior to the date of the meeting at which the actual voting will take place. Therefore, in practice, it is conceivable that a person who happens to be a shareholder of record, by virtue of their name appearing in the register on the record date, may have sold their shares prior to the date of the meeting. In such cases the new owner who has acquired the shares cannot in principle vote, as their name will not be reflected in the register. To get over this problem, the seller(s) of the shares can give a proxy to the buyer(s).

It is not realistic to expect a large percentage of the shareholders of large companies to attend the annual meetings in order to be physically present to cast their votes. Thus, in practice, companies choose to send a proxy statement to absentee shareholders along with a ballot, prior to the scheduled date of the meeting. The shareholders are expected to mark their preferences and return the ballot prior to the date of the meeting. A typical proxy statement will include information on the individuals seeking appointment or reappointment as directors, and details of any resolutions for which the opinions of the shareholders are being sought, which is consequently the raison d'être for the vote. Once the ballots are received from the absentee shareholders, they will be collated, and a person appointed by the firm will cast the votes as directed by the shareholders who have submitted the ballots.

In practice there is a critical reason why companies require shareholders to attend meetings or to send proxies if they are unable to be physically present. This is because a *quorum* is required before any business can be transacted. That is, a minimum number of shares must be represented at the meeting, either by the holders in person or in the form of proxies.

DIVIDENDS

As explained earlier, shareholders are residual claimants. Consequently, they cannot demand dividends from the firm; that is, dividends, unlike interest payments to creditors, are not a contractual obligation. That is, the payment of dividends is not mandatory, and the decision to pay or not to pay is entirely at the discretion of the board of directors of the company. Companies usually declare a dividend when they announce their results for a period. In the United States, since results are typically declared on a quarterly basis, dividends are also announced every quarter. In the United Kingdom most companies pay their annual dividends in two stages.

A dividend declaration is a statement of considerable importance. It is an affirmation by the company that its affairs are on track, and that it has adequate resources to reinvest in its operations as well as to reward its shareholders.

In the context of a dividend payment, there are four dates that are important. The first is what is termed as the *declaration date*. It is the date on which the decision to pay a dividend is declared by the directors of the company, and the amount of the dividend is announced. The dividend announcement will mention a second date called the *record date*. The significance of this date is the same as we have seen earlier for voting. That is, only those shareholders whose names appear as of the record date on the register of shareholders will be eligible to receive the forthcoming dividend.

A third and extremely critical date is what is termed as the *ex-dividend date*, which is specified by the stock exchange on which the shares are traded. The relationship between the record date and the ex-dividend date depends on the settlement cycle. The term *settlement cycle* refers to the duration between the date of a sale transaction and the date on which securities are received by the buyer and cash is received by the seller. The import of the ex-dividend date is that an investor who purchases shares on or after the ex-dividend date will not be eligible to receive the forthcoming dividend. Thus the ex-dividend date will be set a few days before the share transfer book is scheduled to be closed, in order to help the share registrar complete the administrative formalities.

Quite obviously, the ex-dividend date will be such that transactions prior to that date will be reflected in the register of shareholders as on the record date, whereas transactions on or after that date will be reflected in the books only after the record date. It is therefore easy to surmise the relationship between the two dates. Assume that an exchange follows a T+3 settlement cycle; that is, it takes three business days after the trade date to fully consummate the trade. Obviously, if the trade were to take place three days before the record date or earlier, then the transfer will be reflected as on the record date. Consequently, the ex-dividend date in such cases must be two business days before the record date.

The NYSE, for instance, follows a T+3 settlement cycle. Hence, on the NYSE the ex-dividend date for an issue is specified as two business days prior to the record date announced by the firm.

Prior to the ex-dividend date, the shares are said to be traded on a cum-dividend basis, which means that the right to receive the dividend is inherent in the shares. Therefore, an investor who acquires the share on a cum-dividend basis is entitled to receive the dividend. On the ex-dividend date, the shares begin to trade ex-dividend, which connotes that potential buyers will no longer be eligible to receive the next dividend if they were to acquire the share. This is because it is too late for buyers' names to figure in the register as of the record date, and consequently dividends will go to the parties selling the shares.

On the ex-dividend date, the shares ought to in theory decline by the amount of the dividend, if we assume there is no other information with implications for the share value that permeates the market. Thus, if the cum-dividend price is $75 per share at the close of trading on the day prior to the ex-dividend date, and the quantum of the dividend is $3.50 per share, then from a theoretical standpoint the market should open with a price of $71.50 on the ex-dividend date.

Finally, we have a date called the *distribution date*, which is purely of academic interest. This is the date on which the dividends are actually paid or distributed.

Dividend Yield

The annual dividend yield is defined as the annual dividend amount divided by the current share price, expressed in percentage terms.

$$\text{Dividend Yield} = \frac{\text{Dividend}}{\text{Price}} \times 100\%$$

For instance, take the case of a company that has reported a dividend of $2.50 per quarter over the past financial year. Assume that the current market price of the shares is $80. The dividend yield is:

$$\frac{2.50 \times 4}{80} \times 100 = 12.50\%$$

The dividend yield is a function of the share price as well as the quantum of the dividend. Yields are generally lower for profitable companies as compared to companies in financial difficulty. If the profits and thus the dividends of a company are expected to increase over time, then the yield will be relatively lower. This is because the market will place a higher value on the shares of such companies. On the other hand, companies perceived as having a lower potential for growth will have a relatively higher dividend yield. Yields are also a function of the liquidity of a scrip. Potential buyers of a stock that is thinly traded are likely to require a higher rate of return, which will manifest itself as a lower price. Consequently, the yield for such stocks will be relatively higher. It is not necessary that a company that promises a steady growth pattern of dividends will be characterized by a dividend yield that will steadily increase over time. This is because a growing dividend stream will also lead to higher share prices. The net result on the dividend yield is therefore ambiguous.

It is not necessary that the dividends that are declared in a year be less than the profits earned by the firm. Companies are allowed to pay dividends out of profits retained in earlier years. Consequently a company with relatively low profits can declare a high dividend. Similarly, a loss-making firm too can declare a dividend. Companies generally try to maintain a steady growth rate in dividends. Ideally, the growth rate of dividends should be greater than or equal to the prevailing rate of inflation. In years of financial hardship a company may be forced to cut its dividend payout. Such cuts, however, can send unwarranted distress signals to the shareholders, and if the current financial situation is perceived as a temporary aberration, the firm, despite its difficulties, may opt to keep the dividend at a steady level by dipping into profits retained in earlier years.

Dividend Reinvestment Plans

Dividend reinvestment plans, referred to by the acronym DRIPs, are schemes that allow the shareholders to opt to have the cash dividends automatically reinvested in additional shares of stock. Members can directly acquire shares from the company and consequently do not need to route the order through a broker.[1] The plans are typically administered by large banks that usually send a report every quarter to the participating investors stating how much dividend has been paid; how many additional shares have been acquired in the process of reinvestment; and the total number of shares held in the shareholder's account. The plan administrator may levy an annual fee, which will in some cases be paid by the company issuing the shares.

There are two basic types of DRIPs. In some cases the company will acquire shares in the open market and reissue them each time a shareholder expresses his desire to reinvest dividends. These plans are administered by a bank acting in the capacity of a trustee, which will actually buy the shares from the market for the investing shareholder. In these cases the shares are acquired at the prevailing market price.

---

[1]Quite obviously, they stand to gain by way of a saving in brokerage commissions.

Brokerage costs are often paid by the company. The second type of reinvestment plans entails the issue of additional shares directly by the company. In such cases the issuing firms may offer the shares at a discount. Firms can afford to issue shares at below the market price because despite the discount, the shares can be sold at a higher price as compared to an underwritten public issue.

Stock Dividends

A stock dividend is a dividend that is distributed in the form of shares of stock rather than in the form of cash. The issue of additional shares is without requiring any monetary contribution from the investors, as a consequence of which such a corporate action is referred to as a *bonus share issue* in some markets. A stock dividend entails the transfer of funds from the reserves and surplus account to the share capital account. This is known as the *capitalization of reserves*. The net result is that funds are transferred from an account that belongs to the shareholders to another account that is also theirs.

Hence, from a theoretical standpoint, stock dividends do not create any value for an existing shareholder. For instance, assume that a shareholder owns 1,000 shares of a firm which has issued a total of 500,000 shares. So, this individual owns 0.20% of the firm. Now assume that the firm announces a 20% stock dividend, or 1 additional share for every five existing shares. If so, it will have to issue 100,000 shares of which this investor will receive 200. Hence after the issue of the additional shares, the investor will be in possession of 1,200 shares, which is 0.20% of the total number of shares issued by the firm, which is 600,000. Thus, the investor's percentage stake in the company remains unaltered.

From the perspective of the company, the issue of the new shares does not connote any changes in the asset base of the firm. Nor does it signal any enhancements to the earnings capacity of the firm. All that has happened is an accounting transaction. It is as if an investor has two bank accounts, one with Citibank and the other with JPMorgan Chase. What has happened is that we have debited one account and credited the other, without increasing or decreasing the investor's wealth in the process.

The share price should theoretically decline after a stock dividend is declared. Let us go back to our illustration and assume that the share price prior to the stock dividend was $60 per share. The ex-dividend price, P, should be such that

$$500,000 \times 60 = 600,000 \times P$$

$$\Rightarrow P = \$50$$

A stock dividend is usually declared when a firm wants to reward its shareholders without having to face an external outflow of cash. In practice there could be various reasons why the firm wishes to conserve cash. One reason could be that the firm is short of funds. Or else it could be that the available cash is required for productive investments.

Sometimes a company may declare a stock dividend prior to the payment of a cash dividend. The implications for the share price may be analyzed with the help of a numerical example.

Silverline Technologies has 500,000 shares outstanding, and the price is $60 per share. The firm announces a stock dividend of 20% and a cash dividend of $4.00 per share. The company also declares that the new shares that come into existence by virtue of the stock dividend will be eligible for the cash dividend.

The cum-stock dividend cum-cash dividend price is obviously $60. Hence the market value of the firm is

$$500,000 \times 60 = \$30,000,000$$

Because the stock dividend in theory is value neutral, in principle the market capitalization of the firm after the stock dividend should remain at $30,000,000. Thus, the theoretical price of ex-stock dividend ex-cash dividend shares will be

$$(30,000,000 - 4.00 \times 600,000) \div 600,000 = \$46$$

TREASURY STOCK

The term *Treasury Stock* refers to shares that were at one point in time issued to the public, but which have subsequently been reacquired by the firm.

These shares are held by the company and can subsequently be reissued, for instance, if and when employees were to exercise their stock options. Unlike the shares issued by the firm that are held by shareholders, Treasury shares carry no voting rights, are ineligible for dividends, and are not included in the denominator used for computation of the earnings per share (EPS).

Why do companies repurchase shares? One motivation could be that the directors of the firm are of the opinion that the market is undervaluing the stock, and consequently they would like to prop up the share price by creating greater demand. For a given level of profitability a buyback program will increase the earnings per share. And if the *dividends per share* (DPS) were to be kept constant, it would also reduce the total amount of dividends that the company needs to declare. Buyback is also a potent tool for fighting a potential takeover by corporate raiders. By reducing the shares in circulation, the current management can acquire greater control.

There are also situations where a company is generating a lot of cash but is unable to identify profitable avenues for investment, that is, it is unable to identify projects with a positive *net present value* (NPV). One way of dealing with such a situation is to declare an extraordinary dividend. But in many countries, shareholders are taxed for cash dividends at the normal income tax rate, which could be significant for investors in higher tax brackets. On the other hand, if investors were to sell their shares back to the firm at a price that is higher than what they paid to acquire them, the profits will be construed as capital gains, which in most countries are taxed at a lower rate.

ACCOUNTING FOR TREASURY STOCK

When a company buys back its own shares from the market, there are two ways of accounting for it, namely the cash method and the par value method. Assume that on 1 January 20XX, a company had issued 100,000 shares with a par value of $5 and a price of $8 each. Cash would have been debited with 800,000; common stock would have been credited with 500,000; and additional paid in capital would have been credited with 300,000.

Now, three years hence, the company decides to buy back 20,000 shares at a price of $9.50 each. Under the cash method, cash will be credited with $20,000 \times 9.50 = \$190,000$. A contra liability account called Treasury Stock would be debited with $190,000. Unlike share capital, which will have a credit balance, a contra liability account will have a debit balance.

If, however, the company were to use the par value method, it would proceed as follows. The Treasury Stock account will be debited with the par value of 20,000 shares, which is $100,000. The additional paid-in capital will be debited with $4.50 per share, which is the difference between the repurchase price and the par value and will amount to $90,000. Cash will once again be credited with $190,000.

SPLITS AND REVERSE SPLITS

An *n:1* stock split means that *n* new shares will be issued to the existing shareholders in lieu of one existing share. For instance, a 5:4 split means that a holder of four existing shares will receive five shares after the split, without having to invest any more funds. From a mathematical standpoint this is exactly analogous to a 25% stock dividend. However, despite this equivalence, a stock split is operationally different from a stock dividend. While stock dividends entail the capitalization of reserves, stock splits do not. What happens in the case of a split is that the par value of existing shares is reduced and the number of shares outstanding is correspondingly increased. The net result is that the issued capital remains unchanged. For instance, take the case of a company which has issued 100,000 shares with a face value of $100. If it were to announce a 5:4 stock split, the number of shares issued would increase to 125,000, while the par value would stand reduced to $80.

Why do companies split their shares? In practice, companies generally go in for such a course of action if, in the perception of management, the share price of the firm has become too high. While in theory there is nothing wrong with the stock price being at a relatively high level, companies wanting to attract a broad class of investors will try to ensure that their scrip is within an affordable price range for small and medium investors. It is difficult to categorically state as to what a high price is, and what constitutes an affordable price range. But in practice it is believed that most managers have a feel for what is the popular price range for their stock. In other words, they are believed to be aware of the price range within which their stock should trade, if it is to attract adequate attention from investors. Historically investors have normally traded in round lots, or board lots, which is usually defined as a bundle of 100 shares. Anything less than a round lot is referred to as an odd lot. Round lots had a lot of significance when physical share certificates were the norm. In those circumstances special procedures were often required for odd lots, because only an investor with an odd lot was likely to be interested in another trader with a similar lot. It must be pointed out, however, that with the advent of dematerialized or scrip-less trading, this distinction does not carry any significance. Psychologically, though, many investors are still comfortable trading in round lots. At very high share prices, small and medium investors may not be able to afford round lots. Thus, one of the motives that has been expounded to justify stock splits is the desire to ensure that even small investors can buy round lots of the firm's shares.

The opposite of a stock split is a reverse split or a consolidation. The difference between an *n:m* split and an *n:m* reverse split is that in the first case *n* will be greater than *m*, whereas in the second case it will be less. For instance, assume that the company, which has 100,000 shares outstanding with a par value of $100, announces a 4:5 reverse split. It will subsequently have 80,000 shares outstanding, each of which will have a par value of $125. Companies are likely to go in for such a course of action if their managements perceive that their stock prices are too low. Exchanges like the NYSE discourage the listing of securities consistently trading at very low prices. This is because such prices have a tendency to attract inexperienced traders with unrealistic price expectations who could get their fingers burned. This is referred to as the *penny stock trap*. For instance, take the case of a share that is trading at $1. A naïve investor may buy it in the belief that a mere 50 cents increase in the price will amount to a 50% return on investment. What such investors fail to realize is that such a gain is highly improbable for a company in the doldrums.

In practice, stock splits will usually result in a reduced dividend per share. This is because, given that the number of shares on which dividends have to be paid is a multiple of the number of shares outstanding prior to the split, most companies will have little option but to reduce the magnitude of the dividend per share. In many cases, however, companies will increase the aggregate dividends. This may be best understood with the help of an example. Take the case of a company that was paying a dividend of $2.50 per share. Assume it announces a 5:4 split. The post-split dividend may be fixed at $2.20 per share, so that holders of four shares prior to the split – who would ordinarily have been entitled to a dividend of $10 – will now be entitled to an aggregate dividend of $11 on the five shares that they possess as a consequence of the split.

EXAMPLE 3.1

We will now illustrate the impact of stock splits and consolidations on the prevailing market price.

Assume that a company has 1,000,000 shares outstanding that are currently trading at $80 per share. The market capitalization is $80,000,000. If it were to announce a 5:4 split, then the market capitalization of 1,250,000 shares after the split will in theory be $80MM. Thus, the theoretical post-split price should be:

$$1,250,000 \times P = 1,000,000 \times 80$$

$$\Rightarrow P = \$64$$

Now consider a 4:5 reverse split. If so, the theoretical market capitalization of 800,000 shares ought to be $80MM. Thus:

$$1,000,000 \times 80 = 800,000 \times P$$

$$\Rightarrow P = \$100$$

Costs Associated with Splits and Stock Dividends

Research by Copeland has found that there are two types of transaction costs that increase following a stock split. Such costs serve to ultimately reduce the liquidity of the stock. First, brokerage fees measured in percentages will increase after a split. Generally, fees for low-priced securities are a larger percentage of the sales price than they are for high-priced securities. For example, an investor will pay a higher commission when buying 100 shares trading at $100 each than when buying 40 shares trading at $250 each. Secondly, Copeland finds that the bid–ask spread, expressed as a percentage of the sales price, rises after a stock split. Thus, it is debatable whether the benefits associated with such corporate actions outweigh the corresponding costs.

PREEMPTIVE RIGHTS

The directors of a company must obtain the approval of existing shareholders if they wish to issue shares beyond what has already been issued earlier. As per the charter or articles of association of some corporations, existing shareholders must be given the first right to buy the additional shares being issued, in proportion to the shares that they already own. Of course, the right to acquire the shares confers them with an option, and does not require a mandatory course of action. Thus, this requirement ensures that existing shareholders have a preemptive right to acquire new shares as and when they are issued.[2] In other words, they have an opportunity to maintain their proportionate ownership in the company. The merits of giving such rights to existing shareholders are debatable. Many people have argued that preemption rules prevent new investors from achieving meaningful stakes in companies, thereby narrowing the shareholder base and increasing dependence on a few investors. Others argue that the right to maintain one's proportional investment is just and fair for the existing shareholders.

Usually, the rights issue is made at a price that is lower than the prevailing market price of the share. If so, then the right acquires a value of its own. The existing shareholders in this case can either exercise their rights and acquire additional shares, or sell the rights to someone else. In most cases the discount from the prevailing market price is set between 10 and 15%. Readers may be surprised to know that rights issues too are usually underwritten. One may wonder as to why there is a need for underwriting, considering that the firm has a captive audience. The reason is that the rights issue must remain open for a specified number of days. During this period, it is conceivable that the market price may fall below the issue price set by the company. In such circumstances, investors would not subscribe to the issue since they can always acquire the shares for a lower price in the secondary market.

What is the value of a right? Let us suppose that a company has 1,000,000 shares outstanding and that shareholders are entitled to purchase one new share for every five shares they are holding; thus, the firm will be issuing 200,000 additional shares. Let us assume that the prevailing market price is $85 per share, and that the additional shares are being issued at $55 per share. The market capitalization of the firm prior

---

[2]In this case we are talking about shares being issued for a monetary consideration.

to the issue is \$85MM. The rights issue is infusing an additional \$11MM into the firm. Thus, the post-issue firm value in theory ought to be \$96MM. This would imply that, considering the fact that 1.2MM shares will be outstanding after the issue, the ex-rights price ought to be such that:

$$P \times 1,200,000 = 96,000,000$$

$$\Rightarrow P = \$80$$

The current shareholders are getting a share worth \$80 at \$55. This implies that the value of the right to acquire one share is \$25. Since the shareholder needs five shares to acquire the right to buy one share, the value of a right is \$5.

Prima facie, it would appear that the issue of additional shares at a discount to their current value would amount to a loss for the existing shareholders. This is because while the cum-rights price is \$85, the ex-rights price is \$5 lower. But there is a fallacy in this perspective. It is important to remember that the shareholders have been given the opportunity to buy new shares at \$55, and that this opportunity compensates for the decline in the price of the share.

For instance, let us consider an investor who is in possession of 100 shares. The value of these shares prior to the rights issue will be \$8,500. If the investor decides to exercise those rights, they can acquire 20 additional shares by paying an additional \$55 for each. The value of the portfolio in this case would be:

$$120 \times 80 = 9,600 = 8,500 + 1,100$$

Thus, the portfolio is worth the original \$8,500 plus the additional amount of \$1,100 that the investor has pumped in. Consequently, there is no loss of value or dilution.

An investor who decides not to exercise their rights can renounce them in favor of another investor. The rights can in this case be sold for \$5 per right. The investor's wealth in the event of such renunciation would be $80 \times 100 + 5 \times 100 = \$8,500$, which is nothing but the original value of the portfolio. Thus, in this case as well, there is no loss of value.

In practice, the ex-rights price may be higher than what we would expect from theory. This could be because the rights issue may be perceived as a signal of information emanating from the firm. In reality, the very fact that the company has chosen to issue additional shares may be construed as an indication of enhanced future profitability. A plausible reason could be that investors believe that the new funds raised will be used for more profitable projects. Another line of argument could be that, considering the fact that cash dividends are usually maintained at existing levels in the medium term, the additional shares from the perspective of the shareholders are a sign of greater profitability from the existing operations of the firm. Both these factors could serve to push up the demand for the firm's shares, and hence may lead to a situation where the ex-rights price, although lower than the cum-rights price, is higher than what is predicted by theory.

When a stock with rights is trading on an exchange it is said to be trading cum-rights. The rights certificates are issued to the shareholders on the *rights record date*. A rights certificate gives the shareholder the right, but not the obligation, to buy additional shares of stock at the subscription price. On an exchange that follows a T+3 settlement cycle, the ex-rights date will be two days before the rights record date. From the time of announcement of the rights issue until the ex-rights date, the rights are attached to the stock. During the ex-rights period the rights are sold separately just like a share of stock. The rights usually expire 4–6 weeks after the ex-rights date. After this point the rights are worthless.

Shareholders receive one right for each share of stock that they own. The number of rights required to acquire one share of stock is obtained by dividing the number of outstanding shares by the number of shares that the firm proposes to issue. For instance, assume that a company has 100,000 shares outstanding, and that it wants to raise $500,000 of capital by issuing rights with a subscription price of $25. Quite obviously it needs to issue 20,000 new shares. Consequently, the number of rights required to acquire one new share is

$$\frac{100,000}{20,000} = 5$$

INTERPRETING STATED RATIOS

Consider a rights issue of one share for every four shares that are being held. In Europe and Asia this will be indicated as a 1:4 rights issue; that is, the first number denotes the additional quantity of the security to be distributed while the second number is the quantity of the underlying security relative to which the additional securities are being issued. Thus, an investor with 2,500 shares would be entitled to an additional 625 shares. In total, that investor will have 3,125 shares if exercising that right.

In the United States, however, this will be indicated as a 5:4 rights issue. The first number denotes the total quantity held after the event while the second number is the quantity relative to which the additional securities are being issued. Thus, an investor who is holding 2,500 shares will have $(2,500 \times 5)/4 = 3,125$ shares if subscribing to the issue.

HANDLING FRACTIONS

Assume that an investor is holding 945 shares of a company that has announced a 5:8 reverse split. This will consequently entitle the investor to 590.625 shares. Quite obviously, one cannot be allocated 0.625 shares of stock. Consequently, the issuer must specify a method to deal with this eventuality. The commonly prescribed methods include the following.[3]

1. Round up the fraction to the next higher whole number. In this case it will be 591 shares.
2. Round up the fraction to the next higher whole number if it is greater than or equal to 0.50. If it is less than 0.50, however, round down to the previous whole number. In this case it will be 591 shares.

---

[3]See Simmons and Dalgleish (2006).

3. Round up the fraction to the next higher whole number if it is greater than 0.50. If it is less than or equal to 0.50, however, round down to the previous whole number. In this case it will be 591 shares.
4. Round down the fraction to the previous whole number. In this case it will be 590 shares.
5. Distribute cash in lieu of the fractional security. If we assume that the company pays out $20 per share, the investor will receive $12.50 in lieu of 0.625 shares.

In those cases where the rounding procedure leads to the previous whole number investors may be given an option to buy a fraction of a share so that they are entitled to the next whole number. For instance, if the practice is to round down to the previous whole number, investors may in this case be given the option to buy 0.375 shares so as to be entitled to 591 shares.

PHYSICAL CERTIFICATES VERSUS BOOK ENTRY

Traditionally, equity shares have been represented by physical certificates, where each certificate represents ownership of a stated quantity of shares. These days, however, in many countries, investors can hold shares as a computer entry or in book-entry form. This facility is provided by organizations known as securities depositories. In the United States the major depository is the Depository Trust and Clearing Corporation (DTCC). In the United Kingdom it is Crest, while in Europe we have Clearstream based in Luxembourg and Euroclear based in Brussels. When shares are held in book-entry form they are said to be either dematerialized or immobilized. In the case of a dematerialized share, there is no physical certificate, and the book entry is the sole means of record. However, in the case of immobilized shares, although a book entry is created, the original physical certificates are kept in safe custody and are not destroyed.

As can be surmised, book entry makes share transfers a lot easier. In the case of physical shares, when a sale is made, the seller's scrip would have to be canceled and one or more new scrips would have to be created. In the case of dematerialized trading, however, all that is required is a debit to the seller's account at the depository and a credit to the buyer's account.

TRACKING STOCK

Tracking stocks, also known as targeted stocks, are issued by many companies in addition to the usual equity shares. A tracking stock tracks the performance of a specific business unit or operating division of a company. Thus, the value of such stock is determined by the performance of this division rather than that of the company as a whole. If the unit or division does well, the tracking stock will rise in value, even though the company as a whole may have underperformed. The converse is also obviously true. Such stocks are traded as separate securities.

Unlike normal equity, tracking stocks usually have limited or no voting rights. If the stock were to pay dividends, the quantum of the dividend would depend on the financial performance of the concerned business unit or division.

REPORT CARDS

Companies issue quarterly and annual reports as mandated by the regulator. Such reports are intended to provide relevant information to the shareholders. Quarterly reports provide shareholders with a summary of the company's performance over the preceding three months. The reports often contain the firm's balance sheet as at the end of the quarter and an income statement for the same period. A copy has to be filed with the market regulator. In the United States, quarterly reports which are filed with the Securities and Exchange Commission (SEC) are called 10Q reports. In addition, at the end of every financial year, US-based companies are required to file an annual report with the SEC called the 10K report.

TYPES OF STOCKS

Most stocks are classified as either growth stocks or cyclical stocks. A cyclical stock is one whose fortunes rise and fall in tandem with the business cycle; that is, the stock price rises during an economic boom and falls during a recession. While this is a feature to some extent of all traded stocks, cyclical stocks are characterized by extreme sensitivity to changes in the business cycle. Two examples of cyclical stocks are automobile stocks and stocks of real estate developers. The reason is that when the economy is on an upward trend, there is a tendency for people to invest in new cars and new houses. However, during a recession, investors tend to postpone the purchase of such durable assets.

The term *growth stocks* is used for the stocks of companies whose sales and earnings have grown faster than those of an average firm and can be reasonably expected to display a similar trend in the future. Investors tend to acquire such stocks in anticipation of capital appreciation. This is because while such firms do pay dividends periodically, they exhibit a marked tendency to retain profits in order to fuel further growth. Unlike cyclical stocks, the performance of such stocks depends more on the quality of the products and the capability of the management teams, and less on economy-wide factors. Stocks of food-and-beverage and pharmaceutical companies usually fall into this category.

Interest-sensitive Stocks

The performance of the equity markets is generally better when interest rates are low. There are two reasons for this. First, most businesses rely to a large extent on borrowed money. In a low interest environment, the financing costs for such firms will go down, and this has obvious implications for their profitability. Second, when rates are low, consumers are likely to borrow more to fund their purchases.

Interest-sensitive stocks are those whose performance is very closely linked to movements in interest rates. These include:

- Utility firms
- Banks
- Brokerage houses
- Insurance companies

RISK AND RETURN AND THE CONCEPT OF DIVERSIFICATION

Consider two securities whose returns are given by the probability distribution shown in Table 3.1.

The expected return is a probability weighted average of returns.

The expected return of asset A is:

$$E(r_A) = 0.10 \times -10 + 0.15 \times -6 + 0.10 \times 0 + 0.25 \times 8 + 0.20 \times 12 + 0.20 \times 20$$

$$= 6.50\%$$

Similarly the expected return of asset B is given by:

$$E(r_B) = 0.10 \times -12 + 0.15 \times 3 + 0.10 \times 8 + 0.25 \times 4 + 0.20 \times 6 + 0.20 \times 12 = 4.65\%$$

The variance is a probability-weighted average of squared deviations from the mean or the expected value. The variance of asset A's return is given by:

$$\sigma_A^2 = 0.10 \times (-10 - 6.50)^2 + 0.15 \times (-6 - 6.50)^2 + 0.10(0 - 6.50)^2$$

$$+ 0.25 \times (8 - 6.50)^2 + 0.20 \times (12 - 6.50)^2 + 0.20 \times (20 - 6.50)^2 = 97.95$$

Similarly, the variance of asset B's return is given by:

$$\sigma_B^2 = 0.10 \times (-12 - 4.65)^2 + 0.15 \times (3 - 4.65)^2 + 0.10(8 - 4.65)^2$$

$$+ 0.25 \times (4 - 4.65)^2 + 0.20 \times (6 - 4.65)^2 + 0.20 \times (12 - 4.65)^2 = 40.5275$$

The square root of the variance is known as the standard deviation. In this case $\sigma_A = 9.8970$ and $\sigma_B = 6.3661$. The return, the expected return, and the standard deviation have the same unit of measure, in this case, percentage.

When we have more than two assets, we need to assess the way the assets move with respect to each other. For this purpose, we compute two statistics, *covariance* and *correlation*. The covariance is the probability weighted average of the product of the deviation from the mean for the two variables.

TABLE 3.1 Asset Returns

Probability	Return on Asset A	Return on Asset B
0.10	−10%	−12%
0.15	−6%	3%
0.10	0%	8%
0.25	8%	4%
0.20	12%	6%
0.20	20%	12%

In this case:

$$\text{Covariance}(r_A, r_B) = 0.10 \times (-10 - 6.50)(-12 - 4.65) + 0.15 \times (-6 - 6.50)$$
$$\times (3 - 4.65) + 0.10 \times (0 - 6.50)(8 - 4.65) + 0.25(8 - 6.50)$$
$$\times (4 - 4.65) + 0.20 \times (12 - 6.50)(6 - 4.65) + 0.20$$
$$\times (20 - 6.50)(12 - 4.65) = 49.4750$$

The correlation is obtained by dividing the covariance by the product of the two standard deviations. In this case, the correlation is given by $\rho_{A,B} = 49.4750/(9.897 \times 6.3661) = 0.7853$. The value of the correlation will always lie between -1.00 and $+1.00$.

While studying stocks in isolation we use the variance as a measure of risk. However, as we have studied earlier no rational investor will hold a security in isolation, but will rather hold a well-diversified portfolio. The underlying rationale is that although there is no option but to tolerate exposure to economy-wide risk – what in finance is termed as systematic risk – it is possible to eliminate idiosyncratic or firm-specific risk by holding a well-diversified portfolio. Thus, the relevant measure of risk of an asset is not its variance but its covariance with other assets.

From the Capital Asset Pricing Model (CAPM), the relevant measure of risk in a portfolio context is Beta (β). Beta is defined as the covariance of an asset's return with the rate of return on the market portfolio, divided by the variance of the return on the market portfolio. The market portfolio is a value-weighted portfolio of all assets in the economy.

If we denote the expected return from asset i as $E(r_i)$; the expected return on the market portfolio as $E(r_m)$; and the riskless rate of interest as r_f; then from the CAPM: $E(r_i) = r_f + \beta_i[E(r_m) - r_f]$.

The expected return of a portfolio is a weighted average of the expected returns of the constituent assets. The variance of a portfolio's return is not, however, a weighted average of the variances of its components.

Consider three assets with returns r_1, r_2, and r_3. Consider a portfolio with weights of w_1, w_2, and w_3 in the three assets, where the weights obviously will sum to 1.00.

The expected portfolio return is given by: $E(r_P) = w_1 E(r_1) + w_2 E(r_2) + w_3 E(r_3)$
The portfolio variance is given by:

$$\sigma_P^2 = w_1^2 \sigma_1^2 + w_2^2 \sigma_2^2 + w_3^2 \sigma_3^2 + 2w_1 w_2 \sigma_{1,2} + 2w_2 w_3 \sigma_{2,3} + 2w_1 w_3 \sigma_{1,3}$$

$\sigma_{i,j}$ is the covariance of the returns on assets i and j.
The beauty of the portfolio beta is that it too is a linear combination of the betas of the components.

$$\beta_P = \text{Cov}(r_P, r_m)/\text{Var}(r_m) = \text{Cov}(w_1 r_1 + w_2 r_2 + w_3 r_3, r_m)/\text{Var}(r_m)$$
$$= [w_1 \text{Cov}(r_1, r_m) + w_2 \text{Cov}(r_2, r_m) + w_3 \text{Cov}(r_3, r_m)]/\text{Var}(r_m)$$
$$= w_1 \beta_1 + w_2 \beta_2 + w_3 \beta_3$$

PREFERRED SHARES

Preferred shares, like equity shares, are financial claims that confer ownership rights on the shareholders. The term *preferred* means that such shares have certain associated privileges. In other words, they get preference over equity shareholders in certain respects, as follows:

- Current dividends due on the preferred shares must be paid before any dividends for the year can be declared for the equity shareholders.
- If a company were to file for bankruptcy and be liquidated, the preferred shareholders have to be paid their dues before the balance, if any, can be paid to the equity shareholders. Thus, the pecking order in the event of bankruptcy is: creditors and bondholders, followed by preferred shareholders, followed by equity shareholders.

In general, preferred shares do not carry voting rights. In practice such shareholders may be temporarily conferred with the right to vote if any dividends outstanding have not been paid.

Preferred stocks usually carry a fixed rate of dividend, although there is a type with variable dividends referred to as Adjustable Rate Preferreds (ARPs). The rate may be expressed either in dollar terms or as a percentage. For instance, the term *$7.50 preferred* denotes shares carrying a dividend of $7.50 per share. Another way of expressing the same is to describe the shares as 7.50% preferred stock, assuming that the par value is $100.

Thus, from the standpoint of income distribution, preferred shares are similar to debt securities in the sense that the rate of dividends is fixed and not a function of the profits earned during the year. Unlike bonds, however, preferred stocks represent ownership of the firm and the dividend is not a legal liability, which makes them similar to equity shares. Consequently, such securities have features of both debt and equity. As in the case of equity dividends, preferred dividends must be declared by the directors of the firm.

From the standpoint of capital appreciation, such shares can rise in value. But this is usually caused by declining interest rates in the economy, which leads to a lower required rate of return and is not due to the anticipation of enhanced profitability for the firm, which is the prime driver of equity share prices. Thus, the price of a preferred share is inversely related to the prevailing rate of interest, and consequently behaves like the price of fixed income securities such as bonds and debentures.

Preferred shares offer companies the opportunity to lock in a fixed yet flexible expense. That is, although a fixed dividend is payable on such stocks, like the coupon interest on a bond, the dividends can be deferred if financial pressures preclude the firm from paying them as scheduled. The flexibility from the standpoint of dividends makes such securities similar to equity shares, and can be critical in times of financial distress.

Just like bonds, preferred shares provide leverage to common stockholders. Leverage refers to the ability to magnify returns on equity by using fixed-income securities to partly fund the firm. In the event of higher than anticipated profits, the additional earnings accrue entirely to the equity holders, as the holders of bonds and preferred shares are eligible for fixed payouts. However, in this instance it must be reiterated that although debt securities carry a fixed rate of interest, the bondholders have a legal right to be paid interest and principal when such payments fall due. Consequently, unlike in the case of preferred shares, deferral of such payments is not an option for the firm, no matter how difficult the conditions facing a firm may be.

Callable Preferred Stock

Companies issuing preferred shares in an economic environment characterized by high interest rates need to offer a high rate of dividends to make them attractive to investors. At times management may be of the opinion that although it is imperative to offer a high dividend under present circumstances, the forecast for the future is such that interest rates are headed downwards. If so, the company could issue *callable* preferred stock. As the name suggests, such shares can be prematurely recalled or retired by the company at a predetermined price, unlike conventional or plain-vanilla preferred shares, which are *non-callable*.

The presence of a call provision benefits the issuing firm because it can recall the existing issue if rates were to decline, and reissue fresh shares carrying a lower rate of dividends. If rates were to decline, however, the existing shareholders will be extremely reluctant to part with the shares, as they are earning a higher rate of return. Thus, the call provision works in favor of the issuing firm and against the investors. To sweeten the deal, companies offer callable shares that cannot be recalled for the first few years. The presence of such a feature establishes an assured return for the shareholders for a specified period, while at the same time allowing the issuer to build in the call feature.

Convertible Preferred Shares

A conversion option offers another tool to the issuing firm to sweeten the issue of the preferred shares and lock in a lower rate of dividends. Assume that a company believes that although the current atmosphere is not conducive for issuing equity shares at an attractive price, its prospects are very bright in the medium to long term and thus its equity shares will likely appreciate in value. It has the option of issuing preferred shares with an option to convert subsequently into equity at a prespecified conversion ratio. If investors are convinced that the conversion option is likely to be beneficial, they may accept a lower rate of dividends on the preferred shares than they would otherwise.

EXAMPLE 3.2

Trigyn Solutions has issued convertible preferred stock. Each share is convertible into four equity shares or, in other words, the conversion ratio is 4:1. Let the price of the preferred shares be $\$P_P$ and that of the equity shares be $\$P_E$.

If $P_P = 4P_E$, then the two types of stock are said to be *at parity*. In this case assume that the preferred share is selling at \$80 and equity shares are selling at \$20 each. So we have a situation where the two types of shares are at parity. If parity were to prevail, and the dividend of the equity shares obtained on conversion is greater than the dividend on the preferred share, then under such circumstances the preferred shareholders will normally convert. For instance, assume that the preferred share is paying a dividend of \$7.50 while the equity shares are paying

(continued)

(continued)

a dividend of $2 per share. If preferred shareholders were to convert, they would receive a total dividend of $8 from the four equity shares they would obtain on conversion. In contrast, if they were to hold on to the preferred shares, they would receive only $7.50.

If the preferred share is worth more than the value of the converted equity shares, then we say that the preferred shares are trading above parity. For instance, if the preferred share were to trade at $80 and the equity shares at $18.50 each, then the preferred share is trading above parity.

If the preferred shares were to be trading below parity, this would be tantamount to an arbitrage opportunity. For instance, assume that the preferred share is trading at $80 and that the equity shares are selling at $22 each. An arbitrageur will buy a preferred share for $80 and immediately convert it to equity shares. The four shares the arbitrageur receives can be sold for a consideration of $88, which will clearly lead to an arbitrage profit of $8. As arbitrageurs engage in this activity, the price of the preferred stock will rise due to greater demand, while that of the equity shares will fall, as everyone will be selling them. Eventually parity will be restored and will preclude further arbitrage.

Cumulative Preferred Shares

In the case of noncumulative preferred shares, if the issuing firm were to skip a dividend, then from the standpoint of the shareholder, the dividend lost is lost forever. If the preferred shares were to be cumulative in nature, however, all outstanding dividends, including the current dividend, must be paid before the management can contemplate declaring dividends for the equity shareholders. We will illustrate the difference between cumulative and noncumulative shares with the help of a simple example.

EXAMPLE 3.3

A firm has issued a preferred share with a dividend of $7.50 to Holly, and an equity share to Sandy. We will assume that they are the only two stakeholders in the firm, and that the company has a policy of paying out the entire earnings for the year as dividends.

The earnings for the company over a five-year horizon are shown in Table 3.2.

TABLE 3.2 Earnings Record

Year	Earnings
2000	15.00
2001	2.50
2002	6.50
2003	12.00
2004	22.00

If the preferred share is noncumulative, then the dividends will be distributed as shown in Table 3.3.

TABLE 3.3   Dividend Distribution: The Case of Noncumulative Shares

Year	Earnings	Preferred Dividends	Common Dividends
2000	15.00	7.50	7.50
2001	2.50	2.50	0.00
2002	6.50	6.50	0.00
2003	12.00	7.50	4.50
2004	22.00	7.50	14.50

If the preferred share is cumulative, however, then the dividends will be distributed as shown in Table 3.4.

TABLE 3.4   Dividend Distribution: The Case of Cumulative Shares

Year	Earnings	Preferred Dividends	Common Dividends
2000	15.00	7.50	7.50
2001	2.50	2.50	0.00
2002	6.50	6.50	0.00
2003	12.00	12.00	0.00
2004	22.00	9.00	13.00

Let us examine the entries in Tables 3.3 and 3.4. We will first consider the case of the noncumulative preferred share. In the year 2000 the earnings are $15.00. $7.50 will obviously be paid to the preferred shareholder, which is what is due for the year, and the balance of $7.50 will be paid to the equity shareholder, as we have assumed the firm does not have a policy of retaining any earnings. In 2001 the earnings are $2.50. The entire amount will go to the preferred shareholder, who is eligible for $7.50, but the company does not have adequate funds to pay these dues in full. Obviously, the equity holder will receive nothing under the circumstances. In 2002 earnings are $6.50. The entire amount will go to the preferred shareholder, and once again the equity holder will receive nothing. In 2003 the company earns $12.00. The preferred shareholder will receive $7.50. There is a cumulative deficit of $6.00 from the previous two years, but this need not be factored in since the shares are noncumulative. The equity holder will obviously receive $4.50. In 2004 the company has earnings of $22. It will pay $7.50 to the preferred shareholder, and the balance of $14.50 will be paid to the equity holder.

(continued)

(*continued*)

Now let us turn to the case of the cumulative preferred share. In 2000 the earnings of $15 will be adequate to pay the preferred shareholder what is due, $7.50. The balance of $7.50 will once again go to the equity holder. In 2001 the entire earnings of $2.50 will go to the preferred shareholder and obviously nothing will be paid to the equity shareholder. In 2002 the earnings are $6.50. There is a backlog of $5.00 from the previous year. Consequently, the amount due to the preferred shareholder is $12.50. Since only $6.50 is available, the deficit will be carried forward to the next year. The equity holder will obviously receive nothing. In 2003 the earnings are $12.00. The preferred shareholder is entitled to $7.50 for the year and $6.00 on account of the deficit carried over from the earlier years. Consequently, the preferred shareholder will receive $12.00 and the equity holder will not receive anything. Finally in 2004, out of the earnings of $22 for the year, $9 will go the preferred holder. This represents $7.50 for the current year and the arrears of $1.50 carried over from the previous year. The remaining $13 will go to the equity shareholder.

Adjustable-Rate Preferred Shares

In the case of such securities, the dividend rate is not fixed, but is subject to periodic revision based on a prespecified formula. For instance, the dividend rate may be specified as the T-bond rate plus a spread.

Participating Preferred Shares

Holders of such preferred shares may receive additional dividend payouts over and above what is fixed at the outset. The extra payments may be linked to the performance of the firm based on a predetermined formula, or may be based on the decision of the board of directors, or both. The presence of such a feature can enhance the value of the preferred shares. In practice, however, most preferred shares are nonparticipatory in nature.

DIVIDEND DISCOUNT MODELS

The value of an asset is the present value of all the cash flows that an investor expects to receive from it. Consequently, the value of a financial asset is a function of

- The size of the cash flows
- The timing of the cash flows
- The risk of the cash flows

The magnitude of the cash flow determines the numerator in the pricing equation. The timing of the cash flow is crucial because, as we are aware, money has time value and consequently it matters not only how much we get, but also when we get it. The risk of the cash flows has implications for the discount rate that constitutes the denominator in the pricing equation. For a given cash flow, the greater the risk associated with it, the larger will be the rate at which it is discounted, and consequently the smaller will be the present value.

When it comes to the valuation of a stock, the first question that we need to ask is what are the cash flows for a person who is contemplating the acquisition of a share? Irrespective of his planning horizon, an investor will obviously receive a dividend for each period that he chooses to hold the stock.[4] Second, at the end of his investment horizon, he will have an inflow on account of the sale of the stock. In practice this will be tantamount to either a capital gain or a capital loss.

A GENERAL VALUATION MODEL

We will use the following symbols. Additional variables will be defined as we go along.

- $P_0 \equiv$ Price of the stock at the outset
- $d_t \equiv$ Expected dividend per share at the end of period t
- $P_t \equiv$ Expected price of the stock at the end of period t
- $r \equiv$ Required rate of return for the asset class to which the stock belongs

Let us first take the case of an investor who plans to hold the stock for one period. Obviously

$$P_0 = \frac{d_1}{1+r} + \frac{P_1}{1+r}$$

If we assume that the person who buys the stock after one period also has a one-period horizon, then

$$P_1 = \frac{d_2}{1+r} + \frac{P_2}{1+r}$$

$$\Rightarrow P_0 = \frac{d_1}{1+r} + \frac{d_2}{(1+r)^2} + \frac{P_2}{(1+r)^2}$$

By extending the logic, we arrive at the conclusion that:

$$P_0 = \frac{d_1}{1+r} + \frac{d_2}{(1+r)^2} + \frac{d_3}{(1+r)^3} + - - - - - - - - - -$$

$$= \sum_{t=1}^{\infty} \frac{d_t}{(1+r)^t}$$

From this expression, we conclude that the stock price is the present value of an infinite stream of expected dividends.

---

[4]While this is true in general, there could be periods where the firm decides not to pay a dividend.

THE CONSTANT GROWTH MODEL

In practice, no one can forecast an infinite stream of dividends, hence we need to make an assumption about how the dividends are expected to evolve over time. The simplest approach is to assume that dividends grow at a constant rate year after year.

Let us assume that dividends grow at a constant rate of g% per annum, and that the last declared dividend was d_0. The current price can then be expressed as

$$P_0 = \frac{d_0(1+g)}{1+r} + \frac{d_0(1+g)^2}{(1+r)^2} + \frac{d_0(1+g)^3}{(1+r)^3} + - - - - - - - - - -$$

$$\Rightarrow \frac{P_0(1+r)}{(1+g)} = d_0 + \frac{d_0(1+g)}{1+r} + \frac{d_0(1+g)^2}{(1+r)^2} + - - - - - - - - - -$$

$$\Rightarrow \frac{P_0}{1+g}[r-g] = d_0$$

$$\Rightarrow P_0 = \frac{d_0(1+g)}{r-g} = \frac{d_1}{r-g}$$

This is called the constant growth model or the Gordon growth model. Obviously in order for the cash flow stream to converge, the required rate of return must be higher than the assumed constant growth rate.

As per this model, $P_{t+1} = P_t(1+g)$. Thus, it predicts that the stock price will grow at a constant rate equal to the growth rate of dividends.

EXAMPLE 3.4

Technora has just paid a dividend of $7.50 per share. The required rate of return on the stock is 8% per annum, and dividends are expected to grow at the rate of 5% per annum. What should be the stock price?

The price as per the Gordon model is:

$$P_0 = \frac{d_0(1+g)}{r-g} = \frac{7.50(1.05)}{0.08-0.05}$$

$$= \$262.50$$

THE TWO-STAGE MODEL

The constant growth model assumes a growth rate that stays constant forever. One way of building in a touch of realism is to assume that the stock will display a high growth rate of g_a% per annum for the first A years, and that the growth rate will then settle down to a more modest level of g_n% that will last forever. In other words, at the end of a high-growth period, the stock is similar to one that pays dividends growing at a constant rate. The price of the stock under these assumptions may be then determined as follows.

$$P_0 = \frac{d_1}{1+r} + \frac{d_2}{(1+r)^2} + ---------+ \frac{d_A}{(1+r)^A}$$

$$+ \frac{d_{A+1}}{(1+r)^A(r-g_n)}$$

$$= \frac{d_0(1+g_a)}{1+r} + \frac{d_0(1+g_a)^2}{(1+r)^2} + ---------------+ \frac{d_0(1+g_a)^A}{(1+r)^A}$$

$$+ \frac{d_0(1+g_a)^A}{(1+r)^A} \frac{(1+g_n)}{r-g_n}$$

$$\text{Let } S = \frac{d_0(1+g_a)}{1+r} + \frac{d_0(1+g_a)^2}{(1+r)^2} + ---------------+ \frac{d_0(1+g_a)^A}{(1+r)^A}$$

$$\Rightarrow S = \frac{d_1}{r-g_a}\left[1 - \frac{(1+g_a)^A}{(1+r)^A}\right]$$

$$\Rightarrow P_0 = \frac{d_1}{r-g_a}\left[1 - \frac{(1+g_a)^A}{(1+r)^A}\right] + \frac{d_1(1+g_a)^A}{(1+r)^A}\frac{(1+g_n)}{r-g_n} \times \frac{1}{(1+g_a)}$$

$$= \frac{d_1}{r-g_a}\left[1 - \left(\frac{1+g_a}{1+r}\right)^{A-1}\frac{(g_a-g_n)}{r-g_n}\right]$$

EXAMPLE 3.5

Technora has just paid a dividend of $7.50 per share. Analysts expect that dividends will grow at the rate of 10% per annum for the first eight years, and will then settle down to a constant rate of 5% per annum. The required rate of return on the stock is 8%. What should be the price of the stock as per the two-stage model?

$$P_0 = \frac{7.50(1.10)}{0.08 - 0.10}\left[1 - \left(\frac{1.10}{1.08}\right)^7\left(\frac{0.10 - 0.05}{0.08 - 0.05}\right)\right]$$

$$= -412.50[1 - 1.8951] = \$369.23$$

In this model, the initial growth rate of dividends may be higher than the required rate of return on the stock, but the subsequent constant growth rate cannot be.

THE THREE-STAGE MODEL

A major shortcoming of the two-stage model is that the growth rate suddenly declines at the end of the initial high-growth phase. A more plausible assumption would be that the growth rate gradually declines after the high-growth phase until it reaches its long-run value, and this is precisely what the three-stage model does. It avoids a discrete jump in the growth rate by postulating that dividends grow at a high rate during an initial period, and that the growth rate then declines linearly year after year during an intermediate phase, until it reaches the long-run value, where it remains stable thereafter. We will denote the duration of the high-growth phase as A years, and the duration of the declining growth phase as $B - A$ years. The model may then be stated as:

$$P_0 = \sum_{t=1}^{A} \frac{d_1(1+g_a)^{t-1}}{(1+r)^t} + \sum_{t=A+1}^{B} \frac{d_{t-1}(1+g_t)}{(1+r)^t}$$
$$+ \frac{d_B(1+g_n)}{(1+r)^B(r-g_n)}$$

where

$$g_t = g_a - (g_a - g_n)\frac{t-A}{B-A}$$

during the period $(A + 1) \leq t \leq B$.

EXAMPLE 3.6

Technora has just paid a dividend of $7.50 per share. Dividends are expected to grow at a rate of 10% per annum for the first eight years. The growth rate is then expected to decline linearly for four years until it reaches a constant growth rate of 5% per annum. The required rate of return on the stock is 8% per annum. The question is, what should be the value of the stock? Table 3.5 lists the dividends year wise, and the present value of each dividend.

TABLE 3.5 Valuation of Cash Flows as Per the Three-Stage Model

Year	Dividend	Present Value
1	8.2500	7.6389
2	9.0750	7.7804
3	9.9825	7.9244
4	10.9808	8.0718
5	12.0788	8.2206
6	13.2867	8.3729
7	14.6154	8.5279
8	16.0769	8.6859
9	17.4837	8.7462
10	18.7949	8.7057
11	19.9696	8.5646
12	20.9681	8.3267

$$\frac{d_{12}(1+g_n)}{(r-g_n)(1+r)^{12}} = \frac{20.9681 \times 1.05}{(0.03)(1.08)^{12}}$$

$$= 291.4350$$

$$P_0 = \$391.00$$

THE H MODEL

The H model was developed as an alternative to the three-stage model. In this model, growth begins at a high rate of $g_a\%$ per annum. Unlike the earlier case, however, there is no initial high-growth period of A years. Instead, the growth rate starts declining linearly from the outset over a period of 2H years until it reaches a value of $g_n\%$ per annum. Thereafter, the growth rate remains constant at the long-run value. The value of the share as per this model is given by

$$P_0 = \frac{d_0}{r - g_n}[(1 + g_n) + H(g_a - g_n)]$$

EXAMPLE 3.7

Technora has just declared a dividend of $7.50 per share. The initial growth rate is 10% per annum and is expected to declare linearly over a period of 10 years, until it reaches 5% per annum. The required rate of return on the stock is 8%. What is the price of the stock as per the H model?

$$2H = 10 \text{ years} \Rightarrow H = 5 \text{ years}$$

$$P_0 = \frac{7.50}{0.08 - 0.05}[(1.05) + 5(0.10 - 0.05)]$$

$$= \frac{7.50}{0.03} \times 1.30 = \$325.00$$

STOCK MARKET INDICES

A stock market index is constructed by considering the prices, or the market capitalization, of a predefined basket of securities. The objective of constructing an index is to enable us to track the performance of the securities market. In practice, we cannot meaningfully assess the market by looking at a vector of asset prices or returns. We need one number that will enable us to gauge or track the performance of the market. This explains the faith of the securities industry in a tracking index such as the DOW. An index may be constructed to represent an entire market or a market segment. It is important to select the constituent assets such that they are representative of the market or market segment as the case may be.

PRICE-WEIGHTED INDICES

One way of constructing a market index is by considering only the prices of the constituent stocks. The first step in the construction of an index is the decision regarding the number of securities to be included, and the selection of the specific securities. In the case of a price-weighted index, the current prices of all the component stocks are added up and divided by a number known as the *divisor*.

On the base date, or the date on which the index is being computed for the first time, the divisor can be set equal to any arbitrary value. A very logical way of setting the initial value of the divisor is by setting it equal to the number of stocks chosen for inclusion in the index. In practice, the divisor will be chosen such that the starting value of the index is equal to a nice round number such as 100. Hence, if the aggregate of stock prices on the base date is 25,215, the divisor will be chosen as 252.15 so that the starting value of the index is 100.

The divisor does not have to be adjusted on a day-to-day basis; however, whenever there is a corporate action such as a split/reverse split, a stock dividend, or a rights issue, the divisor will be adjusted as described later. An adjustment is also required when there is a change in the composition of the index, that is, one or more stocks are substituted.

Let us assume that we are standing at the end of day t, and the closing price of the ith stock on the day is $P_{i,t}$. The index level I_t is given by

$$I_t = \sum_{i=1}^{N} \frac{P_{i,t}}{Div_t}$$

where Div_t is the applicable value of the divisor for the day, and N is the number of stocks comprising the index.

EXAMPLE 3.8

Let us assume it is the base date of an index, which has been defined to comprise five stocks. The starting value of the divisor has been chosen to be 5.0. Let the closing prices of these five stocks at the end of the day be as shown in Table 3.6.

TABLE 3.6 Prices of the Constituent Stocks on the Base Date

Stock	Price
3M	80
American Express	55
Coca-Cola	45
IBM	80
Merck	35
Total	295

The end of the day index value will therefore be $295/5 = 59.00$.

On the following day, the prices of the component stocks are assumed to be as shown in Table 3.7.

TABLE 3.7　Prices of the Constituent Stocks on the Following Day

Stock	Price
3M	85
American Express	60
Coca-Cola	48
IBM	85
Merck	40
Total	318

The value of the index on this day will be 318/5 = 63.60, and we will conclude that the market has moved up. If we compare Tables 3.6 and 3.7, we will find that every stock has risen in value. In practice, it is not necessary that all stocks must rise in price for the index to rise or that all of them should decline if the index is to fall.

Changing the Divisor

The divisor has to be adjusted if one or more of the following corporate actions were to occur.

- A split or a reverse split in one or more of the constituent stocks.
- A rights issue if the issue is at a discount to the prevailing market price.
- A stock dividend on one or more of the constituent stocks.
- A change of composition, that is, a replacement of an existing stock(s) by a new stock(s).

We will now illustrate the mechanics of adjusting the divisor by considering a situation where one of the constituent stocks undergoes a split.

We will assume that Coca-Cola undergoes a 3:1 split at the end of the base date. The prices of the constituent stocks at the end of the following day are assumed to be as shown in Table 3.8.

TABLE 3.8　Prices of the Constituent Stocks on the Following Day, Assuming a Stock Split in Coca-Cola

Stock	Price
3M	85
American Express	60
Coca-Cola	16
IBM	85
Merck	40
Total	286

When we compare Table 3.8 with Table 3.7 we find that all the other stocks have the same value at the end of the next day as before, except for Coca-Cola, whose value is one-third of the value it would have had in the absence of the split.

Let us first compute the index without making an adjustment to the divisor. We will get an index value of 286/5 = 57.20, and will conclude that the market has gone down as compared to the base date. However, obviously this is an erroneous deduction, for every stock including Coca-Cola has risen in value as compared to the base date. The perceived decline in the index is entirely due to our failure to take the split into account.

If the index has to continue to be an accurate barometer of the market, then clearly an adjustment needs to be made. The variable that needs to be adjusted is obviously the divisor. In practice we would proceed to adjust the divisor as follows. First, we would list the theoretical post-split values at the end of the day on which the split is declared. The split will affect only the price of the stock whose shares have been split. In this case, the theoretical post-split price of Coca-Cola will be one-third of its pre-split value of $45. This adjustment is reflected in Table 3.9.

TABLE 3.9   Theoretical Post-Split Stock Prices

Stock	Price
3M	80
American Express	55
Coca-Cola	15
IBM	80
Merck	35
Total	265

The new divisor, Div_N, should be such that the index value is the same, whether we use the pre-split prices and the old divisor or the post-split prices and the new divisor. In this case, $265/Div_N$ should equal 59.00. The new divisor is therefore 4.4915. If we were to use this value of the divisor to compute the index level on the following day, we will get a value of 63.68, which is consistent with our earlier observation that the market has risen.

We will continue to use the new divisor until there is another corporate action. The adjustment procedure for a stock dividend is identical to that for a stock split as the two are mathematically equivalent. For instance, if a firm were to declare a stock dividend of 20%, it would be equivalent to a 6:5 split, and we would proceed to adjust the divisor accordingly.

Now we will illustrate the adjustment procedure in the event of a change in composition, with the help of an example. Assume that at the end of the day following the base date, Merck, which has a prevailing market price of $40, is replaced with General Electric, which has a price of $50. The index level prior to the change is 63.68 as computed earlier. The prices of the stocks contained in the reconstituted index will be as shown in Table 3.10.

The new divisor, Div_N, should be such that $296/Div_N = 63.68 \Rightarrow Div_N = 4.6482$

TABLE 3.10 Prices of the Component Stocks
of the Reconstituted Index

Stock	Price
3M	85
American Express	60
Coca-Cola	16
IBM	85
General Electric	50
Total	296

THE IMPORTANCE OF PRICE

A feature of a price-weighted index, which finance theorists opine is one of its weaknesses, is that higher priced stocks tend to have a greater impact on the index level than lower priced components. Let us take the data given in Table 3.11 for our five-stock index on a particular day. Assume that the divisor is 5.0.

The index level is 310/5 = 62.00.

Consider two possible situations for the following day, as depicted in Table 3.12. In Case A, IBM's price has gone up by 20%, whereas in Case B, Merck's price has gone up by 20%.

In the first case the index value is 65.60, which represents an increase of 5.81% as compared to the previous day. However, in the second case the index value is 63.20,

TABLE 3.11 Prices of the Constituent Stocks
on a Given Day

Stock	Price
3M	85
American Express	60
Coca-Cola	45
IBM	90
Merck	30
Total	310

TABLE 3.12 Prices on the Following Day: Two
Different Scenarios

	Case A Price	Case B Price
3M	85	85
American Express	60	60
Coca-Cola	45	45
IBM	108	90
Merck	30	36
Total	328	316

which represents an increase of only 1.94% as compared to the previous day. Quite obviously, a change of 20% in the price of IBM, which is a high-priced stock, has had a greater impact than a similar change in the price of Merck, which is priced considerably lower.

In finance, the importance accorded to a company is based on its market capitalization and not on its price. A model like the Capital Asset Pricing Model is consistent with this viewpoint, for it defines the *market portfolio* as a market capitalization–weighted portfolio of all assets. Thus, a price-weighted index can in a sense be construed as a less than perfect barometer of the stock market.

VALUE-WEIGHTED INDICES

A value-weighted index is theoretically more sound, for it takes into consideration the market capitalization of a component stock and not merely its price.

Let us assume that we are standing on day t, and that the starting or base date of the index is day b. We will use $P_{i,t}$ and $P_{i,b}$ to denote the market prices of the ith stock on days t and b respectively, and $Q_{i,t}$ and $Q_{i,b}$ to denote the number of shares outstanding on those two days.

On the base date, the index can be assigned any arbitrary value. We will assign a value of 100. The level of the index on day t is then defined as

$$\frac{1}{Div_t} \left(\frac{\sum_{i=1}^{N} P_{i,t} Q_{i,t}}{\sum_{i=1}^{M} P_{i,b} Q_{i,b}} \right) \times 100$$

Div_t represents the value of the divisor on day t. In the case of a value-weighted index, the divisor is always assigned a value of 1.0 on the base date. Subsequently it will be adjusted as and when required. However, unlike in the case of the divisors used for price-weighted indexes, the divisor need not be adjusted for a stock split or a stock dividend, as we shall shortly see.

EXAMPLE 3.9

We will consider the same five companies that we used earlier and their prices are given in Table 3.13. The difference is that we will now also consider the number of shares issued by each firm.

TABLE 3.13 Prices, Number of Shares Outstanding, and Market Capitalization of the Components of a Value-weighted Index on the Base Date

Stock	Price (P)	# of Shares (Q)	Market Capitalization
3M	85	780,000,000	66,300,000,000
American Express	60	1,250,000,000	75,000,000,000
Coca-Cola	45	2,425,000,000	109,125,000,000
IBM	85	1,635,000,000	138,975,000,000
Merck	35	2,220,000,000	77,700,000,000

The total market value is

$$\sum_{i=1}^{5} P_i Q_i = 467{,}100{,}000{,}000$$

Now suppose that on the following day, the prices and number of shares are as depicted in Table 3.14.

TABLE 3.14   Prices, Number of Shares Outstanding, and Market Capitalization of the Components of a Value-weighted Index on the Following Day

Stock	Price (P)	# of Shares (Q)	Market Capitalization
3M	90	780,000,000	70,200,000,000
American Express	65	1,250,000,000	81,250,000,000
Coca-Cola	50	2,425,000,000	121,250,000,000
IBM	90	1,635,000,000	147,150,000,000
Merck	40	2,220,000,000	88,800,000,000

The total market value is

$$\sum_{i=1}^{5} P_i Q_i = 508{,}650{,}000{,}000$$

The value of the index on this day is therefore

$$\frac{508{,}650{,}000{,}000}{467{,}100{,}000{,}000} \times 100 = 108.8953$$

Our conclusion would therefore be that the market has moved up.

Changing the Divisor

In the case of a value-weighted index, there is no need to adjust the divisor if one of the components of the index were to undergo a split or a reverse split, or if a firm that is present in the index were to declare a stock dividend. This is because, from a theoretical standpoint, such corporate actions are value neutral and do not have any impact on the market capitalization. However, if there is a rights issue, whether at the prevailing market price or at a discount, a follow-on public offering, or a share buyback, the divisor will have to be adjusted. This is because all these corporate actions will lead to a change in the market capitalization of the security.

In the case of a stock split or a stock dividend the share price will decline, whereas in the case of a reverse split the share price will rise. In the first two cases the number of shares outstanding will rise, whereas in the last case it will decline. The changes in the number of shares outstanding will exactly offset the price change such that there is no impact on the market capitalization. We will now give an illustration of this phenomenon.

EXAMPLE 3.10

Assume that 3M has a market price of 90, and that the number of shares outstanding is 780,000,000. Now consider the case of a 20% stock dividend. The share price will immediately decline to $90 \times 780,000,000/936,000,000 = \$75$. The market capitalization before the stock dividend is

$$90 \times 780,000,000 = 70,200,000,000$$

which is the same as the market capitalization after the dividend, which is

$$75 \times 936,000,000 = 70,200,000,000$$

The divisor, however, would have to be modified whenever there is a change in the composition of the index. Let us assume that the prices and number of shares of the companies constituting the index are as shown in Table 3.14, at the end of a particular day. Now assume that Merck, with a price of $40 and number of shares outstanding equal to 2,220,000,000, is replaced with General Electric, which has a price of $50 and number of shares outstanding equal to 10,500,000,000. The market capitalization of the component stocks after the change will be as depicted in Table 3.15.

TABLE 3.15   Market Capitalization of the Component Stocks of the Reconstituted Index

Stock	Price (P)	# of Shares (Q)	Market Capitalization
3M	90	780,000,000	70,200,000,000
American Express	65	1,250,000,000	81,250,,000,000
Coca-Cola	50	2,425,000,000	121,250,000,000
IBM	90	1,635,000,000	147,150,000,000
General Electric	50	10,500,000,000	525,000,000,000

The total market capitalization after the change is 944,850,000,000. The new divisor, Div_N, should be such that

$$\frac{1}{Div_N} \times \frac{944,850,000,000}{467,100,000,000} \times 100 = 108.8953$$

$$\Rightarrow Div_N = 1.8576$$

CHANGING THE BASE PERIOD CAPITALIZATION

In the event of a change in its composition, one of the ways of handling the situation, as we have just seen, is by changing the divisor. In such cases the base period market capitalization will always stay frozen at its initial level.

A different but equivalent approach, however, is adopted in the case of certain value-weighted indices. In such cases, the divisor is not recomputed in the event of a change in composition. In other words it is always maintained at its initial level of 1.00. What is done in practice in such cases is that the base period market capitalization is adjusted to reflect the change in the composition of the index.

Let us take the data depicted in Table 3.15. If we denote the modified base period capitalization by BPC_N, then it should be such that

$$\frac{944,850,000,000}{BPC_N} \times 100 = 108.8953$$

$$\Rightarrow BPC_N = 867,668,301,600$$

For all subsequent calculations, the new value will be used for the base period capitalization until there is another change in the composition of the index. Mathematically the two approaches are equivalent because the denominator in the index computation formula consists of the product of the divisor and the base period market capitalization. Thus, we can keep either one constant and adjust the other.

EQUALLY WEIGHTED INDICES

An equally weighted index offers yet another alternative for tracking the performance of a market. In the case of such indices, as in the case of price-weighted indices, we consider only the prices of the component stocks.

Let us look at an index consisting of N component stocks. The value of the index on day t is defined as

$$I_t = I_{t-1} \times \frac{1}{N} \sum_{i=1}^{N} \frac{P_{i,t}}{P_{i,t-1}}$$

The ratio of the prices, $P_{i,t}/P_{i,t-1}$ may be expressed as $(1 + r_{i,t})$ where $r_{i,t}$ is the arithmetic rate of return on the ith stock between day t and day $t - 1$. Therefore

$$\frac{1}{N} \sum_{i=1}^{N} \frac{P_{i,t}}{P_{i,t-1}} = \frac{1}{N} \sum_{i=1}^{N} (1 + r_{i,t})$$

$$= 1 + \frac{1}{N} \sum_{i=1}^{N} r_{i,t} = 1 + \bar{r}_t$$

where $\bar{r}_t$ is the arithmetic average of the returns on all the component stocks between day $t - 1$ and day t. Thus

$$I_t = I_{t-1} \times (1 + \bar{r}_t)$$

In other words, the value of the index on a particular day is its value at the point in time at which it was previously computed, multiplied by one plus the average arithmetic rate of return on all the stocks constituting the index, for the period.

TRACKING PORTFOLIOS

In practice, investors often seek to hold a basket of securities that imitates or mirrors the behavior of a stock market index. The method of forming such a tracking or mimicking portfolio would obviously depend on the method adopted to compute the index being tracked.

Imitating an equally weighted index is fairly simple. The investor has to put an equal fraction of his wealth in all the assets that constitute the index. Consider an investor with an initial wealth of $\$W$ who is seeking to track an index consisting of N stocks. Obviously the investor will have to invest an amount of W/N in each security.

Tracking a price-weighted index too is fairly straightforward. An investor who seeks to do so must acquire an equal number of shares of each of the companies present in the index.

Finally, we come to the task of forming a portfolio to track a value-weighted index. In practice this is the most complex task because to imitate such an index, we must invest a fraction of our wealth in each asset that is equal to the ratio of the market capitalization of that particular asset to the total market capitalization of all the assets that constitute the index.

Rebalancing a Tracking Portfolio

Once we set up a tracking portfolio it does not mean that we can sit back and watch the portfolio automatically track the index in question. In the case of every index, irrespective of its mode of computation, there will arise circumstances when the tracking portfolio will have to be rebalanced.

Equally Weighted Portfolios

In practice, an equally weighted tracking portfolio needs to be rebalanced very frequently, virtually on a daily basis. This is because – unless it were to be the case that none of the component stocks has undergone a change in price from one day to the next – an index that is equally weighted on a particular day will no longer be equally weighted on the following day. We will now give a detailed example as to why an equally weighted portfolio will require rebalancing with the sheer passage of time.

Take the case of an investor who has a corpus of $600,000 and decides to form an equally weighted portfolio consisting of the four stocks whose prices are shown in Table 3.16.

Because the investor has $600,000, we will have to invest $150,000 in each of the four stocks: 3,000 shares of General Electric; 1,500 shares of 3M; 3,750 shares of Merck; and 1,200 shares of IBM. If we assume that the index value is 100, then the portfolio is worth 6,000 times the index.

TABLE 3.16 Prices of the Stocks Constituting an Equally Weighted Index at the Time of Formation of the Portfolio

Stock	Price
General Electric	50
3M	100
Merck	40
IBM	125

Let us assume that on the next day, the prices of the companies are as shown in Table 3.17.

The amounts invested in the stocks will be $120,000, $187,500, $187,500, and $120,000 respectively. The total portfolio value is $615,000, of which 19.51% each is in General Electric and IBM, and 30.49% each is in 3M and Merck.

Quite obviously the portfolio is no longer equally weighted, in which case 25% of the investor's wealth would be in each asset. If the weights have to be reset to 0.25 each, then the investor would rebalance by selling off a part of the holdings in 3M and Merck and investing the proceeds in General Electric and IBM.

In practice we would proceed as follows. The total value of the portfolio is $615,000, which means that the investor needs to have $153,750 in each stock. To accomplish this, the investor would buy 843.75 shares of General Electric and 337.50 shares of IBM, and sell 270 shares of 3M and 675 shares of Merck.

The inflow on account of what is being sold is $270 \times 125 + 675 \times 50 = \$67,500$.

The outflow on account of what is being bought is $843.75 \times 40 + 337.50 \times 100 = \$67,500$.

Thus we have demonstrated the investor can rebalance at zero net cost. It can be verified that the amount invested in each company is $153,750.

The new index level is $100 \times (1 + \bar{r}_t)$.

$$\bar{r}_t = \frac{(-0.20 + 0.25 + 0.25 + -0.20)}{4} = \frac{0.10}{4} = 0.025$$

Therefore the new value of the index is 102.50. The total value of the portfolio is $615,000, which is 6,000 times the value of the index. Hence the portfolio continues to mimic the index.

TABLE 3.17 Prices of the Stocks Constituting an Equally Weighted Index on the Following Day

Stock	Price
General Electric	40
3M	125
Merck	50
IBM	100

Price-weighted Portfolios

Now let us turn our attention to a portfolio that is constructed to track a price-weighted stock market index. Such a portfolio has to be rebalanced whenever there is a split or a reverse split, a stock dividend, a rights issue at a discount, or a change in the index composition. In other words, whenever circumstances warrant a change in the divisor used to compute the index, we need to rebalance the tracking portfolio.

Let us consider a price-weighted index consisting of the four stocks depicted in Table 3.16. Assume that the divisor is equal to 4.0, which would mean that the index level is

$$\frac{50 + 100 + 40 + 125}{4.0} = 78.75$$

Let us form a tracking portfolio by buying 2,000 shares of each of the constituent stocks. The value of our tracking portfolio will be:

$$2,000 \times (50 + 100 + 40 + 125) = \$630,000 = 8,000 \times 78.75$$

Hence our portfolio is worth 8,000 times the index.

Consider a situation where 3M undergoes a 2:1 split, which means that its post-split theoretical value will be \$50. The new divisor, Div_N, should be such that

$$\frac{50 + 50 + 40 + 125}{Div_N} = 78.75$$

$$\Rightarrow Div_N = 3.3651$$

In order to ensure that our portfolio continues to mimic the index, we need to rebalance in such a way that our portfolio value remains unchanged. Let the number of shares of each stock held before the split be denoted by N_O, and the number of shares required after the split by N_N. If the value of our tracking portfolio is to remain unchanged, it should be the case that

$$N_0 \times Div_o \times I_t = N_N \times Div_N \times I_t$$

$$\Rightarrow N_N = \frac{N_o \times Div_o}{Div_N}$$

In our example, the number of shares of each stock required after the split is

$$\frac{2,000 \times 4.0}{3.3651} = 2,377.3439$$

If we assume that fractional shares can be bought and sold, we will have to buy 377.3439 shares of General Electric, Merck, and IBM, and sell 1,622.6561 shares of 3M.[5]

The inflow on account of what is sold is $1,622.6561 \times 50 = \$811,32.805$.

---

[5]Remember that we would have 4,000 shares of 3M after the split.

The outflow on account of what is being bought is $377.3439 \times (50 + 40 + 125) =$ $811,28.938.

Once again, if we ignore transactions costs, we can rebalance at zero net cost. The difference that we get between the inflow and the outflow is entirely due to rounding errors.

Rights Issues

Let us now consider the case of rebalancing a price-weighted portfolio to factor in a rights issue. Consider the four stocks given in Table 3.17. We will assume that the divisor at the outset is 4.0 and the index level is 78.75. To form a tracking portfolio the investor has acquired 2,000 shares of each company.

Assume that Merck announces a 1:10 rights issue at a price of $39 per share. The ex-rights price will decline from 50 to 49, and the aggregate value of the four stocks will decline from 315 to 314. The new number of shares required to track the price-weighted index is given by

$$N_N = (N_o \times Div_o)/Div_N = (2000 \times 4) \times 78.75/314 = 2,006.3694$$

There are two possibilities. The investor may renounce those rights. Because the investor owns 2,000 shares, they have the right to acquire 200 shares, and the right to acquire a share is worth $10. Thus, the investor would receive $2,000 if renouncing the rights. The outflow on account of the extra shares acquired is:

$$6.3694 \times (49 + 100 + 40 + 125) = \$2,000$$

Thus, the inflow from the renounced rights is exactly equal to the outflow. The other possibility is that the investor acquires 200 shares of Merck by paying $7,800, keeping 6.3694 shares, and selling the balance at $49 each. The *net* inflow $= 49 \times 193.6306 - 7,800 = 1,687.90$. This will be exactly sufficient to acquire 6.3694 shares of each of the other three companies.

$$6.3694 \times (100 + 40 + 125) = 1,687.89$$

Value-weighted Portfolios

Consider four stocks, whose prices and number of shares outstanding are shown in Table 3.18.

The total market capitalization is $20,000,000. Assume that the base period market capitalization is $16,000,000 and that the current divisor is 1. The index level is therefore 125.00.

TABLE 3.18　Components of a Value-weighted Index

Stock	Price (P)	# of Shares(Q)	Market Capitalization
MRF	20	200,000	4,000,000
J.K. Tyres	80	50,000	4,000,000
Apollo Tyres	50	200,000	10,000,000
Viking Tyres	20	100,000	2,000,000

Let us consider the case of investors who have an endowment of $500,000, and who wish to create a portfolio to track the index. In order for their portfolio to mimic the index, they must have

$$\frac{4,000,000}{20,000,000} \times 500,000 = \$100,000 \text{ in } MRF \text{ stock,}$$

$$\frac{4,000,000}{20,000,000} \times 500,000 = \$100,000 \text{ in } J.K. \text{ Tyres stock,}$$

$$\frac{10,000,000}{20,000,000} \times 500,000 = \$250,000 \text{ in Apollo Tyres stock,}$$

$$\text{and } \frac{2,000,000}{20,000,000} \times 500,000 = \$50,000 \text{ in Viking Tyres stock.}$$

Consequently, the investors must buy 5,000 shares of MRF, 1,250 shares of J.K. Tyres, 5,000 shares of Apollo Tyres, and 2,500 shares of Viking Tyres. In general, the number of shares of the ith stock is given by

$$\frac{Q_i}{\sum P_i Q_i} \times W$$

where W is the initial wealth. The total portfolio value in this case is 4,000 times the index value of 125.00.

Now assume that Viking Tyres is replaced by Ceat, which has a share price of $70 and has 100,000 shares outstanding. The total market capitalization of the four components of the index will now be $25,000,000. The divisor will have to be adjusted in such a way that the index level remains unchanged. That is

$$\frac{1}{Div_N} \times \frac{25,000,000}{16,000,000} \times 100 = 125$$

$$\Rightarrow Div_N = 1.25$$

In order for the portfolio to remain value weighted, the investor must have

$$\frac{4,000,000}{25,000,000} \times 500,000 = \$80,000 \text{ in } MRF \text{ stock,}$$

$$\frac{4,000,000}{25,000,000} \times 500,000 = \$80,000 \text{ in } J.K. \text{ Tyres stock,}$$

$$\frac{10,000,000}{25,000,000} \times 500,000 = \$200,000 \text{ in Apollo Tyres stock, and}$$

$$\frac{7,000,000}{25,000,000} \times 500,000 = \$140,000 \text{ in Ceat stock.}$$

Thus, the investor requires 4,000 shares of MRF, 1,000 shares of J.K, 4,000 shares of Apollo, and 2,000 shares of Ceat. This means that he will have to sell 1,000 shares of MRF, 250 shares of J.K, 1,000 shares of Apollo, and 2,500 shares of Viking. All the shares of Viking have to be sold because it is no longer a part of the index. He will also have to buy 2,000 shares of Ceat. The number of shares of the *i*th stock is once again given by

$$\frac{Q_i}{\sum P_i Q_i} \times W$$

The inflow $= 1,000 \times 20 + 250 \times 80 + 1,000 \times 50 + 2,500 \times 20 = \$140,000$.

The outflow $= 2,000 \times 70 = \$140,000$.

Thus, if we ignore transactions costs, then once again we can rebalance at zero net cost. The portfolio value after rebalancing will be \$500,000, which is 4,000 times the index level of 62.50.

HANDLING A RIGHTS ISSUE

Consider the data given in Table 3.18. Assume that Apollo Tyres announces a 1:4 rights issue at a price of \$25 per share. The ex-rights price will be:

$$\frac{(50 \times 200,000 + 25 \times 50,000)}{250,000} = \$45$$

The price and market capitalization data, post rights, is as shown in Table 3.19. The aggregate market capitalization is 21.25MM dollars.

Let us first assume the investors renounce their rights. They will get \$20 for the right to acquire a share. Because they have 5,000 shares of Apollo, they have the right to buy 1,250 shares.

The value of the portfolio after the rights issue is:

$$5,000 \times 20 + 1,250 \times 80 + 5,000 \times 45 + 2,500 \times 20 = \$475,000$$

The inflow from the sale of rights is:

$$1,250 \times 20 = \$25,000$$

Thus the total capital available is \$500,000.

TABLE 3.19 Components of a Value-weighted Index

Stock	Price (P)	# of Shares(Q)	Market Capitalization
MRF	20	200,000	4,000,000
J.K. Tyres	80	50,000	4,000,000
Apollo Tyres	45	250,000	11,250,000
Viking Tyres	20	100,000	2,000,000

The amount of capital required to be invested in each constituent firm after the rights issue can be computed as follows:

$$\frac{4,000,000}{21,250,000} \times 500,000 = \$94,117.645 \text{ in } MRF \text{ stock,}$$

$$\frac{4,000,000}{21,250,000} \times 500,000 = \$94,117.645 \text{ in } J.K. \text{ Tyres stock,}$$

$$\frac{11,250,000}{21,250,000} \times 500,000 = \$264,705.88 \text{ in Apollo Tyres stock, and}$$

$$\frac{2,000,000}{21,250,000} \times 500,000 = \$47,058.82 \text{ in Viking stock.}$$

The total investment is $500,000.
The outflow on account of what is being bought is:

$$250,000 - 264,705.85 = \$14,705.88$$

The inflow from the three firms whose shares are being sold is:

$$(100,000 - 94,117.645) + (100,000 - 94,117.645) + (50,000 - 47,058.82)$$

$$= \$14,705.90$$

Thus, the portfolio can be rebalanced at zero net cost.

What if the investors were to exercise their rights and buy 1,250 shares at $25 each? The amount of funds required is $31,250. The value of the shares will be $(5,000 + 1,250) \times 45 = \$281,250$.

The investment required in Apollo Tyres is $264,705.88. Thus $281,250 - 264,705.88 = 16,544.12$ will be released when the surplus shares are sold.

The inflow from the other three firms whose shares are being sold is:

$$(100,000 - 94,117.645) + (100,000 - 94,117.645) + (50,000 - 47,058.82)$$

$$= \$14,705.90$$

Thus, the total funds released $= 16,544.12 + 14,705.90 = \$31,250.02$, which is exactly equal to the amount required to subscribe to the rights issue.

THE FREE-FLOATING METHODOLOGY

The traditional method of computing a value-weighted index entails the use of the market capitalization of the constituent stocks, where the market capitalization is defined as the price of the share multiplied by the total number of shares issued by the company. In recent years, this approach has come under criticism from those who propound that the appropriate number of shares used to compute the market capitalization should be those that are *freely floating*. The free-floating methodology entails the calculation of the market capitalization of a stock as the share price multiplied by the number of shares that are freely available for trading in the market.

Obviously, for a widely held firm, the free-floating market capitalization will be high and will be close to or even equal to its total market value. For closely held companies, however, the free-floating market capitalization may be considerably less than the full market value. One of the arguments advanced against using the full market capitalization to compute the index value is that those index constituents that have a relatively smaller percentage of shares available for trading may be vulnerable to sharp price fluctuations. Thus not only will a price move in such an illiquid stock cause the index to move sharply, but such stocks will also be vulnerable to manipulation by speculators. Therefore, defining the index on the basis of free-floating shares can help ensure that the impact of underlying market movements is reflected in a better fashion.

WELL-KNOWN GLOBAL INDICES

The most famous index is undoubtedly the Dow Jones Industrial Average (DJIA), popularly known as the *Dow*. It is a price-weighted average of 30 stocks.

The Nikkei Index, which is a barometer of the Japanese stock market, is also price weighted and includes 225 large Japanese companies. The Standard & Poor's 500 Index (S&P 500) and the Nasdaq 100 index are both value weighted.

MARGIN TRADING AND SHORT-SELLING

The term *buying stock on margin* refers to a process of investment where the investor funds the acquisition of the stock by borrowing a part of the required funds from the broker. As can be surmised, the ability to raise a loan to fund a share purchase will enable investors to acquire more shares than what their own funds will permit.

TERMINOLOGY

The minimum percentage of the securities' market value that has to be deposited by the customer is called the *margin rate*. The difference between the market value of the securities and the minimum amount that has to be deposited by the customer is called the *loan value*. Thus, the loan value represents the maximum amount that can be borrowed from the broker. The loan value expressed as a fraction of the market value is referred to as the *loan rate*. Obviously, the margin rate, which is the minimum that the investor has to deposit, and the loan rate, which is the maximum that the investor can borrow, will therefore always be equal to 100%. The actual amount that is borrowed from the broker is called the *broker's loan* or is referred to as a *debit balance*. The term *debit balance* indicates that investors are indebted to the broker, and consequently owe the broker money. The difference between the market value and the debit balance is called the *owner's equity*. The owner's equity represents the amount that the investor will be entitled to if the securities are immediately liquidated and the broker is repaid the amount due.

EXAMPLE 3.11

We will illustrate these terms with the help of an example. Clients want to purchase 200 shares of ABC stock, which is currently trading at $45 per share. The margin rate is 50%. That is, regulations stipulate that the clients should put up at least 50% of the cost from their own funds. We will assume that they invest the minimum amount required.

The market value of 200 shares is $9,000. The margin rate is 50%, which implies that a minimum of $4,500 has to be deposited by the investor. Hence, the maximum amount that they can borrow from the broker is $4,500. Thus the loan value of the position is $4,500. The loan rate which is the loan value expressed as a fraction of the market value is 50%. The debit balance, which represents the amount borrowed from the broker, is obviously $4,500.

The position may be depicted in a T-account format as shown in Figure 3.1.

Liabilities	Assets
Broker's Loan $4,500	200 Shares @ $45 = $9,000
Owner's Equity $4,500	

FIGURE 3.1

Now let us assume that the share price increases to $50. The market value of the securities will be $10,000. The debit balance will stay at $4,500 as nothing further has been borrowed. If the position is immediately liquidated, the investors will be eligible to withdraw $5,500. Thus, the owner's equity is $5,500. As per the requirement, the owner's equity must be at least 50% of the market value, which in this case is $5,000. In this case we say that the investors have excess equity of $500. There is another way of perceiving the excess equity. The loan value of the position is 50% of 10,000, which amounts to $5,000. However, the debit balance is only $4,500. The difference between the loan value and the debit balance will also be equal to the excess.

What can the investors do with the excess? They can either withdraw it as cash or use it to acquire more securities. If the investors were to withdraw the excess, the funds will be provided by the broker. When that happens, the debit balance will increase by the amount and the owner's equity will decline by an equivalent amount. In this example the owner's equity will decline to $5,000 and the debit balance will increase to $5,000. This is consistent with the stipulation that a maximum of 50% of the market value of the securities can be borrowed. The situation is depicted in Figure 3.2.

Liabilities	Assets
Broker's Loan $5,000	200 Shares @ $50 = $10,000
Owner's Equity $5,000	

FIGURE 3.2

What if the investors were to desire to use their excess to acquire more securities? The excess equity of $500 can support an acquisition of $1,000 worth of shares, because the requirement is that at least 50% of the value of the acquisition must be the owner's contribution. In this case, the broker will advance $1,000 to enable the investors to purchase the securities. The market value of the securities will be $11,000. The owner's equity will remain at $5,500 and the debit balance will increase to $5,500. Consequently the requirement that not more than 50% of the value of the securities can be borrowed has been complied with. Figure 3.3 illustrates this situation.

Liabilities	Assets
Broker's Loan $5,500	220 Shares @ $50 = $11,000
Owner's Equity $5,500	

FIGURE 3.3

Thus, in this case an excess equity of $500 represents the ability to buy additional securities worth $1,000. This is referred to as the *buying power* of the excess equity. The buying power of a position may be defined as: Buying Power = Excess Equity/Margin Rate.

EXAMPLE 3.12

(Magnifying Returns)

Consider the case of an investor called Martin, who has $5,000 at his disposal and is desirous of acquiring shares of ABC, which are currently available at a price of $50 each. We will assume that the margin rate is 50%.

(continued)

(*continued*)

If Martin were to purely trade on a cash basis, that is, if he were to acquire securities only up to the limit permitted by his own funds, he could acquire 100 shares of stock. If he were to trade on margin, however, he could borrow up to a maximum of $5,000, since the margin rate is given to be 50%, and he can then purchase 200 shares.[6]

What is the advantage of margin trading? Just the way the assumption of debt enables the equity holders of a firm to obtain leverage, margin trading allows the investor to obtain *leverage*. That is, by using borrowed capital to partly fund the transaction, investors can magnify the returns on investment. As we have seen earlier, though, leverage is a *double-edged sword*. This can be illustrated clearly by continuing with our example on Martin.

We will first analyze a pure cash trade, with the help of different scenarios for the price at the end of a week, which we will assume is Martin's investment horizon.

CASE A: THE MARKET RISES

The market price of ABC at the time of disposal is $62. The 100 shares that Martin owns will therefore be worth $6,200. The return on investment is:

$$\frac{(6{,}200 - 5{,}000)}{5{,}000} \times 100 = 24\%$$

CASE B: THE MARKET DECLINES

The market price of ABC a week hence is $42. The shares are obviously worth only $4,200 and hence the rate of return is:

$$\frac{(4{,}200 - 5{,}000)}{5{,}000} \times 100 = -16\%$$

Let us now consider the situation where Martin chooses to exert the full borrowing power of the capital at his disposal and indulge in margin trading. With $10,000 in hand, he can acquire 200 shares of ABC. Let us examine the consequences from the standpoint of the rate of return.

---

[6]Because of the 50% margin requirement, he can borrow an amount up to the funds at his disposal.

CASE A: THE MARKET RISES

Assume that the share price rises to \$62. The value of 200 shares will be \$12,400. After returning the amount borrowed from the broker, Martin will be left with \$7,400. The rate of return is:

$$\frac{(7,400 - 5,000)}{5,000} \times 100 = 48\%$$

CASE B: THE MARKET DECLINES

But what if the price was to decline to \$42 per share? The value of 200 shares will be \$8,400. After returning the amount borrowed, Martin will be left with \$3,400. The rate of return is consequently:

$$\frac{(3,400 - 5,000)}{5,000} \times 100 = -32\%$$

As can be seen, trading on the margin has doubled the rate of return. This is true irrespective of whether the trade has led to a profit or to a loss.

INTEREST AND COMMISSIONS

In our preceding illustration, we ignored two major real-life issues. The first is that in practice the broker will charge interest on the amount borrowed by Martin. The second factor to be considered is that in practice investors will have to pay commissions twice: when acquiring the shares and when disposing of them. When these facets are factored in, the result will be a reduction in the percentage of profit in the event of a rise in the market price, and an increase in the percentage of loss in the event of an adverse price change.

Margin interest income is a significant source of revenue for brokers and dealers. The normal practice is for the broker to obtain a loan from a bank, by pledging the securities as collateral. The rate charged by commercial banks for such loans is called the *broker call money rate*, which is usually about 1% less than the *prime rate*, which is the rate at which a commercial bank lends to its best clients. The reason why the loan rates are lower for such transactions is that the borrower, in this case the broker, is providing very liquid or marketable securities. The broker will usually add a mark-up to the call money rate before extending a loan to a client. In practice, the lowest rates ordinarily go to clients who have the largest debit balances or, in other words, bigger borrowers pay less. The level of trading undertaken by the borrower is also a factor while determining the rate of interest charged by the broker. A customer with a very active account may be able to negotiate a lower rate of interest, because the additional income generated by way of commissions will more than compensate the broker for the concession made by way of a lower rate of interest.

Let us assume that the broker charges Martin an interest of 10% per annum on the amount borrowed. We will reexamine the consequences of a price increase and a price decline, assuming that the account is kept open for a period of three months.

CASE A: THE MARKET RISES

Once again consider a situation where the terminal stock price is $62. The 200 shares bought by Martin are worth $12,400. As he has borrowed $5,000, he needs to repay $5,125, which represents the repayment of principal plus interest for three months. The rate of return is:

$$\frac{(12,400 - 5,125 - 5,000)}{5,000} \times 100 = 45.50\%$$

Thus the assumption of an interest payment, which is consistent with a real-life transaction, leads to a reduction of 2.50% in returns.

CASE B: THE MARKET DECLINES

Now consider a situation where the terminal stock price is $42. After repaying the lender, the customer will be left with $3,275. The rate of return is:

$$\frac{(8,400 - 5,125 - 5,000)}{5,000} \times 100 = -34.50\%$$

Compared to the earlier case, our loss has been increased by 2.50%. Thus, interest charges mitigate profits and magnify losses.

Commissions have a similar impact on the rate of return obtained by the investor, that is, they mitigate profits and magnify losses.

MAINTENANCE MARGIN

As we have seen, if the stock price were to rise, it will lead to an increase in the owner's equity. The investor can either withdraw the excess equity as cash, or use it to acquire more shares. However, it is not necessary that the stock price should always rise. In practice, the price can always decline and we need to consider the consequences of the same. Losses will lead to a reduction in the owner's equity, and sustained losses can lead to a significant reduction in the equity level. To protect themselves, brokers will fix a threshold level called the maintenance margin level. If, due to adverse market movements, the account were to become under-margined, the investor may eventually receive a notice for additional margin from the broker, which is referred to as a *margin call*. If the investor were to fail to respond to such a call, which in essence is a demand for additional collateral, the broker is at liberty to liquidate all or a part of the securities in the account.[7] The objective of prescribing a maintenance margin level is obviously to protect the broker's investment.

Let us take the case of an investor who acquires 200 shares of ABC at $75 each, by borrowing $7,500. Assume that the broker has fixed a maintenance margin level of 25%. The issue is, how low will the price of the stock fall, before a margin call is

---

[7]Remember, the securities have been pledged as collateral by the investor.

triggered off? Let us denote this price by P. At this price the owner's equity must be exactly 25%. So, obviously it must be that:

$$(200P - 7,500)/200P = .25$$

$$\Rightarrow 200P = 50P + 7,500$$

$$\Rightarrow P = 7,500/150 = \$50$$

At this point, the T-Account would look as shown in Figure 3.4.

Liabilities	Assets
Broker's Loan $7,500	200 Shares @ $50 = $10,000
Owner's Equity $2,500	

FIGURE 3.4

If the stock price were to decline below $50, a call would be issued demanding an immediate deposit of new funds or securities to raise the equity to a level higher than 25%. In practice a margin call must be met on demand.

SHORT-SELLING

Investors who anticipate a bull phase, or in other words expect the stock market to rise, will seek to acquire stocks in anticipation of being able to sell them subsequently at a higher price. The principle being followed is *buy low and sell high*. Some investors may decide to take additional risk by using leverage, which is tantamount to margin trading.

Short sellers have an opposite viewpoint regarding the market. They are bearish and anticipate a decline in the market. Their objective is therefore to *sell high and buy low*. Short-selling in practice requires such investors to sell stocks that they do not own. You may wonder how investors can sell something that they do not possess. The answer is they can always borrow shares from a third party and sell them. In practice short sellers borrow securities from brokers. Short-selling is also a form of margin trading, the difference being that margin trading entails the borrowing of cash while short-selling requires the borrowing of securities.

A broker obtains the right to borrow securities from a client by appropriately wording the margin agreement. Such a clause is known as a *customer loan consent*. Before executing a short sale transaction, the broker has to seek and receive an authorization from the stock loan department, stating that the security is indeed available for the purpose of the short sale. Security availability can change on a day-to-day basis.

Consequently, in practice, short sale orders are accepted only as *day orders*. That is, they are valid only for the day on which they are placed. If such an order were to remain unexecuted at the end of the trading day on which it is placed, it would stand canceled automatically. A client who seeks to keep the order active on the following day would have to rebook the order.

When an investor borrows and sells a share, the proceeds will be credited to the investor's account. At some point in time, the shares will have to be purchased and returned to the broker. This is called *covering the short position*. If the price at this point of time is lower than the original purchase price, then the investor stands to make a gain. Otherwise, if the price has risen, the investor will have a loss.

In principle, traders have the freedom to keep the position open for as long as they desire. At times, however, the lenders of the shares may seek to call away the stock that they have lent. In such a situation, the broker will try and borrow the securities from a fresh source. However, if unable to do so, the broker will be left with no option but to request the investor to close out or cover the short position.

Let us analyze the transaction from the standpoint of the trader who lends the share. The investors or brokers who part with shares to facilitate the sale by the short seller do not actually sell the shares. They merely lend them to another party to facilitate a sale. Take a situation where a cash dividend is declared on the underlying stock during the period of the short sale. The firm will pay the dividend to the party who has acquired the shares from the short seller, because at any one point in time a share can have only one legal owner. The lender of the share, however would demand the payment of an equivalent amount. The lender has merely lent the shares, and should not consequently lose entitlement to the payout. Consequently, the short sellers have to compensate the lenders for such lost income from their personal funds. Similarly, if the stock were to undergo an $n{:}1$ split during the period of the short sale, the lender will be entitled to receive n shares when the position is closed, per share that was lent at the outset. There is one right, however, that is irretrievable from the standpoint of the lender. If there is a meeting of shareholders during the period of the short sale, the lender loses the right to vote, for this is one entitlement that the borrower of securities cannot compensate. It must be remembered that a short sale creates two long positions, the "real" long position held by the buyer who takes delivery of the stock from the short seller and a "phantom" long position that is held by the person who has lent the stock.

As we explained earlier, short-selling is also a form of margin trading, because the investor is borrowing shares from the broker. Consequently, rules similar to margin trading apply to short sales, and such transactions too are governed by the same regulations in the United States.

Traders who engage in margin trading must deposit at least 50% of the cost of the shares from their pocket. This margin is required because the market may subsequently decline, and brokers must have adequate assets to recover their loan. In the case of a short sale, the investor borrows a share and sells it. The investor is required to have enough funds to reacquire the stock subsequently in order to cover the position. Thus, the account must at all times have adequate funds to facilitate the reacquisition of the shares. Because the price may rise after the short sale, investors who are selling short must deposit additional funds over and above what they receive in the form of sale proceeds. As per regulations, a short seller must make the same deposit that would be required if the stock were to be purchased on margin. That is, the short seller must offer at least 50% of the sale proceeds as additional collateral. This deposit, plus the proceeds of the short sale, would show up as a credit balance in their account. We will illustrate this with the help of a numerical example.

EXAMPLE 3.13

Nick decides to sell short 100 shares of ABC, which is currently trading at $50 per share. Obviously, he is anticipating a falling market. He will receive $5,000 when he sells the shares. He will have to deposit this amount, plus an additional 50%, which in this case is $2,500, with the broker. His account position may be represented as shown in Figure 3.5.

Liabilities	Assets
100 Shares @ $50 = $5,000	Credit Balance $7,500
Owner's Equity $2,500	

FIGURE 3.5

Now assume that the value of the shares drops to $40. The credit balance will remain at $7,500, while the value of the shares will be only $4,000. Consequently, the position will now have an equity of $3,500. As per the requirement, the necessary margin is $2,000. Thus, there is an excess equity of $1,500. The excess equity can either be withdrawn in the form of cash, or it can be used for additional shorting. If the balance is withdrawn, the account position will look as shown in Figure 3.6.

Liabilities	Assets
100 Shares @ $40 = $4,000	Credit Balance $6,000
Owner's Equity $2,000	

FIGURE 3.6

The other possibility is that the excess equity of $1,500 can be used to short additional shares. Since the margin requirement is 50%, the shorting power of the

(continued)

(*continued*)

excess is $3,000. Consequently, in this case 75 more shares can be shorted. The position will then look as shown in Figure 3.7.

Liabilities	Assets
175 Shares @ $40 = $7,000	Credit Balance $10,500
Owner's Equity $3,500	

FIGURE 3.7

The credit balance in a short account provides collateral for the shares which have been sold short. They are not *free credit balances,* in the sense that they cannot be removed from the account. So typically, they will not earn any interest for the short seller. Any interest earned will accrue to the brokerage firm. Consequently, stock loan departments of brokerage firms are usually very profitable. However, institutional clients may demand that the brokerage firm share the interest that it will earn on the credit balance. Such a payment by a brokerage firm is referred to as a *short interest rebate*.

MAINTENANCE OF A SHORT POSITION

A short position is inherently more risky than a long position. This is because the worst thing that can happen when one buys a security is that the securities can become totally worthless. Due to the limited liability feature, the price of a share has a lower bound of zero.

In the case of a short sale, however, what has been loaned is a stock. While stocks have a lower bound, they do not have an upper bound. In other words, there is no limit on how high the share price can rise. Since the short seller is required to acquire the stock at the prevailing market value, at the time of covering the short sale, the maximum possible loss, in principle, is infinite.

Brokers take this higher risk aspect of short sales into consideration by setting the maintenance margin requirement for such transactions at higher levels.

Let us assume that the maintenance level is 30%. How do we compute the corresponding trigger for a margin call? Assume that Nick has sold 100 shares of ABC at $65 and has deposited an initial margin of $3,250. Let the price corresponding to a 30% margin level be denoted by P. Therefore

$$(9{,}750 - 100P)/100P = .30$$

$$\Rightarrow 9{,}750 - 100P = 30P$$

$$\Rightarrow P = 975/13 = 75.00$$

SHORTING AGAINST THE BOX

This entails establishing a short position in a security that the investors already own. In other words, the investors have no intention of delivering the stock that they are holding, and instead seek to borrow the security to facilitate delivery. Why would a trader resort to such a course of action? Typically, traders go in for such a strategy to defer any unrealized capital gains for tax purposes while at the same continuing to protect the magnitude of the capital gain. We will illustrate this with the help of an example.

EXAMPLE 3.14

Let us assume that we are on 15 December 20XX. In March of the same year we had acquired a stock for $800, and it is currently worth $1,200. If we were to sell it immediately, we would have a capital gain of $400. If we assume that the tax rate is 15%, we would have a post-tax profit of $340. Now consider a situation where we are anticipating a capital loss after a few months from another source, which in principle can be set off against this capital gain to reduce or even avoid our tax liability. If so, we may want to defer the sale. But this entails a risk. If we postpone the sale, we may end up with a reduced capital gain or even a capital loss, depending on how the share price moves in the interim. In such a situation we can defer the capital gain while continuing to protect its quantum by engaging in a short sale.

If we were to engage in a short sale, any change in the value of the existing long position would be exactly offset by an equal and opposite change in the value of the newly established short position. Consequently, the net result would be a freeze on the capital gain of $400. For instance, if the share price were to rise to $1,500 after six months, the capital gain on the long position would increase to $700; however, the short position would lead to a loss of $300. The net result would be an overall capital gain of $400.

THE RISK FACTOR

In general, over a medium- to long-term horizon, stock prices have a tendency to drift upwards. This is because even if the performance of the company were to remain stagnant, its share price should rise over a period of time to compensate owners for the effects of inflation. Thus, the long-run direction of the market is upwards. Short-selling represents an effort to profit from a falling market. Thus, it is tantamount to betting against the overall direction of the market.

Due to the limited liability feature, a long position entails finite losses and potentially infinite profits. Short sales, however, entail finite profits and infinite losses. Consequently, while profits are capped at 100%, potential losses cannot be capped.

In a rising market a situation could develop where a large number of short sellers attempt to close out their positions after witnessing a rapid price increase. This can in practice cause prices to quickly spiral upwards. This phenomenon is known as a *short squeeze*. Usually, the root cause of such an event is the availability of news relevant to the security. But, at times, a trader who notices a high short interest will attempt to induce a squeeze by placing a large buy order. If the corresponding price rise were to lead to the covering of positions by short sellers, the trader who placed the buy order may be able to exit the market with a handsome profit.

THE ECONOMIC ROLE OF SHORT SALES

Many market analysts have viewed short sales as a major cause of market downturns. However, short-selling undoubtedly contributes positively to the functioning of a free market system. It provides liquidity and drives down the prices of overvalued securities to realistic levels. If a security is perceived to be undervalued, traders will assume long positions to take advantage of the anticipated price rise. On the other hand, if a security were perceived as overvalued, the freedom to short sell is imperative to ensure that prices can be driven down to a fair or true value.

THE UPTICK RULE

A tick is the minimum price increment or variation observable in the market. In other words, it is the smallest amount by which two prices can differ. It is usually set by exchange regulations. In the United States, until the year 2000, the tick size was one-sixteenth of a dollar, or 6.25 cents. Now the system has been decimalized, and the tick size is 0.01 dollars, or 1 cent.

The minimum tick size on the Tokyo Stock Exchange is a function of the share price and is depicted in Table 3.20.

Traders classify prices by their relation to previous prices. The price is said to be on an uptick if the current price is higher than the last price, on a downtick if it is lower, and on a zero tick if it is the same. Zero tick prices are further classified depending on the last different price observed. A zero tick price is said to be on a zero downtick if the last different price observed was higher, and on a zero uptick if the last different price observed was lower. We will illustrate these concepts using an example, as shown in Table 3.21.

TABLE 3.20   Tick Sizes on the TSE

Price	Tick Size
P ≤ 2000 yen	1 yen
2000 < P ≤ 3000 yen	5 yen
3000 < P ≤ 30,000 yen	10 yen
30,000 < P ≤ 50,000 yen	50 yen
50,000 < P ≤ 100,000 yen	100 yen
100,000 < P ≤ 1,000,000 yen	1,000 yen
P > 1,000,000 yen	10,000 yen

TABLE 3.21 Illustration of Uptick, Downtick, and Zero Tick

Previous to Last Price	Last Price	Current Price	Term
72	72	72.10	Uptick
72	72	71.90	Downtick
72.10	72	72	Zero Downtick
71.90	72	72	Zero Uptick

On certain exchanges, short sales are permitted only on an uptick or a zero uptick. This is because sustained short-selling in a declining price environment can cause the market to crash.

CHAPTER 4

Bonds

INTRODUCTION

Bonds and debentures, which we have already introduced, are referred to as fixed-income securities. They are called this because once the rate of interest is set at the onset of the period when it is due to be paid, interest is not a function of the profitability of the firm. For this reason, all bonds, including floating-rate bonds that entail the resetting of interest at the commencement of each interest payment period, are called fixed-income instruments. Interest payments are therefore contractual obligations, and failure to pay what was promised at the start of an interest computation period is tantamount to default.

A bondholder is a stakeholder in a business but is not a part owner of the business. Bondholders are entitled only to the interest that was promised and to repayment of principal at the time of maturity and do not partake in the profits of the firm. As we discussed earlier, bonds may be unsecured or secured. Unsecured debt is referred to as a debenture in the United States, and the term connotes that no specific asset(s) have been earmarked as collateral for the securities. In the case of secured debt, however, the issuer sets aside as collateral specific assets on which the investors have a claim in the event of default. Debt securities may be negotiable or nonnegotiable. A negotiable security is one that can be traded in the secondary market, whereas a nonnegotiable security cannot be endorsed by the holder in favor of another investor. Bank accounts are classic examples of nonnegotiable securities, for if investors were to open a term deposit with a commercial bank, they can always withdraw the investment and pay a third party, but they cannot transfer the ownership of the deposit.

The most basic form of a debt security is referred to as a plain-vanilla bond. It is an IOU that promises to pay a fixed rate of interest every period, which is usually every six months in the United States, and to repay the principal at maturity. Floating-rate bonds are similar except that the interest rate does not remain constant from period to period but fluctuates with changes in the benchmark to which it is linked. There are also bonds with embedded options. Convertible bonds can be converted to shares of stock by the investor. Callable bonds can be prematurely retired by the issuing company, while putable bonds can be prematurely surrendered by the bondholders in return for repayment of the principal.

Bonds provide equity shareholders with leverage. Here is a detailed illustration. Company ALPHA is entirely equity financed and has issued shares worth $1,000,000. Company BETA has raised the same amount of capital, half in the form of debt and the other half in the form of equity. The debt carries interest at the rate of 6% per annum.

Let us consider two situations, the first where both companies make a profit of $250,000 from operations, and the second where they both make a loss of $250,000. We will assume that the firm does not have to pay tax to keep matters simple.

PAT stands for profit after tax and represents what the shareholders are entitled to.

ROI is the return on investment for shareholders.

As we can see from Table 4.1, the presence of debt in the capital structure creates leverage. The profit for the shareholders is magnified from 25% to 44% when a firm is financed 50% with debt. On the other hand, any loss incurred is also magnified – in this case, from –25% to –56%. Thus, as we saw in the case of margin trading, leverage is a double-edged sword. It can also be seen from the case of BETA that the incurrence of a loss does not give the flexibility to the firm to avoid or postpone the interest due to bondholders. Thus, interest on bonds is indeed a contractual obligation.

Bonds also provide the issuing firm with a tax shield. This is because while interest on debt is a deductible expense for figuring the tax liability of a company, dividends on equity shares is not. Consequently, interest payments reduce the tax liability for the firm or, in other words, give it a tax shield. Here is an illustration using the same data as above. Both firms are assumed to have a profit of $250,000 and the applicable tax rate is assumed to be 30%.

PBT stands for Profits Before Tax.

PAT stands for Profits After Tax.

Let us analyze the last row of Table 4.2. If company BETA had been a zero-debt company like ALPHA, its shareholders would have been entitled to an income of $175,000. Because it has paid interest, though, the shareholders have received only $154,000, which is $21,000 less. Thus, from the standpoint of shareholders of BETA, they have effectively paid an interest of $21,000. So, what explains the missing $9,000, for we know that BETA did pay $30,000 to its bondholders? The answer is that by allowing the firm to deduct the interest paid as an expense prior to computing tax, the country's tax authority has forgone taxes to the extent of $9,000. Thus, the tax authority has effectively provided a subsidy to the company. The tax shield, as we term it, is equal to the product of the tax rate and the interest paid; in this case it is $0.30 \times 30,000 = \$9,000$.

If the rules were changed and interest on debt was no longer tax deductible, BETA would have to pay tax on $250,000 and the PAT, which is what belongs to the

TABLE 4.1 Illustration of Leverage

	Case-A	**Case-A**	**Case-B**	**Case-B**
	Firms Make a Profit	Firms Make a Profit	Firms Make a Loss	Firms Make a Loss
	ALPHA	BETA	ALPHA	BETA
Profits from Operations	250,000	250,000	(250,000)	(250,000)
Less Interest	0	(30,000)	0	(30,000)
PAT	250,000	220,000	(250,000)	(280,000)
ROI	25%	44%	–25%	–56%

TABLE 4.2   Illustration of a Tax Shield

	ALPHA	BETA
Profit from Operations	250,000	250,000
Interest	NIL	30,000
PBT	250,000	220,000
Tax	(75,000)	(66,000)
PAT	175,000	154,000

shareholders, would be only $145,000. In this situation, the shareholders will feel the full burden of the interest paid by the firm.

In many countries interest received from bonds is taxable at the hands of the receiver, whereas dividends received from shares are not. The reason is that since the interest is being paid out of pre-tax profits, it is not being taxed at the level of the firm. However, dividends on equity is not a tax-deductible expense for the firm and, to prevent it from being taxed twice, it is not taxed at the hands of the shareholders.

TERMS USED IN THE BOND MARKET

Face Value

The face value, also known as

> *Par value*
>
> *Redemption value*
>
> *Maturity value*
>
> *Principal value*

is the principal amount underlying the bond. It was the amount raised by the issuer from the first holder and is the amount repayable by the issuer to the last holder. We will denote it by the symbol M.

Term to Maturity

This is the time remaining in the life of the bond as measured at the point of evaluation. It may be perceived as the length of time after which the debt shall cease to exist, and the borrower will redeem the issue by repaying the holder. It may also be viewed as the length of time for which the borrower has to make periodic interest payments on the debt. The words *maturity*, *term*, and *term to maturity* are used interchangeably. We will assume that we are stationed at time zero and will denote the point of maturity by T. Thus, the number of periods until maturity is T, which is normally measured in years.

Coupon

The contractual interest payment made by the issuer is called a coupon payment. The name came about because in the earlier days, bonds were issued with a booklet of post-dated coupons. On an interest payment date, the holder was expected to detach the relevant coupon and claim his payment.

The coupon may be denoted as a rate or as a dollar value. We will denote the coupon rate by c. The dollar value, C, is therefore given by $c \times M$. Most bonds pay interest on a semiannual basis and consequently the semiannual cash flow is $c \times M/2$.

Consider a bond with a face value of $1,000, which pays a coupon of 8% per annum on a semiannual basis. The annual coupon rate is 0.08. The semiannual coupon payment is $0.08 \times 1,000/2 = \$40$.

Yield to Maturity

Like the coupon rate, the yield to maturity is an interest rate. The difference is that while the coupon rate is the rate of interest paid by the issuer, the yield to maturity (YTM) is the rate of return required by the market. At a given point in time, the yield may be greater than, equal to, or less than the coupon rate. The YTM will be denoted by y and is the rate of return that a buyer will get if he were to acquire the bond at the prevailing price and hold it to maturity. We will shortly see that the YTM of a bond is equivalent to the concept of the Internal Rate of Return (IRR) used in capital budgeting. As in the case of the IRR, the YTM computation assumes that all intermediate cash flows are reinvested at the YTM itself.

VALUATION OF A BOND

To value a bond, we will first assume that we are standing on a coupon payment date. That is, we will assume that a coupon has just been received and the next coupon is exactly six months or one period away. If T is the term to maturity we have N coupons remaining where $N = 2T$.

We will receive N payments during the life of the bond, where each payment or cash flow is equal to $C/2$. This payment stream constitutes an annuity. The present value of this annuity is:

$$
\frac{\frac{C}{2}}{\frac{y}{2}} \times \left[1 - \frac{1}{\left(1 + \frac{y}{2}\right)^N} \right]
$$

The terminal payment of the face value is a lump-sum payment. Since we are discounting the cash flows from the annuity on a semiannual basis, this payment too needs to be discounted on a similar basis. Thus, the present value of this cash flow is:

$$
\frac{M}{\left(1 + \frac{y}{2}\right)^N}
$$

Thus, the price of the bond is given by:

$$
P = \frac{\frac{C}{2}}{\frac{y}{2}} \times \left[1 - \frac{1}{\left(1 + \frac{y}{2}\right)^N} \right] + \frac{M}{\left(1 + \frac{y}{2}\right)^N}
$$

As can be seen the YTM is the discount rate that makes the present value of the cash flows from the bond equal to its price. The price of a bond is like the initial investment in a project. The remaining cash flows are similar to the inflows from the project. Consequently, the YTM is exactly analogous to the IRR.

EXAMPLE 4.1

Infosys Technologies has issued bonds with 10 years to maturity and a face value of $1,000. The coupon rate is 8% per annum payable on a semiannual basis. If the required yield in the market is equal to 9%, what should be the price of the bond?

The periodic cash flow is $0.08 \times 1,000/2 = \$40$. Thus, the present value of all the coupons is:

$$\frac{\frac{80}{2}}{\frac{0.09}{2}} \times \left[1 - \frac{1}{\left(1 + \frac{0.09}{2}\right)^{20}}\right] = \$520.3175$$

The present value of the face value is:

$$\frac{1,000}{\left(1 + \frac{0.09}{2}\right)^{20}} = \$414.6429$$

Thus, the price of the bond is $520.3175 + 414.6429 = \$934.9604$.

PAR, PREMIUM, AND DISCOUNT BONDS

In the preceding illustration, the price of the bond is less than its face value. Such bonds are said to be trading at a discount to the par value and are therefore referred to as *discount* bonds. If the price of the bond were to be greater than its face value, then it would be said to be trading at a premium to its face value and would consequently be referred to as a *premium* bond. If the price is equal to the face value, then the bond is said to be trading at *par*.

The relationship between the price and the face value depends on whether the YTM is greater or less than the coupon. Consider the pricing equation:

$$P = \frac{\frac{C}{2}}{\frac{y}{2}} \times \left[1 - \frac{1}{\left(1 + \frac{y}{2}\right)^N}\right] + \frac{M}{\left(1 + \frac{y}{2}\right)^N}$$

$$= \frac{\frac{cM}{2}}{\frac{y}{2}} \times \left[1 - \frac{1}{\left(1 + \frac{y}{2}\right)^N}\right] + \frac{M}{\left(1 + \frac{y}{2}\right)^N}$$

$$= \frac{cM}{y} + \frac{M}{\left(1 + \frac{y}{2}\right)^N} \times \left[1 - \frac{c}{y}\right]$$

If $c = y$, $P = M$. In other words, if the coupon is equal to the YTM, the bond will always trade at par.

Why would a bond sell at a premium or at a discount? The price of a bond is the present value of all the cash flows emanating from it. If the yield is equal to the coupon, then the rate of return being demanded by investors is exactly equal to the rate of return being offered by the issuer, and consequently the bond will sell at par.

Now take a case where the yield is less than the coupon. For instance, assume that the coupon is 10% per annum while the yield is 8% per annum. An investor would be willing to pay more than its face value for it. In practice, the price would be bid up to a level where the YTM is exactly equal to 8% per annum. Finally, consider a case where the YTM is greater than the coupon. Assume that the coupon is 8% per annum while the yield is 10% per annum. Investors in these circumstances would be willing to pay only a price that is less than the face value. In practice the price would be driven down to a level where the YTM is exactly equal to 10%.

EVOLUTION OF THE PRICE

Let us consider the change in the price of a bond from one coupon date to another, assuming that the YTM remains constant.

Note: C is the annual coupon in currency terms and c is the annual coupon rate in percentage terms. Thus $C = c \times M$.

The price of a bond with N coupons remaining is:

$$P = \frac{\frac{C}{2}}{\frac{y}{2}} \times \left[1 - \frac{1}{\left(1 + \frac{y}{2}\right)^N}\right] + \frac{M}{\left(1 + \frac{y}{2}\right)^N}$$

The price when there are $N - 1$ coupons left is given by:

$$P = \frac{\frac{C}{2}}{\frac{y}{2}} \times \left[1 - \frac{1}{\left(1 + \frac{y}{2}\right)^{(N-1)}}\right] + \frac{M}{\left(1 + \frac{y}{2}\right)^{(N-1)}}$$

Thus the price change between successive coupon periods is given by:

$$\Delta P = \frac{\frac{C}{2}}{\frac{y}{2}} \times \left[\frac{1}{\left(1 + \frac{y}{2}\right)^N} - \frac{1}{\left(1 + \frac{y}{2}\right)^{(N-1)}}\right]$$

$$+ M \times \left[\frac{1}{\left(1 + \frac{y}{2}\right)^{(N-1)}} - \frac{1}{\left(1 + \frac{y}{2}\right)^N}\right]$$

$$= \frac{M}{\left(1 + \frac{y}{2}\right)^N} \times \left[\frac{y}{2} - \frac{c}{2}\right]$$

Obviously if $y = c$, then $\Delta P = 0$. Thus, if the YTM were to remain constant, the price of a par bond will continue to remain at par as we go from one coupon date to the next. If the yield is greater than the coupon, then $\Delta P > 0$. Thus, a discount bond will steadily increase in price as we go from one coupon date to the next. In the case of a premium bond, the price will steadily decline as we go from one coupon date to the next.

This is called the Pull to Par effect. The reason is the following. As we go from one coupon date to the next, one coupon drops out of the pricing equation, which pulls down the price. On the next coupon date, however, the face value is discounted for one period less, which pulls up the price. For par bonds, the two effects neutralize each other, and the price remains unchanged. For premium bonds, the first effect dominates, and the price steadily declines as we approach maturity. For discount bonds, however, the second effect dominates, and the price steadily increases from one coupon date to the next.

EXAMPLE 4.2

Consider a bond with 10 years to maturity and a face value of $1,000. Assume that the YTM is 8% per annum while the coupon is 6% per annum. The bond will sell at a discount. The price can be calculated to be $864.10. Now let us move one period ahead to a time when there are only 9.5 years left. The price can be calculated to be $868.66. As expected, the price has increased.

Now consider the same bond but assume that the coupon is 10% per annum. This bond will sell at a premium. The price when there are 20 coupons left is $1,135.90. Six months later, if the yield were to remain constant, the price will be $1,131.34. As expected, the price has declined.

ZERO-COUPON BONDS

Unlike a plain-vanilla bond, which pays coupons at periodic intervals, zero-coupon bonds, also known as deep discount bonds, do not pay any interest. Such instruments are always traded at a discount to the face value, and the holder at maturity will receive the face value. For instance, consider a zero-coupon bond with a face value of $1,000 and 10 years to maturity. Assume that the required yield is 8% per annum. The price may be computed as follows.

$$\frac{1,000}{(1.04)^{20}} = \$456.39$$

Notice that we have chosen to discount at a rate of 4% for 20 half-yearly periods, and not at 8% for 10 annual periods. The reason is that in practice a potential investor will have a choice between plain-vanilla bonds and zero-coupon bonds. To draw meaningful inferences, it is imperative that the discounting technique be common. Since the cash flows from plain-vanilla bonds are usually discounted on a semi-annual basis, we choose to do the same for zero-coupon bonds.

A zero-coupon bond will never sell at a premium. It will always trade at a discount except at the time of maturity, when it will trade for the face value. That does not mean that buyers of such a bond will always experience a capital gain. If they were to buy and hold it to maturity, then obviously they will have a capital gain. But if they choose to sell it prior to maturity they may well end up with a capital loss as we shall demonstrate.

EXAMPLE 4.3

Alex bought a zero-coupon bond when there were 10 years to maturity. The prevailing yield was 10% per annum. Today, that is, a year later, the YTM is 12% per annum. The purchase price was $\dfrac{1,000}{(1.05)^{20}} = \$376.89$. The price at the time of sale can be shown to be $350.34. Thus, in this case the investor has a capital loss of $26.55.

VALUING A BOND IN BETWEEN COUPON DATES

Thus far we have assumed that we are valuing the bond on a coupon date. That is, the next coupon is exactly one period away. Now let us consider a more realistic situation where the price of the bond is sought to be calculated in between coupon dates.

Consider the timeline depicted in Figure 4.1.

As you can see, the length of time between "0" and "1" is less than one period, whereas the other coupon dates are spaced exactly one period apart.

To value the bond at time "0" we will proceed in two steps. First let us value the bond at time "1." At this point in time, we will get a cash flow of C/2. There are $N-1$ coupons left after this and the face value is scheduled to be received $N-1$ periods later. The present value of the remaining cash flows at this point in time is:

$$\frac{\frac{C}{2}}{\frac{y}{2}} \times \left[1 - \frac{1}{\left(1 + \frac{y}{2}\right)^{(N-1)}}\right] + \frac{M}{\left(1 + \frac{y}{2}\right)^{(N-1)}}$$

Thus, the price of the bond at time "1" is:

$$P_1 = \frac{C}{2} + \frac{\frac{C}{2}}{\frac{y}{2}} \times \left[1 - \frac{1}{\left(1 + \frac{y}{2}\right)^{(N-1)}}\right] + \frac{M}{\left(1 + \frac{y}{2}\right)^{(N-1)}}$$

$$= \frac{\frac{C}{2}}{\frac{y}{2}} \left[\frac{\left(1 + \frac{y}{2}\right)^{N} - 1}{\left(1 + \frac{y}{2}\right)^{N-1}}\right] + \frac{M}{\left(1 + \frac{y}{2}\right)^{N-1}}$$

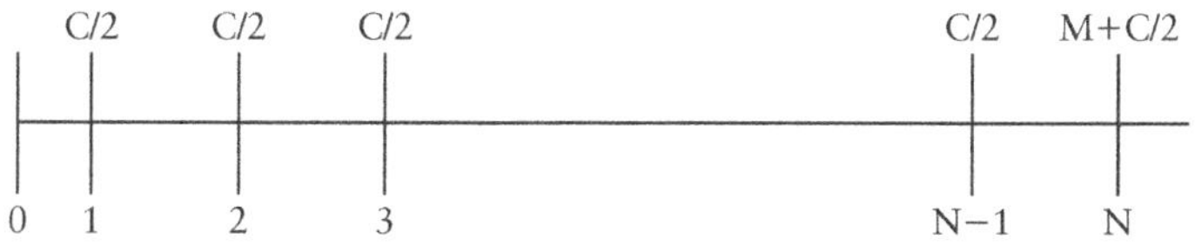

FIGURE 4.1   Cash Flows from a Plain-Vanilla Bond

Let us denote the length of time between "0" and "1" by the symbol k. Obviously $k < 1$. Discounting back P_1 for k periods we get:

$$P_0 = \left[\frac{\frac{c \times M}{2}}{\left(1 + \frac{y}{2}\right)^k} \times \frac{\left[\left(1 + \frac{y}{2}\right)^N - 1\right]}{\left(\frac{y}{2}\right)\left(1 + \frac{y}{2}\right)^{N-1}} \right] + \frac{M}{\left(1 + \frac{y}{2}\right)^{N-1+k}}$$

DAY-COUNT CONVENTIONS

When valuing a bond between coupon dates the key issue is the calculation of the fractional first period. Unfortunately, there is no unique method for computing this period. Different markets, and at times different products in the same market, follow different conventions. A method of computation of the fractional period is called a *day-count convention*.

ACTUAL-ACTUAL

We will illustrate a convention known as the actual-actual approach. This is used for Treasury bonds in the United States. Let us go back and analyze the fractional period. In order to compute the fraction, we need to define the numerator and the denominator. The numerator is the number of days between the valuation date and the next coupon date. The denominator is obviously the number of days between the previous coupon date and the next coupon date.

As per the actual-actual method we have to actually count the exact number of days in both the numerator as well as the denominator. We will illustrate it with the help of an example.

EXAMPLE 4.4

Let us assume that we are standing on 21 May 20XX and that we have a bond maturing on 15 May (20XX+20). The face value is $1,000; the coupon rate is 6% per annum payable semiannually; and the YTM is 8% per annum. The coupon dates are 15 May and 15 November.

The numerator in this case is the period between 21 May and 15 November. The number of days is calculated month-wise as shown in Table 4.3. The principle is that we include either one of the starting or the ending dates, but not both.

TABLE 4.3 Calculation of the Numerator

Month	# of Days
May	10
June	30
July	31
August	31
September	30
October	31
November	15
Total	178

The denominator is the period between 15 May and 15 November. In this case it is 184 days as shown in Table 4.4.

TABLE 4.4 Calculation of the Denominator

Month	# of Days
May	16
June	30
July	31
August	31
September	30
October	31
November	15
Total	184

In practice, if we were to count the actual number of days between two dates six months apart, we will always get a number between 181 and 184. There are only four possibilities: 181, 182, 183, and 184.

The actual-actual method is denoted in short form as Act/Act and is pronounced as Ack/Ack by Wall Street traders. Let us now use it to derive the price of the bond on 21 May 20XX. The number of coupons remaining as of this day is obviously 40. The value of the fractional first period is $178/184 = 0.9674$.

The price of the bond is therefore:

$$P_0 = \left[\frac{\frac{0.06 \times 1,000}{2}}{\left(1 + \frac{0.08}{2}\right)^{0.9674}} \times \frac{\left[\left(1 + \frac{0.08}{2}\right)^{40} - 1\right]}{\left(\frac{0.08}{2}\right)\left(1 + \frac{0.08}{2}\right)^{39}}\right] + \frac{1,000}{\left(1 + \frac{0.08}{2}\right)^{40-1+0.9674}}$$

$$= \$803.0939$$

THE TREASURY'S APPROACH

The Treasury uses a slightly different method to compute the prices of its bonds, with the difference being that it uses simple interest for the fractional period. The Treasury's formula may be stated as:

$$P_0 = \left[\frac{\frac{c \times M}{2}}{\left(1 + k \times \frac{y}{2}\right)} \times \frac{\left[\left(1 + \frac{y}{2}\right)^{N} - 1\right]}{\left(\frac{y}{2}\right)\left(1 + \frac{y}{2}\right)^{N-1}}\right] + \frac{M}{\left(1 + k \times \frac{y}{2}\right)\left(1 + \frac{y}{2}\right)^{N-1}}$$

In this case, the price obtained by the Treasury will be $803.0738. The price that is computed by the Treasury for a given bond will always be lower than the value determined by Wall Street. This is because simple interest gives a higher discount rate for fractional periods as compared to compound interest.

CORPORATE BONDS

Corporate bonds in the United States are priced using a different day-count convention known as 30/360 NASD. As per this convention, the denominator, or the time period between two successive coupon dates, is always taken to be 180 days. That is, every month is assumed to consist of 30 days. The numerator, in order to compute the fractional period, is determined as follows.

Let us define the start date as $D_1 = (month_1, day_1, year_1)$ and the end date as $D_2 = (month_2, day_2, year_2)$. The numerator is calculated as:

$$360(year_2 - year_1) + 30(month_2 - month_1) + (day_2 - day_1)$$

There are some additional rules which may have to be applied depending on the circumstances.

1. If $day_1 = 31$, then set it equal to 30.
2. If day_1 is the last day of February, whether 28 or 29, then set it equal to 30.
3. If day_1 is 30 or has been set equal to 30 based on the two rules listed above, then if $day_2 = 31$, set it equal to 30.

Let us take the case of the bond maturing on 15 May (20XX+20). The valuation date as per our assumption is 21 May 20XX. The numerator for the fractional period is given by:

$$360(20XX - 20XX) + 30(11 - 5) + (15 - 21) = 174$$

The value of the fractional period is $174/180 = 0.9667$.
The value of the bond is therefore:

$$P_0 = \left[\frac{\frac{0.06 \times 1,000}{2}}{\left(1 + \frac{0.08}{2}\right)^{0.9667}} \times \frac{\left[\left(1 + \frac{0.08}{2}\right)^{40} - 1\right]}{\left(\frac{0.08}{2}\right)\left(1 + \frac{0.08}{2}\right)^{39}} \right] + \frac{1,000}{\left(1 + \frac{0.08}{2}\right)^{40-1+0.9667}}$$

$$= \$803.1150$$

As can be seen the day-count convention does have an impact, albeit a minor one, on the price.

ACCRUED INTEREST

The value of the bond as calculated by us using the appropriate day-count convention is referred to as the *full* or the *dirty* price. This is the price that is payable by the buyer to the seller. The price includes a component called the accrued interest, which we will now explain.

When a bond is sold between two coupon dates, the next coupon will go to the buyer of the bond. The seller, having held the security for a fraction of the coupon period, is entitled to a part of the next coupon payment. This fraction of the next coupon that belongs to the seller is termed as the accrued interest. The bond pricing equation that we have just used automatically factors in the accrued interest, for it discounts all the forthcoming cash flows, from the perspective of the buyer, until the date of sale. The partial derivative of the dirty price with respect to the length of the fractional period is negative. The shorter the time remaining until the next coupon, the higher will be the accrued interest, keeping all the other variables constant; hence the higher is the dirty price.

The method for computing the accrued interest is a function of the day-count function. Let us take the case of the Treasury bond. On 21 May 20XX, it has accrued interest for 6 days. The total length of the coupon period is 184 days.[1]

The accrued interest is therefore:

$$\frac{0.06 \times 1{,}000}{2} \times \frac{6}{184} = \$0.9783$$

The dirty price less the accrued interest is referred to as the *clean price*. In this case it is $803.0939 − 0.9783 = $802.1156.

The significance of the clean price may be demonstrated as follows. Let us consider the value of the bond on the previous coupon date, that is 15 May 20XX, assuming that the YTM is 8% per annum. The price comes out to be $802.0722.

On 15 May there is no difference between the clean price and the dirty price, since interest accrual for the next period is yet to commence. As can be seen, if the YTM is assumed to be constant, the dirty price changes by $1.0217, which amounts to more than a dollar, whereas the clean price changes only by $0.0434. Thus in the absence of a change in yield, the clean price remains relatively constant in the short run.

Look at the situation from the perspective of a bond market analyst, who knows that yield changes induce price changes. From an analysis of dirty prices, however, the analyst will be unable to discern how much of the perceived change is due to a movement in the required yield, and what is due to the change in accrued interest. Thus analysts look at prices that are not contaminated with accrued interest, or what we term as clean prices. For this reason, quoted prices in bond markets are always clean prices. However, a trader who buys a bond has to pay the full price or the dirty price. Hence when a bond is bought, the accrued interest has to be computed and added to the quoted price in order to determine the amount payable.

NEGATIVE ACCRUED INTEREST

One interesting question is, can the accrued interest be negative? Let us analyze the possible reason why accrued interest may be negative. Accrued interest represents the amount that the sellers of the bond are entitled to by virtue of the fact that they have held the bond for a part of the coupon period. Consequently, the buyer has to compensate them with this amount. Thus, negative accrued interest would correspond to

---

[1]Remember, we are using the actual-actual day-count convention.

a situation where the seller has to compensate the buyer, and such a case can arise when the bond trades *ex-dividend*.

Certain bonds trade on an ex-dividend basis close to the coupon date. We know that bonds pay coupons and not dividends, and consequently the term ex-dividend is a bit of a misnomer. But the implication is the same. Until the ex-dividend day a bond will trade cum-dividend. That is, the buyer will be entitled to the next coupon. On the ex-dividend day, however, the bond will begin to trade ex-dividend, which implies that the next coupon will go to the seller and not the buyer. However, a buyer who acquires the bond on or after the ex-dividend day is entitled to the pro-rata interest for the number of days remaining until the next coupon date. In such a situation, the seller has to share a part of the interest received with the buyer, which leads to a situation where the accrued interest is negative.

Let us consider a corporate bond maturing on 15 May (20XX+20). Assume that we are on 8 November 20XX, which is an ex-dividend date. The dirty price, just before the bond goes ex-dividend, is:

$$P_0 = \left[\frac{\frac{0.06 \times 1,000}{2}}{\left(1 + \frac{0.08}{2}\right)^{0.0380}} \times \frac{\left[\left(1 + \frac{0.08}{2}\right)^{40} - 1\right]}{\left(\frac{0.08}{2}\right)\left(1 + \frac{0.08}{2}\right)^{39}} \right] + \frac{1,000}{\left(1 + \frac{0.08}{2}\right)^{40-1+0.0380}}$$

$$= \$832.9078$$

The moment the bond goes ex-dividend the price will drop by the present value of the next coupon, because the buyer is no longer entitled to it. Thus, the ex-dividend dirty price is:

$$832.9078 - \frac{30}{(1.04)^{0.0380}} = \$802.9525$$

Notice that the dirty price will fall by the present value of the coupon and not by the coupon itself. This is because there is a week remaining until the next coupon and we consequently need to discount the cash flow.

The accrued interest as of 8 November 20XX is:

$$\frac{0.06 \times 1,000}{2} \times \frac{177}{184} = \$28.8587$$

Thus the ex-dividend clean price is 832.9078 – 28.8587 = \$804.0491. As can be seen, the ex-dividend clean price is greater than the ex-dividend dirty price by \$1.0966. This is the negative accrued interest and corresponds to the accrued interest for the remaining week, which is:

$$\frac{0.06 \times 1,000}{2} \times \frac{7}{184} = \$1.1413$$

YIELDS

The yield, or the rate of return from a bond, can be computed in a variety of ways. We have already referred to the YTM, which we will discuss in further detail shortly. There are a number of other yields measures that we will examine as well.

THE CURRENT YIELD

The current yield is very simple to compute, although technically it leaves a lot to be desired. It is commonly reported in practice, however, because of the ease with which it can be calculated.

To compute the current yield, we simply take the annual coupon payment (irrespective of the frequency with which the coupon is paid) and divide it by the current market price. Thus

$$CY = \frac{\text{Annual Coupon Interest}}{\text{Price}}$$

One question is, should the price used be the clean or the dirty price? If the clean price were to be used, then the current yield will change only when there is a change in the YTM. But if the dirty price were to be used, the current yield using the dirty price will be lower than the value obtained using the clean price, if we were to calculate it prior to the ex-dividend date. This is because the dirty price in this period will be higher than the clean price. Besides, even if the YTM were to remain constant, the current yield will steadily decline along with the increase in the dirty price. In the ex-dividend period, however, the value of the current yield that we get with the dirty price will be higher than what we would get with the clean price, because the dirty price will be lower than the clean price. In this period too, if the YTM were to remain constant, the dirty price will steadily increase and consequently the current yield will steadily decline. Thus in practice if we were to plot the current yield versus the dirty price for a given YTM, we would get a sawtooth pattern.

Why do we say that the current yield is an unsatisfactory yield measure? Consider the case of investors who have a one-year investment horizon. They will get a coupon of $C in the course of the year. If we assume that P_0 was the price they paid at the outset to acquire the bond, then their interest yield for the year is the same as the current yield as defined by us. But even if the investors were to have a one-year horizon, they will sell the bond at the end of the year, unless of course it were to mature at that time. They will experience a capital gain or a loss.[2]

If the investors had a longer-term horizon, they would get additional coupons. These can be reinvested to earn income. Besides, when multiple cash flows are involved, time value of money will enter the picture. All these facets of yield computation are totally ignored by the current yield measure.

EXAMPLE 4.5

Consider a bond with a face value of $1,000, and a coupon of 8% per annum payable semiannually. Assume that the current price is $950.

The annual coupon is $80. Thus the current yield = 80/950 = 0.084211 ≡ 8.4211%.

---

[2]Even if the bond were to mature after a year, there will be a capital gain or a loss.

SIMPLE YIELD TO MATURITY

The simple yield to maturity, also known as the Japanese Yield, as it is a key yield measure used in Japan, factors in the capital gain or loss that investors will get. However, it assumes that the bond will be held to maturity and that capital gains/losses occur evenly over the life of the bond. In other words, it builds in the assumption that capital gains and losses occur on a straight-line basis.

Consider the case of investors who buy the bond at a price P. If they hold it to maturity, they will get back the face value, M. The capital gain/loss over the investment horizon is given by $M - P$. If the bond is bought at a discount, there will be a capital gain; otherwise there will be a capital loss. If we assume that we are standing on a coupon date and that there are N coupons left, obviously there are $N/2$ years remaining until maturity. The capital gain/loss amortized on a straight-line basis is obviously

$$\frac{M - P}{\frac{N}{2}}$$

The simple YTM is given by:

$$\text{Simple YTM} = \frac{C}{P} + \frac{M - P}{\frac{N}{2} \times P}$$

Thus, for discount bonds, the simple yield to maturity will be greater than the current yield, whereas for premium bonds it will be lower. For par bonds, the two will obviously be equal.

One of the shortcomings of the Japanese yield is that it fails to take into account that investors in bonds can reinvest the coupons received by them in order to earn interest on such interest. This has the potential to significantly increase the returns from holding a bond, as we shall soon demonstrate.

EXAMPLE 4.6

Consider a bond with a face value of $1,000 that pays coupons at the rate of 7.25% per annum. Assume that the current price is $925 and that there are 10 years to maturity. The Japanese yield is given by:

$$\text{Japanese Yield} = \frac{0.0725 \times 1,000}{925} + \frac{1,000 - 925}{10 \times 925}$$

$$= 0.07838 + .0081 = 0.086486 \equiv 8.6486\%$$

YIELD TO MATURITY

The Yield to Maturity (YTM) is the internal rate of return of a bond. It is that single discount rate[3] that makes the present value of the cash flows from a bond equal to its price. The bond pricing equation is a nonlinear equation. Because there is only a

---

[3] The key term is "single."

single change of sign in the cash flows, from Descartes' rule of signs we know that there will be a single positive real root. The pricing formula gives us a polynomial of degree "N," assuming that the bond has N coupons remaining. To solve it, we generally require a computer program, but we can get fairly close with the Approximate Yield to Maturity (AYM) approach, which we shall demonstrate. We will show subsequently that it is a very simple matter to compute the YTM for zero-coupon bonds, and bonds with only two coupons remaining.

APPROXIMATE YIELD TO MATURITY

Consider a bond with a face value of M, a current price of P, an annual coupon of C, and with N coupons remaining until maturity.

The current investment in the bond is P. An instant before the bond matures the investment in the security is M. Thus the average investment is $(M + P) \div 2$.

The annual capital gain/loss computed by amortizing on a straight-line basis is

$$\frac{M - P}{\dfrac{N}{2}}$$

as we have seen in the case of the Japanese Yield.

The approximate YTM is defined as:

$$\text{AYM} = \frac{C + \dfrac{M - P}{\frac{N}{2}}}{\dfrac{M + P}{2}}$$

The numerator in the expression represents the annual income for the investor, assuming of course that capital gains/losses are realized on a straight-line basis. The denominator, as we have explained, is the average investment during the life of the bond.

Once the approximate yield is computed, we need to choose an interest rate band such that the upper limit gives a lower price than the observed price while the lower limit gives a higher price. The exact YTM is then obtained using linear interpolation.

EXAMPLE 4.7

Consider a bond with a price of $925. The coupon is 7% per annum and the face value is $1,000. There are 10 years to maturity and the bond pays coupons on a semiannual basis.

$$\text{AYM} = \frac{70 + \dfrac{1,000 - 925}{\frac{20}{2}}}{\dfrac{1,000 + 925}{2}}$$

$$= 0.08052 \equiv 8.052\%$$

Let us choose a band of 7.75%–8.25%. The prices at the two extremes are 948.4675 and 915.9929. In this case the actual price lies in between the two extreme

(continued)

(*continued*)

prices. At times, however, we may end up choosing the interest rate band in such a way that the actual price is either higher than both the extreme values or lower than both. In such cases we have to redefine the band so that one of the corresponding prices is higher than the actual price while the other is lower.

Now let us interpolate: 8.25%–7.75% corresponds to a price difference of 915.9929 – 948.4675. Thus 8.25% – y^* should correspond to a price difference of 915.9929 – 925, where y^* is the true YTM.

$$0.0825 - 0.0775 \equiv 915.9929 - 948.4675$$

$$0.0825 - y^* \equiv 915.9929 - 925$$

If we take the ratio of both and solve for y^*, we get

$$\frac{0.005}{0.0825 - y^*} = \frac{-32.4746}{-9.0071}$$

$$\Rightarrow y^* = 0.081113 \equiv 8.113\%$$

We can calculate the price corresponding to a YTM of 8.1113% to verify the accuracy. It comes out to be $924.86.

ZERO-COUPON BONDS AND THE YTM

It is simple to determine the YTM for a zero-coupon bond, given its price, as the following example will illustrate.

Consider a bond with 10 years to maturity and a face value of $1,000. Assume that the current price is $475. The pricing equation is[4]

$$475 = \frac{1,000}{\left(1 + \frac{y}{2}\right)^{20}}$$

$$\Rightarrow \left(1 + \frac{y}{2}\right)^{20} = 2.105263$$

$$\frac{y}{2} = 0.037923 \Rightarrow y \equiv 7.5847\%$$

ANALYZING THE YTM

To better appreciate the mathematics underlying the YTM, let us consider the sources of return for investors who buy the bond at the prevailing market price and hold it to maturity.

---

[4]As explained earlier, we are pricing the bond based on 20 half-years to maturity and not on 10 years.

They will obviously get N coupons, where each coupon is equal to $\$C/2$. Each time they get a coupon they can reinvest at the market yield prevailing at that time in an asset of the same risk class. And finally, when the bond matures, they will be repaid the face value. The cash flows from the coupon payments constitute an annuity. When these cash flows are reinvested, they will earn interest. The important thing is the future value of these cash flows at the time the bond matures, which can be computed by the standard annuity formula. Let us assume that each cash flow can be reinvested at a periodic (six-monthly) rate of $r/2\%$. For ease of exposition, we will assume that r is the same for each cash flow, or in other words, that the reinvestment rate is a constant. This is not a necessary assumption and is made purely to facilitate the presentation of the argument.

The future value of the coupons as calculated at the time of maturity is given by

$$\frac{\frac{C}{2}}{\frac{r}{2}}\left[\left(1+\frac{r}{2}\right)^{N}-1\right]$$

Thus the total cash flow at maturity is

$$M+\frac{\frac{C}{2}}{\frac{r}{2}}\left[\left(1+\frac{r}{2}\right)^{N}-1\right]$$

From the bond pricing equation

$$P=\frac{\frac{C}{2}}{\frac{y}{2}}\times\left[1-\frac{1}{\left(1+\frac{y}{2}\right)^{N}}\right]+\frac{M}{\left(1+\frac{y}{2}\right)^{N}}$$

When can we make a claim that we have received a yield of $y/2$ per period over N periods? Only if the terminal cash flow is equal to the initial investment compounded at $y/2$ for N periods.

In other words, we can claim that we have obtained a semiannual yield of $y/2$ if

$$P\times\left(1+\frac{y}{2}\right)^{N}=\frac{\frac{C}{2}}{\frac{y}{2}}\times\left[\left(1+\frac{y}{2}\right)^{N}-1\right]+M$$

$$=\frac{\frac{C}{2}}{\frac{r}{2}}\left[\left(1+\frac{r}{2}\right)^{N}-1\right]+M$$

The implication is that in order to receive a periodic yield of $y/2$ over N periods, we need to satisfy two conditions. First, the investor must hold the bond until the maturity date. Second, $y/2$ must equal $r/2$. In other words, each intermediate cash flow obtained during the life of the bond (coupon) must be reinvested at the YTM prevailing at the time of acquisition of the bond.

Let us now analyze the consequences of relaxing this assumption.

THE REALIZED COMPOUND YIELD

We will now relax one of the two assumptions made in the previous section. We will continue to assume that the bond will be held until maturity, but we will no longer take it for granted that each coupon is reinvested at the YTM. Rather, we will assume a specific rate r, at which the coupons are assumed to be reinvested.

The following example illustrates the approach adopted to compute what is termed as the *realized compound yield*.

EXAMPLE 4.8

Consider the bond with a face value of $1,000 and 10 years to maturity. The price is $925 and the coupon is 7% per annum paid semiannually. The YTM obtained by us was 8.1113%.

Now assume that each cash flow can be reinvested at 7% per annum, or at 3.50% per six-monthly period.

The future value of the coupons is

$$\frac{\frac{70}{2}}{\frac{0.07}{2}}\left[\left(1 + \frac{0.07}{2}\right)^{20} - 1\right] = 989.7889$$

The terminal cash flow is $1,000 + 989.7889 = \$1,989.7889$.

The initial investment was $925. The rate of return over 20 periods is given by

$$925\left(1 + \frac{i}{2}\right)^{20} = 1,989.7889 \Rightarrow i \equiv 7.8085\%$$

This return is called the realized compound yield. It can be done on an ex-ante basis, as we have just done, by assuming a rate(s) at which the reinvestment will take place, or on an ex-post basis by plugging in the actual rate(s) at which the cash flows were reinvested.

In this illustration, the realized compound yield is less than the YTM. That is because the reinvestment rate assumed by us is less than the YTM. If we had assumed a reinvestment rate higher than the YTM, we would have obtained a RCY greater than the YTM.

REINVESTMENT AND ZERO-COUPON BONDS

The inability to reinvest at a rate of return assumed at the outset is referred to as reinvestment risk. For coupon-paying bonds, reinvestment risk is a critical feature. Zero-coupon bonds are devoid of reinvestment risk as there are no coupons to be reinvested. Thus, in order to obtain a rate of return equal to the YTM for a zero-coupon bond, we have to satisfy only one condition: we should hold the bond to maturity.

THE HOLDING PERIOD YIELD

Now we will relax both the assumptions we made earlier in order to compute the YTM. The first change, as we did in the case of the RCY, is that we will explicitly assume a rate at which the coupons are reinvested. Second, we will no longer assume that the bond is held to maturity but will assume an investment horizon shorter than the time to maturity. The corresponding yield measure is termed as the *horizon yield* or the *holding period yield*.

The consequence of the second assumption is that it is no longer necessary that an investor will receive the face value at the end of the investment horizon. The investor will receive the market price at that time, which may be more or less than the face value, depending on the YTM prevailing at that time.

Since we need to compute the sale price prior to maturity, we need to make an assumption about the YTM that is likely to prevail at that time, if we are computing the holding period yield on an ex-ante basis.[5]

Let us consider the data that we used to compute the RCY. We will assume, however, that the investor has a horizon of eight years or 16 semiannual periods. We will assume that the bond can be sold at a YTM of 7.50% at the end of eight years. At that point in time, it will be a two-year bond. The corresponding price is $990.8715.

The future value of the reinvested coupons is given by[6]

$$\frac{\frac{70}{2}}{\frac{0.07}{2}}\left[\left(1 + \frac{0.07}{2}\right)^{16} - 1\right] = 733.9860$$

Thus, the terminal cash flow is $990.8715 + 733.9860 = 1{,}724.8575$.
The rate of return over the eight-year period is given by

$$925\left(1 + \frac{i}{2}\right)^{16} = 1{,}724.8575 \Rightarrow i \equiv 7.9425\%$$

TAXABLE EQUIVALENT YIELD

Certain bonds are exempt from income taxes. In the United States both the federal and state governments are empowered to levy such taxes. In order to deal with a situation where a comparison is sought between a bond whose interest is taxable and another whose income is tax free, we need to compute the taxable equivalent yield (TEY) of the tax-free bond.

The computation of the TEY depends on the applicable taxes. Let us first consider a municipal bond which gives a yield of 6.00%. The bond is exempt from federal income tax, which we will assume is 25%. The TEY is given by

$$\text{TEY} = \frac{6.00}{1 - 0.25} = 8.00\%$$

---

[5]On an ex-post basis we will obviously know the selling price.
[6]Notice that we have taken the coupons only for the first 16 periods.

The implication is that an investor should be indifferent between a taxable bond that yields 8% and the tax-free municipal bond which yields 6%. If the taxable bond were to yield more than 8%, that would be preferable. On the other hand, if it were to yield less than 8%, the investor would prefer the municipal bond.

To make the computation more precise we need to account for the fact that both the bonds attract state income tax. This per se does not warrant an adjustment since both the bonds will be equally affected. For a bond that attracts both federal and state income taxes, however, the state tax can be deducted from the federal tax bill. This calls for the following adjustment.

Let us assume that the federal rate is 25% and the state tax rate is 8%. The adjusted federal rate is given by:

$$0.25 - 0.25 \times 0.08 = 0.23$$

The TEY of the municipal bond is therefore:

$$\text{TEY} = \frac{6.00}{1 - 0.23} = 7.7922\%$$

The rationale for this correction is the following. Someone who earns $100 in income will have to pay $8 by way of state tax. The federal tax is applicable only on $92. So, the effective federal tax rate is: $0.92 \times 0.25 = 0.23 \equiv 23\%$.

Now consider a situation where the municipal bond is exempt from both federal as well as state taxes. To make the necessary adjustment we need to compute the combined tax rate for a bond which is subject to both taxes. In our case it is 23% + 8% = 31%.

The TEY of the municipal bond in such a situation is given by

$$\text{TEY} = \frac{6.00}{1 - 0.31} = 8.6957\%$$

There can be a situation where the taxable bond, which is being compared with the municipal bond, is subject to federal taxes but not to state taxes. If so, we need to compute the TEY of the taxable bond and compare it with that of the municipal bond.

Assume that a T-bond with a coupon of 6.90% is being compared with a municipal bond which is exempt from both state and federal taxes. The TEY of the T-bond is:

$$\text{TEY} = \frac{6.90}{1 - 0.08} = 7.50\%$$

This TEY should be compared with the TEY of the municipal bond, and the bond that offers the higher TEY will be deemed to be superior.

CREDIT RISK

Credit or default risk is the risk that the coupons and/or principal may not be paid as scheduled. Except for Treasury securities, which are backed by the full faith and credit of the federal government, all debt securities are subject to default risk, and differ only with respect to the degree of the associated risk. When a bond is issued, the borrower will release a prospectus with detailed information about its financial health and creditworthiness; however, most investors lack the required skill sets to draw meaningful conclusions from analyzing such documents. In order to give confidence to potential investors about the quality of the issue, issuers have the securities rated by credit rating agencies. These agencies specialize in evaluating the credit quality of a security issue. They not only provide a rating prior to the issue, but also continuously monitor the health of the issuer throughout the life of the security and modify their recommendations as and when required. The rating accorded to a particular issue is based on the financial health of the issuer and the quality of its management team. In the case of secured bonds, it also depends on the quality of collateral that has been specified.

The three main rating agencies in the United States are:

Moody's Investors Service

Standard and Poor's (S&P)

Fitch Ratings

There are two categories of rated securities: investment grade and speculative grade. Investment-grade bonds are of higher quality and carry a lower credit risk. Non-investment grade, also known as speculative grade or *junk bonds*, carry a higher risk of default. Because a riskier security must offer a higher rate of return to compete with better rated securities, junk bonds carry a high coupon. Thus, investors are cautioned that they are investing at their own risk. If nothing were to go wrong, investors will walk away with higher returns.

The ratings scales adopted by the three rating agencies are depicted in Tables 4.5 and 4.6.

As discussed, the agencies may revise their ratings during the life of the security. If a rating change is being contemplated, they will signal their intentions. S&P will place the security on *Credit Watch*. Moody's will place the security on *Under Review*, while Fitch will place it on *Rating Watch*.

TABLE 4.5 Investment Grade Ratings

Credit Risk	Moody's Ratings	S&P's Ratings	Fitch's Ratings
Highest Quality	Aaa	AAA	AAA
High Quality	Aa	AA	AA
Upper Medium	A	A	A
Medium	Baa	BBB	BBB

TABLE 4.6 Speculative Grade Ratings

Credit Risk	Moody's Ratings	S&P's Ratings	Fitch's Ratings
Somewhat Speculative	Ba	BB	BB
Speculative	B	B	B
Highly Speculative	Caa	CCC	CCC
Most Speculative	Ca	CC	CC
Imminent Default	C	C	C
Default	C	D	D

BOND INSURANCE

A company seeking a better rating can have its issue insured in order to enhance credit quality. In such cases, the issuer will have to pay a premium to the insurance company. But this cost will be passed on to investors in the form of a lower coupon. In the case of insured bonds, the timely payment of promised cash flows is guaranteed by the insurance company. Thus, the rating of such issues would depend on the financial health of the insurer. Clearly it would make sense to get an issue insured only by a company that enjoys a better reputation than the issuer.

In the case of such bonds, the credit quality of the issuer will be appraised by two entities: the rating agency and the insurance company.

EQUIVALENCE WITH ZERO-COUPON BONDS

Consider a bond with a face value of $1,000 and two years to maturity. Assume that the coupon is 7% per annum, payable on a semiannual basis. This bond will give rise to five cash flows as per the schedule shown in Table 4.7.

Consider the first cash flow. It is like the maturity value of a zero-coupon bond with a face value of $35, maturing after six months. Similarly, the second cash flow is like the maturity value of a zero-coupon bond with a face value of $35, maturing after 12 months. Thus, the plain-vanilla bond is like a portfolio of five zero-coupon bonds. This is true for any plain-vanilla bond. If the bond has N coupons remaining until maturity, it is equivalent to a portfolio of $N + 1$ zero-coupon bonds.

SPOT RATES

Consider the two-year bond that we just discussed. It is equivalent to a portfolio of five zeroes. Each of the zeroes must have its own yield to maturity. The yield to maturity of a zero-coupon bond, for a given time to maturity, is referred to as the *spot rate* for that period. Thus, the price of the plain-vanilla bond may be expressed as

$$P_0 = \frac{35}{(1 + s_1)} + \frac{35}{(1 + s_2)^2} + \frac{35}{(1 + s_3)^3} + \frac{1,035}{(1 + s_4)^4}$$

TABLE 4.7 Cash Flows from a Two-Year Bond

Time Period	Cash Flow
6-M	$35
12-M	$35
18-M	$35
24-M	$35
24-M	$1,000

The traditional pricing equation, based on the YTM, states that

$$P_0 = \frac{35}{\left(1 + \frac{y}{2}\right)} + \frac{35}{\left(1 + \frac{y}{2}\right)^2} + \frac{35}{\left(1 + \frac{y}{2}\right)^3} + \frac{1,035}{\left(1 + \frac{y}{2}\right)^4}$$

Since a plain-vanilla bond is a portfolio of zeroes, the correct way to price it is by discounting each cash flow at the corresponding spot rate. When we value the cash flows by discounting at the YTM, we are using an average discount rate to capture the effect of the various spot rates. Thus, the YTM of a bond is a complex average of the underlying spot rates.

THE COUPON EFFECT

The YTM is subject to what we call a coupon effect. Consider two one-year bonds, both with a face value of $1,000. Bond A pays coupons at the rate of 7% per annum, while bond B pays a coupon at the rate of 10% per annum. Assume that the six-month spot rate is 6% per annum, while the one year spot rate is 7.25% per annum.

The price of bond A is

$$\frac{35}{(1.03)} + \frac{1,035}{(1.03625)^2} = 33.9806 + 963.8540 = \$997.8346$$

The YTM may be calculated as

$$997.8346 = \frac{35}{\left(1 + \frac{y}{2}\right)} + \frac{1,035}{\left(1 + \frac{y}{2}\right)^2}$$

If we solve the quadratic equation, we get $y = 7.2283\%$.
Now consider bond B. The price is given by

$$\frac{50}{(1.03)} + \frac{1,050}{(1.03625)^2} = 48.5437 + 977.8229 = \$1,026.3666$$

The YTM comes out to be 7.2197%.
Why is it that bond A has a higher YTM than bond B? The price of one-period money is 6% per annum while that of two-period money is 7.25% per annum. Clearly, two-period money is more expensive. Bond A has

$$\frac{35}{(1.03) \times 997.8346} = 3.4054\%$$

of its value locked up on one-period money. Bond B on the other hand has

$$\frac{50}{(1.03) \times 1,026.3666} = 4.7297\%$$

of its value locked up in one-period money. Since bond B has a greater percentage of its value locked up in one-period money, which in this case is cheaper, it is not surprising that its YTM is lower than that of bond A. Thus, the YTM, which is a complex average of spot rates, is a function of the coupon rate of a bond, for a given term to maturity, which is what we term the coupon effect.

BOOTSTRAPPING

In practice we will not have price data for zero-coupon bonds expiring exactly one period apart. In other words, we will not be in a position to compute the spot rates directly from the observable prices. Bootstrapping is a technique for obtaining spot rates from price data for plain-vanilla bonds.

Consider the information given in Table 4.8. All the bonds have a face value of $1,000 and pay a coupon of 7% per annum on a semiannual basis.

The one-period spot rate is given by

$$985 = \frac{1,035}{\left(1 + \frac{s_1}{2}\right)} \Rightarrow s_1 = 10.1523\% \text{ per annum}$$

We know that

$$950 = \frac{35}{\left(1 + \frac{s_1}{2}\right)} + \frac{1,035}{\left(1 + \frac{s_2}{2}\right)^2}$$

Substituting for s_1 we get $s_2 = 12.5146\%$ per annum. Similarly, using the pricing equation for the 18-M bonds and substituting for s_1 and s_2, we can compute s_3, and by extending the logic we can find s_4. This is the essence of bootstrapping.

FORWARD RATES

Consider a person with a two-period investment horizon. He can directly invest in a two-period zero-coupon bond. Or else he can invest in a one-period bond and roll over his investment. The second approach is obviously fraught with risk, for we cannot predict at the outset as to what the one-period rate will be after one period. It

TABLE 4.8 Prices of Plain-Vanilla Bonds with Varying Times to Maturity

Term to Maturity	Price
6-M	985
12-M	950
18-M	925
24-M	900

may be possible, however, to enter into a forward contract at the outset which locks in a rate for the one-period investment after one period. The rate implicit in such a contract is referred to as the forward rate of interest. We will denote it as f_1^1. The subscript indicates is that it is for a loan to be made after one period, while the superscript indicates that the loan is for one period. To rule out arbitrage it must be the case that

$$\left(1 + \frac{s_2}{2}\right)^2 = \left(1 + \frac{s_1}{2}\right)\left(1 + \frac{f_1^1}{2}\right)$$

For instance, if the one-period rate is 8% per annum while the two period rate is 8.50% per annum, then

$$(1.0425)^2 = (1.04)\left(1 + \frac{f_1^1}{2}\right) \Rightarrow f_1^1 = 0.090012$$

Thus, the one-period forward rate is 9.0012% per annum. In general, the forward rate symbol for an $m - n$ period loan to be made after n periods is f_n^{m-n}.

The relationship between the n period spot rate and the m period spot rate is given by

$$\left(1 + \frac{s_m}{2}\right)^m = \left(1 + \frac{s_n}{2}\right)^n \times \left(1 + \frac{f_n^{m-n}}{2}\right)^{m-n}$$

THE YIELD CURVE AND THE TERM STRUCTURE

The plot of the YTM versus the time to maturity of the bond is referred to as the Yield Curve. On the other hand, a plot of the spot rate versus the term to maturity of the bond is called the Term Structure of Interest Rates. The term structure is also known as the Zero-Coupon Yield Curve. The two will coincide if the yield curve is flat. A flat yield curve means that all the spot rates are identical. Obviously since the YTM is an average of spot rates, the YTM in such circumstances will be the same as the spot rate.

While plotting the yield curve or the term structure, it is important to ensure that the data being used pertains to bonds of the same risk class. That is, if one of the bonds is AAA, then all the bonds in the data set must be AAA, meaning that we should compare apples with apples and should not mix up data for AAA bonds with that of T-bonds.

SHAPES OF THE TERM STRUCTURE

In practice the term structure may take a variety of shapes. The commonly observed shapes are:

- Upward Sloping or Rising
- Downward Sloping or Inverted
- Humped
- U-Shaped

Rising yield curves will have a positive slope; that is, short-term yields will be lower than long-term yields. On the other hand, inverted yield curves are characterized by a negative slope; that is, short-term yields are higher than long-term yields. Humped yield curves tend to have lower rates at the short and long ends of the spectrum, and higher rates in between; the curve initially rises, peaks at the middle of the maturity spectrum, and then gradually slopes downward. U-shaped yield curves have the opposite shape; the rates are higher at the short and long ends of the spectrum and tend to be low in between. Such curves are characterized by a curve that declines initially, reaches a trough at the middle of the maturity spectrum, and then gradually slopes upwards.

THEORIES OF THE TERM STRUCTURE

A variety of theories have been expounded to explain the various observed shapes of the yield curve.

The Pure or Unbiased Expectations Hypothesis

This popular theory states that the implied forward rates computed using current spot rates are nothing but unbiased estimators of future spot rates. As per this theory, therefore, long-term spot rates are geometric averages of expected future short-term rates. This hypothesis can be used to explain any shape of the yield curve. Let us take an upward sloping curve. The expectations hypothesis would explain it with the argument that the market expects spot rates to rise. If rates are expected to rise, then holders of long-term bonds will be perturbed because the prices of such bonds are expected to decline, and they will be confronted with the possibility of a capital loss. Such investors will start selling long-term bonds and buying short-term bonds. This will lead to an increase in long-term yields and a decrease in short-term yields. The net result would be an upward-sloping yield curve.

Now consider an inverted yield curve. This would be consistent with the view that the market expects future spot rates to fall. If so, investors will seek to sell short-term bonds and invest in long-term bonds, which will push up short-term yields and lead to declining long-run yields. The net result will be an inverted yield curve.

A humped yield curve would be consistent with the expectations that investors expect short-term rates to rise and long-term rates to fall.

The expectation of the future direction of the market is primarily a function of the expected rate of inflation. If the market expects inflationary pressures in the long run, the yield curve will be upward sloped. However, if inflation rates are expected to decline in the long run, then the curve will be negatively sloped.

THE LIQUIDITY PREMIUM HYPOTHESIS

This hypothesis argues that the forward rate is not equal to the expected spot rate but is greater than the expectation of the future spot rate. The difference between the forward rate and the expectation of the future spot rate is termed the *liquidity premium*. This theory argues that because lenders generally prefer to lend short-term, they must be suitably compensated if induced to lend for longer terms. This compensation takes the form of a premium for a loss of liquidity. As per this hypothesis, the yield curve should invariably be upward sloping, reflecting the investors' preference for liquidity. A declining yield curve, however, can be explained by postulating that future spot rates may sharply decline, causing long-term rates to be lower than short-term rates, the liquidity premium notwithstanding.

THE MONEY SUBSTITUTE HYPOTHESIS

Per this theory short-term bonds are essentially a substitute for cash. Investors generally hold only short–term bonds because of the lower perceived risk. This drives up the demand for such securities and pushes down the yield. This explains low yields at the short end of the maturity spectrum. As far as the other end is concerned, borrowers tend to issue long-term debt, which implies that they will have to access the capital market less frequently, which minimizes the costs associated with borrowing. This leads to an excess supply at the longer end of the maturity spectrum and consequently pushes up the yield.[7]

THE MARKET SEGMENTATION HYPOTHESIS

The theory postulates that the market is made up of a wide variety of investors and issuers. Each class of investors or issuers has its own requirements, and consequently tends to focus on a particular range of the maturity spectrum. This theory argues that the segments of the market are compartmentalized and there are no interrelationships between them.

The observed shape of the yield curve, as per this theory, depends on the demand-supply dynamics within the market segment, and activities in a given segment have no implications for any other part of the curve. For instance, the need to constantly manage their cash leads to a situation where commercial banks primarily focus on the short end of the curve. On the other hand, institutions such as insurance companies and pension funds, whose liabilities are primarily long-term, tend to focus on the long end of the market.[8] In practice there is relatively less demand for medium-dated bonds. Thus, according to this theory, yields will be relatively low at the short and long ends of the maturity spectrum and high in the middle of the term structure, which is consistent with what we call a humped yield curve.

THE PREFERRED HABITAT THEORY

A slight modification of the market segmentation hypothesis, this theory proposes that while investors do tend to concentrate on their chosen market segment, they can be persuaded to hold securities from other segments by offering them suitable inducements. For instance, while banks generally operate at the lower end of the spectrum,

---

[7]See Choudhry (2004).
[8]See Choudhry (2004).

an increase in yields of long-dated bonds may sometimes be adequate to persuade them to hold such securities. Similarly, an increase in short-term rates may encourage pension funds and insurance companies to invest in that segment, an area of the market which they would otherwise avoid.

THE SHORT RATE

A short rate of interest is a future spot rate of interest that may evolve over time. It is usually represented as a single period rate, for the shortest period of time considered by the model under consideration. In our previous discussions, we have assumed that the shortest time period corresponds to six months.

At a given point in time we will have a vector of spot rates corresponding to various intervals of time. This vector can be used to derive a unique vector of current forward rates, as explained earlier. We cannot state with certainty, however, what the spot rate will be at a future point in time, for it may take on one of several values, each of which will have an associated probability of occurrence.

At the current instant the one-period spot rate will be equal to the one-period forward rate, which will be equal to the short rate. If we look at a longer time horizon, however, these rates will in general not be equal to each other.

EXAMPLE 4.9

The tree for the evolution of short rates that we describe here is based on the Ho and Lee model, and was originally presented in Parameswaran (2009).[9] The details behind the derivation are beyond the scope of this book. The derivation assumes the term structure depicted in Table 4.9.

TABLE 4.9   Vector of Spot Rates

Period	Spot Rate
1	6.00%
2	5.80%
3	6.05%
4	5.90%

In Figure 4.2, at each node there is a 50% probability of reaching the upper state at the end of the current period, and an equal probability of reaching the lower state. The current one-period spot rate is 6%, which is equal to the current short rate. At the end of the period there is a 50% chance that the short rate will be 6.5983% and an equal probability that it will be 4.5983%. Similarly, at the end of two periods, the short rate can take on one of three possible values, while at the end of three periods it can take on one of four possible values.

---

[9] *Futures and Options: Concepts and Applications* by Sunil Parameswaran.

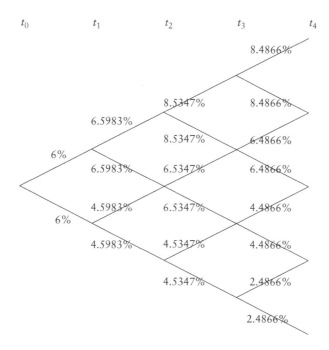

FIGURE 4.2 Evolution of the Short Rate

FLOATING RATE BONDS

Floating-rate notes and bonds, also referred to as floaters, are debt securities whose coupons are reset periodically based on a reference or benchmark rate. Typically, the coupon on such a security is defined as

Benchmark Rate + Quoted Margin

For instance, consider a security whose coupon is specified as

The 5-year T-note rate + 75 basis points

In this case, the reference rate is the yield on a 5-year T-note and the quoted margin is 75 b.p. It should be noted that the quoted margin need not always be positive. For instance, a floater may have a coupon rate specified as

The 5-year Benchmark rate − 50 basis points

In the case of a default risk-free floating-rate bond, the price of the security will always reset to par on a coupon date, although in between two coupon dates, it may sell at a premium or at a discount.

For instance, consider a floater with a coupon equal to the 5-year T-bond rate. Assume that there are two periods to maturity. The price of the bond at the end of the first coupon period will be given by

$$P_{T-1} = \frac{M + \frac{c_{T-1}}{2} \times M}{\left(1 + \frac{y_{T-1}}{2}\right)}$$

where c_{T-1} is the coupon rate one period before maturity, and y_{T-1} is the required yield one period before maturity. On the coupon reset date, the YTM will be equal to the coupon since we have assumed that there is no default risk implicit in the security. Consequently, any change in the required yield, as reflected by the YTM at that point in time, will also be reflected in the coupon that is set on that day. We know that if the yield is equal to the coupon, then the bond should sell at par. Thus $P_{T-1} = M$.

The price at the outset is given by

$$P_{T-2} = \frac{P_{T-1} + \frac{c_{T-2}}{2} \times M}{\left(1 + \frac{y_{T-2}}{2}\right)}$$

$$= \frac{M + \frac{c_{T-2}}{2} \times M}{\left(1 + \frac{y_{T-2}}{2}\right)}$$

Once again at $T-2$, $c_{T-2} = y_{T-2}$ and consequently $P_{T-2} = M$. This logic can be applied to a bond with any number of coupons remaining to maturity.

In between two coupon dates, however, the price of such a floater may not be equal to par. Consider the valuation of the note at time $T-2+k$. The price is given by

$$P_{T-2+k} = \frac{P_{T-1} + \frac{c_{T-2}}{2} \times M}{\left(1 + \frac{y_{T-2+k}}{2}\right)}$$

$$= \frac{M + \frac{c_{T-2}}{2} \times M}{\left(1 + \frac{y_{T-2+k}}{2}\right)}$$

While c_{T-2} was set at time $T-2$, and is equal to y_{T-2}, y_{T-2+k} is determined at time $T-2+k$ and will reflect the prevailing 5-year T-note yield at that point in time. In general, y_{T-2+k} need not equal c_{T-2} and may be higher or lower. Consequently, in between two coupon dates, a floater may sell at a premium or at a discount.

Now let us consider the case of floaters characterized by default risk. In this case it is not necessary that the risk premium required by the market be constant over time. For instance, assume that when the bond was issued the required return was equal to the 5-year T-note rate + 75 b.p. The coupon was set equal to this rate and the bond was sold at par. 6-M hence, the issue is perceived to be more risky and the required return in the market is the 5-year T-note rate + 95 b.p. The coupon, however, will be reset at the prevailing T-note rate + 75 b.p. Hence this issue will not reset to par at the next coupon date.

SIMPLE MARGIN

A margin measure is essentially a yield spread measure, and such measures are used to evaluate the returns from a floater. There are various types of margins that can be computed in practice. We will consider a measure known as the *simple margin*.

If a floater trades at a premium or a discount, then the premium/discount needs to be factored in while computing the return. If the floater trades at a discount, then we need to account for the accretion of the discount over the life of the floater. On the contrary, if the floater trades at a premium, we need to factor in the amortization of the premium over the life of the security. The formula for the simple margin is

$$\text{Simple Margin} = \left[\frac{100 \times (100 - P)}{T_m} + \text{Quoted Margin} \right]$$

P is the market price (clean price) of the floater, as a percentage of par, and T_m is the remaining time until maturity. If it is not an integer, we need to invoke a day-count assumption. The quoted margin must be expressed in basis points and not percentage terms.

EXAMPLE 4.10

A floater is trading at a price of $98.25. It has two years and nine months to maturity. If we assume a 30/360 day-count convention, the time to maturity is 2.75 years. The quoted margin is 95 basis points.

The simple margin is

$$[100 \times (100 - 98.25)] \div 2.75 + 95 = 158.64 \text{ basis points}$$

BONDS WITH EMBEDDED OPTIONS

We will consider three types of bonds with embedded options: callable, putable, and convertible bonds. All these bonds give either the issuer or the lender an option. As we have seen, an option gives the holder the right to take a course of action. Since no one will give away a right for free, the holder has to pay a price or a premium to the seller of the option. Consequently, in the case of bonds with embedded options, if the option is with the issuer, then the issuer must pay for it, and consequently the price of the bond will be less than that of a plain-vanilla bond. But if the option is with the lender, then it will manifest itself as a higher price as compared to that of a plain-vanilla bond.

CALLABLE BONDS

Such bonds contain a call option, that is, they give the issuer the right to call away the bond from the lender prior to maturity. In the case of such bonds, issuers can change the maturity of the bond by prematurely recalling it. When will such a bond be recalled? Clearly, when market interest rates are declining. Under such circumstances, the issuer can recall the existing bonds and replace them with a fresh issue with a lower coupon due to the changed circumstances.

The call provision works against lenders. This is because they may have to part with the bond when the market rates are falling, which is precisely a situation where they desire to hold on to the bonds and keep earning a high coupon. To compensate for this, lenders will demand a higher yield as compared to that of a plain-vanilla bond of the same credit quality. This will manifest itself as a lower price. Thus, whether we view it from the issuer's perspective or the lender's, a callable bond must sell at a lower price as compared to an otherwise similar plain-vanilla bond.

Such bonds may be *discretely callable* or *continuously callable*. A discretely callable bond may be recalled only at certain prespecified dates, for instance, at the coupon dates over a portion of the bond's life. A continuously callable bond may be called at any time after it becomes callable.

As we have just mentioned, a bond may be recalled only when it becomes callable. This implies that it may not be callable right from the outset. In practice, issuers generally specify a call protection period, which is a period of time during which the bond may not be recalled irrespective of what happens to the market rate of interest. Thus, a discretely callable bond can usually be recalled on any coupon payment date after the call protection period ends, while a continuously callable bond may be recalled at any time from the end of the call protection period until the maturity date of the bond. Bonds with a call protection period are referred to as *deferred callable bonds* and serve to provide holders with relatively greater certainty.

The price at which the bond can be recalled is referred to as the *call price*. In many cases a bond may be recalled at par by an issuer. But at times the issuer may specify a call premium. That is, the issuer will pay a value higher than the face value of the bonds if and when the issue is recalled. The call premium is usually set equal to one year's coupon.

Holders of callable bonds are extremely vulnerable to reinvestment risk. The likelihood that they will experience a return of cash increases in a falling interest rate environment means that they will have to face the specter of reinvesting their corpus at a lower rate of interest. Secondly, the potential for price appreciation in a falling rate environment is relatively limited as compared to a plain-vanilla bond. Why do bond prices increase in value? Because yields are declining in the market. But in the case of callable bonds this is precisely the situation where the bond can be recalled, which means the buyer of such bonds in a falling interest rate environment is constantly exposed to the risk of having to part with it at the call price. This aspect is referred to as price compression.

YIELD TO CALL

In the case of callable bonds, it is a normal practice to compute the yield to call (YTC). That is, for a given call date, all the cash flows from the current point in time until the call date are specified, and the discount rate that makes the present value of these cash flows equal to the dirty price of the bond is computed. The cash flows will be the coupons scheduled to be paid on or before the call date, and the call price.

The price at which the bond is recalled may in certain cases vary with the call date; that is, the call price may be a function of the call date.

The formula for the YTC, assuming that the bond is callable after N^* coupons have been paid, may be stated as

$$P = \frac{\frac{C}{2}}{\frac{y_c}{2}} \times \left[1 - \frac{1}{\left(1 + \frac{y_c}{2}\right)^{N^*}} \right] + \frac{M^*}{\left(1 + \frac{y_c}{2}\right)^{N^*}}$$

This looks similar to the pricing equation corresponding to the YTM calculation. But there are two key differences. First, M^*, which is the call price, need not equal the face value. Second, N^*, the number of coupons until the call dates, will be $\leq N$.

EXAMPLE 4.11

Consider a bond with 20 years to maturity and a face value of $1,000. Assume that the coupon rate is 7% per annum and that the current price is $925. The first call date is eight years away, and if called, the issuer will pay one year's coupon as the call premium. The YTC can be computed from the following equation.

$$925 = \sum_{t=1}^{16} \frac{35}{\left(1 + \frac{y_c}{2}\right)^t} + \frac{1,070}{\left(1 + \frac{y_c}{2}\right)^{16}}$$

The solution comes out to be 8.9503%.

PUTABLE BONDS

In the case of a putable bond, the holders have a put option. That is, they can prematurely return the bond to the issuer and claim the face value. Such an option would obviously be exercised when the market interest rates have risen. Under such circumstances the holders can return the old bonds, which are yielding a relatively lower coupon, and use the proceeds to buy bonds yielding a higher coupon. Since the option in these cases is with the holders, they have to pay for it. This will manifest itself as a higher price as compared to that for a plain-vanilla bond carrying the same coupon. Thus, a putable bond will sell for a lower yield as compared to a plain-vanilla bond.

Consider the relative coupons for plain-vanilla, callable, and putable bonds for a given risk class. The callable will have to offer the highest coupon, while the putable can be issued at the lowest coupon. After the issue, if we were to compare bonds with and without call/put options for a given coupon rate, the callable will have the lowest price or the highest yield, while the putable will have the highest price or the lowest yield.

The yield to put is typically defined as the discount rate that makes the present value of the cash flows from the bond equal to its price, assuming that the bond is held to the first put date.

CONVERTIBLE BONDS

Such bonds allow holders to convert the debt securities into shares of stock of the issuer. The number of shares that investors will receive if they were to convert the bond is known as the *conversion ratio*. For instance, consider a bond with a face value of $1,000 that can be converted to 50 shares of stock. The conversion ratio is obviously 50. The *conversion price* is the face value divided by the conversion ratio. In this case it is $20. The conversion value is the value of the shares if the bond were to be converted immediately. If we assume that the current share price is $22.50, the conversion value is $1,125.

The minimum value of a convertible is the greater of the conversion value and the value that will be obtained if the bond were to be valued under the assumption that it is a plain-vanilla bond. The latter value is termed as the *straight value* of the bond.

EXAMPLE 4.12

Consider a convertible bond with a face value of $1,000 and five years to maturity. Assume that the coupon is 7% per annum payable on a semiannual basis, and that the conversion ratio is 50.

If the current stock price is $21, the conversion value is $1,050. If we assume that the YTM of a plain-vanilla bond with the same risk is 8% per annum, the straight value will be $959.45. Since 1,050 is greater than 959.45, the price of the convertible must be $\geq$ $1,050.

But what if the YTM of a comparable bond were to be 5%? The straight value will be $1,087.52. In this case the value of the convertible must be $\geq$ $1,087.52.

USING SHORT RATES TO VALUE BONDS

Let us consider a segment of the interest rate evolution tree that we referred to earlier. See Figure 4.3.

Consider a plain-vanilla bond maturing at t_2, with a face value of $100, paying a coupon of 6% per annum on a semiannual basis. At time t_2 there are three possible nodes. At each node the payoff will be $103.

The value of the bond at the upper node at t_1 is:

$$\frac{103}{\left(1 + \dfrac{0.065983}{2}\right)} = 99.7104$$

Similarly the value at the lower node at t_1 is

$$\frac{103}{\left(1 + \dfrac{0.045983}{2}\right)} = 100.6851$$

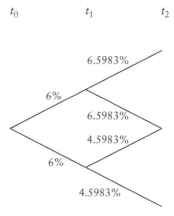

FIGURE 4.3 A Segment of the Short-Rate Tree

Given a node, the probability on an up move is equal to that of a down move, which in turn is equal to 50%, we can compute the value of the bond at t_0 as

$$\frac{0.5 \times (3 + 99.7104)}{1.03} + \frac{0.5 \times (3 + 100.6851)}{1.03} = 100.1920$$

Now let us consider a callable bond, which we will assume can be called back at the face value.[10] Since the value at the upper node at t_1 is less than the call price, the bond will not be recalled. At the lower node, however, the value is higher than the call price and hence the issuer would like to exercise the call option. Thus, the price of the callable bond at t_0 may be computed as

$$\frac{0.5 \times (3 + 99.7104)}{1.03} + \frac{0.5 \times (3 + 100)}{1.03} = 99.8594$$

As can be seen, the presence of the call option leads to a reduction in the bond value. Now consider a bond with a put option. Holders will exercise it only if the value of the bond is less than its face value, assuming that they have the right to put it back at the face value. If so, the value at t_0 is given by

$$\frac{0.5 \times (3 + 100)}{1.03} + \frac{0.5 \times (3 + 100.6851)}{1.03} = 100.3326$$

For obvious reasons, the put option makes the bond more valuable.

---

[10]In other words, there is no call premium.

PRICE VOLATILITY

It is common knowledge that prices of long-term bonds are more sensitive to a change in yield than comparable short-term bonds. This can be easily explained. The present value of a cash flow is given by $\frac{CF_t}{(1+r)^t}$.

The further away the cash flow – that is, the larger the value of t – the greater will be the impact of a change in the discount rate. Because long-term bonds have more cash flows coming at distant points in time, their prices are more volatile; however, subsequently a second fact was noticed. For a given term to maturity, a zero-coupon bond was more price sensitive than any coupon-paying bond with the same term to maturity. This was perplexing, as the bonds have the same term to maturity.

Frederick Macaulay came up with the concept of *duration* to explain this phenomenon. The crux of the idea is the following. A plain-vanilla bond, as we have seen earlier, is a portfolio of zero-coupon bonds. Each of these component zeroes will have its own term to maturity. When we state that a plain-vanilla bond has a term to maturity of T years, we are considering the term to maturity of only the last of the component zeroes. Macaulay argued that the effective term to maturity of a plain-vanilla bond ought to be a weighted average of the terms to maturity of each of the component zeroes. The weight attached to a cash flow, he postulated, should be the present value of the cash flow divided by the price of the bond. Because the price of a bond is the sum of the present values of all the cash flows received from it, the weights defined by Macaulay will add up to one. Thus, the Macaulay duration of a bond may be defined as

$$\sum_{t=1}^{N} \frac{CF_t \times t}{P \times \left(1 + \frac{y}{2}\right)^t}$$

Following is an example of the computation of duration for a plain-vanilla bond.

EXAMPLE 4.13

Consider a bond with a term to maturity of five years and a face value of $1,000. Assume that the coupon is 7% per annum, and that the YTM is 9% per annum. The computation of the duration is shown in Table 4.10.

TABLE 4.10 Computation of Duration

Time Period	Cash Flow	Present Value of Cash Flow	Weight	Weight × Time
1	35	33.49282	0.036371	0.036371
2	35	32.05055	0.034805	0.069609
3	35	30.67038	0.033306	0.099917
4	35	29.34965	0.031872	0.127486
5	35	28.08579	0.030499	0.152495
6	35	26.87635	0.029186	0.175114
7	35	25.71900	0.027929	0.195503
8	35	24.61148	0.026726	0.213810
9	35	23.55165	0.025575	0.230178
10	1035	666.4652	0.723732	7.237320
	TOTAL	920.8728	1.000000	8.537804

The price of the bond is \$920.8728. The weighted average term to maturity, which we term as the duration of the bond, is 8.537804 semiannual periods or 4.26892 years. Thus, although the bond has a stated term to maturity of five years, its effective term to maturity is only 4.26892 years. It should now be clear why a five-year zero-coupon bond will be more price sensitive. It is because in the case of the zero, as there is a single cash flow, there is no difference between its stated term to maturity and its effective term to maturity. Thus, irrespective of the value of T, a T-year zero will always have a higher duration than a T-year plain-vanilla bond, and will therefore be more price sensitive.

A CONCISE FORMULA

For a plain-vanilla bond, we can derive a concise expression for the duration. Let us first redefine a few variables.

$$c \equiv \textbf{semiannual coupon rate}$$
$$y \equiv \textbf{semiannual YTM}$$

It can be shown that the duration of a bond is given by

$$D = \frac{1+y}{y} - \frac{(1+y) + N(c-y)}{c[(1+y)^N - 1] + y}$$

Using the data that we considered for the illustration in the example,

$$D = \frac{1.045}{0.045} - \frac{(1.045) + 10(0.035 - 0.045)}{0.035[(1.045)^{10} - 1] + 0.045} = 8.5378$$

DURATION AND PRICE VOLATILITY

The rate of change of the percentage change in price with respect to yield is a function of the duration of the bond. The relationship may be expressed as

$$\frac{\frac{dp}{P}}{dy} = -\frac{D}{\left(1 + \frac{y}{2}\right)}$$

In this expression D is the duration of the bond expressed in years.

The expression $\frac{D}{\left(1+\frac{y}{2}\right)}$ is referred to as the modified duration of the bond, D_m.

We know that for a finite price change, the percentage change in price is $\frac{\Delta P}{P}$. In the limit we can express it as dP/P. Thus, the rate of change of the percentage change in the price with respect to the yield is equal to the modified duration of the bond. Thus, it is duration, and not the term to maturity, that is an accurate measure of interest rate sensitivity.

It must be pointed out that the duration of a bond should be technically perceived as a measure of interest rate sensitivity. It cannot always be perceived as a measure of the effective average life of the bond.

PROPERTIES OF DURATION

1. The duration of a bond generally increases with its term to maturity. There are two reasons for this.[11] First, the principal repayment is a major component of the bond's present value, and consequently has a significant impact on its duration. As the time to maturity is increased, the repayment of principal is postponed, which serves to increase the duration. Second, as compared to a short-term bond, a long maturity bond has cash flows arising at later points in time, which serves to increase the duration.

    The duration of par and premium bonds will always increase with the time to maturity; however, there could be situations where, if a bond is trading at a substantial discount, the duration may decline as the term to maturity increases.
2. The duration of a bond is inversely related to its coupon rate. There are two reasons for this. First, high coupon bonds have greater amounts of cash flow occurring prior to the maturity date. This serves to reduce the relative impact of the principal repayment on duration.

    Second, discounting has less impact on the earlier cash flows as compared to greater cash flows. The greater the coupon, the more is the relative present value of the earlier cash flows, which serves to reduce the duration of the security.
3. Duration is inversely related to the YTM of the bond. Duration is computed by weighting the times to maturity of each coupon payment by its contribution to the present value of the bond. The higher the discount rate, the lower is the present value of a cash flow. However, increasing the discount rate has a greater impact on long-term cash flows as compared to shorter-term cash flows. Consequently, the relative weightage of shorter-term cash flows is increased as we increase the YTM, which serves to bring down the duration of the bond.

DOLLAR DURATION

The dollar duration of a bond is defined as the product of the modified duration of the bond and its price. In the illustration in Example 4.13, the price of the bond was $920.8728 and its modified duration was 4.0851 years. Consequently, the dollar duration is $920.8728 \times 4.0851 = 3,761.8574$.

CONVEXITY

The price-yield relationship for a plain-vanilla bond is convex in nature. Duration is a measure of the first derivative and varies along with yield. To factor in the convex nature, or curvature, of the bond we need to compute the second derivative.

---

[11] See Livingston (1990).

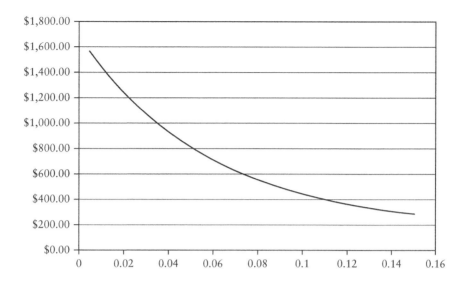

FIGURE 4.4 The Price-yield Relationship

Figure 4.4 illustrates the price-yield relationship for a plain-vanilla bond. The bond was assumed to have 10 years to maturity, a face value of $1,000, and a coupon of 7% per annum payable semiannually.

From the Taylor series expansion, we can state that

$$dP = \frac{dP}{dy}dy + \frac{1}{2}\frac{d^2P}{dy^2}(dy)^2 + \text{h.o.t.}$$

$$\Rightarrow \frac{dP}{P} = \frac{dP}{dy}\frac{dy}{P} + \frac{1}{2}\frac{d^2P}{dy^2}\frac{(dy)^2}{P} + \frac{\text{h.o.t}}{P}$$

where h.o.t. stands for *higher order terms*.

The first term on the RHS captures the duration effect. The second expression is the convexity effect. The convexity of a bond is defined as $\frac{d^2P}{dy^2}\frac{1}{P}$. Thus the percentage price change due to the convexity effect is

$$\frac{1}{2} \times \text{convexity} \times (dy)^2$$

The convexity can be computed as $\sum_{t=1}^{N} \frac{CF_t}{\left(1+\frac{y}{2}\right)^{t+2} P} \times t(t+1)$.

In Table 4.11, we will now calculate for the five-year bond with a coupon of 7%.

TABLE 4.11 Computation of Convexity

Time Period	Cash Flow (CF$_t$)	$\dfrac{CF_t}{\left(1+\frac{y}{2}\right)^{t+2}P}$	t × (t+1)	$\dfrac{CF_t}{\left(1+\frac{y}{2}\right)^{t+2}P} \times t(t+1)$
1	35	0.033306	2	0.066612
2	35	0.031872	6	0.191229
3	35	0.030499	12	0.365989
4	35	0.029186	20	0.583715
5	35	0.027929	30	0.837868
6	35	0.026726	42	1.122503
7	35	0.025575	56	1.432220
8	35	0.024474	72	1.762130
9	35	0.023420	90	2.107811
10	1,035	0.662743	110	72.90174
			TOTAL	81.37182

The convexity in half-years is 81.37182. The convexity in annual terms can be obtained by dividing this number by 4.[12] In this case the annual convexity is 20.3430.

Now consider a finite change of 100 b.p. in the annual YTM. The price at a YTM of 10% is \$884.1740. The percentage price change is

$$\frac{884.1740 - 920.8728}{920.8728} = -0.039852 \equiv -3.9852\%$$

The percentage price change as captured by duration is $-D_m \times dy$. The modified duration of the bond is

$$\frac{8.5378}{2 \times 1.045} = 4.0851$$

Thus, the price change as captured by duration is $-4.0851 \times 0.01 = -0.040851 \equiv -4.0851\%$

The price change due to the convexity effect is $0.5 \times 20.3430 \times (0.01)^2 = 0.001017 \equiv 0.1017\%$.

Thus, the percentage price change as captured by both the factors combined is $-4.0851\% + 0.1017\% = -3.9834\%$. As we can see, the result is fairly close to the exact percentage price change, and a combination of duration and convexity does a better job than duration alone.

A CONCISE FORMULA

There is a closed-form expression for computing the convexity of a plain-vanilla bond. It may be stated as

$$\frac{1}{P}\left\{ \frac{2C}{y^3}\left[1 - \frac{1}{(1+y)^N}\right] - \frac{2CN}{y^2(1+y)^{N+1}} + \frac{N(N+1)\left(M - \frac{C}{y}\right)}{(1+y)^{N+2}} \right\}$$

---

[12]In general, we have to divide by the square of the frequency of compounding.

where as before $C \equiv$ periodic, in our case semiannual, coupon $y \equiv$ semiannual YTM, and $N \equiv$ number of coupons remaining until maturity.

In our illustration, $C = \$35$; $y = 0.045$; $N = 10$; and $P = \$920.8728$. Substituting for the variables, we get convexity $= 81.3718$.

DOLLAR CONVEXITY

The dollar convexity of a bond is equal to its convexity multiplied by its price. In our illustration the price is 920.8728, and the convexity is 20.3430. Thus the dollar convexity is 18,733.3150.

PROPERTIES OF CONVEXITY

The following properties are valid for the convexity of plain-vanilla bonds.[13]

1. As the YTM increases, the convexity decreases, and vice versa. This property of option-free bonds is referred to as positive convexity.
2. For a given value of the YTM and time to maturity, the lower the coupon, the greater is the convexity of the bond. Thus, for a given yield and time to maturity, a zero-coupon bond will have the highest convexity.
3. For a given value of the YTM, *and modified duration,* the lower the coupon, the lower is the convexity of the bond. Thus, for a given yield and modified duration, a zero-coupon bond will have the lowest convexity.

IMMUNIZATION

Consider the case of a pension fund that promises to pay a return of 4.9688% per annum compounded semiannually, on an initial investment of $100,000, after eight years. If the fund invested the corpus in a bond, it would be exposed to two types of risks. The first is reinvestment risk, or the risk that the cash flows received at intermediate stages may have to be invested at lower rates of interest. The second, called price or market risk, is the risk that interest rates could increase, causing the price of the bond to fall at the end of the investment horizon. The two risks obviously work in opposite directions. Therefore the issue is whether there is a bond that will ensure that the terminal cash flow will be equal to the amount required to satisfy the liability, irrespective of whether rates rise or fall. The process of protecting a bond portfolio against a change in the interest rate is termed as *immunization.*

We are considering a simple immunization strategy where we have to immunize a portfolio required to satisfy a single liability. There are two conditions that we need to satisfy in such cases. First, the present value of the liability should be equal to the amount invested in the bond at the outset. Second, the duration of the bond should be equal to the investment horizon.

---

[13]See Fabozzi (1996).

Consider a bond with a face value of $1,000 and 10 years to maturity. Assume that the coupon rate is equal to the YTM and is equal to 4.9688% per annum. It can be shown that the duration is eight years.

Now consider a one-time change in interest rates right at the outset. Assume that the interest rate increases from 4.9688% per annum to 5.50% per annum. The terminal value of the coupons from the bond at the end of eight years is given by

$$100 \times \frac{24.844}{.0275}[(1.0275)^{16} - 1] = \$49,101.6306$$

The price at which 100 bonds can be sold, if the YTM for two-year bonds after eight years is 5.50% per annum, is $100 \times 990.0681 = \$99,006.8080$. The total terminal cash flow is $148,108.4386. Table 4.12 gives the terminal cash flow for various values of the interest rate.

Analysis

As can be seen, the income from reinvested coupons steadily increases with the interest rate while the price of the bond at the time of sale steadily decreases with the interest rate. When there is no change in the rate, the terminal cash flow from the bond is exactly adequate to meet the liability. In all the other cases, there is a surplus. Thus, under all circumstances, the terminal cash flow from the bond is adequate to

TABLE 4.12   An Immunized Portfolio

Interest Rate (annualized)	Cash Flow from Reinvested Coupons	Proceeds from Sale of Bonds	Terminal Cash Flow per Bond	Terminal Cash Flow from 100 Bonds	Deviation
0.010	412.7639	1078.394	1491.1576	149,115.76	1026.28
0.015	420.6656	1068.094	1488.7601	148,876.01	786.53
0.020	428.7544	1057.921	1486.6752	148,667.52	578.04
0.025	437.0349	1047.871	1484.9056	148,490.56	401.08
0.030	445.5118	1037.943	1483.4544	148,345.44	255.96
0.035	454.1900	1028.134	1482.3244	148,232.44	142.96
0.040	463.0744	1018.445	1481.5190	148,151.90	62.42
0.045	472.1701	1008.871	1481.0415	148,104.15	14.67
0.049688	480.8948	1000.000	1480.8954	148,089.48	0.00
0.050	481.4823	999.4131	1480.8948	148,089.54	0.06
0.055	491.0163	990.0681	1481.0844	148,108.44	18.96
0.060	500.7776	980.8346	1481.6122	148,161.22	71.74
0.065	510.7716	971.7112	1482.4829	148,248.29	158.81
0.070	521.0043	962.6962	1483.7005	148,370.05	280.57
0.075	531.4813	953.7881	1485.2694	148,526.94	437.46
0.080	542.2087	944.9853	1487.1940	148,719.40	629.92
0.085	553.1925	936.2864	1489.4789	148,947.89	858.41
0.090	564.4392	927.6898	1492.1290	149,212.90	1123.42
0.095	575.9551	919.1942	1495.1493	149,514.93	1425.45
0.100	587.7467	910.7981	1498.5448	149,854.48	1765.00

meet the liability. Thus, if the pension fund were to invest in an asset whose duration is equal to the time to maturity of its liability, then the funds received will always be adequate to meet the contractual outflow. To meet this requirement, certain conditions must be satisfied. First, the amount invested in the bonds must be equal to the present value of the liability. In this case, since the bond is assumed to be selling at par, we need to invest in 100 bonds. Second, the duration of the asset must equal the maturity horizon of the liability. Third, there must be a one-time change in the interest rate, right at the very outset. Fourth, there must be a parallel shift in the yield curve.

TREASURY AUCTIONS

The Treasury issues T-bills, T-notes, and T-bonds by way of auctions. The auction procedure is described in detail in the next chapter on *money market securities*. Here we will illustrate two auctions of notes and bonds to describe the salient features.

EXAMPLE 4.14

(Issue of a 5-year T-note)

Consider the following details.

- Interest Rate = 2.5000%
- High Yield = 2.6050%
- Price = 99.510730
- Accrued Interest = None
- Issue Date = March 31, 2010
- Maturity Date = March 31, 2015
- Original Issue Date = March 31, 2010
- Dated Date = March 31, 2010

This is an issue of a new security with a maturity of five years. Consequently, the issue date is the same as the original issue date, March 31, 2010. The maturity date is five years after the issue date because the security has a lifespan of five years. The dated date is the first date from which coupons begin to accrue, and in this case is the same as the issue date.

The auction cleared at a YTM of 2.605%. That is, the quotes were arranged in ascending order of bids (yields), and the highest bid at which some securities were awarded was 2.605%. The coupon was unknown at the outset since this was a new issue. The Treasury will set the coupon after rounding down the market yield to the nearest multiple of 0.125, which in this case is 2.5000%. The issue price may be determined as follows.

$$P = \frac{1.25}{0.013025}\left[1 - \frac{1}{(1.013025)^{10}}\right] + \frac{100}{(1.013025)^{10}} = 99.510730$$

EXAMPLE 4.15

Reopening of a 30-year T-bond

Consider the following details.

- Interest Rate = 4.6250%
- High Yield = 4.7700%
- Price = 97.692939
- Accrued Interest = 7.53798
- Issue Date = April 15, 2010
- Maturity Date = February 15, 2040
- Original Issue Date = February 16, 2010
- Dated Date = February 15, 2010

This is a reopening of an existing Treasury security. That is, on February 16, 30-year T-bonds were issued. On April 15 a fresh issue was made of 29-year and 10-month bonds with the same coupon. That is, the auction added to the supply of securities that were already available in the market. This is the import of the word *reopening*.

Thus, the issue date is two months after the original issue date. February 15 was a market holiday. Consequently, while the dated date is February 15, the original issue date is February 16.

The auction cleared at 4.77%. The coupon was known from the outset, for the security was already in existence. The accrued interest and price may be computed as follows. The number of days from the dated date until the issue date is 59. The total number of days in the coupon period is 181. Thus, the accrued interest per $1,000 of face value is given by:

$$\text{AI} = \frac{46.25}{2} \times \frac{59}{181} = \$7.537983$$

The clean price may be determined as follows. The fractional period until the next coupon is $122/181 = 0.6740$. The dirty price is given by:

$$P_0 = \left[\frac{\frac{0.04625 \times 100}{2}}{\left(1 + 0.6740 \times \frac{0.0477}{2}\right)} \times \frac{\left[\left(1 + \frac{0.0477}{2}\right)^{60} - 1\right]}{\left(\frac{0.0477}{2}\right)\left(1 + \frac{0.0477}{2}\right)^{59}} \right] +$$

$$\frac{100}{\left(1 + 0.6740 \times \frac{0.0477}{2}\right)\left(1 + \frac{0.0477}{2}\right)^{59}} = \$98.4467$$

The clean price is = $98.4467 − $0.7538 = $97.6929.

WHEN ISSUED TRADING

The when-issued (WI) market is a market for forward trading of a bond whose issue has been announced but has not yet taken place. Trades in this market take place from the date of announcement of a forthcoming auction of government securities until the actual issue date of the securities. The WI market helps potential bidders to gauge the market's interest in the security prior to the actual auction. This will obviously have ramifications for the bidding strategies of market participants and consequently will have a bearing on the outcome of the auction.

Traders can take both long and short positions in the WI market, with settlement being scheduled for the issue date. Thus, trades in this market represent forward contracts with the issue date being the settlement date. On and before the date of the auction, the issues trade on a yield basis. The actual price in dollars can be established only after the Treasury sets the coupon. For instance, a 5-year T-note is quoting in the WI market at 5%. If the coupon is set at 4.875, the price of the security will be 99.4530; however, if the coupon is set at 5.125, the price will be 100.547. Starting with the day after the auction, securities in the WI market are quoted on a price basis, since the coupon has already been established.

PRICE QUOTES

Bond prices are always quoted per $100 of face value. The reason is the following. Consider two bonds, one with a face value of $1,000 and another with a par value of $2,000. Assume that both securities are quoting at $1,500; the first is a premium bond and the second a discount bond. This cannot be discerned, however, from the observed price unless the corresponding face value is also specified. On the other hand, if the price were to be expressed for a par value of $100, any value less than 100 would signify a discount bond while a value more than 100 would connote a premium bond.

In the US market prices are quoted as a percentage of par plus 32nds. For instance, consider a quote of 97-08. This does not mean a price of $97 and 8 cents per $100 of face value. What it means is that the price per $100 of face value is $97 + 8/32$ or $97.25. So if we were to buy bonds with a face value of $1MM, the amount payable will be $1,000,000 \times 97.25/100 = \$972,500$.

The quoted prices are always clean prices. Thus, to compute the exact amount payable by the buyer, the accrued interest has to be calculated as per the prescribed convention and added to the clean price.

STRIPS

STRIPS is an acronym for Separate Trading of Registered Interest and Principal of Securities. As the name suggests, these represent zero-coupon debt securities created by selling the entitlement to each cash flow from the mother security separately. For, as we have seen earlier, a conventional bond is a portfolio of zero-coupon bonds.

Thus a 10-Year T-note can be stripped into 21 zero-coupon securities, where the first 20 represent the respective coupon payments and the last represents the face value. The US Treasury does not strip eligible securities; however, a trader who holds a Treasury note or bond can seek to have the issue converted into the coupon and principal components. The request can be made at any point in time before the maturity date of the security. Once stripped, each zero-coupon component can be traded separately. Each component will have a unique CUSIP number. In practice, all interest-based strips that mature on the same day are assigned a common CUSIP number, irrespective of the mother bond from which they are created. However, principal strips that mature on a given day are assigned different CUSIP numbers.

Just as a Treasury note or a bond can be stripped, it can also be reconstituted. That is, a trader who holds the entire set of component zeroes can have the original or parent Treasury security regenerated.

Why is the STRIPS program popular? As we have seen, immunization strategies require the matching of the duration of the assets of the institution with that of its liabilities. Unlike coupon-paying bonds, whose duration is constantly changing, zero-coupon bonds always have a duration equal to their remaining term to maturity. Thus, zeroes are invaluable for implementing such a strategy. Besides, while a 30-Year note will have a duration substantially less than 30 years, by stripping it into 61 component securities, we can create zeroes with durations ranging from 6 months to 30 years.[14]

When a bond is stripped, the zeroes created from the coupons are referred to as C-STRIPs, while those derived from the principal are termed as P-STRIPs. The availability of P-STRIPs is higher than that of C-STRIPs corresponding to a coupon date.

EXAMPLE 4.16

Consider a T-bond with a face value of $1,000, and a coupon of 4.50% per annum, paid semiannually. Assume that 500,000 bonds are issued, and that all C-STRIPs and P-STRIPs have a face value of $1,000. The magnitude of the cash flow on each coupon date is:

$$1,000 \times 500,000 \times 0.045 \times 0.50 = \$11,250,000$$

Thus 11,250 C-STRIPs can be issued corresponding to each coupon date. However 500,000 P-STRIPs can be issued.

INFLATION INDEXED BONDS

A plain-vanilla bond does not provide protection against inflation. The coupons are fixed in currency terms, and thus with the passage of time the purchasing power of payments received from these bonds steadily declines. There are bonds, however, whose cash flows are determined by the prevailing inflation rates; in this case, the

---

[14]See Sundaresan (2009).

cash flow is higher when the rate of inflation is high, and lower when the rate is low. The objective is to ensure that, in real terms, the rate of return is reasonably constant. In the United States, the Treasury issues TIPS, or Treasury Inflation-Protected Securities.

Protection against inflation may be offered in one of two ways. The first method entails the adjustment of coupons, keeping the face value constant. This is equivalent to a floating-rate bond; that is, the coupon rate is high when inflation is high and low when the change in the price level is low. Such securities are termed *Coupon-Linkers* or *C-Linkers* for short. The alternative is to keep the coupon rate constant and adjust the principal periodically for inflation to get an adjusted principal. In such cases, a fixed coupon rate is paid on the adjusted principal. These securities are termed *Principal-Linkers* or *P-Linkers*. With both security types, the cash flows per period are variable and related to the rate of inflation.

Usually, the rate of inflation will be positive, and consequently cash flows will increase. At times, however, we may have a deflationary situation, where the purchasing power of money actually increases and the rate of inflation will be negative. In such a situation, the adjusted principal for a P-Linker may be less than the original par value at maturity. If so, most governments will pay back the original par value or the terminal-adjusted principal, whichever is higher. In the case of a C-Linker, if there is a sharp decline in the price level and the inflation adjusted rate is negative, most issuers pay a coupon of zero.

EXAMPLE 4.17

We will first illustrate a P-Linker and then a C-Linker. Consider the following inflation related data. Table 4.13 reports the Price Index Level at the end of every year, the rate of inflation for the year, and the index ratio for the year. If we denote the price index at time t by I_t, the inflation for the year is $(I_t - I_{t-1})/I_{t-1}$. The index ratio for the year is I_t/I_0, that is, the ratio of the index at the end of the year, and the index value at the very beginning.

TABLE 4.13   Index Levels, Inflation Rates, and Index Ratios

Time	Price Index	Inflation Rate	Index Ratio
0	100.0000	–	
1	104.0000	4.00%	1.04000
2	98.8000	−5.00%	0.98800
3	104.9750	6.25%	1.04975

Consider a three-year P-Linker with a face value of $1,000, which pays a coupon of 5% per annum on the adjusted principal. The nominal and real cash flows are depicted in Table 4.14.

(continued)

(continued)

TABLE 4.14   Cash Flows for a P-Linker

Time	Adjusted Principal	Nominal Cash Flow	Real Cash Flow
0	1,000.00	(1,000)	(1,000)
1	1,040.00	52.0000	50
2	988.00	49.4000	50
3	1,049.75	1,102.2375	1,050

The adjusted principal at a point in time is the original principal multiplied by the prevailing index level. The nominal cash flow is the adjusted principal multiplied by the coupon rate. The real cash flow is the nominal cash flow divided by the index ratio for that point of time.

Now let us consider a three-year C-Linker with a face value of 1,000 and a real coupon rate of 4.20% per annum. The inflation rate, the adjusted coupon, and the nominal cash flow for each period are depicted in Table 4.15.

TABLE 4.15   Cash Flow for a C-Linker

Time	Inflation Rate	Adjusted Coupon	Nominal Cash Flow
0	–	–	(1,000)
1	2.50%	6.70%	67.00
2	–5.75%	0.00%	0.00
3	4.80%	9.00%	1,090.00

The inflation for the first year is 2.50%. Thus, the adjusted coupon rate is the prescribed coupon rate of 4.20% plus the rate of inflation. In the second year the inflation rate is negative. If we add the prescribed coupon, the adjusted coupon is –1.55%, thus the adjusted coupon is set to zero. In the final year, the inflation is 4.80%, thus the adjusted coupon is 9.00%.

COMPUTING PRICE GIVEN YIELD AND VICE VERSA IN EXCEL

If we are on a coupon date, we can compute the price given the YTM by using the PV function in Excel, and the YTM given the price by using the RATE function in Excel. Quite obviously, on a coupon date, the dirty price will be equal to the clean price.

We will illustrate the use of the functions with the help of an example.

EXAMPLE 4.18

TISCO has issued a bond with a face value of $1,000, and five years to maturity. The coupon rate is 3.8% per annum paid semiannually and the YTM is 4.2% per annum.

The required inputs for the PV function are:

Rate = 0.021 (the annual YTM divided by two)

Nper = 10 (the number of years multiplied by two)

Pmt = −19 (the semiannual coupon in dollars)

Fv = −1,000 (the face value)

Type: Is not required

$$PV(0.021, 10, -19, -1000) = 982.13$$

Now assume that this bond has a price of 964. What is the corresponding YTM?

The required inputs for the RATE function are:

Nper = 10

Pmt = −19

Pv = 964

Fv = −1,000

Type: Is not required

Guess: Is not required

$$Rate(10, -19, 964, -1000) = 2.3072\%$$

Note that Pv, which is the price, is an investment, whereas Pmt, or the periodic coupon, and Fv, the terminal face value, are inflows. Hence Pmt and Fv should have the same sign, while Pv should have the opposite sign.

This is a semiannual value, since the coupon and the YTM have been specified in semiannual terms. The annual YTM is 2.3072 × 2 = 4.6144%.

If we arc between two coupon dates, we need to use the PRICE function to compute the price of a bond given its YTM, and the YIELD function to compute the YTM of a bond given its price. The PRICE function gives the clean price of the bond. Hence to compute the dirty price, we need to separately calculate and add the accrued interest using the ACCRINT function.

The YIELD function returns the YTM given the clean price. Hence if we have the dirty price of the bond, we need to compute and subtract the accrued interest to convert it to the clean price, before invoking the YIELD function. Here are some examples.

EXAMPLE 4.19

Assume we are on 21 September 2020. A bond with a face value of $1,000 was issued on 15 May 2016 and is scheduled to mature on 15 May 2045. The coupon is 4.2% per annum paid semiannually, and the YTM is 4.8% per annum. Compute the clean and dirty prices using the PRICE and ACCRINT functions.

The price on the next coupon date, 15 November 2020, may be computed as follows. On a coupon date we can invoke the PV function. However, there will be a coupon received on that day, which must be added.

$$PV(0.024,49,-21,-1000) + 21 = \$935.1032$$

Let us assume an Actual/Actual day-count convention. The number of days between 15 May 2021 and 15 November 2021 is $16+30+31+31+30+31+15 = 184$.

The number of days between 21 September 2020 and 15 November 2021 is $9+31+15 = 55$.

The fractional period remaining is $55/184 = 0.2989$.

Thus the dirty price on 21 September is given by PV(.024,0.2989,,−935.1032) = $928.4978.

The accrued interest is $[(184-55)/184] \times 21 = 14.7228$.

Thus the clean price is $928.4978 - 14.7228 = 913.7750$.

Now let us use the PRICE function in Excel. The parameters are:

Settlement

Maturity

Rate

Yld

Redemption

Frequency

Basis

The settlement and maturity date have to be input using the DATE function in Excel. In our case the corresponding inputs are Date(2020,09,21) and Date(2045,05,15). The rate is the annual coupon rate and yield is the annual YTM. The redemption is the percentage of the face value that will be returned at maturity. Thus, in most cases it will be 100. It is not the par value, which is $1,000 in this case. Hence, the answer obtained will be for a face value of 100, and consequently the answer will have to be multiplied by 10 to obtain the price for a face value of 1,000. The frequency will be entered as 2, since coupons are being paid semiannually, which is why the coupon rate and the yield are being entered as annual values. The basis represents the day-count convention and the value for the Actual-Actual convention is 1.

Price(Date(2020,09,21),Date(2045,05,15),0.042,0.048,100,2,1) × 10 = $913.7745.

The accrued interest function requires the following parameters.

Issue: This is the previous coupon date

First_interest: This is the next coupon date

Settlement: Is the settlement date

Rate: Is the annual coupon rate

Par: Is the actual par value

Frequency: Is 2 for bonds paying semiannual coupons

Basis: Is 1 for Actual/Actual

Calc_method: Is not required

Accrint(Date(2020,05,15),Date(2020,11,15),Date(2020,09,21),0.042,1000,2,1) = $14.7228.

If we are given the price, we can compute the YTM using the YIELD function. Assume that the quoted price of the bond in the previous example is 90.9375. Quoted prices are per $100 of face value and are always clean prices. The Yield function requires the following parameters.

Settlement: This is the settlement date

Maturity: This is the maturity date

Rate: This is the annual coupon rate

Pr: This is the clean price per $100 of face value

Redemption: Is 100, that is, 100% of par

Frequency: Is 2 for a bond paying semiannual coupons

Basis: Is 1 for Actual/Actual

Yield(Date(2020,09,21),Date(2045,05,15),0.042,90.9375,100,2,1) = 4.8327%. There is no need to multiply this by 2, because we have given the frequency of coupons as 2, and thus the function automatically returns the annual YTM value.

COMPUTING DURATION IN EXCEL

Excel has a function for computing the duration of a bond. The required parameters are:

Settlement: This is the settlement date to be input using the Date function.

Maturity: This is the maturity date to be input using the Date function.

Coupon: This is the annual coupon rate.

Yield: This is the annual YTM.

Frequency: This is 2 for bonds paying semiannual coupons.

Basis: This represents the day-count convention.

Let us use the earlier data.
Duration(Date(2020,09,15),Date(2045,05,15),0.042,0.048,2,1) = 14.8915 years. Because the frequency has been specified as 2, the function returns the duration value in terms of number of years.

CHAPTER 5

Money Markets

INTRODUCTION

The money market is an important segment of the debt market of countries with active financial markets. Debt markets exist so that parties in need of funds can interact with those seeking to deploy surplus funds. Thus there are two key constituents of such markets, those who are ready to borrow money by issuing securities, called borrowers or issuers, and those willing to lend in the process of acquiring securities, called lenders or holders. But all debt market transactions are not comparable. Clearly there is a difference between a 20-year term loan negotiated by a company with its bank, a 30-year mortgage loan negotiated by a home buyer with a savings and loan institution, and a three-month bank loan that is arranged by a corporation with its bank to fund its inventories.

The purpose for which money is borrowed varies from borrower to borrower. And, in the case of the same borrower it may vary from transaction to transaction. A company may be negotiating a term loan to facilitate the construction of a factory; in this case, the company needs capital for a relatively long period of time. At the same time, however, the company may need an overdraft from its bank to pay outstanding wages. The first is a capital market transaction, whereas the second is clearly a short-term or current account transaction.

The different motives for borrowing funds lead to the creation of different types of debt securities that vary with respect to their magnitude, tenor, and risk features. Our focus here is on the *money market*, or the market for short-term credit. Loans in the money market have an original term to maturity of one year or less. In the case of debt securities, we need to make a distinction between the original term to maturity of a security and its actual or current term to maturity. The original term to maturity is the instrument's time to maturity when issued. Clearly, it cannot change after the issue is made. On the other hand, the actual or current term to maturity is the term remaining to maturity at the point of consideration; as we know, with the passage of time the actual term to maturity will keep declining. The *capital market*, in contrast to the money market, is an arena where securities with an original term to maturity of more than one year are issued and traded.

The money market consists of transactions to meet short-term cash needs. It is an arena where parties with temporary cash surpluses are given an opportunity to interact with those who have temporary cash deficits. The first category of people are potential investors in money market securities, while the second category are potential issuers of such securities. Participants in the money market include corporations, financial institutions, and governments. The nature of transactions ranges from overnight deals to those with a maturity of as long as one year, although some markets are occasionally characterized even by intraday transactions.

Why does an economy require a money market? The reason is that in real life, for most individuals and institutions, inflows and outflows of cash will rarely be synchronized. Take the case of the federal or central government of a country. Such entities raise income primarily in the form of tax revenues; however, such income is lumpy in nature and is never received as uniform or predictable cash flows. The problem is that a government has to make payments throughout the year in the form of wages, pension payments, and other budgeted expenditure. There will be times when the government is flush with tax revenues. At such times, the government needs to deploy the surplus funds meaningfully until they are required. At other times when the availability of cash is low related to budgeted expenses, the same government will need to raise funds on a short-term basis. The same is true for a corporation. When there is a surge in sales-related revenues, the firm's checking account will show a healthy credit balance. As it starts spending on supplies, wages, taxes, and other annual items of expenditure, however, it may find it suddenly needs funds urgently to cover a short-term deficit. At such times, it will need to negotiate for a temporary line of credit such as an overdraft, or resort to the issue of other money market securities, as we shall see. Thus, the key feature of a money market is its ability to help governments and businesses bridge the gap between their receipts and expenditure; in other words, it facilitates what is called *liquidity management.*

Why is there so much significance attached to the ability of these entities to borrow and lend for relatively short durations? The reason is that money is a very perishable commodity. When idle cash is not invested the holder incurs an opportunity cost in the form of interest income that is forgone, and income that is forgone is lost forever. When large amounts of funds are involved, the lost income can be substantial. Take, for instance, the case of an institution that has 12MM dollars available overnight. If we assume that the interest rate is 12% per annum and that the year consists of 360 days, which is a common assumption in the case of money market securities, the loss if the funds are kept idle is:

$$12,000,000 \times 0.12 \times \frac{1}{360} = \$4,000$$

For a week that amounts to $28,000 of lost income. Similar analogies can be given from the hotel and airline industries. If the New York Hilton has 20 unoccupied rooms on a given day, then that lost revenue is lost forever; obviously, the hotel cannot accommodate two guests in a room on a subsequent day. Similarly, if British Airways were to fly from New York to London with 10 empty seats, then that lost income is lost forever.

It must be mentioned that an entity is not usually a permanent borrower or lender in the money market. A corporation may issue commercial paper to borrow a large amount of money. It may subsequently reenter the market as a lender, due to a sudden surge of cash receipts. Also, there are institutions that simultaneously operate on both sides of the market. Take the case of a large commercial bank like Citibank. At any point in time, it will be issuing negotiable certificates of deposit and borrowing federal funds, activities that warrant its classification as a borrower. At the same time, however, it is likely to make short-term loans to satisfy the working capital needs of its corporate clients. One institution that is usually on the demand side of the money market is the government. The US Treasury is the largest of all money market borrowers worldwide at any point in time.

Investors in the money market seek to keep their temporary surpluses gainfully invested without compromising on credit risk or liquidity. Because cash inflows and outflows cannot be perfectly anticipated, liquidity becomes paramount because players may seek to enter and exit the market in a sudden, unpredictable fashion. From the standpoint of such parties, it is imperative that the market be characterized by the presence of plenty of active buyers and issuers of securities who can facilitate transactions without a major price impact. Safety is important because investments are made for short periods and may need to be liquidated at any time to meet future cash requirements. For this reason, money market investors are especially sensitive to default risk. Even the slightest perception of a decline in credit quality can bring the market to a standstill. Rose gives two significant examples from the US money market.[1] In 1970 the Penn Central Transportation Company defaulted on its commercial paper. Immediately, the paper market came to a grinding halt because of the investors' reluctance to subscribe to the paper of even highly rated companies. A second significant incident was the 1984 failure of the Continental Illinois Bank and its subsequent need for government support.[2] This led to an immediate increase in the rates of all bank negotiable certificates of deposit, because of a fear among market players that all banks had become more risky.

Money market securities, like other debt securities, are in principle vulnerable to interest rate risk; however, the prices of such securities are relatively more stable over time. Thus, although such securities do not offer prospects for significant capital gains, neither do they raise the specter of significant capital losses. There are essentially two reasons for this. First, interest rate movements over relatively short periods of time tend to be moderate. Second, the price impact due to a given interest rate change is greater the longer the term to maturity of the cash flow being affected.

Similarly, default risk is minimal in the money market. This is because the ability to borrow in such markets is restricted to well-established institutions with impeccable credit ratings, usually from multiple rating agencies.

The money market is extremely liquid and can absorb large volumes of transactions with only relatively small effects on security prices and interest rates. Consequently, it is possible for borrowers to issue large quantities of securities at short notice, often in a matter of minutes. The market consists of a wide network of securities dealers, brokers, and banks. There is a large volume of interbank trading, which is often brokered. Money market dealers also assume large positions in securities, and access the market both to acquire such securities and to fund these acquisitions. Brokers in these markets have access to good and accurate information, and consequently provide traders with the latest information on the best available prices and rates. Such intermediaries also facilitate the maintenance of confidentiality in the market, for large institutions will be unwilling to disclose their identity prior to the trade, for fear that such information may tend to influence the

---

[1]See Rose (2000).
[2]See Rose (2000).

eventual outcome. In the case of brokered transactions, however, the intermediary will reveal the principal's identity to the counterparty only after the deal has been wrapped up.

Such brokers provide up-to-date indicative interest rates to the market via information service providers such as Reuters. Typically, rates are quoted for all freely convertible currencies. They charge a standard commission for their services. But large clients can often negotiate the rates payable.

The market is dominated by active traders who are consistently looking out for arbitrage opportunities. They will move money in an instant from a corner of the market that is offering a lower yield to another corner offering a higher yield. The market is overseen by the Federal Reserve in the United States, and by other central banks in their respective countries. There is no central trading arena for money market securities and the market is totally OTC. Participants negotiate trades over the phone or through computer networks. Speed is of the essence because money, as we have seen, is highly perishable. Consequently, most trades are consummated in a matter of minutes, and at times even in seconds.

Money markets may be securities market dominated or bank dominated. In a securities-dominated market most borrowing and lending is through open market trading of financial instruments. In a bank-dominated market, bank borrowing and lending is at the center of most transactions. Markets in Western economies are largely securities dominated while Asian markets, like those in Japan and Korea, tend to be largely bank dominated. Bank-dominated money markets have a potential weakness: they are more vulnerable to pressures from the government, particularly in countries where the banking sector is characterized by substantial government ownership or control. This raises the possibility of bad loans and thus has the potential to impede the development of financial markets in such countries.

MARKET SUPERVISION

Money markets are overseen by the respective central banks. The major central banks in the world are listed in Table 5.1.

THE FEDERAL RESERVE SYSTEM

The Federal Reserve system consists of 12 district Federal Reserve Banks. These are identified by the cities in which they are located. The 12 banks are listed in Table 5.2.

TABLE 5.1   Major Central Banks

The Federal Reserve
The European Central Bank
The Bank of England
The Bank of Japan
The Swiss National Bank
The Bank of Canada
The Reserve Bank of Australia
The Reserve Bank of New Zealand

TABLE 5.2   The District Federal Reserve Banks

Federal Reserve Bank of Boston
Federal Reserve Bank of New York
Federal Reserve Bank of Philadelphia
Federal Reserve Bank of Cleveland
Federal Reserve Bank of Richmond
Federal Reserve Bank of Atlanta
Federal Reserve Bank of Chicago
Federal Reserve Bank of St. Louis
Federal Reserve Bank of Minneapolis
Federal Reserve Bank of Kansas City
Federal Reserve Bank of Dallas
Federal Reserve Bank of San Francisco

The Fed sets and implements the monetary policy of the United States, which has implications for interest rates in the economy, and for the rate of inflation. Considering the importance of the United States in the global financial markets, the actions of the Fed resonate beyond the borders of the country.

The Fed sets and targets two important interest rates in the economy. The first is the discount rate, which is actually set by the Fed. This is the rate at which banks borrow from the central bank. Clearly, the greater the discount rate, the higher will be the rates charged by commercial banks for extending credit. The second rate, which is targeted by the Fed, is the fed funds rate. This is the rate at which banks extend loans, typically overnight, to other depository institutions.

KEY DATES IN THE CASE OF CASH MARKET INSTRUMENTS

There are three key dates in the case of such instruments.

- Transaction date
- Value date
- Maturity date

The transaction date is the date on which the terms and conditions of a financial instrument such as the term to maturity, transaction amount, and price are agreed upon. In other words, it is the date on which the counterparties enter into a contract with each other.

The value date is the date on which the instrument starts to earn or accrue a return. The value date may or may not be the same as the transaction date. If the two dates are the same, then the transaction is said to be for *same day value* or *value today*. In other cases, the value date will be the following business day. Transactions with such a feature are said to be for *next-day value* or *value tomorrow*. Finally, there are markets and transactions where the value date will be two business days after the transaction date. A transaction with such a feature is referred to as a *spot transaction* and is said to be for *spot value*.

The maturity date is the date on which the instrument ceases to accrue a return. The maturities of money market instruments are often fixed not by agreeing to a specific date of maturity, but by agreeing to a term to maturity, which will be a number of weeks or months after the value date. For instance, assume that today is 21 June 20XX. A bank will usually quote an interest rate for a one-month deposit rather than for a deposit with a specific maturity date in the following month. The date on which the one-month deposit will mature is then fixed according to market convention. Many money markets follow two conventions.[3]

- The Modified Following Business Day Convention
- The End/End Rule

THE MODIFIED FOLLOWING BUSINESS DAY CONVENTION

This convention consists of the following three rules.

1. Maturity is set for the same date as the value date. For instance, if the value date is 21 June 20XX, the maturity date for a three-month deposit will be 21 September, and that for a six-month deposit will be 21 December.
2. If the maturity date as per the first rule, however, happens to be a non-business day, then it will be moved to the following business day. Take the case of a three-month deposit with a value date of 21 June 20XX. Under normal circumstances the maturity date would be 21 September 20XX. But if 21 September was a Saturday, then the maturity date would be Monday, 23 September 20XX, assuming of course that this day is not a market holiday.
3. If the following business day, according to the second rule, was to fall in the next calendar month, then the maturity date would be moved back to the last business day of the maturity month. Consider a one-month deposit with a value date of 31 July 20XX. The maturity date as per the first rule will be 31 August 20XX. Assume that 31 August is a market holiday. According to the previous rule the maturity date should be taken as the following business day. In this case, however, the following business day will fall in September, the next calendar month. Consequently, the maturity date will be moved back to the last business day of August, which we will assume is 29 August.

THE END/END RULE

This rule states that if the value date is the last business day of the current calendar month, then the maturity date will be the last business day of the relevant calendar month. For example, take a one-month deposit with a value date of 31 May. It will mature on 30 June, assuming that it is a business day. Similarly, a one-month deposit with a value date of 30 June will mature on 31 July, assuming once again that it is a business day.

---

[3]See Comotto (1998).

A one-month deposit with a value date of 31 January will mature on 28 or 29 February depending on whether or not it is a leap year. But a one-month deposit with a value date of 28 or 29 February will mature on 31 March. However if the maturity date as per this rule were to be a holiday, then the modified following business day convention would apply; that is, the maturity date will be taken as the last business day of the maturity month.

THE INTERBANK MARKET

The interbank market is a market for large or wholesale loans and deposits. As the name suggests, it is primarily an arena for borrowing and lending deals between commercial banks, with tenors less than or equal to one year.[4]

Why is there a need for an interbank market? On any given day, certain commercial banks will have a surplus of funds while others will be confronted with the specter of a deficit. An institution whose inflow on account of deposits exceeds the outflow on account of loans and security purchases will see a surge in its reserves. On the contrary, banks whose demand for funds on account of client loan requests and the acquisition of securities exceeds the availability of funds by way of deposits will face a depletion of reserves. The term *reserves* refers to the balance that a commercial bank has on deposit with the regional Federal Reserve Bank in the United States, and in general refers to the balance that a bank must maintain with its central bank due to statutory requirements. Such reserve balances do not earn any interest for banks with a surplus. Thus, it is prudent for banks with surpluses to lend to those with a deficit, despite the fact that interest rates for such transactions tend to be relatively low. While the loan of funds is a manifestation of lending institutions' desire to keep idle resources productively invested, on behalf of borrowers, it also reflects the fact that they cannot leave the shortfall in reserves uncovered, due to statutory regulations. Loans made in the interbank market are unsecured.

Currently the reserve requirement in the United States is nil. In principle, central banks require commercial banks to hold reserves to ensure that they can meet unexpected withdrawal requests. In countries with a prescribed reserve requirement, a decrease in the reserve percentage frees up money for the banks to make fresh loans and investments. On the other hand, an increase in the reserve ratio curtails the banks' ability to deploy funds.

TYPES OF LOANS

Overnight Money: The term refers to money that is borrowed/lent on a given banking day and is scheduled to be repaid on the next banking day. Weekend money is the term used to describe loans that are made on Friday with repayment scheduled for the following Monday. Interest on weekend money, however, is payable for a period of three days.

Call Money: This term refers to deposits for an unspecified term on a day-to-day basis. The lender can call back the funds at any time and will be repaid on the same day.

---

[4]In debt markets the word *tenor* is used for maturity of a security.

Notice Money: This is money lent with a short notice of withdrawal, for example, with seven days' notice.

Term Money: This is money lent or deposited for a fixed period such as a week or a month.

Intraday Money: The term refers to money that is lent and repaid on the same day. Borrowing takes place in the morning of the business day and repayment is scheduled for the same afternoon.

LIBOR

LIBOR is an acronym for London Interbank Offer Rate. It may be defined as the rate at which a top-rated bank in London is prepared to lend to a similar bank. It is the main benchmark rate in the London interbank market. In practice LIBOR is quoted for a number of tenors: 1 month, 2 months, 3 months, 6 months, and 12 months. Thus, there are several LIBOR rates that are quoted at any point in time, and any quotation must be prefixed by its term to maturity. Every bank in London will quote its own LIBOR rate for each tenor. But usually the rates quoted by competing banks are identical, with some minor differences observed occasionally.

While LIBOR is the globally recognized benchmark for loans granted by a top-rated depository institution to parties with a high credit rating, highly rated banks and companies can often borrow short-term at a rate below the prevailing LIBOR. On the other hand, institutions with a lower credit rating may have no option but to borrow at a rate above LIBOR.

LIBID

LIBID is an acronym for the London Interbank Bid Rate. It is the rate that a bank in London with a good credit rating is prepared to pay for funds deposited with it by another highly rated London bank. LIBID, just like LIBOR, is quoted for a number of tenors. Whereas LIBOR represents the rate that a bank seeking to borrow in the interbank market has to pay on a loan availed by it, LIBID is the rate that a bank with surplus funds will have to accept on funds it has deposited with another bank. LIBID will be lower than LIBOR. Although the size of the spread between the two rates can vary, the difference is usually just a few basis points for the same tenor.

In an interbank transaction, the rate that is agreed upon will often be somewhere between LIBID and LIBOR and is often the average of the two rates. Some depository institutions therefore use LIMEAN, which is an arithmetic average of the LIBID and the LIBOR, as the reference rate for their interbank transactions.

SONIA

SONIA is an acronym for the Sterling Overnight Index Average. This index tracks actual market overnight funding rates. It is the rate paid by banks for unsecured transactions in the British Sterling Pounds market, and it provides traders and financial institutions with an alternative to LIBOR as a benchmark. SONIA is the weighted average rate to four decimal places of all unsecured sterling overnight transactions brokered in London by member firms of the Wholesale Markets Brokers' Association (WMBA) with all counterparties in a minimum deal size of £25 million. The index is a weighted average of overnight deposit rates for each business day. Each rate in the average is weighted by the principal amounts of deposits which were taken on that day.

The Bank of England is the administrator of this benchmark. In 2018 the BoE took over the calculation and publication of SONIA. The definition of SONIA was expanded to include not just bilateral overnight unsecured transactions, but also those arranged via brokers. It is reported on the day following the day to which it relates, at 9 AM London time. The delay in the announcement allows the BoE to account for a higher volume of activity.

TRANSITIONING FROM LIBOR

The Financial Conduct Authority (FCA), the market regulator in the United Kingdom, has announced that banks do not need to quote LIBOR after 2021. In November 2020 the Federal Reserve asked banks to stop writing contracts using LIBOR by the end of 2021. The Intercontinental Exchange (ICE), which reports the LIBOR on a daily basis, will stop publishing one-week and two-month LIBOR after December 31, 2021. It has specified that all contracts using LIBOR must be wrapped up by June 30, 2023.

Similar alternatives have been proposed for the LIBOR in other markets. These are:

- Secured Overnight Financing Rater (SOFR) in the United States. This is a secured rate that covers multiple overnight repo market segments. Unlike SONIA, SOFR is a secured rate.
- Swiss Average Rate Overnight (SARON) in Switzerland. It is a secured rate that reflects interest paid on interbank overnight repos.
- Tokyo Overnight Average Rate (TONAR) in Japan. It is an unsecured rate that captures the overnight call money market.
- European Short-Term Euro Rate (ESTER) in the European Union. It is an unsecured rate that captures overnight wholesale deposit transactions.

In explaining the need to move away from the LIBOR, the FCA cited a lack of activity in the underlying interbank markets as a key concern. It argued that because an active market does not exist, even the best-run benchmark cannot be used as a measure of it.

INTEREST COMPUTATION METHODS

For interbank loans and some money market instruments, interest is payable on the principal value of the instrument. That is, interest is paid at the end of the loan period, along with the repayment of principal to the investor. On the other hand, securities like Treasury bills and commercial paper are what we term as discount securities.

That is, they are issued at a discount to their principal value and repay the principal at maturity. Clearly these are analogous to zero-coupon bonds. We will illustrate the difference between the two with the help of an example.

EXAMPLE 5.1

Let's first focus on the add-on approach. Consider a loan of $100 that is made at a rate of 4% per annum for a period of 90 days. The day-count convention is Actual/360. So, the interest repayable at the end, along with the principal, is 100 × 0.04 × 90/360 = $1. Hence a loan of $100 is retuned as $101. The annualized rate of return is $(1 \div 100) \times (360 \div 90) \times 100 = 4\%$.

Now assume that the loan was made on a discount basis. The amount lent at the outset will be 100 − 1 = $99, and the amount repaid will be $100. The annualized rate of return is $(1 \div 99) \times (360 \div 90) \times 100 = 4.0404\%$.

In the discount approach, the actual rate of interest will always be higher than the quoted rate.

For interbank loans, interest is computed and paid along with the principal. The method of calculating the interest differs according to the currency under consideration. Interest on most currencies including the US dollar and the euro is calculated on the assumption that the year has 360 days and is based on the ACT/360 day-count convention. This means that the interest payable on a loan for T days with a principal of P and carrying an interest rate of r is:

$$P \times \frac{r}{100} \times \frac{T}{360}$$

For certain currencies, however, like the sterling, interest is calculated on the assumption of a 365-day year and is said to be based on an ACT/365 day-count convention. Consequently, the formula for computing interest is:

$$P \times \frac{r}{100} \times \frac{T}{365}$$

EXAMPLE 5.2

A bank makes a loan of €10 MM from 15 July till 15 October at an interest rate of 5.75% per annum. The number of days is = 16 + 31 + 30 + 15 = 92. Notice that although the loan is for three months we consider the actual number of days in the period, and do not automatically take the period as consisting of 90 days. The interest is given by:

$$10,000,000 \times \frac{5.75}{100} \times \frac{92}{360}$$

$$= \text{euros } 146,944.44$$

EXAMPLE 5.3

A bank makes a loan of \$7.5 MM for a period of one year (365 days) at an interest rate of 5.25% per annum. The interest is given by:

$$7,500,000 \times \frac{5.25}{100} \times \frac{365}{360}$$

$$= \$399,218.75$$

Notice that because the actual number of days exceeds 360 and even though the quoted rate is 5.25%, the rate paid on a simple interest basis is:

$$\frac{399,218.75}{7,500,000} \times 100 = 5.3229\%$$

EXAMPLE 5.4

A bank makes a loan of £7.5 MM for a period of 180 days at an interest rate of 4.95% per annum. The interest is given by:

$$7,500,000 \times \frac{4.95}{100} \times \frac{180}{365}$$

$$= £183,082.19$$

TERM MONEY MARKET DEPOSITS

A term money market deposit is a short-term deposit, with a maximum maturity of one year, that is placed with a bank or a security house. Such deposits carry a fixed rate of interest, and the rate is linked to the prevailing LIBOR for the same term. Interest is usually paid along with the principal when the deposit matures. These deposits are nonnegotiable, that is, they cannot be sold to another party by the depositor prior to maturity. Depositors can usually break or terminate the deposit prematurely; that is, they have the option to withdraw their money prior to expiration. However, this feature may carry an attached penalty.

Such deposits can be placed in any of the major currencies and settlement happens on the same day for domestic deposits, and in two working days for eurocurrency deposits.

MONEY MARKET FORWARD RATES

Let s_1 be the quoted spot rate for an A-day loan and s_2 the spot rate for a B-day loan where $B > A$. If rates are quoted on an add-on basis,

$$\left[1 + \frac{s_1 \times A}{360}\right] \times \left[1 + \frac{f \times (B - A)}{360}\right] = \left[1 + \frac{s_2 \times B}{360}\right]$$

where f is the forward rate for a B − A day loan, as fixed at the outset.

If the rates are quoted on a discount basis, however, the forward rate is the solution to the following equation.

$$\left[1 - \frac{s_1 \times A}{360}\right] \times \left[1 - \frac{f \times (B - A)}{360}\right] = \left[1 - \frac{s_2 \times B}{360}\right]$$

In the case of loans on an add-on basis, the forward rate is

$$\frac{(s_2 B - s_1 A)}{360 + s_1 A} \times \frac{360}{B - A}$$

However, in the case of loans on a discount basis, the forward rate is given by

$$\frac{(s_2 B - s_1 A)}{360 - s_1 A} \times \frac{360}{B - A}$$

$360 - s_1 A$ will always be less than $360 + s_1 A$. Thus the forward rate that is obtained for a given set of spot rates will always be greater in the case of loans that are made on a discount basis.

EXAMPLE 5.5

Assume that the spot rate for a 90-day loan is 2.4% per annum, while that for a 198-day loan is 3.2% per annum. The forward rate for a 108-day loan after 90 days is given by

$$\left[1 + \frac{0.024 \times 90}{360}\right] = \left[1 + \frac{f \times 108}{360}\right] = \left[1 + \frac{0.032 \times 198}{360}\right]$$

$$\Rightarrow f = 3.8436\%$$

if we assume that rates are quoted on an add-on basis. If we were to assume, however, that rates are quoted on a discount basis,

$$\left[1 - \frac{0.024 \times 90}{360}\right] \times \left[1 - \frac{f \times 108}{360}\right] = \left[1 - \frac{0.032 \times 198}{360}\right]$$

$$\Rightarrow f = 3.8900\%$$

FEDERAL FUNDS

Federal funds are the principal means of making payments in the money market in the United States. By definition, the term *federal funds* refers to money that can be immediately transferred from the buyer to the seller or from the lender to the bor-rower. The term *federal funds* came into use in earlier years when the principal way of effecting an immediate fund transfer was by debiting the reserve account held by the buyer/lender at its regional Federal Reserve bank and crediting the reserve account maintained by the seller/borrower at its regional Federal Reserve bank. Such transac-tions are instantaneous and can be effected in a matter of seconds in practice. Today, however, the fed funds market is broader in scope than just the funds available with Federal Reserve banks in the form of reserves held by depository institutions. It is a common practice for all banks to maintain deposits with large correspondent banks in major financial centers. These deposits may also be transferred readily from the account of one bank to that of another.

Large corporate borrowers tend to route their financial dealings through large banks in the major money market centers, in particular New York City. For such money center banks, therefore, the demand for loans and investments made by their clients inevitably exceeds the quantum of funds at their disposal. On the other hand, for smaller banks located in rural or semiurban areas in a state like Alabama, the availability of funds due to deposits by the local population will usually exceed the demand for funds at the local level.

An increase in deposits consequently leads to an increase in the availability of fed funds, whereas loans made and securities purchased manifest themselves as a reduction in the availability of such funds. Most lenders tend to make overnight loans of fed funds. This is because the availability of excess reserves tends to vary daily, and in a fairly unpredictable fashion. The lending of such funds is termed as a sale, while the borrowing of such funds is referred to as a purchase.

In the United States, the Federal Reserve does not impose a fed funds rate on banks. It sets an interest rate band as a target; currently the prescribed interval is 0 to 0.25%. The band prescribed by the Federal Reserve provides a corridor of reference for commercial banks. The central bank, however, indirectly influences the fed funds rate by increasing or decreasing the money supply. By increasing the money supply the central bank can cause the fed funds rate to decline. On the other hand, a contraction in the money supply will cause rates to rise.

FEDERAL FUNDS VERSUS CLEARINGHOUSE FUNDS

Federal funds transfers operate very differently from the payment mechanism used in the capital market. When a money market dealer acquires securities from another party, it will immediately instruct its bank to effect a transfer of funds from its account to the account held by the selling institution at its bank. The buyer's bank will contact its regional federal reserve bank and request the Fed to debit its reserve account, and credit the reserve account held by the seller's bank at the same or possibly a different district federal reserve bank. All 12 federal reserve banks maintain an *interdistrict set-tlement account* in Washington D.C. Thus, transfers between regional federal reserve banks take place by decreasing the share of the buyer's bank and augmenting the share of the seller's bank. In practice, these transactions are so quick that the seller of securities has funds available for immediate use on the day of the transaction. Con-sequently, federal funds are referred to as *immediately available funds*.

On the other hand, consider the conventional method of payment that is used in most transactions. The buyer will either issue a check favoring the seller or, for personal transactions, pay by credit card and then subsequently issue a check to pay the credit card bill. Funds transferred by means of checks are referred to as *clearinghouse funds* because once the buyer writes a check it goes to the seller's bank, which forwards that check eventually to the depository institution upon which it was drawn, and transfers between the two depository institutions are processed and reconciled through a central processing center known as a clearinghouse. Clearinghouse funds are not acceptable in money markets because speed is of the essence. Compared to federal funds, it takes at least a day to clear local checks and longer for outstation checks, which is far too slow for a money market transaction, because no interest can be earned until the check is collected.

CORRESPONDENT BANKS: NOSTRO AND VOSTRO ACCOUNTS

It is common practice for banks to maintain accounts with other banks. For instance, foreign banks have accounts with banks in the United States. Within the United States, banks located in smaller towns and cities tend to have relationships with larger banks in cities like New York and Chicago. Such arrangements are referred to as correspondent banking relationships. The bank that maintains an account is referred to as the respondent bank, while the bank that offers the account maintenance facility is referred to as the correspondent bank. Correspondent banks facilitate check clearing and collection, foreign exchange transactions, and other activities. They also participate in loan syndication. For many small banks, the demand for loans at the local level is often in excess of the available deposits, and at times may exceed the bank's legal lending limit. Syndication helps surmount these barriers, in addition to helping in risk diversification.

From the standpoint of a bank, a *nostro* is its account of its money that is being held by another bank, whereas a *vostro* is its account of the money of another bank being held by it. For instance, assume that Barclays Bank is holding an account with Citibank in New York City. Barclays would refer to this account as its nostro. Citibank, on the other hand, would term it a vostro account. A nostro account with a credit balance is an asset, and in this case will show up on the asset side of Barclays' balance sheet. Seen from the perspective of a vostro account, a credit balance signifies that the bank is holding the assets of another institution, and consequently is the manifestation of a liability. On the contrary, a vostro with a debit balance would signify that the bank has made a loan to the counterparty, and would therefore be tantamount to an asset.

TREASURY BILLS

Treasury bills are short-term debt securities issued by the federal government. The US Treasury bill rates set the benchmark for the rates on other money market securities. The reasons why T-bills carry the lowest yield for a given tenor are the following. First, they are totally devoid of credit risk, as they are backed by the full faith and credit of the federal government. Second, they are highly liquid. Third, income from such securities is exempt from state income tax. In the United States, unlike in many other countries, state governments are empowered to levy income tax. The governments follow a guideline of mutual reciprocity. That is, federal securities are exempt from state income tax and vice versa.

By law, T-bills in the United States must have an original maturity of one year or less. Regular series bills are issued routinely every week or month by way of competitive auctions. Four-week, eight-week, three-month, and six-month bills are auctioned every week and one-year bills are sold usually once a month. Of the four maturities, the six-month bills provide the largest amount of revenue for the US Treasury. On the other hand, cash management bills are issued only when the Treasury has a special need due to low cash balances. Such bills have maturities ranging from as short as a few days to as long as six months. They give maximum flexibility to the Treasury because they can be issued as and when required. The money raised through these issues is used by the Treasury to meet any temporary shortfalls.

T-bills are sold by an auction process. The Treasury entertains both competitive and noncompetitive bids. Large investors submit competitive bids, wherein they indicate not only the quantity sought, but also the minimum yield they are prepared to accept. The yield in this case refers to the discount yield for the bill being auctioned. Noncompetitive tenders, on the other hand, are submitted by small investors who agree to accept the yield at which securities are auctioned off, whatever that yield may be. Thus, such bidders have to only indicate the quantities sought by them. Generally, the Treasury fills all noncompetitive tenders.

Besides being traded in the United States, T-bills issued by the US Treasury are actively traded in other major financial centers like London and Tokyo. Thus, the market for such securities operates virtually round the clock. The globalization of the market is characterized by the presence of non-US dealers in the US market, as well as by the activities of American dealers in markets outside the country.

REOPENINGS

Every T-bill issue is identified with a unique CUSIP number.[5] Some issues are, however, a reopening of an existing issue. That is, the new issue is identical in all respects to an issue that is already trading in the secondary market. For instance, the three-month bill issued three months after the issuance of a six-month bill is considered a reopening of the six-month bill. In this case, the new issue is given the same CUSIP number. For a given maturity, the most recently issued securities are referred to as on-the-run, while those issued earlier are referred to as off-the-run. On-the-run securities generally trade at slightly lower yields because they are more liquid. The reason for this is that for some time after the issue of such bills, there tends to be active trading in the secondary market. Thereafter most securities pass into the hands of investors who choose to hold them until maturity. Consequently, off-the-run securities are less liquid, which explains the higher yield.

Cash management bills are issued via a standard auction process; however, they are irregular with respect to their term to maturity and auction schedule. If a cash management bill were to mature on the same day as a regular bill, which is usually a Thursday, then it is said to be on-cycle. In this case, the issue is considered to be

---

[5]CUSIP is a securities identification code used in the United States and Canada. It stands for Committee on Uniform Securities Identification Procedures.

a reopening, and is consequently allotted the same CUSIP. If it were to mature on a different day, however, it would be said to be off-cycle, and would carry a different CUSIP number.

YIELDS ON DISCOUNT SECURITIES

In the market for fixed income securities, there are different ways of computing the yield on an instrument. It is very important for an investor to be conversant with the various methods used for calculation, and the relationship between the corresponding yields, in order to understand the various instruments that are available.

NOTATION

We will define the following symbols. The corresponding terms will become clear as we proceed.

$d \equiv$ quoted yield on a discount security like a T-bill.

$D \equiv$ discount from the face value in dollars.

$V \equiv$ face value of the discount security.

$T_m \equiv$ time left to maturity in days.

$P \equiv$ price of the discount security.

$y_{365} \equiv$ Bond Equivalent Yield, of a discount security, with $T_m < 182$ days.

$y_{360} \equiv$ Money Market Yield, of a discount security, with $T_m < 182$ days.

$y_c \equiv$ Bond Equivalent Yield, of a discount security, with $T_m > 182$ days.

DISCOUNT RATES AND T-BILL PRICES

The quoted yield on a T-bill is a discount rate, which is used to determine the difference between the price of a T-bill and its face value. For the purpose of calculation, the year is treated as if it has 360 days.

If d is the quoted yield for a T-bill, with a face value of $\$V$ and having T_m days to maturity, the dollar discount D is given by

$$D = V \times d \times \frac{T_m}{360}$$

Given the discount, the price may be calculated as

$$P = V - D$$

Alternatively, the price may be directly computed from the discount rate as follows.

$$P = V - D = V - V \times d \times \frac{T_m}{360}$$

$$= V \left[1 - \frac{d \times T_m}{360} \right]$$

We will illustrate these concepts with the help of an example.

EXAMPLE 5.6

A T-bill with 90 days to maturity and a face value of $1,000,000 has a quoted yield of 4.8%. What is the price in dollars?

$$D = 1,000,000 \times 0.048 \times \frac{90}{360} = \$12,000$$

The price is given by

$$P = V - D = 1,000,000 - 12,000 = \$988,000$$

EXAMPLE 5.7

A one-year bill (364 days) has just been issued at a quoted yield of 5.4%. What is the corresponding price in dollars?

$$D = 1,000,000 \times .054 \times \frac{364}{360} = \$54,600$$

The price is given by

$$P = V - D = 1,000,000 - 54,600 = \$945,400$$

THE BOND EQUIVALENT YIELD (BEY)

The objective of calculating the Bond Equivalent Yield, also known as the Coupon Equivalent Yield, is to compute a yield measure that facilitates comparisons between the rate of return on discount securities like T-bills, and capital market debt instruments like coupon-paying bonds. The procedure used to compute the BEY depends on whether the discount instrument under consideration has less than six months left to maturity, or more. The reason is the following. A bill with less than six months to maturity will be compared with a bond with less than six months to maturity. The latter is also a zero-coupon instrument like the bill. However, a bill with more than six months to maturity has to be compared with a bond with more than six months to maturity. Such a bond will pay a coupon prior to maturity, and consequently the mode of comparison needs to be different.

CASE A: $T_M < 182$ DAYS

The bond equivalent yield for a T-bill with less than 182 days to maturity is just the equivalent rate of return on a simple interest basis, computed under the assumption that the year has 365 days.

The bond equivalent yield for a T-bill with a given discount rate will always be greater than the stated discount rate. The reason is the following. Yield, or the rate of return obtained by an investor, is always computed with respect to the price paid for the security. Thus, the rate of return on an asset that is bought for P, and which pays the face value V at maturity, is given by

$$\frac{(V - P)}{P}$$

As we have seen earlier, for a discount security, the yield that is computed in this manner will always be greater than:

$$\frac{(V - P)}{V} = \frac{D}{V}$$

which is the dollar discount expressed as a fraction of the face value. Thus, if a T-bill is bought at a price corresponding to a given discount rate, and is held to maturity after acquisition, then the rate of return earned by the investor will always be greater than the quoted discount rate.

The BEY in this case is defined as

$$y_{365} = \frac{(V - P)}{P} \times \frac{365}{T_m}$$

It can be directly computed given the quoted yield, using the following equation.

$$y_{365} = \frac{(V - P)}{P} \times \frac{365}{T_m} = \left(\frac{V}{P} - 1\right) \times \frac{365}{T_m}$$

$$= \left[\frac{V}{V\left[1 - \frac{d \times T_m}{360}\right]} - 1\right] \times \frac{365}{T_m}$$

$$= \left[\frac{360}{360 - d \times T_m} - 1\right] \times \frac{365}{T_m}$$

$$= \frac{d \times 365}{360 - d \times T_m}$$

We will now give an illustration for computing the BEY.

EXAMPLE 5.8

A T-bill with a face value of $1,000,000 and 90 days to maturity has a quoted yield of 4.75%. What is the bond equivalent yield?

The price is given by

$$P = V\left[1 - \frac{d \times T_m}{360}\right]$$

$$= 1,000,000 \times \left[1 - \frac{0.0475 \times 90}{360}\right] = \$988,125$$

The bond equivalent yield is given by

$$i_{365} = \frac{(V-P)}{P} \times \frac{365}{T_m}$$

$$= \frac{(1000000 - 988{,}125)}{988{,}125} \times \frac{365}{90}$$

$$= 0.048738 \equiv 4.8738\%$$

THE MONEY MARKET YIELD

The BEY can be converted to a money market yield, that is, yield on a 360-days basis, by multiplying by 360/365. Thus

$$y_{360} = \frac{d \times 365}{360 - d \times T_m} \times \frac{360}{365}$$

$$= \frac{d \times 360}{360 - d \times T_m}$$

EXAMPLE 5.9

Take the case of the T-bill with a face value of $1,000,000 and 90 days to maturity, which has a quoted yield of 4.75%. The money market yield is:

$$\frac{0.0475 \times 360}{360 - 0.0475 \times 90}$$

$$= 0.048071 \equiv 4.8071\%$$

CASE B: $T_M > 182$ DAYS

A conventional coupon-paying bond with a time to maturity that is greater than 182 days (half a year) will make a coupon payment before it matures. It is inappropriate to compare the simple yield on a discount security with the YTM of a bond, because the bond will yield an interest payment before maturity, but the discount security will not. To facilitate a comparison between the BEY for a discount instrument, such as a T-bill, with more than 182 days to maturity and the yield to maturity (YTM) for the bond, the T-bill must be treated as if it too would pay interest after six months, and that interest is paid on this intermediate interest for the remaining period left to maturity.

Let us denote the BEY in this case by y; y is given by the following equation.

$$P\left(1 + \frac{y}{2}\right)\left(1 + \frac{y}{2}\left\{\frac{T_m - \frac{365}{2}}{\frac{365}{2}}\right\}\right) = V$$

The logic is as follows. The future value of P at the end of six months will be

$$P\left(1 + \frac{y}{2}\right)$$

The future value of this expression as calculated on the date of maturity must equal the face value. The compounding factor for the remaining period, on a simple interest basis, is

$$\left(1 + \frac{y}{2} \times \frac{T_m - \frac{365}{2}}{\frac{365}{2}}\right)$$

Therefore

$$P\left(1 + \frac{y}{2}\right)\left(1 + \frac{y}{2}\left\{\frac{T_m - \frac{365}{2}}{\frac{365}{2}}\right\}\right) = V$$

The expression for y is:[6]

$$\frac{-\frac{2T_m}{365} \pm 2\sqrt{\left(\frac{T_m}{365}\right)^2 - \left(\frac{2T_m}{365} - 1\right)\left(1 - \frac{V}{P}\right)}}{\frac{2T_m}{365} - 1}$$

We will obviously discard the negative root and retain the positive. The calculation of the BEY for a T-bill with a time to maturity greater than six months can be illustrated with the help of the following example.

EXAMPLE 5.10

Consider a T-bill with 270 days to maturity and a face value of $1,000,000, which has a quoted yield of 5.25%. What is the bond equivalent yield?
    The price of the bill is

$$1,000,000 - 1,000,000 \times 0.0525 \times \frac{270}{360} = \$960,625$$

---

[6]The derivation is given in the Appendix at the end of this chapter.

Therefore

$$y_c = \frac{\dfrac{-2 \times 240}{365} \pm 2\sqrt{\left(\dfrac{240}{365}\right)^2 - \left(\dfrac{2 \times 240}{365} - 1\right)\left(1 - \dfrac{1000000}{960,000}\right)}}{\dfrac{2 \times 240}{365} - 1}$$

$$= \frac{-1.315068 + 2\sqrt{(.432351) - (.315068)(-.041667)}}{.315068}$$

$$= .0629 \equiv 6.29\%$$

HOLDING PERIOD RETURN

Take the case of an investor who buys a bill at a discount rate of d_1, when there are T_{m1} days left to maturity, and sells it at a discount rate of d_2, when there are T_{m2} days left to maturity. The holding period return is given by:

$$\text{HPR} = \frac{(P_2 - P_1)}{P_1} \times \frac{365}{(T_{m1} - T_{m2})}$$

$$= \frac{\left(1 - d_2 \times \dfrac{T_{m2}}{360}\right) - \left(1 - d_1 \times \dfrac{T_{m1}}{360}\right)}{\left(1 - d_1 \times \dfrac{T_{m1}}{360}\right)} \times \frac{365}{(T_{m1} - T_{m2})}$$

$$= \frac{(d_1 T_{m1} - d_2 T_{m2})}{360 - d_1 T_{m1}} \times \frac{365}{(T_{m1} - T_{m2})}$$

On a 360-day basis, we would state the equivalent return as:

$$= \frac{(d_1 T_{m1} - d_2 T_{m2})}{360 - d_1 T_{m1}} \times \frac{360}{(T_{m1} - T_{m2})}$$

EXAMPLE 5.11

A bill with 180 days to maturity is bought at a yield of 6%. It is sold 30 days later at a yield of 5.80%. The holding period return is:

$$\text{HPR} = \frac{(0.06 \times 180 - 0.0580 \times 150)}{360 - 0.06 \times 180} \times \frac{365}{30} = 0.0732 \equiv 7.32\%$$

VALUE OF AN 01

Money market participants are always interested to know the price sensitivity of a security with respect to changes in the yield. In particular, they seek to know how much the price would change if the yield were to change by 1 basis point.

For a T-bill this is given by:

$$P_{01} = 0.0001 \times V \times \frac{T_m}{360}$$

Consider the bill with 90 days to maturity that is quoting at 5%.

$$P_{01} = 0.0001 \times 1,000,000 \times \frac{90}{360} = \$25$$

CONCEPT OF CARRY

The term *carry* may be defined as:[7] "The interest income received on the security being financed minus the interest expense incurred in financing the security."

The carry may be positive or negative.

CONCEPT OF A TAIL

What is a *tail*? Trading-glossary.com defines a tail as follows: "Calculating the yield at which a future money market security (one available some period hence) is purchased when that future security is created by buying an existing instrument and financing the initial portion of its life with a Term repo."

A term repo is a collateralized loan that is usually backed by a government security. We will study it in detail shortly. Here is an illustration.

EXAMPLE 5.12

Stanley & Co., a brokerage house in New York, is funding the acquisition of a 108-day bill using a 45-day term repo. The quoted rate for the bill is 4.8% while the rate for the repo is 4.56%. The initial cost of the bill is:

$$1,000,000 \left[1 - 0.048 \times \frac{108}{360} \right]$$

$$= 985,600$$

---

[7]See Stigum and Robinson (1996).

The funding cost is:

$$985,600 \times 0.0456 \times \frac{45}{360}$$

$$= 5,617.92$$

At the end of 45 days the brokerage house will be holding 63-day bills. The cost of this bill is:

$$985,600 + 5,617.92 = \$991,217.92$$

This corresponds to a dollar discount of \$8,782.08, which translates into a discount rate of:

$$\frac{8,782.08}{1,000,000} \times \frac{360}{63}$$

$$= 0.050183 \equiv 5.0183\%$$

Thus, the transaction would be attractive from the brokerage house's standpoint only if it were to be of the view that the 63-day bill could be sold 45 days hence at a discount rate that is lower than 5.0183%.

T-BILL RELATED FUNCTIONS IN EXCEL

If we are given the discount yield and the time till maturity of a T-bill, we can compute its price using the TBILLPRICE function. Conversely, if we are given the price, we can compute the discount yield using the DISC function in Excel. For a T-bill we can use the TBILLYIELD function to compute the money market yield, and the TBILLEQ function to compute the bond equivalent yield. As discussed earlier, there are two formulas for computing the bond equivalent yield, and Excel will automatically use the appropriate formula, depending on whether the bill has less or more than 182 days till maturity. We will now illustrate these functions with suitable examples.

TBILLPRICE

The required parameters are:

- Settlement: This is the settlement date, which has to be entered in the YYYYM-MDD format using the DATE function.
- Maturity: This is the maturity date, which too has to be entered using the DATE function.
- Discount: This is the quoted yield.

EXAMPLE 5.13

The settlement date is 10 May 2021, and the maturity date is 21 July 2021. The quoted yield is 1.60%. The price may be computed as follows.

TBILLPRICE(Date(2021,05,10),Date(2021,07,21),0.016) = 99.68

This may be verified as follows. The time till maturity is $21 + 30 + 21 = 72$. $72/360 = 0.20$.

The price per $100 of face value is $100 \times (1 - 0.016 \times 0.20) = 99.68$.

TBILLYIELD

The required parameters are:

- Settlement
- Maturity
- Pr: This is the price per hundred dollars of face value

For the bill that we just considered: TBILLYIELD(Date(2021,05,10),Date(2021,07, 21),99.68) = 0.0160514 = 1.60514% per annum. This can be verified as follows. The discount is 0.32. Thus the money market yield is $(0.32/99.68) \times (360/72) = 1.6051\%$.

TBILLEQ

This function is used for computing the bond equivalent yield. The parameters are:

- Settlement
- Maturity
- Discount

TBILLEQ(Date(2021,05,10),Date(2021,07,21),0.016) = 1.62743.

Because the bill has less than 182 days till maturity the bond equivalent yield is equal to the money market yield multiplied by 365/360.

$$1.6051 \times (365 \div 360) = 1.6274$$

DISC

This function is used for computing the quoted yield given the price. The parameters are:

- Settlement
- Maturity
- Pr
- Redemption
- Basis

The price is per $100 of face value and so the redemption value should be given as 100. The basis represents the day-count convention. For the Actual/360 convention it is 2.

Assume the price for the bill discussed above is 96.60. What is the corresponding discount rate?

$$DISC(Date(2021\ 05\ 10), Date(2021\ 07\ 21), 99.6, 100, 2) = 0.02$$

This can be verified as follows. The discount is 0.40:

$$(0.40/100) \times (360/72) = 0.02$$

TREASURY AUCTIONS

Bills are arranged in descending order from the highest price, if it is a price-based auction, or in ascending order from the lowest yield, if it is a yield-based auction. All competitive bids are required to be submitted to three decimal places. The minimum denomination for T-bills is $100, and bills are issued in multiples of $100 thereafter. Noncompetitive bidders cannot submit bids for bills with a face value in excess of $5MM. No competitive bidder can be awarded more than 35% of the amount on offer. The highest yield at which some bills are awarded is called the stop-out yield or high yield. No investor who has bid more than the stop-out yield will be awarded any bills. Once bills are acquired by successful bidders, however, many of them will be sold right away in the secondary market. This will afford the unsuccessful bidders a second chance to acquire the bills. All bills are these days being issued only in book-entry form. In other words, a computerized record of ownership is maintained in Washington D.C. and at the Federal Reserve banks, and no physical certificates are issued.

TYPES OF AUCTIONS

There are two types of auctions, uniform price/yield auctions and discriminatory price/yield auctions. We will illustrate the difference between the two with the help of an example.

EXAMPLE 5.14

Assume that four bids, shown in Table 5.3, have been received by the Treasury, which is auctioning $10 billion worth of securities. Assume that no noncompetitive bids have been received.

Obviously, Alfred and Chris will get 100% of the quantities sought by them. When it comes to David, however, the Treasury will have only $2bn left to allot. Thus, he will get 50% of the quantity sought by him. The stop-out yield or high yield in this case is 1.275%. Paula will get no securities and therefore is said to be *shut out* of the auction.

(continued)

(continued)

TABLE 5.3   Bids in Ascending Order of Yield

Bidder	Bid	Amount in bn.
Alfred	1.245	4.00
Chris	1.260	4.00
David	1.275	4.00
Paula	1.280	2.50

In the case of a discriminatory auction, each of the successful bidders will be allotted securities at his bid. Thus, Alfred will have to pay based on a discount rate of 1.245%, Chris at a rate of 1.260%, and David at a rate of 1.275%. However, in the case of a uniform price/yield auction, all successful bidders will be allotted at the market clearing yield, which in this case is 1.275%. Obviously, those who have bid less will have no objections to accepting a higher yield.

RESULTS OF AN AUCTION

On 23 April 2009, the Treasury issued 91-day bills with a maturity date of 23 July 2009. The high yield was 0.135%. All bids at lower yields were accepted in full. The high yield corresponds to a price of:

$$100 - 100 \times 0.00135 \times \frac{91}{360} = \$99.965875$$

The bond equivalent yield corresponding to this price is:

$$\frac{(100 - 99.965875)}{99.965875} \times \frac{365}{91}$$

$$= 0.00137 \equiv 0.137\%$$

The median rate was 0.11%. That is, 50% of the amount of accepted competitive bids was tendered at or below this rate. The low rate was 0.050%. That is, 5% of the amount of accepted competitive tenders was tendered at or below this rate. At the high rate, 59.26% of the quantity demanded at that rate was awarded.

The total competitive bids were for $85,359,617,000. The amount accepted was $26,110,257,000. The total noncompetitive bids were for $1,889,862,600. All noncompetitive bids were accepted in full. The total bids, both competitive and noncompetitive taken together, were for $87,249,479,600, and the total amount accepted was $28,000,119,600. The ratio of what was sought to what was eventually awarded is called the bid to cover ratio. In this case it was:

$$87,249,479,600/28,000,119,600 = 3.116$$

Of the total competitive bids, bids for $72,064,000,000 were received from primary dealers, a topic to which we will turn next.

PRIMARY DEALERS AND OPEN MARKET OPERATIONS

The money market depends heavily on the buying and selling activities of securities dealers. The term *primary dealer* simply means that the dealer firm is qualified to trade securities directly with the Federal Reserve Bank of New York.

The significance of the New York Fed may be understood as follows. The Federal Reserve periodically conducts open market operations. Such operations refer to the buying and selling of securities in the secondary market, as an instrument of monetary policy. The acquisition of government securities by the Fed adds reserves to the banking system, while the sale of such securities is tantamount to a depletion of reserves. The decisions pertaining to such operations are taken by a body known as the Federal Open Market Committee (FOMC). The New York Fed is permanently represented on this body, because New York is the world's largest money market, and all decisions taken by the FOMC are ultimately implemented by the New York Fed.

Primary dealers may be commercial banks or brokerage houses. Foreign-owned institutions are permitted to be primary dealers in the United States. All primary dealers must have a minimum level of capital. These norms are imposed to ensure that such dealers are in a position to undertake large-scale transactions with the Fed. Primary dealers are required to participate actively in both open market operations and fresh Treasury auctions. They are also expected to serve as a source of information for the Fed from the standpoint of formulating and implementing monetary policy.

REPURCHASE AGREEMENTS

Securities dealers need to fund their security purchases, whose values are far in excess of what their own funds will permit. One source of funds is demand loans from the banking sector. Another source is a repurchase agreement, or repo. Under such an arrangement, the dealer sells securities to a lender with a concomitant commitment to buy back the securities at a later date at the original sale price plus interest. Thus, a repo is nothing but a borrowing arrangement that is collateralized by marketable securities. Many repos are overnight transactions; that is, the funds are returned in exchange for the collateral on the following business day. Longer-term repos for a fixed length of time are referred to as *term repos. Continuing contracts* are repos that carry no explicit maturity date but may be terminated on short notice by either party. Lending institutions find the repo market to be a relatively convenient and low-risk outlet for investing short-term cash surpluses.

Repos were first introduced by the Federal Reserve as a tool for conducting open market operations to regulate the supply of money in the economy.[8] While securities dealers undertake such transactions to fund their positions, the FED uses them as a monetary policy tool. Today, repos are a major constituent of money market operations worldwide in both developed capital markets and markets in emerging economies. The securities used in repo transactions are typically government securities such as T-bills and T-bonds. However, highly rated corporate debt securities may also be pledged as collateral. Here is an example of a repurchase transaction.

---

[8]See Choudhry (2001).

EXAMPLE 5.15

A dealer wishes to borrow by pledging government securities with a face value of $5MM. The current market price is 100-05 and the accrued interest is $2.50 per $100 of face value. Thus, the dirty price of the bond is:

$$5,000,000 \times \frac{\left[100 + \dfrac{5}{32} + 2.5\right]}{100}$$

$$= \$5,132,812.50$$

The loan carries an interest of 4.8% per annum and is repayable after 45 days. Thus, the amount payable at maturity, when the collateral is taken back, is:

$$5,132,812.50 \times \left[1 + \frac{4.8}{100} \times \frac{45}{360}\right] = \$5,132,812.50 + 30,796.875$$

$$= \$5,163,609.375$$

REVERSE REPOS

Buyers of bonds enter into repo agreements to fund their purchases. The lender receives what is known as *general collateral*, which implies that the securities pledged are indistinguishable from the point of view of their function as collateral. The advantage for the lender is that the transaction constitutes a secured loan, with a return that is at times higher than what is available on a bank deposit. Because repos constitute a secured transaction, the general collateral rate is below the prevailing LIBOR, and often below the prevailing LIBID.

The motivation for the party lending money is the following. When entering into a short sale transaction, the party will require bonds for delivery and will also have cash for investment. A reverse repo is a mechanism for investing the cash and simultaneously acquiring the security required for delivery. If the bond desired by the lender of cash is in short supply or is what is termed in market parlance as *being on special*, then the repo rate, or the rate paid by the borrower of funds, may be considerably below the rate for transactions backed by general collateral. From the standpoint of the securities seller, the cash received can usually be invested at a rate higher than the repo rate, particularly when the collateral is on special.

As can be seen, from the perspective of the borrower of cash, such transactions are termed as repos, whereas from the point of view of the lender of cash they are termed as reverse repos. Market makers engage in both kinds of transactions. A dealer in search of cash will do a repo while a dealer in search of securities will do a reverse repo.

A bond-trading house may acquire bonds by financing its purchase via a repurchase transaction. The acquired securities will be sold with an agreement for future repurchase, and the proceeds obtained will be used to pay off the party who sold the bonds to the trading house. The scheduled repurchase of the bonds can be timed to coincide with the sale of bonds to other investors at a profit by the trading house, assuming that the anticipated decline in yield were to materialize.

GENERAL COLLATERAL VERSUS SPECIAL REPOS

The rate on a repo is a function of the underlying security pledged as collateral. Most issues are viewed as *general collateral*; that is, they are perceived as being close substitutes for each other, and consequently the repo rate for transactions backed by such securities is the same for all securities in this category. There could be, however, other securities for which the repo rate may be lower and, as discussed, such securities are said to be on special. Unlike the general collateral rate, which is common for all securities in that class, special repo rates are issue specific. Consequently, different issues on special will have their own associated repo rates.

Why would a security be on special? A party may require a specific security because he needs to cover a short position in it, or perhaps requires it for delivery under a futures contract – if the security in question has become the cheapest to deliver. You will understand the concept of the cheapest to deliver security when we study futures contracts in the next chapter. In such cases, the security being offered is not just collateral; it is the prime motivation for the transaction. Thus, the repo rate in these cases is a function of the demand and supply for the security and, if it is in short supply, the repo rate could be considerably less than the general collateral rate.

MARGINS

In principle, both the parties to a repo face credit risk. From the standpoint of the lender, the risk is that the collateral may decline in value due to an increase in the yield and may prove to be insufficient to recover the investment if the borrower were to default. From the borrower's perspective, the risk is that the collateral may appreciate in value due to a fall in the yield, and the lender may consequently be reluctant to return it in order to reclaim his cash.

There is no strategy that will simultaneously reduce the risk for both parties. Lenders can protect themselves by seeking margins. That is, they may lend an amount that is less than the current market value of the securities. The higher the margin, the greater will be the protection. Borrowers, in principle, can protect themselves by seeking a reverse margin. That is, they can demand a loan amount that is in excess of the market value of the collateral. Clearly, both parties cannot protect themselves at the same time. In practice, it is the lender who receives margin. The rationale is that the lender is giving away a more liquid asset, as cash is always more liquid than any security that is offered as collateral for the loan.

Thus, to protect the lender from the specter of an under-collateralized loan, the borrower is required to provide securities with a market value in excess of the amount of money borrowed. The difference between the market value of the securities and the loan amount is called the margin, or *haircut*. The size of the haircut depends on the following factors.

- The credit quality of the collateral
- The time to maturity of the collateral
- The term to maturity of the repo

In practice the lender will set a threshold level for the value of the collateral called the *maintenance margin* level. If the securities were to fall in value and a situation were to arise where their current market value is lower than the maintenance level, the borrower will be required to provide additional securities with a market value sufficient to make up the deficit. On the other hand, if the securities were to rise in value, the borrower may ask for extra cash or a partial return of collateral.

There are two ways in which the haircut can be applied, as Example 5.16 illustrates.

EXAMPLE 5.16

(Initial Margins)

A pension fund that is prepared to offer bonds with a face value of $25 MM enters into a three-day repurchase agreement with a bank. The collateral is T-bonds with a coupon of 6% and a market price of $95 per $100 of face value. The haircut is 1.25%. Accrued interest is $2 per $100 of face value. The repo rate is 7.50% per annum.

The loan amount may be calculated in either of two ways.

$$1. \text{Method-1: Loan amount} = 25,000,000 \times \frac{97}{100} \times 0.9875$$

$$= \$23,946,875$$

$$2. \text{Method-2: Loan amount} = 25,000,000 \times \frac{97}{101.25}$$

$$= \$23,950,617.28$$

Thus, if x is the percentage of the haircut, the lender may either multiply the dirty price by $1 - x$, or else divide it by $1 + x$.

Both are acceptable methods of applying a haircut, and it is up to the lender to choose the method that he wishes to adopt. The amount of the loan and the amount to be repaid will obviously depend on the method adopted.

The amount repayable at maturity is, assuming that method-1 is used to compute the loan amount:

$$23,946,875 \left[1 + 0.075 \times \frac{3}{360} \right] = \$23,961,841.80$$

SALE AND BUYBACK

In a standard repurchase transaction, or what is termed as a *classic repo*, the price at which the collateral is sold is the same as the price at which it is repurchased, as the interest is separately computed and paid. Of course, the amount that is repaid at maturity will be greater than the loan amount, because it will incorporate the interest in addition to the principal. Any coupons paid on the underlying collateral during the life of the repo will be handed over to the borrower as and when they are received by the lender. This is because, although technically borrowers cease to be the legal owners they continue to be the beneficial owners.

In a sale and buyback transaction too, the securities are sold at the outset accompanied with an agreement for forward repurchase. Thus, such a transaction also entails the transfer of ownership; however, there are some critical differences between the two transactions. Unlike a repo, which is technically a single transaction, a sale and buyback is a combination of two distinct cash market trades. Sale and buyback does not involve the maintenance of margins. Thus, there is no requirement on the part of the borrower to provide additional collateral if the security were to decline in value. Clearly, there is greater credit risk for the lender in such circumstances. Second, unlike in the case of a classic repo where any coupons paid during the life of the transaction are immediately passed on to the borrower, in a sale and buyback transaction, the coupon is factored into the price at which the security is repurchased. Third, classic repos often allow substitution of securities; that is, the borrower can substitute the collateral that was initially offered with a similar security. Sale and buyback transactions do not have a clause for substitutions. Finally, repos are covered by standard legal contracts developed by the industry. There is, however, no such standard documentation for sale and buyback deals. From the standpoint of the borrower, such a transaction is referred to as a sale and buyback, whereas from the perspective of the lender, it is termed as buy and sell-back transaction.

COLLATERAL

The securities that are offered as collateral should be placed in a custodial account at a bank. When the loan is repaid, the borrower's liability will be canceled and the securities will be returned to him. This method ensures safety for the party who is lending. However, it was found that dealers were not always following this norm. This led to a situation in the United States where many depository institutions lost money because the dealers who borrowed from them went out of business, and they could not easily take possession of the collateral. Subsequently, the federal authorities have imposed strict guidelines for dealers entering into such transactions.

REPOS AND OPEN MARKET OPERATIONS

The Federal Reserve undertakes repurchase and reverse repurchase transactions with primary dealers. These transactions constitute an important component of the monetary policy instruments employed by the Fed. A repo represents a collateralized loan made by the Fed to primary dealers. Thus, repos are used by dealers to borrow funds from the Fed. On the other hand, a reverse repo transaction entails the borrowing of funds by the Fed from the primary dealers. Typically, these are overnight transactions, but the Fed can undertake operations with longer terms to maturity.

From a monetary policy standpoint, a repo temporarily adds reserve balances to the banking system, while a reverse repo transaction temporarily drains such balances from the system. However, this is only true for transactions involving the central bank. Transactions not involving the central bank do not affect total reserves in the banking system.

Repurchase and reverse agreements are operations that are undertaken by the trading desk at the New York Fed, which in turn implements monetary policy decisions taken by the Federal Open Market Committee (FOMC). When the Fed does a repo, funds are credited to the dealer's commercial bank. This enhances the level of reserves in the banking system. At maturity, in return for the amount lent plus interest, the Fed transfers the collateral back to the dealer. This automatically neutralizes the extra reserves that were created by the original transaction. Thus, such operations that are undertaken by the Fed have a short-term, self-reversing effect on bank reserves.

Reverse repos are similar from the standpoint of their impact on reserves. In such transactions, the Fed sends collateral to the dealer's clearing bank, in return for the funds. This action reduces the availability of reserves in the banking system. At the time of maturity of the contract, the dealer returns the collateral back to the Fed, which then returns with interest the funds that were initially borrowed. This automatically restores the reserves reduced by the original transaction.

NEGOTIABLE CDs

A CD is an interest-bearing receipt for funds left with a depository institution for short periods of time. CDs are usually issued at par and pay interest explicitly, although banks also issue discount CDs that are similar to T-bills in structure. Payment is made in federal funds on the day of maturity. Banks and other institutions issue many types of CDs, but true money market CDs are negotiable instruments that can be resold before maturity and are typically issued with a face value of $1MM. CDs issued to retail investors are nonnegotiable and consequently not classified as money market instruments. CDs issued in the United States, and Eurodollar CDs, usually have an original maturity that is less than or equal to one year and pay interest at maturity. The day-count convention is Actual/360, and the rate of interest is referred to as the coupon rate. The interest rate on a money market CD is slightly less than that on a standard time deposit of the same tenor, because the instrument is negotiable.

NOTATION

$N \equiv$ the number of days from the time of issue till the time of maturity, which is the original term to maturity or OTM

$T_m \equiv$ the number of days from the settlement date till the maturity date, which is the actual term to maturity or ATM

$c \equiv$ the coupon rate

$y \equiv$ quoted yield

$V \equiv$ the face value of the CD or the principal amount

$P \equiv$ the dirty price of the CD

The amount payable at maturity is given by:

$$V \times \left[1 + c \times \frac{N}{360}\right]$$

In Example 5.17 we demonstrate the computation of the maturity value. Example 5.18 illustrates how to compute the yield given the price, while Example 5.19 illustrates the converse.

EXAMPLE 5.17

Consider a CD with 180 days to maturity that has just been issued with a face value of $1MM and a coupon rate of 4.5%. The amount that the holder will receive at maturity is equal to:

$$1{,}000{,}000 \times \left[1 + 0.045 \times \frac{180}{360}\right]$$

$$= 1{,}022{,}500$$

Quoted yields on CDs are yields on a simple interest basis. Thus, if the dirty price of the CD is $P, then the quoted yield y is given by:

$$y = \left(\frac{V \times \left[1 + c \times \dfrac{N}{360}\right] - P}{P}\right) \times \frac{360}{T_m}$$

EXAMPLE 5.18

A CD with an original term to maturity of 180 days and a face value of $1,000,000 was issued with a coupon rate of 4.80%. The current term to maturity is 144 days, and the CD is quoting at a price of $1,000,000. What is the corresponding yield?

The maturity value is given by:

$$1{,}000{,}000 \times \left[1 + 0.048 \times \frac{180}{360}\right]$$

$$= \$1{,}024{,}000$$

(continued)

(*continued*)

The yield is given by:

$$\frac{(1,024,000 - 1,000,000)}{1,000,000} \times \frac{360}{144}$$

$$= 0.06 \equiv 6\%$$

If we are given the yield, we can obviously compute the price. The expression for the price is given by:

$$y \times \frac{T_m}{360} = \frac{V \times \left[1 + c \times \frac{N}{360}\right]}{P} - 1$$

$$\Rightarrow P = \frac{V \times \left[1 + c \times \frac{N}{360}\right]}{\left[1 + y \times \frac{T_m}{360}\right]}$$

EXAMPLE 5.19

A CD with an original term to maturity of 180 days and a face value of $1,000,000 was issued with a coupon of 5.2%. The current term to maturity is 108 days, and the quoted yield is 5.6%. What is the dirty price?

$$P = \frac{1,000,000 \times \left[1 + 0.052 \times \frac{180}{360}\right]}{\left[1 + 0.056 \times \frac{108}{360}\right]}$$

$$= \frac{1,026,000}{1.0168} = \$1,009,048$$

The price of the CD can be decomposed into the clean price plus the accrued interest. The accrued interest on CDs is given by:

$$AI = V \times c \times \frac{N - T_m}{360}$$

In the above example, the accrued interest is given by:

$$1,000,000 \times 0.052 \times \frac{(180 - 108)}{360}$$

$$= \$10,4000$$

Thus, the clean price is 1,009,048 − 10,400 = $998,648.

COST OF A CD FOR THE ISSUING BANK

The actual cost of a CD from the standpoint of an issuing bank is usually greater than the coupon rate. There are two reasons for this. First, in most cases banks have to maintain reserves. Second, bank deposits are often insured up to specified amounts. The effect of these factors may best be illustrated with the help of an example.

EXAMPLE 5.20

Bank Alpha has issued a CD with a coupon of 6.3%. The bank has to maintain 10% reserves with the central bank, which are non-interest-bearing. Thus, if the bank were to raise a deposit of $100, it would be paying 6.3% interest on $90 of usable money. This automatically raises the effective cost of the deposit to:

$$\frac{6.30}{90} = 0.07 \equiv 7\%$$

Assume that the bank has to pay an insurance premium of 7.5 b.p. The overall cost of the deposit is therefore:

$$0.07 + 0.00075 = 0.07075 \equiv 7.075\%$$

TERM CDs

Term CDs have a maturity in excess of one year at the time of issue, and usually pay coupons on a semiannual basis. The price of the instrument is the present value of all the cash flows to be received from it, as of the settlement date, where the discounting is done using the quoted yield. The procedure is analogous to the valuation of a bond, where the coupons and the face value are discounted at the YTM, with certain differences.

First, the amount of interest in a coupon period is not $\frac{c \times V}{2}$ as in the case of a bond. The interest in this case is given by:

$$\text{Interest} = c \times V \times \frac{N_i}{360}$$

where N_i is the number of days in the ith coupon period. Thus, the coupon will vary from period to period.

The second difference is that we do not discount the kth cash flow by $\left(1 + \frac{y}{2}\right)^k$ where y is the YTM of the security. In the case of term CDs, the discounting is based on the actual number of days in the coupon period and is effected on a simple interest basis. We will illustrate the valuation of a term CD with the help of an example.

EXAMPLE 5.21

A CD with a coupon rate of 4.8% was issued on 1 July 2019. It is scheduled to mature on 30 June 2021. On 1 September 2019 the quoted yield is 5%. What should be its current price?

The first step is to calculate the number of days in each coupon period as well as the number of days from the date of settlement to the first coupon. The length of each period is given in Table 5.4.

TABLE 5.4 Day-Counts for Valuing the Term CD

Start Date	End Date	# of Days
1 July 2019	1 January 2020	184
1 January 2020	1 July 2020	181
1 July 2020	1 January 2021	184
1 January 2021	30 June 2021	180
1 September 2019	1 January 2020	122

To value the security, we start with the cash flow at maturity. This is discounted back to the penultimate coupon date. The coupon payment at this point of time is added to the present value obtained in the previous step. The sum is then discounted back to the previous coupon date. This procedure is repeated until we reach the settlement date.

In our example, the cash flow at maturity is:

$$1,000,000 \times \left[1 + 0.048 \times \frac{180}{360}\right] = \$1,024,000$$

The present value of this on 1 January 2021 is:

$$\frac{1,024,000}{\left[1 + 0.05 \times \frac{180}{360}\right]}$$

$$= 999,024.39$$

The coupon due on 1 January 2021 is:

$$1,000,000 \times 0.048 \times \frac{184}{360} = 24,533.33$$

The amount to be discounted to the previous coupon date is:

$$999,024.39 + 24,533.33 = \$1,023,557.72$$

The present value on 1 July 2020 is:

$$\frac{1,023,557.72}{\left[1 + 0.05 \times \dfrac{184}{360}\right]}$$

$$= 998,051.95$$

The coupon due on 1 July 2020 is:

$$1,000,000 \times 0.048 \times \frac{181}{360} = 24,133.33$$

The amount to be discounted to the previous coupon date is:

$$998,051.95 + 24,133.33 = \$1,022,185.28$$

The present value on 1 January 2020 is:

$$\frac{1,022,185.28}{\left[1 + 0.05 \times \dfrac{181}{360}\right]}$$

$$= 997,118.82$$

The coupon due on 1 January 2020 is:

$$1,000,000 \times 0.048 \times \frac{184}{360} = 24,533.33$$

The amount to be discounted to the settlement date is:

$$997,118.82 + 24,533.33 = \$1,021,652.15$$

The present value on 1 September 2019 is:

$$\frac{1,021,652.15}{\left[1 + 0.05 \times \dfrac{122}{360}\right]}$$

$$= 1,004,629.27$$

This is the dirty price of the CD as of 1 September 2019. The accrued interest as of this day is:

$$1,000,000 \times 0.048 \times \frac{62}{360} = \$8,266.67$$

Thus, the clean price is:

$$1,004,629.27 - 8,266.67 = \$996,362.60$$

The interest rate on a large negotiable CD is set by negotiations between the issuing institution and its customer and generally reflects prevailing market conditions. Thus, like the rates on other money market securities, rates rise in periods when funds are hard to come by and fall in periods characterized by easy availability of funds.

For the issuing banks, CDs increase the average cost of funds as well as their volatility; however, banks have no choice but to offer such instruments because otherwise they face the specter of lost business. The cash management departments of major corporations have become increasingly aware of the various profitable outlets for their short-term surpluses. Prior to the introduction of the negotiable CD, banks found that their biggest corporate customers were reducing their deposits and buying T-bills, repos, and other money market instruments. The negotiable CD was developed in order to attract the lost deposits back into the banking system.

CDs VERSUS MONEY MARKET TIME DEPOSITS

In the case of a conventional time deposit, investors will deposit a sum of money with a bank for a stated period of time. They will be paid interest at a specified rate. At the end of the deposit period, they can withdraw the original sum deposited plus the interest. In the case of a CD, however, depositors will be typically issued a bearer security. While they are entitled to claim the deposit with interest at the end of the deposit period, they can always sell the security prior to maturity in the secondary market. In the process, ownership of the underlying deposit will be transferred from sellers to buyers. CDs have one major advantage over a conventional money market deposit, namely liquidity. A money market deposit cannot be easily terminated until it matures. If investors wish to withdraw the funds prior to maturity, they will often have to pay a penalty in terms of a lower rate of interest. In contrast, CDs can be liquidated at any time at the prevailing market rate. Thus, these instruments are attractive for investors who seek the high interest rates offered by time deposits but who are reluctant to commit their money for the full term of the deposit.

COMMERCIAL PAPER

Every year several large corporations borrow billions of dollars in the money market through the sale of unsecured promissory notes known as commercial paper. Such instruments are issued by large corporations and bought principally by other large corporations. In terms of volumes issued and traded, such paper is the single largest instrument issued in the US money market.

By definition, such paper consists of short-term unsecured promissory notes issued by well-known companies that are financially strong and carry high credit ratings. The word *unsecured* connotes that the issuer is not pledging any collateral to back these securities, and that buyers can only depend of the liquidity and earning power of the issuer from the standpoint of repayment. The funds raised in this manner are normally used for current account transactions, such as purchase of raw materials, payment of accrued taxes, meeting wage and salary obligations, and other short-term expenditure, rather than for capital account transactions or, in other words, long-term investments. These days, however, a substantial number of paper issues are used to provide *bridge financing* for long-term projects. This works as follows. If the prevailing interest rates in the market are high, a company may issue commercial paper to fund a long-term investment. Subsequently, if rates decline as anticipated, long-term debt can be issued to retire the existing paper. In these instances, issuing companies usually plan to convert their short-term paper into more permanent financing when the capital market looks more favorable.

Most issuers of paper enjoy a high credit rating; however, to reduce investor risk, borrowers nearly always secure a line of credit at a commercial bank for a small fee or in return for a compensating deposit. But the line of credit cannot be used to directly guarantee payment if the company goes bankrupt, and the bank may renege on the credit line if it perceives the borrower's credit quality has significantly deteriorated. Thus, many issuers also take out irrevocable letters of credit prepared by their banks. Such a letter of credit makes a bank unconditionally responsible for repayment if the corporation defaults on its paper.

LETTERS OF CREDIT AND BANK GUARANTEES

A letter of credit (LC) is a document issued by a bank, called the issuer or opener, at the behest of a client, referred to as the applicant, in favor of a named beneficiary, declaring that it will effect payment of a stated sum of money for certain specified good or services, against presentation of a predefined set of documents. Such instruments are very common in international trade transactions, although they may be occasionally used for domestic deals as well. There are two categories of LCs: commercial LCs and standby LCs. The first type of LC is used to cover the movement of goods, whereas standby LCs are used for other financial arrangements. While a commercial LC is a direct instrument of payment, a standby LC is a guarantee that is invoked only if there is default in the primary settlement process or performance, including the failure to pay.[9]

Another instrument used to provide reassurance to a beneficiary is what is known as a bank guarantee. There is, however, a difference between the two instruments from the standpoint of the position of the bank relative to the applicant and the beneficiary. A letter of credit is a bank's direct undertaking to the beneficiary. That is, when the shipment of goods occurs under a letter of credit, the issuing bank does not wait for the buyer to default or, in other words, for the seller to invoke the undertaking, before making the payment to the beneficiary. On the other hand, a bank guarantee is an undertaking stating that in the event of the inability or unwillingness of the buyer to make payments to the seller, the bank, as the guarantor to the transaction, would pay the supplier. Thus, a bank guarantee comes into play only when the buyer fails to pay the supplier. In this case, the supplier is expected to first seek to have the claim honored by the buyer and not the bank. Thus, a bank guarantee is a contingent guarantee. In the case of an LC, however, the principal liability is that of the issuing bank. It must first pay on submission of the predefined set of documents and then collect the amount from its client. Thus, an LC substitutes the bank's creditworthiness for that of its client.

---

[9]See Bose (2006).

Hence, a bank guarantee is riskier for the supplier and less risky for the bank. An LC is less risky for the seller, but riskier for the bank. In both cases, however, the bank accepts full liability for the specified amount.

What then is a standby letter of credit? A standby LC is a written obligation on the part of the issuing bank to pay the beneficiary on behalf of its client, if the client does not pay the beneficiary. This sounds very much like the definition of a conventional bank guarantee. So is there a difference between the two? The answer is that in certain countries, banking legislation forbids depository institutions from assuming guarantee obligations of third parties. To overcome this legal hurdle, banks have created the instrument known as the standby LC, which is based on the uniform customs and practices for documentary credits (UCPDC), the protocol that applies for standard LCs.

There are two major types of commercial paper: direct paper and dealer paper. The main issuers of direct paper are large finance companies and bank holding companies that deal directly with the investors, rather than using securities dealers as an intermediary. Such companies, which regularly extend installment credit to consumers and large working capital loans and leases to business firms, announce the rates they are currently paying on various maturities of their paper. Investors select maturities that most closely match their expected holding periods and buy the securities directly from the issuer. Such borrowers have an ongoing need for huge amounts of short-term money, possess top credit ratings, and have established working relationships with major institutional investors in order to place new issues regularly.

Directly placed paper must be sold in large volume to cover the substantial costs of distribution and marketing. Issuers of direct paper do not have to pay dealers' commissions, but they must operate a marketing division to maintain constant contact with active investors. These companies also have to pay fees to banks for supporting lines of credit, to rating agencies that rate their issues, and to agents such as trust companies that collect funds and disburse payments.

The other major variety of commercial paper is dealer paper issued by security dealers on behalf of their corporate customers. Dealer paper is issued mainly by firms that borrow less frequently than companies that issue direct paper. The issuing company may sell the paper directly to the dealer, who will buy it less a discount and commissions, and then resell it at the highest possible price in the market. Alternatively, the issuing company may bear all the risk, with the dealer agreeing only to sell the issue at the best price available less commissions. This is referred to as a best-efforts transaction.

One reason for the market's rapid growth is the high quality of most paper. Many investors regard such paper as a high-quality substitute for T-bills and other money market instruments. The second factor is the expanding use of credit enhancements in the form of standby letters of credit, indemnity bonds, and other irrevocable payment guarantees. Such paper usually carries the higher credit rating of the guarantor rather than the lower credit rating of the issuer. Consequently, despite paying the guarantor's fee, the issuer can still save on interest costs.

YANKEE PAPER

Paper that is issued in the United States by foreign firms is called Yankee paper. Foreign issuers find that they can often issue Yankee paper at a cheaper rate than what it would cost them to borrow outside the United States. Foreign borrowers, however, must generally pay higher interest costs than US companies of comparable credit rating. That is, Yankee paper generally carries a higher yield than US paper of the same credit quality. This is because an American investor will demand higher returns considering the difficulty of gathering information on a foreign firm.

There are several advantages for companies with good ratings that are in a position to tap the paper market. Generally, rates on high-quality paper are less than on bank loans. Moreover, the effective rate on bank loans is even higher than what is quoted, because corporate borrowers usually are required to keep a percentage of the loan in the form of a deposit with the bank. This compensating balance is generally 15–20% of the loan amount. For instance, if a company borrows 100 MM USD at 8% with a compensating balance of 20%, the effective rate on the loan will be

$$\frac{8,000,000}{80,000,000} \equiv 10\%$$

CREDIT RATING

It is extremely difficult to market unrated paper. Generally, commercial paper bearing ratings from at least two agencies is preferred by investors.

MOODY'S RATING SCALE

Moody's uses the following rating scale for short-term taxable instruments like commercial paper.

Prime-1: Superior ability to repay short-term debt obligations.

Prime-2: Strong ability to repay short-term debt obligations.

Prime-3: Acceptable ability to repay short-term obligations.

Not Prime: These do not fall within any of the prime rating categories.

Prime-1, Prime-2, and Prime-3 are all investment-grade ratings.

S&P'S RATING SCALE

Standard & Poor's rates issues on a scale from A-1 to D. Within the A-1 category an issue can be designated with a plus sign. This indicates that the issuer's ability to meet its obligation is extremely strong. Country risk and currency of repayment of the obligor to meets its obligation are factored into the credit analysis and are reflected in the issue rating.

A-1: Issuer's capacity to meet its financial commitment on the obligation is strong.

A-2: The issuer is susceptible to adverse economic conditions; however, the issuer's capacity to meet its financial commitment is satisfactory.

A-3: Adverse economic conditions are likely to weaken the issuer's capacity to meet its financial commitment on the obligation.

B: Has significant speculative characteristics. The issuer currently has the capacity to meet its financial obligation but faces major ongoing uncertainties that could affect its financial commitment.

C: The issue is currently vulnerable to nonpayment and is dependent upon favorable business, financial, and economic conditions for the obligor to meet its financial commitment.

D: The issue is in payment default. Obligation not made on due date and grace period may not have expired. The rating is also used upon the filing of a bankruptcy petition.

A-1, A-2, and A-3 are all investment-grade ratings.

FITCH'S RATING SCALE

Fitch's short-term ratings indicate the potential level of default within a 12-month period. A "+" or "−" may be appended to the F1 rating to denote relative status within the category.

F1: Best quality grade. Indicates strong capacity of obligor to meet its financial commitment.

F2: Good quality grade. Indicates satisfactory capacity of obligor to meet its financial commitment.

F3: Fair quality grade: Adequate capacity of obligor to meet its financial commitment, but near-term adverse conditions could affect the obligor's commitments.

B: Of speculative nature. Obligor has minimal capacity to meet its commitment and is vulnerable to short-term adverse changes in financial and economic conditions.

C: Possibility of default is high. Financial commitment of the obligor is dependent upon sustained, favorable business and economic conditions.

D: The obligor is in default as it has failed on its financial commitments.

Short-term debt issues given a top-grade credit rating by both S&P and Moody's are referred to as A1/P1 debt. A1/P1 paper will sell at the finest rates.

BILLS OF EXCHANGE

Before we go on to study the nature of a bankers' acceptance, which is a key constituent of the money market, let us first analyze the concept of a bill. As per the English Law of Contracts, the definition of a bill of exchange is:[10] "An unconditional order in writing, addressed by one person to another, signed by the person giving it,

---

[10]See Palat (2006).

requiring the person to whom it is addressed to pay on demand or at a fixed or determinable future time a sum certain in money or to the order of a specified person, or to the bearer."

The parties to a bill are the following.

Drawer: The drawer is the party who makes out the bill of exchange. A bill of exchange is drawn by the person who will be paid.

Drawee: The party who is directed to pay by the drawer. A bill of exchange is always drawn on the person who is ordered to pay. Thus, the drawee is the party who owes the money, and to whom the bill is addressed.

There are two categories of bills of exchange: bank bills and trade bills. A trade bill is drawn by one nonbank company on another, typically demanding payment for a trade debt. A bank bill, on the other hand, is a bill that is drawn on and payable by a commercial bank.

Bills may be classified as sight bills and time, term, or usance bills. A sight bill has to be honored on demand, that is, the drawer is expected to pay on sight. In the case of a term bill, however, the specified amount is payable on a future date that is mentioned on the bill. There are three ways in which the due date for payment of a term bill may be specified.

1. Payment to be made on a stated date.
2. Payment to be made after a stated period after the bill is sighted, where the date of sighting is the date on which the drawee signs on it, indicating his acceptance.
3. Payment to be made after a stated period from the date of the bill.

For a bill with a future payment date, the drawee will sign his acceptance across the face of the bill and return it either to the drawer or to his bank. When such a bill is accepted by the debtor, it becomes a promise to pay or an IOU. Since a bill represents an undertaking to pay a stated amount at a future date, it is a form of short-term finance for the debtor. The holder of the bill therefore effectively gives credit to the debtor, and the accepted bill represents a zero-coupon security.

The drawer may hold the bill until maturity and present it to the drawee for payment, or may sell it in the money market at any time prior to its maturity date. A bill of exchange can thus be transferred by a simple endorsement. An authorized signatory of the drawer will sign the back of the bill and give it to the buyer. The seller of the bill in the secondary market gives up the right to eventual payment on the maturity date, in return for an immediate payment from the person who is acquiring the bill. The purchaser of the bill consequently acquires the right to receive payment on the maturity date. A common feature of the secondary market for all categories of bills is that the market price of the instrument will always be less than the amount that is payable at maturity. Thus, bills are discount instruments that are always traded at a discount to their face values.

The ability of a holder of a bill to sell it at a reasonable price depends on the credit quality of the drawee and on the existence of a liquid secondary market. In the case of trade bills, it would obviously depend on the financial status of the two companies concerned. Financial institutions will buy only the finest trade bills in the market, that is, bills in which both companies have a high credit standing. Bank bills, for obvious reasons, are more easily marketable than most trade bills. The secondary market is provided by banks and other institutions dealing in the money market. Bills are purchased extensively and held as short-term investments by banks and nonbanking institutions, and market makers are able to operate a liquid two-way market for accepted bills.

A bill of exchange is doubly secured. That is, if the drawee fails to honor it on presentation, the holder may look to the drawer for payment. A common form of a bank bill is a bankers' acceptance, whereby a bank accepts a bill on behalf of a customer and promises to pay the bill at maturity.

DOCUMENTS AGAINST PAYMENT (DAP) VERSUS DOCUMENTS AGAINST ACCEPTANCE (DAA) TRANSACTIONS

In the case of a transaction that is based on a sight bill, the buyer or its bank must pay before it will be handed over the shipping documents. These documents are required to take possession of the goods and are termed as bills of lading for shipments by sea, and airway bills for shipments by air. Hence the term *documents against payment*.

If the seller is offering credit to the buyer, however, the buyer or its bank has to sign its acceptance on the document, and the shipping documents will be released immediately. Hence the term *documents against acceptance*.

ELIGIBLE AND NONELIGIBLE BANK BILLS

Bank bills may be classified as eligible or noneligible. The term *eligibility* refers to the willingness of the government to deal in the bills in the secondary market. Thus, an eligible bill is one that the government or government agency will agree to buy. Eligibility depends partly on the bill's original term to maturity. The government will not buy bills with an original term to maturity greater than a specified number of days. Eligibility also depends on the identity of the bank. The government will buy bills of only those banks present on their list of eligible banks. Eligible bank bills are more highly rated and attract smaller and finer rates of discount. In the United States, eligible bank bills are those that the Federal Reserve will be willing to purchase.

BUYING AND SELLING BILLS

A company has drawn a bill on HSBC for $5,000,000 with a maturity of 150 days. The bank has accepted it and the drawer has sold it to Barclays at a discount of 5.25%. Now, 30 days hence, Barclays has sold the bill to ABN Amro at a discount of 4.75%. The rate of return for Barclays may be computed as follows:

The purchase price is given by:

$$5,000,000\left[1 - \frac{5.25}{100} \times \frac{150}{360}\right]$$

$$= \$4,890,625$$

The sale price is given by:

$$5{,}000{,}000 \left[1 - \frac{4.75}{100} \times \frac{120}{360} \right]$$

$$= \$4{,}920{,}833.33$$

The profit is:

$$4{,}920{,}833.33 - 4{,}890{,}625 = \$30{,}208.33\$\$$$

The return on investment on a 360-day year basis is:

$$\frac{30{,}208.33}{4{,}890{,}625} \times \frac{360}{30} \equiv 7.41\%$$

BANKERS' ACCEPTANCE

A bankers' acceptance is a term bill that is drawn on a bank by a seller of merchandise. If the bank honors the bill, it will stamp "Accepted" on its face, thereby signaling its willingness to pay at the end of the stated credit period. A bankers' acceptance is a very popular instrument in international trade transactions because most exporters are uncertain of the credit standing of the importer to whom the goods are being shipped. Such exporters, however, are usually quite content to rely on acceptance financing by a well-reputed domestic or foreign bank.

The creation of a bankers' acceptance may be best illustrated with the help of an example.

EXAMPLE 5.22

IBM is shipping six mainframe computers to Kim and Company in Seoul and is prepared to grant three months' credit to the buyer. The Korean importer will approach their bank in Seoul, First National Bank of Korea, for a line of credit. Once the bank approves a line of credit it will issue a letter of credit (LC) in favor of IBM. The bank in Seoul will send it to its correspondent bank in the United States, known as the advising bank. The advising bank may or may not confirm the LC. If it were to confirm the LC, then IBM can be assured that it will make the payment, even if the Seoul-based importer or the Korean bank were to default. As per the LC, IBM can draw a term bill for a specified amount against the bank, provided that the shipping documents are sent to the bank. On receipt, the bank will check to see that the draft and any accompanying documents are correctly drawn and will then stamp "Accepted" on its face. In this way, a banker's acceptance is created.

In this case, IBM must wait for three months in order to be paid; however, a situation may arise when it needs the funds immediately. It may therefore seek to

(continued)

(*continued*)

have the bill discounted by its bank in the United States. The American bank that has acquired the bill from IBM may hold it as an asset, or sell it in the secondary market. At the end of the stipulated period, which is three months in this case, the party who is holding it at that point in time will present it to the bank in Seoul in return for payment.

When a bank wishes to trade an acceptance in the secondary market, the rate of discount applicable is determined by the current rate on acceptances of similar maturity. The yield on bankers' acceptances is usually only slightly higher than the rate on T-bills because banks that issue such acceptances are normally large and have a good reputation from the standpoint of credit risk. The discount rate on an acceptance is also comparable with the rate on a CD, because both instruments are unconditional obligations of the issuing bank.

Most bankers' acceptances are with recourse transactions. This can be best illustrated with the help of an example.

EXAMPLE 5.23

Fujitsu has sold a high-performance machine to a company in the United States. The corresponding bill has been accepted by First Midland Bank in New York. Fujitsu subsequently gets the bill discounted by Hitachi. When the bill matures, Hitachi approaches the bank for payment, only to find that the bank has failed. If the transaction were to be without recourse, it would be Hitachi's bad luck. However, if it were to be a with-recourse transaction, then Hitachi can demand payment from Fujitsu.

ACCEPTANCE CREDITS

An acceptance credit facility is a form of fundraising option that is made available to a company with the assistance of a commercial bank. In this case, a client of a bank will draw up bills on the bank up to a specified credit limit. The bank will accept the bills, and the drawer can have them discounted in the market to obtain funding. The advantage is that, because a well-known commercial bank has accepted these bills, the drawer can get better terms while having them discounted, due to the higher credit standing of the bank. This is an option for working capital financing for companies in some markets.

EUROCURRENCY DEPOSITS

What is a Eurocurrency? It is a freely convertible currency deposited outside the country to which it belongs. Thus, dollars deposited outside the United States are

Eurodollars. Japanese yen deposited outside Japan are Euroyen. The large majority of such deposits are held in Europe, but these deposits have spread worldwide; Europe's share of the total is declining. Among the most important non-European centers for Eurocurrency trading are the Bahamas, Canada, the Cayman Islands, Hong Kong, Panama, and Singapore.

We will now illustrate how a Eurocurrency deposit arises. Siemens has exported equipment to a party in Dallas and has invoiced in dollars. Subsequently, a bill for 1MM USD is sent to the American party, which pays by issuing a check in US dollars. Let us assume that the check is deposited with Citibank in New York, where Siemens has an account. After the check clears, Siemens' account in New York will be credited with 1MM dollars. Thus, Siemens has a dollar-denominated asset of the same magnitude. This is not, however, a Eurodollar deposit because the deposit of dollars has been placed with a bank in the United States, where the dollar is the official unit of currency.

Assume that a few days later, Siemens decides to transfer the funds to Deutsche Bank in Frankfurt, where it is being offered a better rate of return on a term deposit. Instead of converting the funds into euros, however, it decides to keep them in US dollars. Once the funds are transferred, Siemens will receive a confirmation for a dollar deposit of $1MM from the bank in Frankfurt. But the dollars per se will not be transferred to Europe. Deutsche Bank will have a correspondent bank in the United States, say Wells Fargo, that will be credited with the dollars once the funds are transferred from Citibank.

Now we have a Eurodollar deposit in the form of a $1MM term deposit with Deutsche Bank in Frankfurt. This is because Siemens' deposit has been accepted and recorded on the books of Deutsche Bank in US dollars, although the official currency of Germany is the Euro.

As can be seen, the total amount of dollar deposits in the US banking system has not changed, nor has the quantum of reserves maintained by US banks with the Federal Reserve. Thus, the creation of a Eurodollar deposit does not lead to a situation where the money actually leaves the United States. All that happens is that the ownership of money is transferred across international borders.

Most Eurocurrency deposits are short-term deposits, ranging from call money to term deposits with up to a year to maturity. Call deposits are analogous to demand deposits placed with banks in the United States. Euro CDs are also common. The difference between a term deposit and a CD is that the latter is a negotiable instrument. For a US bank, Euro CDs often offer a lower cost alternative to domestic CDs, because they are exempt from reserve requirements, and the need to have them insured. There is also a market for Eurocurrency interbank loans, which is the equivalent of the Fed funds market.

APPENDIX

We will derive the expression for y, given that

$$P\left(1+\frac{y}{2}\right)\left(1+\frac{y}{2}\left\{\frac{T_m-\frac{365}{2}}{\frac{365}{2}}\right\}\right)=V$$

From the above expression, when we expand the terms we get,

$$P+\frac{Py}{2}+\frac{Py}{2}\times\frac{2T_m-365}{365}+\frac{Py^2}{4}\times\frac{2T_m-36}{365}=V$$

$$\Rightarrow y^2\times\frac{P}{4}\times\frac{2T_m-365}{365}+y\times\frac{P}{2}\times\left(1+\frac{2T_m-365}{365}\right)+(P-V)=0$$

This is a quadratic equation of the form,

$$ax^2+bx+c=0$$

The roots are given by,

$$\frac{-b\pm\sqrt{b^2-4ac}}{2a}$$

Substituting the appropriate values for a, b, and c, and simplifying, we get,

$$\frac{\dfrac{-2T_m}{365}\pm 2\sqrt{\left(\dfrac{T_m}{365}\right)^2-\left(\dfrac{2T_m}{365}-1\right)\left(1-\dfrac{V}{P}\right)}}{\dfrac{2T_m}{365}-1}$$

Forward and Futures Contracts

INTRODUCTION

In order to understand forward and futures contracts, let us commence our discussion with an illustration of a spot transaction. Assume that we are standing on 15 May 20XX and that we wish to buy 100 shares of ABC. We will go to an exchange like the NYSE and place a buy order for 100 shares of ABC stock. The order will be matched with a sell order placed by another party, assuming that a suitable counterparty is available, and a trade will be executed for 100 shares. Such a transaction is termed as a cash or a spot transaction. This is because as soon as a deal is struck between the buyer and the seller, the buyer has to immediately make arrangements for the cash to be transferred to the seller, while the seller has to ensure that the right to the asset in question, in this case shares of ABC, is immediately transferred to the buyer.

Now consider a slightly different situation. Assume that on 15 May 20XX we wish to enter into a contract to acquire 100 shares of ABC on 15 August 20XX, and that a counterparty exists who is willing to sell the shares on that day. If so, we can enter into a contract that entails the payment of cash on 15 August against delivery of shares on the same day. The difference as compared to the earlier transaction is that no money need be paid by the buyer at the time of negotiating the contract, and neither does the seller need to transfer rights to the underlying asset on that day. The actual exchange of cash for the asset will take place on the transaction date specified in the contract, which in this case is 15 August. Such a contract is termed as a forward contract, for it entails the negotiation of terms and conditions in advance for a trade that is scheduled to take place on a future date.

In a forward contract, at the time of negotiating the deal the two parties have to agree on the terms at which they will transact on the future date. The following need to be clearly spelled out: (1) the underlying asset, in this case shares of ABC; and (2) the contract size, in this case 100 shares. The delivery date and the transaction venue should also be agreed upon. In our illustration the delivery date is 15 August, and we will assume that the venue for the exchange is New York City. Finally, the price at which the deal will be consummated on 15 August should also be fixed at the time of negotiating on 15 May. Let us assume that the price that is agreed upon is $80 per share.

A forward contract is termed as a commitment contract, for it represents an unconditional commitment to buy the underlying asset on the part of the buyer and an equivalent commitment to sell on the part of the seller. If the buyer were to renege by not paying the contractual amount on 15 August, it would be tantamount to default. Similarly, if the seller were to refuse to part with the shares on that day, it would be construed as default.

In every forward contract there will be a party who agrees to buy the underlying asset and a party who agrees to sell the underlying asset. The first party is termed as the buyer or the *long*, while the counterparty is designated as the seller or the *short*.

A forward contract is a customized or a private or an OTC contract. The term *OTC*, which stands for Over-the-Counter, connotes that such trades are not executed on an organized exchange. That is, a forward contract such as the one that we have described will not take place on an exchange like the NYSE. Such contracts are negotiated privately between a potential buyer and a potential seller. They are referred to as customized agreements because the two parties are at liberty to specify any terms and conditions that they can mutually agree upon. Let us consider the forward contract on shares of ABC. We have specified the underlying asset as shares of ABC. In practice the asset could be shares of any other stock, or even a nonfinancial product such as gold or wheat. The contract size has been assumed to be 100 shares. This too was arbitrarily fixed. While two parties, say Alfred and Colin, may agree to transact in 100 shares of ABC stock, two others, say Molly and Patsy, may agree on 175 shares of ABC stock. The transaction date has been set as 15 August 20XX. There is no sanctity about this date, and the potential buyer and seller are at liberty to arrive at any transaction date by consensus. Finally, we have assumed that the location for the trade is New York City. This was chosen arbitrarily as well, and the two parties may agree on any location of their choice. Thus, in the case of a forward contract all features such as the underlying asset, the quantum of the underlying asset, the date of delivery, and the place of delivery are arrived at by bilateral discussions between the potential buyer and the seller. Needless to say, the transaction price that is fixed at the outset is also determined by a process of negotiation between the two parties.

In these contracts there is obviously a major risk of default. Let us analyze the rationale. Assume that Alfred agrees to acquire 500 shares of ABC from Bob on 15 August 20XX. The agreement is entered into on 15 May 20XX and the price is fixed at $80 per share. On 15 August there are two possibilities. The market price for a cash or spot transaction may be less than 80 or more than 80. If the price were to be less than $80 per share, Alfred would be unwilling to pay $80 per share if he can get away with it. Thus, if the spot price on the scheduled transaction date were to be less than the forward price, the long will have an incentive to renege. But what if the spot price on 15 August were to be more than $80 per share? If so, the seller will be unwilling to sell the asset for the contracted price. In other words, if the spot price on the scheduled date were to be greater than the forward price, the short has an incentive to default. Thus, default risk is an integral part of such contracts. It is for this reason that forward contracts are primarily between institutional parties such as commercial banks, investment banks, large corporations, and insurance companies. Such parties have the resources and skills to assess the credibility of a potential counterparty. Forward contracts are extremely popular in the foreign exchange market where importers and exporters routinely enter into such transactions with commercial banks.

Now let us turn our attention to another product known as a futures contract. It too is a commitment contract that is written on an underlying asset; however, it is offered by an organized futures exchange and is not an OTC product. The most famous futures exchange in the world is the CME Group based in Chicago, and we will illustrate such contracts with an example from this exchange.

Consider the corn futures contract on this exchange. Each contract is for 5,000 bushels of the commodity. Quite obviously the contract can be used only by traders who wish to transact in multiples of 5,000 bushels. The exchange specifies three deliverable grades: #1 Yellow; #2 Yellow; and #3 Yellow. Thus, transactions are feasible in only the specified grades. The contract months available are March, May, July, September, and December. Thus, if two traders wish to transact on 15 August 20XX, as we assumed in our earlier illustration, they cannot use these contracts. The last delivery date as per the specifications of the exchange is the second business day following the last trading day of the delivery month, and the last trading date is the business day prior to the 15th calendar day of the contract month. Consider the futures contracts expiring in July 20XX. The last trading day is Wednesday 14 July, and the last delivery date is Friday the 16th of July. Hence if two parties desire to effect delivery on the 25th of July 20XX, then such contracts are unsuitable.

As can be deduced from this example, futures contracts are standardized contracts. That is, unlike forward contracts where the terms and conditions are set based on bilateral negotiations, in futures contracts there is a third party that specifies the permitted terms and conditions. This third party is the futures exchange. Such an exchange may be a stand-alone entity such as the CME Group, or it may be a division of a stock exchange. The exchange will specify the following features in the case of a futures contract.

The contract size: In our illustration it is 5,000 bushels. Thus, traders can take positions only in multiples of this amount.

The allowable grades: In our illustration the exchange has specified three allowable grades for corn. Thus, transactions in any other variety of the product are ruled out.

The allowable locations: In some cases, the exchange will specify more than one location where the underlying asset can be delivered. Thus, delivery has to be made at only the locations specified in the contract.

The delivery date/window: The exchange may specify a specific date on which delivery can be made. In practice it is more common to specify a delivery window. Thus, delivery can be made only between the start and end dates specified by the exchange. In the case of corn futures, the first delivery date is the first business of the expiration month, which is 1 July 20XX for the July contract. The last delivery date is the second business day following the last trading day of the delivery month, which is 16 July 20XX.

What are the consequences of such standardization? First, it reduces transactions costs. The cost of negotiating a customized agreement where each clause has to be drafted after painstaking negotiations will be much higher. Second, the trading volumes and the liquidity of futures contracts is much higher since only a few types of contracts are eligible for trading for each underlying product.

The futures exchange will have an associated entity known as a clearinghouse. The clearinghouse will position itself as the counterparty for each of the two original parties to the trade. That is, once a trade is consummated between a buyer and a seller, the clearinghouse will intervene and position itself as the effective seller from the standpoint of the buyer, and as the effective buyer from the perspective of the seller. Thus, the link between the two original parties is severed by the clearinghouse. It must be noted that neither of the parties to the trade actually trades with the clearinghouse. The clearinghouse intervenes and positions itself as a central counterparty only after the trade is consummated. The clearinghouse essentially reduces the risk of default for the two parties to the trade. Once the clearinghouse enters the picture, each of the two parties has to only worry about the strength and integrity of the clearinghouse and not about the original counterparty. The clearinghouse also makes it easier to offset the transaction.

What is offsetting? The term *offsetting*, also referred to as the assumption of a counterposition, entails the taking of a short position by a trader who has previously gone long, or by the taking of a long position by an investor who has earlier gone short.

A forward contract is a customized contract between two parties. Thus, a party who is seeking to offset or abrogate an existing position has to approach the original counterparty and have the agreement canceled. For instance, assume that Sterling Infotech, a software company based in Bangalore, has entered into a forward contract with HSBC to sell 250,000 USD to the bank after three months at a rate of INR 75.0000 per dollar. But one month after entering into the contract Sterling finds that its US customer has gone bankrupt and the receivable in dollars will not materialize. Sterling then has to approach the bank and have the original agreement canceled.

The cancellation of a futures position, however, is a lot easier and does not require the canceling party to approach the party with which it traded initially. Assume that Ray, a trader in Kansas City, has gone long in 100 futures contracts on wheat, with a counterparty in Des Moines. In this case, the order would have been routed through an exchange like the CME Group. The bilateral auction process on such exchanges is such that the trading parties would not even be aware of their counterparty's identity. Assume that two weeks after the transaction, Ray wishes to offset his long position. All he has to do is to contact a broker and have a sell order placed for 100 futures contracts on wheat. This time, the counterparty with whom the trade is effected need not be the party in Des Moines with whom he had originally traded, and in practice could be anybody who wishes to go long at that instant. Let us assume that this time the party who trades with Ray is based in Bloomington. As far as the records of the clearinghouse are concerned, they will reflect the fact that Ray had initially gone long in 100 contracts on wheat, and that he has subsequently gone short in 100 contracts on the same asset. His net position after the second transaction will be nil, and consequently he has no further obligations from the standpoint of giving or taking delivery.

To offset a futures position, the offsetting order must be on the same underlying asset, and for a contract expiring in the same month. For instance, if Ray had initially gone long in wheat futures expiring in September, he should subsequently go short in futures on the same underlying commodity, which are scheduled to expire in the same expiration month, September. The price at which the original trade was consummated need not be the same as the price at which the offsetting order is placed. Thus, Ray may exit the market with either a profit or a loss. If we assume that he went long at $4.25 per bushel and that he subsequently offset at $4.95 per bushel, his profit/loss will be:

$$100 \times 5,000 \times (4.95 - 4.25) = \$350,000$$

There are two reasons why futures contracts are easy to offset. First, contracts on the underlying product, in this case wheat, have to be designed as per the specifications of the exchange. In this case each contract has to be for 5,000 bushels, with the same allowable grade/grades, and with the same delivery schedule. Thus, the nature of Ray's initial contract with the party in Des Moines will be identical to that of the subsequent offsetting contract with the party in Bloomington. Second, once Ray's initial trade is consummated, the link between him and the counterparty in Des Moines is broken because the clearinghouse has subsequently positioned itself as the effective counterparty to the trade. On the other hand, forward contracts are typically for nonstandard sizes, products, and delivery dates. Consequently, they can be offset only with the approval of the original counterparty. In addition, the identity of this party remains critical for there is no intervening entity, such as a clearinghouse.

The clearinghouse provides both original counterparties with a guarantee against the specter of default. The issue is, how can such a guarantee be implemented in practice? In order to ensure that neither party has to worry about the possibility of default on the part of the other, the clearinghouse will estimate the potential loss for each party and collect it in advance. This deposit is referred to as a *margin* and is a performance guarantee or good-faith deposit. The rationale is that if a party were to default after providing such a margin, then the funds held by the clearinghouse will be adequate to take care of the interests of the counterparty. In a futures contract, both parties have a commitment to perform, and the possibility of default exists for both a priori. Consequently, both the long and the short are required to deposit margins immediately after the trade. The margin that is deposited at the outset is referred to as the *initial margin*.

If a margin is collected at the very outset, it need not imply that both parties will be protected against default until the very end. What would happen, for instance, if a major price move led to a substantial erosion of margin for one of the two parties, thereby putting the counterparty at risk once again? Thus there is a need to period- ically assess the level of margin posted by a party and make adjustments for prior profits and losses. To understand how the mechanism works in practice, we need to introduce the concepts of *marking to market*, and *maintenance/variation margins*.

The loss or gain accruing to a party to a futures trade arises over a period of time. As a result, there is a need to periodically compute the gain/loss for a party and adjust the margin position accordingly. In practice, futures exchanges do this at the close of trading every day, a procedure called marking to market. While marking to market, the clearinghouse will compute the profit for a party from the time the contract was previously marked to market. Gains will be credited to the margin account and losses will be debited. Futures contracts are marked to market for the first time on the day that the position is entered into. Subsequently they are marked to market on every business day until the contract expires, or is offset by the party, if that were to happen earlier. The principle for computing the profit/loss is the following.

Assume that traders have gone long in a contract at a price of F_0. Assume that the price at the end of the day is F_1. If they were to offset at the end of the day, it would be tantamount to agreeing to sell the underlying asset, which they had earlier agreed to buy at F_0, at a price of F_1. If $F_1 > F_0$, they will obviously have a profit; if not, they will have a loss. While marking to market, the clearinghouse will compute the profit/loss assuming that the party is offsetting and will credit/debit the margin account accordingly. Because the party has not actually expressed a desire to offset, however, the clearinghouse will reopen the position at the price at which the offset was assumed to have taken place.

Thus, rising futures prices lead to profits for the long, while declining prices lead to losses. It can be logically deduced that the situation for the shorts is exactly the opposite; rising futures prices will lead to losses, while falling prices will imply profits.

All futures contracts are marked to market every day. The price used for this purpose is referred to as the *settlement price*. This may be the closing price for the day, although many exchanges use a volume-weighted average of prices observed during the last phase of trading for the day. If a contract is inactive, the clearinghouse may set the settlement price equal to the average of the bid and ask quotes for the product.

Once a contract is marked to market, the gain for one of the counterparties is realized from the standpoint of price movements until that instant. Thus, if the counterparty were to subsequently default, the clearinghouse has the resources to protect the interests of the party who has realized a gain. A series of negative price movements due to rising prices from the standpoint of the shorts or falling prices from the point of view of the longs, however, could erode the amount of funds available in the margin account significantly, thereby defeating the very purpose of requiring the party to post margins. To protect the counterparty against this eventuality, exchanges specify a threshold level termed as the *maintenance margin*. This is set at a level below that of the initial margin.

If adverse price movements were to lead to a situation where the balance in the margin account declines below the maintenance level, the clearinghouse will issue what is termed a *margin call*. This is a request to the party to top up the funds in the margin account to take the balance back to the initial level. The funds deposited in response to a margin call are referred to as *variation margin*. A margin call always has a negative connotation, as it is an indication that the party has suffered a significant loss. While initial margins may be deposited in the form of cash or cash-like securities, variation margins must always be deposited in the form of cash. A cash-like security is a liquid marketable security. In practice the broker will apply a haircut while evaluating the value of the security to protect himself against a sharp unanticipated loss. The reason why variation margins must always be in the form of cash is that unlike initial margins, which represent a performance guarantee, a variation margin represents an actual loss suffered by the trader. In practice traders have to maintain a margin account with their respective brokers while brokers have to maintain margin accounts with the clearinghouse. The margin that a broker deposits with the clearinghouse is referred to as a *clearing margin*. These accounts are adjusted on a daily basis for gains and losses, in exactly the same manner that a client's account with a broker is adjusted.

We will now provide a detailed illustration to depict how the marking to market mechanism works in practice. Assume that the initial margin is $5,000 while the maintenance margin is $3,750. The two traders entered into the contract at a price of $4.50 per bushel of wheat, where each contract is for 5,000 bushels. The observed prices over the next four days are as shown in Table 6.1.

TABLE 6.1   Observed Futures Prices

Time	Contract Price
0	4.50
1	4.35
2	4.15
3	4.20
4	4.25

TABLE 6.2 Margin Account of the Long

Time	Price	Account Balance	Day's Gain/Loss	Total Gain/Loss	Variation Margin
0	4.50	5,000	—		
1	4.35	4,250	(750)	(750)	
2	4.15	3,250	(1,000)	(1,750)	1,750
3	4.20	5,250	250	(1,500)	
4	4.25	5,500	250	(1,250)	

The impact on the margin accounts of the long and the short respectively are given in Tables 6.2 and 6.3.

Let us analyze Table 6.2. At the end of the first day the change in price as compared to the initial transaction price is −0.15. Falling prices lead to a loss for the long. In this case the loss is 0.15 × 5,000 = \$750. This is the loss for the day that has caused the margin account balance at the end of the day to decline to \$4,250, after the loss is debited. The price at the end of the following day is \$4.15. As compared to the previous day's settlement price, the price has declined by a further 20 cents per bushel. This amounts to a further loss of \$1,000 per contract. When this loss is debited the balance declines further to \$3,250. This leads to a situation where the account balance is below the threshold level of \$3,750. Consequently, a margin call will go out. To comply with it the trader must deposit an additional \$1,750 to take the balance back to the initial level of \$5,000. The following day the price increases by 5 cents per bushel. The long will make a profit of \$250. The cumulative loss will be \$1,500. The margin account balance will be \$5,250. The following day the price again rises by 5 cents a bushel. The day's profit will once again be \$250. The cumulative loss will be \$1,250 and the account balance will be \$5,500. This can be deduced as follows.

$$5,000 \text{ (Initial Deposit)} + 1,750 \text{ (Variation Margin)}$$

$$- 1,250 \text{ (Cumulative Loss)} = \$5,500$$

The margin account for the short is depicted in Table 6.3. The corresponding entries are self-explanatory.

As we can see, the cumulative gain/loss for the long is exactly equal to the loss/gain for the short. Thus, futures contracts are *zero-sum games*. That is, taken together the profit/loss for the long and the short is always zero.

TABLE 6.3 Margin Account of the Short

Time	Price	Account Balance	Day's Gain/Loss	Total Gain/Loss	Variation Margin
0	4.50	5,000	—		
1	4.35	5,750	750	750	
2	4.15	6,750	1,000	1,750	
3	4.20	6,500	(250)	1,500	
4	4.25	6,250	(250)	1,250	

MARKING TO MARKET FOR A TRADER IN PRACTICE

Traders in practice carry over open positions to the next business day. They may also trade multiple times during a day, buying and selling futures contracts on the same underlying asset. Here is a detailed example.

EXAMPLE 6.1

Arthur Joseph was long in 225 futures contracts at the end of yesterday. The settlement price yesterday was 124, and the contract multiplier is 20. Today he first went short in 80 contracts at a price of 126.50. Subsequently he went long in 120 contracts at 130. Toward the close of the day he once again went short in 60 contracts at 132. The settlement price at the end of the day is 128. The cumulative cash flow from marking to market may be computed as follows. We compute the profit/loss of yesterday's carried over position, and each of today's trades, with respect to today's settlement price.

Carried Over Position: $225 \times 20 \times (128 - 124) = 18{,}000$

Today's First Trade: $80 \times 20 \times (126.5 - 128) = -2{,}400$

Today's Second Trade: $120 \times 20 \times (128 - 130) = -4{,}800$

Today's Third Trade: $60 \times 20 \times (132 - 128) = 4800$

Cumulative cash flow from marking to market at the end of the day is $15,600.

DELIVERY OPTIONS

In practice the right to choose the deliverable grade and location are given to the short. The short also has the right to initiate the process of delivery. What this means is that a long cannot seek delivery of the underlying asset and will have to wait to be chosen by the exchange to take delivery in response of a declaration of intent by a short. What this also means is that longs who do not desire to take delivery will quit the market by offsetting prior to the commencement of the delivery period. For if they were to keep their positions open, they could be called upon to take delivery without having the right to refuse.

PROFIT DIAGRAMS

Rising futures prices lead to profits for holders of long positions, while falling futures prices lead to profits for holders of short positions. Take the case of two parties who traded at time 't' and hold their positions until time 'T', which is the point of expiration. The profit for the long is: $F_T - F_t$. In general, if a trade is initiated at a price of F_t and offset at time t^*, at a price of F_{t^*}, the profit for the long is $F_{t^*} - F_t$. Thus, once a position is set up, the profit for the long increases dollar for dollar with an increase in the terminal futures price.

The profit for the short may be expressed as $F_t - F_T$, or in general as $F_t - F_{t^*}$. Thus, once a short position is set up, the profit increases dollar for dollar with a decrease in the terminal futures price. The profit diagrams for both long and short positions are therefore linear. We depict the diagrams in Figures 6.1 and 6.2.

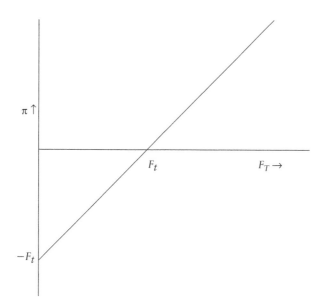

FIGURE 6.1   Profit Profile – Long Futures

In Figure 6.1, π represents the profit, which is shown along the Y-axis. The terminal futures price is shown along the X-axis. The maximum loss occurs when the terminal futures price is zero, and is equal in magnitude to the initial futures price F_t. Thus, as it is for a holder of a long spot position, the maximum loss is limited. In this case it is equal to the futures price prevailing at the outset. The maximum profit, as in the case of a long spot position, is unlimited because the terminal futures price has no upper bound. The position breaks even if the terminal futures price is equal to the initial futures price, or in other words, the price remains unchanged. Consequently, the holder of a long futures position faces the specter of potentially infinite profits. However, his loss is capped at the initial futures price. Thus, as in the case of trades in the cash market, long futures positions are intended for investors who are bullish about the market.

The profit diagram for a short futures position is also linear, but is downward sloping, as depicted in Figure 6.2.

In this case, the maximum profit occurs when the terminal futures price is zero and is equal in magnitude to the initial futures price. The maximum loss is obviously unlimited, because the terminal futures price has no upper bound. Thus holders of short positions, like investors who establish short positions in the spot market, are confronted with the prospect of finite profits but infinite losses. Quite obviously such investors too are bearish in nature, for they stand to make profits if the prices were to decline.

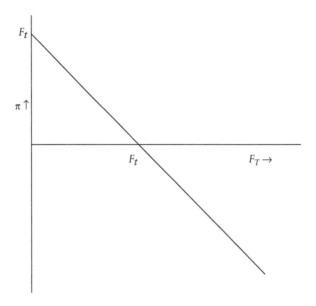

FIGURE 6.2   Profit Profile – Short Futures

VALUE AT RISK

To estimate the required margin, the clearinghouse needs to assess the potential loss for a party. Now, the loss from a futures contract does not arise all of a sudden but rather is accumulated over a period of time, as the futures price fluctuates from trade to trade in the market. In practice exchanges use a statistical technique known as *Value at Risk (VaR)* to estimate the potential loss over a given time horizon. The value at risk of a portfolio is an estimate of the loss over a specified time horizon for a given probability level. For instance, if the 95% value at risk of a portfolio over a one-day horizon is $7,500, it implies that there is only a 5% chance that the loss from the portfolio will exceed this amount over a one-day horizon. Quite obviously the estimate of the loss is a function of the specified probability level as well as the time horizon over which the loss is sought to be measured. That is, for a given probability level, the estimated loss over a three-day horizon will be different from the estimate for a one-day horizon. And, for a given time horizon the 95% VaR estimate will be different from the 99% VaR estimate. Consequently, a VaR number is meaningless until it is accompanied by the corresponding probability percentage and the time horizon. It must be remembered that the value at risk of a portfolio is not the maximum loss it can suffer over a given time period. In practice the value of a portfolio can always go to zero over any specified horizon, however small. Consequently, the maximum loss that a portfolio can suffer is its entire current value.

To illustrate how the VaR is computed in practice let us demonstrate the application of a method called RiskMetrics developed by JP Morgan. The volatility of the underlying asset on a given day is computed as an exponential moving average. The formula is given by:

$$\sigma_t^2 = \lambda \sigma_{t-1}^2 + (1 - \lambda) r_t^2$$

σ is the value of the standard deviation or the volatility of the rate of return and r is the return for the day. In practice, a value of 0.94 is recommended for λ. Let us consider futures contracts on a stock index such as the S&P 500. The return for day t is defined as $r_t = \ln(I_t/I_{t-1})$, where I_t is the level of the index on day t. Consider a short futures position. We know that shorts will lose if the futures price were to rise. We can state with 99% confidence that the return will lie within +2.33 standard deviations. In practice, in order to account for the fat tails of the observed return distribution, a limit of +3 standard deviations is often taken. Thus, for a short position the upper limit is taken as $+3\sigma$.

Therefore

$$\ln\left(\frac{I_{t+1}}{I_t}\right) = 3\sigma_t^{*}$$

$$\Rightarrow \left(\frac{I_{t+1}}{I_t}\right) = e^{3\sigma_t^{*}}$$

$$\Rightarrow I_{t+1} = I_t[1 + e^{3\sigma_t^{*}} - 1]$$

Hence if we know I_t, we can say with the stated level of confidence that the percentage change in the futures price will be less than or equal to $[e^{3\sigma_t^{*}} - 1] \times 100$.

Similar logic will show that the percentage decline in the futures price, which has pertinence for a long futures position, will be less than or equal to $[1 - e^{-3\sigma_t^{*}}] \times 100$.

We will illustrate the application of this methodology with the help of an illustration.

EXAMPLE 6.2

Assume that $\sigma_{t-1} = 3.25\%$, while $r_t = 2.5\%$. If so, then

$$\sigma_t^2 = 0.94 \times 0.0325 \times 0.0325 + (1 - 0.94) \times 0.0250 \times 0.0250 = 0.001030375$$

$$\Rightarrow \sigma_t = 0.032099 \equiv 3.2099\%$$

So, the percentage margin for a short position is $[e^{3 \times 0.032099} - 1] \times 100 = 10.1086\%$.

Assume that the futures price at the end of the day is 5,000 and that the contract multiplier is 50. Thus, the required margin for the following day is:

$$50 \times 5,000 \times 0.101086 = \$25,271.50$$

THE EXPECTED SHORTFALL

The expected shortfall is the expected loss given that the loss exceeds the value at risk. The computation of the VaR and ES, given the distribution of losses for an investment, is given in Example 6.3.

EXAMPLE 6.3

Consider the following probability distribution of losses for an investment.

Loss	Probability
−4000	0.075
−2500	0.125
−1000	0.100
−250	0.125
1250	0.150
1750	0.175
2250	0.200
2750	0.025
3500	0.025

In the table, negative values are gains and positive values are losses. The probability that the loss will exceed 2250 is only 5%. Thus, we say that the 95% value at risk over a one-day horizon is 2250. There are two possible outcomes for losses exceeding 2250, both of which are equally probable.

Thus, the expected shortfall is $0.50 \times 2750 + 0.50 \times 3500 = 3{,}125$.

SPOT-FUTURES EQUIVALENCE

Consider a futures contract that is entered into an instant prior to the specified delivery time. It is no different from a spot contract, as it requires the short to make delivery immediately and the long to accept immediate delivery. Thus, the futures price at the time of expiration of the contract must be exactly equal to the spot price, to preclude arbitrage. That is, as the time of expiration approaches, the spot and futures prices must converge with each other.

Let us examine the consequences if the futures price were not to be equivalent to the spot price at the time of contract expiration. There are two possibilities: the futures price may be higher or lower.

We will first consider the case where the futures price is higher. Assume that ABC is trading at $80 per share on the stock exchange and that ABC futures are trading at $82 on the futures exchange. Each futures contract is for 100 shares of stock.

Arbitrageurs will acquire 100 shares in the spot market and immediately go short in a futures contract. They can obviously take delivery at $80 in the spot market and simultaneously give delivery at $82 in the futures market. Thus, they have a costless assured profit of $2 per share or $200 per contract awaiting them. To preclude such an arbitrage opportunity, we require that the futures price must be less than or equal to the spot price at expiration.

The futures price, however, cannot be less than the spot price, for this situation too will give rise to an arbitrage opportunity. For instance, assume that the spot price of ABC is $80, while the futures price is $77.50. Arbitrageurs will short sell the stock and simultaneously go long in the futures contract. They will get $80 per share when they take the short position. They can immediately cover the short position by taking delivery under the futures contract at $77.50. Thus there is an arbitrage profit of $2.50 per share or $250 per contract. To rule out both forms of arbitrage it is imperative that the futures price converge to the spot price at the time of expiration.

PRODUCTS AND EXCHANGES

Futures contracts are available on a variety of financial assets and commodities. There was a time when the bulk of trading activity was in commodity-based products. Subsequently trading action has picked up considerably in contracts based on financial assets, such as stock indices, bonds, and foreign currencies, although many commodity derivative contracts continue to be very active. The newest derivatives on financial assets are single stock or individual stock futures.

Financial products on which contracts are traded include bonds such as T-notes and T-bonds, and money market securities such as Eurodollars. Contracts are traded on a variety of stock indices such as the Dow Jones Industrial Average, the Standard & Poor's 500, and the Nikkei 225. Foreign exchange products, based on the currencies of G-10 countries and of emerging markets, are also actively traded.

Derivative exchanges in the developed countries are characterized by large trading volumes for most of their products, and consequently attract attention from traders across the world. Emerging markets have picked up considerably in recent years, however, and offer attractive trading opportunities for both domestic market participants as well as cross-border traders. The derivatives markets have been characterized by a series of high-profile mergers in recent years. Prominent mergers include: CME with CBOT; NYSE with Euronext; NASDAQ with OMX; and BM&F with Bovespa.

CASH-AND-CARRY ARBITRAGE

An arbitrage strategy that is implemented for taking advantage of an overpriced futures contract is termed a cash-and-carry arbitrage. It entails the assumption of a long position in the spot market coupled with a short position in the futures market. If the futures contract is scheduled to expire immediately, the profit is $F_T - S_T$. But if there is time left for the maturity of the contract, the arbitrage profit may be expressed as $F_t - S_t \times (1 + r)$, where r is the interest rate for the period from t until T.[1] The interest cost is the market rate of interest if the arbitrageurs are borrowing to fund the acquisition in the spot market; otherwise it is an opportunity cost if they are deploying their own funds.

REVERSE CASH-AND-CARRY ARBITRAGE

Such an arbitrage strategy comes into play when the futures contract is underpriced. It entails the assumption of a short position in the spot market coupled with a long position in the futures market. If the futures contract is slated to expire immediately,

---

[1]That is, r is not an annualized rate.

the profit is $S_T - F_T$. But if the maturity date of the contract is in the future, the profit may be expressed as $S_t \times (1 + r) - F_t$.

REPO AND REVERSE REPO RATES

Consider a cash-and-carry arbitrage strategy. It requires arbitrageurs to go long at a price S_t, in order for an assured payoff of F_t at the time of expiration. Thus the rate of return is given by

$$\frac{F_t - S_t}{S_t}$$

and is termed as the *Implied Repo Rate (IRR)*. If the contract were to be fairly priced, then this rate will be exactly equal to the riskless rate. However, if the contract were to be overpriced, then this will exceed the riskless rate. Consequently, cash-and-carry arbitrage is profitable if the contract is overpriced, or equivalently if the IRR is greater than the borrowing rate.

Now let us consider reverse cash-and-carry arbitrage. The arbitrageurs will indulge in a short sale at a price S_t, knowing at the outset that they will eventually have to cover at a price F_t. Thus, their funding rate is

$$\frac{F_t - S_t}{S_t}$$

which is referred to as the *Implied Reverse Repo Rate (IRRR)*. If the contract were to be fairly priced, then this rate will be exactly equal to the riskless rate. If the contract were to be underpriced, however, then this rate will be less than the riskless rate. Thus, reverse cash-and-carry arbitrage is profitable if the contract is underpriced or if the IRRR is less than the lending rate.

SYNTHETIC SECURITIES

Cash-and-carry arbitrage entails an initial investment in return for an assured payoff at the time of expiration of the futures contract. Thus, it is akin to an investment in a zero-coupon security such as a Treasury bill. Consequently, the artificial security created by such an arbitrage strategy is referred to as a synthetic T-bill. Quite obviously reverse cash-and-carry arbitrage is equivalent to a short position in a synthetic T-bill.

We can therefore state that: Spot – Futures = Synthetic T-bill

That is, a long position in the spot market, coupled with a short position in a futures contract, is equivalent to a long position in an artificial T-bill. Thus, if we have a natural position in any two of the three assets, then the third can be synthetically created.

VALUATION

The futures price is a function of the spot price, the interest rate, the time until expiration, and any payouts made by the underlying asset. We will start by analyzing the futures price of an asset that is not scheduled to make any payouts during the life of the contract.

We know that cash-and-carry arbitrage is ruled out if $F_t \leq S_t(1 + r)$, and that reverse cash-and-carry arbitrage is precluded if $F_t \geq S_t(1 + r)$. Hence, to rule out both forms of arbitrage it must be the case that $F_t = S_t(1 + r) = S_t + rS_t$. Thus the futures price in an arbitrage-free setting should be equal to the cost of acquisition of the asset, and the funding cost for the duration of the contract. This relationship is referred to as the *cost of carry*. In Example 6.4 we show how the no-arbitrage futures price is determined.

EXAMPLE 6.4

Assume that shares of ABC are currently trading at $80 and that futures contracts are available with six months to expiration. The borrowing/lending rate for a six-month period is 6% per annum. The no-arbitrage futures price is therefore:

$$80 \times (1.03) = \$82.40$$

THE CASE OF ASSETS MAKING PAYOUTS

Now assume that ABC is expected to make a payout of $2.50 after three months. Let us analyze the impact on both forms of arbitrage. Cash-and-carry arbitrage requires the trader to borrow and acquire the asset and go short in the futures contract. If the asset were to make a payout during the life of the contract, the effective carrying cost will stand reduced. The cost of funding the purchase of the security is rS_t. If we denote the future value of the payout, as computed at the point of expiration of the futures contract by I, then the effective carrying cost is $rS_t - I$. The reason why we need to compute the future value of the payout is the following. The interest cost is incurred at the point of expiration of the futures contract. In order to be consistent with the principles of time value of money, the magnitude of the payout too should be measured at this point. If the payout has occurred prior to the expiration date of the contract, it will obviously need to be compounded until the point of expiration. Thus, to rule out cash-and-carry arbitrage we require that $F_t \leq S_t \times (1 + r) - I$.

Now let us analyze reverse cash-and-carry arbitrage. The arbitrageur would have short sold the asset and invested it in the market, while simultaneously going long in the futures contract. The income from the investment proceeds of the short sale is rS_t. However, if there were to be a payout from the asset, then the interest income will stand reduced, because the short seller, as explained earlier, will have to compensate the party who is lending the asset for any lost income. Thus, the net proceeds from the investment is $rS_t - I$. Thus, to rule out reverse cash-and-carry arbitrage we require that

$$F_t \geq S_t \times (1 + r) - I$$

Hence to rule out both forms of arbitrage in the case of contracts on assets that make a payout, we require that $F_t = S_t \times (1 + r) - I$. Here are numerical illustrations of how arbitrage profits can be earned if this condition is violated.

EXAMPLE 6.5

Assume that ABC is trading at $80 in the spot market and that six-month contracts on the stock are trading at $81. The stock is scheduled to pay a dividend of $2 after three months, and the riskless rate of interest is 6% per annum. The no-arbitrage futures price is $80 \times (1.03) - 2 \times (1.015) = \$80.37$. Thus, the contract is clearly overpriced.

   An arbitrageur will buy the stock by borrowing $80 and will simultaneously go short in a futures contract. After three months he will receive a dividend which can be reinvested until the expiration date of the contract. The cash inflow at expiration is:

$81(from delivery under the futures contract)

+ $2.03 (from the reinvested dividend)

The cash outflow at the same point of time is 82.40 due to repayment of the amount borrowed with interest. Thus, there is an arbitrage profit of $0.63.

EXAMPLE 6.6

Assume that all the other variables have the same values as Example 6.5, except for the futures price, which we will assume is $79.50. Arbitrageurs will short sell the stock and invest the proceeds. After three months they will be required to compensate the lender of the security with the amount of the dividend. We will assume that this amount can be borrowed at the riskless rate. At the point of expiration, they will need to take delivery under the futures contract and repay the amount borrowed to pay the dividend.

   Cash inflow = $80 \times 1.03 = 82.40$

   Cash outflow = $2 \times 1.015 + 79.50 = 81.53$

   Profit = $82.40 - 81.53 = \$0.87$

PHYSICAL ASSETS

Unlike financial assets, physical assets do not make payouts; however, the acquirers of such assets have to expend resources for storing and possibly insuring such assets. Let us denote the total cost incurred in holding such assets by Z. A cost is nothing but a negative income. Thus, if we replace the variable I in the pricing equation for assets making a payout with Z, we get the relationship for physical assets that is

$$F_t = S_t \times (1 + r) + Z$$

   And yet the issue is not so straightforward. First we need to make a distinction between assets that are held for the purpose of investment and those that are held for consumption purposes. This has implications for the ability to short sell the asset. Financial assets such as stocks and bonds are held for investment reasons. Holders of such assets will have no problems in lending such assets to facilitate a short sale, if the asset is returned at the end of the period for which they intend to hold it, and if they are compensated for any income that they would have received had they continued to hold it. Precious metals like gold and silver are also usually held for investment purposes. An agricultural product like wheat or corn, however, may be held for other reasons. A wheat mill owner may choose to hold it in stock to avoid problems of short supply due to unanticipated events such as a natural calamity or a rainfall failure. Such assets will in these circumstances not be parted with to facilitate short sales. We term such assets as consumption or convenience assets and say that the holders are receiving a convenience value. The convenience value is like an implicit dividend; however, it cannot be quantified for (1) it cannot be objectively measured, and (2) it varies from holder to holder. Before we proceed to discuss the pricing of futures contracts on physical assets let us introduce the concept of quasi-arbitrage.

We know that a long spot position plus a short futures position is equivalent to a long position in a T-bill-like security, which we have termed as a synthetic T-bill. The variables can be repositioned to show that a synthetic position in any of the three products – the underlying asset, the futures contract, or the riskless asset – can be taken if we have natural positions in the remaining assets. A strategy that is designed to take a synthetic position in a product, because the perceived returns are greater than what traders would get were they to take a natural position in it, is termed as a quasi-arbitrage strategy.

Let us now consider cash-and-carry arbitrage. It requires traders to go long in spot and short in futures. This per se should pose no problems irrespective of whether the asset is a pure asset, like gold or silver, or a convenience asset, like wheat. Thus, overpricing of the futures contract is ruled out; however, the reverse cash-and-carry argument may be needed to be supplanted with a quasi-arbitrage argument to rule out an underpriced futures contract, as the following illustration will demonstrate.

EXAMPLE 6.7

A metal product is trading at $250 per ounce. Futures contracts are available with six months to maturity, at a price of $260. The riskless rate is 8% per annum. The storage cost for six months is $10, which is assumed to be payable at the end of the contract.

Take the case of arbitrageurs who go short in the spot market and long in a futures contract. The future value of the proceeds from the short sale will be $260, which will be just adequate to take delivery under the futures contract. So in order for them to make an arbitrage profit, the party who lent the asset to facilitate the short sale must share some of the storage costs that they have saved due to the fact that they chose not to hold the asset. The rationale is that under normal circumstances the short seller would have been required to compensate the lender of the assets for any income forgone. Logically, therefore, when it comes to the saving of expenses, the lender of the asset should share the gain with the short seller. However, in practice this is extremely unlikely. Therefore, to rule out reverse cash-and-carry arbitrage we need to consider the activities of quasi-arbitrageurs.

Take the case of a party who already owns an ounce of the metal. They can sell it for $250 and invest the proceeds at 8% per annum for six months. Simultaneously they can go long in a futures contract. At the end of six months the asset will be back in their possession, and they would have saved $10 in the process by way of saving of storage costs. Thus, quasi-arbitrage is indeed a profitable activity in such circumstances, and a combination of conventional cash-and-carry arbitrage and reverse cash-and-carry quasi-arbitrage will ensure that the asset is neither underpriced nor overpriced.

The situation can be different, however, in the case of a convenience asset. Conventional cash-and-carry arbitrage will help ensure that the contract is not overpriced. Traders may be unwilling to indulge in either reverse cash-and-carry arbitrage or quasi-arbitrage because they are getting a convenience value from the asset. Thus, all that we can state in the case of such assets is that $F_t \leq S_t \times (1 + r) + Z$. That is, while the contract cannot be overpriced, what looks like underpricing may not be exploitable in practice.

NET CARRY

The net carry for an asset that makes no payouts may be expressed as $NC = r$, while for assets making a payout it is $r - \dfrac{I}{S_t}$. For assets that entail the payment of storage costs we can express it as $NC = r + \dfrac{Z}{S_t}$. Thus, in all cases we can state that $F_t = S_t \times (1 + NC)$. If, however, the asset were to yield a convenience value, we can state the futures price as: $F_t = S_t \times (1 + NC) - Y$. Y, the variable that equates the two sides, is termed as the marginal convenience value.

BACKWARDATION AND CONTANGO

If the futures price is in excess of the spot price, or if the price of the nearby futures contract is lower than that of the more distant contract, then we say that the market is in *contango*. If, however, the futures price is less than the spot price, or if the nearby contract is priced higher than the more distant contract, then we say that the market is in *backwardation*. Let us first consider financial assets.

$$F_t = S_t \times (1 + NC)$$

The net carry may be positive or negative, depending on whether the interest cost dominates the income from the security, or is dominated by it. Thus, the market may be in backwardation or in contango.

For physical assets held for investment purposes, the net carry will always be positive. Consequently, such assets will always be in contango. Convenience assets may be in backwardation or in contango. For such assets:

$$F_t = S_t \times (1 + NC) - Y$$

The net carry will be positive. If the effect of the net carry were to dominate, the market will be in contango. However, if the convenience yield is substantial, then

TABLE 6.4   Illustration of a Contango Market

Contract	Price
Spot	$100.00
3-M Futures	$107.50
6-M Futures	$112.50
9-M Futures	$118.00
12-M Futures	$122.00

TABLE 6.5   Illustration of a Backwardation Market

Contract	Price
Spot	$100.00
3-M Futures	$ 97.50
6-M Futures	$ 92.50
9-M Futures	$ 88.00
12-M Futures	$ 82.00

the market may be in backwardation. Tables 6.4 and 6.5 represent two illustrations showing markets in backwardation and contango respectively. In practice it is not necessary that a market should steadily be in backwardation or in contango. For instance, while a three-month contract may be priced higher than the spot, which is what we would associate with a contango market, a six-month contract may be priced lower than the three-month contract, thereby displaying backwardation.

THE CASE OF MULTIPLE DELIVERABLE GRADES

We have shown that the futures price must converge to the spot price of the underlying asset. But in the case of contracts on certain commodities, multiple grades are permitted for delivery. The question in this case is, which spot price will the futures price converge to, as each eligible grade of the underlying asset will have its own spot price?

Before we go on to answer this question, let us deal with the issue of the spot-futures ratio. In the case of contracts where there is only one eligible grade for delivery, any arbitrage strategy that entails the assumption of a futures position until the time of expiration requires spot-futures positions in the ratio of 1:1. That is, the number of units in which a long or a short position is taken in the spot market must be identical to the number of units of the underlying asset represented by the position taken in the futures market. If multiple grades are permitted for delivery, however, then this will typically not be the case. There are two possible ways of price compensation when multiple grades have been specified for delivery. These are referred to as multiplicative price adjustment and additive price adjustment respectively.

In the case of contracts where a multiplicative price adjustment system has been specified, the short will receive $a_i F_T$ if he were to deliver grade 'i' where a_i is the adjustment factor for the grade. One grade will be designated as the par grade, for which the adjustment factor will be 1.0. For premium grades the adjustment factor will be greater than 1.0, while for discount grades it will be less than one. The cash inflow for an arbitrageur who chooses to initiate a cash-and-carry arbitrage strategy at time t with a short position in 'h' futures contracts will be $a_i F_T + h(F_t - F_T)$. To make the cash flow from this strategy riskless we need to eliminate the term involving 'T,' which implies that $h = a_i$. Thus, the number of futures contracts required is equal to the adjustment factor of the grade in which the trader has taken a long spot position.

The profit from the arbitrage strategy is $a_i F_t - S_t(1 + r)$. To rule out arbitrage we require that the profit be zero, which implies that $F_t = \frac{S_t \times (1 + r)}{a_i}$. Because there are multiple grades, this condition clearly cannot prevail for all grades simultaneously. The most preferred grade for which this condition will prevail is called the cheapest to deliver grade (CTD). In technical terms, we say that the futures price prior to expiration will be equal to the delivery-adjusted no-arbitrage futures price of the CTD grade, where the no-arbitrage futures price is $S_t \times (1 + r)$. For all the other grades, which we will denote in general by 'j,' it must be the case that $F_t < \frac{S_t \times (1 + r)}{a_j}$. The no-arbitrage condition at expiration is obviously $F_T = S_T/a_i$. Thus, the futures price will converge at the time of expiration of the contract to the delivery-adjusted spot price of the CTD grade where the delivery-adjusted spot price of a grade is S/a. For all the other grades 'j,' the delivery-adjusted spot price will obviously be higher. Thus, the CTD grade at expiration is the grade with the lowest delivery-adjusted spot price.

The multiplicative system of price adjustment is used for contracts like Treasury Bond futures. Consider the September 2018 futures contract. The CTD bond is a 5% coupon bond maturing on 15 May 2047. Its adjustment factor is 0.8642.

On September 15, which is an allowable date for delivery, the futures price (per dollar 100 of face value) is 96-08. The accrued interest per \$100 of face value is \$1.6984. Thus, the price payable by the long is:

$$96.25 \times 0.8642 + 1.6984 = \$84.87765$$

Now let us consider the system of additive price adjustment, which is used for contracts on agricultural commodities with multiple deliverable grades. In the case of such contracts, the short will receive $F_T + a_i$, if he were to deliver grade i where a_i is the adjustment factor for the grade. One grade will be designated as the par grade for which the adjustment factor will be 0.0. For premium grades the adjustment factor will be positive, while for discount grades it will be negative. The cash inflow for an arbitrageur who chooses to initiate a cash-and-carry arbitrage strategy at time t with a short position in 'h' futures contracts will be $F_T + a_i + h(F_t - F_T)$. To make the cash flow from this strategy riskless we need to eliminate the term involving 'T,' which implies that $h = 1$. Thus the appropriate spot-futures ratio for such contracts is 1:1, as it is for contracts that do not offer a choice with respect to the eligible grade.

The profit from the arbitrage strategy is $F_t + a_i - S_t(1 + r)$. To rule out arbitrage we require that the profit be zero, which implies that $F_t = S_t \times (1 + r) - a_i$. As there are multiple grades, this condition once again cannot prevail for all grades simultaneously. The most preferred grade for which this condition will prevail is called the cheapest to deliver grade (CTD). Thus, as in the case of multiplicative adjustment, the futures price prior to expiration will be equal to the delivery-adjusted no-arbitrage futures price of the CTD grade, where the no-arbitrage futures price is $S_t \times (1 + r)$. For all the other grades, which we will denote in general by 'j,' it must be the case that $F_t < S_t \times (1 + r) - a_j$. The no-arbitrage condition at expiration is $F_T = S_t - a_i$. Thus, the futures price will converge at the time of expiration of the contract to the delivery-adjusted spot price of the CTD grade where the delivery-adjusted spot price of a grade is $S - a$. For all the other grades 'j,' the delivery-adjusted spot price will obviously be higher. Thus, the CTD grade at expiration is once again the grade with the lowest delivery-adjusted spot price.

RISK ARBITRAGE

In the preceding case we stated that the futures price prior to expiration will converge to the delivery-adjusted no-arbitrage futures price of the CTD grade. For all other grades we can state that $F_t < \frac{S_t \times (1 + r)}{a_j}$ or $F_t < S_t \times (1 + r) - a_j$. The issue is that if the futures price is lower than the delivery-adjusted no-arbitrage futures price for a grade, then why can we not implement a reverse cash-and-carry arbitrage strategy to earn a costless, riskless profit. The answer is that such strategies are not riskless.

Let us analyze the cash-and-carry strategy for contracts on a commodity where the additive/multiplicative price adjustment systems are used. Arbitrageurs would have gone long in the required number of units in the spot market and assumed a short position in the futures market. Since they hold the short position in futures, they have the prerogative to decide as to which grade they should choose to deliver. If the maximum profit is likely to be obtained by delivering the grade in their possession, then they will choose to deliver that grade. If, however, they were of the opinion that any other grade is likely to lead to a larger cash flow if delivered, then they would choose to dispose of the grade in their possession in the spot market and acquire the required number of units of the grade that will lead to optimal profits if delivered. Consequently, while arbitrageurs may realize the profits that they have been anticipating from the outset, they can only earn more if circumstances were to change.

Reverse cash-and-carry arbitrage, however, is different. It requires arbitrageurs to go long in futures and short in the spot. In this case the right to choose the deliverable grade is with the counterparty and not the arbitrageurs. There is no guarantee that the counterparty will choose to deliver the grade that the arbitrageur has sold short. If they choose to deliver a different grade because it is optimal for them, then the arbitrageurs will realize a lower profit than anticipated. Thus, while implementing a reverse cash-and-carry strategy, arbitrageurs may end up realizing a lower profit, which in practice may even be a loss, and can never earn more than what they were anticipating at the outset. It is for this reason that reverse cash-and-carry arbitrage under such circumstances is termed as *risk arbitrage*. We will now demonstrate these arguments, first with the multiplicative adjustment system, and then with the additive adjustment system.

THE CASE OF MULTIPLICATIVE ADJUSTMENT

Consider the case of arbitrageurs who have gone long in one unit of grade 'i' of the asset and short in a_i futures contracts. Assume that at the point of expiration, another grade 'j' has become more profitable to deliver. If so, they will sell the unit of grade 'i' that they possess in the spot market and acquire a_i units of grade 'j' to satisfy their delivery commitments under the futures contract. Let us consider their cash flows.

Inflow from sale of grade 'i' = $S_{i,T}$

Marking to market profit/loss = $a_i(F_t - F_T)$

Cost of acquisition of grade 'j' = $a_i S_{j,T}$

Inflow from delivery under the futures contract = $a_i \times a_j F_T$

$$\text{Net cash flow} = S_{i,T} + a_i \times a_j F_T + a_i(F_t - F_T) - a_i S_{j,T}$$

$$= a_i F_t + (S_{i,T} - a_i F_T)$$

$$= a_i F_t + a_i \left[\frac{S_{i,T}}{a_i} - \frac{S_{j,T}}{a_j} \right]$$

$$> a_i F_t$$

We have used the fact that $a_j F_T = S_{j,T}$ and that 'j' is the CTD grade and so $\frac{S_{i,T}}{a_i} > \frac{S_{j,T}}{a_j}$.

Thus the arbitrageurs will never earn a profit that is less than what they anticipated at the outset.

Now let us turn to reverse cash-and-carry arbitrage. It would have been initiated by short selling one unit of grade "i" and going long in a_i futures contracts. Assume that at the point of expiration, another grade "j" has become more profitable to deliver. If so, the arbitrageurs will acquire one unit of grade "i" to cover their short position and sell a_i units of grade "j" which they would receive under the futures contract in the spot market. Let us consider their cash flows.

Outflow on account of acquisition of grade "i" = $S_{i,T}$

Marking to market profit/loss = $a_i(F_T - F_t)$

Proceeds from sale of grade "j" = $a_i S_{j,T}$

Outflow due to acquisition under the futures contract = $a_i \times a_j F_T$

$$\text{Net cash flow} = a_i S_{j,T} + a_i(F_T - F_t) - S_{i,T} - a_i \times a_j F_T$$

$$= a_i(F_T - F_t) - S_{i,T}$$

$$= a_i \left[\frac{S_{j,T}}{a_j} - \frac{S_{i,T}}{a_i} \right] - a_i F_t$$

We know that $\frac{S_{i,T}}{a_i} > \frac{S_{j,T}}{a_j}$. Thus, the net outflow can be greater than what was anticipated at the outset but not less. Thus, reverse cash-and-carry arbitrage is fraught with danger and is consequently termed as risk arbitrage.

THE CASE OF ADDITIVE ADJUSTMENT

Consider the case of cash-and-carry arbitrage. That is, the arbitrageurs have gone long in one unit of grade 'i' of the asset and short in one futures contract. Assume that at the point of expiration, another grade 'j' has become more profitable to deliver, and that consequently they decide to sell their unit of grade 'i' in the spot market and acquire one unit of grade 'j' to satisfy their delivery commitments under the futures contract. Let us consider their cash flows.

Inflow from sale of grade 'i' $= S_{i,T}$

Marking to market profit/loss $= (F_t - F_T)$

Cost of acquisition of grade 'j' $= S_{j,T}$

Inflow from delivery under the futures contract $= F_T + a_j$

The net cash flow $= S_{i,T} + F_T + a_j + (F_t - F_T) - S_{j,T}$

$$= F_t + a_i + [S_{i,T} - a_i - (S_{j,T} - a_j)]$$

Because grade 'j' is the CTD, we know that $(S_{i,T} - a_i) > (S_{j,T} - a_j)$. Thus, the net inflow may be higher than anticipated but never less. Using similar arguments, we can demonstrate that reverse cash-and-carry arbitrage in the case of a contract for which additive adjustment has been prescribed is also a case of risk arbitrage.

EXAMPLE 6.8

Futures contracts on a commodity permit three grades for delivery, Red, White and Blue. Each contract is for 5,000 bushels of the underlying asset. White is the par grade. Red can be delivered at a discount of 2 cents per bushel, while Blue can be delivered at a premium of 2 cents per bushel.

Assume that futures contracts are available with six months to maturity. The riskless rate is 8% per annum. The spot prices for the three grades are as depicted in Table 6.6.

TABLE 6.6 Spot Prices Prior to Expiration

Grade	Price
Red	3.2500
White	3.2800
Blue	3.3000

Let us compute the delivery-adjusted no-arbitrage futures price for each of the three grades. For Red it is: $3.2500 \times 1.04 - (-0.02) = 3.4000$. We can similarly show that it is 3.4112 for White and 3.4120 for Blue. Red is clearly the CTD grade, and the futures price must be equal to 3.4000 to rule out arbitrage.

Now assume that the spot prices and the delivery-adjusted spot prices at expiration are as shown in Table 6.7.

(continued)

(continued)

TABLE 6.7 Spot Prices and Delivery-Adjusted Spot Prices at Expiration

Grade	Price	Delivery-adjusted Spot Price
Red	3.3900	3.4100
White	3.4000	3.4000
Blue	3.4500	3.4300

Thus at expiration, White is the CTD grade.

EXAMPLE 6.9

Consider the data in the previous illustration. Assume that the futures price six months prior to expiration is 3.4075. The contract is obviously overpriced. Take the case of an arbitrageur who goes long in 5,000 bushels of Red and goes short in one futures contract. The futures price at expiration will be the delivery-adjusted spot price of the CTD grade, which in this case is 3.4000.

If the arbitrageurs were to deliver the grade in their possession, they will receive: $3.4000 - 0.02 = 3.3800$. Their profit/loss from marking to market will be $(3.4075 - 3.4000)$ per bushel. Thus, the net amount receivable for 5,000 bushels is:

$$5,000 \times [3.3800 + 0.0075] = \$16,937.50$$

The amount repayable on account of the loan taken to acquire the 5,000 bushels at the outset is $5,000 \times 3.2500 \times 1.04 = \$16,900$.

Thus, the profit from the strategy is $37.50, which is equal to $5,000 \times 0.0075$, where 0.0075 represents the extent to which the contract was mispriced at the outset.

Now consider a situation where the arbitrageurs decide to sell the 5,000 bushels of Red in their possession and acquire 5,000 bushels of White to fulfill their commitments under the contract.

The inflow from the sale of 5,000 bushels of Red = $5,000 \times 3.3900 = \$16,950$.
The cost of acquisition of 5,000 bushels of White = $5,000 \times 3.4000 = \$17,000$.
The profit from marking to market = $5,000 \times (3.4075 - 3.4000) = 37.50$.
The amount receivable when delivery is made under the contract = $5,000 \times 3.4000 = \$17,000$.

Thus, the net inflow = $16,950 - 17,000 + 37.50 + 17,000 = \$16,987.50$.

The amount repayable on account of the loan taken at the outset is $16,900. Thus, the profit is $87.50. Consequently, the profit from a cash-and-carry strategy in the case of commodities for which multiple grades are permitted for delivery can be greater than what was anticipated at the outset, but cannot be less.

Now let us turn to reverse cash-and-carry arbitrage. Assume that the futures price at the outset is 3.3925 per bushel. The traders will have to short sell 5,000 bushels of Red and go long in a futures contract. We will first compute their profits under the assumption that they are asked to take delivery of Red at maturity.

The inflow from the initial investment of the short sale proceeds = $5,000 \times 3.2500 \times 1.04 = 16,900$.

The cost of taking delivery under the futures contract = $5,000 \times 3.3800 = \$16,900$.

The profit/loss from marking to market = $5,000 \times (3.4000 - 3.3925) = \$37.50$.

Thus, the overall profit is $37.50, which corresponds to the mispricing of the contract at the outset.

Let us now turn to a situation where the arbitrageurs are asked to take possession of White.

They will have to acquire 5,000 bushels of Red, which will cost: $5,000 \times 3.3900 = \$16,950$.

The proceeds from the sale of 5,000 bushels of White acquired under the contract = $5,000 \times 3.4000 = \$17,000$.

The cost of taking delivery under the futures contract = $5,000 \times 3.4000 = \$17,000$.

The profit/loss from marking to market = $5,000 \times (3.4000 - 3.3925) = \$37.50$.

The proceeds from the investment of the short sale proceeds = $16,900.

The overall profit = $-16,950 + 17,000 - 17,000 + 16,900 + 37.50 = \$(12.50)$.

Thus, instead of the anticipated profit of $37.50, they have ended up with a loss of $12.50. This is why reverse cash-and-carry arbitrage under such circumstances is said to be fraught with risk.

TRADING VOLUME AND OPEN INTEREST

Trading volume refers to the number of contracts traded during a given time interval. In practice we are usually concerned with the volume for a given trading day that is from the commencement of trading in the morning until the close of the market. Every trade that is consummated during the day adds to the trading volume for that day. Take the case of Mitch, who goes long in 250 contracts on wheat with Doug. The addition to the trading volume for the day is obviously +250. A trade will always serve to increase the observed volume for the time period.

Open interest refers to the number of open positions at any point in time. Every long position must be matched by a corresponding short position. Consequently, open interest may be measured as the total number of open long positions at a given point in time, or equivalently as the total number of open short positions. A trade may lead to an increase or a decrease in the open interest or may leave it unchanged as we will demonstrate.

Assume that Mitch took a long position in 250 contracts on wheat last week and that Doug also had a prior short position in 200 contracts on the commodity. The two parties now execute a trade in 100 contracts wherein Mitch takes a long position and Doug takes a short position. The number of open long positions increases by 100 as a consequence of the trade. Equivalently the number of open short positions also increases by 100. Thus, the impact of the trade is to increase the open interest by 100 contracts. Hence if a trade results in an establishment of new positions by both the parties who enter into it, the open interest will rise.

Now consider a situation where Mitch goes long in 100 contracts with Kirk, who takes a short position. Assume that Kirk previously had a long position in 200 contracts. The impact of the trade is to increase the number of total open long positions by 100 as seen from Mitch's perspective; however, the trade simultaneously results in a decline of the open interest by 100 contracts since Kirk is partially offsetting his position. Thus, the net impact on open interest is nil. So, if a trade results in the opening of a position by a party by trading with a counterparty who is offsetting, the open interest will remain unchanged.

Finally, consider a situation where Mitch takes a short position in 100 contracts by trading with Doug, who takes a long position. The consequence of the trade is that Mitch's long position is reduced by 100 contracts. Simultaneously the trade has resulted in a decrease of 100 in Doug's short position. Thus, the open interest will decline by 100 contracts in this case. Therefore, if a trade results in the offsetting of existing positions by both the parties, open interest will decline.

Thus, while a trade will always lead to an increase in the trading volume for a day, its impact on the open interest will depend on the prior positions held by the counterparties.

A high trading volume for a day is symptomatic of a highly liquid market. Open interest, on the other hand, is an indicator of high future liquidity, because the higher the open interest, the greater is the potential for offsetting transactions.

EXAMPLE 6.10

Consider the following trades on a given day:

Name of Long	# of Contracts	# of Short
Cathy	200	Maureen
Cindy	300	Molly
Cathy	250	Monica
Maureen	450	Cindy
Cindy	300	Carol

Let us consider the open interest trade by trade. After the first trade the open interest is 200. In the second trade, no one is offsetting and consequently the open interest after the trade is 500. In the third trade, no one is offsetting and consequently the open interest after the trade is 750. The fourth trade may be analyzed as follows. Maureen is offsetting 200 contracts and Cindy is offsetting 300 contracts. Thus in 200 contracts the two offset each other and the open interest will decline by 200. In 100 more contracts Maureen is replacing Cindy and consequently there is no change in the open interest. Since the trade is for 450 contracts, the increase in open interest is 150. Thus, the open interest after the trade is 700. After the fourth trade Cindy was short in 150 contracts. She is now going long in 300 contracts with Carol, who does not have a prior position. Thus, the open interest increases by 150 contracts. The final open interest at the end of the day is therefore 850. This can be verified by reconciling the transactions client-wise:

Client	Long	Short	Net
Cathy	200+250 = 450		+450
Cindy	300+300 = 600	450	+150
Maureen	450	200	+250
Molly		300	−300
Monica		250	−250
Carol		300	−300

Now consider the last column. Items with a plus sign are long positions and those with a minus sign are short positions. Thus, the open interest is the number of long positions open or the number of short positions open, which is 850.

DELIVERY

Both forward and futures contracts may set forth terms for delivery, but the two types of contracts differ in several respects. First, the majority of forward contracts that come into existence are actually settled by delivery. On the other hand, the majority of futures contracts are offset prior to maturity. In practice, a small number of futures contracts, ranging from 2 to 5%, are actually settled by delivery.

Second, in the case of a forward contract the party who went short at the outset will end up delivering to the party with whom they traded initially. As explained earlier, there is no intervention in the case of such contracts by an agency such as a clearinghouse, and consequently the link between the two original counterparties very much remains intact. In the case of a futures contract, however, the link between the two counterparties is snapped by the clearinghouse immediately after the trade. Subsequently one or both counterparties may exit the market by taking a counterposition. Hence, when a short expresses the desire to make delivery, the exchange has to locate a party to whom they can deliver. In practice the long who is chosen to accept delivery is the party with the oldest outstanding long position.

Third, futures contracts are marked to market on a daily basis. The cash flow, for a long position, on a given day is $F_t - F_{t-1}$. If we aggregate the cash flows, we get $\sum_{t=1}^{T}[F_t - F_{t-1}] = F_T - F_0$. In order to ensure that the price paid by the long is what was contracted at the outset, they should pay a price P, such that after accounting for the cash flows from marking to market they effectively end up paying F_0.

$$P - [F_T - F_0] = F_0 \Rightarrow P = F_T$$

Thus, the price at which delivery is made under a futures contract is the terminal futures price, which, as we have seen earlier, is no different from the terminal spot price.

In the case of a forward contract, however, there is no marking to market. Hence the price that is paid by the long at the time of delivery is the price that was contracted at the outset.

CASH SETTLEMENT

All futures contracts do not mandate the delivery of the underlying asset. Stock index futures contracts, for instance, do not, for it is extremely cumbersome to deliver a large basket of securities (the S&P 500 is composed of 500 stocks) in exactly the same proportions as they are present in the index. Contracts such as index futures are cash settled. That is, they are marked to market one last time at the close of trading on the expiration day, and all positions are declared closed. Both the long and the short will exit the market with their profit/loss, but without taking delivery. The cash flow for the long will be $F_t - F_0$, while that for the short will be $F_0 - F_t$. Cash settlement may at times be the prescribed mechanism in markets where there is a perceptible risk of manipulation or the potential to create artificial shortages. Exchanges in many developing economies therefore prescribe cash settlement as the norm for many contracts.

HEDGING AND SPECULATION

There are two categories of traders in futures contracts: hedgers and speculators. The former take positions in futures contracts to reduce or eliminate their exposure to risk on account of a spot market position. The latter consciously seek to take an exposure to risk in the futures market in anticipation of gains.

The rationale for hedging may be explained as follows. Take the case of traders who own 5,000 bushels of wheat they are planning to sell after a month. Their worry is that the price of the product may fall in the spot market by the time the delivery date arrives. They can, however, go short in a futures contract at the prevailing futures price F_t. If so, they can be assured of being able to sell at this price, no matter what the spot price of wheat may be on the expiration date of the contract. In this argument we are assuming that the planned date of sale of the commodity coincides with the expiration date of the futures contract. In practice this may not be the case. If the wheat were to be sold before the delivery date of the contract on a date t^*, the traders would have to sell the asset in the spot market at a price S_{t^*}, and collect their profit/loss from marking to market in the futures market. The net inflow will be:

$$S_{t^*} + (F_t - F_{t^*}) = F_t + (S_{t^*} - F_{t^*})$$

$S_{t^*} - F_{t^*}$ is referred to as the basis. Thus, the risk for the hedger is the risk of variation in the basis. If the trader had not hedged, he would have received S_{t^*}. The risk of variation in the spot price is termed as *price risk*. Hence hedging replaces price risk with the more acceptable risk of variation in the price difference between the spot and the futures price, which is termed as *basis risk*.

Now let us take the case of traders who are short in the spot market. The term connotes that they have a prior commitment to buy. For instance, a company in Bangalore may have imported mainframe computers from the United States and may have a commitment to pay in USD after a month. The risk is that the rupee price of the US dollar may rise or, in other words, that the US dollar may appreciate. Such traders can go long in the futures market in order to hedge. If the date of acquisition of dollars were to coincide with the expiration date of the futures contracts, the dollars can be acquired at the initial futures price F_t. If not, the dollars can be bought in the spot market, and the profit/loss from marking to market can be collected. In this case, the outflow will be:

$$-S_{t*} + (F_{t*} - F_t) = -F_t - (S_{t*} - F_{t*})$$

The magnitude of the cash inflow for a short hedger is $F_t + b_{t*}$, while the magnitude of the outflow for a long hedger is also $F_t + b_{t*}$. The short hedger therefore stands to benefit from a rising basis, while the long hedger stands to profit from a falling basis. We know that traders with short futures positions stand to benefit from falling futures prices while those with long futures positions stand to gain from rising futures prices. The basis itself may be construed as a price, for it is but the difference of two prices, or a synthetic price. Consequently, we say that the short hedger is long the basis while the long hedger is short the basis.

On the day of expiration, the basis will be zero, for $b_T = S_T - F_T = 0$, because the futures price must converge to the spot price when the contract itself is scheduled to expire. A hedge without any inherent basis risk is termed as a *perfect hedge*. Thus, one of the key requirements for a perfect hedge is that the date of termination of the hedge must coincide with the expiration date of the futures contract. In the case of a perfect hedge a short hedger can be assured of receiving the futures price that was prevailing when the hedge was set up, while a long hedger can be guaranteed that he can acquire the asset by paying the futures price that was prevailing when he took a long position.

There is another key requirement for a perfect hedge. Let us consider the cash inflow for a short hedger, who is long in Q units of the asset and short in N futures contracts where each contract is for C units of the underlying asset. Thus the futures position represents Q_f units of the underlying asset, where $Q_f = NC$. The cash inflow is: $QS_T + NC(F_t - F_T)$. For this to be equal to QF_t, we require that $Q = NC = Q_f$. Thus the hedge ratio must be 1:1, which implies that the quantity being hedged must be an integer multiple of the size of the futures contract.

Let us summarize the conditions for a perfect hedge.

1. The first and the most basic condition is that futures contracts must be available on the asset whose price is being sought to be hedged.
2. The date of sale/purchase of the underlying asset must coincide with the expiration date of the futures contract.
3. The number of units of the underlying asset must be an integer multiple of the contract size.

In practice, condition-1 is likely to be satisfied in many cases; however, condition-2 is not. Take, for instance, a commodity on which contracts expiring in March, May, July, September, and December are available. Assume that the contracts expire on the 21st of the respective months, whereas the hedger would like to terminate the hedge on the 15th of July. The May contract is not appropriate as it will leave the trader open to price risk for the period from May until July. July contracts are not usually suitable because futures contracts can exhibit erratic price movements in the expiration month. Consequently, a hedger who seeks to buy or sell in July would like to avoid exposure to this contract. Thus, the choice is between the September and December contracts. In practice, the further away the expiration month, the greater is the basis risk. The reason is as follows.

The spot price, as well as the futures price, is being influenced by the same economic factors. The spot price represents the current market price, whereas the futures price is the price for a transaction at a future point in time. If the termination date of the hedge is close to the expiration date of the futures contract, then both the markets will be discovering the price of the product for virtually the same point in time. Consequently, the prices will converge such that the difference or the basis is more predictable.[2] Consequently the September contract is likely to expose the trader to a lower basis risk than the December contract. Hence in practice, when the transaction date does not coincide with the expiration date of the futures contract, the hedger will choose a contract which is slated to expire soon after the month in which the hedge is being terminated.

ROLLING A HEDGE

In the preceding argument we assumed that the hedger would choose the September futures contract. Let us assume that the futures position was taken on 21 April. On that day, however, the September contracts may not have commenced trading. Or they may be so illiquid as to deter investors who seek to enter and exit the market at a price that is close to the true or fair value of the asset. In such cases, it is conceivable that hedgers will first go short in the May contract. Since they would like to avoid exposure to the contract in its expiration month, they are likely to offset the position at the end of April and go short in July contracts. Finally, toward the end of June, they are likely to offset the July contracts and take a short position in September contracts. On 15 July they will sell the underlying asset in the spot market and offset the September futures position. Such a hedging strategy is known as a *rolling hedge*.

TAILING A HEDGE

Consider a perfect hedge. We know that a short hedger will receive the spot price prevailing at the time of termination of the hedge, and then collect the total profit/loss from marking to market. The profit/loss from marking to market on a given day 't' is $F_{t-1} - F_t$. This can be reinvested if it is a profit, or financed if it is a loss, until the maturity date so as to yield $(F_{t-1} - F_t)(1 + r)^{t^* - t}$. The cumulative profit/loss from a futures

---

[2]See Koontz and Purcell (1999).

position equivalent to Q_f units is $Q_f \sum\limits_{t=1}^{t^*} [F_{t-1} - F_t](1 + r)^{t^*-t}$. This will in general not be equal to $Q_f[F_0 - F_{t^*}]$. To make it so, we should have a position in

$$Q_{f,t} = \frac{Q_f}{(1 + r)^{t^*-t}}$$

futures contracts at the beginning of day 't.' Thus, we would have to start with a quantity less than Q_f and increase our position steadily at the end of each day. Consequently, if we were to start with Q_f units rights from the outset, we would be over-hedging. Overhedging will inflate the profit when there is a profit but will magnify the loss when there is a loss. The process of periodically adjusting the futures position in order to account for the effect of marking to market is termed as *tailing*. In practice the futures position is not usually adjusted daily but only periodically, for each adjustment entails the incurrence of transactions costs.

THE MINIMUM VARIANCE HEDGE RATIO

We know that the cash flow for a short hedger is:

$$QS_{t^*} + Q_f(F_t - F_{t^*})$$

If $t^* = T$, then $S_{t^*} = S_T = F_{t^*} = F_T$, and we should set $Q_f = Q$ such that the total revenue is QF_t, an amount about which there is no uncertainty. Thus, in order to obtain a perfect hedge under such circumstances, we need to set $Q_f = Q$, or in other words we need a hedge ratio of 1:1.

In general, however, the revenue from the hedged position is:

$$\begin{aligned} R &= QS_{t^*} + Q_f(F_t - F_{t^*}) \\ &= QS_{t^*} + hQ(F_t - F_{t^*}) \\ &= QS_t + (S_{t^*} - S_t)Q - (F_{t^*} - F_t)hQ \\ &= QS_t + (\Delta S - h\Delta F)Q \end{aligned}$$

where h is obviously the hedge ratio.

At the outset, we know Q, S_t, and h. In order to minimize risk we need to minimize the variance of the revenue using the only variable in our control, which is h.

$$\begin{aligned} \text{Var}\,[R] &= \text{Var}[QS_t + (\Delta S - h\Delta F)Q] \\ &= Q^2\text{Var}[\Delta S - h\Delta F] \end{aligned}$$

Let us denote Var(ΔS) by σ_s^2 and Var(ΔF) by σ_f^2. The correlation between the two variables is ρ. If we minimize the variance of R with respect to h, we get $h = \rho\frac{\sigma_s}{\sigma_f}$.

ESTIMATION OF THE HEDGE RATIO AND THE HEDGING EFFECTIVENESS

Consider the following statistical relationship.

$$\Delta S = \alpha + \beta \Delta F + \varepsilon$$

To estimate the parameters, we can run a linear regression with ΔF as the independent variable and ΔS as the dependent variable. The minimum variance hedge ratio is given by the slope coefficient β. The R^2 of the regression is a measure of the hedging effectiveness. If the basis risk is equal to the price risk, there will be no risk reduction and the R^2 will be zero. However, if there is a perfect hedge, then the R^2 will be 1.0. Thus, in practice we will get a value between 0 and 1.0.

CROSS-HEDGING

Sometimes it may so happen that there are no suitable futures contracts on the product whose price is sought to be hedged. It could be because there is no contract on the commodity in which we are interested. Otherwise, it could be the case that while contracts are available, they are so illiquid that the hedger does not have the confidence to take a position. Under such circumstances, the trader may choose to hedge by taking a futures position in a closely related commodity, where, by the term closely related, we mean a commodity whose price is highly positively correlated with that of the commodity that we are interested in. The use of futures contracts on a closely related commodity is termed as *cross-hedging*.

The revenue for the short hedger under such circumstances is: $S_{t^*} + [F^*_t - F^*_{t^*}]$, where S and F represent the spot and futures prices of the commodity the revenue from which is sought to be hedged, and S^* and F^* are the spot and futures prices of the closely related commodity that is being used for cross-hedging.

This can be expressed as $F^*_t + (S^*_{t^*} - F^*_{t^*}) + (S_{t^*} - S^*_{t^*})$. The basis therefore consists of two components. $(S^*_{t^*} - F^*_{t^*})$ is the basis if the asset being hedged is the same as the asset underlying the futures contract. The second term, $(S_{t^*} - S^*_{t^*})$, is the basis that arises due to the fact that the two assets are different. If $t^* = T$, then the first term will drop out and the basis for a cross-hedge will be $(S_{t^*} - S^*_{t^*})$.

SPECULATION

Futures contracts can be used for speculation. Take the case of traders who are bullish about the market. If so, they can go long in a futures contract at the prevailing spot price. If the market were to rise, they can either take delivery at expiration and sell the commodity at the prevailing spot price, which by assumption is higher, or they can offset their position prior to expiration and exit the market with a cumulative profit from marking to market.

EXAMPLE 6.11

Rob is of the opinion that corn will trade at (at least) $3.95 per bushel after a month. The current futures price for a one-month contract is $3.40. Let us assume that he goes long in 5 futures contracts where each contract is for 5,000 bushels.

Now assume that the price one month hence is $4.05 per bushel. Rob can take delivery under the contract at $3.40 and sell the commodity immediately at $4.05. His profit is:

$$5,000 \times 5 \times (4.05 - 3.40) = \$16,250$$

EXAMPLE 6.12

Now assume that two weeks after Rob went long, the spot price is $4.00. The futures price assuming that the cost of carry model is applicable, and that the interest rate is 6.5% per annum, is $4.00 \times (1 + 0.065 \times 2/52) = \$4.01$.[3] Rob will have a cumulative profit from marking to market of

$$5,000 \times 5 \times (4.01 - 3.40) = \$15,250$$

Futures contracts can also be used by bears for speculation. To put their viewpoint regarding the market into operation they need to go short in futures contracts, as the following two examples illustrate.

EXAMPLE 6.13

Holly is of the opinion that wheat will decline in price over the next two months. Futures contracts with two months to expiration are currently quoting at $4.95 per bushel. Assume that Holly goes short in 5 contracts, each of which is for 5,000 bushels.

Consider a situation where the price after two months is $4.25 per bushel. Holly can buy spot at this price and immediately deliver under the futures contract at $4.95. Her profit is:

$$5,000 \times 5 \times (4.95 - 4.25) = \$17,500$$

---

[3] The contract at this point in time has two weeks remaining until expiration.

EXAMPLE 6.14

Now assume that one month after Holly goes short, the spot price is $4.00 and that the futures price[4] is $4.00 \times (1 + 0.06 \times 1/12) = \$4.02$.

If Holly were to offset at this point in time, she can walk away with a profit of

$$5,000 \times 5 \times (4.95 - 4.02) = \$23,250$$

Thus, futures contracts can yield substantial profits for both bulls and bears if they make the right calls on the movement of the market. If they were to make an error of judgment, however, their losses can be substantial, as the following examples involving bulls will illustrate.[5]

EXAMPLE 6.15

Assume that Rob goes long in 5 corn futures contracts when the futures price is $3.40 per bushel. A month later when the contract expires, the prevailing spot price is $2.50 per bushel. If Rob were to take delivery under the futures contract and offload the corn in the spot market, he would incur a loss of:

$$5,000 \times 5 \times (2.50 - 3.40) = \$(22,500)$$

EXAMPLE 6.16

Assume that Rob goes long in corn futures when the futures price is $3.40. Instead of going up, however, the spot market crashes to $2.00 after two weeks, which corresponds to a futures price of $2.005 per bushel. If Rob were to exit at this point in time, he would have incurred a loss of:

$$5,000 \times 5 \times (2.005 - 3.400) = \$(34,875)$$

LEVERAGE

Bulls have a choice between a long spot position and a long futures position from the standpoint of speculation, whereas bears have a choice between a short spot position and a short futures position.

---

[4]We have assumed that the interest rate is 6% per annum.
[5]Similar illustrations can be designed for bears who choose to speculate with futures.

Futures positions offer the benefit of leverage to a speculator. As we have seen earlier, a position may be said to be levered if a small price movement in the underlying asset has a disproportionately large impact on the rate of return.

Why do we say that a futures position is levered? Take the case of a trader who goes long in a futures contract on a commodity by depositing $5,000 as the initial margin. Let the initial futures price be $5.00 per bushel and assume that the contract size is 5,000 bushels. Consider a price increase of $0.40 per bushel. The profit per contract will be $2,000, which amounts to a return of 40% on the initial margin deposit. If the trader had taken a spot position at a price equal to the initial futures price, however, the investment would have been $25,000, and a profit of $2,000 would amount to a return of only 8%. Thus, the leverage inherent in a futures contract helps magnify the rate of return. However, as we are aware, leverage is a double-edged sword. That is, losses if any will also be magnified. A price decline of $0.40 per bushel would amount to a –40% return on the futures position, but to a loss of only 8% on a spot position.

CONTRACT VALUE

When a forward contract is entered into, neither the short nor the long has to pay a price to enter into it. The price at which the underlying asset is scheduled to be bought/sold at a future date as per the contract is referred to as the *delivery price* of the contract. The delivery price is set in such a way that the contract value at inception is zero. That is, the two equal and offsetting obligations ensure that neither party has to pay the other to take a position.

The delivery price remains fixed once a contract is sealed. However, the price for a fresh contract will keep fluctuating over time. The price that is applicable if a forward contract were to be sealed at a particular instant is referred to as the forward price. If a contract were to be sealed, the prevailing forward price will be the delivery price of the contract. But an instant later the forward price will typically change.

Although the value of a contract will be zero at inception, such contracts will accrue value as time elapses. Consider a long forward position taken at a point of time in the past, when the forward price was K. This forward price would have been set as the delivery price of the contract. Now, a few periods later, the prevailing forward price is F. If the party who had originally gone long were to offset, they would have to do so by going short at a price F. The two offsetting positions would lead to a cash flow of $F - K$ at the time of expiration of the contract. The current value of the contract is the present value of this cash flow. As we have seen earlier, rising prices will lead to profits for the longs, while falling prices will lead to losses. Thus, if the forward price at a point in time were to be higher than the delivery price of the contract, a long forward position will have a positive value. If the price were to have declined after a contract was entered into, however, a long position will have a negative value. The situation will be exactly the opposite for shorts. Falling prices will lead to positive contract values while rising prices will lead to negative values. Example 6.17 shows how to compute the value of a preexisting forward contract.

EXAMPLE 6.17

A four-month forward contract was taken a month ago with a delivery price of 100. Today the forward price for a three-month contract is 106.15. Assume that the rate of interest is 10% per annum. The value of a long position is:

$$\text{Value} = \frac{F - K}{(1 + r)} = \frac{106.15 - 100}{1.025} = \$6$$

The value of a short position is:

$$\text{Value} = \frac{K - F}{(1 + r)} = \frac{100 - 106.15}{1.025} = -\$6$$

As can be seen, a contract is always a zero-sum game. The value for a short is exactly the negative of the value for a long.

What about the value of a futures contract? Such contracts too will have a zero value at inception. At the end of each day, starting with the trade date, the contract will be marked to market. Marking to market is nothing but the settlement of built-up value since the time that the contract was previously marked to market. The party with a positive value will have their margin account credited while the counterparty's margin account will be debited. Thus, the only time that a futures contract acquires value is in the intervening period between two successive marking to market dates. Each time the contract is marked to market, the value will revert back to zero.

FORWARD VERSUS FUTURES PRICES

In general, the forward price will not be equal to the futures price for contracts on the same underlying asset and with the same expiration date. The reason is that futures contracts are periodically marked to market, while forward contracts are not.

It can be shown that if the interest rate is a constant and is equal for all maturity periods, then there will be no difference between the forward price and the futures price. In reality, however, interest rates are a random variable; that is, they are stochastic in nature. Therefore, in practice the forward price will differ from the futures price.

The rationale is the following. If interest rates were to be positively correlated with futures prices, rising prices will lead to a situation where the long, who will have a profit under such circumstances, can invest profits from marking to market at high rates of interest. Clearly, falling futures prices will lead to a situation where the longs have to finance their losses at a lower rate of interest. Thus, an interest rate that is positively correlated with futures prices is beneficial for the longs. Therefore, longs will have to pay more under such circumstances, which means that the futures price will be higher than the forward price. The positive correlation has no consequences for a forward contract since there is no concept of marking to market. Thus, under such circumstances, futures prices will be higher than forward prices.

On the other hand, if futures prices were negatively correlated with interest rates, then rising futures prices would correspond to a situation where the longs are investing their profits at lower rates of interest, while declining prices will obviously mean that they are financing their losses at higher rates of interest. Consequently, under such circumstances the futures price will be lower than the forward price.

HEDGING THE RATE OF RETURN ON A STOCK PORTFOLIO

Index futures can be used to lock in the rate of return on a stock portfolio. The number of futures contracts required to set up a risk-minimizing hedge can be shown as:

$$\beta_p \frac{P_t}{I_t}$$

β_p is the beta of the portfolio whose risk is sought to be hedged. P_t is the current market value of the portfolio being hedged, and I_t is the present index level in dollars.

EXAMPLE 6.18

Consider a stock portfolio that is currently worth 5MM USD. The S&P 500 index is quoted at 400 and the lot size (contract multiplier) is 250. Thus the value of the index is terms of dollars is $400 \times 250 = \$100,000$.

If the portfolio beta is 1.40, then the hedger needs to go short in the following number of contracts:

$$1.40 \times \frac{5,000,000}{100,000} = 70$$

Assuming that the stocks in the index are not scheduled to pay any dividends during the life of the futures contract, the pricing condition required to preclude both forms of arbitrage is:

$$F_t = I_t \left[1 + r \times \frac{(T - t)}{360} \right]$$

where $T - t$ is the time remaining until the expiration date of the futures contract.

If we were to assume that there are 90 days until expiration, and that the interest rate is 7.20% per annum, the corresponding futures price is:

$$F_t = 400 \times [1 + 0.072 \times 0.25] = 407.20$$

We will consider two illustrations, the first where the index rises, and the second where it declines.

EXAMPLE 6.19

The index value 90 days hence is at 425. The return on the index is $\frac{(425 - 400)}{400} \equiv$ 6.25%.

The riskless rate for 90 days is $7.20 \times 0.25 = 1.80\%$

(continued)

(*continued*)

Thus the rate of return on the portfolio is

$$1.80 + 1.40(6.25 - 1.80) = 8.03\%$$

The terminal value of the portfolio is $5,000,000 \times 1.0803 = \$5,401,500$. The profit/loss from the futures position is:

$$70 \times 250 \times (407.20 - 425) = \$(311,500)$$

The net value of the asset is $5,401,500 - 311,500 = 5,090,000$. The rate of return is

$$\frac{90,000}{5,000,000} \times 100 \times \frac{360}{90} = 7.20\%$$

The portfolio has earned the riskless rate of return over a period of 90 days, because the futures contracts have completely eliminated the exposure to market risk.

EXAMPLE 6.20

Now assume that the index is at 375 after 90 days. The rate of return is −6.25%. The portfolio return is:

$$1.80 + 1.40(-6.25 - 1.80) = -9.47\%$$

The terminal value of the portfolio is: $5,000,000 \times (1.00 - 0.0947) = \$4,526,500$.
The futures profit/loss is: $70 \times 250 \times (407.20 - 375.00) = \$563,500$.
Thus, the net value of the asset is $4,526,500 + 563,500 = \$5,090,000$. As expected, we have once again locked in the riskless rate for 90 days.

CHANGING THE BETA

Stock index futures can be used to change the beta of a stock portfolio. Assume that a portfolio has a beta of β_0, and that we wish to change it to β_T. The number of futures contracts required is given by:

$$N = (\beta_T - \beta_0)\frac{P_t}{I_t}$$

Thus, if we wish to increase the beta, we should go long in futures contracts, whereas if we wish to decrease the beta, a short position will be required.

EXAMPLE 6.21

Investors are holding a portfolio worth $5MM. The current beta is 1.40 and they wish to increase it to 1.80. The index is currently at 400 and the index multiplier is 250. Since the beta is being sought to be increased, a long futures position is required. The number of contracts required is:

$$(1.80 - 1.40)\frac{5,000,000}{400 \times 250} = 20$$

PROGRAM TRADING

Program trading is a market term for stock index arbitrage. It refers to cash-and-carry and reverse cash-and-carry arbitrage strategies implemented with the help of index futures contracts. If potential arbitrageurs were of the opinion that the futures contract is overpriced, they would go in for a cash-and-carry strategy by buying the stocks contained in the index and taking a short position in index futures. On the other hand, if they were of the opinion that the contract is underpriced, they would short sell the stocks contained in the index and take a long position in index futures.

Index arbitrage therefore requires traders to take simultaneous long or short positions in a large basket of securities.[6] Given the magnitude of the task, computer-based programs are indispensible for implementing such strategies, and hence the origin of the term *program trading*.

EXAMPLE 6.22

A value-weighted index is based on four stocks whose current prices and numbers of shares outstanding are given in Table 6.8.

TABLE 6.8   Prices, Number of Shares Outstanding, and Market Capitalization

Company	Price	# of Shares Outstanding	Market Capitalization
Avery	25	400,000	10,000,000
Avon	40	100,000	4,000,000
Aliph	50	200,000	10,000,000
Alize	100	160,000	16,000,000

Assume that the base period market capitalization is 25,000,000 and that the divisor is 1.0. The index level is:

$$\frac{40,000,000}{25,000,000} \times 100 = 160$$

(continued)

---

[6]The S&P 500 is composed of 500 stocks.

(*continued*)

We will assume that the contract multiplier is 25.

Consider a futures contract that is scheduled to expire after 90 days. Assume that none of the constituent stocks is scheduled to pay a dividend during this period, and that the riskless rate is 8% per annum.

The no-arbitrage futures price is given by:

$$F = 160 \times \left[1 + 0.08 \times \frac{90}{360}\right] = 163.20$$

Assume that the futures contract is priced at 167.50. The contract is clearly overpriced. Arbitrageurs decide to invest $1,000,000 in the stocks constituting the index and go short in the required futures contracts. They will have to invest:

$$\frac{10,000,000}{40,000,000} \times 1,000,000 = \$250,000 \text{ in Avery}$$

$$\frac{4,000,000}{40,000,000} \times 1,000,000 = \$100,000 \text{ in Avon}$$

$$\frac{10,000,000}{40,000,000} \times 1,000,000 = \$250,000 \text{ in Aliph}$$

$$\frac{16,000,000}{40,000,000} \times 1,000,000 = \$400,000 \text{ in Alize}$$

Thus, they will acquire 10,000 shares of Avery, 2,500 shares of Avon, 5,000 shares of Aliph, and 4,000 shares of Alize. The number of futures contracts required is:[7]

$$\frac{1,000,000}{160 \times 25} = 250$$

At the time of contract expiration, the futures price will be set equal to the spot index value at that time, since index futures are always cash settled.

Assume that share prices after 90 days are as shown in Table 6.9.

TABLE 6.9 Prices, Number of Shares Outstanding, and Market Capitalization on the Expiration Date

Company	Price	# of Shares	Market Capitalization
Avery	30.00	400,000	12,000,000
Avon	45.00	100,000	4,500,000
Aliph	57.50	200,000	11,500,000
Alize	137.50	160,000	22,000,000

---

[7]The index has a beta of 1.0.

The index value on this date will be:

$$\frac{50,000,000}{25,000,000} \times 100 = 200$$

The gain/loss from the futures position is: $(167.50 - 200) \times 25 \times 250 = \$(203,125)$.

The cash inflow when the shares are sold is:

$$10,000 \times 30.00 + 2,500 \times 45 + 5,000 \times 57.50 + 4,000 \times 137.50 = \$1,250,000$$

The repayment of the amount borrowed at the outset with interest entails an outflow of

$$1,000,000 \times [1 + 0.08 \times 0.25] = 1,020,000$$

The net cash flow is: $1,250,000 - 1,020,000 - 203,125 = 26,875$.

This is equivalent to $250 \times 25 \times 4.30$, where 4.30 is the difference between the quoted futures price of 167.50 and the no-arbitrage price of 163.20. The profit will always be independent of the stock prices prevailing at expiration, for we have assumed that arbitrageurs can sell the shares in the market at the same prices as those used to compute the index value at expiration.

Now let us turn to reverse cash-and-carry arbitrage. Assume that all the variables have the same value as assumed above, except for the initial futures price, which we will assume is 158.50. Arbitrageurs will short sell the shares required to realize a cash flow of $1MM, which they will lend out at 8% per annum. Simultaneously they will go long in 250 futures contracts. At expiration they will buy back the shares required to cover the short position.

Cash inflow from the initial investment $= 1,000,000 \times [1 + 0.08 \times .0.25] = 1,020,000$.

Profit/loss from the futures market $= 250 \times 25 \times [200 - 158.50] = \$259,375$.

Cost of acquisition of the shares required to cover the short position is $1,250,000.

The net cash flow $= 1,020,000 + 259,375 - 1,250,000 = \$29,375$.

This is equal to $250 \times 25 \times 4.70$, where 4.70 is the difference between the no-arbitrage futures price of 163.20 and the quoted price of 158.50.

STOCK PICKING

Stock pickers are traders who believe that they have the uncanny ability to spot underpriced and overpriced stocks. The rate of return on an asset may be expressed as:

$$r_i = r_f + \beta_i[r_m - r_f] + \varepsilon_i + \alpha_i$$

As per the CAPM, ε_i, which is the return due to unsystematic risk, has an expected value of zero. α_i is what is termed as the abnormal return. If the asset is fairly priced, then α_i will have a value of zero. But if the asset is underpriced or overpriced, then it will have a non-zero value. For underpriced stocks the abnormal return will be positive, whereas for overpriced stocks it will be negative.

Stock pickers who take positions based on their hunch about the stock being mispriced need to guard against adverse movements in the market as a whole. For there is always a risk that even if the anticipated abnormal return were to material-ize, adverse market movements could wipe out the profits, leading to a lower profit or even a loss.

Take the case of traders who believe that a stock is underpriced and that they will get an abnormal return of 0.75% if they were to buy it. Assume that the nonsystematic risk is zero, that the beta of the stock is 1.25, and that the riskless rate is 2.75%.

It could so happen that while the expected abnormal return is translated into reality, the market moves down by say 4%. The return from the stock will be:

$$2.75 + 1.25[-4.00 - 2.75] + 0.75 = -4.9375\%$$

Thus the overall market movement has resulted in a situation where, despite the fact that traders made the right call, they ended up with a negative rate of return.

We will now illustrate how stock pickers can use index futures to capture abnor-mal returns.

EXAMPLE 6.23

Assume that the trader invests $10 MM in the stock and goes short in index futures. If we assume that the current index value is 160, the corresponding futures price will be 164.40.

The required number of futures contracts, assuming a contract multiplier of 25 is:

$$1.25 \times \frac{10,000,000}{160 \times 25} = 3,125$$

If we assume that none of the component stocks are scheduled to pay a divi-dend during the life of the contract, a –4% rate of return on the market corresponds to an index level of 153.60. The rate of return on the stock is –4.9375%, which cor-responds to a terminal portfolio value of $10,000,000 \times [1 - 0.049375] = \$9,506,250$.

The profit/loss from the futures market is:

$$3,125 \times 25 \times [164.40 - 153.60] = \$843,750$$

The total net worth of the trader is $9,506,250 + 843,750 = \$10,350,000$, which implies a return of 3.50%. This return corresponds to the riskless return of 2.75% plus the abnormal return of 0.75%.

EXAMPLE 6.24

Now assume that the trader believes that the abnormal return will be –0.75%. The trader will have to short sell the stock and go long in futures contracts. We will assume that all the other variables have the same values as in the above illustration.

Assume that the market rises by 4%. The rate of return on the stock will be:

$$2.75 + 1.25[4.00 - 2.75] - 0.75 = 3.5625\%$$

The terminal value of the portfolio will therefore be:

$$10{,}000{,}000 \times [1.00 + 0.035625] = 10{,}356{,}250$$

A 4% increase in the market means that the terminal index level will be 166.40. The profit/loss from the futures market will be:

$$3{,}125 \times 25 \times [166.40 - 164.40] = \$156{,}250$$

The proceeds of the short sale can be invested at the outset to yield:

$$10{,}000{,}000 \times [1 + 0.0275] = \$10{,}275{,}000$$

The net cash flow will be:

$$10.275{,}000 + 156{,}250 - 10{,}356{,}250 = \$75{,}000$$

This amount represents the abnormal return of 0.75%.

PORTFOLIO INSURANCE

Index futures contracts can in principle be used to remove the entire risk inherent in a portfolio, thereby ensuring that it earns the riskless rate of return. In practice, however, portfolio managers may not like to convert the entire portfolio into a riskless position. That is, they may choose to convert a fraction of the portfolio into an effective riskless security using index futures contracts, while continuing to hold the balance in its current form. The riskless fraction will earn the riskless rate of return. The risky component's value will be market determined and, in a worst-case scenario, can go to zero. Therefore, in practice there will be a floor on the overall value of the portfolio. The returns on the portfolio may exceed this floor value but cannot be less.

An investment strategy using futures contracts to partially hedge the risk of a stock portfolio is referred to as *portfolio insurance*. In practice, fund managers will constantly monitor the market and either increase or decrease the percentage of investment in the riskless component. That is, the proportion of equity to synthetic debt will be periodically changed. At any point in time, if a greater level of insurance were needed, then more futures contracts would be sold. Such an asset management strategy is referred to as *dynamic hedging*.

EXAMPLE 6.25

Assume that a fund manager is holding a stock portfolio worth 5MM USD, with a beta of 1.20. The current level of the index is 160, and the contract multiplier is 25. Futures contracts are available with 90 days to expiration, and the riskless return for this period is 2.75%.

(continued)

(*continued*)

The no-arbitrage futures price is:

$$160 \times [1 + 0.0275] = 164.40$$

Assume that the manager wants to use a short futures position to convert 3MM USD worth of equity to synthetic debt. The number of futures contracts required is:

$$1.20 \times \frac{3,000,000}{160 \times 25} = 900$$

Assume that 18 days later, the index is at 200. The corresponding futures price will be:

$$200 \times \left[1 + 0.11 \times \frac{72}{360}\right] = 204.40$$

Since the market has increased by 25%, the rate of return on the portfolio over 18 days is:

$$0.55 + 1.20 \times [25 - 0.55] = 29.89\%$$

Hence the value of the portfolio is: $5,000,000 \times [1+0.2989] = \$6,494,500$.
The profit/loss from the futures position is:

$$900 \times 25 \times [164.40 - 204.40] = \$(900,000)$$

Thus the total value of the hedged portfolio is: $6,494,500 - 900,000 = \$5,594,500$.

If the 3MM USD had been perfectly hedged, the value of the overall position after 18 days would have been:

$$2,000,000 \times [1 + 0.2989] + 3,000,000 \times 1.0055 = \$5,614,300$$

Why is it that we were to unable to obtain a perfect hedge? It is because while the futures contracts had 90 days to expiration at the outset, we opted to terminate the hedge after 18 days.

The performance of the hedge may be analyzed as follows. The basis at the end is equal to the basis at the outset. Consequently, the hedge will lock in the initial spot value of the index. Thus, for the 3 MM that we hedged, it is equivalent to a market return of zero. Hence the rate of return is $= 0.55 + 1.2 \times (0 - .55) = 0.11\%$. Hence the value is $3,000,000 \times 0.9989 = 2,996,700$. The value of the unhedged component is $2,000,000 \times 1.2989 = 2,597,800$. The total value is $2,996,700 + 2,597,800 = 5,594,500$.

Because the portfolio value has increased by $594,500, the manager may opt to expose a greater proportion of the funds to market risk. Let us assume that the manager decides to insure the value of $2.75 MM. This will require:

$$1.20 \times \frac{2,750,000}{200 \times 25} = 660 \text{ contracts}$$

IMPORTANCE OF FUTURES

Futures contracts provide economic benefits in a number of ways. First, they facilitate reallocation of risk. All traders in the market do not have an identical appetite for risk. Hedgers seek to avoid risk while speculators consciously seek to take risk. Futures contracts enable the transfer of risk from those who do not want to bear it to those who consciously seek to take risky positions in anticipation of gains.

Second, futures markets facilitate price discovery. The informational accuracy of asset prices is imperative for ensuring the success of a free market economy. When new information enters the market, it typically percolates into the futures markets a lot faster. This is because taking a long futures position requires the deposit of a relatively small margin, as compared to a long stock position where the entire value has to be deposited up front. In addition, from the standpoint of bears, taking a short futures position is a lot easier in practice than short selling the underlying asset. Consequently, trading volumes in derivative markets tend to be high. This has two major consequences: (1) transactions costs in such markets tend to be much lower as compared to spot markets, and (2) these markets are characterized by a high degree of liquidity.

Futures contracts play a critical economic role by enabling markets to be more efficient. Because trading in such markets is relatively easier, new information with an implication for prices typically permeates such markets first. As there is a pricing relationship between spot and futures markets, this will initially manifest itself as an arbitrage opportunity. The activities of arbitrageurs will, however, quickly ensure that the spot markets too reflect the new information.

Finally, futures markets are a very potent tool for speculators, both bulls and bears. The freedom to speculate is imperative for the effective functioning of the free market system. Futures contracts are attractive for speculators because positions can be taken by depositing relatively smaller amounts. Besides, as explained earlier, they are a vital tool for those seeking to go short.

CHAPTER 7

Options Contracts

INTRODUCTION

Forward and futures contracts, which we examined earlier, are commitment contracts. That is, once an agreement is reached to transact at a future point in time, noncompliance by either party would be tantamount to default. In other words, having committed to the transaction, the long – whom we have defined as the party who has agreed to acquire the underlying asset – must buy the asset by paying the pre-fixed price to the short. At the same time, the short is obliged to deliver the underlying asset in return for the payment.

Now let us turn our attention to contracts that give the buyer the right to transact in the underlying asset. The difference between a right and an obligation is that a right needs to be exercised if it is in the interest of holders and need not be exercised if it is not beneficial for them. An obligation, on the other hand, mandates them to take the required action, irrespective of whether they stand to benefit or not. Contracts to transact at a future point in time, which give buyers the right to transact, are referred to as options contracts, for they are being conferred an option to perform. When it comes to bestowing a right, there are two possibilities. Buyers can be given the right to acquire the underlying asset or they can be given the right to sell the underlying asset. Consequently, there are two categories of options: call options and put options. A call option gives the buyers of the option the right to buy the underlying asset at a predecided price, whereas a put option gives them the right to sell the underlying asset at a pre-fixed price. The prespecified price in the contract is termed as the strike price or the exercise price.

Let us first consider call options. Clearly, holders will exercise their right to purchase the underlying asset only if the prevailing spot price at the time of exercise is higher than the exercise price. In such a situation, however, the counterparty, who has sold the option, would be unwilling to transact if they could get away with it. The only way that we can ensure compliance on the part of the sellers of the option is by imposing an obligation on them. Consequently, call options give buyers the right to buy the underlying asset and impose a contingent obligation on the sellers. The term contingent indicates that the sellers will have an obligation to perform if and when the buyers exercise their right.

The same rationale applies for put options. The buyers of the option will choose to sell the underlying asset only if the prevailing spot price at the time of exercise is less than the exercise price of the option. Once again, the sellers of the put option will be unwilling to take delivery under such circumstances if they can avoid it. Consequently, there is once again a need to impose an obligation on the sellers of the put. Thus, both call and put options give a right to the option buyers and impose a contingent obligation on the sellers. Contracts for transactions scheduled at a future point in time may impose an obligation on both parties, as do forward and futures contracts, or they may grant a right to one party while imposing an obligation on the counterparty, as do options contracts.

The party who buys the options contract, whether it is a call or a put, is referred to as the option buyer or the long. The counterparty who sells the options contracts is termed as the option writer or the short. The implication is that the short has written the options contract.

From the standpoint of the date of exercise, there are two possibilities. The scheduled transaction date may be either the only point in time at which the holders of the option can exercise their right, or it may represent the last point in time at which they can exercise the option. Consequently, we have two types of call options and two types of put options. Call and put options that permit the holders to exercise only at the point of expiration of the contract are referred to as European options. Contracts that give the holders the flexibility of exercising on or before the expiration date of the option are referred to as American options. If we were to compare options contracts which are equivalent in all other respects, an American option will be more valuable than a European option.

The strike price or exercise price represents the price at which the underlying asset can be bought if a call is exercised, and the price at which it can be sold if a put option is exercised. The option itself, however, carries an attached price tag, which is called the option price or the option premium. This is the price that the option buyers have to pay to the option sellers at the outset, for conferring them the right to transact. Thus, unlike in the case of forward and futures contracts, where the two equal and opposite obligations ensure that neither party has to pay the other at the outset, options contracts require buyers to pay an up-front price. This is required for both calls and puts, whether the option is European or American. While the strike price enters the picture only if the option is exercised, the premium payable at the outset is nonrefundable and represents a sunk cost.

While forward contracts are OTC products, and futures contracts are exchange traded, options can be of both types. Options exchanges offer standardized contracts, and customized contracts can be privately negotiated by corporations and financial institutions. We have once again used the terms *standardization* and *customization*, which refer to the terms and conditions of the contract. In the case of an options contract the critical terms are the exercise price, the expiration date, and the contract size. In the case of OTC options, the two parties are at liberty to fix any strike price and contract size and choose any desirable expiration date. As in the case of a forward contract, these terms will have to be finalized by way of bilateral negotiations. In the case of exchange-traded options contracts, however, the exchange will fix these parameters. For instance, on the CBOE a stock options contract is for 100 shares. Thus, transactions are possible only in multiples of 100. Contracts expire on the third Friday of the month. The last day of trading is the third Friday of the month, or the preceding business day if the third Friday is a holiday. Thus, stock options contracts expiring on any other day of the month cannot be traded on the exchange. The exchange will also specify the allowable exercise prices. Traders are at liberty to enter into contracts with one of the allowable exercise prices, but cannot choose a price that is not permitted by the exchange. Exchange-traded stock options are American in nature while options based on stock indices may be either European or American.

NOTATION

We will use the following symbols to depict the various variables.

- $t \equiv$ today, a point in time before the expiration of the options contract
- $T \equiv$ the point of expiration of the options contract
- $S_t \equiv$ the stock price at time t
- $S_T \equiv$ the stock price at the point of expiration of the options contract
- $I_t \equiv$ the index value at time t
- $I_T \equiv$ the index value at the point of expiration of the options contract
- $X \equiv$ the exercise price of the option
- $C_t \equiv$ a general symbol for the premium of a call option at time t, when we do not wish to make a distinction between European and American options
- $P_t \equiv$ a general symbol for the premium of a put option at time t, when we do not wish to make a distinction between European and American options
- $C_T \equiv$ a general symbol for the premium of a call option at time T, when we do not wish to make a distinction between European and American options
- $P_T \equiv$ a general symbol for the premium of a put option at time T, when we do not wish to make a distinction between European and American options
- $C_{E,t} \equiv$ the premium of a European call option at time t
- $P_{E,t} \equiv$ the premium of a European put option at time t
- $C_{A,t} \equiv$ the premium of an American call option at time t
- $P_{A,t} \equiv$ the premium of an American put option at time t
- $C_{E,T} \equiv$ the premium of a European call option at time T
- $P_{E,T} \equiv$ the premium of a European put option at time T
- $C_{A,T} \equiv$ the premium of an American call option at time T
- $P_{A,T} \equiv$ the premium of an American put option at time T
- $r \equiv$ the riskless rate of interest per annum

EXERCISING OPTIONS

Let us first consider contracts that are delivery settled. For the purpose of exposition, we will focus on European options although the underlying rationale applies to American options as well, with the difference being that such options may possibly be exercised prior to the expiration date.

Take the case of a call options contract on XYZ stock. Each contract is for 100 shares. Let the exercise price be $\$X$ and the option premium be C_t. Option premiums are always quoted on a per-share basis in practice. So, the premium for the contract is $100C_t$. At the time of entering into the trade, the buyers of the contract will have to pay $\$100C_t$ to the sellers for giving them the right to transact. On the expiration date of the contract there could be two possibilities. The prevailing stock price S_T may be greater than X or less than X. Obviously the buyers will choose to exercise only if $S_T > X$. If they decide to exercise, they will pay $100X$ to the sellers, who in turn will deliver 100 shares to them.

Now consider the case of put options on the same stock. Let us denote the premium per share by P_t. Buyers will have to pay the writer $100P_t$ at the outset. Obviously, it would make sense to sell a share at a price X only if the prevailing market price were to be lower. Consequently, a European put option will be exercised only if the terminal stock price S_T is less than X. If the holders were to exercise, they would have to deliver 100 shares to the writer, who in turn will have to pay $100X$ to them. In the case of both contracts – that is, calls and puts – the initial premium is nonrefundable if market movements were to be such that the option holders choose not to exercise their right. Let us now consider numerical illustrations to reinforce the concepts.

EXAMPLE 7.1

Consider a call options contract on ABC with an exercise price of $85, which is scheduled to expire on 21 July 20XX. Assume that today is 1 June 20XX, and that the premium is $6.25 per share. The option is bought by Ron from Pete.

Right at the outset, Ron will have to pay $6.25 \times 100 = \$625$ to Pete. This represents the option premium, which is nonrefundable. On 21 July there are two possibilities. The stock price may be more than $85, say $95, or it may be less than $85, say $70. If the terminal price is $95, it would clearly make sense for Ron to exercise the option and acquire the shares at a price of $85. If the terminal price were to be $70, however, it would make no sense to exercise the option and Ron will simply allow it to expire without exercising it. The last action clearly demonstrates the difference between a futures contract and an options contract. Because an options contract is not a commitment contract, holders need not perform if it is not in their interest.

Assuming that the terminal stock price is $95, Ron will pay $85 \times 100 = \$8,500$ to Pete in return for the 100 shares. If he does not want to hold the shares, he can immediately sell them to realize a profit of $9,500 − \$8,500 = \$1,000$. After taking into account the premium paid at the outset, the profit is $375. But if the terminal stock price is $70, the options will not be exercised and the loss for Ron is $625, which represents the premium paid at the outset.

EXAMPLE 7.2

Let us consider the information in the preceding example but assume that the options are puts with an option premium of $3.00. If Ron were to buy the options from Pete, he would have to pay $300 at the outset. This is a nonrefundable payment. On 21 July the stock price, we will assume, can be either $95 or $70. It would not make sense to sell the shares for $85 if the market price per share were $95. Thus, in this case Ron would allow the options to expire worthless and forfeit the initial payment of $300. If the terminal stock price were to be $70, however,

(continued)

(*continued*)

it would make sense to sell the shares at $85. If Ron has the shares, he would be willing to sell. Otherwise, he would be willing to buy the shares from the market and exercise the option. His profit in this case would be $8,500 − $7,000 = $1,500, or $1,200 if we were to take the up-front premium paid into account.

Thus, a call will be exercised if $S_T > X$; otherwise, it would be allowed to expire worthless. Therefore the payoff at expiration is $Max[0, S_T − X]$. The profit is $Max[0, S_T − X] − C_t$. On the other hand, a put will be exercised if $S_T < X$, and would otherwise be allowed to expire. Thus the payoff at expiration is $Max[0, X − S_T]$, while the profit is $Max[0, X − S_T] − P_t$.

Now let us look at the cash flows from the perspective of the writer.

EXAMPLE 7.3

Consider call options on ABC with an exercise price of $45. Assume that the premium is $3.25 per share. If the terminal stock price were to be $52, then the options will be exercised. The payoff for the writer is:

$$100 \times (45 − 52) = (700)$$

The profit is
$$100 \times (45 − 52) + 100 \times 3.25 = (375)$$

In symbolic terms, the payoff can be expressed as $(X − S_T)$ or $−(S_T − X)$. The profit is $−(S_T − X) + C_t$.

If the terminal spot price was $40, however, then the options would not be exercised, and the writer would get to keep the premium of $375. Thus, the writer's profit in this case is C_t.

Thus the payoff for a call writer may be expressed as $−Max[0, (S_T − X)] = Min[0, X − S_T]$. The profit for the writer is therefore $Min[0, X − S_T] + C_t$.

Using similar logic, it can be demonstrated that the payoff for a put writer is $Min[0, S_T − X]$ while the profit is $Min[0, S_T − X] + P_t$.

Thus, options, like futures contracts, are zero-sum games. The profit/loss for the holders is exactly equal to the loss/profit for the writers. Let us consider the profit for call holders, which is $Max[0, S_T − X] − C_t$. The maximum profit is unbounded, as the terminal stock price has no upper bound. Thus, there is no cap on the potential profit for call holders; however, their maximum loss is restricted to the premium paid at the outset. That is, the worst-case scenario from the standpoint of the holders is that the options are not exercised and they lose the entire premium. This once again illustrates the difference between an options contract and a commitment contract. For the call writers, the maximum loss is unbounded, for the stock price has no upper bound; however, the maximum profit is restricted to the premium received at the outset. Thus, the best possibility from the standpoint of the writers is that the options are not exercised and they consequently get to retain the premium paid by the holders. Therefore, while call holders face the specter of infinite profits and finite losses, call writers face the possibility of infinite losses and finite profits.

The profit for put holders is $\text{Max}[0, X - S_T] - P_t$. Thus, the holders stand to gain if the asset price declines. The lowest possible stock price, because of the limited liability feature, is zero. Hence, the maximum profit for put holders is $X - P_t$. Their maximum possible loss is once again the premium that they pay at the outset. Thus, put holders face finite profits as well as finite losses. For writers the profit is $\text{Min}[0, S_T - X] + P_t$. From their standpoint, therefore, the maximum loss is $P_t - X$, while the maximum profit is P_t. Once again, as in the case of the call writers, the best situation that put writers can hope for is that the options are not exercised thereby enabling them to retain the premium received at the outset.

Thus, the maximum loss for an option holder is the premium, while the maximum gain for the option writer is the premium. Because of the limited liability feature of stocks, both put buyers and put writers face the specter of finite profits and finite losses. In the case of calls, however, holders may have unbounded gains, while writers may have unbounded losses. The. maximum loss for the former is the premium, which also represents the maximum profit for the latter.

MONEYNESS

If the current asset price is greater than the exercise price of a call option, then the option is said to be *in the money (ITM)*. But if the spot price is less than the exercise price, then the call is said to be *out of the money (OTM)*. If the two were exactly equal, then the option is said to be *at the money (ATM)*.

Symbolically:

- $S_t > X \Rightarrow$ ITM call and OTM put
- $S_t = X \Rightarrow$ ATM call and ATM put
- $S_t < X \Rightarrow$ OTM call and ITM put

For put options, it is just the opposite. If the spot price of the asset is greater than the exercise price of the option, then the put is said to be *out of the money*. If, however, the spot price is less than the strike price of the option, then we would say the put is *in the money*. And if the spot price is equal to the strike price, the put option would be said to be *at the money*.

An option, whether it is a call or a put, would be exercised only if it is in the money. Prior to the expiration date, however, it is not necessary that an option be exercised if it is in the money, for the holder may like to wait in anticipation of the contract going deeper into the money. At expiration, of course, an in-the-money contract will be exercised.

EXAMPLE 7.4

Call and put options on ABC are available with exercise prices of $45, $50, and $55. The current stock price is $50. In the case of calls, the contract with a strike of 45 is in the money; that with a strike of 50 is at the money; and the one with

(continued)

(*continued*)

a strike of 55 is out of the money. For puts it is just the reverse. The put with an exercise price of 45 is out of the money; that with an exercise price of 50 is at the money; while the contract with an exercise price of 55 is in the money. Thus, if a call with a given exercise price and expiration date is in the money, a put with the same exercise price and expiration date will be out of the money, and vice versa.

EXCHANGE-TRADED OPTIONS

An exchange-traded options contract is standardized, as discussed earlier. That is, the contract size, the allowable exercise prices, and the allowable expiration dates are specified by the exchange. Thus, while an infinite number of OTC options contracts can be designed, there will only be a finite number of exchange-traded products available at any point in time. We will now discuss how the allowable exercise prices and expiration dates are fixed by the exchange.

When the exchange declares a new asset to be eligible to have options written on it, it will assign the asset to a quarterly cycle. There are three possible cycles: January, February, and March. The January cycle comprises the following months: January, April, July, and October. The February cycle comprises: February, May, August, and November. The March cycle comprises: March, June, September, and December.

At any point in time, the allowable contract months are:

- The current month
- The following month
- And the next two months of the cycle to which the underlying asset has been assigned

Here is an illustration.

EXAMPLE 7.5

Assume that today is 28 July 20XX, which is the fourth Friday of the month. The July 20XX contracts would have ceased trading on 21 July. Assume that the asset has been assigned to the January cycle. The available contracts on 28 July will be August 20XX contracts, which represent the current month; the September 20XX contracts, which represent the following month; and October 20XX and January 20(XX + 1) contracts, which represent the two months from the January cycle after September 20XX. When the August contracts expire, September will automatically become the current month. October will be the following month. As far as the next two months from the cycle are concerned, January 20(XX + 1) will already exist. Consequently, contracts expiring in April 20(XX + 1) will be declared to be eligible for trading. When the September contracts expire, October will automatically become the current month. So, November contracts that represent the next month will need to be introduced. The next two months from the cycle, namely January 20(XX + 1) and April 20(XX + 1), will already exist. Similarly, when the October contracts expire, December 20XX contracts will have to be introduced. And when the November contracts expire, July 20(XX + 1) contracts will have to be permitted.

In addition to these contracts, the CBOE offers contracts on both individual stocks and stock indices with up to three years to maturity. These contracts are termed as *Long Term Equity Anticipation Securities* or *LEAPS*. These contracts expire on the third Friday of January each year.

Now let us turn our attention to the permitted exercise prices. At any point in time there will always be a contract that is at the money or near the money. In addition, there will be other contracts which are in or out of the money to various extents. When contracts for a new calendar month are listed, two strike prices that are closest to the prevailing price of the stock will be chosen. The CBOE usually follows the rule that the interval formed by these two strike prices should be $2.50 if the stock price is less than $25; $5.00 if the stock price is between $25 and $200; and $10.00 if the stock price exceeds $200. Subsequently, based on the movement in the price of the underlying asset, additional exercise prices may be permitted for trading. Thus, at a given point in time, contracts with many different exercise prices will be trading for a particular expiration month. Of course, not all contracts will be equally active.

OPTION CLASS AND OPTION SERIES

All options contracts on a given asset that are of the same type, that is, calls or puts, are said to belong to the same option class, irrespective of the exercise price or expiration date. For instance, an ABC call with $X = \$80$ and a maturity of January 20XX would be said to belong to the same class as an ABC call with $X = \$85$ and a maturity of February 20XX.

All the contracts that belong to the same class, and have the same exercise price and expiration date, are said to belong to the same option series. Thus an ABC call option contract with $X = \$80$ and a maturity of January 20XX that is executed at 10:30 a.m. on a given day is said to belong to the same series as another call with $X = \$80$ and a maturity of January 20XX that is executed at 11:00 a.m. on that day.

FLEX OPTIONS

Before the CBOE introduced exchange-traded options, the only way to trade options was in the OTC market. While standardized options contracts have their own benefits, for many institutional traders OTC options are more attractive as they provide greater flexibility from the standpoint of contract design. Consequently, the exchanges were required to design contracts specifically targeted at such investors in order to prevent them from opting for OTC products. Their response was FLEX options, where FLEX stands for FLexible EXchange.

Such options combine the features of exchange-traded and OTC products. On the one hand, as in the case of OTC products, these contracts permit traders to choose their own contract terms, such as exercise price and expiration date. On the other hand, these contracts are cleared by the clearing corporation, which eliminates the counterparty risk that is associated with OTC products.

CONTRACT ASSIGNMENT

When traders with a long position declare their intention to exercise, a counterparty has to be found to give delivery in the case of calls, and to take delivery in the case of puts. As in the case of futures contracts, it is not necessary that the party who originally traded with the holder of option should still have an open short position. This is because they could have exited the market at a prior point in time by taking a counterposition.

When holders wish to exercise, they will inform their brokers, who will convey their declaration of intent to the clearinghouse by placing an exercise order. In most cases, there will be many different brokers through whom traders would have taken short positions in the contract being exercised. The clearinghouse will have to choose one of them. Typically, the clearing firm chosen by the clearinghouse will have multiple clients who have written options with the same exercise price and expiration date. The clearing firm will consequently have to choose one such writer to deliver the stock in the case of calls, or to accept delivery in the case of puts. The writer who is chosen to perform in such a fashion is said to be assigned.

ADJUSTING FOR CORPORATE ACTIONS

Exchange-traded options have to be adjusted for corporate actions such as stock splits and stock dividends. Take, for instance, a 20% stock dividend. If the current share price were to be S_t, post-split the price in theory ought to be $5/6 \times S_t$. The terms of the options contract would be adjusted as follows. The exercise price will be modified to $5/6 \times X$. and the contract size will be changed to $6/5 \times 100 = 120$. Similarly, if a firm were to announce an $n{:}m$ split, the contract size will be increased from 100 to $n/m \times 100$, and the exercise price will be modified to $m/n \times X$.

EXAMPLE 7.6

Consider an equity option contract with a contract size of 100 and an exercise price of $75. Assume that the underlying stock pays a 20% stock dividend. If so, the terms of the contract will be altered as follows. The contract size will be increased to 120, and the exercise price will be changed to $62.50.

EXAMPLE 7.7

Consider an equity options contract with a contract size of 100 and an exercise price of $75. Assume that the firm announces a 5:4 split. If so, the following adjustments will be made to the terms of the contract. The contract size will be increased to 125. And the exercise price will be reduced to $60.

NONNEGATIVE OPTION PREMIA

Neither European nor American options can ever have a negative premium. That is, no rational trader will pay you for giving you a right. The acquirer of the right has to pay the party who is offering the right. A negative option premium, which would imply that the writer has to pay the holder, will be a classic case of arbitrage. Because, if an option were to have a negative premium, a rational trader will buy the option and pocket the premium. If the option were to subsequently end up in the money, the trader stands to make an additional profit. Otherwise, if the option were to end up out of the money, the trader need not take any action and consequently does not face the specter of a cash outflow. This is clearly a case of arbitrage.

INTRINSIC VALUE AND TIME VALUE

The intrinsic value of an option is the extent to which it is in the money, if it is in the money, else it is equal to zero. That is, in-the-money options will have a positive intrinsic value, whereas at-the-money and out-of-the money options will have a zero intrinsic value. This is true for calls as well as puts; that is, by definition, the intrinsic value of an option cannot be negative.

Thus, for calls:

I.V. = $\text{Max}[0, S_t - X]$ and for puts: I.V. = $\text{Max}[0, X - S_t]$

The difference between the current option premium and the current intrinsic value is referred to as the time value or the speculative value of the option. Because out-of-the money options have a zero intrinsic value, their entire premium represents their time value. And because an option cannot have a negative premium, such options will always have a nonnegative time value. In-the-money options may or may not have a negative time value, as we will demonstrate shortly.

EXAMPLE 7.8

Call options on ABC are available with a premium of $7.25. The current stock price is $105, and the exercise price of the contracts is $100. The intrinsic value is $(105 - 100) = \$5$. The time value is $7.25 - 5.00 = \$2.25$.

EXAMPLE 7.9

Consider a put option contract with an exercise price of $80, and a premium of $2.75. Assume that the current stock price is $84. The I.V is: Max[0, 80 − 84] = 0.

Thus the entire premium of $2.75 represents the speculative or time value of the option.

TIME VALUE OF AMERICAN OPTIONS

American calls and puts cannot have a negative time value, for it would be tanta-mount to arbitrage. This is because if the time value is negative, a trader can acquire the option and immediately exercise it to realize a riskless profit. The rationale does not apply to European options, because they cannot be exercised immediately. Thus, for an American call:

$$C_{A,t} \geq \text{Max}[0, S_t - X]$$

and for an American put:

$$P_{A,t} \geq \text{Max}[0, X - S_t]$$

Out-of-the-money American options cannot have a negative time value for an options contract cannot have a negative premium. We will now demonstrate with the help of numerical examples that in-the-money American calls and puts also cannot have a negative time value.

EXAMPLE 7.10

Consider a stock that is currently trading at $100. Call options with an exercise price of $95 are trading at $4. The intrinsic value is $5. Thus, the time value is obviously −1. We will demonstrate that this amounts to an arbitrage opportunity.

Consider the following strategy. Buy a call and immediately exercise it. The initial outflow is 4 × 100 = $400. The options can immediately be exercised to yield a cash inflow of 5 × 100 = $500. Thus, there is obviously an arbitrage profit of $100.

EXAMPLE 7.11

Consider a stock that is currently trading at $80. Put options with an exercise price of $85 are currently trading at $3.50. This too is a manifestation of arbitrage, for the time value is −1.50.

Consider the following strategy. Buy a put contract. The initial outflow will be $350. Exercise the options immediately. The inflow will be $500. Thus, there is a riskless profit of $150.

TIME VALUE AT EXPIRATION

All options, European or American, calls or puts, must have a zero time value at expiration. That is, the premium of an option at expiration must be equal to its intrinsic value. Violation of this condition will amount to arbitrage as the following examples will demonstrate.

EXAMPLE 7.12

Take the case of a stock trading at $100. Call options with an exercise price of $95, which are scheduled to expire immediately, are quoting at $5.50. Because the intrinsic value is $5, the option has a positive time value, which can be exploited by an arbitrageur as follows. A trader who notices these prices will write a call option, which will lead to a cash inflow of $5.50 for the trader. Because the option is in the money, and is scheduled to expire immediately, the counterparty will exercise, and consequently the arbitrageur will have an outflow of $5.00. The difference of $0.50 per share is clearly an arbitrage profit. Thus, options cannot have a positive time value at the time of expiration.

EXAMPLE 7.13

A stock is trading at $100. Call options with an exercise price of $90, which are scheduled to expire immediately, are quoting at $8.50. Because the intrinsic value of the option is $10, the time value is –1.50. Such a situation too can be exploited by an arbitrageur.

   A trader who notices these prices will buy a call option, which will entail a cash outflow of $8.50. Because it is in the money, the trader will immediately exercise it for an inflow of $10. The difference of $1.50 is clearly an arbitrage profit. Therefore, options cannot have a negative time value at expiration.

PUT-CALL PARITY

The put-call parity relationship for European options on a non-dividend-paying stock may be stated as follows.

$$C_{E,t} - P_{E,t} = S_t - \frac{X}{(1+r)^{T-t}}$$

To prove this consider the following strategy. Buy the stock at the prevailing price; sell a call with an exercise price of X and a time to maturity of $T - t$; buy a put with the same exercise price and expiration date; and borrow the present value of the exercise price. The strategy and its implications in terms of current and future cash flows is depicted in Table 7.1.

   Let us analyze the entries in Table 7.1. The first column represents the transactions that form components of the overall strategy. The second column depicts the

TABLE 7.1   Illustration of Put-Call Parity: Strategy 1

Action	Initial Cash Flow	Terminal Cash Flow If $S_T > X$	If $S_T < X$
Buy the Stock	$-S_t$	S_T	S_T
Sell the Call	$C_{E,t}$	$-(S_T - X)$	0
Buy the Put	$-P_{E,t}$	0	$X - S_T$
Borrow the P.V. of X	$\dfrac{X}{(1+r)^{T-t}}$	$-X$	$-X$
Total	$-S_t + C_{E,t} - P_{E,t} + \dfrac{X}{(1+r)^{T-t}}$	0	0

cash flow corresponding to each transaction. If an asset results in a cash inflow, the initial cash flow will be shown with a positive sign, whereas if it results in a cash out-flow, the initial cash flow will have a negative sign. When an asset is bought there will be an outflow, whereas when an asset is sold there will be a cash inflow. Similarly, when funds are borrowed there will be an inflow, whereas when funds are lent there will be a cash outflow.

The third and fourth columns depict the cash flows at the time of expiration of the option. The variable of relevance is the terminal stock price and its level with respect to the exercise price of the options. There are two possibilities, that is, the stock price may be more than the exercise price or it can be less than it. Irrespective of the stock price, the stock can be sold at the prevailing stock price. If the call is in the money, it will be exercised by the counterparty, whose cash flow will be $S_T - X$, so the arbitrageur's cash flow will be $-(S_T - X)$. If the put is in the money, it will be exercised by the arbitrageur, who will receive $X - S_T$. Finally, because the present value of X has been borrowed at the outset, there will be an outflow of $X at the time of the expiration of the option, because the borrowed amount has to be returned with interest.

As can be seen from Table 7.1, the net cash flow at the point of expiration of the options is zero, irrespective of whether the terminal stock price is above the exercise price or below it. Thus, to rule out arbitrage we require that the initial cash flow be nonpositive, because if we have a cash inflow at the outset, followed by no further outflows, then it would clearly be a case of arbitrage. Therefore, to rule out arbitrage, we require that:

$$-S_t + C_{E,t} - P_{E,t} + \frac{X}{(1+r)^{T-t}} \leq 0$$

If, however, $-S_t + C_{E,t} - P_{E,t} + \dfrac{X}{(1+r)^{T-t}} < 0$, then we can make an arbitrage profit by simply reversing the above strategy, as demonstrated in Table 7.2.

If as assumed earlier that $-S_t + C_{E,t} - P_{E,t} + \dfrac{X}{(1+r)^{T-t}} < 0$, then the initial cash flow in this case will be positive, whereas the terminal cash flows irrespective of the value of the stock price will continue to be zero.

TABLE 7.2 Illustration of Put-Call Parity: Strategy 2

Action	Initial Cash Flow	Terminal Cash Flow	
		If $S_T > X$	If $S_T < X$
Short Sell the Stock	S_t	$-S_T$	$-S_T$
Buy the Call	$-C_{E,t}$	$(S_T - X)$	0
Sell the Put	$P_{E,t}$	0	$-(X - S_T)$
Lend the P.V. of X	$-\dfrac{X}{(1+r)^{T-t}}$	X	X
Total	$S_t - C_{E,t} + P_{E,t} - \dfrac{X}{(1+r)^{T-t}}$	0	0

Hence to ensure the total absence of arbitrage, we require that:

$$-S_t + C_{E,t} - P_{E,t} + \frac{X}{(1+r)^{T-t}} = 0$$

$$\Rightarrow C_{E,t} - P_{E,t} = S_t = \frac{X}{(1+r)^{T-t}}$$

This relationship is referred to as *put-call parity*. The expression that we have derived is valid only for European options on a non-dividend-paying stock. We will subsequently derive the equivalent expression for European options on a dividend-paying stock.

We will now consider the arbitrage strategies that can yield a profit if this relationship were to be violated. First assume that $C - P > S - \text{PV}(X)$. There are three possibilities: the call may be overpriced, and/or the put may be underpriced, and/or the stock may be underpriced. Anything that is perceived as being overpriced must be sold, while an asset that is thought to be underpriced must be bought. Thus, to exploit such a situation, the call must be sold, and the stock and put must be bought. The acquisition of the stock can be funded by using borrowed money.

On the other hand, what if $C - P < S - \text{PV}(X)$? The possibilities are that the call is underpriced, and/or the put is overpriced, and/or the stock is overpriced. Thus, to exploit this situation, the stock must be sold short, the put must be sold, while the call must be bought.

EXAMPLE 7.14

ABC is currently trading at $80. European call and put options with a year to maturity are selling at $7.75 and $1.25 respectively. The stock is not scheduled to pay any dividends during the life of the options contracts. The exercise price of the options is $80 and the riskless rate is 8% per annum.

The difference between the call and put premiums is $6.50; however, the stock price minus the present value of the exercise price is only $5.9259. Thus, there is

(continued)

(continued)

an obvious violation of put-call parity. We can exploit the situation by adopting the first arbitrage strategy that we considered earlier. That is:

- Buy the stock
- Sell the call
- Buy the put
- Borrow the present value of the exercise price

The initial cash flow is $-80 + 7.75 - 1.25 + 74.0741 = 0.5741$. This is clearly an arbitrage profit because the subsequent cash flows are guaranteed to be zero, irrespective of the terminal value of the stock price.

EXAMPLE 7.15

Consider the data used in the previous example. Assume that the calls are priced at \$6.25 each while the other assets, namely the put and the stock, have the same values as assumed before. The difference between the call and put premiums is $6.25 - 1.25 = \$5$. The difference between the stock price and the present value of the exercise price is 5.9259 as before. The arbitrage strategy used above will not yield a profit in this case. But the second strategy used to demonstrate put-call parity will. That is, we need to:

- Short sell the stock
- Buy the call
- Sell the put
- Lend the present value of the exercise price

The initial cash flow is: $80 - 6.25 + 1.25 - 74.0741 = \$0.9259$. This is an arbitrage profit because the subsequent cash flows, if the strategy were to be implemented, are guaranteed to be zero.

IMPLICATIONS FOR THE TIME VALUE

$$C = P + S - PV(X) = P + (S - X) + [X - PV(X)]$$

If the call is in the money, the time value is $P + [X - PV(X)]$, which cannot be negative. If the call is at or out of the money, the entire premium consists of time value. Because the premium cannot be negative, nor can the time value. Thus, European calls on a non-dividend-paying stock will always have a positive time value, except at expiration when they will have a zero time value.

Now let us consider puts.

$$P = C - S + PV(X) = C + (X - S) + [PV(X) - X]$$

If the put is at or out of the money, the entire premium consists of time value, and consequently the time value cannot be negative. If the put is in the money, the time value is $C + \{PV(X) - X\}$. C cannot be negative; however, $PV(X) - X$ is negative. Hence the time value can be negative if the call premium is very low, which would mean that the call is substantially out of the money. If so, a put with the same exercise price will be substantially in the money. Thus, deep in-the-money European puts on a non-dividend-paying stock may have a negative time value.

Rationale: For a given intrinsic value, the longer the wait until exercise, the greater is the interest earned on the exercise price for a European call holder. Thus, the longer the term to maturity of the option, the greater is the premium.

In the case of puts for a given intrinsic value, however, the longer the wait to receive the exercise price, the greater is the interest lost from the inability to invest. This could lead a situation where the time value is negative. For instance, if the stock price is close to zero, the holder would love to exercise immediately; however, the European nature of the option prevents him from doing so. The longer the wait under these circumstances, the greater is the loss for the put holder. Thus, deep in-the-money European put options on a non-dividend-paying stock may have a negative time value.

PUT-CALL PARITY WITH DIVIDENDS

Let us now consider European call and put options on a stock with an exercise price of $\$X$ and $T - t$ periods to maturity. Assume that the stock will pay a dividend of $\$D$ at a time t^*, where $t < t^* < T$. The put-call parity relationship for such options may be stated as:

$$C_{E,t} - P_{E,t} = S_t - \frac{D}{(1 + r)^{t^* - t}} - \frac{X}{(1 + r)^{T - t}}$$

To prove this, consider the strategy depicted in Table 7.3.

It is very similar to the strategy used earlier to demonstrate the put-call parity relationship for a non-dividend-paying stock. The difference is that the stock we have bought is scheduled to pay a known dividend at time t^*. To make the net cash flow at this point in time equal to zero, we assume that the trader borrows the present value of this dividend at the outset. Because the dividend is scheduled to be paid at t^*, the present value is $\frac{D}{(1 + r)^{t^* - t}}$.

As can be seen from Table 7.3, the cash flows at all subsequent points in time are guaranteed to be zero. Hence, to rule out arbitrage we require that the initial cash flow be nonpositive. If the initial cash flow were to be negative, however, we can reverse the above strategy and make arbitrage profits. Consequently, to rule out all forms of arbitrage, we require that:

$$C_{E,t} - P_{E,t} = S_t - \frac{D}{(1 + r)^{t^* - t}} - \frac{X}{(1 + r)^{T - t}}$$

This can be extended to the case of multiple dividends.

TABLE 7.3 Illustration of Put-call Parity for a Dividend-paying Stock

Actions	Initial Cash Flow	Intermediate Cash flow	Terminal Cash flow If $S_T > X$	If $S_T < X$
Buy the Stock	$-S_t$	D	S_T	S_T
Sell the Call	$C_{E,t}$		$-(S_T - X)$	0
Buy the Put	$-P_{E,t}$		0	$X - S_T$
Borrow the P.V. of D	$\dfrac{D}{(1+r)^{t^*-t}}$	$-D$		
Borrow the P.V. of X	$\dfrac{X}{(1+r)^{T-t}}$		$-X$	$-X$
Total	$-S_t + C_{E,t} - P_{E,t}$ $+\dfrac{D}{(1+r)^{t^*-t}} + \dfrac{X}{(1+r)^{T-t}}$	0	0	0

IMPLICATIONS FOR THE TIME VALUE

$$C = P + S - PV(D) - PV(X) = P + (S - X) + [X - PV(X)] - PV(D)$$

If the option is at or out of the money, the time value cannot be negative. For in-the-money calls, however, the time value is $P + [X - PV(X)] - PV(D)$. The put premium cannot be negative and neither can the difference between the exercise price and its present value. But the third term, $-PV(D)$, will be less than zero. Hence if P is very low and D is high, the call option may have a negative time value. If P is very low, the put will be substantially out of the money, which would mean that the call will be substantially in the money. Thus, deep in-the-money European calls on a dividend-paying stock may have a negative time value. There are conflicting forces at work here. The longer the exercise is delayed, the greater the income earned from investing the exercise price. If there is a large dividend before exercise, however, the holder may like to exercise and receive the dividend, which can then be reinvested. The longer the term to maturity of the option, the greater is the lost interest due to the inability to reinvest the dividend. The larger the magnitude of the dividend, the more is the lost interest. Thus, European in-the-money calls on a dividend-paying stock may have a negative time value.

Now consider puts. $P = C - S + PV(D) + PV(X) = C + (X - S) + PV(D) + [PV(X) - X]$.

Once again, at-the-money and out-of-the-money puts cannot have a negative time value. For an in-the-money put, the time value is $C + PV(D) + [PV(X) - X]$. The first two terms are nonnegative while the third is negative. If C is very low, which means that the put is substantially in the money, the time value, as in the case of puts on a non-dividend-paying stock, may be negative. For a given set of a parameters, the lower the magnitude of the dividend, the greater the likelihood of the time value being negative.

A VERY IMPORTANT PROPERTY FOR AMERICAN CALLS

We will now demonstrate that an American call on a non-dividend-paying stock will never be exercised early, that is, prior to expiration. In other words, an American call on a non-dividend-paying stock is exactly equivalent to a European call on the same stock.

Consider the strategy outlined in Table 7.4.

Assume that the initial cash flow is positive. That is:

$$S_t - \frac{X}{(1 + r)^{(T-t)}} - C_t > 0$$

$$\Rightarrow C_t < S_t - \frac{X}{(1 + r)^{(T-t)}} > 0$$

In the table, the initial cash flow has been assumed to be positive. The cash flows at the time of expiration of the option will be nonnegative, as can be seen, whether the option is in the money or out of it. The cash flow at the intermediate point in time t^*, however, looks to be negative. Let us analyze this.

First, why are we concerned with the situation at a time prior to expiration? The reason is that this proof is intended to be common for both European and American options. And whenever we seek to present a result for American options, we need to factor in the consequences of early exercise. In this strategy arbitrageurs have bought the call. If they were to prematurely exercise it, it will lead to an overall cash outflow. Because the option is in their control, however, they will obviously never exercise it early in such circumstances. Thus, we do not have to consider the possibility of a negative cash flow prior to expiration. Hence irrespective of the subsequent movements in the stock price, this strategy will give rise to nonnegative cash flows. So, to rule out arbitrage, the initial cash flow must be nonpositive. Thus:

$$C_t \geq S_t - \frac{X}{(1 + r)^{T-t}}$$

TABLE 7.4   Lower Bound for Call Options

Actions	Initial Cash Flow	Intermediate Cash flow If $S_{t^*} > X$	Terminal Cash flow If $S_T > X$	If $S_T < X$
Short Sell the Stock	S_t	$-S_{t^*}$	$-S_T$	$-S_T$
Buy the Call	$-C_t$	$(S_{t^*} - X)$	$(S_T - X)$	0
Lend the P.V. of X	$-\dfrac{X}{(1 + r)^{T-t}}$	$\dfrac{X}{(1 + r)^{T-t^*}}$	X	X
Total	$S_t - C_t - \dfrac{X}{(1 + r)^{T-t}}$	$\dfrac{X}{(1 + r)^{T-t^*}} - X < 0$	0	$X - S_T > 0$

But what if $S_t - \dfrac{X}{(1+r)^{T-t}} < 0$? Then we can state that $C_t > 0$, for we know that an option cannot have a negative premium. Thus, combining the two conditions we can state that:

$$C_t \geq \text{Max}\left[0, S_t - \frac{X}{(1+r)^{T-t}}\right]$$

We know that an American option must trade at least for its intrinsic value. That is: $C_t > \text{Max}[0, S_t - X]$. But if $C_t \geq \text{Max}\left[0, S_t - \dfrac{X}{(1+r)^{T-t}}\right]$, then this condition will be automatically satisfied. Thus, the condition that we have just derived gives us a tighter lower bound for the premium of an option prior to expiration. Based on this result, we can draw some important conclusions about an American call on a non-dividend-paying stock.

- An in-the-money American call will always have a positive time value except at expiration. We know that the time value of all options must be zero at expiration. From our result, however, if we assume that $S_t > X$, prior to expiration, then:

$$C_{A,t} \geq S_t - \frac{X}{(1+r)^{T-t}} \geq S_t - X$$

- Obviously, an American call on a non-dividend-paying stock will never be exercised early. If holders were to exercise such an option when it is in the money, they will get the intrinsic value of the option. If they were to offset their long position by taking a counterposition, however, they will get the premium, which, as we have just demonstrated, will be greater than the intrinsic value. Thus, traders who desire to get out of a long call position would rather offset than exercise prior to maturity.
- An American call on a non-dividend-paying stock must have the same premium as a European call on the same asset, with the same exercise price and expiration date. Why is an American call generally priced higher than a European call on the same asset, and with the same features? It is because the American call gives the trader the flexibility to exercise early. If, however, an option is never going to be exercised prior to maturity, then the early exercise feature will have no value, and no rational investor will pay for it. Thus, an American call on a non-dividend-paying stock must sell for the same premium as an otherwise similar European call on the same stock.

EARLY EXERCISE OF OPTIONS: AN ANALYSIS

Consider the position of investors who own a call option on a stock and have cash equal to the exercise price of the option. If they were to exercise at time t, they would get one share of stock. If the stock price were to remain constant, which would be tantamount to assuming a constant intrinsic value, the longer the wait, the greater the interest earned on the exercise price. Thus, irrespective of the intrinsic value, holders would like to wait as long as they can, which means they will wait until expiration.

Thus, under no circumstances is it beneficial to exercise an American call on a non-dividend-paying stock prior to expiration. Hence, a trader who acquires such an option will either offset it before expiration or hold it to maturity and exercise it if it is in the money.

American puts may, however, be exercised prior to expiration. Assume that a put is substantially in the money and that the market is convinced that it will finish in the money. Holders will rather exercise than wait, for if they were to exercise, they would get the exercise price, which can be immediately invested to earn the riskless rate. Waiting is suboptimal for it will delay the cash inflow and amount to a loss of interest income. In such a situation, offsetting will not be beneficial because no potential counterparty will be willing to pay a positive time value for the option.

PROFIT PROFILES

We will now depict the profit diagrams for the four basic option positions, that is:

- Long call
- Short call
- Long put
- Short put

The payoff from a long call is $Max[0, S_T - X]$, while the profit is $Max[0, S_T - X] - C_t$. Consider a stock currently trading at $100. Call and put options with an exercise price of $100 are currently trading at $9.50 and $5.60 respectively. The payoffs and profits for the options for various values of the terminal stock price are given in Table 7.5.

The profit diagrams are as depicted in Figures 7.1 and 7.2.

The payoffs and profits for short call and put positions are as shown in Table 7.6.

TABLE 7.5   Payoffs and Profits for Long Call and Put Positions

Terminal StockPrice	Payoff for Call	Profit for Call	Payoff for Put	Profit for Put
50	0	−950	5,000	4,440
60	0	−950	4,000	3,440
70	0	−950	3,000	2,440
80	0	−950	2,000	1,440
90	0	−950	1,000	440
94.40	0	−950	560	0
100	0	−950	0	−560
109.50	950	0	0	−560
110	1,000	50	0	−560
120	2,000	1,050	0	−560
130	3,000	2,050	0	−560
140	4,000	3,050	0	−560
150	5,000	4,050	0	−560

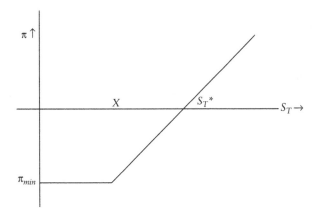

FIGURE 7.1 Profit Diagram for a Long Call Position

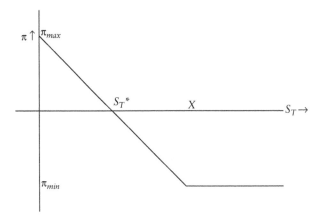

FIGURE 7.2 Profit Diagram for a Long Put Position

TABLE 7.6 Payoffs and Profits for Short Call and Put Positions

Terminal StockPrice	Payoff for Call	Profit for Call	Payoff for Put	Profit for Put
50	0	950	−5,000	−4,440
60	0	950	−4,000	−3,440
70	0	950	−3,000	−2,440
80	0	950	−2,000	−1,440
90	0	950	−1,000	−440
94.40	0	950	−560	0
100	0	950	0	560
109.50	−950	0	0	560
110	−1,000	−50	0	560
120	−2,000	−1,050	0	560
130	−3,000	−2,050	0	560
140	−4,000	−3,050	0	560
150	−5,000	−4,050	0	560

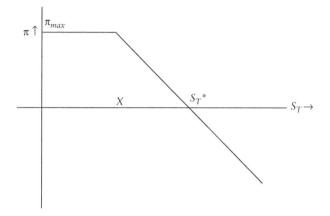

FIGURE 7.3   Profit Diagram for a Short Call Position

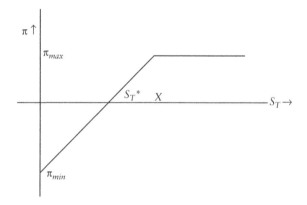

FIGURE 7.4   Profit Diagram for a Short Put Position

SPECULATION WITH OPTIONS

Traders can use options contracts for speculation. Bulls can take a long position in call options or short positions in put options. In either case, they stand to make a profit if they are right, and the market does rise. Figure 7.3 depicts the profit profile for a short call position while Figure 7.4 depicts the equivalent profile for a short put position.

EXAMPLE 7.16

A stock is currently trading at $100. Call options with six months to expiration and an exercise price of $100 are trading at $10.90. Traders are of the view that the market will rise over the next six months, and consequently decide to speculate by taking a long position in five contracts.

(continued)

(*continued*)

Assume that the stock price after six months is 122. If so, the options will be exercised, and the profit from five contracts will be:

$$5 \times 100 \times (122 - 100) - 5 \times 100 \times 10.90 = \$5,550$$

If the stock price were to fall and reach a value of $90 after six months, however, the contracts will be allowed to expire worthless. The loss in this case will be the premium paid at the outset, which is:

$$5 \times 100 \times 10.90 = \$5,450$$

Thus, the difference between speculating with options versus speculating with futures is that in the case of an options contract, a speculator who goes long in an option cannot lose more than the premium paid at the outset.

EXAMPLE 7.17

Consider the data used in the previous illustration. Assume that the stock price rises to $110 after a few weeks and that the corresponding value of the option is $16.65. The traders can offset their position and exit with a profit. In this case the profit will be:

$$5 \times 100 \times (16.65 - 10.90) = \$2,875$$

EXAMPLE 7.18

Bulls can also use a short position in put options to speculate. Assume that put options with an exercise price of $100 and six months to expiration are trading at $6.00. Traders decide to sell five contracts. If they read the market correctly and the stock price after six months is more than $100, the counterparty will not exercise the options. The profit for the speculator is the premium received at the outset, which is:

$$5 \times 100 \times 6.00 = \$3,000$$

EXAMPLE 7.19

Consider the data used in the previous illustration. Assume that a few weeks after the position is taken the stock price rises to $110 and the put premium falls to $2.70. The traders can offset their position by going long in puts and exit the market with a profit. The profit in this case is:

$$5 \times 100 \times (6.00 - 2.70) = \$1,650$$

In the case of speculators who take short positions in options, the losses can be significant, as the following example illustrates.

EXAMPLE 7.20

Richard, who is bullish about the market, takes a short position in five put options contracts when the premium is $6.00. A few weeks later the stock price falls dramatically to $25, and the option premium rises to $71. The loss for the trader if he were to offset would be:

$$5 \times 100 \times (6.00 - 71.00) = -32{,}500$$

Bears can also use options to speculate. In their case, they will have to use a long position in put options or a short position in call options.

HEDGING WITH OPTIONS

Call and put options can be used to hedge the risk associated with spot positions. We will study two hedging strategies, using calls to hedge a short spot position, and using puts to hedge a long spot position.

Using Call Options to Protect a Short Position

Call options can be used to hedge the risk associated with a short spot position. To implement the strategy, the trader needs to acquire a call option for every share that is sold short. The profit from the short spot position is $S_t - S_T$. The profit from the long call is $\text{Max}[0, S_T - X] - C_t$. Thus, the total profit is equal to:

$$S_t - S_T + \text{Max}[0, S_T - X] - C_t$$

If the option were to expire in the money, the call will be exercised. The total profit in this case will be: $S_t - X - C_t$. This represents the minimum profit from the position. If the option were to expire out of the money, however, the call will expire worthless, and the profit will be: $S_t - S_T - C_t$. The break-even stock price is given by:

$$S_t - S_T^* - C_t = 0 \Rightarrow C_t = S_t - S_T^*$$

The maximum profit will arise if the stock price were to attain a value of zero, and will be equal to $S_t - C_t$. Thus, the hedged position puts a cap on the loss in the event of an adverse market movement, but enables the trader to benefit from a positive market movement.

EXAMPLE 7.21

Assume that the initial stock price is $100. Call options with an exercise price of $100 and six months to expiration are available at a premium of $10.90. Traders

(continued)

(continued)

decide to hedge their short stock position by buying a call option. The profit for various values of the terminal stock price is shown in Table 7.7.

TABLE 7.7 Profit from the Hedged Position for Various Values of the Terminal Stock Price

Terminal Stock Price	Cash Flow from Short Stock	Cash Flow from Option	Profit from Strategy
10	9,000	0	7,910
20	8,000	0	6,910
30	7,000	0	5,910
40	6,000	0	4,910
50	5,000	0	3,910
60	4,000	0	2,910
70	3,000	0	1,910
80	2,000	0	910
89.10	1,090	0	0.00
90	1,000	0	−90
100	0	0	−1,090
110	−1,000	1,000	−1,090
120	−2,000	2,000	−1,090
130	−3,000	3,000	−1,090
140	−4,000	4,000	−1,090
150	−5,000	5,000	−1,090
160	−6,000	6,000	−1,090

Thus, the maximum loss is capped at $1,090. The break-even point is 89.10, which is $100 - 10.90 = S_t - C_t$. The position leaves the trader with the opportunity to take advantage of price movements on the downside.

Using Put Options to Protect a Long Spot Position

Similarly, put options can be used to protect a long spot position from price risk. In this case, hedgers have to buy one put option for every stock that they acquire. The profit from the long stock position is: $S_T - S_t$. The profit from the long put position is: $\text{Max}[0, X - S_T] - P_t$. Thus the profit from the overall position is: $S_T - S_t + \text{Max}[0, X - S_T] - P_t$. If the terminal stock price were to be below the exercise price, the puts will be exercised, and the overall profit will be $X - S_t - P_t$. This represents the maximum loss from the position. If the option were to end up out of the money, the profit will be $S_T - S_t - P_t$. The break-even point is given by $S_{T*} = S_t + P_t$. There is obviously no upper limit on the profit. Once again, the hedge puts a cap on the loss, while permitting traders to take advantage of favorable market movements.

EXAMPLE 7.22

Consider a stock that is trading at $100. Put options with an exercise price of $100 and six months to expiration are trading at $6.00. Traders decide to hedge their long stock position by buying a put option. The profit for various values of the terminal stock price is shown in Table 7.8.

TABLE 7.8 Profit from the Hedged Position for Various Values of the Terminal Stock Price

Terminal Stock Price	Cash Flow from Long Stock	Cash Flow from Option	Profit from Strategy
10	−9,000	9,000	−600
20	−8,000	8,000	−600
30	−7,000	7,000	−600
40	−6,000	6,000	−600
50	−5,000	5,000	−600
60	−4,000	4,000	−600
70	−3,000	3,000	−600
80	−2,000	2,000	−600
90	−1,000	1,000	−600
100	0	0	−600
106	600	0	0.00
110	1,000	0	400
120	2,000	0	1,400
130	3,000	0	2,400
140	4,000	0	3,400
150	5,000	0	4,400
160	6,000	0	5,400

Thus, the maximum loss is capped at $600. The break-even point is 106, which is $100 + 6 = S_t + P_t$. The position leaves the trader with the opportunity to take advantage of price movements on the upside.

VALUATION

Options, unlike futures contracts, cannot be priced by ruling out simple cash-and-carry and reverse cash-and-carry arbitrage strategies. The value of an option depends on the probability that it will finish in the money, and on the payoff if it does so. Consequently, to price an option, we need to make an assumption about the process for the evolution of the price of the underlying asset over time. The pricing formula obtained would depend on the price process that is postulated. In some cases, we will arrive at precise mathematical formulae, or what we term as closed-form solutions, while in other cases the best we can do is to come up with a numerical approximation.

The price of an option, irrespective of the price process assumed, is a function of the following variables.

The Price of the Underlying Asset: Because the option is based on the underlying asset, its price will depend on the price of the underlying asset. Keeping all the other variables constant, the higher the price of the underlying asset, the higher will be the value of a call option, and the lower will be the value of a put option.

The Exercise Price: The partial derivative of the option premium with respect to the exercise price will be negative for call options and positive for put options, as is to be expected. That is, the higher the exercise price, ceteris paribus, the lower will be the call premium and the higher will be the put premium.

Dividends: When a stock goes ex-dividend, the share price will decline immediately. Because the call premium is positively related to the stock price, the larger the dividend, the lower will be the call premium. Similar logic tells us that the larger the dividend, the higher will be the put premium. It must be clarified that the only dividends of consequence are those that are scheduled to be paid during the life of the options contract.

Volatility: In finance we typically assume that investors are risk averse. That is, for a given level of expected returns, the greater the risk as measured by the standard deviation or variance, the lower will be the utility. Options, however, are different. Both calls and puts, being contingent contracts, protect the holders from price movements on one side while permitting them to take full advantage of movements on the other side. This is because the worst that can happen to call holders is that they will lose the option premium, no matter how low the stock price may go. Similarly, irrespective of the increase in the stock price, a put holder can never lose more than the premium. Thus, the higher the volatility the greater will be the values of both call and put options.

Time to Maturity: Most options are what are termed as *wasting assets*, that is, keeping all the other variables constant, their value steadily erodes over time. Most options, with the exception of certain European options, have a positive time value prior to expiration. At the point of expiration, as we have seen earlier, all options must have a zero time value to rule out arbitrage. Thus, most options will experience a steady decline of value over time, if the other variables that influence the price remain constant.

The Riskless Interest Rate: Take the case of an investor who has adequate funds to acquire a stock at its prevailing price. One alternative would be to buy a call option and invest the balance at the riskless rate. The higher the interest rate, the more attractive will be the second course of action. Consequently, the higher the interest rate, the greater will be the demand for the call, and hence the greater will be the premium of a call option.

To draw a conclusion for put options, let us look at the issue from the perspective of an investor who owns the underlying asset and is contemplating its sale. One alternative is to buy a put option and thereby lock in a minimum price for the asset. The higher the prevailing rate of interest, the more enticing will be the prospect of an immediate sale followed by reinvestment of the sale proceeds. Consequently, the higher the interest rate, the lower will be the demand for put options, and the lower will be the value of a put option.

THE BINOMIAL OPTION PRICING MODEL

This model assumes that given a state of nature characterized by a price S_t, at the end of the next period the asset price may either go up to uS_t or go down to dS_t, where u is obviously greater than 1.0, while d is less than 1.0. Because the asset can only take on one of two possible values at the end of every time period, the model is termed as the *binomial model*.

We will first consider the one-period case; that is, we will assume that we are at time $(T - 1)$, where T is the scheduled expiration date of the option. The evolution of the asset price may be depicted as shown in Figure 7.5.

Our objective is to find the option premium at $(T - 1)$. We have to commence our computation from the point of expiration, because that is the instant at which we know what the payoff from the contract will be. Thus, in the binomial model, we always start by considering the cash flows from the option at the point of expiration.

If the upstate is reached, the payoff from a call option will be $C_u = \text{Max}[0, uS_t - X]$, whereas if the downstate is reached, it will be $C_d = \text{Max}[0, dS_t - X]$.

Consider a portfolio consisting of α shares of stock and a short position in a call option. α is termed as the hedge ratio. The current value of the portfolio is $\alpha S_t - C_t$, where C_t is the unknown call premium that we are seeking to derive. Next period, in the upstate the portfolio will be worth $\alpha uS_t - C_u$, while in the downstate it will be worth $\alpha dS_t - C_d$. We will choose the hedge ratio in such a way that the payoff in the upstate is the same as that in the downstate. That is:

$$\alpha uS_t - C_u = \alpha dS_t - C_d$$

$$\Rightarrow \alpha S_t(u - d) = C_u - C_d$$

$$\Rightarrow \alpha = \frac{C_u - C_d}{S_t(u - d)}$$

This portfolio by construction is riskless because the payoff is identical in both states of nature. To rule out the prospect of arbitrage, it must therefore earn the riskless rate of return. That is:

$$\alpha uS_t - C_u = \alpha dS_t - C_d = (\alpha S_t - C_t)r$$

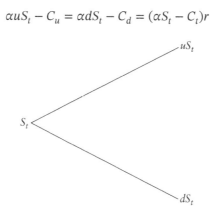

FIGURE 7.5 Stock Price Tree for the One-period Case

where r is one plus the riskless rate per period.[1]

Therefore

$$\alpha u S_t - C_u = (\alpha S_t - C_t)r$$

$$\Rightarrow \left(\frac{C_u - C_d}{S_t(u-d)}\right) \times uS_t - C_u = \left(\frac{C_u - C_d}{S_t(u-d)}\right) \times rS_t - C_t r$$

$$\Rightarrow \left(\frac{C_u - C_d}{u-d}\right) \times (u-r) - C_u = -C_t r$$

$$\Rightarrow C_t = \left(\frac{C_u\left(\dfrac{r-d}{u-d}\right) + C_d\left(\dfrac{u-r}{u-d}\right)}{r}\right)$$

Let $\dfrac{r-d}{u-d} = p$. Therefore, $\dfrac{u-r}{u-d} = 1 - p$

$$\Rightarrow C_t = \left(\frac{pC_u + (1-p)C_d}{r}\right)$$

p and $(1-p)$ are referred to as risk-neutral probabilities. Thus, the value of the option as per this model is a probability-weighted average of the option values in the up and down states.

EXAMPLE 7.23

Assume that the current stock price is $80, and that every period the price may go up by 25% or down by 25%. That is $u = 1.25$ and $d = 0.75$. We will assume that the riskless rate is 10% per period.

Consider a call option with an exercise price of $80 and one period to expiration.

$$C_u = \text{Max}\,[0,100 - 80] = 20 \quad \text{and} \quad C_d = \text{Max}\,[0,60 - 80] = 0$$

$$p = \frac{r-d}{u-d} = \frac{1.10 - 0.75}{1.25 - 0.75} = 0.70; 1 - p = 0.30$$

$$C_t = \frac{0.70 \times 20 + 0.30 \times 0}{1.10} = \$12.7273$$

---

[1]The symbol r is generally used to denote the riskless rate of return. In the binomial model, however, the standard practice is to use it to denote one plus the riskless rate. In this context, r represents the periodic rate of interest, which need not necessarily be an annual rate.

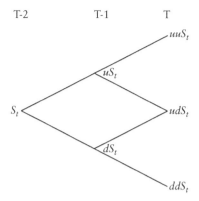

T-2   T-1   T

FIGURE 7.6   Stock Price Tree for the Two-period Case

THE TWO-PERIOD MODEL

In the preceding exposition we assumed that the stock price will move just once prior to the expiration of the option. In general, the asset price will move many times before the expiration of the options contract. The arguments used for the one-period case can be extended to value an option in a multi-period framework.

Let us assume that the current stock price is S_t, and that there are two periods left until the expiration date of the option. The evolution of the stock price is depicted in Figure 7.6.

As we did in the one-period case, we know the payoffs at expiration. Let us step back one period from T to $T-1$, to compute the option price. As this is a one-period problem, we can state that

$$C_u = \frac{pC_{uu} + (1-p)C_{ud}}{r}$$

$$C_d = \frac{pC_{ud} + (1-p)C_{dd}}{r}$$

We know the values of C_{uu}, C_{ud}, and C_{dd}, because they represent the payoffs at the three nodes corresponding to the expiration date of the option. Once we have computed the values of C_u and C_d, we can once again invoke the one-period model to evaluate C_t, which is the value of the option at $T-2$. This is the basis on which we will solve the multi-period option pricing problem. That is, we start at expiration, and repeatedly invoke the one-period logic to compute the value of the option at a node corresponding to a previous point in time. We will now present the solution for the two-period problem using the data in Example 7.24.

EXAMPLE 7.24

Assume that the current stock price is $80, and that every period the stock price may move up or down by 25%. The riskless rate will be assumed to be 10%.

(continued)

(*continued*)

p and $(1 - p)$ are obviously 0.70 and 0.30. Consider a call option with two periods to expiration. We will first depict the stock price tree (Figure 7.7).

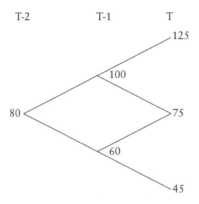

T-2	T-1	T

FIGURE 7.7 Stock Price Tree for the Two-period Example

$$C_{uu} = \text{Max}[0,125 - 80] = 45$$

$$C_{ud} = \text{Max}[0,75 - 80] = 0$$

$$C_{dd} = \text{Max}[0,45 - 80] = 0$$

$$C_u = \frac{0.70 \times 45 + 0.30 \times 0}{1.10} = 28.6364$$

$$C_d = \frac{0.70 \times 0 + 0.30 \times 0}{1.10} = 0$$

$$C_t = \frac{0.70 \times 28.6364 + 0.30 \times 0}{1.10} = \$18.2231$$

VALUATION OF EUROPEAN PUT OPTIONS

Let us consider the one-period case first. Define $P_u = \text{Max}[0, X - uS_t]$ and $P_d = \text{Max}[0, X - dS_t]$. The option premium at a prior point in time may be computed as a probability-weighted average of the payoffs at expiration, where the risk-neutral probabilities have the same definition as before. When we extend the theory to the multi-period case, we once again start at the expiration date of the option and work backwards, one step at a time, by repeatedly invoking the one-period model. Example 7.25 demonstrates the valuation process for a two-period put option.

EXAMPLE 7.25

Consider the data used in the previous illustration, but assume we are dealing with a put option with two periods to expiration.

$$P_{uu} = \text{Max}[0, 80 - 125] = 0$$

$$P_{ud} = \text{Max}[0, 80 - 75] = 5$$

$$P_{dd} = \text{Max}[0, 80 - 45] = 35$$

$$P_u = \frac{0.70 \times 0 + 0.30 \times 5}{1.10} = 1.3636$$

$$P_d = \frac{0.70 \times 5 + 0.30 \times 35}{1.10} = 12.7273$$

$$P_t = \frac{0.70 \times 1.3636 + 0.30 \times 12.7273}{1.10} = \$4.3388$$

VALUING AMERICAN OPTIONS

The binomial model can be easily extended to value American options. At each node we have to compare the model value, obtained by working backwards from the following point in time, with the intrinsic value of the option. If the intrinsic value is greater than the model value, we use it to compute the option premium for subsequent calculations. The rationale is that if the model value is lower than the intrinsic value at a particular node, then the holders will choose to exercise it early. If they do not wish to hold the option, then obviously early exercise will occur. This is because although offsetting is an alternative for such investors, it will not be optimal because potential buyers will not pay more than the model value for the option, since buyers can always replicate the option at the model value. Thus, early exercise is superior to taking a counterposition under such circumstances. Even if the holders were to desire to continue holding the option, it would be more profitable to exercise it, realize the intrinsic value, and replicate it at a cost lower than the intrinsic value.

We demonstrate the valuation of an American put option in Example 7.26.[2]

EXAMPLE 7.26

Let us use the data that we considered in the previous illustration. We will now assume that we are dealing with an American put option with two periods to expiration.

(continued)

---

[2]An American call on a non-dividend-paying stock will obviously never be exercised early.

(continued)

$$P_{uu} = \text{Max}[0, 80 - 125] = 0$$

$$P_{ud} = \text{Max}[0, 80 - 75] = 5$$

$$P_{dd} = \text{Max}[0, 80 - 45] = 35$$

$$P_u = \frac{0.70 \times 0 + 0.30 \times 5}{1.10} = 1.3636$$

The intrinsic value is zero. Therefore, we will use the model value while working backwards.

$$P_d = \frac{0.70 \times 5 + 0.30 \times 35}{1.10} = 12.7273$$

The intrinsic value is $20, which is greater than the model value. Thus, early exercise is optimal at this node and we need to use the intrinsic value to work backwards.

$$P_t = \frac{0.70 \times 1.3636 + 0.30 \times 20}{1.10} = \$6.3223$$

As is to be expected, the American put is priced higher than the European put. We need to check for the possibility of early exercise at time $T - 2$ as well. In this case, the option is at the money and thus early exercise is not an issue.

IMPLEMENTING THE BINOMIAL MODEL IN PRACTICE

While illustrating the binomial model we have arbitrarily assumed values for u, d, and consequently p. In practice, these parameters are chosen such that the moments of the discrete-time asset price process correspond to the moments of the lognormal distribution. The significance of the lognormal distribution is that it is the price process assumed by Black and Scholes in order to derive their option pricing model.

If σ is the standard deviation of the rate of return on the underlying asset, i is the annual riskless rate, and Δt is the length of a period in the binomial process being modeled, as measured in years, the normal practice is to set

$$u = e^{\sigma\sqrt{\Delta t}}; \ d = e^{-\sigma\sqrt{\Delta t}}; \ r = e^{i\Delta t}$$

EXAMPLE 7.27

A stock is currently priced at $80. A six-month call option is available with an exercise price of $80. The riskless rate is 8% per annum and the volatility of the rate of return is 25%. If we model the stock price evolution process as a four-period binomial model, then $\Delta t = 0.125$. Consequently

$$u = e^{0.25\sqrt{0.125}} = 1.0924; \ d = e^{-0.25\sqrt{0.125}} = 0.9154; \ r = e^{0.08 \times 0.125} = 1.01005$$

$$p = \frac{1.01005 - 0.9154}{1.0924 - 0.9154} = 0.5347 \text{ and } 1 - p = 0.4653$$

THE BLACK-SCHOLES MODEL

Black and Scholes derived closed-form solutions for the values of European call and put options on non-dividend-paying stocks by assuming that stock prices follow a log-normal process. The Black-Scholes formula for a European call option may be stated as follows.

$$C_{E,t} = S_t N(d_1) - X e^{-r(T-t)} N(d_2)$$

The formula for European put options is

$$P_{E,t} = X e^{-r(T-t)} N(-d_2) - S_t N(-d_1)$$

In these formulae

$$d_1 = \frac{ln\left(\frac{S_t}{X}\right) + \left(r + \frac{\sigma^2}{2}\right)(T-t)}{\sigma\sqrt{(T-t)}}$$

and $d_2 = d_1 - \sigma\sqrt{(T-t)}$.

$N(X)$ is the cumulative probability distribution function for a standard normal variable.

EXAMPLE 7.28

A stock is currently priced at $80. European call and put options are available with 4.5 months to expiration and an exercise price of $80. The stock is not scheduled to pay any dividends during the life of the options contract. The riskless rate of interest is 8% per annum and the volatility of the rate of return is 25%.

Thus $S_t = X = \$80$; $T - t = 0.375$; $r = 0.08$; $\sigma = 0.25$.

$$d_1 = \frac{ln\left(\frac{80}{80}\right) + \left(0.08 + \frac{(0.25)^2}{2}\right)0.375}{0.25\sqrt{0.375}}$$

$$= \frac{0.04172}{0.1531} = 0.2725$$

$$d_2 = 0.2725 - 0.1531 = 0.1194$$

$N(d_1)$ and $N(d_2)$ may be computed using linear interpolation if we have a table for the standard normal distribution. Otherwise, if we have access to Excel, we can use the NORMSDIST function. $N(0.27) = 0.6064$ and $N(0.28) = 0.6103$. Thus

$$N(0.2725) = 0.6064 + (0.6103 - 0.6064)\frac{0.0025}{0.01} = 0.6074$$

(continued)

(*continued*)

N(0.11) = 0.5438 and N(0.12) = 0.5478. Therefore

$$N(0.1194) = 0.5438 + (0.5478 - 0.5438)\frac{0.0094}{0.01} = 0.5476$$

$$C_{E,t} = 80 \times 0.6074 - 80e^{-0.08 \times 0.375} \times 0.5476 = \$6.0787$$

N(-X) = 1 - N(X). Thus N(-0.2725) = 1 - 0.6074 = 0.3926 and N(-0.1194) = 1 - 0.5476 = 0.4524. Thus

$$P_{E,t} = 80e^{-0.08 \times 0.375} N(-0.1194) - 80N(-0.2725) = \$3.7144$$

PUT-CALL PARITY

Put-call parity is a relationship that must be satisfied if arbitrage is to be ruled out. Consequently, it is independent of the model that is used to price the options and we would therefore expect the Black-Scholes model to satisfy it. We will now demonstrate that the formula indeed satisfies the put-call parity condition.

$$
\begin{aligned}
C_{E,t} &= S_t N(d_1) - Xe^{-r(T-t)} N(d_2) \\
&= S_t[1 - N(-d_1)] - Xe^{-r(T-t)}[1 - N(-d_2)] \\
&= Xe^{-r(T-t)} N(-d_2) - S_t N(-d_1) + S_t - Xe^{-r(T-t)} \\
&= P_t + S_t - Xe^{-r(T-t)}
\end{aligned}
$$

INTERPRETATION OF THE BLACK-SCHOLES FORMULA

The option price as per the formula is independent of the risk preferences of traders. If the attitude toward risk is indeed irrelevant, the simplest approach to valuation would entail the assumption that all investors are risk neutral. A risk-neutral investor would value any asset as the present value of the expected payoff, where the discount rate used will be the riskless rate.

From the Black-Scholes formula for call options:

$$
\begin{aligned}
C_{E,t} &= S_t N(d_1) - Xe^{-r(T-t)} N(d_2) \\
&= e^{-r(T-t)} \left[S_t e^{r(T-t)} N(d_1) - XN(d_2) \right]
\end{aligned}
$$

Thus $[S_t e^{r(T-t)} N(d_1) - XN(d_2)]$ is the expected payoff from the option at the time of expiration as perceived by a world of risk-neutral investors.

$S_t e^{r(T-t)} N(d_1)$ is the expected value of a variable, once again in a risk-neutral world, that has a value equal to S_T if the option is exercised and a value of zero otherwise. $XN(d_2)$ is the expected outflow on account of the exercise price. Because the exercise price has to be paid only if the option is exercised, $N(d_2)$ is the probability that the option will be exercised. In other words, $N(d_2)$ is the probability that the option will end up in the money, that is, the odds that $S_T > X$.

For a put option

$$P_{E,t} = Xe^{-r(T-t)}N(-d_2) - S_tN(-d_1)$$

$$= e^{-r(T-t)}[XN(-d_2) - S_te^{r(T-t)}N(-d_1)]$$

Using similar logic $S_te^{r(T-t)}N(-d_1)$ is the expected value of a variable that will be equal to S_T if $S_T < X$ and will be zero otherwise. Obviously, $N(-d_2)$ is the probability that the put will end up in the money and will consequently be exercised.

THE GREEKS

The option price is a function of many different variables that we have discussed earlier. The rate of change of the option premium with respect to these variables is denoted by Greek symbols. Hence this part of option valuation theory is referred to as *The Greeks*.

The partial derivative of the option price with respect to the price of the underlying asset is termed as *delta*. For a call option, delta will always be between zero and one. For deep out-of-the-money options, delta will be close to zero, while for deep in-the-money options it will be close to one. Delta itself is a function of several variables, including the price of the underlying asset. Consequently, delta will change as the asset price changes, and a given value of delta is valid only for an infinitesimal change in the price of the asset.

Even if the asset price were to remain constant, delta will change with the passage of time. As the time to expiration nears, delta will tend toward one if the call is in the money and will tend toward zero if the option is out of the money. Put options have a delta between zero and minus one.

The rate of change of delta with respect to the price of the underlying asset is termed as the *gamma* of the option. Gamma is positive for both calls and puts and tends to be at its highest when the option is close to the money.

The rate of change of the option premium with respect to the volatility of the rate of return is termed as *vega*. Because volatility will be perceived positively by both call and put holders, vega will be positive for both types of options.

The time decay of the option is denoted by *theta*. That is, theta is the negative of the partial derivative of the option premium with respect to the time remaining until maturity. Most options, with the exception of certain European options, are wasting assets; that is, their time values will steadily approach zero as expiration approaches. Because the time value at expiration must be zero for all options, theta will be negative for most options. Certain European options may have a negative time value prior to expiration. In such cases, theta will be positive because the time value must increase so as to attain a value of zero at expiration.

The rate of change of the option premium with respect to the riskless rate of interest is termed as *rho*. As discussed earlier, rho will be positive for call options and negative for put options.

From the put-call parity relationship for European options on a non-dividend-paying stock:

$$C_{E,t} = P_{E,t} + S_t - Xe^{-r(T-t)}$$

Thus, we can make the following assertions:

1. The delta of a call will be equal to one plus the delta of a put.
2. The gamma of call and put options will be equal.
3. The vega of both call and put options will be equal.
   If options were to be priced as per the Black-Scholes model, the expressions for the Greeks will be as follows.
   1. The call delta will be $N(d_1)$ and the put delta will be $-N(-d_1)$
   2. The gamma for both calls and puts will be $\dfrac{n(d_1)}{S_t \sigma \sqrt{T-t}}$
   3. Vega for both calls and puts will be $S_t n(d_1)\sqrt{T-t}$
   4. The theta for a call will be $-rXe^{-r(T-t)}N(d_2) - S_t n(d_1)\dfrac{\sigma}{2\sqrt{T-t}}$

   The theta for a put will be $rXe^{-r(T-t)}N(d_2) - S_t n(d_1)\dfrac{\sigma}{2\sqrt{T-t}}$
4. The rho for a call will be $X(T-t)e^{-r(T-t)}N(d_2)$ while that for a put will be $-X(T-t)e^{-r(T-t)}N(-d_2)$.

OPTION STRATEGIES

Options contracts can be used to implement various trading strategies. We will discuss two types of strategies, *spreads* and *combinations*. We will look at three categories of spreads, namely *bull spreads*, *bear spreads*, and *butterfly spreads*, and two types of combinations, *straddles* and *strangles*.

Bull Spreads

Bull spreads lead to a profit for the trader if the stock price were to rise; hence the name. It can be implemented using both call and put options. A bull spread, whether set up with calls or puts, sets a cap on both the loss and the profit from the strategy.

Let us first analyze a spread using calls. We will denote the two exercise prices by X_1 and X_2 where $X_1 < X_2$. The strategy requires the trader to buy an option with a lower exercise price and sell an option with a higher exercise price. Because the lower the exercise price, the higher will be the option premium, this strategy involves a net investment. The payoff from the strategy at expiration for various values of the terminal stock price is depicted in Table 7.9.

The minimum payoff is zero while the maximum payoff is $X_2 - X_1$. If we denote the initial investment by ΔC, then the maximum loss is $-\Delta C$, while the maximum profit is $X_2 - X_1 - \Delta C$. The break-even stock price is $X_1 + \Delta C$.

TABLE 7.9 Payoffs from a Bull Spread with Calls

Terminal Price Range	Payoff from Long Call	Payoff from Short Call	Total Payoff
$S_T < X_1$	0	0	0
$X_1 < S_T < X_2$	$S_T - X_1$	0	$S_T - X_1$
$S_T > X_2$	$S_T - X_1$	$-(S_T - X_2)$	$X_2 - X_1$

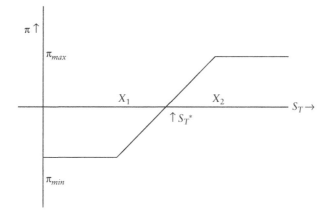

FIGURE 7.8 Profit Profile: Bull Spread

The profit diagram may be depicted as shown in Figure 7.8.

A bull spread can also be created using puts. The trader has to buy the put with the lower exercise price and sell the put with the higher exercise price. Because the put premium increases with the exercise price, the inflow from the option that is sold will be higher than the outflow on account of the option that is bought. Consequently, a bull spread with puts will lead to a cash inflow at inception. The payoff from the strategy at expiration for various values of the terminal stock price is depicted in Table 7.10.

The minimum payoff is $X_1 - X_2$ and the maximum payoff is zero. If we denote the initial inflow as ΔP, then the maximum loss is $X_1 - X_2 + \Delta P$ and the maximum profit is ΔP. The break-even stock price is $X_2 - \Delta P$.

TABLE 7.10 Payoffs from a Bull Spread with Puts

Terminal Price Range	Payoff from Long Put	Payoff from Short Put	Total Payoff
$S_T < X_1$	$X_1 - S_T$	$-(X_2 - S_T)$	$X_1 - X_2$
$X_1 < S_T < X_2$	0	$-(X_2 - S_T)$	$S_T - X_2$
$S_T > X_2$	0	0	0

EXAMPLE 7.29

Denise has bought a call option on ABC with an exercise price of $95 for $9.68 and sold an option on the same stock with an exercise price of $100 for $6.68. Both options have 110 days to maturity. The initial investment is: $100 \times (9.68 - 6.68)$ = $300. The maximum loss is obviously $300. The maximum profit is: $100 \times (100 - 95) - 300 = \$200$. The break-even stock price is: $95 + 3 = 98$. The payoffs and profits for various values of the terminal stock price are depicted in Table 7.11.

TABLE 7.11   Profit from the Bull Spread

Stock Price	Payoff from Long Call	Payoff from Short Call	Payoff from the Spread	Total Profit/ Loss
75	0	0	0	(300)
80	0	0	0	(300)
85	0	0	0	(300)
90	0	0	0	(300)
95	0	0	0	(300)
96	100	0	100	(200)
97	200	0	200	(100)
98	300	0	300	0
100	500	0	500	200
105	1,000	(500)	500	200
110	1,500	(1,000)	500	200
115	2,000	(1,500)	500	200
120	2,500	(2,000)	500	200
125	3,000	(2,500)	500	200

EXAMPLE 7.30

Chris has bought a put option on ABC with an exercise price of $95 for $2.42 and sold a put on the same stock with an exercise price of $100 for $4.30. Both options have 110 days to expiration. The initial cash inflow is: $100 \times (4.30 - 2.42) = \$188$. This is also the maximum profit. The maximum loss is: $100 \times (95 - 100) + 188 = -\$312$. The break-even stock price is: $100 - 1.88 = 98.12$.

Bear Spreads

Bear spreads lead to a profit for the trader if the stock price were to decline; hence the name. It can be implemented using both call and put options. A bear spread, whether set up with calls or with puts, sets a cap on both the loss and the profit from the strategy.

Let us first analyze a spread using calls. We will denote the two exercise prices by X_1 and X_2 where $X_1 < X_2$. The strategy requires the trader to sell an option with a

TABLE 7.12 Payoffs from a Bear Spread with Calls

Terminal Price Range	Payoff from Long Call	Payoff from Short Call	Total Payoff
$S_T < X_1$	0	0	0
$X_1 < S_T < X_2$	0	$-(S_T - X_1)$	$X_1 - S_T$
$S_T > X_2$	$S_T - X_2$	$-(S_T - X_1)$	$X_1 - X_2$

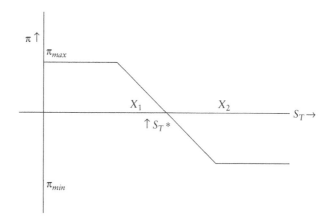

FIGURE 7.9 Profit Profile: Bear Spread

lower exercise price and buy an option with a higher exercise price. Because the lower the exercise price, the higher will be the option premium, this strategy involves a cash inflow at inception. The payoff from the strategy at expiration for various values of the terminal stock price is depicted in Table 7.12.

The maximum payoff is zero while the minimum payoff is $X_1 - X_2$. If we denote the initial inflow by ΔC, then the maximum profit is ΔC, while the maximum loss is $X_1 - X_2 + \Delta C$. The break-even stock price is $X_1 + \Delta C$.

The profit diagram may be depicted as shown in Figure 7.9.

A bear spread can also be created using puts. The trader has to sell the put with the lower exercise price and buy the put with the higher exercise price. Because the put premium increases with the exercise price, the outflow on account of the option that is bought will be higher than the inflow on account of the option that is sold. Consequently, a bear spread with puts will lead to a cash outflow at inception. The payoff from the strategy at expiration for various values of the terminal stock price is depicted in Table 7.13.

TABLE 7.13 Payoffs from a Bear Spread with Puts

Terminal Price Range	Payoff from Long Put	Payoff from Short Put	Total Payoff
$S_T < X_1$	$X_2 - S_T$	$-(X_1 - S_T)$	$X_2 - X_1$
$X_1 < S_T < X_2$	$(X_2 - S_T)$	0	$X_2 - S_T$
$S_T > X_2$	0	0	0

The minimum payoff is zero and the maximum payoff is $X_2 - X_1$. If we denote the initial investment as ΔP, then the maximum loss is $-\Delta P$ and the maximum profit is $X_2 - X_1 - \Delta P$. The break-even stock price is $X_2 - \Delta P$.

EXAMPLE 7.31

Denise has sold a call option on ABC with an exercise price of $95 for $9.68 and bought an option on the same stock with an exercise price of $100 for $6.68. Both options have 110 days to maturity. The initial cash inflow is: $100 \times (9.68 - 6.68) = \$300$. This is the maximum profit from this strategy. The maximum loss is: $100 \times (95 - 100) + 300 = -\$200$. The break-even stock price is: $95 + 3 = 98$. The payoffs and profits for various values of the terminal stock price are depicted in Table 7.14.

TABLE 7.14 Profit from the Bear Spread

Stock Price	Payoff from Long Call	Payoff from Short Call	Payoff from the Spread	Total Profit/ Loss
75	0	0	0	300
80	0	0	0	300
85	0	0	0	300
90	0	0	0	300
95	0	0	0	300
96	0	(100)	(100)	200
97	0	(200)	(200)	100
98	0	(300)	(300)	0
100	0	(500)	(500)	(200)
105	500	(1,000)	(500)	(200)
110	1,000	(1,500)	(500)	(200)
115	1,500	(2,000)	(500)	(200)
120	2,000	(2,500)	(500)	(200)
125	2,500	(3,000)	(500)	(200)

EXAMPLE 7.32

Chris has sold a put option on ABC with an exercise price of $95 for $2.42 and bought a put on the same stock with an exercise price of $100 for $4.30. Both options have 110 days to expiration. The initial investment: $100 \times (4.30 - 2.42) = \$188$. This is also the maximum loss. The maximum profit is: $100 \times (100 - 95) - 188 = \$312$. The break-even stock price is: $100 - 1.88 = 98.12$.

Butterfly Spread

A butterfly spread requires options with three different exercise prices. To set up a long butterfly spread with calls, the trader will take a long position in an in-the-money call and an out-of-the-money call, and take a short position in two at-the-money calls. A butterfly spread can also be set up using put options, as we shall shortly demonstrate.

We will denote the exercise prices by X_1, X_2, and X_3 where $X_1 < X_2 < X_3$. The exercise prices are generally chosen so that the middle price is an arithmetic average of the other two prices. That is $X_2 = (X_1 + X_3)/2$.

The Convexity Property

Consider three exercise prices X_1, X_2, and X_3 such that $X_2 = wX_1 + (1 - w)X_3$.

The convexity property states that the call and put premiums for the options with the corresponding exercise prices will be such that

$$C_2 \leq wC_1 + (1 - w)C_3 \text{ and } P_2 \leq wP_1 + (1 - w)P_3$$

Thus, it can be demonstrated that a butterfly spread will always require an initial investment which we will denote by ΔC. The payoffs from the strategy at expiration are depicted in Table 7.15.

The minimum payoff is zero and arises if the terminal stock price is either below the lowest of the exercise prices or above the highest. In either case the profit is $-\Delta C$. This is the maximum potential loss from the strategy. The maximum profit is realized when $S_T = X_2$. There are two break-even prices: $X_1 + \Delta C$ and $X_3 - \Delta C$.

The profit diagram is depicted in Figure 7.10.

TABLE 7.15 Payoffs from a Long Butterfly Spread

Terminal Price Range	Payoff from Call with $X = X_1$	Payoff from Call with $X = X_3$	Payoff from Calls with $X = X_2$	Total Payoff
$S_T < X_1$	0	0	0	0
$X_1 < S_T < X_2$	$S_T - X_1$	0	0	$S_T - X_1$
$X_2 < S_T < X_3$	$S_T - X_1$	0	$-2(S_T - X_2)$	$X_3 - S_T$
$S_T > X_3$	$S_T - X_1$	$S_T - X_3$	$-2(S_T - X_2)$	0

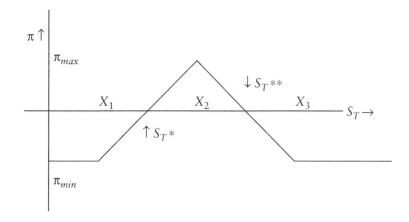

FIGURE 7.10 Profit Profile: Butterfly Spread

A butterfly spread can also be set up using put options. The strategy requires an investor to buy an in-the-money put and an out-of-the-money put, and sell two at-the-money puts, where the exercise prices are such that $X_1 < X_2 < X_3$, and $X_2 = (X_1 + X_3)/2$. The strategy will entail an initial investment of ΔP, which also represents the magnitude of the maximum loss. Once again, the maximum loss will be realized if the terminal stock price is below the lowest exercise price or above the highest. The two break-even prices are $X_1 + \Delta P$ and $X_3 - \Delta P$.

EXAMPLE 7.33

Meg Foster decides to set up a butterfly spread using call options on ABC. The exercise prices and corresponding premiums of the options chosen by her are given in Table 7.16.

TABLE 7.16   Premiums for Call Options

Exercise Price	Option Premium
80	12.80
90	6.01
100	2.20

The initial investment is $100 \times (12.80 + 2.20 - 2 \times 6.01) = \$298$. Thus, the maximum loss is –\$298. The maximum profit is realized when the stock price is \$90 and is equal to $100 \times (90 - 80 - 2.98) = \$702$. The two break-even prices are \$82.98 and \$97.02. The payoffs and profits for various values of the terminal stock price are depicted in Table 7.17.

TABLE 7.17   Profit from the Butterfly Spread

Stock Price	Payoff from Call with X = 80	Payoff from Call with X = 100	Payoff from Calls with X = 90	Total Payoff	Total Profit/ Loss
70	0	0	0	0	(298)
75	0	0	0	0	(298)
80	0	0	0	0	(298)
82.98	298	0	0	298	0
85	500	0	0	500	202
90	1,000	0	0	1,000	702
95	1,500	0	(1,000)	500	202
97.02	1,702	0	(1,404)	298	0
100	2,000	0	(2,000)	0	(298)
105	2,500	500	(3,000)	0	(298)
110	3,000	1,000	(4,000)	0	(298)
115	3,500	1,500	(5,000)	0	(298)
120	4,000	2,000	(6,000)	0	(298)

TABLE 7.18   Payoffs from a Long Straddle

Terminal Price Range	Payoff from Call	Payoff from Put	Total Payoff
$S_T < X$	0	$X - S_T$	$X - S_T$
$S_T > X$	$S_T - X$	0	$S_T - X$

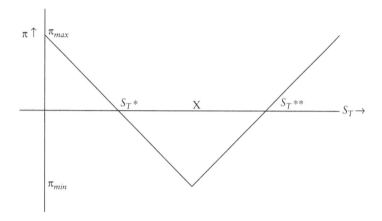

FIGURE 7.11   Profit Profile: Straddle

A Straddle

A long straddle requires the investor to buy a call and a put option on the same asset. Both options must have the same exercise price and expiration date. The initial investment is $C_t + P_t$. The call option will be in the money if the stock were to rise in value, while the put will be in the money if the stock were to decline in value. Thus, a straddle will pay off in both a bull and bear market. Consequently, it is a suitable strategy for an investor who is anticipating a large price move, but is unsure about its direction. The payoff at expiration is depicted in Table 7.18.

The maximum payoff is unlimited if $S_T > X$, and consequently so is the maximum profit. The profit increases dollar for dollar with the stock price. In the other direction the maximum payoff is X, because the stock price cannot decline below zero. Thus, the maximum profit in this price range is $X - C_t - P_t$. The lowest payoff is zero, which occurs if $S_T = X$. Hence the maximum loss is $-(C_t + P_t)$. There are two break-even points: $X - C_t - P_t$ and $X + C_t + P_t$. The profit diagram may be depicted as shown in Figure 7.11.

EXAMPLE 7.34

Gene Altman buys a call and a put option on ABC with an exercise price of $90, and 110 days to expiration. The respective premiums are $6.01 and $3.87. Thus, the initial investment is $988, which is also the maximum potential loss from the strategy.

(continued)

(continued)

In the price range $S_T > X$, the profit is $S_T - 99.88$. The maximum profit is unbounded, and the break-even stock price is 99.88. In the price range $S_T < X$, the profit is $80.12 - S_T$. The maximum profit in this region is 80.12. The break-even price is 80.12. The payoffs and profits for various values of the terminal stock price are depicted in Table 7.19.

TABLE 7.19   Profit from a Long Straddle

Stock Price	Payoff from Call	Payoff from Put	Total Payoff	Total Profit/Loss
70	0	2,000	2,000	1,012
75	0	1,500	1,500	512
80	0	1,000	1,000	12
80.12	0	988	988	0
85	0	500	500	(488)
90	0	0	0	(988)
95	500	0	500	(488)
99.88	988	0	988	0
100	1,000	0	1,000	12
105	1,500	0	1,500	512
110	2,000	0	2,000	1,012
115	2,500	0	2,500	1,512

A Strangle

A strangle is similar to a straddle in the sense that it requires the trader to buy a call and a put on the same asset, and with the same expiration date. The difference is that the two options are chosen with different exercise prices. If we denote the exercise price of the call as X_1, and that of the put as X_2, there are two possibilities, that is, $X_1 > X_2$, and $X_1 < X_2$. Thus, there are two types of strangles: out-of-the-money strangles and in-the-money strangles.

Let us first consider an out-of-the-money strangle. The payoff is depicted in Table 7.20.

If $S_T < X_2$, the profit is $X_2 - S_T - C_t - P_t$. The maximum profit in this region is $X_2 - C_t - P_t$, which is also the magnitude of the break-even stock price. If $X_2 < S_T < X_1$, the payoff is zero and the loss is equal to the initial investment.

TABLE 7.20   Payoffs from an Out-of-the-money Long Strangle

Terminal Price Range	Payoff from Call	Payoff from Put	Total Payoff
$S_T < X_2$	0	$X_2 - S_T$	$X_2 - S_T$
$X_2 < S_T < X_1$	0	0	0
$S_T > X_1$	$S_T - X_1$	0	$S_T - X_1$

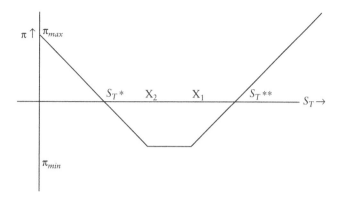

FIGURE 7.12   Profit Profile: Strangle

TABLE 7.21   Payoffs from an In-the-money Long Strangle

Terminal Price Range	Payoff from Call	Payoff from Put	Total Payoff
$S_T < X_1$	0	$X_2 - S_T$	$X_2 - S_T$
$X_1 < S_T < X_2$	$S_T - X_1$	$X_2 - S_T$	$X_2 - X_1$
$S_T > X_2$	$S_T - X_1$	0	$S_T - X_1$

This represents the maximum possible loss for this strategy. If $S_T > X_1$, the profit is $S_T - X_1 - C_t - P_t$. The maximum profit in this region is unbounded. The second break-even price is $X_1 + C_t + P_t$. The profit diagram is depicted in Figure 7.12.

Now let us consider an in-the-money strangle. The payoffs are shown in Table 7.21.

If $S_T < X_1$, the profit is $X_2 - S_T - P_t - C_t$. The maximum profit in this region is $X_2 - P_t - C_t$, which is also the magnitude of the break-even stock price. If $X_1 < S_T < X_2$, the profit is $X_2 - X_1 - P_t - C_t$. This represents the maximum loss from the strategy. Finally, if $S_T > X_2$, the profit is $S_T - X_1 - P_t - C_t$. The profit is unbounded is this region. The corresponding break-even stock price is $X_1 + P_t + C_t$.

We will now give a numerical illustration of an out-of-the-money strangle.

EXAMPLE 7.35

Gene Altman buys a call and a put option on ABC with 110 days to expiration. The call has an exercise price of $100, while the put has an exercise price of $90. The respective premiums are $2.20 and $3.87. Thus, the initial investment is $607, which is also the maximum potential loss from the strategy. In the price range $S_T > 100$, the profit is $S_T - 106.07$. The maximum profit is unbounded, and the break-even stock price is 106.07. In the price range $S_T < 90$, the profit is $83.93 - S_T$.

(continued)

(continued)

The maximum profit in this region is 83.93. The break-even price is 83.93. The payoffs and profits for various values of the terminal stock price are depicted in Table 7.22.

TABLE 7.22   Profit from a Long Strangle

Stock Price	Payoff from Call	Payoff from Put	Total Payoff	Total Profit/Loss
70	0	2,000	2,000	1,393
75	0	1,500	1,500	893
80	0	1,000	1,000	393
83.93	0	607	607	0
85	0	500	500	(107)
90	0	0	0	(607)
95	0	0	0	(607)
100	0	0	0	(607)
105	500	0	500	(107)
106.07	607	0	607	0
110	1,000	0	1,000	393
115	1,500	0	1,500	893
120	2,000	0	2,000	1,393

FUTURES OPTIONS

A futures option is an option that is written on a futures contract. A call futures option gives holders the right to assume a long position in a futures contract if they were to exercise the option. When such a contract is exercised, a long position is established in the futures contract and the position is immediately marked to market. At this stage the holders have two options. They can either deposit the margin required to support the long futures position or they can offset the futures contract. When a call futures option is exercised by the holders, a short position in the futures contract is established for the writers of the contract, whose position will also be marked to market, and they will be confronted with the same two choices. That is, they can either deposit the margin required to maintain the futures position, or offset it.

If we denote the current futures price by F_t and the exercise price of the option by X, the contract will be exercised only if $F_t > X$. When the contract is marked to market there will be an inflow of $F_t - X$, which is nothing but the intrinsic value of the contract. What is the rationale for marking the contract to market upon exercise? The options contract gives holders the right to assume a long futures position upon exercise. When a futures position is established, it will obviously be at the prevailing futures price F_t. To ensure that the position is effectively at the exercise price, the price difference must be paid to the holders.

EXAMPLE 7.36

Benny has acquired a call futures option with an exercise price of $100. Each contract is for 100 units of the underlying asset and the current futures price is $106. If the option is exercised, a long position would be established in the futures contract and the holders would receive a cash flow of $100 \times (106 - 100) = \$600$.

A put futures option gives holders the right to assume a short position in a futures contract if they were to exercise the option. Simultaneously a long position in the futures contract will be established for the writer. Both the contracts will be marked to market, and as in the case of the call, they can either post the required margin, or offset their positions. If we denote the current futures price by F_t, the put will be exercised only if $F_t < X$. As in the case of the call, there will be an immediate cash inflow of $X - F_t$.

EXAMPLE 7.37

Mike has bought a put futures option. The exercise price is $100 and the current futures price is $93.50. Each contract is for 100 units of the underlying asset. If the put were to be exercised, a short position will be established in the futures contract and the holder will receive a cash flow of $100 \times (100 - 93.50) = \$650$.

PUT-CALL PARITY

The put-call parity condition for European futures options is:

$$C_{E,t} = P_{E,t} + (F_t - X)e^{-r(T-t)}$$

THE BLACK MODEL

The Black Model is applicable for pricing European options on futures contracts. In the case of European options scheduled to expire at the same time as the underlying futures contracts, the Black Model states that:

$$C_{E,t} = e^{-r(T-t)}[F_t N(d_1) - X N(d_2)]$$

$$\text{and } P_{E,t} = e^{-r(T-t)}[X N(-d_2) - F_t N(-d_1)]$$

The variables d_1 and d_2 may be expressed as follows.

$$d_1 = \frac{\ln\left(\frac{F}{X}\right) + \left(\frac{\sigma^2}{2}\right)T}{\sigma\sqrt{T-t}}$$

$$d_2 = d_1 - \sigma\sqrt{T-t}$$

EXAMPLE 7.38

A futures contract with 4.5 months to expiration is currently trading at $95. European call and put options with the same time to expiration are available with an exercise price of $90. The riskless rate is 10% per annum and the volatility is 25% per annum.

$$d_1 = \frac{ln\left(\frac{95}{90}\right) + \left(\frac{0.25 \times 0.25}{2}\right)0.375}{0.25\sqrt{0.375}}$$

$$= \frac{0.0658}{0.1531} = 0.4298$$

$$d_2 = 0.4298 - 0.1531 = 0.2767$$

$$N(0.4298) = 0.6663; N(0.2767) = 0.6090$$

$$C_{E,t} = e^{-0.10 \times 0.375}[95 \times 0.6663 - 90 \times 0.6090] = 8.1761$$

$$P_{E,t} = e^{-0.10 \times 0.375}[90 \times 0.3910 - 95 \times 0.3337] = 3.3601$$

CHAPTER 8

Foreign Exchange

INTRODUCTION

The market for the sale and purchase of currencies is an OTC market. That is, there is no organized exchange on which currencies are traded. The largest players in the market are commercial banks. These banks typically provide two-way quotes for a number of currencies; that is, they will quote a bid rate for buying a particular currency and an ask rate for selling the currency. The difference between the two rates, which is called the spread, is a source of profit for the dealer. In the major money centers of the world, some nonbank dealers and large multinational corporations may also don the mantle of dealers. The market in which these entities operate is referred to as the interbank market. The transactions sizes are typically very large, usually of the magnitude of several million US dollars. The retail market for foreign exchange, in which tourists typically transact in the form of currency notes and travelers checks, is characterized by transactions of much smaller magnitudes, and the corresponding bid–ask spreads are also larger.

An exchange rate is the price of one country's currency in terms of that of another. In any bilateral trade there has to be a buyer and a seller. In the foreign exchange market, the words *buy/sell*, or *purchase/sale*, are always used from the dealers' perspective. When dealers buy a foreign currency from a client, they will pay out the equivalent in terms of the domestic currency. On the other hand, when dealers sell a foreign currency, they will take the equivalent amount in terms of domestic currency from the client.

EXAMPLE 8.1

Golden Circle in Sydney has exported canned food to Singapore and has been paid in Singapore dollars. The bank presents the check to Commonwealth Bank seeking the equivalent amount in Australian dollars. From the standpoint of the bank, this represents the acquisition of a foreign currency, which in this case is the Singapore dollar. Consequently, this is a purchase transaction.

EXAMPLE 8.2

An expatriate manager working in Sydney has saved 250,000 AUD and wants to remit the amount to New York in the form of US dollars. Consequently, he goes to the bank seeking a transfer to the United States. From the standpoint of the bank, this represents a sale of foreign currency, which in this case is the US dollar. Consequently, this is a sale transaction.

CURRENCY CODES

Every currency has a three-character code assigned by the International Standards Organization (ISO). The codes for some of the globally important currencies are given in Table 8.1.

TABLE 8.1 Symbols for Major Currencies

Country	Currency	Symbol
Australia	Dollar	AUD
Brazil	Real	BRL
Canada	Dollar	CAD
China	Renminbi Yuan	CNY
Czech Republic	Koruna	CAK
European Monetary Union	Euro	EUR
Hong Kong	Dollar	HKD
Hungary	Forint	HUF
India	Rupee	INR
Israel	Shekel	ILS
Japan	Yen	JPY
Malaysia	Ringgit	MYR
Mexico	Peso	MXN
New Zealand	Dollar	NZD
Norway	Krone	NOK
Poland	Zloty	PLN
Russia	Ruble	RUB
Singapore	Dollar	SGD
South Africa	Rand	ZAR
South Korea	Won	KRW
Sweden	Krona	SEK
Switzerland	Franc	CHF
Thailand	Baht	THB
UK	Pound Sterling	GBP
USA	Dollar	USD

BASE AND VARIABLE CURRENCIES

While quoting the rate of exchange between two currencies, the obvious practice is to keep the number of units of one currency fixed while making changes in the number of units of the other to reflect changes in the rate of exchange. The currency whose units remain invariant is referred to as the *base* currency while the other is termed as the *variable* currency. The practice in the foreign exchange market is to show the ISO codes for the two currencies involved as ABC–XYZ or ABC/XYZ where the first code refers to the base currency and the second to the variable currency. For instance, a quote of 0.8125 USD/EUR or 0.8125 USD–EUR denotes a quote of € 0.8125 per US dollar. Thus, in this quote the US dollar is the base currency while the euro is the variable currency.

DIRECT AND INDIRECT QUOTES

While quoting the exchange rate for a currency it is obviously possible to quote the rate by designating the domestic currency as the base currency or by specifying the foreign currency as the base currency. Exchange quotes where the domestic currency is the variable currency and the foreign currency is the base are referred to as *direct* quotes. Thus, in London 0.6750 USD–GBP is a direct quote. On the other hand, if the exchange rate were to be specified with the domestic currency as the base currency and the foreign currency as the variable currency, it would be deemed to be an *indirect* quote. Thus, a quote of 1.425 GBP–USD in London would be an example of an indirect quote.

The reason why we have two systems may be explained as follows. Take the case of a commodity such as wheat. We typically quote the price as dollars per unit of the commodity and not as the number of units of the commodity per dollar. Thus, the standard quote will be something like $5.00 per bushel of wheat and not 0.2000 bushels per dollar. In the currency market, however, we are dealing with two currencies. Consequently, either quoting convention is equally valid; that is, a quote in London may be USD–GBP or GBP–USD. We will briefly consider the indirect method because it is important that readers understand the principle; however, all our illustrations in this chapter will use the direct method.

EUROPEAN TERMS AND AMERICAN TERMS

If an exchange rate were to be quoted with the US dollar as the base currency, then it would be called a quote as per European terms. Thus, a quote of 0.6750 USD–GBP in London would represent a rate as per European terms. An exchange rate with the US dollar as the variable currency, however, will be categorized as a quote as per American terms. For instance, a quote of 1.2500 EUR–USD in NYC would represent a quote as per the American convention. Obviously direct quotes in the United States would be per American terms while indirect quotes will be per European terms. In other countries, quotes for the US dollar where the dollar is represented as the base currency would be termed as *European-style quotes* while those where the dollar is represented as the variable currency would amount to *American-style quotes*.

BID AND ASK QUOTES

Let us first consider direct quotes. Consider a quote of 1.2250–1.2375 EUR–USD. The first term represents the rate at which dealers are willing to buy euros from a client, and the second is the rate at which they are willing to sell euros to the client.

If dealers have to remain profitable, the rate at which they are prepared to buy the foreign currency – the bid – should be lower than the rate at which they are willing to sell the foreign currency – the ask or offer. Thus, in the case of direct quotes, the bid rate will always be lower than the ask rate.

Now consider a quote of 0.8195–0.8075 USD–EUR. Once again, the first term represents the rate at which dealers are prepared to buy euros from the client, and the second term is the rate at which they are willing to sell euros to a party. Obviously, when acquiring euros from a client, they would want to acquire more per dollar. On the other hand, when selling euros, they would like to part with less per dollar. Thus, it is not surprising that in the indirect quotation system the bid is higher than the ask.

You may still be wondering why the bid is higher than the ask in the case of indirect quotes. The reason is as follows. In a normal price quote, the bid is the rate for buying the base item, while the ask is the rate for selling the base item, both from the dealer's perspective. For instance, a stock broker may quote 80.15 – 80.30 for shares of ABC stock. Thus, if buying shares from a client, the broker will pay 80.15 per share, whereas if asked to sell shares to a client, the broker will charge 80.30 per share.

In a direct foreign exchange quote, the bid is the rate for buying the base currency and the ask is the rate for selling the base currency. Thus, we get the standard result that the bid is lower than the ask. In an indirect quote, however, the bid is the rate for buying the variable currency and the ask is the rate for selling the variable currency. Hence, the bid is higher than the ask. Unlike commodities and other financial assets, in foreign exchange markets both quoting conventions are legitimate.

APPRECIATING AND DEPRECIATING CURRENCIES

If the value of a currency increases in terms of another currency, then it is said to have appreciated. On the other hand, if the value of a currency declines in terms of another, then it is said to have depreciated. It should be noted that appreciation or depreciation of a currency is with respect to another currency. Thus, statements like "the US dollar has appreciated" have no meaning. In order to be meaningful, the currency with respect to which it has appreciated or depreciated should also be specified; for example, "The US dollar has appreciated with respect to the Australian dollar."

Consider a quote of 1.2250 EUR–USD in NYC. It is obviously a direct quote. If the rate increased to 1.2305 EUR–USD, it would mean that a euro is worth more in terms of dollars. If, however, the rate decreased to 1.2180 EUR–USD, it would mean that a euro is worth less in terms of dollars. An increase in the quote would consequently imply that the euro has appreciated or that the US dollar has depreciated. On the contrary, if the rate declined, it would signify that the euro has depreciated or that the US dollar has appreciated. Thus, in the case of direct quotes, a rising value signifies a depreciating home currency and an appreciating foreign currency, whereas a decline in the rate signifies the opposite.

Now let us consider indirect quotes. Take a quote of 0.8125 USD–EUR. If the rate increases, it would signify that the dollar is worth more in terms of euros, and therefore that the dollar has appreciated or equivalently the euro has depreciated. On the other hand, a fall in the rate would signify that the dollar is worth less in terms of the euro, which would consequently be construed as a depreciation of the dollar with respect to the euro. Hence, in the case of indirect quotes, a rising value signifies an appreciating home currency, whereas a decline in the rate connotes a depreciating home currency.

This does appear confusing at first glance that an increase in the quoted rate connotes a depreciating US dollar in NYC if rates are quoted directly, but it signifies an appreciating dollar if rates are quoted indirectly. The best way to clear up the confusion is to perceive the two currencies involved as base and variable currencies. An increase in the quote always means that the variable currency has depreciated, while a decrease in the quote always means that the variable currency has appreciated. In the case of a direct quote in NYC, the US dollar is the variable currency. Thus, a rising quote with respect to a currency like the euro signifies a depreciating dollar and an appreciating euro, while a declining rate connotes the opposite. On the other hand, in the case of an indirect quote in NYC, the US dollar is the base currency. In this case, a rising quote with respect to a currency like the euro signifies a depreciating euro or an appreciating dollar. A declining value in the case of an indirect quote in NYC would imply a depreciating dollar and an appreciating foreign currency.

What are the implications of an appreciation or depreciation of the US dollar with respect to the euro? An appreciation of the dollar would mean that the price of the euro in terms of dollars has gone down. Consequently, imports from the EU would be more attractive for Americans while imports from the United States would be less attractive for EU consumers. Conversely, a depreciating dollar would lead to a decline in imports from the EU into the United States while boosting US exports to the EU.

CONVERTING DIRECT QUOTES TO INDIRECT QUOTES

Consider a quote of 1.2250–1.2375 EUR–USD offered by Citibank in NYC. It is obviously a direct quote. Consider the bid of 1.2250. If the dealers are prepared to buy euros at dollars 1.2250 per euro, it obviously means they are prepared to sell dollars at $1/1.2250 = 0.8163$ euros per dollar. Similarly, the ask rate of 1.2375 is equivalent to a rate of 0.8081 euros per dollar. Thus, the equivalent indirect quote is 0.8163–0.8081 USD–EUR.

The direct quote of 1.2250–1.2375 will have an equivalent direct quote in Frankfurt, where a direct quote will be in terms of euros per dollar. The bid for a dealer in Frankfurt, however, will be a rate for buying US dollars while the ask rate will be a rate for selling dollars. Thus, the equivalent direct quote in Frankfurt is 0.8081–0.8163 USD–EUR.

Thus, to convert a direct quote in a market to an indirect quote in the same market, take reciprocals on both sides. To convert a direct quote in a market to the equivalent direct quote for the foreign currency in its home market, take reciprocals on both sides and interchange the numbers.

POINTS

Consider a quote of 1.2235–1.2295 EUR–USD. Exchange rate quotations in interbank markets are given up to four decimal places. Thus the last digit corresponds to 1/10,000th of the variable currency. The last two digits in such quotes are called *points* or *pips*. The first three digits of a quote are known as the *big figure*. In this case, the big figure is 1.22 and the spread is 60 points.

In the case of certain currencies, the quotes are given up to two decimal places only. Consequently, in such cases a point or pip is 1/100th of the variable currency. For instance, consider a quote of 95.75–96.95 USD–JPY. The spread is 120 points.

RATES OF RETURN

Let S_0 be the exchange rate for US dollars in terms of the euro as quoted in Frankfurt. Assume that a year later the exchange rate is S_1 USD–EUR. The rate of return for a European trader who acquires a dollar is given by

$$r_d = \frac{(S_1 - S_0)}{S_0}$$

Now consider the issue from the perspective of an American trader who acquires a euro. The price of a euro in terms of the dollar is obviously $1/S_0$ EUR–USD. Thus the rate of return for the trader is

$$r_f = \frac{\left(\frac{1}{S_1} - \frac{1}{S_0}\right)}{\frac{1}{S_0}}$$

$$= \frac{(S_0 - S_1)}{S_1}$$

$$= \frac{-r_d}{(1 + r_d)}$$

Thus the percentage change in return depends on the perspective that we take. We have considered the European trader to be the domestic investor and the American trader as the foreign investor. It can be demonstrated that

$$(1 + r_d) = \frac{1}{(1 + r_f)}$$

Thus, one plus the rate of return for a domestic investor is the reciprocal of one plus the rate of return for a foreign investor.

EXAMPLE 8.3

Consider the following quotes for the US dollar on two different dates.

1 January 20XX: 0.8000 USD–EUR

31 December 20XX: 0.8125 USD–EUR

The rate of return for a European investor is

$$r_d = \frac{(0.8125 - 0.8000)}{0.8000} = 0.015625 \equiv 1.5625\%$$

The rate of return for a European investor is positive because the dollar has appreciated against the euro.

The rate of return for an American trader is

$$r_f = \frac{-0.015625}{1 + 0.015625} = -0.015385 = -1.5385\%$$

The return is negative because the euro has depreciated against the dollar.

THE IMPACT OF SPREADS ON RETURNS

Assume that the quoted rates for the US dollar in Frankfurt at the beginning and end of a year are as follows.

1 January 20XX: S_{b0}–S_{a0} USD–EUR

31 December 20XX: S_{b1}–S_{a1} USD–EUR

A European trader can acquire a dollar on 1 January at a price of S_{a0}, and can sell it after a year at S_{b1}. The rate of return is

$$r_d = \frac{(S_{b,1} - S_{a,0})}{S_{a,0}}$$

An American trader can acquire a euro on 1 January at $1/S_{b,0}$. A year later the euro can be sold to realize $1/S_{a1}$ dollars. The rate of return is

$$r_f = \frac{\left(\dfrac{1}{S_{a,1}} - \dfrac{1}{S_{b,0}}\right)}{\dfrac{1}{S_{b,0}}}$$

$$= \frac{(S_{b,0} - S_{a,1})}{S_{a,1}}$$

EXAMPLE 8.4

Consider the following rates in the Frankfurt interbank market.

1 January 20XX: 0.8000–0.8075 USD–EUR

31 December 20XX: 0.8100–0.8175 USD–EUR

The rate of return for a European investor is:

$$r_d = \frac{(0.8100 - 0.8075)}{0.8075} = 0.003096 \equiv 0.3096\%$$

The rate of return for an American investor is

$$r_f = \frac{(0.8000 - 0.8175)}{0.8175} = -0.021407 \equiv -2.1407\%$$

ARBITRAGE IN SPOT MARKETS

We will consider three types of arbitrage in foreign exchange spot markets: one-point arbitrage, two-point arbitrage, and three-point (or triangular) arbitrage. Let us first look at one-point arbitrage.

ONE-POINT ARBITRAGE

Consider the following quotes in NYC on a given day.

> Citibank: 1.2225–1.2280 EUR–USD
>
> HSBC: 1.2285–1.2340 EUR–USD

Take the case of an arbitrageur who has 1,000,000 US dollars. The arbitrageur can buy 1,000,000/1.2280 or 814,332.25 euros from Citibank. This can immediately be sold to HSBC at the bid rate of 1.2285 to yield 1.2285 × 814,332.25 = $1,000,407.17. Clearly there is an arbitrage profit of 407.17 dollars.

Consider another situation.

> Citibank: 1.2225–1.2280 EUR–USD
>
> HSBC: 1.2180–1.2220 EUR–USD

In this case an arbitrageur can acquire 1,000,000/1.2220 or 818,330.61 euros from HSBC. This can immediately be sold to Citibank at its bid rate of 1.2225 to yield $1,000,409.17. Thus, once again there is an arbitrage profit of 409.17 dollars.

Such potential for arbitrage will exist as long as the quotes from competing banks do not overlap by at least one point. Consider the following quotes.

> Citibank: 1.2225–1.2280 EUR–USD
>
> HSBC: 1.2280–1.2340 EUR–USD

> Or

> Citibank: 1.2225–1.2280 EUR–USD
>
> HSBC: 1.2185–1.2225 EUR–USD

Obviously, there is no scope for arbitrage in either of these two cases.

TWO-POINT ARBITRAGE

Consider the following quote in NYC on a given day.

> Citibank: 1.2225–1.2280 EUR–USD

On the same day BNP Paribas in Paris is quoting 0.8185–0.8220 USD–EUR.

This also represents an arbitrage opportunity although it is not obvious at first glance. Consider the following strategy. Borrow 1,000,000 euros and acquire 1,222,500 USD in NYC. The currency can immediately be sold in Paris to yield 1,000,616.25 euros. Obviously, there is an arbitrage profit of 616.25 euros. What is the cause in this case?

The equivalent direct quote in Paris for Citibank's quote in NYC is 0.8143–0.8180. This is not overlapping with the quote given by BNP, and we know that the two quotes must overlap by at least one point to rule out arbitrage. This kind of an arbitrage opportunity is called a two-point arbitrage. Clearly, two-point arbitrage is a manifestation of one-point arbitrage executed across two markets.

TRIANGULAR ARBITRAGE

Consider the following quotes in Tokyo and NYC respectively.

Bank of Tokyo: 125.00 EUR–JPY

112.50 USD–JPY

Citibank: 1.1250 EUR–USD

Consider the following strategy. Borrow 1 MM yen in Tokyo and acquire 8,000 euros. The euros can be sold in NYC to yield 9,000 USD. The USD can then be sold in Tokyo to yield 1,012,500 JPY. Obviously, the strategy yields an arbitrage profit of 12,500 JPY. This kind of arbitrage, which entails the use of three currencies, is termed as *triangular arbitrage*.

There are two ways of acquiring a currency. In this case, USD can be acquired in Tokyo by paying Japanese yen. Or euros can be acquired in Tokyo using Japanese yen, which can subsequently be sold in NYC to yield dollars. The first transaction, which is based on a direct yen for dollar exchange, can be termed as the *natural rate*. The second may be termed as the *synthetic rate*. To rule out arbitrage, the natural rate must be equal to the synthetic rate. If we assume that the Tokyo market is fairly priced, then the rate that must prevail in NYC to rule out arbitrage is

$$112.50 = 125/X \Rightarrow X = 125/112.50 = 1.1111 \text{ EUR–USD}$$

Now let us make matters more realistic by introducing bid–ask spreads. Consider the following rates in Tokyo.

124.25–125.50 EUR–JPY

111.75–112.50 USD–JPY

The issue is what should be the rates in NYC to rule out triangular arbitrage.

Let us depict the two rates as: $S_b – S_a$ EUR–USD where the subscripts denote bid and ask respectively.

Consider an arbitrageur who borrows 1 MM USD and sells it in Tokyo to yield 111.75MM JPY. This can be used to acquire $111,750,000/125.50 = 890,438.25$ euros in Tokyo. The euros can be sold in NYC to yield $S_b \times 890,438.25$ USD. The condition to preclude arbitrage is therefore

$$S_b \times 890,438.25 \leq 1,000,000 \Rightarrow S_b \leq 1.1230 \text{ EUR–USD}$$

S_b may be termed as the *natural bid rate*.
The no-arbitrage condition is that

$$1,000,000 \times (\text{USD–JPY})_{\text{bid}} \times 1/(\text{EUR–JPY})_{\text{ask}} \times S_b \leq 1,000,000$$

$$\Rightarrow S_b \leq (\text{EUR–JPY})_{\text{ask}} \times 1/(\text{USD–JPY})_{\text{bid}} = (\text{EUR–JPY})_{\text{ask}} \times (\text{JPY–USD})_{\text{ask}}$$

Consider the RHS, which represents an indirect way of acquiring euros using US dollars, as it requires the acquisition of Japanese yen using dollars followed by the acquisition of euros using yen. Thus, it can be termed as a *synthetic ask rate* for euros in terms of USD. Hence the no-arbitrage condition is

$$S_b \equiv (EUR\text{–}USD)_{bid} \leq (EUR\text{–}USD)_{synthetic\ ask}$$

In other words, the natural bid should be less than or equal to the synthetic ask.

We can derive a similar condition for the natural ask. Take the case of a trader who borrows 1MM Yen and acquires dollars in Tokyo. He will get $1,000,000/112.50 = 8,888.8889$ USD. This can be used to acquire $8,888.8889 \times 1/S_a$ euros in NYC. The euros can be sold in Tokyo to yield $8888.8889 \times 124.25 \times 1/S_a$ Japanese yen. The no-arbitrage condition is that:

$$8888.8889 \times 124.25 \times 1/S_a \leq 1,000,000$$
$$\Rightarrow S_a \geq 1.1044\ EUR\text{–}USD$$

Thus, the no-arbitrage condition is that

$$[1,000,000/(USD\text{–}JPY)_{ask}] \times (EUR\text{–}JPY)_{bid} \times 1/S_a \leq 1,000,000$$
$$\Rightarrow S_a \geq (EUR\text{–}JPY)_{bid} \times (JPY\text{–}USD)_{bid}$$

The RHS represents an indirect way of acquiring US dollars using euros for it requires the acquisition of Japanese yen using euros followed by the acquisition of US dollars using yen. Thus, it can be termed as a *synthetic bid rate* for euros in terms of USD. Hence the no-arbitrage condition is

$$S_a = (EUR\text{–}USD)_{ask} \geq (EUR\text{–}USD)_{synthetic\ bid}$$

In other words, the natural ask should be greater than or equal to the synthetic bid. Of course, the natural ask must be greater than the natural bid.

CROSS RATES

As we have just seen, a bid for euros in terms of the dollar can be generated by multiplying the $(EUR\text{–}JPY)_{bid}$ by the $(JPY\text{–}USD)_{bid}$. Similarly the ask for euros in terms of the dollar can be generated by multiplying the $(EUR\text{–}JPY)_{ask}$ by the $(JPY\text{–}USD)_{ask}$. The bid and ask rates for a pair of currencies that are arrived at by using rates relative to a third currency are referred to as cross rates. In our illustration, the common currency was the Japanese yen, which was the base currency with respect to the USD and the variable currency with respect to the euro. Thus, in order to compute cross rates from two given quotes where the common currency is the base rate in one quotation and the variable currency in the other, we need to multiply the two quoted bid rates to arrive at the cross bid and multiply the two quoted ask rates to arrive at the cross ask.

Sometimes, however, the common currency may be either the base currency with respect to both the other currencies, or the variable currency with respect to both. In such cases, the cross rate may be generated using the following logic.

Assume that a bank in NYC is quoting the following rates.

1.2225–1.2295 EUR–USD

0.6225–0.6350 AUD–USD

In this case, the USD is the variable currency in both cases. Consider the synthetic $(EUR-AUD)_{bid}$. It requires the trader to sell euros and buy USD and then sell USD to buy AUD. A dealer selling a euro will get 1.2225 USD. A dealer selling one USD will get 1/0.6350 AUD. Thus the synthetic $(EUR-AUD)_{bid} = 1.2225/0.6350 = 1.9252 = (EUR-USD)_{bid} \div (AUD-USD)_{ask}$.

Now consider the synthetic ask. In order to buy euros, the trader can buy US dollars by selling Australian dollars and then sell the US dollars to acquire a euro. A trader selling an Australian dollar will get 0.6225 USD. The USD price for buying a euro is 1.2295. Thus, in order to buy a euro using Australian dollars, the trader requires 1.2295/0.6225 AUD or 1.9751 EUR-AUD. Therefore the synthetic $(EUR-AUD)_{ask} = (EUR-USD)_{ask} \div (AUD-USD)_{bid}$. Thus, in order to arrive at a spot rate from two other rates which have a common variable currency, we need to divide opposite sides of the quotes. In this case, the synthetic EUR-AUD bid rate is obtained by dividing the EUR-USD bid rate by the AUD-USD ask rate. Similarly, the EUR-AUD ask rate is obtained by dividing the EUR-USD ask rate by the AUD-USD bid rate.

Now let us consider a situation where the common currency is the base currency in both cases. Assume that the following quotes are available.

0.8225–0.8375 USD–EUR

1.5225–1.5350 USD–AUD

Consider the synthetic EUR-AUD bid. A trader selling a euro will get 1/0.8375 USD. That can be sold to get $1.5225 \times 1/0.8375 = 1.8179$ AUD. Thus, the EUR-AUD bid is equal to the USD-AUD bid divided by the USD-EUR ask. Now consider the EUR-AUD ask rate. To buy a US dollar the trader requires 1.5350 AUD. With one USD the trader can acquire 0.8225 euros. Thus, to acquire one euro the trader requires 1.5350/0.8225 = 1.8663 AUD. Thus, the EUR-AUD ask rate is equal to the USD-AUD ask divided by the USD-EUR bid. Hence, once again, to arrive at a spot rate from two other rates that have a common base currency, we need to divide opposite sides of the quotes.

MARKET RATES AND EXCHANGE MARGINS

Market rates, or interbank rates, are rates that are confronted by foreign exchange dealers. When quoting rates to retail customers, the dealers will apply a margin. Thus the bid–ask spread for the dealer will be greater than the prevailing spread in the interbank market. Here is an illustration.

EXAMPLE 8.5

Bank Aruba is quoting rates to retail clients for the USD. The mid-market rate is 0.8200 USD–EUR. The bank applies a margin of 0.25% in both directions. Thus, if it is selling dollars to a client, it will quote a rate of $0.8200 \times (1+0.0025) = 0.8221$ USD–EUR. If the bank is buying from a client, however, it will quote a rate of $0.8200 \times (1-0.0025) = 0.8180$ USD–EUR.

VALUE DATES

Spot market transactions have a value date of two business days after the trade date. For instance, if a spot transaction occurs on a Monday, the value date will be Wednesday. The market for the purchase and sale of foreign currencies with a delivery date that is more than two business days after the trade date is referred to as the forward market. The delivery dates for forward contracts, as is the case for money market transactions, are based on the modified following business day convention and the end-to-end rule.

For instance, assume that we are on 5 March 20XX, and that the spot value date is 7 March. A 1-month forward contract will have a value date of 7 April, while a 3-month forward contract will have a value date of 7 June. If the value date was a holiday, then the delivery would be moved to the next business day. As in the case of the money market, if moving the value date forward due to a market holiday were to result in a situation where it falls in the subsequent calendar month, then it would be moved back to the last business day of the same calendar month. For instance, assume that we are on 29 July 20XX. The spot value date is 31 July while the value date for a 1-month forward contract is 31 August. If 31 August were to be a Sunday, the value date for the contract will be 29 August.

As per the end-to-end rule, if the spot value date is the last business day of a month, then the forward value date will be the last business day of the corresponding month. For instance, if 31 July were to be the spot value date, then a 2-month forward contract will have a value date of 30 September.

THE FORWARD MARKET

In most foreign exchange markets the standard maturities for forward contracts are one week, two weeks, and one, two, three, six, nine, and 12 months. Countries like the United States have an active currency futures market. Foreign currencies, however, are one product where the volume of forward contract transactions is much higher than the trading volumes in futures markets.

If the forward rate for a maturity exceeds the spot rate, then we say that the foreign currency is trading at a premium. If the forward rate is less than the spot rate, however, then the foreign currency would be said to be trading at a discount. If the two rates were to be equal, then the currency would be said to be trading flat. Consider Example 8.6.

EXAMPLE 8.6

Consider the following rates that are observed in NYC on a given day.

Spot: 1.2225–1.2275 EUR–USD

1-month Forward: 1.2325–1.2405 EUR–USD

Spot: 0.7250–0.7305 AUD–USD

1-month Forward: 0.7165–0.7235 AUD–USD

Spot: 0.8815–0.8855 CAD–USD

1-month Forward: 0.8815–0.8855 CAD–USD

The euro is trading at a forward premium; the Australian dollar at a forward discount; and the Canadian dollar is trading flat.

OUTRIGHT FORWARD RATES

Forward contracts that are undertaken in isolation are referred to as outright forward contracts, and the corresponding quotes are referred to as outright forward rates. An outright forward contract has a single leg. For instance, Bank ABC buys one million USD one month forward, or Bank XYZ sells one million euros three months forward. In practice in the interbank market, however, whenever a bank undertakes a forward contract it will be accompanied by a spot transaction in what is termed as a *swap deal*. We will examine swap deals in detail shortly. Unlike an outright forward contract, a swap has two legs.

Outright forward rates have the same properties as spot rates. For instance, if the 1-month rate for the euro is given as 1.2250–1.2325 EUR–USD, then the corresponding rates in terms of USD–EUR are 0.8114–0.8163 USD–EUR where the USD–EUR bid is the reciprocal of the EUR–USD ask and the USD–EUR ask is the reciprocal of the EUR–USD bid.

The rules for calculating cross rates are also the same. For instance, assume that on a given day the following rates are observed in the London market.

3-month Forward: 0.5000–0.5075 USD–GBP

3–month Forward: 0.7500–0.7560 EUR–GBP

The GBP is the variable currency in both cases.

The bid for a 3-month forward contract for euros in terms of the USD is given by $0.7500 \div 0.5075 = 1.4778$ EUR–USD, while the ask rate may be computed as $0.7560 \div 0.5000 = 1.5120$ EUR–USD.

SWAP POINTS

In practice, the forward rates are not quoted directly in the interbank market. Instead, the difference between the forward and spot rates, which is termed as the *forward margin* or *swap points*, is given, and the corresponding outright rates have to be deduced from the data.

Consider the following data.

Spot: 0.5000–0.5075 USD–GBP

1-month Forward Points: 45/75

The numbers 45 and 75 represent the last two decimal places, or what we have termed as *points*. The swap points represent the difference between the forward rate and the corresponding spot rate. It has not been specified, however, whether the points should be added or subtracted in order to arrive at the outright forward rates. So, the issue is whether we add the numbers or subtract them.

It must be remembered that the spot market will have the lowest bid–ask spread and that as we negotiate contracts for future points in time, the spread will widen. This is because the relative liquidity in the spot market is the highest and the liquidity declines as we go forward in time.

In this case, if we add 45 points on the LHS and 75 points on the RHS, the spread will widen, whereas if we were to subtract the numbers the spread will narrow. Thus, a quote like 45/75 signifies that the foreign currency is at a forward premium and that the swap points need to be added. Hence the corresponding outright forward rates in this case are 0.5045–0.5150 USD–GBP.

Thus, if the swap points are given as Small Number/Large Number, it connotes that the foreign currency is at a forward premium and that consequently the points need to be added.

Now consider the following situation. On a given day in Frankfurt the rate for the US dollar is given as

Spot: 0.8000–0.8075 USD–EUR

3-Month Swap Points: 95/55

In this case it is obvious that if the forward market were to have a higher spread than the spot market, then we need to subtract the corresponding points from the respective sides. Thus, the equivalent outright forward rates in this case are:

3-Month Forward: 0.7905–0.8020

Thus, the rule is that if the swap points are given as Large Number/Small Number, it connotes that the foreign currency is at a forward discount and consequently the points need to be subtracted.

If the swap points quote were to state *par*, then it indicates that the spot rate and the outright forward rates are identical. Sometimes the swap points may be specified as *x–y* A/P. A/P stands for *around par*. It signifies that the swap points on the LHS should be subtracted while those on the RHS should be added. Consider the following quote.

Spot: 0.8000–0.8005 USD–EUR

1-Month Forward: 9/5 A/P

The corresponding outright rates for a 1-month forward contract are 0.7991–0.8010.

In the absence of the A/P specification, we would subtract 9 pips from the LHS and 5 pips from the RHS. The spread will widen by 4 points. In this case, however, we will subtract 9 pips from the LHS and add 5 pips on the RHS. Thus, the spread will widen by 14 points.

The logic we have used to derive the outright forward rates is valid in the case of direct quotes. In the case of indirect quotes, although the swap points have the same meaning, the treatment is different. Small Number/Large Number implies a foreign currency that is at a forward premium whether rates are quoted directly or indirectly. If the rates are quoted indirectly, however, then the swap points must be subtracted from the respective sides. Similarly, if the swap points are given as Large Number/Small Number, it indicates a foreign currency that is at a forward discount. But if the rates were to be quoted indirectly, then the numbers need to be added. Consider the following illustration.

EXAMPLE 8.7

The following rates are observed in NYC on a given day.

Spot: 123.15–122.50 USD–JPY
1-month Forward: 20/30

The Japanese yen is at a forward premium; however, the points must be subtracted. Thus, the corresponding outright rates are

122.95–122.20 USD–JPY

If, however, the swap points had been given as 30/20, then it would imply that the Japanese yen is at a forward discount. Consequently, the points will have to be added to arrive at the outright rates. The corresponding quote is therefore

123.45–122.70 USD–JPY

BROKEN-DATED CONTRACTS

Most forward contracts are for standard time intervals, such as one month or three months. At times, however, a client may approach a dealer seeking a contract with a nonstandard maturity date, or a date that falls between two standard intervals. Such contracts are referred to as broken-dated contracts, and to compute the applicable rate for such odd periods, a method of linear interpolation is used.

EXAMPLE 8.8

Consider the following rates that are quoted by BNP Paribas in Paris.

Spot: 0.8000–0.8125 USD–EUR
1–M: 40/65
2–M: 60/95

The US dollar is obviously at a forward premium. Assume that today is August 16, 20XX, which is a Wednesday. The spot value date is August 18. Thus, the value date for a 1-month contract is 18 September, while that for a 2-month contract is 18 October.

Assume that a client approaches the bank, seeking to sell dollars on October 9, 20XX, and that none of the three dates involved, that is, 18 September, 9 October, and 18 October, are market holidays.

The number of days between 18 September and 18 October is 30. The number of days between 18 September and 9 October is 21 days, which represents 0.70 months. The premium for a 1-month forward purchase is 40 points, while that

(continued)

(continued)

for a 2-month forward purchase is 60 points. Thus, the swap points for a contract maturing on 9 October may be calculated as:

$$40 + 0.70 \times (60 - 40) = 54 \text{ points}$$

Thus, the outright forward rate for a purchase transaction scheduled for 9 October is:

$$0.8000 + 0.0054 = 0.8054 \text{ USD–EUR}$$

The rate for a sale transaction is $0.8125 + 0.0065 + 0.70 \times (0.0095 - 0.0065) = 0.8211$.

EXAMPLE 8.9

Consider the following quote.

Spot: 0.8000–0.8125 USD–EUR

1-M: 40/80

2-M: 90/30

The USD is at a forward premium for 1-month contracts, and at a discount for a 2-month contracts. What if there is a request for a 1.6-month contract? The difference on the bid side, between one and two months, is $-90 - 40 = -130$ points. Thus, the difference for 0.6 months ought to be $0.6 \times -130 = -78$ points. On the other side, using similar logic, the points ought to be $0.6 \times (-30 - 80) = -66$ points. Thus, the outright forward rate for a 1.6-month forward contract is:

$$0.7962 - 0.8139 \text{ USD–EUR}$$

COVERED INTEREST ARBITRAGE

We will now derive the relationship between the spot rate and the forward rate for a given maturity, using arbitrage arguments. We will denote the spot rates, forward rates, and interest rates using the following symbols. Subsequently we will illustrate our arguments with the help of a numerical example.

Spot: $S_b - S_a$ USD–EUR

3-Month Forward: $F_b - F_a$ USD–EUR

Borrowing/lending rates in Frankfurt (for euros): $r_{db} - r_{dl}$

Borrowing/lending rates in NYC (for dollars): $r_{fb} - r_{fl}$

Note: This is a direct quote for the US dollar in Frankfurt. Consequently, the rate for borrowing/lending euros is the domestic rate, while that for borrowing/lending dollars is the foreign rate.

We will first consider cash-and-carry arbitrage. It entails the acquisition of one unit of the foreign currency and the simultaneous assumption of a short position in a forward contract to sell the foreign currency after three months. In order to buy a US dollar, the arbitrageur will have to borrow S_a EUR. This will be financed at a rate of r_{db}. This dollar can be invested at the rate r_{fl}. This will yield $(1 + r_{fl})$ USD at maturity, which can be sold forward at the outset at a rate F_b. At maturity the amount borrowed in euros will have to be repaid with interest which will entail an outflow of $S_a(1 + r_{db})$. Thus, to rule out arbitrage we require that

$$S_a(1 + r_{db}) \geq F_b(1 + r_{fl})$$

$$\Rightarrow F_b \leq S_a \times \frac{(1 + r_{db})}{(1 + r_{fl})}$$

Now consider a reverse cash-and-carry strategy. It will require the arbitrageur to borrow one US dollar to acquire S_b euros. The amount that is borrowed in dollars will have to be financed at the rate r_{fb}. The euros can be invested at the rate r_{dl}. At the outset the arbitrageur will have to go long in a forward contract to buy $(1 + r_{fb})$ dollars at the rate of F_a. To rule out arbitrage we require that

$$F_a(1 + r_{fb}) \geq S_b(1 + r_{dl})$$

$$\Rightarrow F_a \geq S_b \times \frac{(1 + r_{dl})}{(1 + r_{fb})}$$

A PERFECT MARKET

In a perfect market there will be no bid–ask spreads in either the spot or the forward market, and the borrowing rate for both currencies will be equal to the corresponding lending rates. Thus, in such a scenario $S_a = S_b = S$ and $F_a = F_b = F$. The borrowing/lending rate in Frankfurt will be r_d while that in NYC will be r_f. Thus, the no-arbitrage condition in such circumstances may be stated as

$$F = S \times \frac{(1 + r_d)}{(1 + r_f)}$$

This is termed as the *interest rate parity* condition.

We will illustrate these principles with the help of a numerical example.

EXAMPLE 8.10

The following rates are available in Frankfurt and NYC.

Spot: 0.8000–0.8125 USD–EUR

3-month Forward: 45–95

Thus the outright forward rates are: 0.8045–0.8220 USD–EUR

Borrowing/Lending Rates in the US (per annum): 4.25%/4.00%

Borrowing/Lending Rates in the EU (per annum): 4.75%/4.50%

(continued)

(*continued*)

Let us first check out the condition for cash-and-carry arbitrage.

$$S_a \times \frac{(1 + r_{db})}{(1 + r_{fl})} = 0.8125 \times \frac{(1 + 0.25 \times 0.0475)}{(1 + 0.25 \times 0.04)} = 0.8140$$

The forward bid of 0.8045 is less than this. Consequently, cash-and-carry arbitrage is ruled out.

Now let us check out the condition for reverse cash-and-carry arbitrage.

$$S_b \times \frac{(1 + r_{dl})}{(1 + r_{fb})} = 0.8000 \times \frac{(1 + 0.25 \times 0.045)}{(1 + 0.25 \times 0.0425)} = 0.8005$$

The forward ask of 0.8220 is greater than this. Consequently, reverse cash-and-carry arbitrage is also ruled out.

FOREIGN EXCHANGE SWAPS

It is a common practice for a bank to enter into a foreign exchange swap with a counterparty. Such a transaction entails the purchase or sale of a currency on the spot value date with a simultaneous agreement to sell or purchase the same currency at a future date. That is, it may involve a spot sale accompanied by a forward purchase or a spot purchase accompanied by a forward sale. In some cases, the transaction may entail a purchase/sale for a future date accompanied by a sale/purchase for a longer maturity. These transactions are referred to as *forward to forward swaps*.

In such transactions the key variable is the forward margin or swap points for the foreign currency. The rate for the spot leg per se is irrelevant and in practice the spot purchase or sale may be done at the prevailing bid, or the prevailing ask, or at a rate that is in between. The mechanics of such transactions may be illustrated with the help of a numerical example.

EXAMPLE 8.11

BNP Paribas seeks to sell 1MM euros spot and acquire US dollars for a period of six months. Consequently, it approaches JP Morgan Chase for a swap transaction. The rates in the interbank market are as follows.

Spot: 1.2500–1.2625 EUR–USD

6-M forward: 40/90

The two banks will usually agree on a spot rate between the bid and the ask rates. Let us assume in this case that they agree on a rate of 1.2575. BNP will therefore deliver 1 MM euros to JPMC in exchange for 1,257,500 USD. In the second leg JPMC will be selling euros to BNP. Consequently, the applicable forward margin will be 90 points. Thus BNP will take delivery of 1MM euros after six months at a rate of 1.2665 EUR–USD. This therefore translates to a payable of 1,266,500 USD for the bank.

THE COST

The cost of a foreign exchange swap is a function of the interest rate differential between the two currencies and is defined as the foreign exchange value of the interest rate differential between the currencies for the maturity of the swap. The party who holds the currency that pays a higher interest rate will effectively pay the counterparty, thereby neutralizing the rate differential and equalizing the returns on the two currencies.

Assume that covered interest arbitrage holds and for ease of exposition ignore bid–ask spreads and differential borrowing and lending rates. From the interest rate parity condition, we know that

$$F = S\frac{(1 + r_d)}{(1 + r_f)}$$

$$\Rightarrow \frac{F - S}{S} = \frac{r_d - r_f}{(1 + r_f)}$$

Thus

$$F - S = S \times \frac{r_d - r_f}{(1 + r_f)} \approx S \times (r_d - r_f)$$

$$\Rightarrow S - F = S \times \frac{r_f - r_d}{(1 + r_f)} \approx S \times (r_f - r_d)$$

EXAMPLE 8.12

Assume that the spot rate for the euro is 1.25 EUR–USD. The interest rate in the US market is 4% per annum while that in the EU is 4.80% per annum. Consider a forward contract with six months to maturity. The forward rate, assuming that interest rate parity holds, will be

$$1.2500 \times 1.02/1.024 = 1.2451 \text{ EUR–USD}$$

Consider the following swap transaction. BNP Paribas agrees to sell 1 MM euros to Bank of America at the spot rate and simultaneously agrees to buy back the euros after six months at the forward rate. The near-date transaction requires

(continued)

(*continued*)

BNP to deliver 1MM euros in return for 1.25 MM dollars, while the far-date transaction requires it to buy back 1MM euros by paying 1.2451 MM dollars. Thus, the gain for BNP is

$$1,250,000 - 1,245,100 = \$4,900$$

This can be interpreted as follows. BNP is holding US dollars, the currency that has a relatively lower interest rate, while Bank of America is holding euros, the currency that is paying a relatively higher interest rate. Thus, Bank of America has to make a payment of

$$1,000,000 \times 1.2500 \times (0.048 - 0.04) \times 0.5 \times 1/(1.024) = \$4,882.8125$$

The two amounts are equal except for rounding errors.

THE MOTIVE

What could be the motivation for a swap such as the one undertaken by BNP Paribas with Bank of America? In practice, while banks regularly execute outright forward contracts with their nonbank clients, most interbank transactions entailing the use of forward contracts are done in the form of a foreign exchange swap.

Assume that Bank of America has executed a forward contract with a client to buy 1MM euros six months later. It will thus have a long position in euros six months forward. If the bank were to desire to square off this position, it will have to sell 1 MM euros six months forward. It may not always be easy, however, to locate a counterparty with matching opposite needs, with whom an offsetting outright forward contract can be executed. It is easier in practice to do a swap. In this case the swap will require Bank of America to buy euros spot, and sell the currency six months forward. This creates the required offsetting short forward positions in euros. In the process, however, the bank has created a long spot position in euros. This can be easily offset by selling the euros in the interbank market.[1]

A second reason why banks prefer to do foreign exchange swaps rather than an outright forward is that although an outright forward is influenced by both the spot rate and the difference in the interest rates for the two currencies, a foreign exchange swap is primarily influenced by the interest rate differential. Thus, an outright forward transaction has the effect of combining two related but different markets in a single transaction, which may not be acceptable to the bank, as compared to a swap, which is primarily an interest rate instrument.[2] Speculators do not like financial products where multiple economic variables are intertwined. Consequently, speculators in the foreign exchange market prefer FX swaps to outright forward contracts.

---

[1]See Apte (2006).
[2]See Steiner (2002).

EXAMPLE 8.13

Consider the following data.

Spot: 1.2500 EUR–USD

Interest rate for dollars = 4.00% per annum

Interest rate for euros = 2.80% per annum

A six-month outright forward would be priced at

$$1.2500 \times 1.02/1.014 = 1.2574 \text{ EUR–USD}$$

If the spot rate were to increase to 1.2625, the forward rate would be 1.2700.

If the exchange rate differential were to increase to 2% per annum (assume that the rate for dollars remains at 4% per annum while that for the euro declines to 2% per annum), keeping the spot rate unchanged, the forward rate would be 1.2624.

Thus, a change of 125 points in the spot rate has changed the forward rate by 126 points, while a change of 0.8% in the interest rate differential has changed the rate by 50 points.

Now consider a foreign exchange swap.

$$F - S = S \times \frac{(r_d - r_f)}{(1 + r_f)}$$

$$= 1.2500 \times \frac{(0.02 - 0.014)}{1.014} = 0.0074$$

If the spot rate were to increase to 1.2625, then $F - S = 0.0075$. Thus, the swap price changes by one point. If, however, the interest rate for euros were to decline to 2% per annum, then

$$F - S = 1.2500 \times \frac{(0.02 - 0.01)}{1.01} = 0.0124$$

which corresponds to a change of 50 points. Thus, the swap price is sensitive to interest rate changes but is relatively insensitive to changes in the spot rate. An outright forward contract, on the other hand, is sensitive to both parameters.

INTERPRETATION OF THE SWAP POINTS

Consider the following quote in the foreign exchange market in NYC on a given day.

Spot: 1.2500–1.2625 EUR–USD

1-Month Forward: 50/90

The first figure (the swap points on the left) represents a transaction where the quoting bank is selling the base currency spot and is buying it back one month forward. In this illustration the quoting bank is prepared to offer a premium of 50 points. The second figure (the swap points on the right) represents a transaction where the quoting bank is buying the base currency spot and selling the same one-month forward. In this illustration the quoting bank is charging a premium of 90 points. If we term the spot transaction as the near-date transaction and the forward contract as the far-date transaction, the swap points on the left are for a transaction that entails the sale of the base currency on the near-date and its acquisition on the far-date, while the swap points on the right are for a transaction that entails the purchase of the base currency on the near-date and its subsequent sale on the far-date.[3] This statement should of course be perceived from the standpoint of the quoting bank.

A CLARIFICATION

There is a derivative product known as a *currency swap*. It requires two parties to swap interest rate payments in the two chosen currencies periodically, based on prespecified benchmarks. The principal amounts on the basis of which the interest flows are calculated are always exchanged at the end of the swap; however, there may or may not be an exchange of principal at inception. Here is an illustration.

EXAMPLE 8.14

Commonwealth Bank and Barclays agree to a swap wherein Commonwealth will deliver 1MM AUD to Barclays at the outset in exchange for 500,000 GBP. The exchange is based on the prevailing spot rate of 0.5000 AUD–GBP. As per the agreement, Commonwealth will make payments in British pounds every six months at the LIBOR prevailing at the start of the interest computation period, while Barclays will make payments in Australian dollars at the same frequency at a fixed rate of 8% per annum. The swap has a maturity of five years at the end of which the two banks will swap back the currencies based on the original spot rate.

SHORT-DATE CONTRACTS

A short date transaction may be defined as one for which the value date is before the spot value date. There are two possibilities, *value today* and *value tomorrow*, where tomorrow refers to the next business day. In the foreign exchange markets, three types of one-day swaps are quoted. These are:

- Between today and tomorrow: Referred to as *Overnight* or *O/N*
- Between tomorrow and the next day: Referred to as *tom/next* or *T/N*
- Between the spot date and the next day: Referred to as *spot/next* or *S/N*

---

[3] You will understand the import of this better when we study short-date contracts.

Let us first consider a value tomorrow transaction. An outright sale for a bank, with value tomorrow, may be viewed as a combination of the following transactions: spot sale of euros, accompanied by a swap that includes sale of euros for tomorrow, accompanied by a spot purchase of euros.

Let us assume that the tom/next swap points are given as 25/15. The question is, how do we deal with these points? That is, do we deal with them in the same way as we do for normal forward contracts or is there a difference? Before we proceed, let us reconsider a 1-month forward contract from the standpoint of the quoting bank.

An outright sale one month forward may be viewed as a spot sale accompanied by a swap that entails the spot purchase and forward sale of the base currency. Assume that the swap points are given as a/b. The first number represents a transaction for selling spot and buying forward, while the second number represents a transaction for buying spot and selling forward. Thus, if $a < b$, it implies that the foreign currency is at a forward premium, and we will add the numbers to the respective sides. The rationale here is that if the currency is at a forward premium, the premium that the bank will offer when it buys forward will be less than what it will charge when it sells forward. On the other hand, if $a > b$, it implies that the foreign currency is a forward discount, and we should subtract the numbers from the respective sides. The rationale is that if the currency is at a forward discount, then the discount that the bank will apply when it buys will be larger than what it will offer when it sells. As explained earlier, the swap points on the left are for selling the base currency on the near date and buying it on the far date, whereas the points on the right are for buying the base currency on the near date and selling it on the far date.

Now consider a value tomorrow sale transaction. As we have seen, it may be viewed as a combination of the spot sale of euros accompanied by a swap which entails the spot purchase of euros with the sale of euros for tomorrow. The difference between this swap and the swap corresponding to a 1-month outright forward sale is that this transaction is for the purchase of euros on the far date, whereas in the earlier case it was for the sale of euros on the far date. Thus, in this case, if the swap points are given as a/b, then the points applicable for an outright sale with value tomorrow are the points on the left side, while those applicable for an outright purchase are those on the right side. Remember that the transaction scheduled for tomorrow is the near-date leg while the spot transaction represents the far-date leg.

Now consider a number like 25/15. The implications are that when the bank is buying for value tomorrow it will give a premium of 15 points, whereas when it is selling for value tomorrow it will charge a premium of 25 points. The numbers cannot represent a discount because the bank will not offer a larger discount when it sells as compared to what it levies when it buys. On the other hand, what if the points had been given as 15/20? Clearly, this implies that the bank will apply a discount of 20 points when it buys euros for value tomorrow, while for sale transactions with value tomorrow it will offer a discount of only 15 points.

As can be surmised from the preceding arguments, the way to deal with the swap points in this case is to reverse them and then proceed as before. That is, for a value tomorrow transaction, if the tom/next swap points are given as a/b, we first invert them to obtain b/a. Then if it connotes a smaller number followed by a larger number, we will add the points to the respective sides. If it is a larger number followed by a smaller number, however, we subtract the points from the respective sides. As Steiner points out, the inversion of the swap points is purely from the standpoint of computation. The swap points themselves will not be quoted after inversion.

EXAMPLE 8.15

The following quotes are observed in NYC on a given day.

Spot: 1.2500–1.2600 EUR–USD

T/N: 15/8

If we reverse the swap points, it represents a Small Number/Large Number. Thus, the base currency is obviously at a forward premium. Thus, the rates for a transaction with value tomorrow are

1.2508–1.2615 EUR–USD

Now let us consider the procedure for arriving at a quote for a value today sale transaction. This can be viewed as a combination of three transactions.

1. Sale of euros spot.
2. A swap entailing a sale of euros for value tomorrow accompanied by a spot purchase of euros.
3. A swap entailing a sale of euros for value today accompanied by a purchase of euros for value tomorrow.

The computation of the outright value today rates may be best illustrated with the help of an example.

EXAMPLE 8.16

Consider the following quotes:

Spot: 1.2500–1.2625 EUR–USD

O/N: 15/8

T/N: 12/5

The rates for value today would be computed as:

Bid: 1.2500 + 0.0008 + 0.0005 = 1.2513 EUR–USD

Ask: 1.2625 + 0.0015 + 0.0012 = 1.2652 EUR–USD

Swap points for short-duration transactions like O/N or T/N, may be very small in practice. Often, they may be less than a point and will in practice be expressed either in fractions or as decimals. For instance, consider the following quote for an O/N swap.

$$2\,^1\!/_4 / 1\,^3\!/_4$$

It implies a quote of 2.25/1.75 points. At times the quote may be expressed directly in decimals, that is, as 2.25/1.75. In either case care should be exercised when they are being added to or subtracted from the spot rates.

OPTION FORWARDS

Clients negotiating a forward contract may be uncertain at times about the exact date on which they will have to pay or receive the foreign currency. In such cases, they have the freedom to negotiate a forward contract with the flexibility to transact within a specified time period. For instance, exporters based in Philadelphia may be of the opinion that they will receive a payment in euros sometime between two to three months from the date of negotiation of the forward contract. In such a situation they can negotiate a forward contract with an option to complete the contract on any date during the stated period. The option writer in such cases is the foreign exchange dealer, typically a bank. Dealers will quote a rate for the option forward based on what works out best for them. The implications of this would depend on whether the dealers are buying or selling the foreign currency and on whether the currency is quoting at a premium or a discount. We will illustrate various situations with the help of the following examples.

EXAMPLE 8.17

Raytheon is importing goods from Zurich and is required to make a payment in euros. The company is of the opinion that the payment will have to be made sometime between one and two months from today, although it is unsure about the exact date. Thus, it seeks to negotiate a forward contract with an option to take delivery of the euros at any point in time after one month but before two months.

Assume that the following rates are prevailing in the interbank market.

Spot: 1.2225–1.2350 EUR–USD

1-Month Forward: 30/65

2-Month Forward: 45/95

3-Month Forward: 60/120

The euro is obviously at a forward premium. The relevant exchange rate for the bank is the ask rate, for it is selling foreign currency to Raytheon. If the bank assumes that the contract will be completed after one month, it should charge a premium of 65 points, whereas if it assumes that the currency will have to be sold after two months, it should charge a premium of 95 points. Because the bank is charging a premium, it will charge the higher of the two values. Thus, in this case the rate quoted by the bank will be 1.2350 + 0.0095 = 1.2445 EUR–USD.

EXAMPLE 8.18

Let us continue with the previous example but with a different set of data. Assume that the spot rates are the same but that the euro is at a forward discount and that the swap points are as follows.

1-Month Forward: 65/30

2-Month Forward: 95/45

3-Month Forward: 120/60

In this case if the bank assumes that the deal will be completed after one month, it should offer a discount of 30 points to the client, whereas if it assumes that the currency will have to be sold after two months, it should offer a discount of 45 points. Because the bank is offering a discount, it will offer the lower of the two values. Thus, in this case the rate quoted by the bank will be 1.2350–0.0030 = 1.2320 EUR–USD.

EXAMPLE 8.19

Let us once again take the case of Raytheon and the bank. We will assume that the spot rate remains the same but that the swap points for the various maturities are as follows.

1-Month Forward: 30/65

2-Month Forward: 95/45

3-Month Forward: 120/60

The euro is trading at a premium for a 1-month transaction but at a discount for a 2-month transaction. If the transaction is assumed to be completed after one month, the bank will have to charge a premium of 65 points. If, however, it's assumed that the transaction will take place two months hence, the bank has to offer a discount of 45 points. Because it is selling foreign currency, the bank will charge a premium of 65 points. Thus, the rate quoted by the bank will be 1.2350 + 0.0065 = 1.2415 EUR–USD.

EXAMPLE 8.20

Purovita has exported pet food to the UK and expects to be paid in Pound Sterling sometime between one and two months from today. The current rates in the interbank market are as follows:

Spot: 1.4500–1.4625 GBP–USD

1-Month Forward: 35/75

2-Month Forward: 55/105

3-Month Forward: 80/150

The pound is trading at a forward premium. In this case the bank will be acquiring the foreign currency from the client. Thus, the applicable rate is the spot bid of 1.4500. If the bank assumes that the transaction will be completed after one month, it should offer a premium of 35 points, whereas if it assumes the transaction will be completed after two months, it should offer 55 points. Because it is acquiring the foreign currency, the bank will obviously offer the lower of the two values. Thus, the rate at which the bank will buy will be 1.4500 + 0.0035 = 1.4535 GBP–USD.

EXAMPLE 8.21

Take the case of Purovita, which is expecting to be paid in pounds between one and two months. Assume that the spot rates are the same as earlier but the swap points are as follows.

  1-Month Forward: 75/35

  2-Month Forward: 105/55

  3-Month Forward: 150/80

The pound is obviously trading at a forward discount. If the bank were to assume that the trade will take place after one month, it should apply a discount of 75 points, whereas if it were to assume that the deal will be completed after two months, it should apply a discount of 105 points. Because the bank is buying the foreign currency, it will apply the higher discount of 105 points. Thus, the applicable rate will be 1.4500 – 0.0105 = 1.4395 GBP–USD.

EXAMPLE 8.22

Let us once again take the case of Purovita and the bank. We will assume that the spot rate remains the same but that the swap points for the various maturities are as follows.

  1-Month Forward: 65/30

  2-Month Forward: 45/95

  3-Month Forward: 60/120

The pound is at a discount for a 1-month contract but at a premium for a 2-month contract. If the bank assumes that the transaction will take place after one month, it has to apply a discount of 65 points, whereas if it assumes that the deal will be consummated after two months, it has to offer a premium of 45 points. Because the bank is buying the foreign currency, it will apply a discount of 65 points. Thus, the applicable rate will be 1.4500–0.0065 = 1.4435 GBP–USD.

NONDELIVERABLE FORWARDS

A traditional forward contract entails the acquisition of a foreign currency if a long position is taken, or the delivery of a foreign currency if a short position is taken. In the case of a nondeliverable forward contract there is no need to acquire or deliver a foreign currency. Instead, the two parties simply settle the profit or loss with respect to the prevailing spot rate two business days before the maturity date of the forward contract.

EXAMPLE 8.23

On 15 March 20XX Axis Bank and HSBC agree to a nondeliverable forward contract wherein Axis Bank will acquire 1MM USD three months forward at a rate of 72.2500 USD–INR. On 15 June the two banks agree to settle the difference at a rate of 73.4000 USD–INR. In this case, the dollar has appreciated with respect to the Indian rupee. Consequently, Axis Bank will be entitled to receive

$$1,000,000\,(73.4000 - 72.2500) = 1,150,000 \text{ INR}$$

Nondeliverable forwards can be offset prior to maturity. In this case, the profit/loss may be received/paid either at the original date of maturity of the contract or on the day of offsetting.

EXAMPLE 8.24

On 15 March 20XX Axis Bank and HSBC agree to a nondeliverable forward contract wherein Axis Bank agrees to acquire 1MM USD three months forward at a rate of 72.2500 USD–INR. On 21 May Axis Bank decides to offset the contract with another nondeliverable forward contract with the same maturity date. Assume that the rate on 21 May is 73.1250 USD–INR.

The original contract would have been settled on 17 June. So, one possibility is that the profit/loss, which in this case is

$$1,000,000 \times (73.1250 - 72.2500) = 875,000 \text{ INR}$$

is paid to Axis Bank by HSBC on 17 June.

The other possibility is that the present value of this amount is paid to Axis Bank on 21 May itself. Between 21 May and 17 June there are 27 days. Assume that the interest rate in the Indian market is 8% per annum. If so, the present value of this amount as computed on 21 May is

$$\frac{875,000}{\left(1 + 0.08 \times \dfrac{27}{360}\right)} = 869,781.31 \text{ INR}$$

This amount can be paid by HSBC if the deal were to be settled on 21 May itself.

RANGE FORWARDS

These contracts impose a cap and a floor on the exchange rate. If the spot rate at maturity is higher than the cap, then the rate is set equivalent to it. If the spot rate at maturity is lower than the floor, however, then the applicable rate is the floor. If the spot rate is in between the two bounds, then the applicable rate is the prevailing spot rate.

For instance, assume a party buys a range forward with an upper limit of 0.8225 USD–EUR and a lower limit of 0.8075 USD–EUR. If the rate at maturity is 0.8275 USD–EUR, then the applicable rate will be 0.8225. If the rate at maturity is 0.8025 USD–EUR, however, then the applicable rate is 0.8075. If the terminal spot rate is 0.8185 USD–EUR, then it will be the applicable rate.

FUTURES MARKETS

FOREX futures trading is active on the CME Group. The exchange currently offers futures contracts on a variety of currencies, including the euro, the British pound, and the Japanese yen.

HEDGING USING CURRENCY FUTURES

Futures contracts on foreign currencies may be used by traders to hedge their risks in the spot market. A party who knows that it will be selling a foreign currency in the future will be worried that the currency may depreciate or, in other words, that the price of the currency in terms of the domestic currency may fall. Consequently, it will hedge by going short in futures contracts.

On the other hand, a party that knows it will be acquiring a foreign currency in the future will be concerned that the currency may appreciate, which would mean that the price of that currency in terms of the domestic currency may rise. Such parties will seek to hedge by going long in futures contracts.

We will illustrate buying and selling hedges with the help of numerical examples.

A SELLING HEDGE

EXAMPLE 8.25

Purovita has exported pet food to South Africa and is scheduled to receive 7.5 MM South African rand after 75 days. It decides to hedge the dollar value of its receivable by going short in ZAR futures. On the exchange each futures contract on the rand is for 500,000 ZAR. Thus, the company needs to go short in 15 contracts.

(continued)

(*continued*)

Assume that the rates on 15 January, the day on which the hedge is initiated, are as follows.

Spot: 0.0835–0.0885 ZAR–USD

3-Month Futures: 0.0870–0.0940 ZAR–USD

Because the company needs to go short in futures, the applicable rate is the bid rate of 0.0870. The futures contract is scheduled to expire on 15 April.
Assume that on 1 April the rates in the market are as follows.

Spot: 0.0820–0.0875 ZAR–USD

April Futures: 0.0835–0.0910 ZAR–USD

If the company had not hedged, it would have had to sell the 7.5 MM rand for

$$7,500,000 \times 0.0820 = \$615,000$$

Because it has hedged, however, the proceeds from the spot market will be augmented by the profit/loss from the futures market. In this case the April contracts will have to be offset at the ask rate of 0.0910 ZAR–USD. The cash flow from the market is

$$15 \times 500,000 \times (0.0870 - 0.0910) = -\$30,000$$

Thus, the total cash inflow in dollars is 615,000 – 30,000 = 585,000. The effective exchange rate is therefore

$$585,000 \div 7,500,000 = 0.0780 \text{ ZAR–USD}$$

A BUYING HEDGE

EXAMPLE 8.26

Edgar Royce has imported books from the UK and is due to pay 1.25 MM GBP after 75 days. Each futures contract on the pound is for 62,500 GBP. Consequently, as the company will be buying the foreign currency, it needs to go long in 20 futures contracts.

Assume that the rates on 15 January, the day on which the hedge is initiated, are as follows.

Spot: 1.4500–1.4525 GBP–USD

3-Month Futures: 1.4620–1.4665 GBP–USD

Because the company needs to go long in futures, the applicable rate is the ask rate of 1.4665. The futures contract is scheduled to expire on 15 April.

Assume that on 1 April the rates in the market are as follows.

Spot: 1.4725–1.4750 GBP–USD

April Futures: 1.4775–1.4820 GBP–USD

If the company had not hedged, it would have had to buy 1.25 MM pounds for

$$1,250,000 \times 1.4750 = \$1,843,750$$

Because it has hedged, however, the cash flow in the spot market will be accompanied by the profit/loss from the futures market, which will consequently have implications for the effective rate of exchange. In this case the April contracts will have to be offset at the bid rate of 1.4775 GBP–USD. The cash flow from the futures market is

$$20 \times 62,500 \times (1.4775 - 1.4665) = \$13,750$$

Thus, the total cash outflow in dollars is 1,843,750 – 13,750 = $1,830,000. The effective exchange rate is therefore

$$1,830,000 \div 1,250,000 = 1.4640 \text{ GBP–USD}$$

EXCHANGE-TRADED FOREIGN CURRENCY OPTIONS

NASDAQ OMX PHLX offers options contracts on a number of foreign currencies, with settlement in US dollars. Option premiums are quoted in points where one point is equivalent to $100. For instance, on 15 September 20XX, the Canadian dollar was quoting at 0.8700 CAD–USD. A call options contract with a strike price of 80 cents was quoting at 9.25. Thus, the premium for the contract was 925 USD.

SPECULATING WITH FOREX OPTIONS

A foreign exchange option gives the holder the right to buy or sell a currency. As is the case with other underlying assets, the option may be a call or a put, and both European and American-style options are possible. The number of units of the currency that can be bought or sold per contract will be specified, and both the exercise price and the option premium will be stated in terms of the number of units of the other currency.

EXAMPLE 8.27

The Canadian dollar is quoting at 0.8700 CAD–USD in the spot market. A call option with $X = 80$ and three months to expiration is quoting at 8.50. Thus, the premium per contract is 850 USD. Mitch decides to go long in 100 call options contracts because he expects the Canadian dollar to appreciate. Each contract is for 10,000 CAD.

Assume that three months hence the Canadian dollar is quoting at 0.8975 CAD–USD. Because the contract is in the money it will be exercised and the payoff will be

$$(0.8975 - 0.8000) \times 10,000 \times 100 = 97,500 \text{ USD}$$

Because the premium for 100 contracts was \$85,000, the profit for the option holder is 12,500 USD.

EXAMPLE 8.28

The Canadian dollar is quoting at 0.8700 CAD–USD. A put option with $X = 92.50$ and three months to expiration is quoting at 6.25. Thus, the premium per contract is 625 USD. Janice decides to go short in 100 put options contracts because she expects the Canadian dollar to depreciate.

Assume that three months hence the Canadian dollar is quoting at 0.8550 CAD–USD. The contract is obviously in the money and will be exercised. The payoff will be

$$(0.9250 - 0.8550) \times 10,000 \times 100 = 70,000 \text{ USD}$$

Because the premium for 100 contracts was 62,500 USD, the profit is 7,500 USD.

The Garman-Kohlhagen Model

This is a variation of the Black-Scholes model that was developed to price European options on foreign currencies. In addition to the usual parameters required to calculate an option premium using the Black-Scholes model, the Garman-Kohlhagen model requires us to specify the riskless rate of interest in the foreign country, r_f. As per the model, the price of a European call option is given by

$$C_E = S_t e^{-r_f(T-t)} N(d_1) - X e^{-r(T-t)} N(d_2)$$

where

$$d_1 = \frac{ln\left(\frac{S_t}{X}\right) + \left(r - r_f + \frac{\sigma^2}{2}\right)(T - t)}{\sigma\sqrt{T - t}}$$

and $d_2 = d_1 - \sigma\sqrt{T - t}$.

The price of a European put is given by

$$P_E = Xe^{-r(T-t)}N(-d_2) - S_t e^{-r_f(T-t)}N(-d_1)$$

In Example 8.29 we will demonstrate the computation of option premiums for the euro, using the Garman-Kohlhagen model.

EXAMPLE 8.29

The spot rate for euros in New York is 1.3000 EUR–USD. The riskless rate in the United States is 3% per annum while the rate in the EU is 3.75% per annum. The volatility of the exchange rate is 20%. Consider European call options with an exercise price of 120 and four months to expiration.

$$d_1 = \frac{ln\left(\frac{130}{120}\right) + \left(0.03 - 0.0375 + \frac{(0.20)^2}{2}\right) \times \frac{1}{3}}{0.20\sqrt{\frac{1}{3}}}$$

$$= 0.7293$$

$$d_2 = 0.6138$$

$$N(d_1) = 0.7671 \text{ and } N(d_2) = 0.7303$$

$$C_E = 130e^{-\frac{0.0375}{3}} \times 0.7671 - 120e^{-\frac{0.03}{3}} \times 0.7303 = 11.7202$$

Thus, the premium per contract is 1,172 USD.

Put-Call Parity

The put-call parity relationship for foreign currency options may be expressed as

$$C_{E,t} - P_{E,t} = S_t e^{-r_f(T-t)} - Xe^{-r(T-t)}$$

The Binomial Model

The binomial model can be used to value options on foreign currencies. The only difference is with respect to the definition of the risk-neutral probability p. For currency options, the probability is defined as

$$p = \frac{\frac{r}{r_f} - d}{u - d}$$

In Example 8.30 we will demonstrate the computation of option premiums for the euro, using the binomial model.

EXAMPLE 8.30

Consider a call option on the euro. The current exchange rate is 1.3500 EUR–USD. Every period the exchange rate may go up by 20% or down by 20%. The riskless rate in the US is 4% and the corresponding rate in the EU is 5%. The exercise price of the option is 125, and there are two periods to expiration.

The tree for the evolution of the exchange rate may be depicted as follows (Figure 8.1).

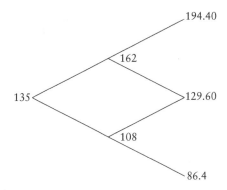

FIGURE 8.1   The Evolution of the Exchange Rate

$$C_{uu,T} = 69.40, C_{ud,T} = 4.60, C_{dd,T} = 0$$

$$p = \frac{\dfrac{1.04}{1.05} - 0.8}{0.4} = 0.4762 \text{ and } (1 - p) = 0.5238$$

$$C_{u,T-1} = \frac{0.4762 \times 69.4 + 0.5238 \times 4.60}{1.04} = 34.094$$

The intrinsic value is 37. So, we will use the intrinsic value for proceeding backwards.

$$C_{d,T-1} = \frac{0.4762 \times 4.60 + 0.5238 \times 0}{1.04} = 2.1063$$

The intrinsic value is zero. Thus, the model value at time $T - 2$ is given by

$$C_{T-2} = \frac{0.4762 \times 37 + 0.5238 \times 2.1063}{1.04} = 18.0026$$

The intrinsic value is 135 – 125 = 10. Thus, the option premium is 18.0026 or 1,800.26 USD per contract.

EXCHANGE RATES AND COMPETITIVENESS

If a currency appreciates, the importers in the home country stand to benefit, whereas if it depreciates, exporters in the home country stand to benefit. Despite a currency movement in their favor, however, producers and consumers may be adversely hit due to a more beneficial currency movement for a competitor in a different country. Here is an illustration.

The euro is quoting in Mumbai at 90.0000 EUR–INR and in Singapore at 1.8000 EUR–SGD. The rupee-Singapore dollar rate is 50.0000 SGD–INR.

A company in India sells a product at 140 euros in Germany. The cost of production in India is 9,000 rupees. Thus, the margin in euros is 40. A company in Singapore sells an identical product for the same price in the EU. Its cost of production is 180 SGD. Thus, it too has a margin of 40 euros.

Now assume that the Indian rupee depreciates to 96.00 EUR–INR, while the Singapore dollar depreciates to 2.00 EUR–SGD. The price of the product remains at 140 euros.

The cost of production in euros for the Indian company is 93.75 euros. Thus, the margin is 46.25 euros. The currency movement has benefited the Indian company.

The cost of production for the Singaporean company is 90.00 euros. Its margin is 50.00 euros. The currency movement is beneficial in this case as well.

Although both companies have benefited from exchange rate movements, the margin for the Singaporean company is greater after the change in the exchange rate. Hence, it can cut its selling price by a greater amount as compared to its Indian competitor, and can potentially increase its market share.

CHAPTER 9

Mortgages and Mortgage-backed Securities

INTRODUCTION

In most developed countries the right to own a home is considered to be virtually a fundamental right. But few people are in a position to pay the cost of acquisition of a home from their own personal funds. Consequently, most of the funds required to buy a home must be borrowed. A loan that is collateralized by real estate property is called a mortgage loan. The lender is called the mortgagee and the borrower is called the mortgagor. In the event of default on the part of the mortgagor, the lender can seize the property and sell it to recover the amount that is owed to it. This is called the right of foreclosure.

MARKET PARTICIPANTS

There are three categories of players in the mortgage market. These are:

* Mortgage originators
* Mortgage servicers
* Mortgage insurers

MORTGAGE ORIGINATION

Who is a mortgage originator? The original lender or the party who first extends a loan to the acquirer of the property is called the mortgage originator. Originators include:

* Thrifts or Savings & Loan Associations
* Commercial Banks
* Mortgage Bankers
* Life Insurance Companies
* Pension Funds

Income for the Originator

Originators get income from various sources. First, when a loan is granted, they will levy an origination fee. The fee is expressed in terms of points where each point is 1% of the borrowed funds. For example, if a lender were to charge 1.5 points on a loan of $200,000, the origination fee will amount to $3,000. Most originators will also levy an application fee and certain processing fees.

The second source of income is the profit that can be earned if and when the mortgage loan is sold by the originator to another party. A mortgage loan is a type of debt, and consequently is vulnerable to interest rate fluctuations. If the interest rate were to decline, such a sale would lead to a gain for the originator. This is called a *secondary marketing profit*. Of course, if interest rates were to rise after the loan is disbursed, the originator will incur a loss when the loan is sold.

If originators were to decide to hold the loan as an asset rather than sell it, they will earn periodic income in the form of interest.

Mortgage Servicing

Every mortgage loan must be serviced. Servicing of a mortgage loan includes the following activities:

- Collection of monthly payments and forwarding the proceeds to the owner of the loan
- Sending payment notices to mortgagors
- Reminding mortgagors whose payments are overdue
- Maintaining records of principal balances
- Administering escrow balances for real estate taxes and insurance purposes
- Initiating foreclosure proceedings if necessary
- Furnishing tax information to mortgagors when applicable

Mortgage servicers include bank-related entities; thrift-related entities; and mortgage bankers.

Escrow Accounts

An escrow account is a trust account held in the name of the homeowner to pay statutory levies like property taxes, and insurance premiums. The maintenance of such an account helps ensure that payments are made when due, for it becomes the lender's responsibility to do so.

In most cases the borrower makes deposits on a monthly basis, along with the loan payment, and the payments accrue at the lender. The amount required to be deposited every month is a function of the cost of insurance and the tax assessment of the property concerned. Consequently, it fluctuates from year to year.

Income for the Servicer

The primary source of income is the servicing fee, which is a fixed percentage of the outstanding mortgage balance. Because the mortgage loan is an amortized loan, where the outstanding principal declines with each payment, the revenue from servicing, in dollar terms, will decline over time. The second source of income arises on account of the interest that can be earned by the servicer from the escrow account that the borrower often maintains with the servicer. The third source of revenue is the float earned on the monthly mortgage payment. This opportunity arises because there is a delay that is permitted between the time the servicer receives the monthly payment and the time that the payment has to be sent to the investor.

Mortgage Insurance

There are two types of mortgage-related insurance. The first type, which is originated by the lender in order to insure against default by the borrower, is called mortgage insurance or private mortgage insurance. It is usually required by lenders on loans with a Loan to Value (LTV) ratio that is greater than 80%. The amount insured will be some percentage of the loan and may decline as the LTV declines.

What is the LTV ratio? Every borrower will have to make a down payment, which is the difference between the price of the property and the loan amount. The LTV ratio is obtained by dividing the loan amount by the market value of the property. The lower the LTV ratio, the greater is the protection for the lender in the event of default by the borrower.

The second type of mortgage-related insurance is acquired by the borrower, usually through a life insurance company, and is typically called *credit life*. This is not required by the lender. Such policies provide for the continuation of mortgage payments after the death of the insured person, so that survivors can continue to live in the house.

Government Insurance and PMI

As we have seen, lenders insist on insurance if the LTV ratio is more than 80%; however, low- to middle-income borrowers may not be in a position to deposit 20% of the value of the property. At the same time, their credit rating makes them ineligible to obtain insurance from private parties. To facilitate the acquisition of properties by this section of society, there are government agencies that provide loan guarantees in lieu of insurance.

Borrowers who are not eligible for loans from these agencies must obtain private mortgage insurance (PMI).

Secondary Sales

Once the loan is granted, the originator can either hold it as an asset, or sell it to an investor who may seek to either hold it as an investment, or may wish to pool many individual mortgage loans and use them as collateral for the issuance of securities. Of course, the issuance of securities backed by a pool of underlying mortgages may be undertaken by the originators themselves. When a mortgage pool is used as collateral for the issuance of a security, it is said to be securitized.

Two federally sponsored credit agencies and many private agencies buy mortgages, pool them, and issue securities backed by the pool to investors. Such agencies are referred to as *conduits*. The two federally sponsored agencies are:

- Federal National Mortgage Association (Fannie Mae)
- Federal Home Loan Mortgage Corporation (Freddie Mac)

Such agencies buy what they call *conforming mortgages*. A conforming mortgage is one that meets the underwriting criteria established by them, from the standpoint of being eligible to be included in a pool for the purpose of being securitized. A conforming mortgage must satisfy three criteria. These are:

- There must be a maximum payment to income (PTI) ratio. The PTI ratio is the ratio of monthly payments (the loan payment plus any real estate tax payments) to the borrower's monthly income. Obviously, the lower the ratio, the greater is the likelihood of the borrower being able to pay as scheduled.[1]
- A maximum LTV ratio
- A maximum loan amount

Mortgages that are nonconforming because they are for amounts in excess of the purchasing limit set by these agencies are termed as *jumbo* mortgages, whereas those which do not meet the underwriting guidelines such as credit quality or loan-to-value ratio are termed as *subprime* mortgages.

RISKS IN MORTGAGE LENDING

Investors who invest in mortgage loans are exposed to four main risks. These are:

- Default risk
- Liquidity risk
- Interest rate risk
- Prepayment risk

Default Risk

Default or credit risk is the risk that the borrower will default. For government-insured mortgages the risk is minimal because the insuring agencies are government sponsored. For privately insured mortgages, the risk can be gauged by the credit rating of the insurance company. For uninsured mortgages, the risk will obviously depend on the credit quality of the borrower.

Liquidity Risk

Mortgage loans tend to be rather illiquid because they are large and indivisible. Thus, while an active secondary market exists for such loans, bid–ask spreads are large relative to other debt instruments.

Interest Rate Risk

The price of a mortgage loan in the secondary market moves inversely with interest rates, just like any other debt security. Moreover, because the loans are for long terms to maturity, the impact of an interest rate change on the price of the mortgage can be significant.

---

[1]The monthly income should be taken as the take-home salary and not as the cost-to-company (CTC).

Prepayment Risk

Most homeowners pay off all or a part of their mortgage balance prior to the maturity date. Payments made in excess of the scheduled principal repayments are called prepayments. Prepayments occur for one of several reasons. First, borrowers tend to prepay the entire mortgage when they sell their home. The sale of the house may be due to:

- A change of employment that necessitates moving
- The purchase of a more expensive home
- A divorce in which the settlement requires sale of the marital residence

Second, if market interest rates decline below the loan rate, the borrower may prepay the loan due to the ability to refinance at a lower rate. Third, in the case of homeowners who cannot meet their mortgage obligations, the property will be repossessed and sold. The proceeds from the sale will be used to pay off the mortgage in the case of uninsured mortgages. For an insured mortgage the insurance company will pay off the balance. Finally, if the property is destroyed by an act of God, the insurance proceeds will be used to pay off the mortgage. The effect of prepayments, irrespective of the reason, is that the cash flows from the mortgage become unpredictable.

In Example 9.1 we illustrate how to take a decision regarding the refinancing of a mortgage loan.

EXAMPLE 9.1

Cindy Hopkins has taken a mortgage loan for $800,000. It is a 10-year mortgage with a nominal interest rate of 12% per annum. Installments are due every six months, and interest is compounded semiannually.

At the end of the first year – that is, just after she has paid the second installment – the interest on housing loans drops to 10.8% per annum. The refinancing fee is 1.75% of the amount being refinanced. If Cindy's opportunity cost of funds is 9.6% per annum, is refinancing an attractive option?

The quantum of the semiannual interest payment is given by:

$$\frac{800{,}000 \times 0.06}{\left[1 - \dfrac{1}{(1 + 0.06)^{20}}\right]}$$

$$= 69{,}747.65$$

From the discussion of amortized loans in Chapter 2, we know that the amount outstanding after the second installment is:

$$\frac{69{,}747.65}{0.06} \times \left[1 - \frac{1}{(1 + 0.06)^{18}}\right]$$

$$= \$755{,}199.90$$

Thus the cost of refinancing is:

$$755,199.80 \times 0.0175 = \$13,216$$

The installment amount if the loan is refinanced is:

$$\frac{755,199.90 \times 0.054}{\left[1 - \dfrac{1}{(1 + 0.054)^{18}}\right]} = 66,638.91$$

Thus the saving every six months for 18 periods is:

$$69,747.65 - 66,638.91 = \$3,108.74$$

The present value of the saving is:

$$\frac{3,108.74}{0.048} \times \left[1 - \frac{1}{(1 + 0.048)^{18}}\right] = \$36,914.46$$

The net saving is:

$$36,914.46 - 13,216 = \$23,698.46$$

Because the net saving is positive, refinancing is an attractive proposition.

OTHER MORTGAGE STRUCTURES

The level payment mortgage, which entails a constant monthly payment for the life of the mortgage, is the most simple of mortgage structures. In practice there are other mortgage loans with more complex features. We will now discuss some of them.

Adjustable-Rate Mortgage (ARM)

In an adjustable-rate mortgage, the interest rate is not fixed for the life of the loan but is reset periodically. Thus, the monthly payments will rise if the interest rate at resetting is higher than it was previously, and will fall if the interest rate declines. The rate on such mortgages is linked to a benchmark such as LIBOR or the rate on Treasury securities. We will illustrate such a mortgage loan, assuming that rates are reset at the end of every year.

EXAMPLE 9.2

Consider a four-year loan with an initial principal of $800,000. Payments are to be made monthly, with the interest rate being reset every year. Assume that the benchmark is LIBOR and that the mortgage rate is LIBOR + 150 b.p. Assume that the values of LIBOR observed over the next three years are as shown in Table 9.1.

TABLE 9.1   Observed Values for LIBOR

Time in Years	LIBOR
0	4.20
1	4.56
2	4.14
3	4.74

The monthly installment for the first year is:

$$\frac{800{,}000 \times 0.00475}{\left[1 - \dfrac{1}{(1 + 0.00475)^{48}}\right]}$$

$$= 18{,}678.19$$

The outstanding balance at the end of the first year is:

$$\frac{18{,}678.19}{0.00475} \times \left[1 - \frac{1}{(1 + 0.00475)^{36}}\right]$$

$$= \$616{,}722.81$$

The monthly installment for the second year is:

$$\frac{616{,}722.81 \times 0.00505}{\left[1 - \dfrac{1}{(1 + 0.00505)^{36}}\right]}$$

$$= 18{,}778.67$$

The outstanding balance at the end of the second year is:

$$\frac{18{,}778.67}{0.00505} \times \left[1 - \frac{1}{(1 + 0.00505)^{24}}\right]$$

$$= \$423{,}442.35$$

The monthly installment for the third year is:

$$\frac{423{,}442.35 \times 0.0047}{\left[1 - \dfrac{1}{(1 + 0.0047)^{24}}\right]}$$

$$= 18{,}698.61$$

The outstanding balance at the end of the third year is:

$$\frac{18{,}698.61}{0.0047} \times \left[1 - \frac{1}{(1 + 0.0047)^{12}}\right]$$

$$= \$217{,}676.16$$

The monthly installment for the fourth year is:

$$\frac{217{,}676.16 \times 0.0052}{\left[1 - \dfrac{1}{(1 + 0.0052)^{12}}\right]}$$

$$= 18{,}758.63$$

The outstanding balance at the end of the fourth year is obviously zero.

Option to Change the Maturity

In the case of certain adjustable-rate mortgages, the borrower may be given the option to keep the monthly installment at the initial level, and have the maturity date altered, every time the rate is reset. Let us see the implications of this for the mortgage discussed in the preceding example.

The outstanding balance after one year is $616,722.81. If we keep the equated monthly payment at $18,678.19, the life of the loan if the rate is reset at 9% is given by:

$$\frac{616{,}722.81 \times 0.0075}{18{,}678.19} = \left[1 - \frac{1}{(1 + 0.0075)^{T}}\right]$$

$$\Rightarrow T = 38.08 \text{ months}$$

Rate Caps

In the case of ARMs, there may be a cap on how much the interest rate may increase or decrease per period. The cap may be a *periodic* cap or a *lifetime* cap. Consider a four-year mortgage with a principal of $800,000. Assume that payments are made monthly and that the interest rate every period is the prevailing LIBOR at the start of the period plus 150 b.p. The values of LIBOR observed over the next three years are as shown in Table 9.2.

Assume that there is a periodic cap of 1.5% and a lifetime cap of 9%. If so, the applicable mortgage rates for each of the periods would be as shown in Table 9.3.

TABLE 9.2　Observed Values for LIBOR

Time in Years	LIBOR	Mortgage Rate
0	4.20	5.70
1	6.00	7.50
2	7.00	8.50
3	8.00	9.50

TABLE 9.3　Mortgage Rates in the Presence of a Cap

Period	Mortgage Rate
0	5.70
1	7.20
2	8.50
3	9.00

Let us analyze the entries in Table 9.3. The starting mortgage rate is 5.70%, which is less than the lifetime cap of 9%. The rate at the end of the first year should be 7.50% in the absence of a periodic cap. Because there is a periodic cap of 1.5%, however, the rate cannot increase by more than 1.5%. Consequently, the rate for the second year is 7.20%, which is the rate for the first year plus 1.5%. The uncapped rate for the third year is 8.50%, which is the same as the capped rate, because 8.50% is only 1.3% more than the rate for the previous year. Finally, the rate for the fourth year in the absence of a cap should be 9.50%. This does not violate the requirement of a periodic cap, because the change is only 1% as compared to the previous year. Because there is a lifetime cap of 9%, however, the rate cannot exceed 9% in any period. Consequently, the rate for the fourth year will be 9%.

Carryovers

The presence of a rate cap may preclude the lender from increasing the coupon rate to the desired level. If, however, there is a carryover provision, the deficit can be carried over to future periods. For instance, consider a mortgage loan with a coupon of LIBOR + 1%, and a periodic cap of 1.25%. If the LIBOR at the outset is 3%, the coupon for the first year is 4%. Assume that the LIBOR at the end of the first year is 4.6%. Thus, the lenders would like to set the coupon at 5.6; however, they are constrained to set it at 5.25%. Thus, there is a deficit of 35 basis points. Assume that at the end of the second year the LIBOR is 4.80%. In the absence of a carryover facility, the coupon for the third year would have been set equal to 5.80%, which is less than the prescribed limit of 6.50%. Because of the carryover provision the coupon would be set at 6.15%, thereby adjusting the deficit that was carried over.

Payment Caps

If the adjustable-rate mortgage were to have a payment cap, there would be a limit on how much the monthly payments can increase or decrease at the end of every period. Let us take the case of the mortgage that we studied in the above example. The mortgage rate for each year is as shown in Table 9.4.

Assume that there is a payment cap of 2%. In the absence of the cap, the monthly payments in every year and the outstanding balance at the end of each year will be as given in Table 9.5.

If there is a payment cap of 2%, however, the monthly payment in the second year cannot exceed:

$$18{,}678.19 \times 1.02 = 19{,}051.75$$

The interest component in the thirteenth month will be:

$$616{,}722.81 \times \frac{0.075}{12}$$

$$= 616{,}722.81 \times 0.00625 = \$3{,}854.52$$

The principal repayment will therefore be only:

$$19{,}051.75 - 3{,}854.52 = \$15{,}197.23$$

as compared to

$$19{,}183.91 - 3{,}854.52 = \$15{,}329.39$$

in the absence of the cap. Thus, the cap leads to a slower repayment of principal. The outstanding balance at the end of the 24th month is given by:

$$616{,}722.81 = \frac{19{,}051.75}{0.00625} \times \left[1 - \frac{1}{(1.00625)^{12}}\right] + \frac{X}{(1.00625)^{12}}$$

$$\Rightarrow X = 427{,}954.71$$

TABLE 9.4 Observed Values for LIBOR

Period	Mortgage Rate	Mortgage Rate
0	4.20	5.70
1	6.00	7.50
2	7.00	8.50
3	8.00	9.50

TABLE 9.5 Monthly Payments & Outstanding Balances

Time in Years	Monthly Payments	Outstanding Balance
1	18,678.19	616,722.81
2	19,183.91	426,313.07
3	19,378.35	222,178.34
4	19,481.38	0

as compared to \$426,313.07 in the absence of the cap. The monthly payment in year three will therefore be:

$$\frac{427{,}954.71 \times \dfrac{0.085}{12}}{\left[1 - \dfrac{1}{\left(1 + \dfrac{0.085}{12}\right)^{24}}\right]} = \$19{,}452.97$$

The cap for the period is:

$$19{,}051.75 \times 1.02 = \$19{,}432.79$$

Thus, the monthly payment in year three will be \$19,432.79.
The outstanding balance at the end of the 36th month is given by:

$$427{,}954.71 = \frac{19{,}432.79}{\dfrac{0.085}{12}} \times \left[1 - \frac{1}{\left(1 + \dfrac{0.085}{12}\right)^{12}}\right] + \frac{X}{\left(1 + \dfrac{0.085}{12}\right)^{12}}$$

$$\Rightarrow X = \$223{,}285.74$$

The monthly payment for year four will therefore be:

$$\frac{223{,}285.74 \times \dfrac{0.095}{12}}{\left[1 - \dfrac{1}{\left(1 + \dfrac{0.095}{12}\right)^{12}}\right]} = \$19{,}578.48$$

Negative Amortization

There are times when a situation could arise wherein the capped monthly payment is less than the monthly interest due for a subsequent month. If so, instead of a reduction in the outstanding balance, the deficit in the interest payment will be added to the outstanding balance, which will cause the principal to increase in value. This is referred to as *negative amortization*. We will illustrate it with the help of an example.

EXAMPLE 9.3

Consider a 30-year adjustable-rate mortgage with an initial loan amount of $800,000. The initial mortgage rate is 7.5%, and payments are to be made on a monthly basis. There is a payment cap of 5%.

The monthly installment for the first year is:

$$\frac{800{,}000 \times 0.00625}{\left[1 - \dfrac{1}{(1 + 0.00625)^{360}}\right]}$$

$$= 5{,}593.72$$

The outstanding balance at the end of the first year is:

$$\frac{5{,}593.72}{0.00625} \times \left[1 - \frac{1}{(1 + 0.00625)^{348}}\right]$$

$$= \$792{,}625.88$$

Assume that the mortgage rate at the end of the year is 9.75%. The monthly payments in the second year, in the absence of a cap would be:

$$\frac{792{,}625.88 \times 0.008125}{\left[1 - \dfrac{1}{(1 + 0.008125)^{348}}\right]}$$

$$= 6{,}849.99$$

Due to the cap, however, the payment has to be:

$$5{,}593.72 \times 1.05 = 5{,}873.41$$

The interest due for the 13th month is:

$$792{,}625.88 \times 0.008125 = 6{,}440.09$$

Thus, there is a deficit of:

$$6{,}440.09 - 5{,}873.41 = 566.68$$

This will get added on to the principal. Consequently, the principal at the end of the 13th month will be:

$$792{,}625.88 + 566.68 = \$793{,}192.56$$

(continued)

(*continued*)

The amortization schedule for the first two years is given in Table 9.6. The evidence of negative amortization is obvious.

TABLE 9.6   Illustration of Negative Amortization

Month	Monthly Installment	Interest Component	Principal Component	Outstanding Balance
0				800000.00
1	5593.72	5000.00	593.72	799406.28
2	5593.72	4996.29	597.43	798808.85
3	5593.72	4992.56	601.16	798207.68
4	5593.72	4988.80	604.92	797602.76
5	5593.72	4985.02	608.70	796994.06
6	5593.72	4981.21	612.51	796381.55
7	5593.72	4977.38	616.34	795765.22
8	5593.72	4973.53	620.19	795145.03
9	5593.72	4969.66	624.06	794520.97
10	5593.72	4965.76	627.96	793893.00
11	5593.72	4961.83	631.89	793261.11
12	5593.72	4957.88	635.84	792625.28
13	5873.41	6440.08	−566.67	793191.95
14	5873.41	6444.68	−571.27	793763.22
15	5873.41	6449.33	−575.92	794339.14
16	5873.41	6454.01	−580.60	794919.73
17	5873.41	6458.72	−585.31	795505.05
18	5873.41	6463.48	−590.07	796095.11
19	5873.41	6468.27	−594.86	796689.98
20	5873.41	6473.11	−599.70	797289.67
21	5873.41	6477.98	−604.57	797894.24
22	5873.41	6482.89	−609.48	798503.72
23	5873.41	6487.84	−614.43	799118.15
24	5873.41	6492.84	−619.13	799737.58

Graduated Payment Mortgage

Young home buyers may not have the disposable income required to qualify for a conventional fixed-rate mortgage; however, many people in this age bracket have the potential to earn substantially more in the coming years. To encourage such parties to take loans, the graduated payment mortgage was designed. Such a mortgage starts with a level of payment that steadily increases every year up to a point, and then remains steady thereafter. We will illustrate it with the help of an example.

EXAMPLE 9.4

Mathew Thomas is being offered a mortgage loan by First National Housing Bank with the following terms. The monthly payment will increase by 5% every year for five years and remain constant thereafter. The mortgage rate is 9.75% per annum for a loan amount of $800,000. What will the payment schedule look like?

Let us denote the monthly payment for the first year by A. Then:

$$800,000 = \frac{A}{0.008125}\left[1 - \frac{1}{(1.008125)^{12}}\right] + \frac{\frac{A \times 1.05}{0.008125}\left[1 - \frac{1}{(1.008125)^{12}}\right]}{(1.008125)^{12}}$$

$$+ \frac{\frac{A \times (1.05)^2}{0.008125}\left[1 - \frac{1}{(1.008125)^{12}}\right]}{(1.008125)^{24}} + \frac{\frac{A \times (1.05)^3}{0.008125}\left[1 - \frac{1}{(1.008125)^{12}}\right]}{(1.008125)^{36}}$$

$$+ \frac{\frac{A \times (1.05)^4}{0.008125}\left[1 - \frac{1}{(1.008125)^{12}}\right]}{(1.008125)^{48}} + \frac{\frac{A \times (1.05)^5}{0.008125}\left[1 - \frac{1}{(1.008125)^{300}}\right]}{(1.008125)^{60}}$$

$$= 11.3896A + 10.8524A + 10.3405A + 9.8527A + 9.3880A + 88.1330A$$

$$= 139.9562A$$

$$\Rightarrow A = 5,716.07$$

The monthly payment values for each year are given in Table 9.7.

TABLE 9.7 Monthly Payments for a GPM

Year	Monthly Payment
1	5,716.07
2	6,001.87
3	6,301.97
4	6.617.07
5	6,947.92
6–30	7,295.31

The monthly payments for the first two years are given in Table 9.8. In this case too, there is negative amortization.

(continued)

(continued)

TABLE 9.8   Amortization Schedule for a GPM

Month	Monthly Installment	Interest Component	Principal Component	Outstanding Balance
0				800000
1	5716.07	6500.00	−783.93	800783.93
2	5716.07	6506.37	−790.30	801574.23
3	5716.07	6512.79	−796.72	802370.95
4	5716.07	6519.26	−803.19	803174.14
5	5716.07	6525.79	−809.72	803983.86
6	5716.07	6532.37	−816.30	804800.16
7	5716.07	6539.00	−822.93	805623.09
8	5716.07	6545.69	−829.62	806452.71
9	5716.07	6552.43	−836.36	807289.07
10	5716.07	6559.22	−843.15	808132.22
11	5716.07	6566.07	−850.00	808982.23
12	5716.07	6572.98	−856.91	809839.14
13	6001.87	6579.94	−578.07	810417.21
14	6001.87	6584.64	−582.77	810999.98
15	6001.87	6589.37	−587.50	811587.49
16	6001.87	6594.15	−592.28	812179.76
17	6001.87	6598.96	−597.09	812776.86
18	6001.87	6603.81	−601.94	813378.80
19	6001.87	6608.70	−606.83	813985.63
20	6001.87	6613.63	−611.76	814597.39
21	6001.87	6618.60	−616.73	815214.13
22	6001.87	6623.61	−621.74	815835.87
23	6001.87	6628.67	−626.80	816462.67
24	6001.87	6633.76	−631.89	817094.56

Growing Equity Mortgages (GEM)

In a growing equity mortgage, the monthly installment increases by a prescribed percentage every year; however, the installment for the first year is the same as that for a plain-vanilla mortgage. Thus, there is no negative amortization in the beginning. In contrast, we may observe negative amortization in the case of a graduated payment mortgage, which too is characterized by increasing periodic payments.

In a GEM the installment increases by a certain percentage; however, the excess payment goes toward prepayment of principal. Consequently, the principal gets paid off faster than in the case of a plain-vanilla mortgage. Thus, while the stated maturity – the time taken for the outstanding balance to go to zero – is equal to the actual maturity observed in practice for plain-vanilla mortgages and graduated payment mortgages, in the case of a growing equity mortgage the principal is fully paid off by an earlier date.

WAC and WAM

All the mortgages that constitute the pool being securitized will not have the same mortgage rate or time to maturity. Thus, it is a common practice in the market for securitized assets to take cognizance of the weighted average coupon rate and the weighted average time to maturity. The weighted average coupon (WAC) of a mortgage pool is determined by weighting the mortgage rate of each loan in the pool by the principal amount outstanding. That is, the weight for each mortgage rate is the outstanding amount of that mortgage divided by the cumulative outstanding amount of all the mortgages in the pool. Similarly, the weighted average maturity (WAM) is found by weighting the remaining number of months to maturity of each of the loans in the pool by the principal amount outstanding. We will illustrate the calculations for a hypothetical pool.

Calculation of WAC and WAM

Assume that a pool consists of 10 mortgage loans. The mortgage rate for each loan and its remaining term to maturity are given in Table 9.9.

The weight to be attached to each of the mortgage rates and terms to maturity, in order to compute the WAC and the WAM, are given in Table 9.10, as are the calculated values of the two variables.

Thus, the WAC for the pool is 6.9265% and the WAM is 301.07 months.

Pass-Through Securities

Mortgage loans are extremely illiquid. Besides, the lender faces significant exposure to credit risk as well as prepayment risk. Thus, making a secondary market for whole

TABLE 9.9 Mortgage Loans, Their Rates, and Times to Maturity

S. No.	Principal Outstanding	Mortgage Rate(r_s)	Term to Maturity (T_s)
1	975,000	6.25%	336
2	925,000	6.50%	324
3	900,000	7.25%	300
4	875,000	7.50%	325
5	825,000	7.00%	350
6	800,000	6.75%	280
7	850,000	6.60%	275
8	910.000	6.95%	250
9	810,000	7.15%	265
10	880,000	7.40%	300
Total	8,750,000		

TABLE 9.10   Calculation of WAC and WAM

S. No.	Weight (w_s)	$r_s \times w_s$	$T_s \times w_s$
1	0.1114	0.6964	37.44
2	0.1057	0.6871	34.25
3	0.1029	0.7457	30.86
4	0.1000	0.7500	32.50
5	0.0943	0.6600	33.00
6	0.0914	0.6171	25.60
7	0.0971	0.6411	26.71
8	0.1040	0.7228	26.00
9	0.0926	0.6619	24.53
10	0.1006	0.7442	30.17
Total	1.0000	6.9265%	301.07

loans is an extremely difficult proposition. It is possible, however, to issue liquid debt securities backed by an underlying pool of mortgage loans. That is, the cash flows stemming from the underlying loans are passed through to the holders of these debt securities, and hence the name. Each holder of a pass-through security is entitled to a pro-rata undivided share of each cash flow that emanates from the underlying pool, as and when the homeowners make monthly payments. Each monthly payment will consist of an interest component, a principal component, and potentially an additional amount on account of prepayment. Any amount that constitutes a prepayment is termed as an *unscheduled principal*, as opposed to the scheduled or expected principal repayment. The mechanics of a pass-through may be illustrated with the help of an example.

EXAMPLE 9.5

Four home loans with a principal of $100,000 each and 30 years to maturity have been pooled. The mortgage rate for two loans is 7.50% per annum, while the rate for the remaining two is 9.00% per annum. One hundred securities backed by these loans have been created. These securities have been distributed as follows: 25 to Alex, 50 to Brown, 15 to Mark, and 10 to David. These securities are identical in all respects and the holder of a security is entitled to 1% of any cash flow that arises from the underlying loans.

The meaning of the term *undivided* may be understood as follows. Alex owns 25% of the securities, which are equivalent to 25% of the underlying collateral, which is tantamount to one loan of $100,000. By virtue of the fact that he has 25% of the securities, however, it cannot be construed that Alex owns one underlying loan in its entirety. All that we can say is that Alex is entitled to 25% of each cash flow that emanates from the underlying pool.

The first month's payment for a loan with a rate of 7.50% is $699.21. This consists of $625 of interest and $74.21 of scheduled principal. For the loan with a rate of 9.00%, the first month's payment will be $804.62, which is composed of $750 of interest and $54.62 of principal.

Thus, the total cash flow from the underlying pool in the first month will be:

$$2 \times 699.21 + 2 \times 804.62 = \$3,007.66$$

Thus, each of the 100 mortgage-backed securities which have been issued is entitled to $30.08 in the first month. Because Alex owns 25 securities, he will receive

$$25 \times 30.08 = \$752.00$$

By the same logic, Brown will receive $1,504.00, Mark will receive $451.20, and David will receive $300.80.

Now assume that each of the four homeowners makes an additional principal payment of $100 at end of the first month. This was not scheduled and consequently is a prepayment. The total cash flow from the underlying loans on account of this prepayment is $400. Thus, each of the mortgage-backed securities will receive $4 more. Because Alex has 25 securities, he will receive $100 extra, which means that his total inflow will be $852.00. By the same logic, Brown will receive $1,704.00, Mark will receive $511.20, and David will receive $340.80.

Cash Flows for a Pass-Through

Assume that the underlying pool consists of four loans of $100,000 each. Each has a rate of 9% and 360 months to maturity. Thus, the WAC will remain constant at 9% and the WAM at any point of time will be equal to the time remaining in the life of the loans. Before we can project the cash flows, we need to consider servicing and guaranteeing fees, and consider the important issue of prepayments.

The cash flow that is passed through to investors in a given period will not in practice be equal to the payment received from the underlying pool. The monthly cash flow for a pass-through is less than the monthly cash flow from the underlying loans by an amount equal to the servicing and guaranteeing fees. Thus, the coupon rate on the pass-through will be less than the mortgage rate of the underlying pool by an amount equal to the servicing and guaranteeing fees. We will assume a servicing fee of 0.5% per annum and a guaranteeing fee of 0.5% per annum. Thus, in our case, the coupon rate of the pass-through will be 8%.

Prepayment Conventions

It is impossible to predict with absolute certainty the monthly cash flow stream that a pass-through holder receives, because the timing and amount of principal that is prepaid is subject to considerable uncertainty. Because a pass-through is a debt security, we need to project the cash flows from it in order to determine its value. Such a projection entails an assumption about the prepayment behavior of the mortgage owners over the life of the pool. The prepayment rate that is assumed is called the *prepayment speed.*

Single Month Mortality Rate

The Single Month Mortality Rate for a given month 't,' SMM_t is defined as:

$$SMM_t = \frac{SP_t - L_t}{SP_t}$$

where SP_t is the scheduled principal outstanding at the end of month 't,' and L_t is the actual principal outstanding at the end of month 't.'

Thus, the actual principal at the end of month 't' is given by:

$$L_t = SP_t[1 - SMM_t]$$

Consider a mortgage with 'N' months to maturity, and a monthly interest rate of 'r.' The original loan balance is given by:

$$L_0 = \frac{A_1}{r} \times \left[1 - \frac{1}{(1+r)^N}\right]$$

where A_1 is the scheduled monthly installment for month 1. The scheduled principal at the end of the first month is given by:

$$SP_1 = L_0 - [A_1 - r \times L_0]$$

$$= L_0 \times (1 + r) - A_1$$

$$= \frac{A_1}{r}\left[1 - \frac{1}{(1+r)^{(N-1)}}\right]$$

The actual balance at time '1' is given by:

$$L_1 = SP_1[1 - SMM_1]$$

$$L_1 = \frac{A_2}{r} \times \left[1 - \frac{1}{(1+r)^{(N-1)}}\right]$$

where A_2 is the scheduled monthly installment for month '2.'

$$\Rightarrow SP_1[1 - SMM_1] = \frac{A_2}{r} \times \left[1 - \frac{1}{(1+r)^{(N-1)}}\right]$$

$$\Rightarrow \frac{A_1}{r}\left[1 - \frac{1}{(1+r)^{(N-1)}}\right][1 - SMM_1] = \frac{A_2}{r} \times \left[1 - \frac{1}{(1+r)^{(N-1)}}\right]$$

$$\Rightarrow A_2 = A_1 \times [1 - SMM_1]$$

Similarly, it can be shown that:

$$A_3 = A_2 \times [1 - \text{SMM}_2]$$
$$= A_1 \times [1 - \text{SMM}_1] \times [1 - \text{SMM}_2]$$

In general, the scheduled monthly installment in month 't' is given by:

$$A_t = A_1 \prod_{i=1}^{t-1} [1 - \text{SMM}_i]$$

If $\text{SMM}_i = \text{SMM} \ \forall \ i$, then:

$$A_t = A_1 \times [1 - \text{SMM}]^{t-1}$$

Let us denote the monthly payment on the original principal, in the absence of prepayments by A. Then we can state:

$$A_t = A \prod_{i=1}^{t-1} [1 - \text{SMM}_i]$$
$$= A \times [1 - \text{SMM}]^{t-1} \text{ if } \text{SMM}_i = \text{SMM} \forall i$$

In the absence of prepayments, the interest and principal components of the tth payment and the outstanding principal at the end of "t" periods are given by:

$$I_t^* = A \times \left[1 - \frac{1}{(1 + r)^{N-t+1}}\right]$$
$$P_t^* = \frac{A}{(1 + r)^{N-t+1}}$$
$$SP_t^* = \frac{A}{r}\left[1 - \frac{1}{(1 + r)^{N-t}}\right]$$

In the presence of prepayments, the actual principal outstanding at the end of '$t - 1$' is given by:

$$L_{t-1} = \frac{A_t}{r} \times \left[1 - \frac{1}{(1 + r)^{N-t+1}}\right]$$

Thus, in the presence of prepayments, the interest and principal components of the tth payment are given by:

$$I_t = A_t \times \left[1 - \frac{1}{(1 + r)^{N-t+1}}\right]$$

and

$$P_t = \frac{A_t}{(1 + r)^{N-t+1}}$$

The scheduled principal at the end of the tth period is given by:

$$SP_t = \frac{A_t}{r}\left[1 - \frac{1}{(1 + r)^{N-t}}\right]$$

We know that

$$A_t = A \prod_{i=1}^{t-1}[1 - \text{SMM}_i]$$

Thus:

$$I_t = I_t^* \prod_{i=1}^{t-1}[1 - \text{SMM}_i]$$

$$P_t = P_t^* \prod_{i=1}^{t-1}[1 - \text{SMM}_i]$$

and

$$\text{SP}_t = SP_t^* \prod_{i=1}^{t-1}[1 - \text{SMM}_i]$$

The actual principal at the end of 't' periods is given by

$$\text{SP}_t \times [1 - \text{SMM}_t]$$

Therefore:

$$L_t = SP_t^* \prod_{i=1}^{t}[1 - \text{SMM}_i]$$

We will now give an illustration of cash flow calculations for a pass-through security with the help of a detailed example.

EXAMPLE 9.6

Consider a pool of four mortgage loans. Each loan has an outstanding principal of $100,000 and 24 months to maturity. The mortgage rate is 9% for each loan. The servicing fee is 0.5% of the outstanding balance, and the guarantor's fee is also 0.5% of the outstanding balance. The SMM is 2.5% for all the months.

The cash flows in the absence of prepayments are given in Table 9.11.

TABLE 9.11 Amortization Schedule in the Absence of Prepayments

Month	Mthly. Pmt.	Serv. Fee	Grot. Fee	Net Int.	Prin. Pmt.	Out. Prin.	Cash Flow
0						400.000	
1	18273.90	166.67	166.67	2666.67	15273.90	384726.10	17940.56
2	18273.90	160.30	160.30	2564.84	15388.45	369337.65	17953.29
3	18273.90	153.89	153.89	2462.25	15503.86	353833.79	17966.12
4	18273.90	147.43	147.43	2358.89	15620.14	338213.64	17979.04
5	18273.90	140.92	140.92	2254.76	15737.29	322476.35	17992.05
6	18273.90	134.37	134.37	2149.84	15855.32	306621.03	18005.17
7	18273.90	127.76	127.76	2044.14	15974.24	290646.79	18018.38
8	18273.90	121.10	121.10	1937.65	16094.05	274552.74	18031.69
9	18273.90	114.40	114.40	1830.35	16214.75	258337.99	18045.10
10	18273.90	107.64	107.64	1722.25	16336.36	242001.63	18058.62
11	18273.90	100.83	100.83	1613.34	16458.88	225542.74	18072.23
12	18273.90	93.98	93.98	1503.62	16582.33	208960.42	18085.94
13	18273.90	87.07	87.07	1393.07	16706.69	192253.72	18099.76
14	18273.90	80.11	80.11	1281.69	16831.99	175421.73	18113.69
15	18273.90	73.09	73.09	1169.48	16958.23	158463.49	18127.71
16	18273.90	66.03	66.03	1056.42	17085.42	141378.07	18141.84
IT	18273.90	58.91	58.91	942.52	17213.56	124164.51	18156.08
18	18273.90	51.74	51.74	827.76	17342.66	106821.85	18170.43
19	18273.90	44.51	44.51	712.15	17472.73	89349.12	18184.88
20	18273.90	37.23	37.23	595.66	17603.78	71745.34	18199.44
21	18273.90	29.89	29.89	478.30	17735.81	54009.53	18214.11
22	18273.90	22.50	22.50	360.06	17868.83	36140.70	18228.89
23	18273.90	15.06	15.06	240.94	18002.84	18137.86	18243.78
24	18273.90	7.56	7.56	120.92	18137.86	0.00	18258.78

Explanation: Mthly. Pmt. ≡ Monthly Payment; Serv. Fee ≡ Servicing Fee; Grnt. Fee ≡ Guaranteeing Fee; Net Int. ≡ Net Interest; Prin. Pmt. ≡ Principal Payment; Out. Prin. ≡ Outstanding Principal

ANALYSIS

Consider the entries for the first month in Table 9.11. The principal outstanding at the beginning of the month is $400,000. The monthly payment due is given by

$$400,000 = \frac{A}{0.0075}\left[1 - \frac{1}{(1.0075)^{24}}\right]$$

$$\Rightarrow A = \$18,273.90$$

(continued)

(*continued*)

The servicing fee is

$$\frac{0.005}{12} \times 400{,}000 = \$166.67$$

The guaranteeing fee for every month is the same as the servicing fee. The net interest to be passed through for the first month is

$$\frac{0.08}{12} \times 400{,}000 = \$2{,}666.67$$

The principal payment for the month is

$$18{,}273.90 - 166.67 - 166.67 - 2{,}666.67 = \$15{,}273.90$$

The total cash flow for the holders of the pass-through securities is

$$2{,}666.67 + 15{,}273.90 = \$17{,}940.57$$

Now let us consider the repayment schedule assuming that the SMM is 2.5% for all months.

ANALYSIS

Let us analyze the entries in Table 9.12. The payment for the first month is the same as in the above case, that is, $18,273.90. The servicing and guaranteeing fees are also the same as those obtained above, for they are based on the same outstanding principal, $400,000. The net interest to be passed through is $2,666.67, which is obviously the same as the value obtained in the absence of prepayments. The scheduled outstanding balance at the end of the first month is

$$400{,}000 - 15{,}273.90 = \$384{,}726.10$$

We have assumed a constant SMM of 2.50%. Thus the prepayment at the end of the first month is $0.025 \times 384{,}726.10 = \$9{,}618.15$. Therefore the actual outstanding principal at the end of the first month is

$$384{,}726.10 - 9{,}618.15 = \$375{,}107.95$$

TABLE 9.12 Amortization Schedule in the Presence of Prepayments

Mt.	Mly. Pmt.	Ser. Fee	Grn. Fee	Net Int.	Sch. Prin. Pmt.	Sch. Out. Prin.	Pre Pmt.	Act. Out. Prin.	CF
0						400.000		400,000	
1	18273.90	166.67	166.67	2666.67	15273.90	384726.10	9618.15	375107.95	27558.72
2	17817.05	156.29	156.29	2500.72	15003.74	360104.21	9002.61	351101.60	26507.06
3	17371.62	146.29	146.29	2340.68	14738.36	336363.24	8409.08	327954.16	25488.12
4	16937.33	136.65	136.65	2186.36	14477.68	313176.48	7836.91	305639.57	24500.95
5	16513.90	127.35	127.35	2037.60	14221.60	291417.97	7285.45	284132.52	23544.65
6	16101.05	118.39	118.39	1894.22	13970.06	270162.46	6754.06	263408.40	22618.34
7	15698.53	109.75	109.75	1756.06	13722.96	249685.44	6242.14	243443.30	21721.15
8	15306.06	101.43	101.43	1622.96	13480.24	229963.06	5749.08	224213.99	20852.27
9	14923.41	93.42	93.42	1494.76	13241.81	210972.18	5274.30	205697.88	20010.87
10	14550.33	85.71	85.71	1371.32	13007.59	192690.29	4817.26	187873.03	19196.17
11	14186.57	78.28	78.28	1252.49	12777.52	175095.51	4377.39	170718.12	18407.39
12	13831.90	71.13	71.13	1138.12	12551.52	158166.60	3954.17	154212.44	17643.80
13	13486.11	64.26	64.26	1028.08	12329.51	141882.93	3547.07	138335.85	16904.67
14	13148.95	57.64	57.64	922.24	12111.43	126224.42	3155.61	123068.81	16189.28
15	12820.23	51.28	51.28	820.46	11897.21	111171.60	2779.29	108392.31	15496.96
16	12499.72	45.16	45.16	722.62	11686.78	96705.53	2417.64	94287.89	14827.03
17	12187.23	39.29	39.29	628.59	11480.07	82807.82	2070.20	80737.62	14178.85
18	11882.55	33.64	33.64	538.25	11277.02	69460.60	1736.52	67724.09	13551.78
19	11585.49	28.22	28.22	451.49	11077.56	56646.53	1416.16	55230.37	12945.21
20	11295.85	23.01	23.01	368.20	10881.62	44348.75	1108.72	43240.03	12358.54
21	11013.45	18.02	18.02	288.27	10689.15	32550.88	813.77	31737.11	11791.19
22	10738.12	13.22	13.22	211.58	10500.09	21237.02	530.93	20706.09	11242.59
23	10469.66	8.63	8.63	138.04	10314.37	10391.73	259.79	10131.93	10712.20
24	10207.92	4.22	4.22	67.55	10131.93	0.00	0.00	0.00	10199.48

Explanation: Mly. Pmt. $\equiv$ Monthly Payment; Ser. Fee $\equiv$ Servicing Fee; Grn. Fee $\equiv$ Guaranteeing Fee; Net Int. $\equiv$ Net Interest; Sch. Prin. Pmt. $\equiv$ Scheduled Principal Payment; Sch. Out. Prin. $\equiv$ Scheduled Outstanding Principal; Pre Pmt. $\equiv$ Prepayment; Act. Out. Prin. $\equiv$ Actual Outstanding Principal; CF $\equiv$ Cash Flow

The total cash flow for the month for the pass-through holders is the sum of the net interest plus the scheduled principal payment plus the prepayment, which in this case is

$$2,666.67 + 15,273.90 + 9,618.15 = \$27,558.72$$

Now let us consider the entries for the second month. The total payment for the month is given by

$$375,107.95 = \frac{A}{0.0075} \left[1 - \frac{1}{(1.0075)^{23}} \right]$$

$$\Rightarrow A = \$17,817.05$$

(continued)

> (*continued*)
>
> The servicing and guaranteeing fees for the second month are
>
> $$\frac{0.005}{12} \times 375{,}107.95 = \$156.29$$
>
> The net interest for the second month is
>
> $$\frac{0.08}{12} \times 375{,}107.95 = \$2{,}500.72$$
>
> The scheduled principal payment for the month is
>
> $$17{,}817.05 - 156.29 - 156.29 - 2{,}500.72 = \$15{,}003.74$$
>
> The scheduled outstanding principal at the end of the month is
>
> $$375{,}107.95 - 15{,}003.74 = \$360{,}104.21$$
>
> The prepayment at the end of the month is $0.025 \times 360{,}104.21 = \$9{,}002.61$. The actual outstanding principal at the end of the second month is therefore
>
> $$360{,}104.21 - 9{,}002.61 = \$351{,}101.60$$
>
> The cash flow for the month that is directed toward the pass-through holders is
>
> $$2{,}500.72 + 15{,}003.74 + 9{,}002.61 = \$26{,}507.06$$
>
> The analysis can be extended along similar lines to the remaining months.

Average Life

Unlike a bond, which repays its principal in the form of a bullet payment at maturity, a pass-through security returns a part of its principal every month. Consequently, it is a common practice to compute the average life of a pass-through security. Let PCF_t be the total principal received at time 't'. PCF_t is obviously the sum of the scheduled principal received at time 't' and the prepayment received at the same point in time. The average life may be defined as

$$\frac{\sum_{t=1}^{T} t \times PCF_t}{L_0}$$

In the case of the pass-through discussed earlier, the average life in the absence of prepayments is 12.8578 months or 1.0715 years. When we assume an SMM of 2.50% per month, however, the average life declines to 10.6677 months, which is equivalent to 0.8890 years. Clearly, the higher the prepayment speed that is assumed, the shorter will be the average life of the security.

Cash Flow Yield

The cash flow yield for a pass-through is the IRR computed using the projected cash flow stream. The result is a monthly rate, which is usually converted to a *bond equivalent* yield to facilitate comparisons with conventional debt securities. If we denote the IRR as i_m, where i_m denotes a monthly rate, then the bond equivalent yield may be expressed as:

$$2[(1 + i_m)^6 - 1]$$

EXAMPLE 9.7

Assume that the pool of four mortgages with a principal of $100,000 each and a coupon of 9% is securitized, and 400 securities are issued. The par value of each security is $1,000 and each security will be eligible for

$$\frac{1}{400}th$$

of each cash flow emanating from the underlying pool. The monthly cash flows for each security assuming an SMM of 2.50% are given in Table 9.13.

TABLE 9.13   Cash Flows for a Security with a Par Value of $1.000

Month	Total Cash Flow from the Underlying Mortgage Pool	Cash Flow for the Pass-Through Security
1	27,558.72	68.90
2	26,507.06	66.27
3	25,488.12	63.72
4	24,500.95	61.25
5	23,544.65	58.86
6	22,618.34	56.55
7	21,721.15	54.30
8	20.852.27	52.13
9	20.010.87	50.03
10	19.196.17	47.99
11	18,407.39	46.02
12	17.643.80	44.11
13	16,904.67	42.26
11	16,189.28	40.47
15	15,496.96	38.74
16	14,827.03	37.07
17	14,178.85	35.45
18	13,551.78	33.88
19	12,945.21	32.36
20	12,358.54	30.90
21	11,791.19	29.48
22	12,242.59	28.11
23	10,712.20	26.78
24	10,199.48	25.50

(continued)

(continued)

The cash flow yield and the corresponding bond equivalent yield for this security are given below for three different price scenarios, and three assumed prepayment speeds in each case.

As can be seen from Table 9.14, the BEY for a pass-through is inversely related to the price of the security, as is the case for a conventional debt security. If the security were to be priced at par, the cash flow yield is equal to the coupon rate, irrespective of the rate that is assumed for prepayment.

TABLE 9.14 Bond Equivalent Yields

Price	SMM	Cash Flow Yield	BEY
1,000	2.5%	0.6667%	8.1349%
1,000	4.0%	0.6667%	8.1349%
1,000	1.0%	0.6667%	8.1349%
975	2.5%	0.9184%	11.2770%
975	4.0%	0.9455%	11.6176%
975	1.0%	0.8927%	10.9543%
1,025	2.5%	0.4243%	5.1459%
1,025	4.0%	0.3987%	4.8323%
1,025	1.0%	0.4487%	5.4452%

A Note

The average life is based on the total principal received every period, that is, the sum of the scheduled principal payment and the prepayment. Thus, it is different from bond duration, and there is no discounting of the principal payments. The cash flow yield is based on the periodic cash flow. The periodic cash flow consists of the net interest payment, that is, the gross interest payment less the servicing and guaranteeing fees, plus the scheduled principal payment, and the prepayment for the month.

Conditional Prepayment Rate

To project the cash flows from a pass-through we need to make an assumption about the prepayment behavior. The prepayment rate that is assumed for a pool of mortgages is called the *conditional prepayment rate* or CPR. The term *conditional* connotes that the rate is conditional on the remaining balance in the pool.

The CPR corresponding to the assumed prepayment speed has to be converted to the equivalent SMM. The formula for conversion is the following:

$$[1 - \text{SMM}]^{12} = 1 - \text{CPR}$$

$$\Rightarrow \text{SMM} = 1 - [1 - \text{CPR}]^{\frac{1}{12}}$$

The rationale for this formula is the following. Prepaying 12 times in a year at the rate of SMM is equivalent to prepaying once a year at the rate of CPR.

PSA PREPAYMENT BENCHMARK

The public securities association (PSA) prepayment benchmark is expressed as a monthly series of annual prepayment rates.[2]

The PSA benchmark assumes that prepayment rates are lower for newly originated mortgages and will then speed up as the mortgages become seasoned. It has been observed that in practice, homeowners are less likely to move in the initial years of the loan. They are also less likely to refinance or make large unscheduled principal repayments. Consequently, the PSA benchmark assumes that the prepayment rate will steadily increase for the first 30 months of the loan, and stabilize thereafter.

The benchmark assumes the following CPR for 30-year mortgages:

- CPR of 0.2% for the first month
- An increase of 0.2% per month for the next 30 months until it reaches 6%
- 6% for the remaining years

This benchmark is called 100% PSA or 100PSA.

Let 't' be the number of months since the mortgage was originated.

$$\text{If } t \le 30; \text{CPR} = 6 \times \frac{t}{30}\%, \text{whereas}$$

$$\text{If } t > 30; \text{CPR} = 6\%$$

Sample calculations for the 100 PSA benchmark are given here:

$$\text{Month 10: CPR} = 6 \times \frac{10}{30} = 2\%$$

$$\text{SMM} = 1 - (1 - .02)^{\frac{1}{12}} = 0.001682 \equiv 0.1682\%$$

$$\text{Months 31–360: CPR} = 6\%$$

$$\text{SMM} = 1 - (1 - .06)^{\frac{1}{12}} = 0.005143 \equiv 0.5143\%$$

Slower or faster prepayment speeds are referred to as a percentage of the standard PSA benchmark. For instance, 50 PSA means one half of the CPR of the PSA benchmark, while 150 PSA means 1.5 times the CPR of the PSA benchmark.

Thus, the case of 150 PSA, the SMM may be calculated as follows:

$$\text{Month 10: CPR} = 1.50 \times 6 \times \frac{10}{30} = 3\%$$

$$\text{SMM} = 1 - (1 - .03)^{\frac{1}{12}} = 0.002535 \equiv 0.2535\%$$

$$\text{Months 30–360: CPR} = 1.50 \times 6\% = 9\%$$

$$\text{SMM} = 1 - (1 - .09)^{\frac{1}{12}} = 0.007828 \equiv 0.7828\%$$

---

[2]This model was developed by the Public Securities Association, which was subsequently renamed as the Bond Market Association (BMA). In 2006 the BMA merged with the Securities Industry Association to form the Securities Industry and Financial Markets Association (SIFMA); however, the prepayment benchmark is still referred to as the PSA benchmark.

It should be noted that 150 PSA does not mean that the SMM for a month is 1.5 times the SMA for the same month under the 100 PSA assumption. It is the CPR for the month that is 1.5 times the CPR under the 100 PSA assumption.

Illustration of 100 PSA

Consider a pass-through backed by a single loan of $100,000 with 360 months to maturity and a mortgage rate of 9% per annum. Assume that there are no servicing or guaranteeing fees. The projected cash flows assuming 100 PSA are given in Table 9.15.

TABLE 9.15   Cash Flows Assuming 100 PSA

Mth.	Mthly. Pmt.	Int. Pmt.	Sch. Prin. Pmt.	Sch. Out. Prin.	Pre Pmt.	Act. Out. Prin.	Cash Flow
1	804.62	750.00	54.62	99945.38	16.67	99928.70	821.30
12	795.75	737.10	58.65	98221.92	198.64	98023.29	994.39
24	767.88	705.98	61.90	94068.57	384.82	93683.75	1152.70
36	724.49	660.61	63.88	88016.81	452.67	87564.14	1177.16
48	681.02	615.34	65.68	81979.09	421.62	81557.47	1102.64
60	640.16	572.62	67.53	76282.30	392.32	75889.98	1032.48
72	601.75	532.31	69.44	70905.39	364.67	70540.72	966.42
84	565.64	494.25	71.39	65828.56	338.56	65490.00	904.20
96	531.71	458.30	73.41	61033.16	313.89	60719.26	845.60
108	499.80	424.33	75.47	56501.65	290.59	56211.06	790.39
120	469.81	392.21	77.60	52217.54	268.56	51948.98	738.37
132	441.63	361.84	79.79	48165.27	247.71	47917.56	689.34
144	415.13	333.09	82.04	44330.24	227.99	44102.25	643.12
156	390.22	305.87	84.35	40698.69	209.31	40489.37	599.53
168	366.81	280.08	86.72	37257.64	191.62	37066.02	558.42
180	344.80	255.63	89.17	33994.90	174.84	33820.06	519.64
192	324.11	232.43	91.68	30898.98	158.91	30740.07	483.02
204	304.66	210.40	94.26	27959.05	143.79	27815.26	448.46
216	286.38	189.46	96.92	25164.92	129.42	25035.49	415.81
228	269.20	169.55	99.65	22506.96	115.75	22391.21	384.96
240	253.05	150.59	102.46	19976.14	102.74	19873.40	355.79
252	237.87	132.52	105.35	17563.90	90.33	17473.57	328.20
264	223.59	115.28	108.32	15262.20	78.49	15183.71	302.09
276	210.18	98.81	111.37	13063.44	67.19	12996.25	277.36
288	197.57	83.06	114.51	10960.45	56.37	10904.08	253.94
300	185.71	67.98	117.73	8946.47	46.01	8900.45	231.73
312	174.57	53.52	121.05	7015.10	36.08	6979.02	210.65
324	164.10	39.64	124.46	5160.32	26.54	5133.78	190.64
336	154.25	26.28	127.97	3376.42	17.36	3359.06	171.62
348	145.00	13.42	131.57	1658.02	8.53	1649.49	153.52
360	136.30	1.01	135.28	0.00	0.00	0.00	136.30

Explanation: Mth. ≡ Month; Mthly. Pmt. ≡ Monthly Payment; Int. Pmt. ≡ Interest Payment; Sch. Prin. Pmt. ≡ Scheduled Principal Payment; Sch. Out. Prin. ≡ Scheduled Outstanding Principal; Pre Pmt. ≡ Prepayment; Act. Out. Prin. ≡ Actual Outstanding Principal

The average life of the pass-through is 12.08 years.

ANALYSIS

Consider the data for the first month. The monthly payment is given by

$$100{,}000 = \frac{A}{0.0075} \times \left[1 - \frac{1}{(1.0075)^{360}} \right]$$

$$\Rightarrow A = \$804.62$$

The interest component for the first month is

$$100{,}000 \times \frac{0.09}{12} = \$750$$

The scheduled outstanding principal at the end of the month is

$$100{,}000 - (804.62 - 750) = \$99{,}945.38$$

The CPR for the first month is 0.2%. Thus, the SMM is

$$1 - (1 - .002)^{\frac{1}{12}} = 0.0001668 \equiv 0.01668\%$$

The prepayment for the month is

$$99{,}945.38 \times 0.0001668 = \$16.67$$

Thus, the actual outstanding principal at the end of the first month is

$$99{,}945.38 - 16.67 = \$99{,}928.71$$

The cash flow for the pass-through is

$$750 + 54.62 + 16.67 = \$821.29$$

Illustration of 200 PSA

Consider a pass-through backed by a single loan of $100,000 with 360 months to maturity and a mortgage rate of 9% per annum. Assume that there are no servicing or guaranteeing fees. The projected cash flows assuming 200 PSA are given in Table 9.16.

TABLE 9.16   Cash Flows Assuming 200 PSA

Mth.	Mthly. Pmt.	Int. Pmt.	Sch. Prin. Pmt.	Sch. Out. Prin.	Pre Pmt.	Act. Out. Prin.	Cash Flow
1	804.62	750.00	54.62	99,945.38	33.38	99,912.00	838.00
12	786.84	728.85	57.99	97,122.15	397.31	96,724.84	1,184.15
24	731.68	672.70	58.98	89,634.10	750.71	88,883.39	1,482.39
36	648.97	591.75	57.22	78,842.54	835.43	78,007.11	1,484.41
48	571.10	516.01	55.08	68,746.86	728.46	68,018.40	1,299.55
60	502.56	149.55	53.112	59,886.42	634.57	59,251.85	1,137.14
120	265.22	221.41	43.81	29,477.80	312.35	29,165.45	577.57
180	139.96	103.77	36.20	13,799.60	146.22	13,653.38	286.19
240	73.86	43.96	29.91	5,830.94	61.79	5,769.15	135.65
300	38.98	14.27	21.71	1,877.81	19.90	1,857.92	58.88
360	20.57	0.15	20.42	0.00	0.00	0.00	20.57

Explanation: Mth. ≡ Month; Mthly. Pmt. ≡ Monthly Payment; Int. Pmt. ≡ Interest Payment; Sch. Prin. Pmt. ≡ Scheduled Principal Payment; Sch. Out. Prin. ≡ Scheduled Outstanding Principal; Pre Pmt. ≡ Prepayment; Act. Out. Prin. ≡ Actual Outstanding Principal

The average life of the pass-through is eight years. As can be seen, the more rapid prepayments lead to a reduction in the average life of the security.

Collateralized Mortgage Obligations

In the case of a pass-through, there is only one class of security that is issued, and every security is entitled to the same undivided share of the cash flows from the underlying pool. The feature of such securities is that prepayments have the same implications for all the security holders.

In real life, however, investors differ with respect to the prepayment exposure and the average security life sought by them. The securitization process can take these preferences into account by creating multiple classes of securities, or what are referred to in MBS parlance as *tranches*. There are clearly specified rules as to how cash flows from the underlying pool are to be directed to the holders of the various tranches. Such securities, with multiple tranches, are referred to as *collateralized mortgage obligations* or *CMOs*. We will introduce the concept by studying a very simple CMO structure known as a sequential pay CMO.

Sequential Pay CMO

Assume that a pool of mortgages consists of four loans with a principal of $100,000 each. Each loan has a maturity of 360 months and a mortgage rate of 9%. The average life of a pass-through, backed by such loans, under the assumption of 100 PSA is 12.08 years, as we have just seen.

Now assume that instead of creating a single type of security like a pass-through, four types of securities known as tranches A to D are created. All principal payments from the underlying pool, both scheduled and unscheduled, will first go to tranche A. During this time, the remaining tranches will continue to earn interest on the outstanding principal. Once tranche A is fully paid off, all subsequent principal payments, scheduled and unscheduled, will be directed to the holders of tranche B. Once again, while tranche B is being paid off, holders of tranches C and D will get interest on their outstanding principal. Extending the logic, the redemption of tranche B will see further principal payments being directed to tranche C, with holders of tranche D getting only the interest due. Finally, once tranche C securities are retired, all further principal payments will be directed to the holders of tranche D.

Let us assume that one security is issued for each tranche, with a face value of $100,000, and that there are no servicing or guaranteeing fees. The cash flow schedules for the four tranches are given in Tables 9.17 to 9.20.

Analysis – Tranche A

Consider the first month. The payment that is received from the underlying pool is

$$400{,}000 = \frac{A}{0.0075} \times \left[1 - \frac{1}{(1.0075)^{360}}\right]$$

$$\Rightarrow A = \$3{,}218.49$$

TABLE 9.17   Amortization for Tranche A

Month	Interest Received	Principal Received	Cash Flow	Outstanding Balance
1	750.00	285.18	1035.18	99714.82
2	747.86	353.50	1101.36	99361.32
10	712.36	895.96	1608.31	94085.02
20	622.99	1543.95	2166.94	81521.67
30	487.00	2127.57	2614.58	62806.32
40	330.88	2026.39	2357.27	42091.53
50	182.18	1930.42	2112.60	22359.64
60	40.49	1839.42	1879.92	3559.90
61	26.70	1830.58	1857.28	1729.32
62	12.97	1729.32	1742.29	0.00

TABLE 9.18   Amortization for Tranche B

Month	Interest Received	Principal Received	Cash Flow	Outstanding Balance
1	750.00	0.00	750.00	100000.00
10	750.00	0.00	750.00	100000.00
20	750.00	0.00	750.00	100000.00
30	750.00	0.00	750.00	100000.00
40	750.00	0.00	750.00	100000.00
50	750.00	0.00	750.00	100000.00
60	750.00	0.00	750.00	100000.00
61	750.00	0.00	750.00	100000.00
62	750.00	92.47	842.47	99907.53
70	655.48	1753.13	2408.61	85644.07
80	526.78	1671.32	2198.11	68566.30
90	404.08	1593.77	1997.85	52283.01
100	287.05	1520.27	1807.32	36752.77
110	175.40	1450.62	1626.02	21936.22
120	68.85	1384.63	1453.48	7795.93
125	17.41	1352.94	1370.35	968.18
126	7.26	968.18	975.44	0.00

TABLE 9.19   Amortization for Tranche C

Month	Interest Received	Principal Received	Cash Flow	Outstanding Balance
1	750.00	0.00	750.00	100000.00
20	750.00	0.00	750.00	100000.00
40	750.00	0.00	750.00	100000.00
60	750.00	0.00	750.00	100000.00
80	750.00	0.00	750.00	100000.00
100	750.00	0.00	750.00	100000.00
120	750.00	0.00	750.00	100000.00
126	750.00	378.53	1128.53	99621.47
140	620.00	1262.90	1882.90	81403.49
160	438.49	1153.77	1592.25	57311.25
180	272.52	1056.02	1328.54	35280.26
200	120.47	968.57	1089.05	15094.36
210	49.20	928.41	977.60	5631.42
215	14.67	909.16	923.83	1047.35
216	7.86	905.38	913.23	141.97
217	1.06	141.97	143.03	0.00

TABLE 9.20   Amortization for Tranche D

Month	Interest Received	Principal Received	Cash Flow	Outstanding Balance
1	750.00	0.00	750.00	100000.00
30	750.00	0.00	750.00	100000.00
60	750.00	0.00	750.00	100000.00
90	750.00	0.00	750.00	100000.00
120	750.00	0.00	750.00	100000.00
150	750.00	0.00	750.00	100000.00
180	750.00	0.00	750.00	100000.00
210	750.00	0.00	750.00	100000.00
217	750.00	759.64	1509.64	99240.36
240	602.36	820.79	1423.15	79493.62
270	427.81	730.43	1158.23	56310.55
300	271.93	654.98	926.90	35601.82
330	131.58	592.44	724.03	16951.79
340	87.77	574.17	661.94	11128.88
350	45.29	557.08	602.37	5482.15
360	4.06	541.13	545.18	0.01

The interest component for the month is

$$400,000 \times 0.0075 = \$3,000.$$

Thus, the scheduled principal for the month is 3,218.49 − 3,000 = \$218.49. This will be directed toward tranche A.

The prepayment for the month is

$$[400,000 - 218.49] \times 0.0001668 = \$66.68$$

This will also be directed to tranche A. Thus, the total principal received by tranche A is

$$218.49 + 66.68 = \$285.17$$

The interest receivable by this security for the month is

$$100,000 \times 0.0075 = \$750.$$

Thus, the total cash flow received by tranche A in the first month is

$$750 + 285.17 = \$1,035.17$$

Now consider the second month. The monthly payment received from the underlying pool is

$$399,714.82 = \frac{A}{0.0075} \times \left[1 - \frac{1}{(1.0075)^{359}}\right]$$

$$\Rightarrow A = \$3,217.95$$

The interest component for the month is

$$399,714.82 \times 0.0075 = \$2,997.86$$

Thus, the scheduled principal for the month is

$$3,217.95 - 2,997.86 = \$220.09$$

The prepayment for the month is

$$[399,714.82 - 220.09] \times 0.0003339 = \$133.41$$

Thus, the total principal for the month is $220.09 + 133.41 = \$353.50$.

The entire amount will obviously be directed toward tranche A. The interest receivable by this tranche for the second month is given by

$$[100,000 - 285.17] \times 0.0075 = \$747.86$$

Thus, the total cash flow that is directed toward tranche A at the end of the second month is $747.86 + 353.50 = \$1,101.36$.

At the end of the 61st month, tranche A has an outstanding principal of $1,729.32. The total principal from the underlying pool at the end of the 62nd month is $1,821.79. Of this $1,729.32 will be directed to tranche A. The balance of $92.47 will be paid to tranche B. Thus the total cash flow received by tranche A in the 62nd month is

$$1,729.32 \times 0.0075 + 1,729.32 = \$1,742.29$$

Analysis – Tranche B

Now let us turn our attention to tranche B. For the first 61 months, tranche B will receive only interest on the outstanding principal of $100,000, which amounts to $750 per month. In the 62nd month this tranche receives $92.47 by way of principal payment, as explained. Thus, the total cash flow for this month is 750 + 92.47 = $842.47. The outstanding principal at the end of the month is 100,000 – 92.47 = $99,907.53. In the 125th month the outstanding principal for this tranche is $968.18. In the 126th month the underlying pool makes a total principal payment of $1,346.71. Thus, in this month tranche B receives $7.26 worth of interest and $968.18 of principal, which amounts to a total cash flow of $975.44. The excess principal, that is, 1,346.71 – 968.18 = $378.53, is directed to tranche C.

Analysis – Tranche C

Let us now consider tranche C. Until the 125th month this tranche receives a monthly cash flow of $750, which represents the interest on an outstanding principal of $100,000. In the 126th month there is a principal repayment of $378.53, as explained. The total cash flow for this month is therefore $1,128.53. At the end of 216 months there is an outstanding principal of $141.97. Thus, in the 217th month this tranche receives an interest payment of $1.06. In this month the total principal received from the underlying pool is $901.61. Thus, after paying $141.97 to tranche C, the excess of $759.64 is directed toward tranche D.

Analysis – Tranche D

Finally, let us analyze the last tranche. Tranche D receives interest on the initial outstanding principal until month 216, which amounts to $750 per month. In month 217 it receives a principal payment of $759.64, as explained. The tranche is fully paid off in month 360.

The average life of the collateral as calculated for a pass-through security based on the pool is 12.08 years; however, each tranche of the CMO has a different maturity and average life. The details are given in Table 9.21.

In the case of a sequential pay CMO, the average life of the mother loan is a weighted average of the average lives of the tranches. The weight attached to a tranche is its original outstanding balance, divided by the cumulative outstanding balances of all the tranches. In our illustration the weight of every tranche is 25%.

$$0.25 \times (36.13 + 92.74 + 168.43 + 282.39) = 144.92$$

TABLE 9.21   Maturity and Average Life of the Securities

Security	Maturity in Months	Average Life in Months
Collateral	360	144.92
Tranche A	62	36.13
Tranche B	126	92.74
Tranche C	217	168.43
Tranche D	360	282.39

EXTENSION RISK AND CONTRACTION RISK

Pass-through securities and CMOs expose investors to prepayment risk. In a declining interest rate environment, prepayments affect security holders in two ways. As they are debt securities, we would expect the price of such securities to rise in a scenario where rates are declining. In the case of mortgage-backed securities, however, holders of underlying loans are likely to prepay and refinance at a lower rate when market rates go down. The overall result is price compression; that is, the rise in price will not be as large as in the case of plain-vanilla bonds. The second adverse consequence for holders of such securities is of course reinvestment risk, as is the case for all debt holders. That is, cash flows that are received in a declining interest rate environment have to be reinvested at lower rates of interest. The risk due to these two adverse consequences is termed as *contraction risk*.

Now let us consider a rising interest rate environment. We would clearly expect the prices of mortgage-backed securities to fall. Unlike in the case of plain-vanilla bonds, however, principal payments are likely to slow down because holders of underlying mortgage loans are less likely to refinance when mortgage rates are rising. This will exacerbate the anticipated price decline. In such a situation, the security holders would like prepayments to be high for it would afford them an opportunity to reinvest larger amounts at high rates of interest. The adverse impact for mortgage-backed securities in a rising interest rate environment is termed as *extension risk*.

ACCRUAL BONDS

In the case of the sequential pay CMO that we just studied, every tranche receives interest every month, based on the principal outstanding for that particular tranche at the beginning of the month. Many sequential pay CMO structures, however, do not require that every tranche should be paid interest every month based on the outstanding principal. In the case of a sequential pay CMO with an *accrual bond*, also termed as a *Z-bond*,[3] however, the Z-bond will not receive any monthly interest until the previous tranches are fully retired. Therefore, the interest for the Z-bond will accrue and be added to its original principal (negative amortization) until the other classes of the CMO have been paid off. In the months prior to the retirement of the penultimate tranche, the interest that would otherwise have been paid to the Z-bond is directed to the tranche receiving principal at that point in time, and thus helps to speed up the repayment of principal.

Let us consider a CMO where tranches A, B, and C are as specified in the preceding illustration; however, the last tranche is an accrual bond. Quite obviously, the inclusion of the Z-bond will reduce the maturity and the average life of each of the three earlier tranches. (See Tables 9.22–9.26.)

Analysis

The cash flows from the underlying pool at the end of the first month are as follows.

Interest = $3,000; Scheduled Principal = $218.49; Prepayment = $66.69

---

[3] Because of its similarities with a zero-coupon bond.

TABLE 9.22 Amortization for Tranche A in the Presence of a Z-bond

Month	Interest Received	Principal Received	Cash Flow	Outstanding Balance
1	750.00	1035.18	1785.18	98964.82
2	742.24	1109.13	1851.36	97855.69
10	660.19	1698.13	2358.31	86326.76
20	508.59	2408.36	2916.94	65403.26
30	305.54	3059.04	3364.58	37679.15
40	77.15	3030.12	3107.27	7256.67
42	31.72	3025.63	3057.35	1203.21
43	9.02	1203.21	1212.23	0.00

TABLE 9.23 Amortization for Tranche B in the Presence of a Z-bond

Month	Interest Received	Principal Received	Cash Flow	Outstanding Balance
1	750.00	0.00	750.00	100000.00
10	750.00	0.00	750.00	100000.00
20	750.00	0.00	750.00	100000.00
30	750.00	0.00	750.00	100000.00
40	750.00	0.00	750.00	100000.00
43	750.00	1820.34	2570.34	98179.66
50	600.57	3012.03	3612.60	77063.95
60	374.98	3004.94	3379.92	46991.80
70	149.54	3009.08	3158.61	16929.01
75	36.61	3015.44	3052.04	1865.71
76	13.99	1865.71	1879.70	0.00

TABLE 9.24 Amortization for Tranche C in the Presence of a Z-bond

Month	Interest Received	Principal Received	Cash Flow	Outstanding Balance
1	750.00	0.00	750.00	100000.00
10	750.00	0.00	750.00	100000.00
20	750.00	0.00	750.00	100000.00
30	750.00	0.00	750.00	100000.00
40	750.00	0.00	750.00	100000.00
50	750.00	0.00	750.00	100000.00
60	750.00	0.00	750.00	100000.00
70	750.00	0.00	750.00	100000.00
76	750.00	1151.35	1901.35	98848.65
80	673.40	3024.71	3698.11	86761.89
90	445.69	3052.16	3497.85	56373.74
100	215.52	3091.80	3307.32	25644.37
109	5.49	731.83	737.32	0.00

TABLE 9.25 Amortization for the Z-Bond

Month	Interest Due	Interest Received	Principal Received	Cash Flow	Outstanding Balance
1	750	0.00	0.00	(750.00)	100750.00
2	755.63	0.00	0.00	(755.63)	101505.63
10	802.17	0.00	0.00	(802.17)	107758.25
20	864.41	0.00	0.00	(864.41)	116118.41
30	931.47	0.00	0.00	(931.47)	125127.18
50	1081.61	0.00	0.00	(1081.61)	145295.69
60	1165.52	0.00	0.00	(1165.52)	156568.10
70	1255.94	0.00	0.00	(1255.94)	168715.05
90	1458.38	0.00	0.00	(1458.38)	195909.25
100	1571.53	0.00	0.00	(1571.53)	211108.38
108	1668.33	0.00	0.00	(1668.33)	224112.42
109	1680.84	1680.84	725.59	2406.43	223386.83
120	1568.85	1568.85	1384.63	2953.48	207795.91
140	1370.00	1370.00	1262.90	2632.90	181403.48
160	1188.49	1188.49	1153.77	2342.25	157311.23
180	1022.52	1022.52	1056.02	2078.54	135280.24
200	870.47	870.47	968.57	1839.05	115094.34
220	730.86	730.86	890.46	1621.32	96557.85
240	602.36	602.36	820.79	1423.15	79493.59
260	483.75	483.75	758.78	1242.53	63740.99
280	373.94	373.94	703.73	1077.66	49154.44
300	271.93	271.93	654.98	926.90	35601.78
320	176.81	176.81	611.96	788.78	22962.97
340	87.77	87.77	574.17	661.94	11128.83
360	4.06	4.06	541.13	545.18	(0.05)

The outstanding principal for each of the four tranches is $100,000. Tranches A, B, and C will therefore receive an interest payment of $750 for the month. The accrual bond will obviously not receive any interest. Tranche A will receive the following amount by way of principal payment

$$3,000 + 218.49 + 66.69 - 750 \times 3 = \$1,035.18$$

Thus, the total cash flow for this tranche is $750 + 1,035.18 = \$1,785.18$. The outstanding principal at the end of the first month is $100,000 - 1,035.18 = \$98,964.82$.

Because the Z-bond does not receive any interest during the month there will be negative amortization. Thus, the outstanding principal for this bond at the end of the first month is $100,750.

Now let us consider the second month. The cash flows from the underlying pool are as follows. Interest = $2,997.86; Scheduled Principal = $220.09; Prepayment = $133.41. Tranche A has an outstanding principal of $98,964.82. Thus, the interest for the month for this tranche is

$$98,964.82 \times 0.0075 = \$742.24$$

Tranches B and C will each receive $750 for the month by way of interest as there has been no principal repayment thus far. The principal repayment that is directed at tranche A for this month is $2{,}997.86 + 220.09 + 133.41 - 742.24 - 750 \times 2 = \$1{,}109.12$. The outstanding principal at the end of the second month is therefore $98{,}964.82 - 1{,}109.12 = \$97{,}855.70$.

Tranche Z will not receive any cash flow during the month. The interest due is $100{,}750 \times 0.0075 = \$755.63$. Thus, the outstanding principal at the end of the second month is $100{,}750 + 755.63 = \$101{,}505.63$.

Now let us turn to the 43rd month. The cash flows from the underlying collateral are as follows: Interest = $2,535.51; Scheduled Principal = $259.71; Prepayment = $1,737.35.

The outstanding principal for tranche A at the end of the 42nd month is $1,203.21. Thus, this tranche will receive a cash flow of $1{,}203.21 \times (1.0075) = \$1{,}212.23$. With this tranche A is retired.

Tranches B and C are entitled to an interest payment of $750 each. Thus, the principal payment that is received by tranche B during this month is $2{,}535.51 + 259.71 + 1{,}737.35 - 1{,}212.23 - 750 \times 2 = \$1{,}820.34$. Thus, the total cash flow that is received by tranche B at the end of this month is $2,570.34. The outstanding principal is $100{,}000 - 1{,}820.34 = \$98{,}179.66$.

Similarly, tranche B is retired at the end of 76 months and tranche C at the end of 109 months. From the 109th month onwards the Z-bond starts receiving repayment of principal. The outstanding principal for the bond at the end of month 108 is $224,112.42. In the 109th month the tranche receives an interest payment of $224{,}112.42 \times 0.0075 = \$1{,}680.84$. It also receives a principal payment of $725.59, which serves to reduce the outstanding principal to $223,386.83. The tranche is fully paid off at the end of the 360th month.

As we can see, the average life of each of the three tranches has reduced due to the presence of the Z-bond. Z-bonds have appeal to investors who are primarily concerned with the specter of reinvestment risk. Because such bonds do not entail the receipt of any cash flows until all the other classes are fully retired, reinvestment risk is totally eliminated until the Z-bond starts receiving its first cash flow.

TABLE 9.26   Maturity and Average Life of the Securities in the Presence of a Z-Bond

Security	Maturity in Months	Average Life in Months
Collateral	360	144.92
A	43	25.06
B	76	59.50
C	109	92.53
Z	360	

FLOATING RATE TRANCHES

Floating rate bonds can be created from a fixed-rate tranche. We will illustrate this using tranche C in the previous illustration, which has a par value of $100,000 and a 9% coupon. In practice, to create a floater we have to simultaneously create an inverse floater.[4] The cumulative principal of the two tranches will in this case be $100,000. There is no rule as to what the principal values of the respective tranches should be as long as their combined par value is $100,000.

Let us assume that the benchmark for the two tranches is the 3-month LIBOR and that we wish to create a floater with a par value of $60,000 and an inverse floater with a par value of $40,000. The coupon on the floater is LIBOR + m basis points while that for the inverse floater is $C - L \times$ LIBOR.

It is a common practice to specify the coupon for an inverse floater as

$$C - L \times \text{Benchmark}$$

C is the cap or maximum interest on the inverse floater while L is referred to as the *coupon leverage*. The concept of a cap can be easily understood. The lower limit for LIBOR is zero. Consequently, the upper limit for the coupon on the inverse floater is C. The coupon leverage measures the rate of change of the coupon of the inverse floater with respect to the benchmark.

We know that the total annual interest available is 9% of 100,000, which is 9000. This is also the maximum interest available for the floating tranche. Thus, the cap on the floater is 9000 ÷ 60000 = 15%. The ratio of floaters to inverses is 3:2, which implies that the coupon leverage for the inverse floater is 1.50. If we assume that the coupon on the floater is LIBOR + 150 b.p., the minimum coupon on the floater is 1.50%, which would be the case if LIBOR were to be zero. The minimum interest on the floater is hence 60,000 × 0.015 = 900. Thus, the maximum interest for the inverse floater is 9,000 – 900 = $8,100. The cap on the inverse is therefore 8,100 ÷ 40,000 = 0.2025 ≡ 20.25%. We can therefore express the coupons of the two tranches as

$$\text{Floater Coupon: LIBOR} + 1.50\%$$

$$\text{Inverse Floater Coupon: } 20.25\% - 1.50 \times \text{LIBOR}$$

The weighted average coupon is

$$0.60 \times (\text{LIBOR} + 1.50) + 0.40 \times (20.25 - 1.50 \times \text{LIBOR})$$

For instance, if LIBOR were to be 7.50%, the weighted average will be

$$0.60 \times 9 + 0.40 \times 9 = 9\%$$

---

[4]While the coupon of a floating rate bond moves up and down with the corresponding changes in the benchmark, the coupon of an inverse floater moves inversely with the benchmark. For instance, an inverse floater may have its coupon specified as 10% – LIBOR. Consequently, if the LIBOR were to rise, the coupon would fall and vice versa.

NOTIONAL INTEREST-ONLY TRANCHE

Let us go back to the sequential pay CMO that we studied earlier. We assumed that the underlying mortgages had a coupon rate of 9% and that each of the four tranches that we created also had a coupon of 9%. In practice, each tranche of a CMO will have a different coupon rate and there will be an excess representing the difference between the interest on the underlying collateral and the coupons on the various tranches. Therefore, it is a common practice to create a tranche that is entitled to receive only the excess coupon interest.[5] Such tranches are referred to as notional interest-only securities.

We will now assume that the underlying collateral has a coupon of 9%, while the four tranches created from it have coupon rates as shown in Table 9.27.

Consider tranche A. It pays a coupon of 7.50%, while the coupon on the collateral is 9%. Thus, there is excess interest of 1.50%. Let us assume that we wish to create a notional interest-only security with a coupon of 8.40%. To find the notional amount on which the interest payable to this security will be calculated, we proceed as follows. An excess interest of 1.50% on $140,000 worth of principal can be used to pay an interest of 8.40% on a principal amount of $25,000. Similarly in the case of tranche B, an excess interest of 1.25% on a principal amount of $84,000 can be used to pay an interest of 8.40% on a principal of $12,500. Tranche C, using the same logic, generates excess interest to support $10,000 worth of principal while the last tranche is capable of servicing a principal of $8,214.2850. Thus, the excess interest generated can service a bond with a principal of $25,000 + 12,500 + 10,000 + 8,214.285 = $55,714.285$. This is the notional principal for the tranche that is scheduled to receive the excess interest. The term *notional* connotes that this principal amount is used merely to compute the interest payable to this class for the month, and that the principal per se is not repaid.

The contribution of a tranche to the notional principal is in general given by the following formula.

$$\text{Notional Amount for an x\% IO Class} = \frac{\text{Par Value of the tranche} \times \text{Excess Interest}}{\dfrac{x}{100}}$$

For instance, in the case of tranche A in the earlier illustration

$$\text{Notional Amount for an 8.40\% IO Class} = \frac{140,000 \times 0.015}{0.0840} = \$25,000$$

TABLE 9.27   Coupon Rates for a Sequential Pay CMO

Tranche	Initial Principal	Coupon Rate
A	140,000	7.50%
B	84,000	7.75%
C	84,000	8.00%
D	92,000	8.25%

---

[5]Note that this tranche is not entitled to any principal payments.

For the first month the IO class will receive a cash flow of

$$0.0840 \times 55,714.285 \times \frac{1}{12} = \$390$$

Let us assume a prepayment speed of 100 PSA. The principal paid to tranche A at the end of the first month will be \$285.18. This will reduce the outstanding principal for this tranche to $140,000 - 285.18 = \$139,714.82$. Thus, the contribution of this tranche to the notional principal for the second month is

$$\frac{139,714.82 \times 0.0150}{0.0840} = \$24,949.08$$

The contributions of the other tranches will not be affected. Consequently, for the second month the notional IO class will receive interest on a principal of

$$24,949.08 + 12,500 + 10,000 + 8,214.285 = \$55,663.36$$

Thus, the interest for this tranche for the second month will be

$$\frac{55,663.36 \times 0.084}{12} = \$389.64$$

INTEREST-ONLY AND PRINCIPAL-ONLY STRIPS

Stripped mortgage-backed securities can be created by directing either all the principal or all the interest to a particular class. The security that is scheduled to receive only the principal is referred to as the *principal-only* or the PO class. The other security is obviously termed as the *interest-only* or IO class.

Let us first consider the PO class. The yield obtained by the security holder will depend on the speed with which the underlying pool generates prepayments. The faster the speed with which prepayments are received, the greater will be the rate of return for holders of such securities. In the case of the IO class holders, however, the desire is to have slow prepayments. This is because, given that such securities do not receive any principal payments, the interest payment income will be higher, the larger the outstanding balance on the underlying pool. This is tantamount to a slower prepayment rate.

PAC BONDS

PAC is an acronym for *planned amortization class*. In the case of such bonds, if the prepayment pattern falls within a prespecified range, then the cash flows received by the security are known.

PAC bonds are not created in isolation. They are accompanied by a category of bonds that are termed as support bonds. It is this category that absorbs the prepayment risk, thereby protecting the PAC bonds against extension risk as well as contraction risk.

To create a PAC bond we need to specify a range of prepayment speeds. These are referred to as the PAC collars. The PAC schedule lists the principal amount payable to the PAC bondholders if the prepayment speed is within the range provided by the lower PAC collar and the upper PAC collar. The schedule is obtained by taking the lower of the principal cash flows generated by the lower collar and the upper collar. Consider the following illustration.

EXAMPLE 9.8

A pool of four mortgage loans of $100,000 each is used to create a PAC bond and a support bond. The lower PAC collar is 100 PSA while the upper collar is 250 PSA. Table 9.28 lists the principal payments from the underlying pool assuming four different prepayment speeds between the lower and upper collars.

TABLE 9.28   Principal Payments for a 100 PSA to 250 PSA Range

Month	At 100 PSA	At 150 PSA	At 200 PSA	At 250 PSA	Minimum Principal Payment
1	285.18	318.57	352.00	385.45	285.18
2	353.50	420.36	487.32	554.40	353.50
3	421.79	522.13	622.71	723.51	421.79
4	490.01	623.83	758.02	892.57	490.01
5	558.13	725.37	893.11	1061.35	558.13
10	895.96	1,227.95	1,560.54	1,893.75	895.96
50	1,930.42	2,553.91	3,066.72	3,477.57	1,930.42
100	1,520.27	1,720.23	1,775.68	1,729.92	1,520.27
101	1,513.14	1,706.67	1,756.27	1,705.78	1,513.14
102	1,506.04	1,693.22	1,737.08	1,681.96	1,506.04
114	1,423.79	1,539.79	1,522.14	1,420.35	1,420.35
150	1,206.84	1,157.52	1,021.39	851.68	851.68
200	968.57	777.74	581.68	412.60	412.60
250	788.87	521.43	326.18	194.79	194.79
300	654.98	348.48	178.44	88.02	88.02
350	557.08	231.79	93.62	36.63	36.63
360	541.13	213.48	81.67	30.24	30.24

ANALYSIS

Until the 113th month, the lowest principal payment is obtained under the assumption of 100 PSA. From the 114th month onward, the lowest principal payment is observed under the assumption of 250 PSA.

The sum total of the principal payments as per the PAC schedule is $278,088.22. This represents the maximum principal for the PAC bonds. For our illustration we have assumed that the PAC bond has a principal of $277,500 while the support bond has a principal of $122,500.

TABLE 9.29 Principal Payments at 150 PSA

Month	Total Principal	Payment to PAC Bond	Payment to Support Bond
1	318.57	285.18	33.39
2	420.36	353.50	66.85
3	522.13	421.79	100.34
4	623.83	490.01	133.82
5	725.37	558.13	167.24
50	2,553.91	1,930.42	623.48
100	1,720.23	1,520.27	199.96
150	1,157.52	851.68	305.85
200	777.74	412.60	365.13
250	521.43	194.79	326.64
300	348.48	88.02	260.46
344	243.49	13.53	229.96
345	241.51	0.00	241.51
350	231.79	0.00	231.79
355	222.46	0.00	222.46
360	213.48	**0.00**	213.48

We will first consider the prepayment scenario corresponding to 150 PSA (Table 9.29).

ANALYSIS

Until the 344th month, the total principal received is in excess of the amount required to satisfy the PAC schedule. The difference is therefore directed to the support bond. In the 344th month the outstanding amount on the PAC bond is $13.53. The total principal received is $243.49. Thus, the excess of $229.96 is directed to the support bond. In subsequent months, because the PAC bond has been fully paid off, the entire principal received is directed to the support bond. The average life of the PAC bond is 98.13 months, while that for the support bond is 156.69 months.

Now let us consider the prepayment scenario corresponding to 250 PSA (Table 9.30).

ANALYSIS

Until the 113th month, the scheduled and unscheduled principal payment, from the underlying collateral based on the assumption of 250 PSA, is greater than the amount required to be directed toward the PAC bond on the basis of the PAC schedule. Consequently, until the 113th month there is a cash inflow for the support bond. From the 114th until the 343rd month, the total principal payment is just adequate to satisfy the PAC schedule. Consequently, the payment directed

(continued)

(*continued*)

TABLE 9.30   Principal Payments at 250 PSA

Month	Total Principal	Payment to PAC Bond	Payment to Support Bond
1	385.45	285.18	100.27
2	554.40	353.50	200.90
3	723.51	421.79	301.72
4	892.57	490.01	402.56
5	1,061.35	558.13	503.23
50	3,477.57	1,930.42	1,547.15
100	1,729.92	1,520.27	209.65
113	1,440.54	1,430.45	10.09
150	851.68	851.68	0.00
200	412.60	412.60	0.00
250	194.79	194.79	0.00
300	88.02	88.02	0.00
344	40.97	13.53	27.44
345	40.22	0.00	40.22
350	36.63	0.00	36.63
355	33.31	0.00	33.31
360	30.24	0.00	30.24

TABLE 9.31   Principal Payments at 0 PSA

Month	Total Principal	Scheduled Payment to PAC Bond	Actual Payment to PAC Bond	Deficit	Cumulative Deficit	Payment to Support Bond
1	218.49	285.18	218.49	(66.69)	(66.69)	0.00
2	220.13	353.50	220.13	(133.37)	(200.06)	0.00
3	221.78	421.79	221.78	(200.01)	(400.07)	0.00
4	223.44	490.01	223.44	(266.57)	(666.64)	0.00
5	225.12	558.13	225.12	(333.01)	(999.65)	0.00
50	315.09	1,930.42	315.09	(1,615.33)	(64,444.79)	0.00
100	457.82	1,520.27	457.82	(1,062.46)	(130,879.07)	0.00
150	665.19	851.68	665.19	(186.49)	(163,337.65)	0.00
161	722.17	727.35	722.17	(5.18)	(164,288.15)	0.00
162	727.59	716.96	727.59	10.63	(164,277.53)	0.00
163	733.05	706.72	733.05	26.33	(164,251.20)	0.00
200	966.49	412.60	966.49	553.89	(152,986.07)	0.00
250	1,404.27	194.79	1,404.27	1,209.48	(108,618.11)	0.00
300	2,040.35	88.02	2,040.35	1,952.33	(29,870.86)	0.00
314	2,265.35	69.61	2,265.35	2,195.74	(735.60)	0.00
315	2,282.34	68.43	804.03	2,213.90	0.00	1,478.30
316	2,299.45	67.28	67.28	2,232.18	0.00	2,232.18
343	2,813.46	41.73	41.73	2,771.73	0.00	2,771.73
344	2,834.56	13.53	13.53	2,821.03	0.00	2,821.03
345	2,855.82	0.00	0.00	2,855.82	0.00	2,855.82
350	2,964.54	0.00	0.00	2,964.54	0.00	2,964.54
355	3,077.39	0.00	0.00	3,077.39	0.00	3,077.39
360	3,194.53	0.00	0.00	3,194.53	0.00	3,194.53

toward the support bond during these months is nil. In the 344th month the total principal received is $40.97. The outstanding balance for the PAC bond is $13.53. Consequently, the payment for the support bond is $27.44. Because the PAC bonds are fully paid off at this stage, in subsequent months all the principal that is received is directed to the support bond.

As is to be expected, the average life of the PAC bond continues to remain at 98.13 months; however, the average life of the support bond falls to 44.07 months. This highlights the protection provided by the support bond. In this case the entire impact of contraction due to the faster prepayment is absorbed by the support bond.

Now let us consider the prepayments at 0 PSA or, in other words, a situation corresponding to no prepayments (Table 9.31).

ANALYSIS

Until the 161st month the total principal received is inadequate to satisfy the PAC schedule. Consequently, the entire principal received is directed toward the PAC bond and the support bond does not receive any payment. The deficit with respect to the PAC schedule is accumulated until the end of the 161st month when it reaches a value of $164,228.15. From the 162nd until the 314th month the entire principal is directed to the PAC bond and the deficit is steadily reduced. At the end

TABLE 9.32   Principal Payments at 400 PSA

Month	Total Principal	Scheduled Payment to PAC Bond	Actual Payment to PAC Bond	Payment to Support Bond	Outstanding for Support Bond
1	485.99	285.18	285.18	200.81	122,299.19
2	756.32	353.50	353.50	402.82	121,896.37
3	1,027.31	421.79	421.79	605.52	121,290.85
4	1,298.44	490.01	490.01	808.43	120,482.42
5	1,569.15	558.13	558.13	1,011.02	119,471.40
40	5,282.47	2,026.39	2,026.39	3,256.08	1,426.02
41	5,160.49	2,016.56	3,734.47	1,426.02	0.00
42	5,041.32	2,006.79	5,041.32		
50	4,181.24	1,930.42	4,181.24		
100	1,289.82	1,520.27	1,289.82		
150	391.27	851.68	391.27		
200	115.53	412.60	115.53		
250	32.57	194.79	32.57		
300	8.42	88.02	8.42		
350	1.77	36.63	1.77		
360	1.23	30.24	1.23		

(continued)

(continued)

of the 314th month the cumulative deficit is $735.60. The scheduled payment for the PAC bond for the 315th month is $68.43. Consequently, a cash flow of $804.03 is directed to the PAC bond. The total cash flow for the month is $2,282.34. Thus $1,478.31 is directed to the support bond. From here on until the 344th month, the principal received is in excess of what is required to satisfy the PAC schedule, and consequently the excess is directed toward the support bond. The principal outstanding for the PAC bond as of the end of month 343 is $13.53. The principal received in month 344 is $2,834.56. Thus $2,821.03 is directed to the support bond at the end of this month. For all subsequent months, the entire principal received is directed to the support bond. The average life of the PAC bond is 214.83 months while that of the support bond is 339.10 months. Thus, although slower prepayment increases the average life of the bonds, the impact on the support bond, as is to be expected, is greater than the impact on the PAC bond.

Finally let us consider a scenario corresponding to 400 PSA (Table 9.32).

ANALYSIS

Until the 40th month the total principal received is in excess of what is required as per the PAC schedule and consequently the excess is directed to the support bond. As of the end of the 40th month the outstanding principal on the support bond is $1,426.02. Thus, in the 41st month this amount is directed to the support bond and the balance is directed to the PAC bond. With this, the support bond is fully paid off. Consequently, in subsequent months the entire principal received is directed to the PAC bond. The average life of the PAC bond is 70.43 months, while that of the support bond is 24.78 months.

CHAPTER 10

Swaps

INTRODUCTION

What exactly is a swap transaction? As the name suggests, it entails the exchanging or swapping of cash flows between two counterparties. There are two broad categories of swaps: interest rate swaps and currency swaps.

In the case of an interest rate swap, all payments are denominated in the same currency. Obviously, the two cash flows being exchanged will be calculated using different interest rates. For instance, one party may compute its payable using a fixed rate of interest, while the other may calculate what it owes based on a market benchmark such as LIBOR. Such interest rate swaps are referred to as fixed-floating swaps. A second possibility is that both payments may be based on variable or floating rates. For instance, the first party may compute its payable based on LIBOR while the counterparty may calculate what it owes based on the rate for a Treasury security. Such a swap is referred to as a floating-floating swap. It should be obvious to the reader that we cannot have a fixed-fixed swap in practice. For example, consider a deal where Bank ABC agrees to make a payment to the counterparty every six months on a given principal, at the rate of 5.25% per annum in return for a counterpayment based on the same principal that is computed at a rate of 6% per annum. Clearly, this is an arbitrage opportunity for Bank ABC, because what it owes every period will always be less than what is owed to it. No rational counterparty will therefore agree to such a contract. Thus, in the case of an interest rate swap, prior to the exchange of interest on a scheduled payment date, there must be a positive probability of a net payment being received for both the parties to the deal.

In the case of an interest rate swap, a principal amount needs to be specified to facilitate the computation of interest. There is no need, however, to physically exchange this principal at the outset. Therefore, the underlying principal amount in such transactions is referred to as a *notional principal*.

Now let us consider a currency swap. Such a contract also entails the payment of interest by two counterparties to each other, the difference being that the payments are denominated in two different currencies. Because there are two currencies involved there are three interest computation methods possible: fixed-fixed, fixed-floating, and floating-floating.

In Example 10.1 we illustrate the mechanics of a fixed-floating interest rate swap.

EXAMPLE 10.1

Consider two banks that are parties to a swap deal. Bank Exotica agrees to pay interest to Bank Halifax at the rate of 6.40% per annum on a principal of $2,500,000. In return, the counterparty agrees to pay Bank Exotica an amount that is computed on the same principal, but which is based on the LIBOR that prevails at the onset of the payment period. Obviously, this is a fixed-floating swap. We will assume that interest is payable at the end of every six months for a period of two years.

Assume that the observed values of LIBOR over a two-year horizon are as depicted in Table 10.1.

TABLE 10.1 6-M Libor as Observed at Six-Monthly Intervals

Time	LIBOR (per annum)
0	6.20%
6-months	6.55%
12-months	6.75%
18-months	6.10%

We will assume that the LIBOR used for computing the interest payable for a period will be the value observed at the start of the period, although the interest per se is payable at the end of the period. This is the common practice in financial markets and is referred to as a system of "determined in advance and paid in arrears." Rarely are we likely to observe a case of "determined in arrears and paid in arrears." The second method obviously entails payment based on the LIBOR prevailing at the end of the period for which the interest is due.

The periodic interest payable by Bank Exotica is:

$$2,500,000 \times 0.064 \times 0.5 = \$80,000$$

This amount will be invariant for the life of the swap. There are two reasons for this. The first is obviously the fact that the bank is paying interest based on a fixed rate. The second is that we are assuming that every six-monthly period corresponds to exactly one-half of a year. In practice the gap between successive interest payment dates may vary and would depend on the day-count convention that is assumed.

The periodic interest that is payable by Bank Halifax will obviously vary because the benchmark rate is variable. The interest payable by the bank for the first period is:

$$2,500,000 \times 0.0620 \times 0.50 = \$77,500$$

Thus, the net transfer at the end of the first six-monthly period is a cash flow of $2,500 from Bank Exotica to Bank Halifax.

The amounts payable by the two banks and the net payment at the end of every period are given in Table 10.2.

TABLE 10.2   Amounts Payable by the Two Counterparties

Time	Payment to Be Made by Bank Exotica	Payment to Be Made by Bank Halifax	Net Payment (to Be Made by Bank Exotica)
6-months	80,000	77,500	2,500
12-months	80,000	81,875	(1,875)
18-months	80,000	84,375	(4,375)
24-months	80,000	76,250	3,750

Consider the last column of Table 10.2. It describes the net payment to be made/received by Bank Exotica. Positive amounts indicate that Bank Exotica will experience a cash outflow; that is, what it owes is more than what it is owed. Amounts in parentheses indicate a net cash inflow, that is, what the bank owes is less than what is owed to it.

EXAMPLE 10.2

Now let us consider a currency swap. Bank Sud Afrique enters into a swap with Bank Oriental with the following terms. The two banks will first exchange South African Rands for US dollars at the rate of 12.50 USD-ZAR. The principal amount in USD is $2,400,000 and is payable by Bank Oriental in exchange for the South African currency. Subsequently every six months Bank Sud Afrique will pay interest at the rate of 4.75% per annum on the principal amount of $2,400,000. Bank Oriental, on the other hand, will pay interest at the rate of 7.25% per annum on the equivalent amount in ZAR. The terms of the deal specify that the two banks will exchange back the currencies at the end of two years, at the original spot rate.

The cash flows payable/receivable by the two banks are depicted in Table 10.3.

TABLE 10.3   Cash Flows for a Fixed-Fixed Currency Swap

Time	Payment by Bank Sud Afrique	Payment by Bank Oriental
0	30,000,000 ZAR	2,400,000 USD
6-months	57,000 USD	1,087,500 ZAR
12-months	57,000 USD	1,087,500 ZAR
18-months	57,000 USD	1,087,500 ZAR
24-months	57,000 USD	1,087,500 ZAR
24-months	2,400,000 USD	30,000,000 ZAR

(continued)

(continued)

CONTRACT TERMS

In swap contracts such as those discussed here, certain terms and conditions need to be specified at the very outset to avoid ambiguities and potential future conflicts.

- Every swap contract must clearly spell out the identities of the two counterparties to the deal. In our first illustration the two counterparties were Bank Exotica and Bank Halifax; in the second they were Bank Sud Afrique and Bank Oriental.
- The tenor of the swap. The tenor or maturity of the swap refers to the date on which the last exchange of cash flows between the two parties will take place. In both our illustrations above the tenor was two years. Unlike exchange-traded products like futures contracts, where the exchange specifies a maximum maturity for contracts on an asset, swaps being OTC products can have any maturity that is agreed upon by bilateral discussions.
- The interest rates on the basis of which the two parties have to make payments should be clearly spelled out. To avoid ambiguities the basis on which the cash inflow and the cash outflow are arrived at for both the counterparties should be explicitly stated.

    In the case of the interest rate swap in Table 10.1, Bank Exotica was a fixed-rate payer with the rate of interest being fixed at 6.40% per annum. Bank Halifax was a floating-rate payer with the amount payable based on the 6-M LIBOR prevalent at the start of the interest computation period.

    For currency swaps we need to specify the currencies in which the two parties will make payments to each other, in addition to the specification of the interest rates to be adopted by them. In our illustration of a currency swap in Table 10.2, Bank Sud Afrique was a fixed-rate payer with the interest payable in US dollars at the rate of 4.75% per annum. Bank Oriental too was a fixed-rate payer, the difference being that it was required to pay interest in South African rands at the rate of 7.25% per annum.
- The frequency with which the cash flows are to be exchanged has to be clearly defined. In our illustrations we assumed that cash flow exchanges would take place at six-monthly intervals. In the market such swaps are referred to as semi-semi swaps. Other contracts may entail payments on a quarterly basis or on an annual basis. The benchmark that is chosen for the floating-rate payment is usually based on the frequency of the exchange. For instance, a swap entailing the exchange of cash flows at six-monthly intervals will specify 6-month LIBOR as the benchmark, whereas a swap entailing the exchange of payments at 3-monthly intervals will specify the 3-month LIBOR as the benchmark. The most popular benchmark in the market is the 6-month LIBOR.
- The day-count convention that is used to compute the interest must be explicitly stated. In our illustration we assumed that every six-month period amounted to exactly one-half of a year. The underlying convention is referred to as 30/360. That is, every month is assumed to consist of 30 days and the year as a whole is assumed to consist of 360 days. Other possibilities include Actual/360 or Actual/365.

> - The principal amounts on the basis of which each party has to figure out the payment to the counterparty must be clearly stated. In the case of interest rate swaps there is obviously only one currency that is involved; however, the magnitude of the principal must still be specified to facilitate the computation of interest. In the case of currency swaps, the two currencies involved and the principal amounts in each have to be specified. That is, the rate of exchange at which the conversion between them is scheduled to be made should be clearly stated.

MARKET TERMINOLOGY

Let us first consider interest rate swaps. As we discussed, there are two possible counterpayments: fixed-floating and floating-floating. A swap where one of the rates is fixed is referred to as a *coupon swap*. On the other hand, a swap wherein both the parties are required to make payments based on varying rates is referred to as a *basis swap*. Thus, the IRS that we considered earlier, where Bank Exotica was required to pay at a fixed rate of 6.40% per annum in exchange for a payment from Bank Halifax that was based on LIBOR, is an example of a coupon swap.

In a coupon swap, the party which agrees to make payments based on a fixed rate is referred to as the *payer*, whereas the counterparty, which is committed to making payments on a floating-rate basis, is referred to as the *receiver*.[1] These terms cannot be used in the case of basis swaps, however, because both the cash flow streams are based on floating rates. In practice it is important to be explicit in order to avoid ambiguities. Thus, for each counterparty, both the rate on the basis of which it is scheduled to make payments and the rate on the basis of which it is scheduled to receive payments should be explicitly stated. For instance, in the case of the interest rate swap that we considered earlier, the terms would be stated somewhat as follows.

Counterparties: Bank Exotica and Bank Halifax

Interest Rate-1: A fixed rate of 6.40% to be paid by Bank Exotica to Bank Halifax.

Interest Rate-2: A variable rate based on the 6-month LIBOR prevailing at the onset of the corresponding six-monthly period, to be paid by Bank Halifax to Bank Exotica.

KEY DATES

There are four important dates for a swap. Consider the two-year swap between Bank Exotica and Bank Halifax. Assume that the swap was negotiated on 10 June 20XX with a specification that the first payments would be for a six-month period commencing on 15 June 20XX; 10 June will be referred to as the *transaction date*.

---

[1] In some swap markets the fixed rate payer is termed as the buyer and the counterparty is termed as the receiver.

The date from which the interest counterpayments start to accrue is termed as the *effective date*. In our illustration the effective date is 15 June.

Our swap by assumption has a tenor of two years and consequently the last exchange of payments will take place on 15 June 20(XX+2). This date will consequently be referred to as the *maturity date* of the swap. We will assume that the four exchanges of cash flows will occur on 15 December 20XX, 15 June 20(XX+1), 15 December 20(XX+1), and 15 June 20(XX+2). The first three dates, on which the floating rate will be reset for the next six-monthly period, are referred to as *reset* or *refixing* dates.

INHERENT RISK

An interest swap exposes both parties to interest rate risk. Let us consider the fixed-floating swap between Bank Exotica and Bank Halifax. For the fixed-rate payer, the risk is that the LIBOR may decline after the swap is entered into. If so, while the payments to be made by it would remain unchanged, its receipts will decline in magnitude. From the standpoint of the floating-rate payer, the risk is that the benchmark, in this case the LIBOR, may increase after the swap is agreed upon. If so, while its receipts would remain unchanged, its payables will increase. A priori we cannot be sure as to whether LIBOR will increase or decline. Consequently, ex ante both the parties to the contract are exposed to interest rate risk.

THE SWAP RATE

What exactly is the swap rate? The term refers to the fixed rate of interest that is applicable in a coupon swap. There are two conventions for quoting the interest rate. The first practice is to quote the full rate in percentage terms. This is referred to as an *all-in price*. In certain interbank markets, however, the practice is to quote the fixed rate as a difference or spread, in basis points, between the fixed rate and a benchmark interest rate. The benchmark that is used is the yield for a government security with a time to maturity equal to the tenor of the swap. The two methods can be best described with the help of an illustration.

EXAMPLE 10.3

Let us consider the interest rate swap between Bank Exotica and Bank Halifax wherein the former agreed to pay a fixed rate of 6.40% per annum. Such a specification is obviously a manifestation of an all-in price for the fixed rate is quoted in full.

Now consider an alternative scenario where the yield to maturity for a two-year T-note is 5.95% per annum. If so, the spread will be quoted as 45 basis points. The implication is that the fixed rate is 45 basis points greater than the yield on a security having the same maturity.

TABLE 10.4 Bid–Ask Quotes for Euro-denominated IRS

Tenor	Bid	Ask
1-Year	1.50%	1.55%
2-Year	1.70%	1.75%
3-Year	1.90%	1.95%
5-Year	2.25%	2.30%
10-Year	2.90%	2.95%
15-Year	3.25%	3.30%
25-Year	3.20%	3.25%

ILLUSTRATIVE SWAP RATES

Consider the hypothetical quotes for euro-denominated interest rate swaps on a given day, as shown in Table 10.4. Assume that the corresponding floating rate is the six-month Euribor.

Such a rate schedule, which is typically provided by a professional swap dealer, may be interpreted as follows. A swap dealer will give a two-way quote wherein the bid is the fixed rate at which he is willing to do a swap that requires him to pay the fixed rate. Obviously the ask represents the rate at which he will do a swap that requires him to receive the fixed rate. Quite obviously the spread must be positive.

DETERMINING THE SWAP RATE

Let us reconsider the coupon swap between Bank Exotica and Bank Halifax. The swap rate was arbitrarily assumed to be 6.40%. We will now demonstrate as to how this rate will be set in practice.

To understand the pricing of swaps, consider an alternative financial arrangement where Bank Exotica issues a fixed-rate bond with a principal of 2,500,000 US dollars and uses the proceeds to acquire a floating-rate bond with the same principal. Assume that the benchmark for the floating-rate bond is the 6-month LIBOR, and that both bonds pay coupons on a semiannual basis. The initial cash flow is zero because the proceeds of the fixed-rate issue will be just adequate to purchase the floating-rate security. Every six months the bank will receive a floating rate of interest based on the 6-month LIBOR on a principal amount of $2,500,000 and will have to make an interest payment for the same principal, based on a fixed rate of interest. When the two bonds mature, the amount received when the bank redeems the principal on the floating-rate bond held by it will be just adequate for it to repay the principal on the bond issued by it. The net cash flow at maturity is therefore zero. Thus, structurally this financial arrangement corresponds to an interest rate swap with a notional principal of $2,500,000 wherein the bank pays a fixed rate of interest every six months in return for an interest stream that is based on the 6-month LIBOR. To ensure that the combination of the two bonds exactly matches the structure of the swap, we need to assume that the bonds also pay coupons based on the same day-count convention, which in this case has been assumed to be 30/360.

TABLE 10.5   Observed Term Structure

Time to Maturity	Interest Rate per Annum
6-months	5.25%
12-months	5.40%
18-months	5.75%
24-months	6.00%

We will now demonstrate how the fixed rate of a coupon swap can be determined. Let us assume that the term structure for LIBOR is as shown in Table 10.5.

These interest rates need to be converted to discount factors, which can be done as follows.[2] The discount factor for the first payment (after six months) is

$$\frac{1}{\left(1 + \dfrac{0.0525}{2}\right)} = 0.9744$$

The remaining discount factors may be computed as follows.

$$\frac{1}{\left(1 + \dfrac{0.0540}{2}\right)^2} = 0.9481$$

$$\frac{1}{\left(1 + \dfrac{0.0575}{2}\right)^3} = 0.9185$$

$$\frac{1}{\left(1 + \dfrac{0.0600}{2}\right)^4} = 0.8885$$

Because we are at the start of a coupon period, the price of the floating-rate bond should be equal to the principal value of $2,500,000. The issue is, therefore, what is the coupon rate that will make the fixed-rate bond have the same value at the outset? Let us denote the annual coupon in dollars by C.

Thus, we require that

$$\frac{C}{2} \times [0.9744 + 0.9481 + 0.9185 + 0.8885] + 2,500,000 \times 0.8885 = 2,500,000$$

$$\Rightarrow \frac{C}{2} = \$74,741.92$$

$$\Rightarrow C = \$149,483.85$$

This obviously implies that the coupon rate is

$$c = \frac{149483.85}{2,500,000} = 0.059794 \equiv 5.9794\%$$

---

[2]The discount factor for a given maturity is the present value of a dollar to be received at the end of the stated period.

TABLE 10.6   Discount Factors as per Market Convention

Time to Maturity	Discount Factor
6-months	0.9744
12-months	0.9488
18-months	0.9206
24-months	0.8929

THE MARKET METHOD

The convention in the LIBOR market is that if the number of days for which the rate is quoted is N, then the corresponding discount factor is given by

$$\frac{1}{\left(1 + i \times \dfrac{N}{360}\right)}$$

For instance, consider the 18-month rate of 5.75%. The corresponding discount factor is

$$\frac{1}{\left(1 + i \times \dfrac{540}{360}\right)} = \frac{1}{\left(1 + 0.0575 \times \dfrac{540}{360}\right)} = 0.9206$$

The vector of discount factors for our example is shown in Table 10.6. The corresponding swap rate is 5.7323%.

VALUATION OF A SWAP DURING ITS LIFE

Let us consider the swap between Bank Exotica and Bank Halifax. Assume that two months have elapsed since the swap was entered into, and that the current term structure of interest rates is as given in Table 10.7. We have used the market method for computing the discount factors.

TABLE 10.7   The Term Structure of Interest Rate After Two Months

Time to Maturity	Interest Rate per annum	Discount Factor
4-months	5.50%	0.9820
10-months	5.80%	0.9539
16-months	6.05%	0.9254
22-months	6.25%	0.8972

The value of the fixed-rate bond can be obtained using the following equation.

$$\frac{C}{2} \times [0.9820 + 0.9539 + 0.9254 + 0.8972] + 2,500,000 \times 0.8972$$

$$= 74,741.92 \times 3.7584 + 2,500,000 + 0.8972$$

$$= \$2,523,910$$

The value of the floating-rate bond may be computed as follows. The next coupon is known for it would have been set at time zero, that is, two months prior to the date of valuation. The magnitude of this coupon is

$$0.0525 \times 2,500,000 \times \frac{1}{2} = \$65,625$$

Once this coupon is paid, the value of the bond will revert back to its face value of 2,500,000. Thus, the value of this bond after four months will be $2,565,625. Consequently, its value today is:

$$2,565,625 \times 0.9820 = \$2,519,444$$

From the standpoint of the fixed-rate payer, the swap is equivalent to a long position in a floating-rate bond that is combined with a short position in a fixed-rate bond. Thus, the value of the swap for the fixed-rate payer is:

$$2,519,444 - 2,523,910 = (\$4,466)$$

That is, because the value of the fixed-rate liability is higher than that of the floating-rate asset, the value of the swap for Bank Exotica, the fixed-rate payer, is negative. What this implies is that if the bank were to seek a cancellation of the original swap, with the consent of the counterparty of course, it would have to pay $4,466 to the counterparty.

From the standpoint of the counterparty, the value of the swap is $4,466. Thus, in the event of cancellation of the contract it will get a cash flow of this magnitude from Bank Exotica.

TERMINATING A SWAP

As we have just seen, one way to exit from an existing swap contract is by having it canceled with the approval of the counterparty. This will entail an inflow or outflow of the value of the swap depending on how interest rates have moved since the last periodic cash flow was exchanged. In market parlance this is known as a *buyback* or *close-out*. In our illustration, Bank Exotica would have to pay $4,466 to Bank Halifax to close out the contract. In practice Bank Exotica will have the option of selling the swap to a party other than Bank Halifax, which is the original counterparty. This would of course require the approval of Bank Halifax. In this case as well, the party who buys the swap from the bank will expect to be paid the value of the swap, which is $4,466 in this case.

Another way for Bank Exotica to exit from its commitment would be to do an opposite swap with a third party. That is, it would have to do a 22-month swap with a party wherein it pays LIBOR and receives the fixed rate. This is known as a *reversal*.

It must be remembered that if it were to do so, there would be two swaps in existence. So, Bank Exotica would be exposed to credit risk from the standpoint of both counterparties.

THE ROLE OF BANKS IN THE SWAP MARKET

In the early years, when the swap market was evolving, it was a standard practice for banks to play the role of an intermediary. That is, they would bring together two counterparties in return for what was termed as an *arrangement fee*. As the market has evolved, such arrangement fees have become extremely rare, except perhaps for contracts which are very exotic or unusual.

These days most banks will don the mantle of a principal party. The reasons why they are required to do so are twofold. The first is that nonbank counterparties are reluctant to reveal their identity when entering into such deals. Consequently, they are more comfortable dealing with a bank while negotiating such contracts. The second reason is that for most parties to such transactions it is easier to evaluate the credit risk while dealing with a bank than while negotiating with a nonbank counterparty. And, as we have seen, swaps being OTC transactions always carry an element of counterparty risk.

In the days when the market was in its infancy, banks would primarily do reversals. That is, they would, for instance, do a fixed-floating deal with a party only if they were hopeful of immediately concluding a floating-fixed deal for the same tenor with a third party. Parties that carry equal and offsetting swaps in their books are said to be running a *matched book*. As we have seen earlier, such parties are exposed to default risk from both the counterparties. These days banks are less finicky about maintaining such a matched position, and in most cases are willing to take on the inherent exposure for the period until they can eventually locate a party for an offsetting transaction.

MOTIVATION FOR THE SWAP

A party to a swap may enter into the contract with a speculative motive or with an incentive to hedge. Such transactions may also be used to undertake what is known as credit arbitrage arising due to the comparative advantage enjoyed by the participating institutions. We will analyze each of these potential uses.

Speculation

Morgan Bank and Brown Brothers Bank are both players in the US capital market, but with different expectations as to where interest rates are headed. Morgan is of the view that rates are likely to steadily decline over the next two years, while Brown Brothers is of the opinion that rates are likely to rise steadily over the same period. Assume that they enter into a coupon swap with a tenor of 2 years wherein Morgan agrees to pay interest at LIBOR every three months on a notional principal of $100MM, while Brown Brothers agrees to pay interest on the same notional principal and with the same frequency, but at a fixed rate of z% per annum.

Quite obviously both parties are speculating on the interest rate. If Morgan is right and rates do decline as it anticipates, Morgan's floating-rate payments are likely to be lower than its fixed-rate receipts, thereby leading to net cash inflows. If Brown Brothers is correct, however, and rates rise steadily as anticipated, its floating-rate receipts are likely to be in excess of its fixed-rate payments, thereby leading to net cash inflows. Because both parties are speculating, ex post one will stand vindicated while the other will have to countenance a loss.

Hedging

Swaps can be used as a hedge against anticipated interest rate movements. Donutz, a company based in Detroit, has taken a loan from First National Bank at a rate of LIBOR + 75 b.p. The company is worried that rates are going to increase and seeks to hedge by converting its liability into an effective fixed-rate loan. One way to do so in practice would be to renegotiate the loan and have it converted to a loan carrying a fixed rate of interest. This may not, however, be easy in real life. There will be a lot of administrative and legal issues and related costs. Consequently, it may be easier in practice for the company to negotiate a coupon swap wherein it pays fixed and receives LIBOR.

Assume that Morgan Bank agrees to enter into a swap with Donutz wherein it will pay LIBOR in return for a fixed interest stream based on a rate of 5.75% per annum.

The net result from the standpoint of Donutz may be analyzed as follows.

- Outflow-1 (Interest on the original loan): LIBOR + 75b.p.
- Inflow-1 (Receipt from Morgan Bank): LIBOR
- Outflow-2 (Payment to Morgan Bank): 5.75%
- Net Outflow: 5.75% + 0.75% = 6.50% per annum

Thus, the company has converted its loan to an effective fixed-rate liability carrying interest at the rate of 6.50% per annum.

COMPARATIVE ADVANTAGE AND CREDIT ARBITRAGE

At times there are situations where, despite being at a disadvantage from the standpoint of interest payments with respect to another party, a party in the market for fixed-rate and variable-rate debt may still enjoy a comparative advantage in one of the two.

For instance, assume that Infosys, a software company based in San Jose, can borrow at a fixed rate of 7.50% per annum and at a variable rate of LIBOR + 125 b.p. IBM is in a position to borrow at a fixed rate of 6% per annum and a variable rate of LIBOR + 60 b.p. Thus, Infosys has to pay 150 b.p more as compared to IBM if it borrows at a fixed rate, but only 65 basis points more if it borrows at a floating rate. We say that although IBM enjoys an absolute advantage from the standpoint of borrowing in terms of both fixed-rate and floating-rate debt, Infosys has a comparative advantage if it borrows on a floating-rate basis.

Assume that Infosys wants to borrow at a fixed rate while IBM would like to borrow at a floating rate. It can be demonstrated that an interest rate swap can be used to lower the effective borrowing costs for both parties, as compared to what they would have had to pay in the absence of it.

Let us assume that IBM borrows 10MM dollars at a fixed rate of 6% per annum, while Infosys borrows the same amount at LIBOR + 125 b.p. The two parties can then enter into a swap wherein Infosys agrees to pay interest on a notional principal of 10MM at the rate of 5.75% per annum in exchange for a payment based on LIBOR from IBM. The effective interest rate for the two parties may be computed as follows.

IBM: 6% + LIBOR − 5.75% = LIBOR + 25 b.p.

Infosys: LIBOR + 125 b.p, + 5.75% − LIBOR = 7.00%

Thus, IBM has a saving of 35 basis points on the floating-rate debt whereas Infosys has a saving of 50 b.p on the fixed-rate debt. What exactly does this cumulative saving of 85 basis points represent? IBM has an advantage of 1.50% in the market for fixed-rate debt and 65 basis points in the market for floating-rate debt. The difference of 85 basis points manifests itself as the savings for both parties considered together.

Now let us introduce a bank into the picture. Assume that IBM borrows at a rate of 6% per annum and enters into a swap with First National Bank wherein it has to pay LIBOR in return for a fixed-rate stream based on a rate of 5.65%. Infosys, on the other hand, borrows at LIBOR + 125 b.p and enters into a swap with the same bank wherein it receives LIBOR in return for payment of 5.85%.

The net result of the transaction may be summarized as follows.

IBM: Effective interest paid = 6% + LIBOR − 5.65% = LIBOR + 35 b.p.

Infosys: Effective interest paid = LIBOR + 125 b.p. + 5.85% − LIBOR = 7.10%

First National Bank: Profit from the transaction = LIBOR − 5.65% − LIBOR + 5.85% = 20 b.p.

The difference in this case is that the comparative advantage of 85 basis points has been split three ways. IBM saves 25 basis points, Infosys saves 40 basis points, and the bank makes a profit of 20 basis points.

It must be pointed out that the transaction that entails a role for the bank is more realistic in practice, as opposed to a deal where the two companies identify and directly enter into a swap with each other.

SWAP QUOTATIONS

The swap rate in the market can be quoted in four different ways.[3] First, there are two possibilities with respect to the interest payments, that is, they may be either on an annual basis or on a semiannual basis. The second issue is that payments may be

---

[3] See Coyle (2001).

settled either on a money market or on a bond market basis, the difference being that the first convention is based on a 360-day year and an Actual/360 day-count convention, while the second is based on a 365-day year and an Actual/365 day-count convention.

Quotes on a semiannual basis can be converted to equivalent values on an annual basis and vice versa. The following examples illustrate the required procedures.

EXAMPLE 10.4

The fixed rate for a swap is given as 7.25% per annum payable semiannually. To convert this to the corresponding value for an annual pay basis, we need to find the effective annual rate. This is given by

$$\left(1 + \frac{0.0725}{2}\right)^2 - 1$$

$$= 0.0738 \equiv 7.38\%$$

Now consider a situation where the fixed rate is quoted as 7.25% per annum payable annually. To convert this to an equivalent rate for a semiannual pay basis, we need to find the nominal annual rate that will yield 7.25% on an effective annual basis if compounding is undertaken semiannually.

This may be calculated as

$$\left(1 + \frac{r}{2}\right)^2 = 1.0725$$

$$\Rightarrow \frac{r}{2} = (1.0725)^{0.50} - 1$$

$$r = 2 \times 0.0356 = 0.0712 \equiv 7.12\%$$

In practice, the fixed rates payable are quoted on a bond basis while floating rates are quoted on a money market basis. To convert from a bond basis to a money market basis, we have to multiply the quote by 360/365, whereas if we were to seek to do the reverse, we should multiply by 365/360.

MATCHED PAYMENTS

Numero Uno Corporation has issued bonds carrying a coupon of 6.25% per annum, and it is of the opinion that market rates could decline. Consequently, it wishes to undertake a swap wherein it has to pay floating and receive fixed. Assume that the bonds pay interest on a semiannual basis and that the swap too entails six-monthly exchange of cash flows. The principal of the bonds is assumed to be 10MM as is the notional principal of the swap.

We will assume that Bank Deux is willing to arrange a swap that is suitable for Numero Uno, but with a swap rate of 5.80% per annum. The company, however, wants a fixed payment of $312,500 to match the cash outflow on account of the bonds issued by it. In practice, Bank Deux would accommodate the request as follows.

Because Numero Uno wants to receive a higher fixed payment, as compared to what it would ordinarily have received, it must compensate the bank in the form of a positive spread with respect to the floating-rate payment that it is required to make. In this case, the difference in the fixed-rate payments is $45,000 per annum, which corresponds to 45 basis points. Thus, the bank will require Numero Uno to make a payment based on a rate of LIBOR + 45 basis points while making the floating counterpayment every six months.

AMORTIZING SWAPS

Unlike a plain-vanilla interest rate swap where the notional principal remains fixed for the life of the swap, in the case of an amortizing swap the principal steadily declines. Let's revisit the data in Table 10.5. We had assumed that the notional principal was $2,500,000. Assume the notional principal declines by $625,000 at the end of every six months. The fixed rate may be determined as follows.

$$[(0.5 \times c \times 2,500,000) + 625,000] \times 0.9744 + [(0.5 \times c \times 1,875,000) + 625,000] \times 0.9481$$

$$+[(0.5 \times c \times 1,250,000) + 625,000] \times 0.9185 + [(0.5 \times c \times 625,000) + 625,000] \times 0.8885$$

$$= 2,500,000$$

The fixed rate comes out to be 5.71% per annum.

EXTENDABLE AND CANCELABLE SWAPS

An extendable swap confers the right to extend the maturity of the swap to one of the two counterparties in a swap. Usually, this right is given to the party paying the fixed rate of interest. Obviously, the party paying the fixed rate will exercise this option in a rising interest rate environment. In such a situation, while this party will continue to pay a fixed rate, the counterpayments it received will steadily increase. Because this party holds an option, it must pay for it. Consequently, the fixed rate in the case of such swaps will be higher than the rate in the case of plain-vanilla interest rate swaps.

A cancelable swap gives one of the counterparties the right to terminate the swap prematurely. If the right is given to the fixed-rate payer, it is called a callable swap, whereas if it is given to the floating-rate payer, it is called a putable swap. A callable swap will be terminated by the fixed-rate payer if rates are expected to decline, whereas a putable swap will be terminated by the fixed-rate receiver if rates are expected to increase. Consequently, the fixed rate for a callable swap will be higher than that of a plain-vanilla swap, whereas the fixed rate for a putable swap will be lower that of a plain-vanilla swap.

SWAPTIONS

A swaption represents an option on a swap. A payer swaption gives the holder the right to enter into a coupon swap as a fixed-rate payer. On the other hand, a receiver swaption gives the holder the right to enter into a coupon swap as a fixed-rate receiver.

The buyer of a swaption has to pay a premium to the writer. The exercise price for such derivatives is an interest rate. A payer swaption will be exercised only if the prevailing swap rate is higher than the exercise price; however, a receiver swaption will be exercised only if the prevailing swap rate is lower than the exercise price. A swaption may be of a European or an American variety.

CURRENCY SWAPS

A currency swap is like an interest rate swap in the sense that it requires two counterparties to commit themselves to the exchange of cash flows at prespecified intervals. The difference in this case is that the two cash flow streams are denominated in two different currencies. The two counterparties also agree to exchange at the end of the stated time period, or the maturity date of the swap, the corresponding principal amounts computed at an exchange rate that is fixed right at the outset.[4]

As we mentioned earlier, because the counterpayments are denominated in two different currencies, there are three possibilities from the standpoint of interest computation. That is, these swaps may be on any of the following bases.

- Fixed rate–fixed rate
- Fixed rate–floating rate
- Floating rate–floating rate

EXAMPLE 10.5

Bank Atlantic and Bank Europeana agree to execute a contract wherein over a period of two years they will exchange cash flows denominated in US dollars and the euro. As per the terms of the agreement, Bank Atlantic will make a payment at the end of every six months denominated in euros, at an interest rate of 4.25% per annum. The payments will be based on a principal amount of 6MM euros. Bank Europeana, on the other hand, will make payments at the same frequency but denominated in dollars and with an interest rate of 5.40% per annum. These payments will be based on a principal of 7.50MM dollars.

At the end of the two-year period, Bank Atlantic will pay 6MM euros to Bank Europeana, which in turn will make a counterpayment of 7.50MM dollars. The implicit exchange rate of 0.8000 USD-EUR is fixed right at the outset and is typically the spot rate of exchange prevailing in the currency market at that point in time.

A currency swap always requires an exchange of principal at the time of maturity; however, there do exist contracts which entail an exchange of principal twice – that is, at inception and at maturity. Such swaps are referred to as *cash swaps*.

---

[4]See Geroulanos (1998).

We will assume that the swap described in the above illustration is a cash swap. Such a contract will typically entail the following transactions.

- Bank Atlantic will borrow 7.50MM USD in New York.
- Bank Europeana will borrow 6.00M euros in Frankfurt.
- Bank Atlantic will transfer the dollars to Bank Europeana in exchange for the equivalent payment denominated in euros.
- On the maturity date of the swap, the principal amounts will be swapped back. In most cases the terminal exchange is based on the exchange rate that was prevailing at the outset, or in other words, the same exchange rate as was used to compute the initial exchange of principal. In our illustration, therefore, we will assume that Bank Atlantic will make a payment of 6MM euros to Bank Europeana after two years, in exchange for a cash flow of 7.50MM dollars. Such a swap where the same amount of principal is exchanged is known as a *par swap*.[5]
- At the end of two years Bank Atlantic would use the dollars received by it to repay the US dollar–denominated loan that it had taken two years prior.
- Bank Europeana would use the euros received by it to repay the loan that it had taken in Frankfurt two years earlier.

As can be perceived from the illustration, a swap transaction such as this enables each party to service the debt of the counterparty. Bank Atlantic has taken a dollar-denominated loan. It will service it using the dollar-denominated payments that it receives every six months from Bank Europeana. Similarly, Bank Europeana has taken a loan denominated in euros, which it will service using the euro-denominated payments it receives periodically from Bank Atlantic.

CROSS-CURRENCY SWAPS

Technically speaking the term *currency swap* is applicable only for transactions that entail the exchange of cash flows computed on a fixed-rate–fixed-rate basis, such as the deal that we have just studied. Currency swaps where one or both payments are based on a floating rate of interest should strictly speaking be termed as *cross-currency* swaps. Within cross-currency swaps, we make a distinction between coupon swaps that are on a fixed-rate–floating-rate basis and basis swaps on a floating-rate–floating-rate basis.

VALUATION

We will explore the mechanics of currency swap valuation by focusing on the swap between Bank Atlantic and Bank Europeana. The swap may be viewed as a combination of the following transactions. Assume that Bank Atlantic has issued a fixed-rate

---

[5]See Geroulanos (1998).

bond in euros with a principal of €6MM and converted the proceeds to dollars at the spot rate of 0.8000 USD-EUR. The proceeds in dollars can be perceived as having been invested in fixed-rate bonds denominated in dollars. From the perspective of the counterparty the transaction may be perceived as follows. Assume that Bank Europeana has issued fixed-rate dollar-denominated bonds with a face value of $7.50MM, converted the proceeds to euros at the prevailing spot rate, and invested the equivalent in euros in fixed-rate bonds in that currency. Thus, every six months Bank Atlantic will receive interest in dollars and pay interest in euros, while Bank Europeana will pay interest in dollars and receive interest in euros. Thus, a currency swap between two parties is equivalent to a combination of transactions in which each party issues a bond in one currency to the other and uses the proceeds to acquire a bond issued by the counterparty. Quite obviously the fixed rate that is applicable in either currency is the coupon rate that is associated with a par bond in that currency, as we have seen in the case of fixed-floating interest rate swaps. Because two currencies are involved, however, we need the term structure of interest rates for both currencies.

Consider the data given in Table 10.8.

The value of the fixed rate for USD may be determined as follows. Consider a bond with a face value of $2.50MM. The coupon for a par bond denominated in USD is given by:

$$\frac{C}{2} \times [0.9792 + 0.9579 + 0.9335 + 0.9158] + 2,500,000 \times 0.9158$$

$$= 2,500,000$$

$$\Rightarrow \frac{C}{2} = \$55,593.70$$

$$\Rightarrow C = \$111,187.40$$

This corresponds to a rate of 4.4475% per annum.

Similarly, we can compute the coupon for a bond denominated in euros.

$$\frac{C}{2} \times [0.9814 + 0.9653 + 0.9535 + 0.9346] + 2,500,000 \times 0.9346$$

$$= 2,500,000$$

$$\Rightarrow \frac{C}{2} = \$42,635.86$$

$$\Rightarrow C = \$85,271.72$$

This corresponds to a coupon of 3.4109% per annum.

TABLE 10.8 Term Structure for US Dollars and the Euro

Time to Maturity	USD-LIBOR	Discount Factor	Euro-LIBOR	Discount Factor
6-months	4.25%	0.9792	3.80%	0.9814
12-months	4.40%	0.9579	3.60%	0.9653
18-months	4.75%	0.9335	3.25%	0.9535
24-months	4.60%	0.9158	3.50%	0.9346

If the swap had been such that the rate for dollars was fixed while that for the payment in euros was variable, then the applicable rate would be 4.4475% for the dollar-denominated payments and LIBOR for the counterpayments. On the other hand, if the rate were to be fixed for the payments in euros and variable for the dollar-denominated payments, the applicable rate would be LIBOR for the payment in dollars and 3.4109 for the payments in euros. Finally, if payments in both currencies were to be on a floating-rate basis, it would be LIBOR for LIBOR.

CURRENCY RISKS

A currency swap, as we would expect, exposes both the parties to currency risk. Let us consider the swap where Bank Atlantic borrows and makes a payment of $7.50MM to Bank Europeana in return for a counterpayment of €6.00MM. The exchange rate for the cash flow swap was 0.8000 USD-EUR.

At maturity Bank Europeana would pay back $7.50MM to the US bank and would receive €6.00 MM in return. Let us assume that in the intervening three years, the dollar has appreciated to 0.8125 USD-EUR. Bank Atlantic would benefit from the fact that the terminal exchange of principal is based on the original exchange rate of 0.8000 USD-EUR. If 6MM euros were to be converted at the prevailing rate of 0.8125 USD-EUR, Bank Atlantic would stand to receive only $7,384,615. Therefore, the counterparty slated to receive the currency that has appreciated during the life of the swap stands to gain from the fact that the terminal exchange of principal is based on the exchange rate prevailing at the outset, while the other party stands to lose. In our illustration, while Bank Atlantic avoids a loss of $115,385 USD, Bank Europeana forgoes an opportunity to save an identical amount.

HEDGING WITH CURRENCY SWAPS

An interest rate swap can be used as a mechanism for hedging foreign currency exposure. Telekurs, a telecom company based in Frankfurt, has issued a Yankee bond for $25MM, carrying interest at the rate of 6% per annum payable semiannually. The bonds have four years to maturity and the company seeks to hedge its exposure to the US dollar-Euro exchange rate, because all its income is primarily denominated in euros. Assume that the current exchange rate is 0.8000 USD-EUR.

The company can use an interest rate swap to hedge its currency exposure. Because it has a payable in US dollars, it needs a contract wherein it will receive cash flow in dollars and make payments in euros. If the company is of the opinion that rates in the eurozone are likely to rise, it can negotiate a swap wherein it makes a fixed-rate-based payment in euros to a counterparty in exchange for a fixed-rate-based income stream in dollars. The dollar inflows should be structured to match the company's projected outflows in that currency. This will lead to a situation where its exposure to the dollar is perfectly hedged.

CHAPTER 11

Mutual Funds, ETFs, and Pension Funds

INTRODUCTION

What is a mutual fund? A mutual fund can be defined as a collection of stocks, bonds, or other securities such as precious metals and real estate that is purchased by a pool of individual investors and managed by a professional investment company.

When investors make an investment in a mutual fund, their money is pooled with that of other investors who have chosen to invest in the fund. The pooled sum is used to build an investment portfolio if the fund is just commencing its operations, or to expand its portfolio if it is already in business. All investors receive shares of the fund in proportion to the amount of money they have invested. Every share that an investor owns represents a proportional interest in the portfolio of securities managed by the fund.

When a fund is offering shares for the first time, known as an IPO, the shares will be issued at par. Subsequent issues of shares will be made at a price that is based on what is known as the Net Asset Value (NAV) of the fund. The Net Asset Value of a fund at any point in time is equal to the total value of all securities in its portfolio less any outstanding liabilities, divided by the total number of shares issued by the firm.

The NAV will fluctuate from day to day as the value of the securities held by the fund changes. On a given day, from the perspective of shareholders, the NAV may be higher or lower than the price that they paid per share at the time of acquisition. Thus, just like the shareholders of a corporation, mutual fund owners share in the profits and losses as well as in the income and expenses of the fund.

PROS AND CONS OF INVESTING IN A FUND

Why would investors prefer to invest in a mutual fund rather than invest directly in financial assets using the secondary markets? First, as compared to a typical individual investor, a mutual fund by definition has a large amount of funds at its disposal. Consequently, given the size of its typical investment, its transactions costs tend to be much lower. Such costs need to be measured not just in terms of the commissions which have to be paid every time a security is bought or sold, but also in terms of the time required to manage a portfolio. To handle a portfolio successfully, an enormous amount of research is required and elaborate records have to be maintained. This is particularly important from the standpoint of investors who seek to build a well-diversified portfolio of financial assets. The costs involved in investing a limited amount of funds across a spectrum of assets can be prohibitive. On the other hand, by investing in the shares of a mutual fund, investors effectively ensure that their money is invested across a pool of assets, while at the same time they are able to take advantage of reduced transactions costs. Yet another feature of mutual funds is that they can afford to employ a team of well-qualified and experienced professionals who can evaluate the merits of investment in a particular asset before committing funds. Most individual investors lack such expertise, and cannot afford to hire the services of people with such skill sets.

Mutual funds diversify their assets by investing in a number of securities. Individual investors can, if they so desire, take diversification one step further by investing in funds promoted by several different investment companies. Most funds engage full-time investment managers who are responsible for obtaining and conducting the needed research and financial analyses required to select the securities that are to be included in the fund's portfolio. Fund managers are responsible for all facets of the fund's portfolio such as: asset diversification; buying and selling decisions; risk-return tradeoffs; investment performance; and nitty-gritty details involved in providing periodic account statements and end-of-the-year tax data to the shareholders.

Liquidity is another of the major benefits of investing in a mutual fund. If the market for a stock or a bond is not very deep, an investor holding such a security may not be able to sell it easily and quickly. It may often be easier to sell the shares of a mutual fund that has invested in such shares and bonds.

Investing in a mutual fund, however, is not without its disadvantages. First, investors in a mutual fund have no control over the cost of investing in the market. As long as they remain invested in a fund, they have to pay the required investment management fees. In practice, such fees must be continued to be paid even though the value of the assets of the fund may be declining. Moreover, mutual funds incur sales and marketing expenditures, which will eventually get passed on to the investors, as you will see shortly. An individual investing alone will obviously not have to incur such costs. Second, when investors invest in securities via the mutual fund route, they are delegating the choice of securities to be held to the professional fund manager. Thus, investors lose the option to design a portfolio to meet their specific objectives. This may not be satisfactory for High-Net-Worth (HNW) investors or corporate investors. In practice, mutual fund managers try to remedy this shortcoming by offering a number of different schemes, which are essentially a family of funds in which each member fund has been set up with a different objective.

The availability of this kind of a choice may itself pose a problem to certain investors. They may once again need expert advice regarding which scheme to select, as in a situation where an investor is contemplating which financial security to invest in.

SHARES AND UNITS

In the United States, mutual funds are set up as companies and issue shares to their investors. In some countries, the funds are set up as trusts and consequently issue units to their investors. We will use the terms *shares* and *units* interchangeably.

OPEN-END VERSUS CLOSED-END FUNDS

In the case of an open-end fund, investors can buy or sell shares of the fund from/to the fund itself at any point in time. The purchase/sale price at which they can transact is called the Net Asset Value (NAV). The NAV of a fund is determined once daily at the close of trading on that day. All new investments into the fund or withdrawals from the fund in the course of a day are priced at the NAV that was computed at the close of that day. As the market prices of the securities in which a fund has invested fluctuate, so will the NAV and the total value of the fund.

The number of shares outstanding at any point in time can subsequently either go up or go down, depending on whether additional shares are issued, or existing shares repurchased. In other words, the *unit capital* of an open-end fund is not fixed but variable. The fund size and its investable corpus will go up if the number of new subscriptions by new/existing investors exceeds the number of redemptions by existing investors. The fund size and corpus, however, will stand reduced if the redemptions exceed the fresh subscriptions.

An open-end fund need not always stand ready to issue fresh shares. Many successful funds stop further subscriptions after they reach a target size. This would be the case if they were to feel that further growth cannot be managed without adversely affecting the profitability of the fund; however, open-end funds rarely deny investors the facility to redeem shares held by them.

Every mutual fund will maintain a cash reserve that is usually about 5% of the total assets of the firm. These funds are reserved to cover shareholders' redemption requests. Should the amount required for redemption exceed the money available, however, the fund manager will have to liquidate some of the securities to obtain the necessary cash.

Closed-end funds, also known as publicly traded investment funds, are similar to open-end funds in the sense that they too provide professional expertise and portfolio diversification; however, such funds make a one-time sale of a fixed number of shares at the time of the IPO. Consequently, their *unit capital* remains fixed. Unlike open-end funds, they do not allow investors to buy or redeem units from/with them. In order to provide liquidity to investors, however, many closed-end funds list themselves on a stock exchange. If a fund were to be listed on an exchange, then investors can buy and sell its shares through a broker, just the way they buy and sell shares of other listed companies. The price of a fund's shares need not be equal to its NAV in this case. The shares may trade at a discount or a premium to the NAV based on the investors' perceptions about its future performance and other market factors affecting its shares' demand or supply. Shares selling below the NAV are said to be *trading at a discount*, while those trading above the NAV are said to be *trading at a premium*. Shares of unlisted closed-end funds can be traded over the counter.

The fund charters of closed-end funds contain what are called *life boat provisions*. These provisions require such funds to take action in cases where the shares are trading at a substantial discount to the NAV, by either buying back the shares via a tender offer or converting the fund to an open-ended structure. If the fund managers fail to respond in an appropriate fashion, dissident shareholders can buy large blocks of shares and initiate a proxy fight in order to either liquidate the assets of the fund or make it open-ended.

A critical feature of such funds is that the subscribers to the IPO bear the entire cost of underwriting and marketing incurred by the fund at the time of the issue. This is because the fund's investable corpus at the outset is equal to the amount raised via the IPO less the issuance costs. Such costs include selling fees paid to the retail brokerage firms that sell the shares to the public. The high commission rates on offer provide a strong incentive to brokers to recommend these funds to their clients. At the same time, because they can reduce the investable corpus substantially, these commissions provide a disincentive to the potential investors from the standpoint of subscribing to the IPO.

PREMIUM/DISCOUNT OF A CLOSED-END FUND

The premium or discount of a fund may be calculated as

$$[\text{Market Price} - \text{NAV}] \div \text{NAV}$$

Thus, if the NAV is $20 and the price in the market is $19, the discount is

$$(19 - 20)/20 \equiv 5\%$$

UNIT TRUSTS

Unit trusts, also known as *unit investment trusts*, are similar to closed-end funds in the sense that they are capitalized only once and consequently their *unit capital* remains fixed. Most unit trusts usually invest in bonds; however, they differ from a conventional mutual fund in one critical respect. Once the portfolio of securities (bonds) is assembled by the sponsor of the unit trust, where the sponsor is usually a brokerage firm or a bond underwriter, the bonds are held until they are redeemed by the issuer of the debt. Thus, there is no trading of the securities that comprise the portfolio held by a unit trust. Usually, the only time the trustee of a unit trust can sell a bond held by the trust is if there is a significant decline in the credit quality of the issue. Due to the lack of active trading, the cost of operating a unit trust is considerably less than the costs incurred by open-end and closed-end funds. Second, most unit trusts have a fixed termination date. And finally, unlike an investor in a mutual fund who is constantly exposed to a changing portfolio composition, an investor in a unit trust knows from the outset the exact composition of the investment portfolio of the trust. In some markets, such funds are referred to as *fixed maturity plans*.

CALCULATING THE NAV

A mutual fund is a common investment vehicle in the sense that the assets of the fund belong directly to the investors. Investors' subscriptions are accounted for as unit capital. The investments made by the fund constitute the assets. In addition, there will be other assets and liabilities.

The net assets of a fund is defined as:

Net Assets = Market Value of Investments + Receivables + Other Accrued Income +

Other Assets − Accrued Expenses − Other Payables − Other Liabilities

The NAV is defined as Net Assets ÷ No. of Units outstanding.
A fund's NAV is affected by four sets of factors:

- Purchase and sale of investment securities
- Valuation of all investment securities held
- Other assets and liabilities
- Units sold or redeemed

The term *other assets* includes any income due to the fund but not received as on the valuation date, for example, dividends that have been announced by a company whose shares the fund is holding, but are yet to be received. Other liabilities have to include expenses payable by the fund, such as custodian fees or even the management fee that is payable to the Asset Management Company (AMC). These income and expenditure items have to be accrued and included in the computation of the NAV.

An AMC may incur many expenses specifically for given schemes and other expenses that are common to all schemes. All expenses should be clearly identified and allocated to the individual schemes. The expenses may be broadly categorized as:

- Investment management and advisory fees
- Initial expenses of launching schemes
- Recurring expenses

EXAMPLE 11.1

A mutual fund in the United States has acquired 1,000 shares of ABC, 2,000 shares of DEF, and 2,000 shares of XYZ. It has issued 20,000 shares to its shareholders. The NAV based on current prices may be calculated as depicted in Table 11.1.

TABLE 11.1   The Fund's Portfolio on a Given Day

Company	# of Shares	Price	Value
ABC	1,000	35	35,000
DEF	2,000	80	160,000
XYZ	2,000	60	120,000
Total	5,000		315,000

NAV = 315,000 ÷ 20,000 = 15.75

Now assume that the prices on the following day are as shown in Table 11.2.

TABLE 11.2   The Fund's Portfolio on the Following Day

Company	# of Shares	Price	Value
ABC	1,000	40	40,000
DEF	2,000	90	180,000
XYZ	2,000	75	150,000
Total	5,000		370,000

$$NAV = 370{,}000 \div 20{,}000 = 18.50$$

The NAV on the following day will depend on how the new investment is deployed at the end of the day, if the fund issues additional shares. For instance, assume that the fund issues 2,000 additional shares at the NAV of 15.75. This will lead to an inflow of 31,500. This can be used to acquire 100 shares of ABC, 200 shares of DEF, and 200 shares of XYZ. If so, the NAV on the following day will be 18.50, because the incoming funds are being used to acquire shares in the existing proportions. See Table 11.3.

TABLE 11.3   The Fund's Portfolio Composition If the Incoming Money Is Deployed in the Existing Proportions

Company	# of Shares	Price	Value
ABC	1,100	40	44,000
DEF	2,200	90	198,000
XYZ	2,200	75	165,000
Total	5,500		407,000

$$NAV = 407{,}000 \div 22{,}000 = 18.50$$

But what if the fund were to acquire 300 shares of ABC, 150 shares of DEF, and 150 shares of XYZ? The NAV on the following day will then be as shown in Table 11.4:

TABLE 11.4   The Fund's Portfolio Composition If the Incoming Money Is Deployed Differently

Company	# of Shares	Price	Value
ABC	1,300	40	52,000
DEF	2,150	90	193,500
XYZ	2,150	75	161,250
Total	5,600		406,750

$NAV = 406{,}750 \div 22{,}000 = 18.4886$. Thus, the NAV on the following day would depend on the deployment of the incoming funds. Redemptions, by existing investors, will have similar consequences.

When a scheme is first launched, the AMC will incur significant expenditure, the benefit of which will accrue over many years. Thus, the entire expenditure cannot be charged to a scheme in the first year itself, and has to be amortized over a period of time; however, issue expenses incurred during the life of a scheme cannot be amortized. The unamortized portion of initial issue expenses shall be included for NAV calculation, and will be classified under *other assets*. Investment advisory fees cannot, however, be claimed on such assets.

COSTS

The costs borne by an investor in a mutual fund can be classified under two heads. The first is what is known as a sales charge or a shareholder fee. This is a one-time charge that is debited to the investor at the time of a transaction, which could be in the form of a purchase, a redemption, or as an exchange of shares of one fund for that of another, which is termed a switch. The amount of the sales charge would depend on the method adopted for distributing the shares. The second category of costs is the annual operating expense incurred by the fund, which is called the expense ratio. The largest component of this expense is the investment management fee. This cost is of course independent of the method adopted for the distribution of shares.

SALES CHARGES

Traditionally there have been two routes for distributing the shares of a mutual fund. They could either be sold using a sales force (or a wholesale distributor) or they could be sold directly. The first method necessarily requires an intermediary, such as an agent, a stockbroker, an insurance agent, or other similar entity, who is capable of providing investment advice to the client and capable of servicing the investment subsequently. This can be construed as an *active* approach, in the sense that the "fund is sold and not bought."

In the case of the direct approach, however, there is no intermediary or salesman who will actively approach the client, provide advice and service, and possibly make a sale. Rather, the client in such a situation will directly contact the fund (usually by calling a toll-free number) in response to an advertisement or information obtained elsewhere. In such cases, little or no investment advice is provided either initially or subsequently. This can therefore be termed as a *passive* approach, in the sense that the "fund is bought and not sold." It must be remembered that even though a fund may adopt a passive approach for selling its shares, it may nevertheless advertise aggressively.

Clearly, the agent-based system comes with an attached cost. The cost is a sales charge which has to be borne by the client, and which constitutes a fee for the services rendered by the agent. The sales charges levied by such funds are referred to as *loads*.

The traditional practice has been to deduct this load up front from the investor's initial contribution at the time of his entry into the fund and pass it on to the agent/distributor. The remainder constitutes the net amount that is investable in the fund in the name of the client. This method is known as *front-end loading*, and the corresponding loads as *front-end* or *entry* loads. Because the amount paid by the investor per share exceeds the NAV of the fund, such funds are said to be "purchased above the NAV."

On the other hand, a mutual fund that sells directly would not incur the payment of a sales charge, because there is no role for an intermediary. Such funds are therefore known as *no-load* mutual funds. In this case, the entire amount paid by investors will be invested in the fund in their name. Consequently, such funds are said to be "purchased at the NAV."

It was thought at one point in time that load funds would become obsolete and that the mutual fund industry would come to be dominated by no-load funds. The underlying rationale for this argument is of course that no rational investor would like to pay a sales charge if the same can be avoided. It was felt that individual investors, given their increasing levels of sophistication, would prefer to make their own invest-ment decisions, rather than rely on agents for advice and service; however, the subse-quent trend has been to the contrary. There are two reasons why load funds continue to be popular with investors.

First, many investors have remained dependent on the counsel, service, and more importantly, the initiative of investment agents. Second, load funds have shown a lot of ingenuity and flexibility in devising new methods for imposing the sales charge that serve the purpose of compensating the agent/distributor, without appearing to be a burden for the investors. These innovations have come in the form of *back-end* loads and *level* loads. Unlike a front-end load, which is imposed at the time of an investor's entry into a fund, a back-end or *exit* load is imposed at the time of redemp-tion of shares. The advantage of this approach is that the entire investment made by the investor is ploughed into the fund without being subject to an up-front deduction.

Yet another variant is the level load. In this case, a uniform sales charge is imposed every year. Consequently, the reported NAVs would be lower than what they would have been in the absence of a sales charge. In this case also, however, the entire amount paid by the investor at the outset would be investable in the securities held by the fund. Level loads appeal to investors who are more comfortable with the concept of an annual fee (so called fee-based planners) rather than commissions, irrespective of whether these are payable at entry or on exit.

The most common form of an exit load is the *contingent deferred sales charge*. This approach imposes a load on withdrawal, which is a function of the number of years that the investor has stayed with the fund. Obviously, the longer an investor stays invested, the lower will be the load on redemption. For instance, a 3,3,2,2,1,1,0 contingent deferred sales charge would mean that a 3% load would be imposed if the shares are redeemed within two years, a 2% load if the shares are redeemed after two years but within four years, and a 1% load if the redemption takes place after four years but within six years. Obviously, there is no sales charge if the redemption occurs at the end of six years or thereafter.

Many mutual fund families often offer their funds with a choice of loading mech-anisms and allow the distributor and the client to pick the method of their choice. Shares subject to front-end loads are usually called *A shares*; those subject to back-end loads are known as *B shares*; while those for which a level load is applicable are known as *C shares*.

In the case of funds with front-end and back-end loads, the declared NAV will not include the load. Thus, in the case of funds that impose a front-end load, investors must add the load amount per share to the NAV per share in order to calculate their purchase price. Similarly, in the case of a back-end load fund, investors have to deduct the load amount per share from the NAV per share in order to know their net sale proceeds.

EXAMPLE 11.2

A fund has a declared NAV of $19.50. The front-end load is 2.5%. The price payable by the investor may be computed in one of two ways. That is, the NAV can be divided by one minus the load, or multiplied by one plus the load.

Method-1: Price payable = 19.50 ÷ 0.975 = 20.0000

Method-2: Price payable = 19.50 × (1.025) = 19.9875

Both are legitimate ways of applying a front-end load.

This can be expressed in a different way as follows. In the absence of the load, an investment of $1,950 would fetch the investor 1,950 ÷ 19.50 = 100.00 units. But with a front-end load it will fetch only

(1,950 × .975) ÷ 19.50 = 97.50 units as per Method-1

And 1,950 ÷ 19.9875 = 97.5610 units as per Method-2

Exit loads too can be levied in two ways. If the load is x%, the NAV can be multiplied by $1 - x$ or divided by $1 + x$. Here is an example.

EXAMPLE 11.3

A fund has a declared NAV of $19.89. The back-end load is 2%. The price receivable by the investor may be computed in one of two ways.

Method-1: Price receivable = 19.89 × 0.98 = 19.4922

Method-2: Price receivable = 19.89 ÷ 1.02 = 19.5000

This can be viewed as follows. In the absence of an exit load, a sale of 100 units would have fetched the investor $1,989. Because of the load, however, he will get only $1,949.22 under Method-1 and $1,950 under Method-2.

The impact of loads can be better appreciated by comparing investments in load and no-load funds with the same NAV.

EXAMPLE 11.4

Assume the NAV is 19.50 and the entry load is 2.50%. The investor invests $1,950. The investor is allotted 97.50 units. In the absence of the load, the investor would obviously have received 100 units. Assume a year later the NAV is 19.89. Without a load the return would have been

$$(1,989 - 1,950) \div 1,950 = 2\%$$

Because of the load the return is $(97.50 \times 19.89 - 1,950) \div 1,950 = -0.55\%$.

Now assume there is no entry load but an exit load. The investor will receive 100 shares at the outset. But when the shares are sold, the investor will get only 19.50 per share. The return is $(1,950 - 1,950) \div 1,950 = 0.00\%$.

EXAMPLE 11.5

In a fund with a contingent deferred sales charge, the longer the investor stays invested, the greater the benefit, assuming a positive rate of return.

For instance, assume that investors acquire a share of a fund at a price of $20 on 1 January 20XX. Assume the NAV after one year is $22. That is, it has increased by 10%. The load structure is such that a 2% exit load is payable if the shares are sold before two years, and a 1% exit load is applicable if the shares are held for two years or longer.

Thus, if the investors sell after one year, they will receive $22 \times 0.98 = 21.56$. The rate of return is $[21.56 - 20] \div 20 = 7.80\%$.

Now assume that the shares are held for two years, and that the exit load after one year is also 2%. We will also assume that the NAV increases by $2 in year two as well. Thus, the NAV after two years is $24. After the load, the amount received is $24 \times 0.98 = \$23.52$. The annual return on a simple interest basis is

$$[23.52 - 20]/(2 \times 20) = 8.80\%$$

Thus, even if the percentage of the load does not change, the return obtained for the same incremental change in the NAV is higher. This is because the load of 2% is applied to the initial investment at the end of the first year, in the earlier case, and at the end of the second year, in the second case.

If the exit load at the end of two years is reduced to 1%, the effect is even more pronounced. The selling price will be $24 \times 0.99 = \$23.76$. The annual return on a simple interest basis is

$$[23.76 - 20]/(2 \times 20) = 9.40\%$$

A load can be charged by open-end and closed-end funds. It should also be remembered that loads represent issue expenses, which are just one component of the expenses incurred by the fund. A mutual fund incurs other expenses, such as the fund managers' fees, which are charged to the investors on an ongoing basis. The impact of such deductions will be reflected in the form of a lower reported NAV.

PRICE QUOTES

Financial sources often publish two prices for a mutual fund. The lower price is what is applicable for an investor who is redeeming shares, while the higher price applies to someone who is acquiring shares. If there is a single price, it means that it is a no-load fund. In the case of funds with an entry load or an exit load, or both, the purchase price will be higher than the sale price.

If we denote the purchase price by B and the sale price by S, the load may be computed as $(B - S)/B$ in the following cases.

Case-1: An entry load of x% is applied as $NAV/(1 - x)$
   Thus $B = NAV/(1 - x)$ and $S = NAV$
   $B - S = xNAV/(1 - x)$ and $(B - S)/B = x$

Case-2: An exit load of x% is applied as $NAV(1 - x)$
   Thus $B = NAV$, while $S = NAV(1 - x)$
   $B - S = xNAV$ and $(B - S)/B = x$

If, however, the entry load is applied as $NAV(1 + x)$ or an exit load as $NAV/(1 + x)$, the formula for the load is $(B - S)/S$.

Case-3: An entry load of x% is applied as $NAV(1 + x)$
   So $B = NAV(1 + x)$ and $S = NAV$
   $B - S = xNAV$ and $(B - S)/S = x$

Case-4: An exit load of x% is applied as $NAV/(1 + x)$
   Thus $B = NAV$ and $S = NAV/(1 + x)$
   $B - S = xNAV/(1 + x)$ and $(B - S)/S = x$

ANNUAL OPERATING EXPENSES

The operating expense is debited annually from the investor's fund balance by the sponsor of the fund. The three main categories of such expenses are the management fee, the distribution fee, and other expenses. These expenses will be mentioned in the prospectus. Thus, it is important to read the prospectus carefully before investing money. Everything else being equal, one should seek funds with low operating expenses.

The management fee, also known as the investment advisory fee, is the fee charged by the investment advisor for managing the fund's portfolio. Sometimes the advisor may be from a different company. If so, the sponsor will pass on some or all of the management fee to the advisor. The fees charged would depend on the type of fund, and as is to be expected, the greater the efforts and skills required to manage the fund, the higher will be the management fee that is charged.

In 1980, in the United States, the SEC approved the imposition of a fixed annual fee called the 12b-1 fee. This is intended to cover distribution costs, including continuing agent compensation and the fund's marketing and advertising expenses. This fee may include a service fee to compensate sales professionals for providing services or for maintaining shareholders' accounts. The amount, which accrues to the selling agent, is to provide an incentive to continue to service the accounts even after having received a transaction-based fee such as a front-end load. This component of the 12b-1 fee is therefore applicable for sales-force-sold load funds and not for directly sold no-load funds. The balance of the 12b-1 fee, which accrues to the fund sponsor, is intended to provide it with an incentive to continue advertising and marketing efforts.

The sum total of the annual management fee, the annual distribution fee, and other annual expenses like the ones described earlier is called the expense ratio.

A fund that tracks an established market index like the S&P 500 is relatively easier to manage as compared to a fund that entails the active implementation of a proactive rebalancing strategy. Thus, it is not surprising that an index fund has the lowest management fee, whereas an actively managed pure stock fund has the highest fee.

SWITCHING FEES

For many years there was no charge for switching from one mutual fund to another within the same family. But these days, some funds have started to charge a flat fee. In many cases, the fee becomes payable once a pre-fixed number of switches for the year is exceeded. These funds justify such charges by arguing that these are being levied to discourage frequent switching. They may have a point because frequent switching of funds increases the administrative costs involved in keeping track of customer accounts. These charges are directly recovered from the shareholder, and do not therefore impact the NAV.

DIVIDEND OPTIONS

Mutual funds usually offer their investors three alternatives from the standpoint of dividends. The first is a dividend option. In this case, the investors periodically get cash inflows, as in the case of equity shares. The second is termed a dividend reinvestment option. In this case, while the fund will declare a dividend, it will not be paid out in the form of cash. What will happen is that an equivalent number of shares, based on the prevailing NAV, will be credited to the investor's account. Thus, the number of shares held by an investor will steadily increase, as the dividends are declared. The third option is termed as the growth option. In this case, no dividends are declared. What happens is that any income and profits earned by the fund are plowed back into the fund. An investor who needs cash can always sell some of the shares in the case of the dividend reinvestment and the growth options.

The option chosen has no consequences for the returns in the first year of investment. But in subsequent years the returns will be different, as we will demonstrate.

In the case of the dividend and dividend reinvestment options, the share prices will fall when a dividend is paid, as is the case for equity shares. Consider an investor who owns Z shares of a mutual fund. The NAV at the outset is N_0. Assume the NAV at the end of the year is N_1. The DPS is $\$D$. If the investor chose the growth option, the value of the portfolio will be $N_1 Z$. If a dividend option is chosen, the ex-dividend NAV is $N_1 - D$. The portfolio value will be $(N_1 - D)Z + DZ = N_1 Z$. In the case of the dividend reinvestment option, the number of additional shares allotted is $DZ/(N_1-D)$. Thus, the value of the portfolio is

$$(N_1 - D)Z + (N_1 - D) \times \frac{DZ}{(N_1 - D)} = N_1 Z$$

Thus, the value of the investment is the same in all three cases.

Now assume that at the end of the following year the NAV is 10% higher than the NAV at the end of the previous year, and that the dividend for the year is D_2. The value of the portfolio in the case of the growth option is $N_2 Z = 1.1 N_1 Z$. If the dividend reinvestment option is chosen, the post dividend NAV at the end of the previous year would be $N_1 - D_1$.[1] Thus, the NAV at the end of the second year is $1.1(N_1 - D_1)$. The number of shares held at the end of the previous year would be

$$\left[Z + \frac{D_1 Z}{(N_1 - D_1)} \right]$$

The dividend for the second year is D_2. The additional number of shares allocated is

$$D_2 \frac{\left[Z + \dfrac{D_1 Z}{(N_1 - D_1)} \right]}{[1.1(N_1 - D_1) - D_2]}$$

The value of the total shares is

$$[1.1(N_1 - D_1) - D_2] \times \left[Z + \frac{D_1 Z}{(N_1 - D_1)} \right]$$

$$+ [1.1(N_1 - D_1) - D_2] \times D_2 \frac{\left[Z + \dfrac{D_1 Z}{(N_1 - D_1)} \right]}{[1.1(N_1 - D_1) - D_2]}$$

$$= 1.1 N_1 Z$$

Thus, the terminal value, after two years, is identical in both cases.

Now consider the dividend option. The number of shares is Z. The dividend in the second year is D_2. Thus, the total dividend is $D_2 Z$. The dividend earned in the first year is $D_1 Z$. Its future value assuming a reinvestment at the rate of $r\%$ is $D_1 Z(1 + r)$. The value of the shares at the end of the second year is $(N_2 - D_2)Z$. Thus, the total value is

$$(N_2 - D_2)Z + D_2 Z + D_1 Z(1 + r) = N_2 Z + D_1 Z(1 + r) = 1.1(N_1 - D_1)Z + D_1 Z(1 + r)$$

$$= 1.1 N_1 Z - 1.1 D_1 Z + D_1 Z(1 + r)$$

In practice, the reinvestment rate for the investor is likely to be less than the 10% growth rate for the mutual fund. Thus, it is likely to be the case that $1.1 N_1 Z - 1.1 D_1 Z + D_1 Z(1 + r) < 1.1 N_1 Z$. Hence the investor stands to get a lower return as compared to the growth and dividend reinvestment options.

---

[1]We are denoting the first year's dividend as D_1, which we had earlier denoted as D.

EXAMPLE 11.6

A mutual fund issues shares at $10 each on 1 January 20XX. On 31 December 20XX the NAV is $15, and the fund declares a dividend of $2.50 per share. The ex-dividend NAV will be $12.50 for the dividend and dividend reinvestment options. If investors opted for the growth option, the return would be $(15 - 10) \div 10 = 50\%$. If they had opted for the dividend reinvestment option, they would receive $2.5 \div 12.50 = 0.20$ shares. The value of their holdings will be $1.2 \times 12.50 = \$15$ and their return for the year will be 50%. Finally let us consider the dividend option. The investors would have a share worth $12.50 and $2.50 in cash, which amounts to a total wealth of $15. Hence, in this case as well, the rate of return is 50%.

Now assume that the NAV increases by 12% by 31 December 20(XX+1) and the dividend at the end of the second year is $1.80. Under the growth option the value of a share will be $15 \times 1.12 = \$16.80$. The rate of return will be $(16.80 - 15.00) \div 15.00 = 12\%$. The return for investors who had opted for the dividend reinvestment option may be computed as follows. The ex-dividend NAV will be $1.12 \times 12.50 - 1.80 = 12.20$. They would have 1.2 shares which would be worth $1.2 \times 12.20 = 14.64$. They will receive $(1.2 \times 1.80) \div 12.20 = 0.1770$ shares extra. The value of these will be $0.1770 \times (1.12 \times 12.50 - 1.80) = 2.16$. The value of their portfolio will be $16.80 and the return is once again 12%.

Finally, let us consider the dividend option. At the end of the first year the investors would have a share and $2.50 in cash. Assume that they can reinvest the cash at 8% per annum. After a year they will have a share plus the future value of the dividend, which is $2.70 and the second dividend of $1.80. The share will be worth $12.20. Thus, the total wealth will be $16.70. Thus, the rate of return is lower, because we have assumed that the cash received at the end of the first year is reinvested at a lower rate than the growth rate of the NAV.

TYPES OF MUTUAL FUNDS

We have examined a general classification of mutual funds as open-end versus closed-end, and as no-load versus load funds. Mutual funds can also be distinguished from each other based on their investment objectives and on the types of securities that they invest in.

Once upon a time, mutual fund investments were perceived to be attractive because of two factors. First, they made it easier to hold a well-diversified portfolio. Second, they operated with the services of professional analysts whose services are by and large inaccessible to individual investors. Today, the industry has become highly specialized and funds offer enormous diversity. Investors can therefore easily choose a fund to meet their specific objectives. This is important because no two investors are exactly alike. Some may be conservative while others may be aggressive. While one person may seek a tax-free investment option, another may be quite prepared to invest in a taxable fund. Besides, while most investors are likely to be content with domestic portfolio options, some may seek to hold globally diversified portfolios.

Categorization by Nature of Investments

Mutual funds may invest in equity shares, bonds, or other fixed-income securities of a long-term nature, or in short-term money market instruments. Consequently, we have equity funds, bond funds, and money market funds. There are also funds that invest in physical rather than financial assets. Hence, we have precious metals funds, real estate funds, and so on.

Categorization by Investment Objectives

Different funds have their own investment objectives and consequently cater to different clienteles. Growth funds invest in order to get capital appreciation in the medium- to long-term. Income funds focus on earning regular income and are less concerned with capital appreciation. Value funds are those that invest in equities perceived to be undervalued, and which are consequently expected to rise in price with the passage of time.

Categorization by Risk Profile

Equity funds have a greater risk of capital loss than debt funds, which seek to protect capital while generating regular income. Money market funds that invest in short-term debt securities are even less exposed to risk as compared to bond funds.

Fund managers can create different types of funds to cater to various investor profiles by mixing investments across categories. For example, equity income funds tend to invest in shares that do not fluctuate much in terms of value, but tend to provide dividends on a steady basis. Utility companies like power-sector companies will constitute suitable investments for such funds. Balanced funds are those that seek to reduce risk by mixing equity investments with investments in fixed-income securities. They can also be perceived as funds that try to strike a balance between the need for capital appreciation and the requirement for steady income.

Now we will go on to discuss specific types of funds.

MONEY MARKET FUNDS

Such funds invest in securities with one year or less to maturity. Typical securities acquired by such funds include Treasury bills, which are issued by the government, certificates of deposit (which are essentially time deposit receipts issued by banks), and commercial paper, which are IOUs issued by companies. These investments are highly liquid and carry relatively low credit risk. Consequently, in some markets they are known as liquid funds. There is also a category of tax-free money market funds that invest only in municipal securities. Thus, the earnings of these funds are exempt from federal taxes, and in certain cases from state income taxes as well.

These funds are ideal for investors seeking stability of principal, high liquidity, check-writing facilities, and earnings that are as high or higher than those available through bank CDs. And, unlike bank CDs, these funds do not come with early withdrawal penalties.

Money market funds usually declare a dividend on a daily basis. Consequently, their NAV stays close to the face value at the time of issue.

While these funds pose a low level of risk, regulators in countries like the United States have sought to provide additional safety by requiring such funds to hold a portfolio whose securities have a weighted average time to maturity, that is, substantially less than one year. Money market securities, it must be remembered, have a maximum time to maturity of one year.

GILT FUNDS

A gilt security is a fixed-income security issued by the government, with a term to maturity of more than one year. In ancient England, government bonds were issued with a border made of gold foil, and hence the name. Gilt funds carry little default risk; however, such securities are subject to interest rate or market risk, in the sense that changes in the interest rate structure in the economy can lead to substantial fluctuations in the values of such assets. As can be appreciated, default risk is not the only risk faced by an investor in bonds.

DEBT FUNDS

These funds, also known as income funds, invest in fixed-income securities issued not only by governments, but also those issued by private companies, banks and financial institutions, and other entities like infrastructure companies and public utilities.

These instruments carry lower risk as compared to equities and tend to provide stable income. Compared to a money market fund, however, a debt fund has greater market risk, as well as credit risk. Compared with gilt funds, on the other hand, these funds have higher credit risk.

Debt funds are known as income funds because their focus is primarily on earning high income, and not on capital appreciation. These funds therefore distribute a substantial part of their surplus to shareholders on a regular basis. We can further subclassify debt funds based on investment objectives.

DIVERSIFIED DEBT FUNDS

A diversified debt fund is defined as one which invests in virtually all types of debt securities issued by entities across all sectors and industries. Although debt securities carry less risk as compared to equities, they nevertheless expose investors to default risk, because they represent contractual obligations on the part of the issuing firm. The advantage of investing in a diversified fund is that the idiosyncratic or firm-specific default risk gets diversified away. Thus, as compared to debt funds that invest only in securities issued by firms in a particular industry or sector of the economy, diversified funds are less risky.

FOCUSED DEBT FUNDS

Such funds tend to invest primarily in debt securities issued by a sector or industry. For instance, there are funds that invest only in corporate bonds and debentures.

There are others that choose to invest in tax-free infrastructure bonds or municipal bonds. There are also funds that invest in mortgage-backed securities.

HIGH YIELD DEBT FUNDS

These funds invest in non-investment-grade bonds, or junk bonds. They expose themselves to a higher degree of default risk, in anticipation of greater returns. Such funds are also known as junk bond funds.

DEBT FUNDS AND BOND DURATION

Bonds offer more safety to investors as compared to equity shares, but that does not mean that such funds carry no risk. Whenever a cash flow from a bond is reinvested, there is risk, due to the fact that interest rates in the market may be low at that point in time. This is called reinvestment risk. The other risk is that when a bond is sold, prevailing market yields may be high. If so, the bond would have to be sold at a low price. This is called market risk or price risk.

We have studied bond duration earlier and know that duration is a measure of the interest rate sensitivity of a bond. The higher the duration of a bond portfolio, the greater is the interest rate risk. In practice bond mutual funds are classified along the following lines. As we go down the list, the duration and interest rate risk increase.

- Ultra-Short Duration Funds
- Short Duration Funds
- Medium Duration Funds
- Long Duration Funds

EQUITY FUNDS

Holders of shares issued by equity mutual funds take on much more risk than those who invest in debt mutual funds. Equity funds by definition invest a major portion of their corpus in shares issued by companies. Such shares may be acquired either through the primary market by participating in an initial public offering, a follow-on public offering, or even through a rights issue, or through the secondary market. The value of an equity share fluctuates in practice due to three types of influences: factors specific to the firm itself; factors characteristic of the industry in which the firm operates; and economy-wide factors. Unlike debt instruments, there is no contractual guarantee in terms of dividend distribution or in terms of the safety of the capital invested. Although debt securities will at best repay the original principal invested, however, there is no limit to the possible capital appreciation when one invests in equities.

AGGRESSIVE GROWTH FUNDS

These funds target high capital appreciation and usually take substantial risks in the process. Their investments are highly concentrated in less researched and highly speculative stocks, which are considered to have more growth potential.

The potential for high returns, however, is accompanied by enhanced volatility of returns, and consequently by a greater level of risk for investors.

GROWTH FUNDS

Such funds also target companies with a high perceived potential for growth; however, the choice of investments made by such funds tend to be in sunrise sectors like information technology, biotechnology, or pharmaceuticals. The difference, as compared to the case of an aggressive growth fund, is that the stocks chosen tend to be less speculative, although they usually represent a relatively new sector of the economy. Growth funds target high capital appreciation over a medium term.

SPECIALTY FUNDS

These funds have a narrow focus and tend to invest only in companies that conform to certain predefined criteria. For instance, there are funds that will not invest in tobacco or liquor companies. Others selectively target specific regions of the world such as Latin America or the ASEAN countries. Having defined their investment criteria, some funds may choose to hold a diversified portfolio, while others may tend to concentrate their investments in a few chosen securities. Obviously, the returns from the latter will be more volatile. Many years ago, certain funds would not invest in companies that did business with South Africa.

SECTOR FUNDS

These are specialty funds that invest only in a chosen sector or industry such as software, pharmaceuticals, or fast-moving consumer goods (FMCG) sectors. As compared to well-diversified funds, these funds carry a higher level of industry-specific risk, if not company-specific risk.

OFFSHORE FUNDS

These funds invest in equities of one or more foreign countries. While international diversification does in principle offer additional opportunities for reducing risk, it also exposes such funds to foreign exchange risk, a factor that is irrelevant for funds that invest solely in domestic securities. A well-diversified offshore fund will invest in more than one country, while a fund with a narrower focus will restrict itself to just a single country.

SMALL CAP EQUITY FUNDS

These funds invest in companies with lower market capitalization as compared to large blue-chip firms. The prices of such firms tend to be more volatile, because the shares are much less liquid. Small cap funds may target aggressive growth or may choose to aim at just a steady level of growth.

Market capitalization is defined as the number of shares outstanding multiplied by the share price. The definition of what constitutes a small cap firm is of course subjective.

OPTION INCOME FUNDS

As the name suggests, these funds write options on securities. Conservative option funds invest in large dividend-paying companies, and then sell options against their stock positions. This strategy ensures a stable income stream on account of two sources: dividend income and premium income.

FUND OF FUNDS

Such a fund is defined as one which invests in other mutual funds. Thus it takes the principle of diversification one level higher. The impact may not be substantial, if the underlying mutual funds themselves are well diversified. The reduction in risk may be perceptible, however, if the underlying funds are narrowly focused.

EQUITY INDEX FUNDS

An index fund tracks the performance of a specific stock market index, such as the Dow Jones Industrial Average or the Standard & Poor's 500 index. Such a fund will invest only in those stocks that constitute the target index, and in exactly the same proportions in which such stocks are present in the index. They can therefore be considered to be mimicking funds. If the index which is being traded represents a large, well-diversified portfolio of assets, then the corresponding fund will have relatively low risk. Such funds reduce operating expenses by eliminating the portfolio fund manager. This is because the stocks in the portfolio rarely change. And even if the relative weights were to change, they will do so in the same way as the weights of the stocks in the index, if the index were to be value weighted. More frequent rebalancing is of course required for funds that track price-weighted or equally weighted indices.

VALUE FUNDS

Growth funds tend to focus on companies with a good or improving prospect for future profits. Their primary aim is therefore capital appreciation. Value funds also seek capital appreciation, but their focus is on fundamentally sound firms that they perceive are undervalued. As compared to growth funds, value funds are usually less risky. Many of these funds tend to invest in a large number of sectors and therefore tend to be diversified; however, value stocks often come from cyclical industries. Shares of cyclical firms may fluctuate more than the overall market in the short run, a phenomenon that can be observed in both bull and bear markets.

EQUITY INCOME FUNDS

These funds invest in companies that give high dividend yields. Their target is high current income with steady, though not spectacular, capital appreciation.

Utility stocks are very popular with such funds. The prices of these stocks do not fluctuate much, but they do provide stable dividends.

BALANCED FUNDS

They hold a portfolio consisting of debt instruments, convertible securities, preference shares, and equity shares. They hold more or less equal proportions in debt/money-market instruments, and equities. These funds have the objective of steady income, accompanied by moderate capital appreciation. They are primarily intended for conservative and long-term investors.

ASSET-ALLOCATION FUNDS

By definition, an equity fund will be primarily invested in equities, whereas a debt fund will have its investments concentrated in fixed-income securities. These funds therefore have a fixed or predetermined asset allocation, in the sense that the relative proportions invested in the various categories of securities is preset and will in general not vary. In practice, however, there are funds that follow a variable allocation policy and will flit in and out of various asset classes, such as equities, debt, money market securities, and even nonfinancial assets. Their choice of an asset class would depend on the fund manager's outlook on the market at a given point in time.

COMMODITY FUNDS

These funds specialize in investing in commodity markets. These investments may be made by directly buying physical commodities, by acquiring shares of commodity firms, or by using commodity futures contracts. Specialized funds in this category will focus their attention on a specific commodity or a group of related commodities (for example, edible oils), while diversified commodity funds will spread their investments over many different commodities. Common examples of such funds include gold funds, silver funds, and platinum funds.

REAL ESTATE FUNDS

These funds either invest in real estate directly or fund real estate developers. Funds that invest in housing finance companies and mortgage-backed securities would also fall in this category.

TAX-EXEMPT FUNDS

A fund that invests in tax-exempt securities is known as a tax-exempt fund. In the United States, municipal bonds yield tax-free income, whereas interest paid on corporate bonds is taxable.

RISK CATEGORIES

Depending on their investment objectives, mutual funds can be grouped into various risk categories.

Low Level Risk Funds

- Money market funds
- US T-bill funds
- Insured bond funds

Moderate Level Risks

- Income funds
- Balanced funds
- Growth & Income funds
- Growth funds
- Short-term bond funds
- Intermediate-term bond funds (taxable and tax-free)
- GNMA funds

High Level Risks

- Aggressive Growth funds
- International funds
- Sector funds
- Specialized funds
- Precious metals funds
- High Yield bond funds
- Commodity funds
- Options funds

THE PROSPECTUS

A prospectus is a formal printed document offering to sell a security. Like equity shares and debt securities, mutual funds too are offered with a prospectus to potential investors. The prospectus is required to disclose important information about the security. As a minimum, it must disclose the fund's financial history, its investment objectives, and information about the management.

There are various ways of obtaining a prospectus. It can be obtained from the broker; however, brokers usually handle only load funds. The prospectus can also be obtained by writing to the investment company. And it can always be ordered by calling the fund's toll-free number.

STRUCTURE OF A MUTUAL FUND

A mutual fund is organized as follows. The shareholders, who are the owners of the fund, are represented by a board of directors. These directors are also known as the trustees of the fund. The board governs the mutual fund. Members of the board may be *interested* or *inside* directors who are affiliated with the fund, or they may be *independent* or *outside* directors not affiliated with the fund in any manner.

The fund's portfolio is managed by an investment adviser or a management company. In practice, the adviser can be an affiliate of a brokerage firm, an insurance company, a bank, an investment management firm, or an independent entity. In addition, many mutual funds will also engage the services of a distributor, whose task it is to sell shares to the public, either directly or through other firms. Such distributors are essentially broker-dealers who may or may not be affiliated with the fund and/or the investment adviser.

The fund is also linked to three external service providers: a custodian, a transfer agent, and an independent public accountant. The role of the custodian is to hold the fund's assets and ensure they are segregated from the accounts of others. Transfer agents perform the task of processing orders at the time of purchase and redemption and transferring securities and cash to the concerned parties. Thus, whenever clients seek to invest in shares or redeem them, they will have to have a transaction with the transfer agent. The agents also collect dividends and coupons and distribute them to the shareholders. The job of the accountant is, of course, to audit the financial statements of the fund.

SERVICES

All mutual funds do not provide the same menu of shareholder services. A complete program of investor services should include at least the following.

Automatic Reinvestment Plan

Most mutual funds offer the option of automatically investing all income and capital gains. This option allows for the easy systematic accumulation of additional shares of the fund. Automatic reinvestment is always a voluntary option. Distributions may always be taken in cash, but the benefits of compounding may be lost. Whether reinvested or taken in the form of cash, however, distributions are subject to certain tax liabilities. In most cases, however, reinvested dividends and capital gains are not subject to loads.

Contractual Accumulation Plan

This kind of a plan requires the investor to commit to purchasing a predetermined fixed dollar amount on a regular basis for a specified period of time. In the case of such plans, the investor gets to decide on the dollar amount, the frequency, and the length of time the plan is to continue. In some countries, these are known as systematic investment plans.

Voluntary Accumulation Plan

In these plans, the shareholder voluntarily purchases additional shares at periodic intervals. Each purchase must meet the fund's minimum investment requirement.

With a voluntary plan, the investor can change the amount invested each time, the frequency of investments, and the duration of the plan.

Check Writing

Many mutual funds, and all money market funds, offer the facility of free check-writing. This option is not available for tax-deferred retirement accounts. There is no restriction on how many checks one may write each month, as long as the account balance is not reduced below the minimum required to maintain the account. Each check should be for an amount greater than or equal to the minimum specified by the fund.

Switching Within a Family of Funds

Most investment companies permit shareholders to switch from one fund to another within the family. Usually all that is required is a telephone call from the investor to the fund's toll-free number. In most cases this feature is offered at no cost. Telephone switching is a strategy whereby the investor attempts to capitalize on the cyclical swings in the stock market. It means keeping a substantial amount in stock funds when the market trend is bullish, and switching most of the investment to a money market fund when the market becomes bearish.

Voluntary Withdrawal Plans

These plans require the shareholder to initiate the request for redemptions whenever they desire to withdraw funds. Shareholders may also establish a plan whereby the fund will redeem a prearranged fixed dollar amount to be wired to the shareholder's bank on a monthly, quarterly, semiannual, or annual basis. In some countries, these are known as systematic withdrawal plans.

INVESTMENT TECHNIQUES

Mutual fund investors may employ a variety of techniques from the standpoint of investment. These include *dollar-cost averaging*, *value averaging*, and a combination of the two approaches.

Dollar-cost Averaging

In this investment technique one must invest the same amount of dollars at regular intervals. Your dollars will buy more shares when the NAV is low, and less when the NAV is high. Over a period of time, the average price paid per share will always be less than the price paid under a strategy where the investor tries to guess the highs and lows. The major disadvantage of this strategy is that it fails to tell you when to buy, sell, or switch. Thus, the valuable benefit of the switching option is completely lost.

EXAMPLE 11.7

Take the case of investors who plan to invest $10,000 during the course of the year, in four equal, quarterly installments. Assume that the NAVs at the beginning of each quarter are $10, $8, $12.5, and $16 respectively. A dollar-cost averaging plan would work as shown in Table 11.5.

TABLE 11.5 An Illustration of Dollar-cost Averaging

Date	Amount	NAV	# of Shares Acquired
January 1	2,500	10.00	250.00
April 1	2,500	8.00	312.50
July 1	2,500	12.50	200.00
October 1	2,500	16.00	156.25
Total			918.75

ANALYSIS

January-1: Investors invest $2,500. Because the NAV is $10, they will get 250 shares.

April-1: Investors invest another $2,500. Because the NAV is $8, they will get 312.50 shares. The total number of shares held is 562.50.

July-1: Investors invest another $2,500. Because the NAV is $12.50, they will get 200 shares. The total number of shares held is 762.50.

October-1: Investors invest another $2,500. Because the NAV is $16, they will get 156.25 shares. The total number of shares held is 918.75.

The average cost of investment is $10,000 \div 918.75 = 10.8844$.
The average NAV is $(10 + 8 + 12.5 + 16)/4 = 11.625$.

Thus, in dollar-cost averaging the average cost of investment will always be lower than the average NAV over the period. The reason is that when we compute the average investment cost, we are giving higher weight to lower NAV values and lower weight to higher NAV values. In contrast, when we compute the average NAV, all values are given the same weights.

Value Averaging

Value averaging is a more sophisticated yet relatively easy means of increasing the value of your investment over time. In our example, let us assume that you want your investment to increase in value by $250 every quarter.

EXAMPLE 11.8

In a value averaging strategy, you will consider the portfolio value at the end of each quarter. If the increase in the balance is exactly $250, which is extremely unlikely, do not do anything. If the increase is less than $250, invest an amount that is adequate to increase the account balance by $250, as compared to the previous quarter. If the increase in the account balance exceeds $250, withdraw the excess balance in the account. Consider Table 11.6.

TABLE 11.6 An Illustration of Value Averaging

Date	Amount	NAV	# of Shares	Account Balance	Additional Investment in Dollars	Additional Investment in Shares
January 1	10,000	10.00	1,000	10,000		
March 31		8.00	1,000	8,000		
April 1	2,250	8.00	1,281.25	10,250	2,250	281.25
June 30		12.50	1,281.25	16,015.625		
July 1	(5,515.625)	12.50	840	10,500	−5,515.625	(441.25)
September 30		16	840	13,440		
October 1	(2690)	16	671.875	10,750	−2,690.00	(168.125)

ANALYSIS

1 January: Investors invest $10,000. Because the NAV is $10, they get 1,000 shares.

31 March: The NAV is $8. Thus, the shares are worth $8,000. The target amount was $10,250. Thus, the investors invest $2,250 to take the balance to the targeted level. At an NAV of $8, they will have to acquire $2,250 \div 8 = 281.25$ units. Thus, on 1 April they will have 1,281.25 units.

30 June: The NAV is $12.50. The shares are worth $1,281.25 \times 12.50 = \$16,015.625$. The target amount was $10,500. Thus, the investors have to sell shares to get $5,515.625. At the prevailing NAV, they need to sell 441.25 units. Thus, on 1 July they will have 840 units.

30 September: The NAV is 16. The shares are worth $840 \times 16 = 13,440$. The target amount was $10,750. Thus, the investors have to sell shares to get $2,690. At the prevailing NAV they need to sell 168.125 units. Thus, on 1 October they will have 671.875 shares.

The Combined Method

One can always combine the features of dollar-cost averaging and value averaging. Investors may wish to invest a fixed amount at the end of every period, and get a targeted appreciation in wealth. For example, let us assume that the investors start with an investment of $1,250 in a money market mutual fund and $1,250 in a stock fund on January 1. Thus, they have invested $2,500 for the quarter. At an NAV of $10, an investment of $1,250 would imply the acquisition of 125 shares. They would like to see the stock fund appreciate by $250 every quarter.

On 31 March, the value of the stock fund will be $1,000, because the NAV by assumption is $8. They would require the stock fund to have a balance of $2,750, which represents the targeted appreciation of $250 and the investment of $1,250 for the quarter. They should now deposit an amount of $750 in the money market fund and $1,750 in the stock fund on April 1. Because the NAV is $8, they will get an additional 218.75 shares of the stock fund. Their total investment in the stock fund corresponds to 343.75 shares. The investment for the quarter is obviously $2,500.

On June 30, the value of the stock fund will be $4,296.875. They would require a balance of $4,250. So, they should invest $2,500 in the money market fund and shift $46.875 from the stock fund to the money market fund on July 1. They will conse-quently have 340 shares in the stock fund after the divestment. The investment for the quarter is obviously $2,500.

On September 30, the value of the stock fund will be $5,440. They would require a balance of $5,750. So, they should invest $310 in the stock fund and put $2,190 in the money market fund on October 1. The total investment for the period is obvi-ously $2,500.

THE TOTAL RETURN

Mutual funds report a statistic called the Total Return. The inherent assumption is that any payouts, by way of dividends or capital gains, are reinvested to acquire addi-tional shares. To calculate the total return for an N-period horizon we need to define the reinvestment factor.

The reinvestment factor for period I, is defined as:

$$R_i = \frac{D_i \times R_{i-1}}{P_i} + 1$$

where

$R_i \equiv$ reinvestment factor for period i. R_0 is obviously 1.0.

$D_i \equiv$ payout for period i.

$P_i \equiv$ NAV at the end of period i.

Consider Table 11.7.

Assume that the dividend payout is $2.50 per share. The reinvestment factor for each year is given in Table 11.8.

The total return is defined as:

$$TR = \frac{NAV_N \times R_N - NAV_0}{NAV_0}$$

where $NAV_t \equiv$ net asset value at time t.

TABLE 11.7 The Year-wise NAVs

Year	Year-End NAV
0	10.00
1	11.00
2	12.50
3	11.50
4	14.00
5	15.00

TABLE 11.8 Evolution of the Reinvestment Factor Through Time

Year	Reinvestment Factor
1	1.2273
2	1.2455
3	1.2708
4	1.2269
5	1.2045

Thus, in our example, the total return is:

$$\frac{15 \times 1.2045 - 10}{10} = 80.6750\%$$

COMPUTATION OF RETURNS

In practice, investors in a mutual fund will not conveniently invest on 1 January of a year and withdraw on 31 December of the same year. They will make multiple investments during the course of the year, and possibly multiple withdrawals as well. If the investors have opted for the dividend option, then they have a choice of taking the payout in the form of cash or reinvesting it back in the fund. In the latter case, there will be no cash receipt, but the number of shares held will increase, which will have implications for future cash flows. In the case of investors who have opted for a dividend reinvestment option, each time a payout is declared, the number of shares held will automatically increase.

We will consider the case of investors who invest at the onset of a calendar year. They receive quarterly dividends and choose to reinvest whatever is received on 31 March and 30 September. The payouts received on 30 June and 31 December are taken in the form of cash.

The NAV at the end of each month and the dividends declared every month are as shown in Table 11.9.

Assume the investors acquire 1,000 shares at the start of the year. At the end of the 4th month, they redeem shares worth $1,650. At the end of the 8th month, they redeem shares worth $1,080. In the 10th month they invest an additional $2,040.

TABLE 11.9 The Dividend Payout and the NAV at the End of Each Month of the Year

Month	Dividend per Share	Month-End-NAV
0	0.00	10.00
1	0.00	10.40
2	0.00	10.75
3	1.05	10.50
4	0.00	11.00
5	0.00	11.60
6	1.20	12.00
7	0.00	11.20
8	0.00	10.80
9	2.12	10.60
10	0.00	10.20
11	0.00	10.60
12	1.25	10.40

TABLE 11.10 The Monthly Cash Flow Schedule for the Investor

Time	Starting Number of Shares	Ending Number of Shares	Cash Flow
0	1,000	1,000	(10,000)
1	1,000	1,000	0.00
2	1,000	1,000	0.00
3	1,000	1,100	0.00
4	1,100	950	1,650
5	950	950	0.00
6	950	950	1,140
7	950	950	0.00
8	950	850	1,080
9	850	1,020	0.00
10	1,020	1,220	(2,040)
11	1,220	1,220	0.00
12	1,220	0.00	14,213

Now let's project the monthly cash flows for these investors. Inflows are positive, and outflows are negative. Dividends that are taken in the form of cash will manifest themselves as inflows. Dividends that are reinvested will have no implications for the cash flow at that point in time, but will influence subsequent cash flows. The monthly cash flows are as depicted in Table 11.10.

Analysis

Month-0: 1,000 shares are acquired at an NAV of 10. Thus, there is an outflow of $10,000.

Months 1 & 2: No transactions and hence no cash flows.

Month-3: Dividends received = $1,000 \times 1.05 = 1,050$. This is reinvested at an NAV of 10.50. Thus, 100 additional shares will be received. There is no cash flow at the end of the period, but the number of shares held, increases from 1,000 to 1,100 because of the reinvestment.

Month-4: Shares worth $1,650 are redeemed. Because the NAV at the end of the month is 11.00, 150 shares have to be sold. Thus, there is an inflow of 1,650 at the end of the month. The number of shares held after redemption is 950.

Month-5: No transactions and hence no cash flows.

Month-6: Dividends received = $1.20 \times 950 = 1,140$. This is taken in the form of cash and hence there is an inflow at the end of this month.

Month-7: No transactions and hence no cash flows.

Month-8: Shares worth $1,080 are redeemed. Because the NAV at the end of the month is 10.80, 100 shares have to be sold. Thus, there is an inflow of 1,080 at the end of the month. The number of shares held after redemption is 850.

Month-9: Dividends received = $850 \times 2.12 = 1,802$. This is reinvested at an NAV of 10.60. Thus, 170 additional shares will be received. There is no cash flow at the end of the period, but the number of shares held increases from 850 to 1,020 because of the reinvestment.

Month-10: An additional 2,040 is invested at an NAV of 10.20. Thus, the number of shares acquired is $2,040 \div 10.20 = 200$. The total number of shares held at the end of the month is 1,220.

Month-11: No transactions and hence no cash flows.

Month-12: Dividends received = $1,220 \times 1.25 = 1,525$. The shares can be sold at the NAV of 10.40, which will yield an inflow of 12,688. The total inflow is 14,213.

We can use the IRR function in Excel to compute the rate of return based on the projected cash flow stream. It comes out to be 4.5864% per month. If we convert the monthly rate to a bond equivalent rate, as we did for pass-throughs, we get a figure of 61.75% per annum.

TAXATION ISSUES

In some countries, the dividends received by an investor from a mutual fund are taxed at the hands of the investor. In other countries the mutual fund may have to pay a dividend distribution tax prior to distribution of the payout. If dividends are added to the income of a shareholder and then taxed, the applicable tax rate will be the marginal rate for the investor. In contrast, if a dividend distribution tax is applicable, the tax burden for all shareholders is identical.

If the NAV at the time of sale is higher than what it was at the time of purchase, a capital gains tax may be payable. The rate of tax may depend on whether the investment was short term or long term. There is no hard-and-fast rule as to what is short and what is long. In some countries, an investment of one year or longer is long term, whereas in some others an investor must have held the shares for at least three years for the gains to be classified as long term.

Capital gains taxes may be applicable after providing an indexation benefit. That is, the initial investment may be indexed to a price index such as the CPI, and the prescribed tax rate is applied to the indexed capital gain. This will obviously reduce the effective rate of tax.

At the level of the fund, income received and capital gains/losses may have tax implications. Once again, the capital gains may be classified as short term and long term.

EXAMPLE 11.9

On 1 January the consumer price index (CPI) is at 100. The NAV of a mutual fund is 12.50, and an investor has acquired 1,000 shares. On 31 December three years later the CPI is at 112.50 and the NAV is 22.50. The capital gain without indexation benefit is $(22.50 - 12.50) \times 1,000 = \$10,000$. If indexation is applicable, the indexed cost of acquisition will be $(12.50 \times 112.50) \div 100 = 14.0625$. Thus, the capital gain, if an indexation benefit is available, is $(22.50 - 14.0625) \times 1,000 = \$8,437.50$.

Mutual fund investors have no control over the size of the distributions from the fund, and hence the timing and amount of taxes payable on their fund holdings is largely out of their control. In particular, if a block of investors was to redeem their shares, it could trigger off a sale of securities by the fund, which could cause capital gains to be realized and could in turn lead to a tax liability for investors who choose to retain their holdings in the fund. New investors may assume a tax liability, even though they may have no gains. This is because shareholders as of the date of record will receive a full year's worth of payout, even though they may have held the shares for only one day. This lack of control over capital gains taxes is one of the major limitations of a mutual fund. It is also one of the reasons attributed for the observed fact that shares of a closed-end fund trade at below the NAV. Here is an illustration.

EXAMPLE 11.10

Consider two investors who invest in the same mutual fund. Bob invested on 1 January 20XX at an NAV of $20. The NAV on 30 December is $40. Mike makes an investment on 30 December at the prevailing NAV. On 31 December the mutual fund declares a dividend of $5 per share. The NAV will obviously decline to $35. Assume investors have to pay a tax of 20% on dividends received from the fund. Thus, Bob will have a share worth $35 and a post-tax cash inflow of $4; he has gained $19 in the course of the year. But Mike, who too has a share worth the same and $4 in cash, has seen an erosion of wealth of $1 in just one day. This erosion is due entirely to the tax and is unrelated to market movements.

ALTERNATIVES TO MUTUAL FUNDS

While mutual funds represent a popular and easily accessible investment tool for most investors, there are alternatives. In this section we will examine some of the alternatives.

Exchange-Traded Funds (ETFs)

Mutual funds, as discussed earlier, have two obvious shortcomings. First, the shares of an open-end fund are priced at, and can be transacted only at, the NAV as calculated at the end of the day. Thus, transactions at intraday prices are ruled out. Second, investors have little control over their tax liabilities. As we discussed, a withdrawal by a group of shareholders can lead to a sale of assets, which can trigger off capital gains taxes for investors who choose to continue to remain invested in the fund.

In response to these perceived shortcomings, exchange-traded funds (ETFs) were introduced in the 1990s. These are open-ended in structure but are traded on stock exchanges just like conventional stocks. They are in a way similar to closed-end funds in the sense that their quoted prices are usually at a small premium to or discount from their NAV. In practice, however, these deviations are limited in the case of ETFs, because of the potential for arbitrage, as we shall shortly demonstrate. Most ETFs are based on popular stock indices. But funds that actively manage portfolios are now available.

The exchange-traded feature of an ETF offers many advantages to the investors. Because ETFs are quoted on stock exchanges, like equity shares and closed-end mutual funds, investors can use a conventional brokerage account to acquire and dispose of shares. Price discovery takes place in a continuous market involving market makers. Potential investors can place a variety of orders like market orders, limit orders, and stop-loss orders. Shares of an ETF can be used for both margin trading and short-selling, as with conventional stocks. ETFs are cheaper than equity mutual funds and even index funds, as measured by their typical expense ratios.

Because ETFs are bought by retail investors through brokers and dealers, all the housekeeping activities pertaining to account management are undertaken by such intermediaries. The fund per se interacts with a small group of brokers and dealers. This brings down the fund management cost considerably.

Conventional mutual funds are much less transparent than ETFs. The former are required to disclose the composition of their portfolios only on a periodic basis, which is typically every quarter. The disclosure is generally made with a lag of a few months. Consequently, investors are not aware of the current composition of the underlying portfolio at any point in time. In contrast, the composition of the underlying portfolio of an ETF is known on a daily basis.

Unlike the shares of an open-end mutual fund, ETF shares cannot be bought from or sold back to the sponsor of the fund. The sponsor, however, will exchange large blocks of ETF shares in kind for the securities of the underlying index plus an amount of cash that represents the accumulated dividends of the fund. This large block of ETF shares is called a *creation unit*. One creation unit is typically equal to 50,000 ETF shares. Broker-dealers will usually purchase creation units from the fund and break them up into individual shares, which will then be offered on the exchange to individual investors. Broker-dealers and institutions can also redeem ETF shares by assembling creation units and exchanging them with the fund for a basket of securities plus cash.

The ETF deals exclusively with a chosen group of institutional investors known as Authorized Participants or APs. To acquire a creation unit, an AP will acquire shares of the individual assets that constitute the portfolio and exchange them with the fund sponsor. Once a creation unit is acquired in this way, the ETF shares can be sold by the AP to investors, with a lot size of one.

The basket of securities required to acquire a creation unit is known as the *creation basket*. The reverse, or the redemption of a creation unit, is also possible. An AP can hand over creation units to the sponsor in exchange for a basket of securities, known as the *redemption basket*.

The sponsor of an ETF will reveal the composition of the creation basket at the start of every trading day. So, the APs know what exactly is required for the acquisition and redemption of creation units.

Thus, if shares of an ETF change hands on a stock exchange, the sponsor of the fund has no role in the process. This is similar to the situation where an investor buys shares of XYZ on the NYSE from another investor. The company that has issued the shares plays no role in the process.

If the price of an ETF share were to diverge significantly from its NAV, then arbitrageurs will step in. If the shares are overpriced, then arbitrageurs will short sell ETF shares and buy creation units from the sponsor to fulfil their delivery obligations. On the other hand, if the shares are underpriced, they will buy ETF shares, assemble them into creation units, and sell them to the sponsor.

ETFs also offer a benefit to investors from the standpoint of taxation, as compared to open-end funds. As illustrated earlier, sale of assets due to a large-scale redemption of shares can lead to capital gains or losses for investors who continue to stay invested. In the case of ETFs, however, the fund can redeem a block of shares by offering the underlying securities in return. This does not constitute a taxable event for the remaining shareholders. Therefore, investors in ETFs are usually subject to capital gains taxes only when they sell their shares in the secondary market at a price higher than the original purchase price. In addition, any cash dividends distributed by ETFs are taxable at the hands of the investor.

The price of an ETF share fluctuates from trade to trade. A potential buyer or seller would like to know if the share price is a fair reflection of the price of the underlying basket of securities. To help investors, ETFs have an arrangement with a third party to compute and publish an intraday value of an ETF share, based on the composition of the creation basket that was disclosed in the morning of that day. This value is published every 15 seconds, and is known as the Intraday Indicative Value (IIV). Others terms for the same include *intraday NAV* and *indication of portfolio value*.

Potential Asset Classes

ETFs may be based on a variety of underlying assets. Prominent asset classes include:

- Equity shares
- Fixed Income Securities
- Commodities
- Foreign Currencies

Segregated (Separately Managed) Accounts

Many high-net-worth (HNW) investors dislike mutual funds because of their inability to control their tax liabilities, their inability to influence investment choices, and the absence of "special service." Money managers offer the facility of separately managed investment accounts for such investors. These are obviously more expensive from the standpoint of the investor as compared to a mutual fund, but they mitigate the problems discussed here. For the money managers, the fee income from such accounts is higher, but so are the service costs.

Pension Plans

A pension plan is a fund that is established for the eventual payment of retirement benefits. The plan may be established or sponsored by (a) a private business entity acting on behalf of its employees – these plans are called corporate or private plans; by (2) federal, state, and local governments acting on behalf of their employees – these are called public plans; and by (3) trade unions acting on behalf of their members. In addition, there are individually sponsored plans that are set up by individuals for themselves.

Pension funds in the United States are essentially financed by contributions by the employer. In some plans, the employer's contribution is matched to some extent by a contribution from the employees. The employer's contributions and a specified amount of the employee's contributions, as well as the earnings of the fund's assets, are tax exempt, provided the plan complies with some governmental regulations. Plans that are given tax exemption are called qualified pension plans. In essence, a pension is a form of employee remuneration for which the employee is not taxed until the funds are withdrawn.

TYPES OF PLANS

There are two basic and widely used types of plans: defined benefit plans and defined contribution plans. There is also a new variant called a cash balance plan, which is a hybrid, in the sense that it combines features of both defined benefit and defined contribution plans.

Defined Benefit Plans

In such plans, the sponsor agrees to make specified payments to qualifying employees beginning at retirement. In the case of death before retirement, some payments are made to nominated beneficiaries. These payments are typically made on a monthly basis. The quantum of the payments is determined by a formula that usually takes into account the length of service of the employee and the earnings. The benefit formula is often based on a fixed percentage of the ending salary for each year of service. From the standpoint of the sponsor, the pension obligation is effectively a debt obligation. Therefore, sponsors of such plans are exposed to the risk that there may be insufficient funds in the plan to satisfy the regular contractual payments that must be made to retired employees.

The employer needs to make a prediction of the future benefits to determine the amount of the contribution. The calculation of the current contributions required to support the promised future payments is made by discounting the projected future cash flows. The entire investment risk in these plans is borne by the employer. That is, as the benefits are assured, the employer faces the risk that the returns on contributions to the plan may not be adequate to make the promised payments.

Actuaries are asked to provide estimates of current pension expenses and the liability of the employer. The following factors are relevant for the computations:

- The age and sex of the employee
- The number of years of service
- The employee's salary
- Anticipated salary increases
- Anticipated employee turnover rates
- Anticipated earnings rate on the plan assets
- Appropriate discount rate

It must be remembered that all estimates involve discretion.

These plans provide an incentive for the employees to stay with the firm until retirement, or at least until the benefits get vested. They also provide an incentive for employees to perform well because the defined benefit is a function of the last salary drawn. The funding status of the plan depends on the difference between the plan assets and the projected benefit obligation.

If the assets exceed the obligation, the plan is said to be overfunded, whereas if the assets are less than the obligation, then the plan is said to be underfunded. If the plan is underfunded, employees may lose earned benefits if the company were to go bankrupt.

A plan sponsor establishing such a plan can use the payments made into the fund to purchase an annuity policy from a life insurance company. Defined benefit plans, which are guaranteed by life insurance companies, are called insured benefit plans. These are not necessarily safer than uninsured plans, because they depend on the ability of the insurance company to make the contractual payments, which is something that cannot be guaranteed.

Benefits become vested when employees reach a certain age and complete enough years of service so that they meet the minimum requirements for receiving benefits upon retirement. The payment of benefits is not contingent upon a participant's continuation with the employer or union. Employees are generally discouraged from quitting, because until the plan is vested, the employee could lose at least the accumulation resulting from the employer's contribution.

Defined Contribution Plans

In the case of such plans, the sponsor is responsible only for making specified contributions into the plan on behalf of qualifying participants and is not responsible for making a guaranteed payment to the employee after retirement. The amount that is contributed in the case of such plans is typically either a percentage of the employee's salary and/or a percentage of the employer's profits.

In this case, the payments made after retirement to qualifying participants would depend on how the assets of the plan have grown over time. In other words, the retirement benefit payments are determined by the performance of the assets in which the contributions made into the plan have been invested. The plan sponsor usually gives the participants various options as to the investment vehicles in which the contributions should be invested.

To the employers, such plans offer the lowest costs and the least administrative problems. The employees also find such plans to be attractive, because they give them some control over how their money is invested. In many cases, participating employees are given an option to invest in one or more of a family of mutual funds.

IRAs

IRA stands for individual retirement account and is a pension plan set up by beneficiaries themselves. Most mutual funds offer tax-deferred retirement plans. These include IRAs and Keogh Plans (meant for the self-employed), The IRA and Keogh plans are subject to certain government regulations. The US government has provided a measure of tax relief for wage earners through IRA and Keogh plans. Both types of plans are intended for individuals. IRA is a personal savings plan that offers tax advantages for setting aside money for one's retirement. In order to qualify one must receive taxable compensation. A Keogh Plan is similar to an IRA, except that it applies to individuals who derive their income from self-employment.

In the case of a traditional IRA, one qualifies for a tax deduction while making a contribution, but taxes must be paid when the money is taken out. Roth IRAs, which became available in 1998, are different. Investors cannot claim a tax deduction on the money that they put in; however, the balance in the account may be withdrawn tax-free at retirement, if the account has been open for at least five years, and the investors have crossed a threshold in terms of age.

CASH BALANCE PLANS

A cash balance plan is basically a defined benefit plan that has some features of a defined contribution plan. It is like a defined benefit plan in the sense that future pension benefits are assured. These benefits are based on a fixed-amount annual employer contribution and a guaranteed annual investment return. Every participant has an account that is credited with a dollar amount periodically, which is generally determined as a percentage of employees' pay. The account is also credited with interest which is linked to some fixed or variable index such as the Consumer Price Index (CPI). Interest is credited at the rate specified in the plan and is not related to the actual investment earnings of the employer's pension trust. Consequently, any gains or losses on the investment accrue to, or are borne by, the employer.

The similarity with a defined contribution plan is that many cash balance plans allow the employee to take a lump-sum payment of vested benefits when terminating their employment with a particular employer, which can then be rolled over into an IRA or to the new employer's plan. In other words, these plans are portable from one employer to another.

Let us say that employees are promised a balance of $600,000 at the time of retirement. Once they retire, employees can take this amount as a lump sum or convert it to an annuity. Every year, the employer will credit the account with a percentage of the annual wage that it pays to the employees. The employer will also credit the account with a fixed percentage of the balance outstanding at the start of the year.

In a defined contribution plan employees will be unsure about the balance in the account at the time of retirement. In the case of a cash balance account, however, they will know it for sure in advance. This feature makes a cash benefit plan resemble a defined benefit plan.

Orders and Exchanges

An order is an instruction to trade that is given by a party who wishes to take a position in an asset. If parties wish to establish a long position, they will issue a buy order, whereas if they desire to go short, they will place a sell order. At the time of placing an order, the security in which the investor wishes to take a position must be clearly identified. This is fairly simple in the case of stocks because most companies usually issue only one type of shares. It must be remembered that some firms may have issued equity shares with differential voting rights, or even nonvoting shares, in which case merely specifying the name of the company will not be adequate. Bonds are more complex. Company XYZ may have issued bonds maturing in 2025 or in 2030. In 2025 there may be an issue maturing in January and possibly one in October. There may be multiple types of bonds maturing in the same month and in the same year, but with different coupons. Thus, XYZ may have bonds maturing in October 2025 with a 5% coupon as well as with a 6% coupon. Hence, if traders wish to buy or sell bonds, they must identify the issuing company and specify the maturity year, the month of maturity, and the coupon rate. Without such a detailed description, the specification may be inadequate. There are certain supranational agencies that may issue bonds with the same month and year of maturity, and the same coupon rate, but with different currencies, say, US dollars and euros. In this case the currency should also be specified by a potential trader.

Derivatives also require more elaborate specification. XYZ company may have futures contracts expiring in January 20XX, February 20XX, and March 20XX. Thus, while placing an order for a futures contract, it is imperative to specify the expiration month, in addition to the identity of the underlying asset. Options are even more complicated from the standpoint of identification. To place an order for options on XYZ, the trader needs to specify the expiration month and the exercise price. That's not all. For each combination of the expiration month and exercise price, there will exist call and put options. Thus, to place a buy or a sell order for an options contract, the trader must spell out the underlying asset, the expiration month, the exercise price, and whether it is a call or a put.

The quantity in which a long or short position is sought to be taken must be clearly spelled out. Most stocks used to trade in what were known as round lots or board lots, where each lot was usually for 100 shares. With the advent of dematerialized securities or scripless trading, however, this requirement has been dispensed with. The quantity that is specified in an order is known as the *order size*.

The price at which an investor is willing to transact is obviously a key feature of the order specification. There are two possibilities. There are investors who will accept any price that a market may offer at the point in time at which the order is placed. Such investors will place what are known as *market orders*. There are others, however, who may have a floor or a ceiling in mind. Traders placing buy orders may seek to specify a price ceiling, that is, a maximum price they are prepared to pay. On the other hand, those placing sell orders may wish to specify a price floor, that is, a minimum price below which they would not like to transact. Traders who specify a floor or a ceiling for the price, place what are known as *limit orders*. Obviously, in the case of market orders, the only parameter that has to be specified is the order size. In the case of limit orders, however, in addition to the quantity, the limit price also has to be specified.

Traders are also required to specify the period of time for which they wish their orders to remain valid. Many exchanges allow only *good today limit orders* or what are known as *day orders*. That is, an order is valid only until the close of trading on the day on which it is placed. If it were to fail to be executed on that day, it would automatically stand canceled. Other exchanges may permit orders to be carried forward; even in such cases the exchange will specify a maximum validity period. Some exchanges permit traders to specify a validity period. These are called *good till days* or GTD orders. Variants include *good this week* orders, and *good this month* orders. Not all brokers may accept such orders, at least not for all clients. There could be situations where traders specify an order with an expiration limit and then forget about it. If it were to go through subsequently, they may call and berate the broker for not informing them about the presence of this order. Clearly, the broker is not at fault. Hence, most brokers will allow only regular clients to specify such orders.

Some traders specify that their orders should be executed on placement or else should be canceled immediately. These are known as *fill or kill* orders. In such cases, the trader will get 100% of the quantity sought, or the order itself will be canceled. Immediate or Cancel orders are similar, but permit partial execution. Thus, if a buy order is placed for 500 shares, and a counterparty is available for only 250 shares, then 250 shares will be bought, and the rest of the order will be canceled. Some traders may allow their order to be filled only if the trade results in the fulfillment of the entire quantity that has been specified; that is, they will not accept a partial match. Such orders are known as *all-or-none* or *all or nothing* orders. The difference between a *fill or kill* and an *all or none* order is that in the case of the former there is either 100% execution or cancellation, whereas in the case of the latter, if 100% execution is not possible, the entire order will be kept pending. The following examples will illustrate these concepts.

EXAMPLE 12.1

Grant Taylor, a trader based in Chicago, has placed a buy order for 80 March 20XX futures contracts on corn. He has specified a price limit of $6.80 per bushel. The order specification states that it is *good this week*. The underlying asset is corn and the expiration month of the futures contract is March 20XX. The order size is 80 contracts. It is a limit order because there is a price limit of $6.80 per bushel. Because it is a buy order, the limit price represents an upper limit or price ceiling. The order is valid for the week in which it is placed. Thus, it will automatically expire at the close of trading on Friday, if it is not executed by then. Quite obviously the exchange in this case allows orders with a validity of more than one day.

> ## EXAMPLE 12.2
>
> Maureen McNally, a trader in Colorado, has placed a buy order for 80 September 20XX call options contracts on XYZ with an exercise price of $75. The specified limit price is $6.50. The asset to which the order pertains is a call options contract on XYZ stock with an exercise price of $75, and which is scheduled to expire in September 20XX. The order size is 80, and the limit price is $6.50 per share. Thus, Maureen is prepared to buy if the option premium is $6.50 or less per share. It must be noted that the price limit in an options order is for the premium of the contract, and not the exercise price. The maximum total premium payable, if the order were to be executed, is $650 per contract, for each stock options contract is on 100 units of the underlying asset, which in this case is shares of XYZ.

> ## EXAMPLE 12.3
>
> Rodney Smith has placed a market order for 200 bonds of ABC Corporation maturing in August 20XX. The coupon rate has been specified as 4.2% per annum. Thus, the security has been adequately identified.

IMPORTANT ACRONYMS

WAP: Weighted Average Price
  If a trade is executed at multiple prices, the WAP will be computed.

LTP: Last Traded Price
  This is the last price at which a trade has taken place.

CMP: Current Market Price
  This is the best bid for sellers and the best ask for buyers.

FOK: Fill or Kill

IOC: Immediate or Cancel

AON: All or None

GTC: Good Till Canceled

GTD: Good Till Days

GTW: Good This Week

GTM: Good This Month

LOB: Limit Order Book

SLB: Stop-Loss Book

MARKET ORDERS AND LIMIT ORDERS

Traders who place market orders are content with the best price that the market has to offer. Obviously, the trading system should be structured in such a way that an order is executed at the best available price from the standpoint of the trader. The best available price for a potential buyer is the lowest of the limit prices of all the limit sell orders that are pending in the market when the market buy order enters. On the other hand, the best available price for a potential seller is the highest of the limit prices of all the limit buy orders that are pending in the market when the market sell order enters. Thus, in order to ensure that buyers are given access to the lowest prices on the sell side, while sellers are given access to the highest prices on the buy side, limit orders that are pending execution are arranged in descending order of price if they are buy orders, and ascending order of price if they are sell orders. This helps ensure that both buyers and sellers will get the best possible price from their perspective.

In practice, limit orders are arranged in the system using two or more priority rules. The primary priority rule is the *price priority rule*. All limit buy orders that are pending execution are sorted in descending order of price, and all limit sell orders that are awaiting execution are sorted in ascending order of price. Thus, an incoming market buy order is assured of execution at the lowest available price on the sell side, whereas an incoming market sell order is guaranteed to be executed at the highest available price on the buy side.

Price priority is the primary criterion that is universally valid across exchanges. Every exchange will have at least one secondary criterion. The secondary criterion that is universally applied is time priority. That is, if two limit orders have the same price limit, the order that came first in a chronological sequence will be accorded priority. Thus, for a given limit price, the orders are arranged in the sequence in which they are received. That is, an order that came in earlier would be accorded priority over an order that came later. Some exchanges also use order size as a priority rule.

THE LIMIT PRICE

For orders placed in connection with stocks and bonds, the limit price represents the highest price that a buyer is prepared to pay, or the lowest price that a seller is prepared to accept. In the case of a futures contract, the specified price limit refers to the futures price. As mentioned earlier, in the case of options, the limit price is for the option premium per unit of the underlying asset.

THE LIMIT ORDER BOOKS

All unexecuted but valid orders need to be stored in the system until they can be matched with an incoming order. The record of such orders is referred to as the *limit order book* (LOB). Prior to the advent of electronic trading, the record was physically maintained in the form of a book of orders. In modern systems everything is maintained in an electronic form. The advantage of the modern system is that with the click of a mouse, a trader can switch from the limit order book for one security to that for another security.

ILLUSTRATION OF A LIMIT ORDER BOOK

Consider the following *limit order book* (LOB) at a given point in time. The book represents the situation for the common stock of XYZ, as at 11:30 a.m. on the morning of 15 July 20XX.

As can be seen, on the buy side the orders have been arranged in descending order of price, whereas on the sell side they have been arranged in ascending order of price. On the buy side both Maureen and Myra have given a limit price of 98.85. Obviously, Maureen's order was placed before Myra's.

The prices specified by traders seeking to buy are known as bids. Conversely, the prices given by those seeking to sell are called offers. The best bid is the highest of the bids in the book. Obviously, it is the best from a seller's perspective. Similarly, the best ask is the lowest of the asks in the book. As can be deduced, it is the best from a buyer's perspective. The difference between the best ask and the best bid is called the bid–ask spread. In our example it is 100.55 – 99.45 = $1.10.

EXAMPLE 12.4

Robert, who sees the limit order book depicted in Table 12.1, places a market buy order for 1,000 shares. 500 shares will be bought at 100.55, another 400 at 100.75, and the final 100 at 100.95. The weighted average price (WAP) may be computed as follows.

$$\text{WAP} = [(500 \times 100.55) + (400 \times 100.75) + (100 \times 100.95)] \div 1,000 = 100.67$$

What if Robert had instead placed a market sell order for 1,000 shares? The WAP will be:

$$\text{WAP} = [(200 \times 99.45) + (250 \times 99.25) + (350 \times 99.05) + (200 \times 98.85)] \div 1,000$$

$$= 99.14$$

TABLE 12.1 Limit Order Book for XYZ Stock at 11:30 a.m. on 15 July 20XX

Trader	Order Size	Limit Price	Limit Price	Order Size	Trader
Mike	200	99.45	100.55	500	Nancy
Mark	250	99.25	100.75	400	Nina
Mathew	350	99.05	100.95	600	Nicole
Maureen	400	98.85	102.25	650	Nick
Myra	500	98.85	102.55	350	Nora
Melanie	600	98.25	102.75	400	Norbert
Melissa	750	98.05	102.95	500	Neville
Molly	800	97.95	103.05	800	Nigel

LIMIT ORDERS VERSUS MARKET ORDERS

Traders who place limit orders are able to control the price at which their order will be executed. A potential buyer who has placed a limit buy order with a limit price of 99.25 can be assured that the eventual price paid will not exceed this limit. Similarly, a potential seller who has placed a limit sell order with a limit price of 101.25 will receive at least this price. However, a trader who places a limit order can never be sure how long it will take for the order to get executed. It could take an inordinately long time for the order to get executed, and there could be circumstances in which the order fails to get executed. This is particularly true for limit orders that are not aggressive. The meaning of aggression may be explained as follows. For buy orders the higher the limit price, the greater is the projected aggression, whereas for sell orders the lower the limit price, the greater is the displayed aggression.

Consider the case of Molly, who is eighth from the top in the list of buy orders. Now assume that Robert gives a market buy order for 1,000 shares. The last traded price will be 100.95. Assume that Roger now gives a market buy order for 750 shares. The last traded price will jump to 102.25. Seeing the price jump to this level, other potential buyers may get more aggressive. That is, they may give limit orders with higher limit prices. For instance, what if Mitch gives a buy order for 300 shares with a limit rice of 99.65, while Marvin gives a buy order for 500 shares with a limit price of 100.05? Due to these two orders, Molly will now be tenth from the top in the list of buy orders.

Thus, if a series of market buy orders keep entering, the last traded price will be steadily pushed upwards. In such situations, if more aggressive limit buy orders were to keep entering, there could be a substantial delay in the execution of a limit order that was placed earlier. The same is true for the other side of the book. If a series of market sell orders were to keep entering, the LTP will be pushed downward. Now if more aggressive limit sell orders were to enter with lower limit prices, a preexisting limit sell order could be pushed behind considerably. In the event of the exchange accepting only day orders, an order like Molly's may not be executed during the course of the day and consequently will have to be canceled.

It is not essential for incoming orders to be market orders for a preexisting limit order to lose its relative position in the queue. A series of aggressive limit orders, either buy or sell orders, could cause the same result to be achieved.

MARKETABLE LIMIT ORDERS

Consider Table 12.1. The best bid is 99.45 and the best ask is 100.55. If potential buyers feel that the best ask price of 100.55 is acceptable, they will place a market buy order. If they feel it is too high, they will place a limit buy order with a lower limit price. Similarly, if potential sellers feel that the best bid price of 99.45 is acceptable, they will place a market sell order. If they feel it is too low, they will place a limit sell order with a higher limit price. Thus, usually, limit buy orders are placed with a limit price that is lower than the best ask, whereas limit sell orders are placed with a limit price higher than the best bid.

There could be situations, however, where traders price their limit order very aggressively. How will such aggression manifest itself? A potential buyer may place an order with a limit price higher than the best ask, or a potential seller may place an order with a limit price lower than the best bid. Such orders are referred to as *marketable limit orders*. Marketable limit orders by definition are those limit orders that are likely to be executed upon submission. In the situation depicted in Table 12.1, a limit buy order with a limit price greater than or equal to 100.55 will be classified as a marketable limit order. Similarly, a limit sell order with a limit price of 99.45 or less will also be classified as a marketable limit order.

Why would anyone wish to place a marketable limit order when they can place a market order? Assume that an investor named William places a limit buy order with a price of 100.60 for 200 shares. His anticipation is that it will be matched with the best sell order and that a trade will result. But what if a market buy order for 1,000 shares enters the system before the limit order is placed? Remember that in today's online trading world, traders throughout the world are watching the action, and an order can always sneak in before we can place our order as planned. In this case, the best ask after the execution of this order will be 100.95. Because William's bid is lower than 100.95, it will stay in the book in the form of a limit buy order with a limit price of 100.60, at the top of the list of buyers. If, however, William had given a market order and the same sequence of events were to have occurred, his order would be matched with the sell order at 100.95, and a trade would result at that price. Thus, if a trader like William were of the opinion that speed matters, but so does price, beyond a point, he may prefer a marketable limit order to a market order.

Thus, with marketable limit orders, in the event that things don't work out as planned, the trader still retains an element of control over the price. But there is a drawback in the case of such orders as compared to market orders. A marketable limit order is, after all, a limit order, and limit orders, marketable or otherwise, are subject to execution uncertainty.

TRADE PRICING RULES

The incoming order is referred to as an *active order*, whereas the orders that are already present in the system are referred to as *passive orders*. The trade price is the limit price of the passive order with which the active order is matched.

Consider the LOB depicted in Table 12.1 Assume that William places a market buy order for 800 shares. 500 will get matched with Nancy at a price of 100.55, and 300 with Nina at 100.75. The WAP will be 100.625. Both Nancy and Nina are passive compared to William. What would happen if William were to issue a marketable limit order with a limit price of 100.80? Once again, 500 will get matched with Nancy and 300 with Nina. The WAP will still be 100.625.

An interesting situation arises when a market order enters the system when the opposite side of the LOB is empty. If we were to wait until a limit order appears on the other side, the passive price rule cannot be applied, as the passive order in this case is a market order. Consequently, in such situations, the market order is usually converted to a limit order with a limit price equal to the last traded price. If it is then matched with an order on the opposite side, a trade will result at this assigned limit price.

EXAMPLE 12.5

Consider the LOB depicted in Table 12.2. The last trade price was 99.75.

Assume that William gives a market buy order for 200 shares. As there is no order on the opposite side, William's order will be converted into a limit buy order with a limit price of 99.75 and will take its place at the top of the buy side

(continued)

(continued)

of the LOB. If a subsequent market sell order for 200 shares or more appears, a trade will result at 99.75. The same would happen if a marketable limit order for 200 shares or more, with a limit price of 99.75 or less, enters the system.

TABLE 12.2 Limit Order Book for a Stock

Trader	Order Size	Limit Price	Limit Price	Order Size	Trader
Mike	200	99.45			
Mark	250	99.25			
Mathew	350	99.05			
Maureen	400	98.85			

It is not necessary that a market order go to the top of the limit order book, if it is converted to a limit order. In the previous illustration, what if the last traded price was 99.15? William's order will be converted to a limit order with this limit price. It will be third in the queue, between Mark and Mathew.

STOP-LOSS AND STOP-LIMIT ORDERS

Stop or *stop-loss orders* are placed by traders who already have a position in the market. At the time of order placement, the traders have no desire to unwind their existing position. However, if market conditions were to suddenly turn adverse, the traders may have a threshold price beyond which they are unwilling to tolerate losses. This desire to cap a trader's loss is why such orders are also termed as stop-loss orders.

Assume that William is short in 400 shares and observes the LOB shown in Table 12.1. The best available price is 100.55. If William is of the opinion that the price is acceptable, he will place a market order. But if he feels it is not high enough to make him buy, and that his threshold price corresponds to 100.95, he could place a stop-loss order with a trigger price of 100.95. For a stop-loss buy order, the trigger will be higher than the best ask. Unlike a market order, or a limit order, the stop-loss order will not directly enter the LOB. It will go to the *stop loss book* (SLB). It will lie dormant there until it is triggered off and, if triggered, will jump into the LOB as a market order.

Now assume that a market buy order for 1,750 shares enters. The LTP will be 102.25. William's order will get triggered off and will go through at 102.25. As can be seen, the eventual trade price is substantially different from the threshold that is specified. This is because once a stop-loss order is triggered off it becomes a market order, and with such orders, traders cannot control the price.

If William wanted to ensure that the execution price is close to his trigger of 100.95, he has the option of placing a *stop-limit order*. This, as the name suggests, is a hybrid between a stop-loss order and a limit order. Thus, two prices have to be specified. The first is the trigger price corresponding to the threshold. The second is the required limit price, if the order were to be triggered off. Obviously, the limit for a stop-loss buy order will be higher than the threshold price for such orders. Such an order, if triggered, will enter the LOB as a limit order. As is the case with all limit orders, however, there is execution uncertainty, if they were to be activated.[1]

Stop-loss and stop-limit orders can be placed by potential sellers as well. Assume that Winnie is long in 500 shares. She would like to sell if the price were to hit or go below 98.75. Assume that she gives a stop sell order with a trigger of 98.75, and that a market sell order for 3,000 shares enters the system. The LTP will be 98.05. Winnie's order will be activated and will become a market sell order. 50 shares will be sold at 98.05 and 450 at 97.95 and the WAP will be 97.96. Once again, the WAP is substantially different from the trigger price of 98.75. This is because once the order was triggered off it became a market order, and the eventual execution price in such cases is uncertain. If Winnie had wanted, she could have given a stop-limit order with a trigger of 98.75 and a limit of say 98.60. In such a situation, she would be assured of a minimum price of 98.60. However, as in the case of a stop-limit buy order, this kind of an order too will lead to execution uncertainty. Obviously, the limit price for a stop-limit sell order will be less than the trigger price.

TRAILING STOP-LOSS ORDERS

In the case of trailing stop-loss orders, the trigger price does not remain fixed, but moves with the market in one direction. Let us consider sell orders first. The trigger price will be specified as a price that is less than the last traded price. The specification can be as a percentage or in dollars. If the market price increases, the trigger will increase along with it. However, if the market price declines, the trigger will remain constant.

For a buy order the trigger will be specified as a price that is greater than the last traded price. Once again, the difference can be as a percentage or in dollars. If the market price declines, the trigger will decline along with it. However, if the market price were to increase, the trigger will remain constant. Here are some examples.

EXAMPLE 12.6

The best bid at a point in time is 99 and the best ask is 101. The last traded price was 100.00. A trader gives a trailing stop sell order as LTP − 2%. Thus, the current trigger is $100.00 \times 0.98 = 98.00$.

Now assume that a market buy order comes and the LTP increases to 101.00. The new trigger will be $101.00 \times 0.98 = 98.98$. This is followed by a market sell order that gets executed at 100.50. The trigger will remain constant at 98.98. The next order is a market sell order that gets executed at 98.75. The stop-loss order will get triggered off and will enter the LOB as a market order.

(continued)

---

[1] If the trigger price is hit, the stop-loss order will be converted to a limit order. Like all limit orders, eventual execution is not a certainty.

(continued)

Now let us consider a trailing stop buy order. The last traded price was 100.00. A trader gives a stop-loss buy order as LTP + \$1.25. Thus, the current trigger is 101.25.

Assume a market sell order comes in and the LTP declines to 99.25. The new trigger will be 100.50. This is followed by a market buy order that gets executed at 99.75. The trigger will remain constant at 100.50. The next order is a market buy order that gets executed at 101.40. The stop-loss order will get triggered off and will enter the LOB as a market order. Trailing stop-loss orders can also be specified with price limits.

MARKET TO LIMIT ORDERS

While an order will typically get filled at multiple prices, which could be very different from each other, a trader may wish to ensure that the order is filled at prices that do not vary much. In such a situation the trader has the option of placing a market to limit or MTL order. The execution of such as order may be illustrated with the help of an example.

EXAMPLE 12.7

Consider the LOB shown in Table 12.3.

TABLE 12.3 Illustration of a Market to Limit Order

Trader	Order Size	Limit Price	Limit Price	Order Size	Trader
Mike	100	99.45			
Mark	200	99.25			
Mathew	200	99.15			

Maureen places a market to limit sell order for 500 shares. 100 shares will be sold at a price of 99.45. The balance of 400 will be converted to a limit sell order with a limit price of 99.45 and will go to the top of the LOB on the right side. Thus, Maureen can be assured that the entire order will go through at a price of 99.45 or less. However, there is a downside to such orders. There is execution uncertainty for the balance of 400 shares, because a limit order always exposes the trader to the specter of execution delays.

EQUIVALENCE WITH OPTIONS

Limit orders may be perceived as options. A limit buy order is a put option, for it gives other traders the right to sell to the trader placing the order. Similarly, a limit sell order is a call option, for it gives other traders the right to buy from the trader placing the order. The limit price that is specified in the order is the strike price of the corresponding option.

There are two key differences between conventional options and the options implicit in limit orders. First, unlike normal options, limit orders represent options with a zero premium, because a trader will not be paid for placing a limit order, which is tantamount to selling an option. Second, a conventional option is a contract between the seller and a particular buyer. In the case of limit orders, however, there is no exclusive owner or buyer. Once the order has been placed, anyone is welcome to come and trade by placing a market order or a marketable limit order.

The question therefore arises as to why someone should offer an option without receiving a premium in return. The rationale is as follows. Traders have an option of placing a market order or a limit order. By placing a limit order, they hope to trade at a better price. Consequently, in such a situation, they may offer an option to others, despite the fact that they will not receive a premium for selling such an option.

VALIDITY CONDITIONS

Traders have the option of specifying a validity instruction to indicate how long their order should remain valid in the event of there being a delay in execution. Such instructions may be appended to any kind of order. However, they are used primarily for limit orders and stop orders (with or without a price limit), for such orders have a tendency to experience delays in execution.

GOOD TILL CANCELED (GTC) ORDERS

If a GTC order is not executed on the day it is entered, it will be carried forward to the following day. Thus, on the following day the LOB at the opening of the market will contain such pending orders. This will happen every day until the trade is executed or canceled. Obviously, such orders cannot remain in the system for an indefinite period of time. Therefore, the exchange will specify a maximum validity period. The order will be automatically canceled if it remains unexecuted at the end of this prescribed time limit.

GOOD TILL DAYS ORDERS

In the case of these orders, the trader can specify the validity period. However, the time limit for such orders cannot exceed the validity period for a GTC order. Thus if a GTC order on a particular exchange has a maximum limit of a month, then this would be the maximum limit for a good till days order. There are different variations of such orders, such as good this week (GTW) and good this month (GTM) orders. The former is valid until the close of trading on Friday of the week in which it is placed, whereas the latter is valid until the close of trading of the last trading day of the month in which it is placed.

ORDERS WITH QUANTITY RESTRICTIONS

A fill or kill order (FOK) is one where the entire order must be filled on submission or the order itself must be canceled. Partial execution is not permissible. On the other hand, an immediate or cancel (IOC) order permits partial execution. In this case, the mandate is to fill whatever is possible and cancel the balance. Here is an illustration.

EXAMPLE 12.8

Consider the LOB shown in Table 12.3. Vincent places a market sell order for 800 shares that is fill or kill. Obviously, the order will be canceled. What if the order had been for 500 shares? It would be filled with a WAP of 99.25. What if Vincent had placed an IOC for 800 shares? 500 shares will be sold with a WAP of 99.25 and the balance of 300 shares will be canceled.

An *all or none* or *all or nothing* (AON) order is another type of order with a quantity restriction. Like an FOK order, it is required to be filled in its entirety or not at all. However, unlike the FOK, it need not be canceled if it cannot be filled, and needs to be kept alive until a suitable match can be found. An AON limit order receives lower priority as compared to a normal limit order with the same limit price but without any such restriction. An AON order may be filled at multiple prices as the following example illustrates.

EXAMPLE 12.9

Consider Table 12.3. Alex gives an AON sell order with a limit price of 99 for 800 shares. It is obviously a marketable limit order which cannot be filled in its entirety. Consequently, it will take its place at the top of the sellers' queue with a limit price of 99. In this case, although the limit price of the sell order is lower than the best bid, execution is infeasible because of the quantity restriction. If the order had been specified for 400 shares with a limit price of 99, 100 shares would have been sold at 99.45, 200 at 99.25, and the balance 100 at 99.15. The WAP will be 99.275. In this case, the entire order has been filled at three different prices.

A POINT ON ORDER SPECIFICATION

In an electronic trading platform, it is important to specify the order correctly to achieve the desired result. If traders were to desire to modify an order subsequently, they will have to cancel the original order and rebook a fresh order. There are two related problems in practice. First, by the time the order is canceled and modified, market conditions may have changed substantially. Second, before traders are able to cancel a preexisting order, it may have gone through. Thus, it is imperative to correctly specify the order right at the outset.

OPEN-OUTCRY TRADING SYSTEMS

Open-outcry systems, also referred to as *oral auctions*, are a type of continuous bilateral auction. They were extremely common in the last century, but have of late been replaced to a large extent by electronic trading systems.

In an oral auction there is a central location at the stock or derivatives exchange where the traders congregate. This location is referred to as a *ring* in a stock exchange and as a *pit* in a derivatives exchange. Traders cry out their bids and offers hoping to entice others who may be willing to take a matching position.

While shouting out their requirements, they will concurrently be listening for orders being shouted out by other traders. A trade will result if a buyer were to accept a seller's offer, or if a seller were to accept a buyer's bid. The consummation of a trade is accompanied by a shout of "take it" if the buyer were to accept an offer, or by a shout of "sold" if the seller were to accept a bid.[2]

Since both buyers and sellers will be shouting out their requirements, it is necessary to distinguish between bids and offers. In most oral auctions the convention is that buyers will call out their limit price first followed by the quantity, whereas sellers will call out their required quantity first followed by their limit price. In certain exchanges, traders have a practice of using a system of hand and finger signals to indicate their limit prices, and the quantities they wish to trade.

The first rule that traders are required to follow on an open-outcry exchange is known as the *open-outcry* rule. This means that whatever the traders have in mind has to be verbally expressed. Once traders express their intention, any other trader standing in the pit may respond. It is a normal practice for traders to take turns in making bids and counter-offers, and offers and counter-bids, before the two parties are able to agree on a price. When a trader expresses the bid or offer, the first counterparty who accepts it gets to make the trade.

As in the case of electronic systems, there are certain priority rules. The principal rule is price priority. That is, a bidder is required to accept the lowest offer, and a seller is required to accept the highest bid. Such a rule is obviously self-enforcing in practice, because an honest buyer will always be on the lookout for the lowest price, while an honest seller will always strive to obtain the highest price.

The price priority rule requires that there should be clarity about the best bid and best offer that are available at a point in time. Obviously inferior bids and offers – bids with prices lower than the best bid, and offers with prices higher than the best offer – will only serve to create confusion. Consequently, most open-outcry systems will not allow a trader to bid below the best bid that is currently available, or offer above the best offer that is currently available. However, a trader may at any time improve upon the best bid by bidding higher, or improve upon the best offer by quoting a lower offer. A trader who does so will obviously attain priority.

The time preference rule in an oral auction, however, is not self-enforcing. This is because from the standpoint of a potential counterparty, it is immaterial as to whose bid or offer is accepted. The sole criterion is that traders should get the best available price. Hence, in such auctions traders who are currently enjoying time preference may have to vocally defend their status. That is, if another party were to bid or offer at

---

[2]See Harris (2003).

the same price, they would have to shout out "That's my bid" or "That's my offer" to ensure that they continue to enjoy priority. Also, in such auctions, bids and offers are valid only for an instant. Hence, if a counterparty is not available, traders may have to repeatedly shout out their order in order to indicate to potential counterparties that they are very much interested in trading.

The trade pricing rule in such auctions is simple. Once a bid or an offer is accepted by another trader, the trade will take place at the price proposed by the trader whose quote was accepted.

ELECTRONIC MARKETS VERSUS OPEN-OUTCRY MARKETS

A system is considered to be successful if the liquidity is high and transactions costs are low. Transactions costs include not just direct transaction costs such as commissions, but also indirect costs such as lost revenues due to illiquidity.

Liquidity in an open-outcry system is supplied by traders called *locals*. These sell-side traders are always ready to buy and sell on their own account. The problem in practice is that a local is restricted at any point in time to a single pit. In a typical derivatives market, different assets trade in different pits. Obviously, locals cannot devote attention to multiple pits at the same time by running back and forth between pits. As a consequence, locals are in practice required to service the traders at their usual pit, even though there may be very little trading activity there.

In contrast, in an electronic system, traders do not face such locational constraints and can effortlessly switch to a different screen displaying the LOB for a different asset, simply with the click of a mouse. Hence, for assets characterized by relatively lower trading volumes, electronic trading is clearly the preferred mode of trading. Thus, most derivatives markets in emerging economies, where the trading volumes are lower, have chosen electronic systems as the mode of trading.

Evidence indicates that even advanced economies are increasingly switching to electronic systems. It must be remembered that exchanges in these countries introduced derivative contracts decades ago. In the earlier years, trading volumes were high for most contracts, because such instruments with their novel features provided opportunities that were simply not available earlier. In most of these cases, trading was active even though the underlying assets were not necessarily very sophisticated. After a point in time, however, the financial instruments on which derivatives have subsequently been introduced tend to be highly specialized. Consequently, the number of traders attracted to such contracts is relatively lower. Thus, derivatives on new instruments are characterized by relatively lower trading volumes, which is causing even established exchanges to switch to screen-based trading systems. Exchanges like the CME Group, which is a pioneer in derivatives trading, continue to use both types of trading platforms.

The older exchanges are also faced with the specter of declining trading volumes. This is to a large extent due to competition from newly established exchanges that embraced modern trading systems from the very outset. In the face of such rivalry, there is little option for the older exchanges but to embrace electronic systems. Electronic systems also play a key role in cross-border trading. Trading across borders is an accepted fact of the modern economy, characterized by the tenets of LPG: Liberalization, Privatization, and Globalization.

Electronic trading platforms are characterized by lower operational costs as compared to open-outcry systems. Screen-based trading platforms typically require less labor, skill, and time. Oral auctions are characterized by higher fixed costs due to the need for relatively larger manpower. The overheads such as building and back-office costs also tend to be higher.

The disadvantages not withstanding open-outcry systems continue to have certain merits of their own. As Sarkar and Tozzi have argued, highly active derivative contracts are better traded on traditional trading platforms, because the traders on such exchanges are more accomplished at executing large and complex orders.[3] Traders in traditional systems also have the advantage that they are well aware of the trading behavior of competitors and counterparties, because the same parties trade with each other virtually every day. Such knowledge is indispensable for predicting the response of counterparties while implementing a trading strategy. In contrast, traders in electronic trading systems are faceless entities, and the counterparties remain unidentified.

Finally, in an oral auction, order revision is relatively simpler because quotes are valid only for an instant after being expressed. In an electronic system, however, modification of an order that has been placed earlier requires the trader to explicitly cancel the prior order. In such a situation, there is always a possibility that the original order will get executed before the change can be effected.

CALL MARKETS

In a continuous market, orders keep coming in when the market is open. They are ranked in the LOB based on the priority rules, and are executed as and when a match is feasible.

In a call market, orders are accumulated for a period in time. At the end of the stipulated period, all the buy and sell orders which have been received are ranked according to price priority. That is, buy orders are arranged in descending order of price and sell orders are arranged in ascending order of price. The market clearing price is determined, and all the orders that satisfy the criteria for execution are executed at the market clearing price. The modalities may vary from market to market. Here is an example based on a major emerging market stock exchange.

EXAMPLE 12.10

The exchange allows traders to submit orders between 9 a.m. and 9:15 a.m. The market is then called, and in this manner the opening price for the day is determined. The following orders have been received in the 15-minute interval on a given day (Table 12.4).

By comparing the demand and supply at each price, we can determine the maximum tradeable quantity, as depicted in Table 12.5.

(continued)

---

[3] See Sarkar and Tozzi (1998).

(continued)

TABLE 12.4 List of Orders Received Prior to the Market Being Called

Order Side	Price	Quantity	Aggregate Demand	Order Side	Quantity	Aggregate Supply
Buy	98.50	2500	38000	Sell	1000	1000
Buy	99.50	3500	35500	Sell	1500	2500
Buy	100.00	4000	32000	Sell	2500	5000
Buy	100.75	2000	28000	Sell	4000	9000
Buy	101.25	3000	26000	Sell	5000	14000
Buy	102.00	6000	23000	Sell	7500	21500
Buy	102.50	8000	17000	Sell	6000	27500
Buy	103.00	4000	9000	Sell	4500	32000
Buy	103.25	3000	5000	Sell	8000	40000
Buy	103.60	2000	2000	Sell	8000	48000

TABLE 12.5 Computation of the Maximum Tradeable Quantity

Price	Aggregate Demand	Aggregate Supply	Maximum Tradeable Quantity
98.50	38000	1000	1000
99.50	35500	2500	2500
100.00	32000	5000	5000
100.75	28000	9000	9000
101.25	26000	14000	14000
102.00	23000	21500	21500
102.50	17000	27500	17000
103.00	9000	32000	9000
103.25	5000	40000	5000
103.60	2000	48000	2000

The maximum tradeable quantity is 21,500 at a price of 102.00. Hence the market clearing price is 102.00. At this price, the quantity demanded is 23,000 while the quantity supplied is 21,500. Assume that market buy orders have been received for 8,000 shares and market sell orders have been received for 12,500 shares. The quantity demanded is 1,500 more than the quantity supplied. Thus these 1,500 shares will be matched with market sell orders. The price will obviously be 102. That leaves 8,000 shares to be bought at the market and 11,000 shares to be sold at the market. Thus 8,000 shares will be transacted at the market clearing price of 102. The remaining 3,000 shares that are sought to be sold cannot be transacted.

The Macroeconomics of Financial Markets

The financial markets are a key component of the economy of a country. Thus, it is not surprising that decisions taken by the government of a country and its central bank have major consequences for the working of such markets. Activities in a country's domestic financial markets are related to activities in foreign markets as well. Thus, decisions taken in one country invariably have implications for the financial markets of other countries.

The policies of significance for a country's financial markets are the fiscal and monetary policies designed and implemented by the federal government and the central bank, respectively. An economy's interest rates, which influence all decisions of significance, are determined by such policies. Trade with foreign countries, foreign investments in the domestic economy, and a country's investments in foreign economies are also influenced by such policies.

ECONOMIC GROWTH

Economic growth is a measure of the expansion of an economy over time. It is measured by comparing the output for a period, such as a year or a quarter, with the output of the previous period.

Output in an economy is referred to as the *gross domestic product* or GDP. We will define the GDP shortly, as well as a related measure known as GNP or *gross national product*. Considering that inflation is a constant feature in life, GDP will increase over time even if the real output remains constant. Consequently, the standard practice is to measure the GDP for a year using the price level of a base year.

GROSS DOMESTIC PRODUCT

GDP is a measure of the output of a country within its borders. The output could be on account of economic activities carried out by its nationals, or by foreign nationals operating in the country. The output refers to the final output, and intermediate products are not counted, for the final output subsumes the same. For instance, assume that a product sold in the market is made by using products X, Y, and Z. The price of the output will reflect the cost of the inputs. Thus, while measuring the GDP for a year, the value of the output is considered and the cost of the inputs is not, for it would amount to double counting.

GDP is determined by the aggregate demand in an economy. The term *aggregate demand* refers to the demand for goods and services in an economy. The greater the aggregate demand, the greater will be the induced production, and consequently the higher will be the GDP.

The aggregate demand can be divided into the following sectors:

- Consumption
- Residential investment
- Capital expenditure by the corporate sector
- Government spending
- Inventories
- Foreign trade

Consumption

We have seen earlier that the economy can be divided into three sectors, one of which is the household sector. Consumption refers to the spending of this sector on goods and services. The term *goods* refers to both durable and nondurable products. The former, such as automobiles, televisions, and computers, are not acquired frequently; the demand for such products tends to be cyclical. Thus, if the economy is facing a downturn and the future looks relatively bleak, people will typically decide to postpone expenditure on durables. They will keep the car or computer for a few more years than they would have otherwise. Consumption of nondurables, however, is steady, because expenditure on food products and drugs and pharmaceuticals cannot be postponed no matter how grim the economic outlook.

In modern economies, services are largely becoming the key components of the consumption in an economy, and both durables and nondurables are losing their relative importance.

The household sector spends out of its income and wealth. If the economy is booming, and people feel that their jobs are secure, they will tend to spend more. A booming economy will be characterized by a booming stock market index such as the Dow Jones Industrial Average and the Standard & Poor's 500 index. Thus, when the stock market is at a healthy level, consumption will tend to be high. However, when faced with the specter of a slowdown or a recession, consumers will tend to be more circumspect, and will cut back on consumption and save more. Consumption is influenced by what is a called a wealth effect. If the stock market is booming, the residents feel that they are more affluent, and consequently tend to spend more. The same holds true for the real estate market. If property prices are rising, homeowners tend to step up consumption.

Real Estate

The investments made in real estate depend on the prevailing level of interest rates in the economy. If the cost of borrowing is high, people are unlikely to take large mortgage loans. It should be noted that we are concerned with newly constructed houses when we talk about the GDP of a country. If Alex sells a house inhabited by him in Detroit to Alice, it does not make a difference to America's GDP.

Capital Expenditure

The business sector spends on capital goods such as machinery, automobiles, and computers. The investments made by this sector on such goods has implications for the output of the country and has a bearing on the future. Thus, capital expenditure is perhaps the most important component of the aggregate demand of an economy. Capital assets stay with the acquiring entity for a number of years and consequently have implications for revenues earned over a period of time. Thus, a high level of capital expenditure in a year is likely to lead to a significant economic growth in future years, which will manifest itself as a higher GDP.

Government Spending

The magnitude of government spending is usually determined by aggregate demand on account of the other factors. If demand is sagging and a slowdown is on the horizon, governments will typically spend more to stimulate the economy. Thus, if a recession is on the horizon, governments will step up their expenditure. Governments can borrow to fund their expenditure by issuing debt, which is termed as deficit financing. But in many countries, legislation has been passed to prevent reckless deficit financing. Consequently, there is a stipulation in many countries that the budget deficit cannot exceed a prescribed percentage of the GDP.

It must be mentioned that while governments spend on goods and services, they also spend on transfer payments, such as social welfare payments. The former is a component of aggregate demand. However, transfer payments merely serve to transfer wealth from one resident to another, and therefore do not constitute a component of aggregate demand.

Inventories

If the level of inventories goes up, it signifies greater economic production. But if inventories decline, it means that output generated in the past is being used for current production. If the level of inventories goes up, it signals a higher GDP for the year. This increase in inventory, however, may manifest itself as a lower output in subsequent years. In contrast, if the level of inventories goes down, it reflects a lower output for the year. Future output is likely to be high, however, because the inventory needs to be replenished. Inventories were of significance when the GDP of countries consisted primarily of goods. In most modern economies, services have become considerably more important than goods, and hence the level of inventories is not as important as it used to be.

Foreign Trade

In today's interconnected world, most countries import and export. Thus, if there is a demand for the products of a country from parties based overseas, it will stimulate production. The term *net export* is used for the difference between exports and imports. A robust economy that produces world-class goods and services may have a positive net export. This will boost employment in the economy and stimulate greater capital expenditure. The ability to export depends on the quality of a country's goods and services and its price competitiveness. A country like the United States imports a lot of manufactured goods, because the domestic price structure is such that imported products are cheaper than locally made products. Asian countries like China and India have taken advantage of their lower labor cost to corner substantial market share in goods and services, respectively. A country like the United States, however, invests heavily in research and development and consequently exports state-of-the-art items such as defense equipment and pharmaceuticals.

GDP VERSUS GNP

GDP measures the output by the residents of a country within its borders, while GNP measures the aggregate output of the nationals of a country, no matter where they are located.

Let us take a country like the United States. Assume US nationals based in the country generate 400 billion dollars of output, while foreign nationals present in the United States generate 300 billion dollars of output. We will say that the United States has a GDP of 700 billion dollars. Assume that US nationals based in the EU generate 150 billion dollars of output while those based in Japan generate 100 billion dollars' worth of goods and services.

We will say the United States has a GNP of $700 + 150 + 100 - 300 = 650$ billion dollars. It should be noted that the 150 billion produced by US residents in the EU will constitute a part of the GDP of that bloc of countries. Similarly, the 100 billion output produced by US residents in Japan will form a part of Japan's GDP.

GDP and GNP do not take into account the wear and tear of capital goods. By making suitable adjustments for the depreciation of capital goods, we can compute the *net domestic product* (NDP) and the *net national product* (NNP).

All the outputs generated in an economy are not necessarily destined for the market. For instance, a country may produce a significant amount of products for the use of its defense forces. This will definitely constitute a part of its GDP, even though it is not destined for the market.

Certain productive activities are not reflected in a country's GDP. For instance, the household sector generates a significant level of output, which is consumed within the family of the producer and not intended for sale. Consequently, it will not be reflected in the country's GDP. Many developing countries have a thriving parallel or underground economy. Such economies may generate significant output. However, for obvious reasons, the output cannot be estimated and included in the country's GDP.

Certain types of output are not included while computing GDP and GNP. Securities transactions, for instance, do not count. Thus, if Alex sells 100 shares of Apple to Andrea, it will not be a part of America's GDP. Social welfare payments and assistance programs do not count. They do not represent a productive activity, for all that the government is doing is taxing Peter to pay Paul. Similarly, certain property transactions are included while others are not. Assume that you build a house worth 500,000 USD in Nashville this year. It will be accounted for while computing America's GDP for the year. If you sell that property to someone three years later for 650,000 USD, it will have no consequences for the GDP in that year.

INFLATION ADJUSTMENT

GDP is based on the current price level in an economy. Inflation, or a steady increase in price levels over the years, is a fact of life in most countries. Thus, even if the real output of an economy were to remain constant, the nominal GDP will increase due to higher prices. Consequently, the GDP level for a year needs to be deflated to facilitate comparisons across years. In practice one year is designated as the base year and its price level is typically assigned a value of 100. Assume that this year's price index is at 125. This year's nominal GDP is 640 billion dollars. The real GDP is $(640 \times 100) \div 125 = 512$ billion dollars.

TRANSNATIONAL COMPARISONS

The GDP of a country is typically denominated in its own currency. Thus, an adjustment is required while comparing output levels across countries. The standard practice is to compute the GDP of every country in US dollars, and then compare.

To convert a country's GDP into a dollar value, we can use either the market exchange rate for that currency or what is called the Purchasing Power Parity (PPP) rate of exchange. The PPP rate measures the price of a standard product in a country vis-à-vis its price in the United States.

For instance, assume that India's rupee is currently being quoted at 75 per USD. Thus, if Indian GDP is 5,625 billion rupees, the equivalent amount in USD will be 75 billion dollars. Assume, however, that a pair of Levi's that costs 25 USD in the United States costs Rs 1250 in India. The PPP-based Rupee-Dollar exchange rate is 50 rupees per dollar. Hence, India's GDP in dollar terms, as computed using a PPP-based exchange rate, is 112.50 billion dollars. In practice, for many emerging economies there can be a significant difference between the market rate of exchange and the PPP rate.

THE BIG MAC INDEX

It has been argued that one of the most standard products in the world is the McDonald's Big Mac burger. Consequently, it has been recommended that the prices of burgers be compared across countries to arrive at the PPP exchange rate. For instance, if a burger that costs 1.50 USD in the United States were to cost Rs 60 in India, the PPP exchange rate will be 40 rupees per dollar.

INFLATION

A booming economy, which signals an economy in heat, will invariably be accompanied by a high level of inflation. Inflation, of course, refers to the change in price level over time. For instance, if a product that cost $100 last year, were to cost $108 this year, we will say that the inflation is 8%. Inflation steadily erodes the purchasing power of money.

A well-known result in economics is the Phillips Curve, which states that the rate of inflation and the level of unemployment are negatively related. Thus, if inflation is high, unemployment will be low and vice versa. Let us analyze the reason.

If an economy is working at close to full capacity, the factors of production would be utilized close to their maximum. Thus, unemployment will be very low. If capacity has to be increased further, it would invariably result in the poaching of labor from other producers. The employees who opt to shift will demand higher wages. If they opt not to shift, they will demand higher wages from their present employers. Rising wage levels will push up the cost of production. Producers will pass on the greater input costs to their consumers. The net result is an increase in price levels across the board, or inflation.

Now consider an economy that is in the throes of a recession. There will be severe layoffs and unemployment will be high. Aggregate demand, however, will be low on account of depressed economic conditions. Price levels will therefore be low, as reflected by low inflation, or possibly even deflation.

A similar analysis can be done for the other major factor of production, namely capital. If multiple entities are vying for scarce capital, the provider of capital will hike the cost or the rate of interest. This too will push up the cost of production, as most companies rely on debt capital to fund the bulk of their operations. Once again, the net result is inflation.

An increase in the cost of labor and capital need not be the sole reason for inflation. In an economy that is doing well, consumption levels are likely to be high. Supply, however, may be unable to keep pace with burgeoning demand. The net result will be an increase in price levels.

Inflation can be a self-fulfilling prophecy in practice. Assume that the workforce of a country is worried about the specter of inflation. It will demand higher wages and salaries. Producers, if they are compelled to concede the demand, will increase the prices of their outputs. Thus, in this case, the worry about inflation has manifested itself in the form of inflation.

Certain extraneous factors may lead to inflation. For instance, OPEC may suddenly decide to cut down the production of crude oil. Oil prices will rise, and will simultaneously pull up the prices of other goods. Or the United States may get involved in a war in an Asian country. This will cause the United States to crank up defense production, and resources could be diverted from civilian to defense uses. The net result could be an increase in price levels.

Why should a policymaker be perturbed by a high inflation level? Corporate expenditure decisions depend on the cost of capital and labor, and on the price of the outputs. High inflation corrupts the decision-making process, for a planner can have faith neither in the prices of the inputs, nor in those of the outputs. Consequently, businesses in such situations have a tendency to postpone capital expenditure that is required to expand, grow, or diversify. This will obviously have consequences for the GDP of a country.

TYPES OF INFLATION

Inflation may be of several types. These are:

- Demand Pull Inflation
- Cost Push Inflation
- Market Power Inflation
- Full Employment Inflation

Demand pull inflation arises in situations where the demand for goods and services outpaces the supply. If credit is easily available, there will be higher demand. Producers may not be able to cater to the growing demand immediately. This will lead to a situation where too much money is chasing too little goods, and the net result is inflation. There is another dimension as well. Reacting to greater demand, producers will increase their demand for the factors of production such as land, labor, and capital. Wage levels and interest costs will rise, leading producers to hike the prices of their output. The consequence, once again, is inflation.

The lack of adequate domestic supply could also lead to greater imports into the country. This will increase the demand for foreign currencies and the local currency will depreciate. This will stimulate exports and reduce imports.

Cost push inflation refers to a situation where the cost structure for producers increases, causing them to hike their prices, even in a situation where demand is stable. For instance, consider a product whose price depends heavily on the price of crude oil. If oil-producing countries cut their output, oil prices will rise, leading to a higher cost of production. We have seen that the Phillips curve predicts that inflation and unemployment are negatively related. Thus, when the economy is booming, inflation should be high and unemployment should be low. In a recession, however, unemployment should be high and inflation levels should be low. But there have been situations where both unemployment and inflation have been high. This is termed as stagflation. This happened in the United States in the 1970s and 1980s. The cause was a rapid increase in oil prices. Since the United States was largely dependent on imported crude oil, US producers saw a significant rise in their input costs, forcing them to hike prices. Stagflation is a manifestation of cost push inflation.

Market power or *profit push inflation* refers to the ability of monopolist producers to hike product costs because they know that consumers do not have an alternative. For instance, Microsoft has a virtual monopoly when it comes to products like MS Office and Windows. Consequently, the company can hike its prices, knowing well that demand is unlikely to be affected.

Wage spiral inflation is a type of market power inflation. In certain countries, trade unions have a lot of political clout and can repeatedly negotiate wage increases with producers. The latter will, after a certain stage, have no alternative but to pass on the increased cost to consumers. The net result is inflation.

Full employment inflation refers to a situation where an economy is operating at full capacity to cater to a high demand level. Producers will have to pay more for inputs such as labor and capital. One way for the government to arrest the increase in price levels in such situations is by encouraging imports. This can be done by reducing customs duties. An inflow of imports will lead to an increased demand for foreign currencies and cause the local currency to depreciate. This will have a positive impact on exports, which once again could push up domestic prices, which had been controlled to an extent by increased imports.

As we have discussed earlier, the fear of inflation can lead to inflation. Anticipating a higher rate of inflation, labor may demand higher wages. Suppliers will factor this into their products costs, which will boost the prices of their outputs. Thus, anticipated inflation may lead to higher actual inflation. This is termed as expectation inflation, for obvious reasons. This kind of inflation can spiral out of control.

INTEREST RATES

Interest is the price of money. People who are willing to postpone current expenditure, the surplus budget units (SBUs), lend to those whose current consumption needs are in excess of their available resources, the deficit budget units (DBUs). The equilibrium interest rate will be such that the supply of capital equals the demand for capital. Interest is the rent paid by the borrower of capital to the lender. For, while the former is using the capital, the latter, to whom it belongs, is deprived of the opportunity to use it himself.

In a recession, unemployment will be high. Insecure people will typically save more. Entrepreneurs are likely to borrow less for capital expenditure purposes. As a consequence of high supply and low demand, interest rates are likely to be low. The prevailing rate of inflation is likely to be low and consequently the inflation risk premium, a key component of the interest rate, will be low.

On the other hand, when an economy is booming, consumer confidence will be high and people will borrow more to spend. Thus, the market for consumer loans will be buoyant. In the prevailing euphoric environment, producers are likely to spend more on capital expenditure. The household sector will save less and spend more. On account of high demand and low supply, interest rates will rise. Worried by the prospect of rising interest rates, lenders will demand an even higher interest risk premium. This will further push up interest rates.

THE FEDERAL BUDGET DEFICIT

The federal or central governments of most countries rely on deficit financing. That is, they spend more than what their revenue in a financial year would warrant. The deficit is reflected by borrowing. In recent years, many legislatures have put a cap on the fiscal deficit as a percentage of a country's GDP. This has helped rein in deficit financing to an extent. The amount of debt outstanding for a sovereign government is called the *public debt* of the country.

Deficit financing can lead to a debt trap. A growing debt level implies an increasing interest rate bill for the federal government. Also, the existing debt has to be paid off in tranches. Thus, to service past debt, a country may need to borrow more and so its public debt will rise. In such a situation, a country may be borrowing to service past borrowings, and not to fund current productive economic activities.

A federal government has three sources of loans. It can borrow from within its borders, from other countries, or from supranational organizations like the World Bank and the International Monetary Fund.

To service debt a government has three options. It can stimulate economy activities, which, if successful, will lead to higher tax revenues, enabling it to pay its lenders. It can hike the tax rates; however, hiking tax rates need not always result in greater revenue for the government. In response to a hike in taxes, a producer may scale back on its operations, or migrate the business activity to another country. A third option is what is termed as debt monetization, or the printing of additional money. This option can give rise to an inflationary spiral in practice.

The budget deficit is correlated with the state of the economy. If the economy is booming, people are less likely to depend on social welfare payments. This brings down the expenditure for the government. Also, in such an environment, tax revenues are likely to be high. On the other hand, when the economic conditions are depressed, social welfare payments will be high and tax revenues are likely to be low. In addition, to kickstart the economy in such situations, governments will step up on capital expenditure. These factors will manifest themselves as a budget deficit.

Certain countries like the United States have a major advantage. The US dollar is a globally acceptable currency that people are willing to hold around the world. Consequently, the United States can run up higher deficits than other countries. It must be remembered that an increasing public debt for a country will result in an increase in the rate at which it can borrow. Worried by the increasing debt burden of a country, prospective lenders will be more circumspect and demand higher rates of interest. A situation may come when a country cannot borrow more and it is forced to default. It must be remembered that in practice, one of the main reasons why a government borrows in a particular year is to pay interest and make principal repayments on debt raised in the past.

MEASURES OF BUDGET DEFICITS

We will define three measures of deficit:

- Revenue Deficit
- Fiscal Deficit
- Primary Deficit

The revenue deficit may be defined as the revenue receipt in a financial year minus the revenue expenditure for the same period. If there is a deficit in a given year, it signals that the earnings of the government are inadequate to finance the annual expenditure. The balance has to be met by capital receipts. That is, the government must either borrow or sell some of its assets. To reduce the revenue deficit, a government can cut back on its expenditure and increase its tax and non-tax revenues. A high revenue deficit fuels future deficits. If the deficit is high, the more the government has to borrow. The more a government borrows, the higher will be its future interest rate payments, which will lead to greater revenue deficits in the future.

The term *fiscal deficit* is the excess of total expenditure, revenue and capital, over total budget receipts, excluding borrowings. Thus, the fiscal deficit is a measure of how much a government needs to borrow in the forthcoming financial year.

There are three reasons why a government may borrow in a financial year. First, to repay principal on past debt issues that are now maturing. Second, to fund the current revenue deficit. Third, to pay interest on debt issued earlier. A government may attempt to bridge the fiscal deficit by borrowing from domestic sources. This option will not lead to an increase in domestic money supply, which would tend to be inflationary. An alternative is deficit financing. The central bank will buy debt securities from the government by printing fresh currency. This will obviously lead to an increase in money supply and can trigger a bout of inflation.

A fiscal deficit does not necessarily mean poor economic management. If a government borrows to create capital assets that will benefit the country in future years, there is nothing negative about it. If, however, a country incurs larger and larger revenue deficits, and keeps borrowing more just to cover them, then this is not a desirable situation.

THE PRIMARY DEFICIT

This is defined as the borrowings for the current year minus the interest payment on account of past debt issues. If the primary deficit is zero, it means that the entire borrowing for the year is to meet interest expenses on account of debt securities issued in the past. If the primary deficit is positive, however, it means that the government is borrowing to fund expenditure or to repay past debt.

FISCAL POLICY

The term *fiscal policy* refers to the expenditure policy of a government and its tax policies. If an economy is in a recession, one way of boosting it is by cutting corporate and personal tax rates. A reduction of the former will increase the profit margins for the producers, which will stimulate them to make fresh investments. If personal tax rates are lowered, consumers will have more spending power and will seek to acquire more goods and services. Both factors will cause the economy to revive. Economic spending by both the business and household sectors has a cascading effect. This is because one party's expenditure is another party's income.

An alternative tool for governments is to increase spending on government-funded infrastructure projects. This too will increase aggregate demand, and can cause an economy to recover by having a cascading or multiplicative effect.

In practice, fiscal policies may offer a government little room for tackling an economy that is slowing down. If the fiscal deficit is high, and particularly when there is a cap on the fiscal deficit, it may not be possible for a government to spend more on capital expenditure. And given the existing deficit level, reducing tax rates will further bring down revenues, and is not an option, either.

BUDGET DEFICITS AND THE CAPITAL MARKET

If the federal government has a high budget deficit, it will lead to an increased demand for capital, which will serve to increase the cost of capital for all players in the market. This will increase the cost of doing business in a country, and will lead to a reduction in capital investments. Also, for a given availability of capital, an increase in the demand for funds by the federal government would mean that there is less capital available for the private corporate sector. This is termed as the *crowding out effect*.

THE ROLE OF THE CENTRAL BANK

The central bank, such as the Federal Reserve in the United States and the Bank of England in the United Kingdom, implements what is termed as *monetary policies*. In the United States, the Federal Reserve targets what is called the Federal Funds or Fed Funds rate. This is the rate at which banks borrow from each other. The other options available to the Fed to control the economy are open market operations and the reserve rate.

Open market operations refers to the buying and selling of government securities by the central bank to influence money supply, and consequently interest and inflation rates. If a central bank wants to increase the money supply, it will acquire government securities from the market. This will increase the money supply. Because the supply is increasing, the price of money, or the interest rate, will decline. Lower interest rates will push down the cost of both consumer and corporate credit and help stimulate the economy.

On the other hand, if an economy is overheating, the central bank will sell government securities and suck money out of the economy. The reduction in money supply will cause interest rates to rise. Companies will cut back on capital expenditure and consumers will spend less. This can cause a heating economy to cool down.

The reserve rate is the percentage of deposits that a commercial bank has to maintain either in the form of approved government securities or as a deposit with the central bank. The consequences may be viewed as follows. Banks are dealers in money, and like all dealers have a bid–ask spread. The bid for a bank is its borrowing rate while the ask is its lending rate. A higher reserve ratio means that a bank has less money to lend. As a consequence, it will lower its deposit rates and hike its lending rates. This will lead to a decline in deposits, and in the case of countries that permit capital outflows, to a flight of capital overseas. On the other hand, an increase in lending rates will lead to a reduced demand for capital by potential investors. This could impede fresh capital expenditure and retard economic growth.

Central banks also do repurchase and reverse repurchase transactions with commercial banks. The repo rate is the rate at which a commercial bank can borrow from the central bank on a collateralized basis. On the other hand, the reverse repo rate is the rate at which the central bank borrows from commercial banks, once again on a collateralized basis. If the central bank increases the repo rate, the cost of borrowing will increase for commercial banks, which will resonate throughout the economy. A decline in the repo rate will lead to greater borrowing by commercial banks, and will ease the availability of credit in the market.

BUDGET DEFICITS AND MONETARY POLICY

If the federal government has a high budget deficit, this means it is spending a lot. This will boost aggregate demand in the economy. The central bank, like the Federal Reserve, may judge this as being inflationary, and act to curb the demand for money by hiking interest rates. The resultant increase in the cost of money can arrest the growth in aggregate demand induced by greater government spending, by reducing both consumer spending and corporate borrowing.

CROSS-BORDER BORROWING

Players in the domestic economy can borrow from lenders in foreign countries as well. If interest rates in a country are attractive, foreigners may seek to lend, as the alternative is to lend at a lower rate in their domestic market. However, cross-border capital flows have a foreign exchange risk. Assume a German bank lent 10 million euros to a US entity when the exchange rate was 1.2125 EUR-USD. Assume the loan is denominated in dollars, and that the corresponding principal in dollars is 12.125 million. The loan is for one year, and at the time of repayment the exchange rate is 1.2255 EUR-USD; that is, the dollar has depreciated. If the borrower pays back 12.125 million USD, the amount received by the lender in Germany will be only 9.8939 million. Thus, if an overseas lender denominates the loan in the foreign currency, it stands to lose from a depreciating foreign currency. Of course, if the foreign currency were to appreciate, the lender would stand to benefit.

For both foreign lenders and exporters based in a foreign country, currency risk is a nonissue if the transaction is denominated in their domestic currency. In practice, importers in advanced economies usually have the market clout to insist that the transaction be denominated in their own currency, which puts the exchange risk burden on the exporter.

If a US entity pays back a loan to a foreign lender, there will be dollars in the hands of the recipient. If the receiver opts to sell the dollars to convert the proceeds to their own currency, the dollar may depreciate due to increased supply.

Now consider a situation where a US entity issues dollar-denominated bonds in a foreign country. This will lead to greater availability of capital in the United States, which could bring down interest rates. Because the foreigners are acquiring dollar debt, there will be a demand for the USD, which would cause an appreciation in its value. This will lead to reduced exports out of the United States, and increased imports into the United States. At some stage, if the debtholders decide to sell on a large scale, bond prices will be depressed, which means that bond yields will go up in the United States.

CENTRAL BANKS AND FOREIGN EXCHANGE MARKETS

The term *open market operations* refers to the buying and selling of government securities by the central bank of a country. The term has another connotation as well. Central banks can buy and sell foreign currencies to arrest the appreciation or depreciation of their home currency.

Assume the US dollar is rapidly appreciating with respect to the British pound and the euro. The Federal Reserve may buy these currencies. This will increase the supply of dollars and help control its appreciation. If the dollar stops appreciating, imports into the United States will come down and exports from it will increase. This will cause greater demand for the dollar relative to other currencies, and may stem the depreciation induced by the central bank. In the process of buying the foreign currencies, the Fed would have injected money into the economy. The increase in the supply of money will bring down interest rates and the price of credit. This will stimulate greater production and may lead to inflation in the medium to long term.

On the other hand, if the US dollar is rapidly depreciating, the Federal Reserve may create demand for the dollar by selling foreign currencies. This will cause the dollar to appreciate. As a consequence, US imports will increase and exports will decline. This will lead to a greater demand for foreign currencies by Americans, and will work to arrest the appreciation of the dollar induced by the central bank. In this case, when the Fed sells foreign currencies, it is reducing the money supply in the domestic economy. This reduced availability of money in the economy will push up interest rates, and can cause the economy to contract due to a higher cost of capital for producers.

STERILIZED AND UNSTERILIZED INTERVENTIONS

As we have seen, foreign currency purchases and sales by a central bank have implications for the domestic money supply. If the central bank acquires foreign currencies, it would have injected money into the economy. On the other hand, if the central bank sells foreign currencies, it would have sucked money out of the economy. Such action by a central bank, without a concomitant action in the money market, is termed as an *unsterilized intervention*.

There is another option available to the central bank. If it acquires foreign currencies, it can sell government securities and mop up the extra money in the system. On the other hand, if it sells foreign currencies, it can buy government securities and inject money into the system to compensate for the contraction caused by the sale of foreign currencies. This kind of intervention, which requires a compensatory intervention in the money market, is termed as a *sterilized intervention*.

EXCHANGE RATES

The demand and supply of foreign currencies may best be illustrated by using an example of two countries, say the United States and Japan. The demand for US dollars arises on account of the following factors. Japanese residents may wish to buy US products and services. Japanese investors may wish to acquire securities in the US money and capital markets. Japanese investors may have borrowed in the past in the United States and need to repay principal and/or interest. It should be noted that the demand for US dollars means the supply of Japanese yen. Thus, for all these reasons, there will be demand for the dollar and the supply of Japanese yen.

Now consider the supply of US dollars; the reasons for this supply are the following. American residents may wish to buy Japanese products and services. American investors may wish to acquire securities in the Japanese money and capital markets. American investors may have borrowed in Japan in the past, and need Japanese yen to repay the principal or to pay interest. Thus, the supply of US dollars translates into a demand for Japanese yen.

Left to itself, the market will find its equilibrium. Now assume that there is a technological revolution in Japan and the demand for Japanese products by Americans surges. Assume that the demand for American products by the Japanese is relatively unaffected. The result will be an increased demand for the yen, which means a greater supply of dollars. The yen will appreciate relative to the dollar. The appreciation will stimulate the demand for US goods and services and, to an extent, dampen the increased demand for Japanese products. The market will find an equilibrium exchange rate by itself.

The currency market that exists in practice is what is called a *dirty float* or a *managed float*. What we have described earlier is a *free-floating market*. In practice, central banks intervene in currency markets to nudge the exchange rates in a particular direction. So, if the dollar is rapidly appreciating, the Bank of Japan may sell dollars from its reserves or the Fed may buy Japanese yen from the market. On the contrary, if the dollar is rapidly depreciating, the Fed may sell Japanese yen, or the Bank of Japan may buy dollars.

There was a time when the currency rates were linked to gold and we had what was called the *gold exchange standard*. Every currency had a fixed value in terms of the dollar, and the dollar had a fixed value in terms of gold. The US government gave an assurance that, on demand, it would freely convert dollars to gold and gold to dollars. There arose a situation when it became obvious that the gold reserves of the United States were not adequate to support the quantum of dollars in circulation. Because the dollar was the central currency, countries other than the United States required large dollar balances to fund their global transactions. This meant that the United States had to run large balance of payment deficits. This implication for a reserve currency is called the *Triffin paradox*.

When it became apparent that the exchange standard was not sustainable, the major currencies began to float. That is, exchange rates began to be determined by free market forces of supply and demand, subject, of course, to periodic interventions by the central banks.

ISSUES WITH A RESERVE CURRENCY

If the US dollar is the reserve currency, other countries would like to have large dollar balances. This would imply that their exports to the United States should exceed their imports from the United States, which implies that the United States should have a large current account deficit. Historically, the US dollar has been acceptable as a reserve currency for the following reasons. First, both World War I and World War II left the United States virtually untouched. Second, the United States has a large domestic economy that can better absorb shocks and disruptions.

Since the rest of the world runs on dollar balances, the Federal Reserve needs to periodically inject dollars into the economy to keep the global economy well oiled. This will increase the money supply in the United States, which will cause domestic inflation to rise. An increase in domestic inflation will make US exports even less competitive, and will lead to greater imports into the United States.

The United States would like a situation where there is high demand for US dollar–denominated bonds. This will push up bond prices, which means that yields will be pushed down, leading to the availability of cheaper capital. But the higher demand for US bonds will lead to an appreciation of the dollar, which will cause US exports to decline and US imports to increase.

Thus, while it sounds impressive to say that a country's currency is the global reserve currency, the consequences are not always desirable. The central bank of the country whose currency is the global reserve has to walk a tightrope between its domestic stakeholders and its overseas audience.

CROSS-BORDER IMPLICATIONS OF CENTRAL BANK ACTIONS

Today's world economies are interconnected. Assume that the Fed wants to jump-start the US economy by reducing interest rates. American producers will have access to cheaper capital. A decline in bond yields, however, will make US debt less attractive for foreign investors, who will move money from the US market to other capital markets. This will cause a reduction in the supply of capital in the United States. US investors may also decide to bypass the US market and invest in other countries offering a higher rate of interest. Due to higher demand for foreign currencies by retreating foreigners and Americans seeking to invest abroad, the dollar will depreciate and other major currencies will appreciate. This will boost US exports and reduce US imports.

If the Fed were to reduce interest rates, the Bank of Japan may also follow suit. This could lead to capital flight from Japan to a third country. This will cause a reduction in the supply of capital in Japan. The Japanese yen will depreciate, which will offset to an extent the appreciation induced by a depreciating US dollar. Japanese exports to the United States will increase, thereby reversing the decline caused by a depreciating dollar. Japanese imports from the United States will decline, thereby reversing the increase caused by a depreciating dollar.

QUANTITATIVE EASING

Quantitative easing (QE) refers to central banks acquiring government and corporate bonds from financial institutions. The increased demand for such securities pushes up their price, which leads to a decline in yields in the market. This brings down the interest rates in the economy, which stimulates borrowings by both the business and household sectors. As a consequence, this in principle can revive a slowing economy.

Quantitative easing has implications for the stock market and the real estate market. If the central bank acquires debt securities from a financial institution, it will leave money in the institution's hands, some of which may find its way to the stock market, because, as a consequence of lower yields on debt, equity may be perceived as a more attractive investment. Increased demand for shares will push up share prices, leading to an increase in wealth for all shareholders. Some of these shareholders may use their wealth to acquire property, which could boost the market for real estate.

Quantitative easing brings down the cost of debt in an economy, for agents in all three sectors: the government, business, and household sectors. However, there is a flipside. Easy availability of money may lead to higher inflation, because if supply does not keep pace, newly acquired money may end up chasing an existing basket of goods.

If quantitative easing is implemented in the United States, interest rates will come down. This will lead to reduced demand for US dollars by foreigners seeking to invest in the US debt market. This will cause the US dollar to depreciate with respect to the currencies of its trading partners. The net result will be an increase in exports out of the United States and a decline in imports into the country, causing the balance of payments situation to improve.

Once the objectives have been met. the central bank can taper quantitative easing. This will cause interest rates to increase. This will lead to a greater investment in debt securities by both domestic and overseas investors. An increase in interest rates in a country will have ramifications for other countries. For instance, if quantitative easing were to taper off in the United States, portfolio investors may divert investments that were planned for an emerging economy like India, to the United States. The demand for US dollars will increase and the demand for the

Indian rupee will decline. Thus, the dollar will appreciate with respect to the rupee. This will boost exports from India to the United States and improve India's balance of trade.

QUANTITATIVE EASING VERSUS OPEN-MARKET OPERATIONS

Quantitative easing leads to an intervention by central banks on a much larger scale, as compared to open-market operations, although both lead to the acquisition of securities by the central bank. The primary focus of open-market operations is to influence interest rates in the economy, whereas the primary focus of quantitative easing is to increase the amount of money in circulation in the economy. In an open-market operation, the central bank primarily acquires short-dated securities from the market. As part of quantitative easing, however, central banks have also acquired medium-term and long-term debt securities. Also, acquisition of privately issued securities may be a part of quantitative easing, a tactic that is absent in an open-market operation.

Interest Rate Derivatives

In this chapter we discuss various interest rate derivatives, both commitment and contingent, such as Forward Rate Agreements, Eurodollar Futures, Caps, Floors, Collars, Captions, and Floortions. We also examine callable and putable bonds, which are bonds with built-in interest rate options.

FORWARD RATE AGREEMENTS (FRAs)

A *forward rate agreement* is a forward contract on an interest rate, such as the six-month LIBOR. Because it is a forward contract, it is traded exclusively over the counter. An FRA represents an agreement between two counterparties to fix a future interest rate. These contracts are cash settled and not delivery settled. There will be a notional principal specified in the agreement, which will be used to compute the terminal cash flow. At maturity, the rate specified in the contract will be invariably different from the prevailing LIBOR. Depending on which is higher, one of the two parties will make a payment to the counterparty. For a potential borrower, the FRA locks in a borrowing rate; for a potential lender, it locks in a lending rate.

In a forward rate agreement, the party who agrees to pay the contract rate is termed the buyer, and the party who agrees to receive the contract rate is termed the seller. Such contracts may be used by hedgers as well as speculators. From a speculative standpoint, traders who are bullish about interest rates will buy FRAs. If the reference rate on the settlement date is higher than the contract rate, then they will receive a cash inflow. If the reference rate is lower, however, then they have to make a cash payment. Similarly, speculators who are bearish about interest rates will sell FRAs. If the reference rate on the settlement date is lower than the contract rate, then they receive a cash inflow. If the reference rate is higher, however, then they have to make a cash payment. We will illustrate this with the help of a numerical example.

EXAMPLE 14.1

Bank ABC has bought an FRA with a contract rate of 3.6% per annum from Bank XYZ. The reference rate is 6-M LIBOR. Assume that the notional principal is $8,000,000 and that the day-count is 30/360. Thus, six months is 180 days. If the

(continued)

(*continued*)

LIBOR on the settlement date is 2.85%, the buyer of the FRA, in this case Bank ABC, will pay

$$8,000,000 \times \frac{180}{360} \times \frac{3.60 - 2.85}{100} = \$30,000$$

to Bank XYZ.

If, however, the LIBOR at settlement is 4.30%, then Bank XYZ will pay

$$8,000,000 \times \frac{180}{360} \times \frac{4.30 - 3.60}{100} = \$28,000$$

to Bank ABC.

Such contracts can also be used by hedgers. Now let's consider a situation where an FRA is used as a hedge.

EXAMPLE 14.2

General Dynamics has borrowed on a floating-rate basis and is worried about the possibility of interest rates increasing. The loan rate is LIBOR + 30 b.p., and interest is determined in advance and paid in arrears. To lock in a borrowing rate, the firm buys an FRA with a contract rate of 3.75%. If the LIBOR on the settlement date is 3.95%, the firm will borrow at 4.25%. Because the reference rate is higher than the contract rate, however, the counterparty will pay 3.95 – 3.75 = 20 basis points, based on the specified principal amount and the prescribed day-count convention. Thus, the effective borrowing cost for the firm is 4.25 – 0.20 = 4.05%, which is the contract rate of 3.75% plus the spread of 30 b.p.

On the other hand, if the LIBOR on the settlement date were to be 3.50%, the company could borrow at 3.80%. It would have to pay 25 basis points to the counterparty, and the effective borrowing cost will once again be 4.05%.

An FRA, like all forward contracts, is a commitment contract, and consequently locks in a rate with absolute certainty. Such contracts can also be used to hedge receivables.

EXAMPLE 14.3

Bank ABC plans to lend at LIBOR + 35 b.p. after six months; however, it is worried about a declining interest rate. It therefore sells an FRA with a contract rate of 3.75%. If the LIBOR on the settlement date is 4%, the bank will lend at 4.35%. Because the reference rate is more than the contract rate, however, it will pay 25 basis points to the counterparty. Thus, the effective lending rate for the bank is 4.35 – 0.25 = 4.10%, which is the contract rate plus the spread. On the other

> hand, if the LIBOR on the settlement date is 3.20%, the bank will lend at 3.55. In this case, it will receive 55 basis points from the counterparty. The effective rate of interest is once again 4.1%, which is the contract rate plus the spread.

An FRA is quoted using two numbers. An 'A × B' FRA implies that settlement is A months from today for a loan or deposit of B − A months. The first date is referred to as the settlement date, and the second is termed the final maturity date.

SETTLING AN FRA

Consider a 6 × 12 FRA. Assume that today is 15 March 2021. The spot settlement date is 17 March 2021, assuming a T + 2 settlement cycle. The settlement date will be six months from 17 March 2021. The reference rate will be fixed two days before the settlement date, or six months from the trade date. The maturity date is six months from the settlement date. There are two possibilities: (1) the cash payment may be made on the settlement date, which is termed an *in arrears FRA*; or (2) the payment may occur on the maturity date, which is termed a *delayed settlement FRA*.[1]

Let's assume that the contract rate is 3.6%, and that the LIBOR on the reference fixing date is 3.1%. We will also assume that the notional principal is 12 MM USD, and that the day-count convention is Actual/360.[2] Assume that the number of days in the six-month period from settlement until final maturity is 182 days.

Because the contract rate is higher than the reference rate, the buyer has to make a payment. The amount due is:

$$12,000,000 \times (0.036 - 0.031) \times (182 \div 360) = \$30,332.40$$

Had the FRA been a delayed settlement contract, the cash flow would occur six months from the settlement date, and the value on the settlement date would be the present value of this amount, determined by discounting at the LIBOR prevailing on the reference fixing date. In our case, the present value would be

$$\frac{30,332.40}{\left(1 + 0.031 \times \dfrac{182}{360}\right)} = \$29,864.36$$

DETERMINING BOUNDS FOR THE FRA RATE

If we are given money market interest rates, we can determine the upper and lower bounds for the FRA rate. Assume that the interest rates in the market are as follows. The lower rate is what the dealer will pay when it borrows, while the higher rate is what it will charge when it lends.

---

[1]See Chance (2001).

[2]For contracts in USD and EUR, the day-count convention is Actual/360, as is the practice in the money market. For transactions in GBP, AUD, CAD, or JPY, the convention is Actual/365.

EXAMPLE 14.4

3-M: 2.80–2.95% per annum

6-M: 2.95–3.15% per annum

The dealer can borrow for 3 months, which we will assume is 90 days at 2.80%. Thus, the amount payable, per dollar borrowed, is

$$1 + 0.028 \times (90 \div 360) = 1.007$$

The dealer can roll over at the unknown FRA rate F for another 90 days. The terminal value will be

$$1.007 \times [1 + F \times (90 \div 360)] = 1.007 \times (1 + 0.25F)$$

The money borrowed can be lent for 180 days. The corresponding future value will be

$$1 + 0.0315 \times (180 \div 360) = 1.01575$$

Because the dealer must make a profit, 1.01575 should be greater than $1.007 \times (1 + 0.25F)$. Thus, F must be less than 3.4756% per annum.

The lower bound for the contract rate of the FRA may be determined as follows. The dealer can borrow for 180 days at 2.95% per annum. The amount payable per dollar borrowed is

$$1 + 0.0295 \times (180 \div 360) = 1.01475$$

The money borrowed can be lent for 90 days at 2.95% The future value is $1 + 0.0295 \times (90 \div 360) = 1.007375$. This loan can be rolled over for another 90 days at F. The terminal value will be

$$1.007375 \times [1 + F \times (90 \div 360)] = 1.007375 \times (1 + 0.25F)$$

For the dealer to make a profit, we require that

$$1.01475 < 1.007375 \times (1 + 0.25F)$$

Thus, F must be greater than 2.9284%. Therefore, the contract rate must be between 2.9284% and 3.4756%.

EURODOLLAR FUTURES

Eurodollars are dollars traded outside the borders of the United States. Eurodollar (ED) futures contracts trade on the IMM in Chicago, which is a part of the CME Group. The underlying interest rate is the London Inter Bank Offer Rate (LIBOR). Each futures contract is for a time deposit with a principal of 1 MM and three months to maturity.

The quarterly cycle for Eurodollar contracts is March, June, September, and December. On the CME, a total of 40 quarterly futures contracts spanning 10 years are listed at any point in time. In addition, the four nearest serial months are also listed. Let us assume that we are standing on June 28, 2021. The four serial months that would be available would be July, August, October, and November 2021. The remaining available months would be September 2021; December 2021; March, June, September, and December of 2022–2030; March 2031; and June 2031.

The price of an ED futures contract is quoted in terms of an IMM index, and implies an interest rate.

$$\text{Quoted ED Futures Price} = 100.00 - \text{Implicit Interest Rate}$$

The implicit interest rate in this case is an actual or add-on interest rate and not a discount rate. Thus, a quoted rate of 3% per annum means that for a 90-day loan with a maturity value of 1 MM, the terminal amount payable or receivable is

$$1,000,000[1 + 0.03 \times (90 \div 360)] = 1,007,500$$

CALCULATING PROFITS AND LOSSES ON ED FUTURES

Assume that the futures price is 97.20. This represents a yearly interest rate of 2.8% per annum or 0.70% per quarter. The implied interest amount is

$$0.007 \times 1,000,000 = \$7,000$$

If the futures price were to fall to 96.80 at the end of the day, then it would represent a quarterly interest payment of $8,000 on a deposit of one million.

Consider a person who goes long in an ED futures contract at 97.20. Such a person is agreeing to lend money at the equivalent interest rate, namely 0.70% per quarter. It must be understood that a long position in ED futures means that the investor is willing to make a term deposit of three months. Thus, it is a lender. If interest rates rise subsequently to 3.20% per annum, that is, the futures price goes down to 96.80, and the contract is marked to market, then the long will lose $1,000. The rationale may be understood as follows. When the contract is marked to market, it is as if the dealer is offsetting by going short, which in this case means that it is agreeing to borrow at 3.20% per quarter. Thus, when the interest rates rise the longs will lose, whereas when the interest rates fall the shorts will lose.

This explains the logic behind quoting futures prices in terms of an index, rather than in terms of interest rates. If futures prices were to be quoted in terms of interest rates, then the longs would gain when the futures prices fall and the shorts would gain when the futures prices rise. This is unlike all other futures markets, where the longs gain when futures prices rise, whereas the shorts gain if futures prices fall. Thus, to make money market futures consistent with other futures markets, we do not quote futures prices in terms of interest rates, but do so in terms of an index. When the index rises, the longs will gain; when it falls, the shorts will gain.

A second reason why futures prices are quoted in terms of an index is to ensure that the bid prices are lower than the ask. In practice, for an investor, the borrowing rate will be higher than the lending rate. Thus, if ED futures were to be quoted in terms of interest rates, the bid will be higher than the ask. For the other products on which futures are available, however, the bid is lower than the ask. Consequently, we express futures prices in terms of an index to ensure that the bid is lower than the ask.

Now consider the case where the ED index changes from F_0 to F_1. The profit for a long is

$$1,000,000 \times \frac{(100 - F_0)}{100} \times \frac{90}{360} - 1,000,000 \times \frac{(100 - F_1)}{100} \times \frac{90}{360}$$

$$= 1,000,000 \times \frac{(F_1 - F_0)}{100} \times \frac{90}{360}$$

The corresponding profit for the short is

$$1,000,000 \times \frac{(100 - F_1)}{100} \times \frac{90}{360} - 1,000,000 \times \frac{(100 - F_0)}{100} \times \frac{90}{360}$$

$$= 1,000,000 \times \frac{(F_0 - F_1)}{100} \times \frac{90}{360}$$

LOCKING IN A BORROWING RATE

Now we will illustrate how borrowing and lending rates can be locked in using ED futures.

EXAMPLE 14.5

Assume that today is 15 July 20XX. Revital is planning to borrow $1 million on 14 September for a period of 90 days. The company is confident that given its rating, it can borrow at LIBOR. It is, however, worried that interest rates may rise before 14 September, which is the last day of trading for the September futures contract. The current September futures price is 97.20. Because the company is planning to borrow money, it requires a short hedge.

Assume that Revital goes short in one September futures contract. We will consider two different scenarios on 14 September, one where the LIBOR is higher as compared to the rate implicit in the futures price, and the other where it is lower.

Let us first assume that the terminal LIBOR is 3.5%.

The interest payable on the loan of 1 MM is

$$0.035 \times 1,000,000 \times (90 \div 360) = \$8,750$$

Gain/loss from the futures market is

$$= 1,000,000 \times \frac{(97.20 - 96.50)}{100} \times \frac{90}{360}$$

$$= 1,750$$

Therefore, the effective interest paid is

$$8{,}750 - 1{,}750 = \$7{,}000$$

$7,000 per quarter is $28,000 per annum. On a principal of $1 million, it translates into a rate of 2.80% per annum, which is the rate implicit in the initial futures price of 97.20.

Now consider the case where the LIBOR at the end is 2.1% per annum. The interest payable is

$$0.021 \times 1{,}000{,}000 \times (90 \div 360) = \$5{,}250$$

Profit/loss from the futures position is

$$= 1{,}000{,}000 \times \frac{(97.20 - 97.90)}{100} \times \frac{90}{360}$$
$$= (1{,}750)$$

Thus, the effective interest paid is

$$5{,}250 + 1{,}750 = \$7{,}000$$

Thus, the company can lock in an interest payable of $7,000, irrespective of the prevailing LIBOR on 14 September. This amount corresponds to a rate of: $(7{,}000 \div 1{,}000{,}000) \times 100 \times (360 \div 90) = 2.80\%$ per annum, which is the rate implicit in the initial futures price of 97.20. Thus, we have a perfect hedge that has locked in the original futures price.

LOCKING IN A LENDING RATE

Here is an example on how to lock in a lending rate.

EXAMPLE 14.6

Assume that today is 15 September 20XX. Mechtronics is planning to lend $5MM on 14 December for a period of 90 days. The company is of the opinion that it can lend at the prevailing LIBOR plus 35 b.p., and wants to lock in a rate using ED futures. 14 December is the last day of trading for the December contract, and the current futures price is 97.80. Because the company wishes to lock in a lending rate, it needs to go long in futures contracts. As the amount being hedged is 5 MM, it needs five futures contracts. As before, we will consider two scenarios for the terminal value of LIBOR.

Let us first consider a case where the terminal LIBOR is 3.25%.

(continued)

(*continued*)

The interest receivable on the loan is

$$0.036 \times 5,000,000 \times (90 \div 360) = \$45,000$$

The profit/loss from the futures position is

$$= 5,000,000 \times \frac{(96.75 - 97.80)}{100} \times \frac{90}{360} = \$(13,125)$$

Thus, the effective interest received is $45,000 - 13,125 = \$31,875$.
This corresponds to an annual interest rate of

$$\frac{31,875}{5,000,000} \times \frac{360}{90} = 0.0255 = 2.55\%$$

2.55 is the rate of 2.20% implicit in the initial futures price of 97.80 plus the spread of 35 basis points.

Now consider a case where the LIBOR is 1.90%.

The interest receivable on the loan is:

$$0.0225 \times 5,000,000 \times (90 \div 360) = \$28,125$$

The profit/loss from the futures position is:

$$= 5,000,000 \times \frac{(98.10 - 97.80)}{100} \times \frac{90}{360} = \$3,750$$

The effective interest received is $28,125 + 3,750 = \$31,875$, which corresponds to an annual rate of 2.55% once again. Thus, the hedge is perfect.

ED futures can be used to hedge short-term loans and deposits for periods that are close to 90 days but are not exactly equal to three months. The inherent assumption is that the N day rate, where N is close to 90, is perfectly correlated with the 90-day rate.

The number of contracts required is N/90 per million dollars being hedged. Here is an illustration.

EXAMPLE 14.7

A party is borrowing 10,000,000 USD on the expiration date of the ED futures contract, for a period of 117 days. Thus, the number of futures contracts required is $10 \times 117/90 = 13$ contracts. Assume the initial futures price is 97.8 while the terminal futures price is 97.

The borrowing cost is $10,000,000 \times 0.03 \times (117 \div 360) = \$97,500$.

The futures profit loss is

$$= 13,000,000 \times \frac{(97.80 - 97.00)}{100} \times \frac{90}{360} = \$26,000$$

Thus, the effective interest paid is 97,500 − 26,000 = \$71,500. This corresponds to an annual interest rate of

$$\frac{71,500}{10,000,000} \times \frac{360}{117} \times 100 = 2.20\%$$

This is the rate implicit in the initial futures price of 97.80.

THE NO-ARBITRAGE PRICING EQUATION

We will now state an expression for the futures price, which will preclude both cash-and-carry and reverse cash-and-carry arbitrage, for a given set of interest rates. Let us denote the day on which we are standing as day 't.' The futures contract is assumed to expire at 'T.' We will denote the Eurodollar rate for a '$T - t$' day loan by s_1 and the borrowing/lending rate for a '$T + 90 - t$' day loan by s_2.

In order to rule out both forms of arbitrage, we require that

$$1,000,000 \times \left[1 + \frac{(100 - F)}{100} \times \frac{90}{360}\right] \times \left[1 + \frac{s_1}{100} \times \frac{T - t}{360}\right]$$

$$= 1,000,000 \times \left[1 + \frac{s_2}{100} \times \frac{T + 90 - t}{360}\right]$$

$$\Rightarrow \left[1 + \frac{(100 - F)}{100} \times \frac{90}{360}\right]\left[1 + \frac{s_1}{100} \times \frac{T - t}{360}\right] = \left[1 + \frac{s_2}{100} \times \frac{T + 90 - t}{360}\right]$$

Here is an illustration.

EXAMPLE 14.8

Assume s_1 is 3.2% per annum while s_2 is 3.6% per annum. Assume $T - t$ is 72 days. The no-arbitrage futures price is

$$\left[1 + \frac{(100 - F)}{100} \times \frac{90}{360}\right] = 1.009738$$

$$\Rightarrow F = 96.1050$$

CREATING A FIXED-RATE LOAN

Assume that Rolta Bank is able to borrow money at LIBOR for three-month periods. Consequently, the interest payable on its liability is variable. The bank, however, has a potential client who wishes to borrow at a fixed rate for a period of one year. Thus, the interest receivable from the proposed asset is fixed in nature. The bank would like to use futures contracts to mitigate the risk arising from the fact that it is borrowing at a floating rate but is lending at a fixed rate. It turns out that ED futures contracts can be used to hedge the funding risk and determine a suitable rate that can be quoted by the bank while negotiating a fixed rate loan. We will illustrate the principle involved with the help of an example.

EXAMPLE 14.9

Renitz, a company based in London, wants a loan for 80 million USD for a period of one year from 15 September 20XX, at a fixed interest rate.

Let us assume that the 90-day LIBOR on 15 September is 2.8% and that December, March, and June contracts are available at 98.1, 97.6, and 97 respectively. For ease of exposition, we will assume that the dates on which the bank will roll over its three-month borrowings, namely 15 December, 15 March, and 15 June, are the same as the dates on which the futures contracts for those months are scheduled to expire. The loan for the first quarter is based on the prevailing 90-day rate, and consequently does not require a futures position. Each ED futures contract is on 1 MM USD and the bank is borrowing at a floating rate. Consequently, it needs a short position in 80 each of the December, March, and June futures contracts.

For the first quarter, the interest expense for the bank is

$$80,000,000 \times 0.028 \times (90 \div 360) = \$560,000$$

The short position in December contracts will lock in a rate of 1.9% for a period of 90 days from December to March. This corresponds to an interest expense of

$$80,000,000 \times 0.019 \times (90 \div 360) = \$380,000$$

In a similar fashion, the short position in March contracts will lock in

$$80,000,000 \times 0.024 \times (90 \div 360) = \$480,000$$

for the 90-day period from March.

The June contracts will lock in the following interest amount for the last quarter.

$$80,000,000 \times 0.03 \times (90 \div 360) = \$600,000$$

Hence the total interest payable by the bank for the 12-month period is:

$$560,000 + 380,000 + 480,000 + 600,000 = \$2,020,000$$

> This corresponds to an annualized interest rate of:
>
> $$\frac{2,020,000}{80,000,000} \times 100 = 2.525\%$$
>
> The bank can now quote a fixed rate to the client, based on this effective cost of funding, after factoring in hedging costs and a suitable profit margin.

30-YEAR T-BOND FUTURES CONTRACTS

The underlying asset is a T-bond with a face value of $100,000. Multiple grades are allowable for delivery. The deliverable grades must, if they are callable in nature, not be callable for at least 15 years from the first day of the delivery month, and if they are not callable in nature, must have a maturity of at least 15 years from the first day of the delivery month. The actual futures price is subject to a conversion factor. At any point in time, the first three months from the March quarterly cycle will be listed. Thus, on June 29, 2021, the available contracts will be September 2021, December 2021, and March 2022.

All the contracts are subject to delivery settlement.

CONVERSION FACTORS

As one can see from the contract specifications, a wide variety of notes and bonds with different coupons and maturity dates will be eligible for delivery under any particular futures contract. The choice as to which bond to deliver will be made by the short, and obviously the price it receives will depend on the bond that it chooses to deliver. If the short were to deliver a more valuable bond, it should receive more than it would if it had delivered a less valuable bond. Thus, in order to facilitate comparisons between bonds, the exchange specifies a conversion factor for each bond that is eligible for delivery. This is nothing but a multiplicative price adjustment system to facilitate comparisons between different bonds that are eligible for delivery.

The conversion factor for a bond is the value of the bond per $1 of face value, as calculated on the first day of the delivery month, using an annual YTM of 6% with semiannual compounding. For the purpose of calculation, the life of the bond is rounded down to the nearest three months. If, after rounding, the bond were to have a life that is an integer multiple of semiannual periods, then the first coupon will be assumed to be paid after six months. After rounding, however, if the life of the bond were not to be equal to an integer multiple of half-yearly periods, then the first coupon will be assumed to be paid after three months and the accrued interest will be subtracted. The following detailed examples will illustrate these principles.

The Invoice Price, which is the price received by the short, is calculated as follows:

$$\text{Invoice Price} = \text{Invoice Principal Amount} + \text{Accrued Interest}$$

$$CF_i \times F \times 100,000 + AI_i$$

where CF_i is the conversion factor of Bond i, F is the quoted futures price per dollar of face value,[3] and AI_i is the accrued interest.

EXAMPLE 14.10

Let us assume that we are short in a September futures contract and that today is 1 September 2021.

Consider a 5% T-Bond that matures on 15 May 2050. This bond is obviously eligible for delivery under the futures contract.

On 1 September, this bond has 28 years and 8.5 months to maturity. When we round down to the nearest three months, we get a figure of 28 years and six months. This is an integer multiple of semiannual periods. Thus, the first coupon is assumed to be paid after six months. The conversion factor may therefore be calculated as follows.

$$CF = \frac{\frac{5}{2}\text{PVIFA}(3,57) + 100\text{PVIF}(3,57)}{100}$$

$$= \frac{67.8773 + 18.5472}{100}$$

$$= 0.8642$$

EXAMPLE 14.11

Instead of the May 2050 bond, consider another bond that is maturing on 15 February 2050 with a coupon of 4.75%. This bond too is suitable for delivery. On 1 September 2021, this bond has 28 years and 5.5 months to maturity. The life of the bond when we round down to the nearest three months is 28 years and three months.

In this case, we assume that the first coupon is paid after three months. The CF can be calculated in three steps as shown below.

▪ First find the price of the bond three months from today, using a yield of 6% per annum.

$$P = \frac{4.75}{2} + \frac{4.75}{2}\text{PVIFA}(3,56) + 100\text{PVIF}(3,56)$$

$$= 2.375 + 64.0430 + 19.1036$$

$$= \$85.5216$$

---

[3]T-Bond futures prices are quoted in the same way as the cash market prices; that is, they are clean prices.

■ Discount the price gotten above for another three months.

$$\frac{85.5216}{(1.03)^{\frac{1}{2}}} = \$84.2669$$

■ Subtract the accrued interest for three months from the price obtained in the second step.

$$AI = \frac{4.75}{2} \times \frac{1}{2} = 1.1875$$

$$CF = \frac{84.2669 - 1.1875}{100} = 0.8308$$

Why do we adopt two different procedures for calculating the *CF*? The *CF* is used to multiply the quoted futures price, which is a clean price. Hence the *CF* should not include any accrued interest. In the first example, the bond has a life that is an integer multiple of semiannual periods after rounding off. Consequently, we need not be concerned with accrued interest. In the second example, however, accrued interest for a quarter is present in the value we get in the second step. Hence, in this case, we need to subtract this interest in order to arrive at the conversion factor.

EXAMPLE 14.12

Calculating the Invoice Price for a T-bond.

Assume that on 15 September 2021 the decision to deliver the 5% bond maturing on 15 May 2050, under the September futures contract, is declared by the short. The actual delivery will obviously take place two business days later, that is, on 17 September, which is T + 2.

The invoice price may be computed as follows. The first step is obviously to calculate the accrued interest. The last coupon would have been paid on 15 May 2021 and the next will be due on 15 November 2021. Between the two coupon dates there are 184 days. Between the last coupon date and the delivery date, there are 125 days. The accrued interest for a T-Bond with a face value of $100,000 is:

$$AI = \frac{0.05}{2} \times \frac{125}{184} \times 100{,}000 = \$1{,}698.3696$$

The futures settlement price on 15 September is assumed to be 98 − 12. This corresponds to a decimal futures price of 98 + 12/32 = 98.375. The conversion factor has already been calculated to be 0.8642.

Invoice Price = 98.375 × 0.8642 × 1,000 + 1,698.3696 = $86,714.0440

INTEREST RATE OPTIONS

Valuing interest rate options requires us to model the evolution of interest rates over time. Equilibrium models of the interest rate attempt to model the rates using economic variables. The problem in practice is that the bond prices predicted by these models do not match the observed bond prices. An alternative is to take the available term structure and derive an interest rate tree that is consistent with the observed spot rates. For the rest of this chapter we will use a tree derived by calibrating a model known as the Ho-Lee model to a given vector of spot rates (Table 14.1).

STATE PRICES

Arrow-Debreu securities, also known as *pure securities*, will pay a dollar if a particular state of nature were to occur. In all other states of nature, however, the payoff

TABLE 14.1 Vector of Spot Rates

Period	Spot Rate
1	6.00%
2	5.80%
3	6.05%
4	5.90%

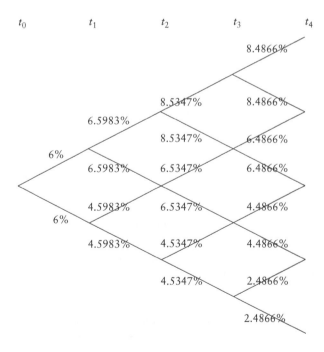

FIGURE 14.1 No-Arbitrage Interest Rate Tree

t_0	t_1	t_2	t_3	t_4
				0.0540
			0.1126	
		0.2349		0.2193
	0.4854		0.3413	
1.0		0.4722		0.3338
	0.4854		0.3446	
		0.2372		0.2258
			0.1160	
				0.0573

FIGURE 14.2   State Price Tree

will be zero. Obviously, each node of a binomial tree represents a particular state of nature. The price at time zero of a pure security that pays off a dollar at a particular node is called the state price of the node. Figure 14.1 depicts the interest rate tree that has been obtained by calibrating the Ho-Lee Model.

At a point in time, a security that pays a dollar in all states of nature is a riskless security. The sum of the prices of all the pure securities for a point in time should be equal to the present value of a dollar, discounted at the riskless rate. Consider the two-period spot rate of 5.80% per annum. Figure 14.2 depicts the state price tree corresponding to the interest rate tree that has been derived.

$$\frac{1}{(1.029)^2} = 0.9444$$

$$0.2349 + 0.4722 + 0.2372 = 0.9443$$

CALLABLE AND PUTABLE BONDS

Consider a two-period bond with a coupon of 8% per annum. The value of this bond is:

$$1{,}040 \times (0.2349 + 0.4722 + 0.2372) + 40 \times (0.4854 + 0.4854) = 982.0720 + 38.832$$

$$= \$1{,}020.9040$$

Now assume that this bond is callable after a period, and if called, a premium of $15 is payable. The value of the bond at the upper node at time t_1 is

$$\frac{1{,}040}{\left(1 + \dfrac{0.065983}{2}\right)} + 40 = 1{,}046.7846$$

If called, the issuer must pay $1{,}000 + 40 + 15 = \$1{,}055$. Thus, the bond will not be called.

The value of the bond at the lower node at time $t1$ is

$$\frac{1,040}{\left(1 + \dfrac{0.045983}{2}\right)} + 40 = 1,056.6262$$

If called, the issuer must pay $1,000 + 40 + 15 = \$1,055$. Thus, the bond will be called. Hence the value of the callable is \$1,046.7846 at the upper node and 1,055 at the lower node. Hence the price at the outset is

$$0.4854 \times (1046.7846 + 1,055) = \$1,020.2062$$

Thus, the value of the call option inherent in the callable bond is

$$1,020.9040 - 1,020.2062 = \$0.6978$$

Now consider a putable bond which can be put back at par. Assume the coupon is 6% per annum. The model value at the upper node is

$$\frac{1,030}{\left(1 + \dfrac{0.065983}{2}\right)} + 30 = 1,027.1040$$

If the bond is put back, the holder will get \$1,030. Thus, the bond will be put back. At the tower node the model value is

$$\frac{1,030}{\left(1 + \dfrac{0.045983}{2}\right)} + 30 = 1,036.8509$$

If the bond is put back, the holder will get 1,030. Thus, the bond will not be put back. Thus, the value of the putable bond at the outset is

$$0.4854 \times (1,030 + 1036.8509) = \$1,003.2494$$

Had it been a plain-vanilla bond the value would have been

$$1,030 \times (0.2349 + 0.4722 + 0.2372) + 30 \times (0.4854 + 0.4854) = 972.6290 + 29.1240$$
$$= \$1,001.7530$$

Thus, the value of the put option inherent in the bond is

$$1,003.2494 - 1,001.753 = \$1.4964$$

CAPS, FLOORS, AND COLLARS

A *caplet* is a call option on an interest rate, while a *floorlet* is a put option on an interest rate. Consider a one-period caplet with an exercise price of 5%. Let the underlying principal be \$5,000,000. Each time period is assumed to be of six months, duration, and we will take it as 0.5 years in order to avoid issues regarding day-count conventions.

At time t_1, the rate may be 6.5983% or 4.5983%. In the first case the caplet will be in the money, whereas in the second case it will be out of the money. The payoff, if it is in the money, is

$$5,000,000 \times (0.065983 - 0.05) \times 0.5 = \$39,957.50$$

In the case of interest rate options, the payoff will occur not when the option expires, but at a point in time when the next interest payment is due. In the above case, the rate as determined at t_1 is applicable for computing the interest due at t_2. Consequently, the caplet will pay off at t_2.

Thus, the value of the caplet at time t_0 may be computed as:

$$0.5 \times \frac{39,957.50}{(1.03)\left(1 + \dfrac{0.065983}{2}\right)} = \$18,777.35$$

A floorlet is a put option on an interest rate. Let us consider a floorlet with the same exercise price and underlying principal as the caplet. The payoff will be zero if the interest rate is 6.5983%, as the option will be out of the money; however, there will be a positive payoff at state if the rate is 4.5983, which is given by:

$$5,000,000 \times [0.05 - 0.045983] \times 0.5 = \$10,042.50$$

This payoff will obviously occur at time t_2. Consequently, the value of the floorlet at t_0 is:

$$0.5 \times \frac{10,042.50}{(1.03)\left(1 + \dfrac{0.045983}{2}\right)} = \$4,765.45$$

A cap is a portfolio of caplets that can be acquired by a borrower who has availed itself of a floating-rate loan in order to protect against an increase in interest rates. Similarly, a floor is a portfolio of floorlets that can be acquired by a lender who has made a loan on a floating-rate basis to protect itself against a decline in interest rates. An interest rate collar is a combination of a cap and a floor. It requires the investor to take a long position in a cap and a short position in a floor.

CAPTIONS AND FLOORTIONS

A *caption* is a financial instrument that gives the holder the right to buy a cap at a future point in time. Consider a company that is likely to borrow funds at a future point in time. In the event that it takes the loan, the prospect of a high rate of interest would be of concern. Consequently, the company may decide to acquire the cap. If, however, it decides not to take the loan, there is no need to acquire the cap. The caption gives the potential borrower the ability to lock in a contract rate in advance for the cap, without taking away its freedom to refrain from exercise if the loan is not taken. If the contract rate in the option is X and prevailing reference rate in the future is K, the caption is exercised if $K > X$. Otherwise, the buyer can allow the caption to expire and acquire a cap at the prevailing contract rate, if it decides to take the loan. In the event of the loan not being availed of, the cap need not be exercised.

Similarly, a *floortion* gives the holder the right to buy a floor at a future point in time. An entity that is likely to make a loan at a future point in time may be interested in such an instrument. A potential lender would be perturbed by the prospect of declining interest rates. If it acquires a floortion, it can exercise if the option is in the money; otherwise, the floortion can be allowed to expire. If the lender decides not to extend the loan, the option can be allowed to expire unexercised. If the contract rate of the floortion is X, and prevailing reference rate in the future is K, the floortion will be exercised if $X > K$. Otherwise, it will be allowed to expire.

Sources and References

CHAPTER 1

Sources & References

Apte, P. G. *International Financial Management*. Tata McGraw-Hill, 2008.

Choudhry, M. *An Introduction to Bond Markets*. Securities Institute, 2001.

Coyle, B. *Overview of the Markets*. Financial World Publishing, 2002.

Dembroski, S. *The Globalization of Financial Markets*. The University of Western Ontario, 1990.

Ferri, M. G. and D.S. Kidwell. *Overview of the Financial System in Selected Topics in Investment Management for Financial Planning*, edited by Fabozzi and Kole. Dow Jones-Irwin, 1985.

Geddes, H. R. *An Introduction to Corporate Finance: Transactions and Techniques*. Securities Institute, 2001.

Geisst, C. R. *A Guide to Financial Institutions*. The Macmillan Press, 1993.

Gibson, N. *Essential Finance*. The Economist, 2004.

Harris, L. *Trading & Exchanges: Market Microstructure for Practitioners*. Oxford University Press, 2003.

Liaw, K. T. *The Business of Investment Banking*. John Wiley & Sons, 1999.

Liaw, K. T. *Capital Markets*. South-Western, 2004.

McInish, T. H. *Capital Markets: A Global Perspective*. Blackwell, 2000.

Resnick, B. G. *The Globalization of World Financial Markets in Advances in Business Financial Management: A Collection of Readings*, edited by P. L. Cooley. Dryden, 1996.

Rose, P. S. *Money and Capital Markets*. McGraw-Hill, 2000.

Saunders, A. and M. M. Cornett. *Financial Institutions Management*. McGraw-Hill, 2003.

Viney, C. *Financial institutions, Instruments and Markets*. McGraw-Hill, 2000.

Websites

adr.com

citissb.com

en.wikipedia.org

www.canadabusiness.ca

www.euromoney.com

invest-faq.com

lbslibrary.typepad.com

www.moneybluebook.com

www.newyorkfed.org

www.poznaklaw.com

www.reuters.com

tse.or.jp

CHAPTER 2

Sources & References

Kellison, S. G. *The Theory of Interest*. Irwin McGraw-Hill, 1991.
Parameswaran, S. K. *Fixed Income Securities: Concepts and Applications*. DeG Press, 2019.
Smith, S. D. and R. E. Spudeck *Interest Rates: Principles and Applications*. Thomson Learning, 1993.

CHAPTER 3

Sources & References

Coyle, B. *Equity Finance*. Financial World Publishing, 2002.
Curley, M. T. *Margin Trading from A to Z*. Wiley, 2008.
Damodaran, A. *Investment Valuation*. Wiley, 1996.
Geddes, H. R. *An Introduction to Corporate Finance: Transactions and Techniques*. Securities Institute, 2001.
Reilly, F. K., and K. C. Brown. *Investment Analysis and Portfolio Management*. Dryden, 2000.
Ross, S. A., R. W. Westerfield, and J. Jaffe. *Corporate Finance*. Irwin McGraw-Hill.
Scott, D. L. *How Wall Street Works*. McGraw-Hill, 1999.
Siegel, D. R. and D. F. Siegel. *Futures Markets*. Dryden, 1990.
Simmons, M. and E. Dalgleish. *Corporate Actions: A Guide to Securities Event Management*. Wiley, 2006.
Taggart, R. A. *Quantitative Analysis For Investment Management*. Prentice Hall, 1996.
Teweles, R. J. and E. S. Bradley. *The Stock Market*. Wiley, 1998.
Weiss, D. M. *After the Trade Is Made*. New York Institute of Finance, 1993.

Websites

Common Stocks, Preferred Stocks – Basic Concepts, http://thismatter.com
Guide to the Markets – Investor's Business Daily, www.investors.com/
Subject: Stocks – Tracking Stock, http://invest-faq.com
www.sec.gov
www.activefilings.com
beginnersinvest.about.com
www.mreic.com
djindexes.com
e-analytics.com
fisonline.net
fool.com
stocks.about.com

CHAPTER 4

Sources & References

Choudhry, M. *An Introduction to Bond Markets*. Securities Institute, 2001.
Choudhry, M. *Analyzing & Interpreting The Yield Curve*. Wiley, 2004.

Fabozzi, F. J. *Bond Markets, Analysis, and Strategies*. Prentice-Hall, 1996.

Garbade, K. D. *Fixed Income Analytics*. MIT Press, 1996.

Livingston, M. *Bonds and Bond Derivatives*. Blackwell, 2004.

Parameswaran, S. K. *Futures and Options: Concepts and Applications*. McGraw-Hill, 2010.

Stigum, M. and F. L. Robinson *Money Market & Bond Calculations*. Irwin, 1996.

Strumeyer, G. *Investing in Fixed Income Securities*. Wiley, 2005.

Sundaresan, S. *Fixed Income Markets and Their Derivatives*. Academic Press, 2009.

Taggart, R.A. *Quantitative Analysis for Investment Management*. Prentice Hall, 2002.

CHAPTER 5

Sources & References

Bose, R. *An Introduction to Documentary Credits*. Macmillan, 2006.

Choudhry, M. *An Introduction to Repo Markets*. Securities Institute, 2001.

Comotto, R. *The Money Market*. Euromoney Publications, 1998.

Coyle, B. *Money Markets*. Financial World Publishing, 2001.

Dodd, R. "Primer on 'Repo' or Repurchase Agreements Market." 2016. http://www.financial policy.org/fpfprimerrepo.htm

Gray, S. *Repo of Government Securities: Handbooks in Central Banking No. 16*. Bank of England, 1998.

Liaw, K. T. *Capital Markets*. Thomson South-Western, 2004.

Palat, R. *Retail Banking*. Executive Excellence Books, 2006.

Rose, P. S. *Commercial Bank Management*. McGraw-Hill Irwin, 2002.

Rose, P. S. *Money and Capital Markets*. McGraw-Hill, 2000.

Steiner, B. *Foreign Exchange and Money Markets*. Butterworth-Heinemann, 2002.

Steiner, R. *Mastering Financial Calculations*. Financial Times Prentice Hall, 1998.

Stigum, M. and A. Crescenzi. *Stigum's Money Market*. McGraw-Hill, 2007.

Stigum, M. and F. L. Robinson. *Money Market & Bond Calculations*. Irwin, 1996.

Websites

www.answers.com

www.bba.org.uk

beginnersinvest.about.com

www.contingencyanalysis.com

www.creditmanagementworld.com

www.ffiec.gov

www.loanuniverse.com

www.malaysiaexports.com

www.newyorkfed.org

www.resources.alibaba.com

www.trading-glossary.com

www.treasurydirect.gov

www.wikipedia.org

www.wmba.org

CHAPTER 6

Sources & References

Chance, D. M. *An Introduction to Derivatives & Risk Management*. South-Western, 2004.

Edwards, F. R. and C. W. Ma. *Futures and Options*. McGraw-Hill, 1992.

Hegde, S. P. and S. K. Parameswaran. *Futures Markets: 200 Questions and Answers*. Wiley, 2007.

Hull, J. *Fundamentals of Futures and Options Markets*. Prentice Hall, 2004.

Kolb, R. W. *Futures, Options, and Swaps*. Blackwell, 2003.

Koontz, S. R. and W. D. Purcell. *Agricultural Futures and Options: Principles and Strategies*. Prentice Hall, 1999.

Lofton, T. *Getting Started in Futures*. Wiley, 2005.

McDonald, R. L. *Derivatives Markets*. Pearson Education, 2006.

Parameswaran, S. K. *Futures and Options: Concepts and Applications*. Tata McGraw-Hill, 2010.

Siegel, D. R. and D. F. Siegel. *Futures Markets*. Dryden, 1990.

Stoll, H. R. and R. E. Whaley. *Futures and Options: Theory and Applications*. South-Western, 1993.

CHAPTER 7

Sources & References

Chance, D. M. *An Introduction to Derivatives & Risk Management*. South-Western, 2004.

Chicago Board Options Exchange: Margin Manual. The CBOE, 2000.

Dubofsky, D. A. *Options and Financial Futures: Valuation and Uses*. McGraw-Hill, 1992.

Figlewski, S., W. L. Silber, and M.G. Subrahmanyam. *Financial Options: From Theory to Practice*. Irwin, 1990.

Hull, J. *Fundamentals of Futures and Options Markets*. Prentice Hall, 2004.

Hull, J. *Options, Futures, and Other Derivatives*. Prentice Hall, 2006.

Kolb, R. W. *Futures, Options, and Swaps*. Blackwell, 2003.

Long-Term Equity Anticipation Securities. The Options Clearing Corporation, 2004.

Option Institute. *Options: Essential Concepts & Trading Strategies*. McGraw-Hill, 1999.

Stoll, H. R. and R. E. Whaley. *Futures and Options: Theory and Applications*. South-Western, 1993.

Understanding Stock Options. The Options Clearing Corporation, 1994.

Understanding Index Options. The CBOE, 2001, www.cboe.com

CHAPTER 8

Sources & References

Apte, P. G. *International Financial Management*. Tata McGraw-Hill, 2006.

Chance, D. M. *An Introduction to Options & Futures*. Dryden, 1991.

Edwards, F. R. and C. W. Ma. *Futures & Options*. McGraw-Hill, 1992.

Logue, D. E. *The WG&L Handbook of International Finance*. South-Western, 1995.

Melvin, M. *International Money and Finance*. Addison Wesley, 1997.

Mobius, M. *Foreign Exchange: An Introduction to the Core Concepts*. Wiley, 2009.

Siegel, D. R. and D. F. Siegel. *Futures Markets*. Dryden, 1990.

Steiner, B. *Foreign Exchange and Money Markets*. Butterworth-Heinemann, 2002.

Websites

www.cmegroup.com
www.nasdaq.com

CHAPTER 9

Sources & References

Davidson, A., A. Sanders, L. Wolff, and A. Ching. *Securitization*. Wiley, 2003.

Fabozzi, F. J. *Bond Markets: Analysis and Strategies*. Prentice Hall, 1996.

Fabozzi, F. J. and F. Modigliani. *Mortgage & Mortgage-Backed Securities Markets*. Harvard Business School Press, 1992.

F. J. Fabozzi, A. K. Bhattacharya, and W. S. Berliner. *Mortgage-Backed Securities*. Wiley, 2007.

Kolev, I. *Mortgage-Backed Securities*. Financial Policy Forum, 2004.

Taff, L. G. *Investing in Mortgage Securities*. St. Lucie Press, 2003.

Websites

en.wikipedia.org
www.fanniemae.com
financecareers.about.com
www.ginniemae.gov

CHAPTER 10

Sources & References

Chance, D. M. *An Introduction to Derivatives & Risk Management*. South-Western, 2004.

Coyle, B. *Currency Swaps*. Financial World Publishing, 2000.

Coyle, B. *Interest-Rate Swaps*. Financial World Publishing, 2001.

Geroulanos, P. *An Introduction to Swaps*. The Securities Institute, 1998.

Hull, J. *Options, Futures, and Other Derivatives*. Prentice Hall, 2006.

CHAPTER 11

Sources & References

Fabozzi, F. J., F. Modigliani, F. J. Jones, and M. G. Ferri. *Foundations of Financial Markets and Institutions*. Pearson Education, 2002.

Jacobs, B. *All About Mutual Funds*. McGraw Hill, 2001.

Johnson, P. W. Jr. *What Is a Mutual Fund?*, https://pwjohnson.com

Hill, J. M., D. Nadig, and M. Hougan. *A Comprehensive Guide to Exchange Traded Funds (ETFs)*. CFA Institute Research Foundation, 2015.

Yanni-Bilkey. *Investment Consulting Exchange-Traded Funds: Understanding the Basics*.

CHAPTER 12

Sources & References

Harris, L. *Trading and Exchanges*. Oxford University Press, 2003.

Kennon, J. *Intro to Stock Trading*. beginnersinvest.com

McInish, T. H. *Capital Markets: A Global Perspective*. Blackwell, 2000.

Sarkar, A. and M. Tozzi. "Electronic Trading on Futures Exchanges." *Derivatives Quarterly* 4, No. 1 (1998).

CHAPTER 14

Sources & References

Babbel, D. F. and C. B. Merrill. *Valuation of Interest-Sensitive Financial Instruments*. Society of Actuaries, 1996.

Buetow, G. W and J. Sochacki. *Term-Structure Models Using Binomial Trees*. AIMR Research Foundation, 2001.

Chance, D. M. *An Introduction to Options & Futures*. Dryden, 1991.

Chance, D. M. *An Introduction to Derivatives & Risk Management*. South-Western, 2004.

Choudhry, M. *An Introduction to Bond Markets*. Securities Institute, 2001.

Choudhry, M. *Analyzing & Interpreting The Yield Curve*. Wiley, 2004.

Edwards, F. R. and C. W. Ma. *Futures & Options*. McGraw-Hill, 1992.

Fabozzi, F. J. *Bond Markets, Analysis, and Strategies*. Prentice-Hall, 1996.

Figlewski S., W. L. Silber, and M. G. Subrahmanyam. *Financial Options: From Theory to Practice*. Irwin, 1990.

Garbade, K. D. *Fixed Income Analytics*. The MIT Press, 1996.

Hull, J. *Fundamentals of Futures and Options Markets*. Prentice Hall, 2004.

Kolb, R. W. *Futures, Options, & Swaps*. Blackwell, 2000.

McDonald, R. L. *Derivatives Markets*. Pearson Education, 2006.

Rendleman, R. J. *Applied Derivatives: Options, Futures and Swaps*. Blackwell, 2002.

Siegel, D. R. and D. F. Siegel. *Futures Markets*. Dryden, 1990.

Stigum, M. and F. L. Robinson. *Money Market & Bond Calculations*. Irwin, 1996.

Index